RACE/GENDER/MEDIA

Considering Diversity across Audiences, Content, and Producers

SECOND EDITION

RACE/GENDER/MEDIA

Considering Diversity across Audiences, Content, and Producers

REBECCA ANN LIND

University of Illinois at Chicago

Allyn & Bacon

Boston   New York   San Francisco
Mexico City   Montreal   Toronto   London   Madrid   Munich   Paris
Hong Kong   Singapore   Tokyo   Cape Town   Sydney

Acquisitions Editor: Jeanne Zalesky
Editorial Assistant: Megan Lentz
Marketing Manager: Suzan Czajkowski
Production Assistant: Maggie Brobeck
Manufacturing Buyer: Renata Butera
Cover Designer: Jayne Conte
Cover Image: Getty Images, Inc.
Electronic Composition: Aptara®, Inc.

Library of Congress Cataloging-in-Publication Data

Race/gender/media: considering diversity, across audiences, content, and producers/[edited by] Rebecca Ann Lind.—2nd ed.
  p. cm.
"This book is a cornucopia of readings and perspectives on the crucial contemporary issues surrounding race, gender, and media. The field is so multi-faceted, with so many interesting perspectives and topics, that one of the biggest challenges with doing a book like this is leaving so much great material out! The best thing about doing a second edition is getting to include new ideas, and things there wasn't room for the first time around."
  ISBN-13: 978-0-205-53735-8
  ISBN-10: 0-205-53735-9
  1. Race relations in mass media.   2. Gender identity in mass media.   I. Lind, Rebecca Ann.
  P94.5.M55R33 2010
  305.8—dc22

                                                                    2008052680

10 9 8 7 6 5 4 3 2 1   RRD-VA   13 12 11 10 09

Allyn & Bacon
is an imprint of

PEARSON

www.pearsonhighered.com

ISBN-13: 978-0-205-53735-8
ISBN-10:   0-205-53735-9

WHY YOU NEED THIS NEW EDITION

This book is a cornucopia of readings and perspectives on the crucial contemporary issues surrounding race, gender, and media. The field is so multifaceted, with so many interesting perspectives and topics, that one of the biggest challenges with doing a book like this is leaving so much great material out! The best thing about doing a Second Edition is getting to include new ideas there wasn't room for the first time around.

It's easy to see why you need this new edition. More than half of the readings are new or updated. The three main sections (Audiences, Content, Production) have been reorganized into seven larger, broader, and more inclusive chapters, and the Second Edition contains more social scientific work, more feminist work, more on new media, and specific new topics such as reality television, diaspora, and fandom. The introduction (Chapter 1) has been updated, as has the epilogue (Chapter 9), which contains a significantly enhanced list of resources.

CONTENTS

CHAPTER THREE

Audience Reception, Use, and Interpretation of Media Content   55

PART II CONTENT 109

CHAPTER FOUR
Journalism, Advertising, and Public Relations 112

CHAPTER FIVE

Film and Entertainment Television   166

CHAPTER SIX
Music and New Media   223

PREFACE

Welcome to the Second Edition of a sampler presenting a wide variety of perspectives that, when taken together, shows just how many ways there are to consider race and gender in the media. This book is designed to make you think critically about these issues and to encourage you to decide which of the ideas and perspectives makes the most sense to you. It's designed to spark your interest and stimulate discussion.

What's new in the Second Edition? Plenty! More than half of the readings are new or updated. The three main sections (Audience, Content, Production) have been totally reorganized to create seven chapters representing broader foci. There are more examples of social scientific work and more feminist works. You'll see more on new media and new readings covering topics such as contemporary film, reality television, advertising/PR, LGBT concerns, diaspora, and fandom.

This collection contains 43 readings by a wide variety of authors representing varied disciplines. They approach the matter of race and gender in the media from rhetorical, social scientific, and critical/cultural perspectives. You won't agree with everything you read, and that's just fine.

As with everything, this book represents a tradeoff. If content is covered in greater depth, there can be less breadth. If greater breadth, there can be less depth. Because I wanted to present as many viewpoints as possible, this book contains many short readings; I emphasize breadth. The readings provide an introduction to the field, a taste of what people are thinking and writing about. If you find something particularly interesting, you can consider it a starting point and then learn much more about it.

This book can be used in both lower- and upper-division courses. The authors have been encouraged to speak with their own voices to better reinforce the fact that the scholarship in this field is diverse.

Because of the number of readings, instructors may choose to emphasize or deemphasize certain things. The book has been designed to contain enough readings so that reading and other assignments can be flexible—depending on the goals of the course, some readings may not be assigned at all.[1] Alternatively, instructors might ask students to learn more about the topic of an especially important reading. Students could be assigned to obtain some of the material referenced by the author, to see whether they can find anything else written by that author, or to search for additional relevant information in the campus library or on the Internet. If desired, students could even become teachers for a time and share what they've learned with the class.

Instructors will have different expectations of students in terms of the items presented in the "It's Your Turn" segment of each chapter. These items can be used or adapted in numerous ways. At the very least, some of the "It's Your Turn" items can provide a basis for fruitful class discussion. Some can become major term projects, on an individual or group level. Some can be handled as traditional assignments. Others can be assigned in lieu of quizzes to encourage students to read and think about the material prior to class. Any of the "It's Your Turn" items that become graded exercises, assignments, or projects could take any number of forms. They could be traditional papers (of varying lengths, determined by the instructor), or complete, full-sentence outlines conveying the essence of the students' ideas (with the expected extent of detail specified by the instructor). They could be traditional oral presentations, or something akin to the "poster session" format that's becoming increasingly popular at scholarly meetings—students could create visual presentations on poster board conveying the essence of their work. If the school has the facilities and the students have the expertise, some "It's Your Turn" items could even result in students producing some audio, video, graphic, or interactive (even online) material. And, as noted earlier, any of these can be done on an individual or small-group basis, or even by the class as a whole.[2]

The chapters comprise multiple readings and are divided into three main parts: Production, Content, and Audience, each of which will be discussed in Chapter 1 (Introduction) as well as in the appropriate section introduction. Because I wanted the emphasis of this book to reflect the overall interests of media students, scholars, and teachers, some sections contain more readings than others. The Content section has the most readings, followed by the Audience section, then Production. Within each section, chapters contain clusters (of varying sizes) of readings, representing thematically coherent emphases. For example, the 23 readings in the Content section are organized into three chapters: Journalism, Advertising, and Public Relations[3]; Film[4] and Entertainment Television; and Music and New Media. These multifaceted chapters are a helpful way to approach a book containing so many readings that are purposely diverse. However, there are other ways to approach and organize this material, so this book also offers alternate tables of contents (see the appendix), although individual instructors might prefer something completely different. The material in this book is nothing if not flexible, so there's no reason not to completely reconsider the order of the material if it helps instructors better meet the goals of their courses.

I hope you come away from this book more aware of precisely what is being presented in the media content that you (and others) consume and that you think about how you (and others) not only make sense of what you see/read/hear but also about how media affects each of us. I hope you have a sense of the varied and complex forces at work in the social organizations within which media content is produced—the social forces providing opportunities or constraints for certain people working in media organizations, inhibiting or encouraging the production and distribution of certain types of messages or content, and even those social forces affecting us as we use the capabilities of new media to make the step from being consumers to producers of mediated content.

I also hope you come away from this book thinking more positively about your role in the entire media system. You aren't a passive victim of what you see—at least, you don't have to be. You can be an active and engaged participant in the process of media use. At the very least, you can decide what media and what content to utilize, and when, and you can critically evaluate the messages as well as the messenger's motives.

I extend my thanks to the students who have enrolled in my courses in race and gender in the media—from first-year students all the way to Ph.D. candidates—for their energy and enthusiasm for the subject, and for what they have taught me. I'd also like to thank Jeanne Zalesky and Karon Bowers of Allyn & Bacon and the reviewers of the first edition. I owe a large debt to my stellar research assistant, Paul Couture, who helped in many ways as I juggled the many pieces of this project. Finally, I'm very grateful to all the contributors to this book. I've made some new friends and built some new connections while corresponding with the authors. Thank you all!

. . . To My Parents & My Students

NOTES

1. When I teach courses using collections containing many readings, I rarely assign everything in the book or packet. Instead, I select a few key items I want to address early in the course, and then I ask each student to select one or two readings/chapters (depending on the number available and the number of students, and striving to have most of the chapters selected). The chapters I select can't be chosen by students, and each of the remaining chapters can't be chosen by more than one student. If each student is selecting two chapters, I hope that they are either similar or different enough to make some kind of coherent whole—in practice, this does get a bit "fuzzy," but it's by no means a severe drawback.

These selections perform two functions. First, they create the list of assigned readings for the term, and in so doing give the students a clear voice in guiding their own learning. Second, they form the basis of an assignment in which each student, informed by the selected chapter, leads the class in a discussion of the chapter content. The length of discussion depends on the number of students in the class as well as the class level; lower-division students have the shortest amount of time, and graduate students have the most. I evaluate these discussions more on preparation than on execution (especially in a lower-level course when students generally have less public speaking experience and aren't as used to nontraditional classroom activities)— if a student has prepared a list of thoughtful questions, which should have filled the required time, the student will earn a good score. I also find it helpful to follow each student-led discussion by posing discussion questions of my own, to ensure that the points I think are most important are indeed raised.

2. Instructors who are new to teaching a course on race and/or gender in the media might find it helpful to look at a chapter I wrote about teaching race and gender in the media; it contains tips from experienced teachers: Lind, R. A. (2003). Race and gender. In M. D. Murray & R. Moore (Eds.), *Mass Communication Education* (pp. 63–77). Ames: Iowa State Press.

Additionally, instructors should acknowledge at the outset that these topics, and certain readings in particular, are sensitive. Your school might have resources for addressing sensitive topics in the classroom, or you might investigate other resources such as those prepared by U.C. Berkeley's Office of Educational Development (http://teaching.berkeley.edu/sensitivetopics.html). Another helpful site is a listserv of women's studies teaching, research, and administration (table of contents at http://userpages.umbc.edu/~korenman/wmst/wmsttoc.html). There you will find discussions on a variety of topics including dealing with sensitive subjects (I and II), teaching about pornography, race/gender/ethnicity, sexuality/sexual orientation, pedagogical issues and strategies, and more.

3. It isn't unusual for these topics to be linked. Many journalism schools offer emphases in advertising, marketing, and public relations.

4. Several readings focus on film—the films themselves, their production, or their reception. Some instructors will find it helpful to show at least part of some of these films during class, although the readings will "work" on a conceptual level even if the students don't know the text.

Still, most students are probably already familiar with *The Lion King, The Devil Wears Prada*, and *The Nanny Diaries*. Many may have seen *Save the Last Dance* (which continues to make the rounds on cable networks), but the main goal of the reading that features that film is to present a framework students can use when approaching other media texts. Even if students haven't seen the film the chapter is still useful—students can approach the framework on a conceptual basis. Alternatively, they can apply the framework to another text instead. Thus, instructors will decide whether and how to incorporate the presentation of any of the media texts discussed in this book.

CHAPTER 1

LAYING A FOUNDATION FOR STUDYING RACE, GENDER, AND THE MEDIA

REBECCA ANN LIND

THE MEDIA MATTER

Ours is a mediated society; much of what we know about, care about, and think is important is based on what we see in the media. The media provides information, entertainment, escape, and relaxation and even help us make small talk. The media can help save lives, and—unfortunately—the media can also encourage people to cause harm to others. For example:

- Linked to the TV powerhouse *American Idol*, the "Idol Gives Back" campaign has raised more than $135 million in two seasons. In 2008, these funds supported the Children's Health Fund, Children's Defense Fund, Make It Right, Save the Children, the Global Fund, and Malaria No More.
- Lucky you! Your e-mail says you'll be handsomely rewarded if you help a sympathetic-sounding family retrieve funds rightfully due them. You may know it's a scam, a high-tech means of obtaining your bank account number and other personal information, but it's still working, with victims losing thousands of dollars.
- The AMBER Alert system uses local radio and TV stations in conjunction with electronic highway signs to rapidly disseminate information about child abductions.
- Videophones are saving the lives of young heart patients who live in communities without pediatric cardiologists. Videophone technology transmits information from outlying hospitals to specialists. Previously, the information was sent by taxi to the specialist—sometimes several hundred miles away!
- A New York City subway clerk was torched and killed after some teens copied what they'd seen in the film *Money Train*. Such "copycat crimes" have occurred frequently enough that they've been the subject of an episode of the A&E series *Investigative Reports*.

If the world is shrinking, and our "village" is becoming global, it's because the media—especially TV—have brought things ever closer to us. The average American household has the television set on more than 8 hours a day. When you consider how averages are calculated, this means that if you—as a busy college student with lots of homework

and perhaps some extracurricular activities, not to mention work and/or family obligations—only have the TV on for about 2 hours, then some other household has it on for
more than 14 hours. Now think about your involvement with other social institutions. How
much time have you spent in the classroom in your entire life? (Because you're in college,
it's a lot more than most Americans). How does that compare to your time spent with TV?
How will that change as you leave the classroom but continue to watch television? How
many hours per day do you spend with your parents (and reflect on others who might not
be as lucky) or with religious leaders? How can the media *not* affect us in some way?

A primary assumption underlying media research is that the media does matter—
what we see, read, and hear does have some type of affect on us. Different types of scholars,
however, approach the matter of media effects differently. Social scientists try to model
their research on the natural sciences and strive to maintain objectivity. They often employ
experimental or survey methodologies testing for precise and narrowly defined media
effects (such as how people's opinions change as a result of media exposure, how people's
perceptions of others or about the world in general are affected by what they see/hear/read,
or whether people behave more aggressively after being exposed to violent media content).

Critical/cultural researchers, on the other hand, reject not only the desirability of maintaining an objective, value-neutral position but also the very possibility of accomplishing such
a goal. As human beings, they argue, we cannot distance ourselves from our social world; indeed, only by immersing ourselves in its practices can we understand them. A subjective interpretation is thus not just desired but required to learn how the media affect the world in which
we live. These are fundamentally different assumptions from those held by most social scientists. The types of media effects that critical/cultural researchers investigate are different, too.
They're much more broadly defined and often address the cumulative effects of a lifetime of
exposure to media content—content that typically represents a limited range of viewpoints,
ideas, and images. Ultimately, the media help maintain a status quo in which certain groups in
our society routinely have access to power and privilege while others do not. Because the
types of questions critical/cultural scholars ask are often different from those posed by social
scientists, these scholars tend to prefer qualitative methodologies such as rhetorical or textual
analysis, interviews, and ethnographic techniques. In addition, critical/cultural scholars extend
their involvement with their research to include the ultimate goal of making the world a better
place. If we can identify the ways in which our social structures function to oppress certain
groups, then we can try to do something to make things more equitable.

This book contains work by both social scientists and critical/cultural scholars, although the latter group dominates. As you explore the readings, see if you can identify
which perspective seems to be guiding the authors and how it affects the questions asked
and the way the answers are sought.

RACE AND GENDER MATTER

Like it or not, we do classify people on the basis of race/ethnicity and gender. Our perceptions of our own and others' identities color all our interactions; they affect our expectations of others, our expectations of ourselves, and others' expectations of us.

According to sociologist Joseph Healey (1995), we make snap judgments about people
(and things). This is necessary, because we live in a complex social world, and we simply

don't have time to ruminate about all the fine points of everything and everyone we encounter. So we constantly categorize people and groups, often on the basis of nothing more than their most "obvious" characteristics—markers of race and gender. Furthermore, the classifications we make affect our behavior toward others.

Why do the markers of race and gender stand out, rather than other attributes? Why are these the "obvious" characteristics by which we categorize others? Healey said this is because "our attention is drawn to the characteristics that have come to identify the dividing lines between groups" (1995, p. 162.) We could classify people according to length of hair, height, or even the size of their feet, but we don't. Ultimately, we rely on these characteristics because we have been taught to do so:

> Our perceptions and impressions in the present are conditioned by the dividing lines that reflect group relations in the past. Our "knowledge" that skin color can be used to judge others and our sensitivity to this characteristic reflects our socialization into a race-conscious society with a long history of racial stratification. (p. 162)

It's the same with gender—we've been socialized into a gender-conscious society that is also stratified (divided in a hierarchical fashion, with some social groups having more of the goods/services valued by society than others) along the lines of gender.

When our generalizations become overly simplistic, when we ignore evidence that they are incorrect, or when they become exaggerated, they have become more than mere "generalizations"; they've become *stereotypes*. Stereotypes reflect our (erroneous) beliefs that the few traits we stress are the most important, and that they apply to all members of the group. They deny the presence and the importance of individual characteristics. Stereotypes are an important component of *prejudice*, which Healey (1995) defined as "the tendency of an individual to think about other groups in negative ways and to attach negative emotions to those groups" (p. 27). Notice the two dimensions of this definition—prejudice has both a cognitive and an emotional element. Stereotypes are at the heart of the cognitive aspect of prejudice. Prejudice can lead to *discrimination*, although it doesn't need to, because even a very prejudiced person can refrain from acting on her or his negative cognitive or emotional response to certain social groups. Discrimination occurs when people are treated unequally just because they belong to a certain group. People can be treated differently for many different reasons, but any time unequal treatment is based on group membership (even the perception of group membership) the behavior is discriminatory. Stereotypes, prejudice, and discrimination reflect *racism* or *sexism* (although both concepts go much deeper than that and are defined differently by different people), depending on whether the stereotypes are rooted in race/ethnicity or gender.

A final word about race and ethnicity: Although both are socially constructed, some people find it helpful to distinguish between race and ethnicity. To those who do, race is primarily defined in terms of physical characteristics and ethnicity in terms of cultural characteristics. Markers of race include skin color and hair (delineating individuals as being of African, Chinese, Japanese, European descent); markers of ethnicity include religious practices, language use, mode of dress, dietary habits, and cuisine (delineating individuals as being Catholic, Hindu, Irish Americans). Those who employ this distinction tend to believe that the meanings attributed to both physical and cultural markers remain socially constructed; they are not propagating biological theories of race, which for good reason have largely been rejected.

AUDIENCE, CONTENT, PRODUCTION: THREE FOCAL POINTS

Our media system is complex and incorporates a variety of interrelated components, each of which experiences many pressures from both within and without. Three of the major elements of the system are the producers, the audience, and the actual media content.[1] The chapters of this book are organized around those three elements.[2] *Production* involves anything having to do with the creation and distribution of mediated messages: how the messages are assembled, by whom, in what circumstances, under what constraints. *Content* emphasizes the mediated messages themselves: what they present, and how; what is included, and by implication, what is excluded. *Audience* addresses the people who engage, consume, or interact with mediated messages: how they use the media, what sense they make of media content, and how they are affected by the media.

The production–content–audience distinction is consistent with commonly used models of communication focusing on the source (or sender), message, channel, and receiver. Scholars have presented these models in a variety of ways and with a variety of additional elements, but at their core they focus on who creates or originates the message (sender/source), how the source has presented the ideas she or he wishes to communicate (message), how the actual message is conveyed (channel), and to whom the message is sent (receiver).[3] These SMCR-type models fit well with the social–scientific approach and all have their roots in the 1940s' work of Harold Lasswell (1948) and Claude Shannon and Warren Weaver (1949). The Shannon and Weaver mathematical model of communication has been most influential in the field.

The production–content–audience distinction is also consistent with how media studies can be approached within the critical/cultural studies perspective. These three realms are usually referred to as *production, text*, and *reception* by critical/cultural scholars and are considered *points of intervention*. Don't let the overt political stance implied by that term escape you—remember the goal of critical/cultural scholars: They want to understand how social structures serve to oppress and repress certain social groups in order to end that oppression.

KEY CONCEPTS AND RECURRING THEMES

As you read this book, you'll begin to notice a pattern of recurring themes. Although these are typically defined when they're presented, it's important that you have a sense of some of the key concepts you'll encounter. In addition, these concepts often inform the readings even if they're not explicitly mentioned. Thinking about these concepts right up front will help frame the readings in a way that should prove beneficial. And speaking of framing . . .

Framing.   Erving Goffman argued in his classic 1974 book that the framing of an event or activity establishes its meaning. In other words, framing is the process by which we make sense of the events around us. Frames are like story lines that allow us to interpret new information in the context of something we already understand. We use frames all the time, without even knowing it. For example, we might say to our friends that a new band is "like Nine Inch Nails with Nelly." Or that a singer is the "new Gwen Stefani." People pitching ideas for films or television shows often frame their ideas in terms of content the networks or studios already know and understand: "It's a Western set in outer space."

Journalists use frames as they prepare news stories, too, whether they know it or not. Despite journalists' quest for the objective presentation of the "facts" to their audiences, Gamson (1989) claimed that "facts have no intrinsic meaning. They take on their meaning by being embedded in a frame or story line that organizes them and gives them coherence, selecting certain ones to emphasize while ignoring others" (p. 157). Because news stories always emphasize some facts over others, we should "think of news as telling stories about the world rather than as presenting 'information,' even though the stories, of course, include factual elements" (p. 157). A story might frame something as an economic or a moral issue, a local issue, or one with far-reaching consequences. A story might emphasize the "horse race" aspects of a political campaign or the important issues and stances held by the candidates. Framing is important, because a great deal of research has shown that the frames employed by the media when telling a story can affect our attitudes and judgments about the issues and people involved in the story—especially, as Gitlin (1980) argued, when people don't have firsthand knowledge of and experience with the issue at hand.

In the case of this book, the information provided in this chapter should frame the readings in such a manner that you're on the lookout for certain concepts and that your understanding of the readings is bolstered by your knowledge of these concepts.

Symbolic Annihilation.   Symbolic Annihilation is a concept often associated with sociologist Gaye Tuchman (whose 1978 work is widely cited, with good reason) but which was presented by George Gerbner in 1972 and George Gerbner and Larry Gross in 1976. The concept is rooted in two assumptions: that media content offers a form of symbolic representation of society rather than any literal portrayal of society, and that to be represented in the media is in itself a form of power—social groups that are powerless can be relatively easily ignored, allowing the media to focus on the social groups that really matter. It's almost like implying that certain groups don't really exist—even though we can't go out and actually annihilate everyone who isn't a straight, White, middle-to-upper-class male, we can at least try to avoid them in our mediated versions of reality. Tuchman (1978) focused on the symbolic annihilation of women, but the concept is applicable to any socially constructed group, whether based on gender, race, sexual orientation, ethnicity, appearance, social class, and so on.

Tuchman argued that through absence, condemnation, and trivialization, the media reflect a social world in which women are consistently devalued. As noted above, when the media consistently fail to represent a particular social group, it becomes easy for us to assume the group either doesn't exist or doesn't really matter. So, if the media consistently present an image of a social world that is (in terms of numbers) dominated by men, Tuchman argued, the media have symbolically annihilated women. But women are not completely absent from media content. Symbolic annihilation also looks for evidence of condemnation or trivialization. Perhaps women are reduced to incompetent childlike beings needing protection from men. Perhaps they're only valuable when they're attractive, young, thin; when they're sexual rather than smart. Perhaps they only function well in the home, getting into all sorts of trouble—some comic, some tragic—when they dare leave the confines of the traditionally acceptable roles of wife and mother. Even when enacting those "appropriate" roles, however, women's contributions may be seen as less valuable than those made by the men of the house. As you're reading the following essays about a variety of social groups falling outside of the straight White middle-to-upper-class male norm—whether it's women, homosexuals, African Americans, Muslims, Sikhs, Latin Americans, Native Americans, or even "White trash"—consider the extent to which, and how, the group might be experiencing a form of symbolic annihilation in the media.

Intersectionality.   The variety of social groups previously noted raises an important issue: No one is a member of just one social group; we are all a product of a combination of experiences and identities, rooted in a variety of socially constructed classifications. The social reality experienced by gay White males, for example, differs from that experienced by White lesbians or by straight White males. The social reality experienced by White women differs from that experienced by Black women. The concept of intersectionality helps us understand the futility of trying to know what it means, for example, to be "Native American." None of us can ever be *only* Native American, *only* female, *only* bisexual, *only* deaf or blind. We all experience multiple identities that combine, or intersect, to help us understand who we are, and who others are, and to help others understand who we are. Our unique combination of identities affects all of our interactions with others. As you read this book, you'll see this is a dominant theme. Notice readings that overtly address intersectionality by acknowledging the interaction of race and gender. Also, see how other readings might be informed by intersectionality even though it may not be a key focal point.

Cultural/Social Identity.   Another concept you'll come across repeatedly, and not only in readings addressing intersectionality is cultural/social identity. We all have the sense that we belong to a particular cultural group (or several such groups), even if we haven't consciously thought about it. The more we've thought about it, though, and the more importance and emotional significance attached to our membership in these groups, the more important this cultural identity is to us. Sometimes a cultural or social identity is so pivotal to us that we never approach any social or communication situation without being aware of ourselves as (for example) a gay man. At other times, an aspect of our identity might hardly be considered.

The way issues of identity are handled can serve to reveal or highlight various social tensions rooted in issues of difference. Think about the character "Pat" originated by Julia Sweeney on *Saturday Night Live*. If gender identity didn't matter, Pat wouldn't be funny. If racial identity didn't matter, we wouldn't care about Michael Jackson's evolving appearance, so we'd never bother making fun of it, and we wouldn't care whether the lightening of his skin was due to vitiligo or personal preference.[4] We wouldn't have people arguing about who is and is not Black, or who has the "right" to employ traditionally Black modes of dress and speech. Members of one social group (in particular the dominant White group) might go so far as to remove someone else's cultural or social identity. We see examples of this every time someone (usually White) say something like, "I don't see Bill Cosby as a Black comedian; he's just a comedian." As you read this book, note how frequently issues of identity are considered, even if the authors don't explicitly use that term.

Social Construction of Reality.   The previous discussion of social identity at least implicitly highlights the fact that identities are negotiated within a social context.[5] Sometimes identities are forced upon people (as in the "one-drop rule," which claimed that any individual with at least one drop of African blood was Black). Sometimes they are rejected (as when people of one social group attempt to "pass" for another, or when acquaintances of someone who has undergone gender reassignment refuse to refer to the person as "he" rather than "she"). But most often we understand and accept what it means in our culture to be male or female, Black, White, Native American, Latino/a, Japanese, Korean, Chinese, and so forth. How do we do this? We learn what it means to be a member of a certain social group through our interactions with others. By consistently being treated in a certain way, we begin to expect to be treated in that way. This is exemplified in the process of engenderment, by which a biological female becomes a socially constructed feminine being and a biological male becomes a socially constructed masculine being. We learn what boys and girls (and later, men and women) act like, do for fun, think is important, are good at, and so on. A similar process is also at work in constructing our ideas about people of various racial and ethnic groups.

The importance of race and gender in our society has nothing to do with physical attributes of race and gender and everything to do with society's interpretation of what it means to be a member of a particular gender or racial/ethnic group. What it *really* means to be a Black man, or a Latina, or a Muslim in our society is entirely dependent on what we *think* it means to be a Black man, or a Latina, or a Muslim. As you read this book, think about what the media are telling us about what it means to be a member of a given social group and how that reflects to us what that group is, does, and values.

Discourse.   Discourse is a concept frequently employed by scholars. It may be used/defined differently by different people, but at the heart of the matter, discourse essentially refers to ways of conceptualizing, discussing, or writing about various social phenomena (such as racism or sexism). Discourses can be seen as interpretive frameworks that have a powerful role in defining the phenomenon of interest, in determining exactly what it is and how it can or should be dealt with—or even whether it should be addressed at all. In a way, the concept of discourse is related to framing. It's probably safe to say that discourse is a more "rich" or "dense" concept that tends to be favored by critical/cultural scholars, while framing is more narrow and tends to be favored by social scientists.

Ideology.   Ideology is one of the concepts that is of fundamental importance to critical/cultural studies, with roots in Marxism. As with discourse, definitions of ideology abound; different scholars approach the concept slightly differently. For our purposes, ideology is best understood as a set of deeply held ideas about the nature of the world and the way the world ought to be. There are many different ideologies, and they all affect the way any given society has been socially constructed. Some ideologies are more repressive or more egalitarian than others. Even within any given society, multiple ideologies can be found, but one ideology is usually accepted by most of the society's members. We call this the *dominant ideology.*

Discovering and articulating a culture's dominant ideology and how it's perpetuated is important to critical/cultural scholars, because if it serves to oppress and repress certain cultural groups, these scholars would like to see it changed. Media perform a pivotal role in perpetuating the dominant ideology, because media texts so often produce and reproduce that ideology. If we (as members of a society) don't see much that represents an alternative way of approaching or understanding our world, it's unlikely we'll embrace an alternative ideology. Because of this, it's vital to examine the way the media represent members of a culture's social groups. In our culture, we should look at media depictions not only of the dominant social group (straight, White, middle-to-upper-class male) but also of the subordinated groups (homosexuals, women, people of color, people of lower economic classes, and the like.)

We should also look at how the media represent groups that explicitly challenge the status quo. The media can ignore such challenges only up to a point—sometimes the groups become so large and well organized that they must be acknowledged. But when they are portrayed in the media, groups challenging the dominant ideology are often represented as deviant, as fringe elements, as disorganized—anything other than offering a viable and beneficial alternative to the way things are. An example of this occurs when the media represent members of the women's movement as hairy-legged, lesbian, man haters who want to destroy the sanctity of the nuclear family. In labor disputes, maybe union negotiators are described as "demanding" while management is "only doing what is logical during the current economic climate." In the early days of the environmental movement, its members were seen as hippies, and called "tree huggers." Members of the women's movement were called "bra burners." These portrayals provide examples of what it means to belong to these groups and in doing so represent to us all the dominant ideology in action. Why should we take these weirdos and their crazy ideas seriously? Again, if that's all we see, that might be all we know.

CRITICAL THINKING AND MEDIA LITERACY

One of this book's goals is to encourage you to think critically about the media. *Critical thinking* has been defined in a variety of ways, but at the very least, it involves "the ability to examine issues rationally, logically and coherently" (Stark & Lowther, 1988, p. 23). However, a fuller definition helps delineate the processes involved more clearly. A group of experts gathered by the American Philosophical Association defined critical thinking as "purposeful, self-regulatory judgment which results in interpretation, analysis, evaluation, and inference, as well as explanation of the evidential, conceptual, methodological, or contextual considerations upon which that judgment is based" (Facione, 1990, p. 2). Essentially, for the type of course using this book, critical thinking boils down to asking and trying to answer the following types of questions (which will take a variety of forms, in part due to whether they're directed at media content, media production, or media audiences): What do I see? What do I think it means? How did it get that way? To what extent is that appropriate, a good thing, or handled effectively? What does this tell me about some aspect of our media system, or our society? And finally, Why do I say that?

Being critical participants in our media system means constantly asking questions and doing our best to answer them in a logical and defensible fashion. We should engage in a systematic but not necessarily linear process of thinking through these issues, defining terms and concepts, looking at and evaluating evidence, considering the pros and cons of various positions, acknowledging underlying assumptions, and justifying our position.

As elements of critical thinking are tailored to fit the media context, the result is a way of thinking that shares a great deal with the idea of *media literacy*. Although the United States falls far behind much of the rest of the developed world in terms of the extent to which media literacy is developed and integrated into the educational system, we are beginning to understand its importance. For example, Wulff (1997) argued that media literacy is a key component in people's ability to participate actively in a democratic society, as well a within a global context.

But what exactly is media literacy? It involves expanding the general concept of "literacy" (the ability to read and write) to what the Aspen Institute called "the powerful post-print media that dominate our informational landscape" (Aufderheide, 1993, p. 1). Media literacy "helps people understand, produce and negotiate meanings in a culture made up of powerful images, words and sounds" (Aufderheide, p. 1). The Institute provided further guidance as to what it actually means to be media literate: "A media literate person: Can decode, evaluate, analyze and produce both print and electronic media. The fundamental objective of media literacy is critical autonomy in relationship to all media" (Aufderheide, p. 1).

According to the Center for Media Literacy's Web site,

A media literate person doesn't know all the answers, but knows how to ask the right questions: Who created this message? Why? How and why did they choose what to include and what to leave out of this message? How is it intended to influence me?

The National Communication Association (1998) developed five standards of media literacy, each of which can be reflected in specific competencies or abilities and as a result are particularly valuable for educational purposes. Here are the standards, with some of their associated competencies:

- *Media literate communicators demonstrate knowledge and understanding of the ways people use media in their personal and public lives.* (Specifically, they "recognize the roles of culture and language in media practices"; "identify personal and public media content, forms, and products"; and "analyze the historical and current ways in which media affect people's personal and public lives"; among other competencies.)
- *Media literate communicators demonstrate knowledge and understanding of the complex relationships among audiences and media content.* (Specifically, they "identify media forms, content, and products"; "recognize that media are open to multiple interpretations"; "explain how media socialize people"; and "evaluate ideas and images in media with possible individual, social and cultural consequences"; among other competencies.)
- *Media literate communicators demonstrate knowledge and understanding that media content is produced within social and cultural contexts.* (Specifically, they "identify the production contexts of media content and products," "identify the social and cultural constraints on the production of media," "identify the social and cultural agencies that regulate media content and products," and "evaluate the ideas and aesthetics in media content and products.")
- *Media literate communicators demonstrate knowledge and understanding of the commercial nature of media.* (Specifically, they "explain how media organizations operate" and "compare media organizations to other social and cultural organizations," among other competencies.)
- *Media literate communicators demonstrate ability to use media to communicate to specific audiences.* (Specifically, they "identify suitable media to communicate for specific purposes and outcomes"; "identify the roles and responsibilities of media production teams"; "analyze their media work for technical and aesthetic strengths and weaknesses"; and "recognize that their media work has individual, social, and ethical consequences"; among other competencies.) (pp. 19–23)

As you read this book, consider these media literacy standards and competencies. Notice how the authors reflect these competencies in their writing. Think about how your responses to the items presented in the "It's Your Turn" section of each reading reflect these competencies. Try to exhibit these competencies as you read/see/hear media content and as you create media content for class or other purposes. You'll probably find that the more you do it, the easier it is to respond in a media literate fashion to the "It's Your Turn" items as well as to the media content you encounter in your day-to-day life. Perhaps it'll even become second nature, which would be good, because a more media-literate media user is a more empowered and less vulnerable media user.

NOTES

1. There are other elements affecting media, such as the legal/regulatory system, but even though regulators could be considered a specialized segment of the audience, this book won't address that part of the process.

2. Classification systems such as the one used here are useful devices to help us organize and make sense of ideas and processes, but they're not perfect—some readings don't fit neatly into a single category. As you read this book, think about the questions posed in item #3 in "It's Your Turn," below.

3. Even though this book doesn't have a special section devoted to the channel of communication, some readings do focus on how the channel of communication might change the relationship of the participants within

the communication process and perhaps even the communication process itself. Note also that one of the alternate tables of contents organizes the readings by medium.

4. Consider the difference between Michael Jackson lightening his skin and the voluntary skin darkening undertaken by Whites everywhere at the beach, in tanning salons, and so on. Why do we not tease Whites for becoming darker, and what does this reveal about the power hierarchy in our society?

5. The social construction of reality concept was first presented by sociologists Peter Berger and Thomas Luckmann (1966). Although it's a little book, it has had a large impact on many disciplines.

IT'S YOUR TURN: WHAT DO YOU THINK? WHAT WILL YOU FIND?

1. At this point, does the social–scientific or the critical/cultural studies approach seem to make more sense to you? Why? What do you think are the strengths and weaknesses of each approach?

2. Consider the term "points of intervention" used within the critical/cultural studies tradition. Why do you think they use that term? Would social scientists ever employ such a term? Why or why not?

3. As you read this book, think about how some readings have been categorized as being about production, content, or audience—do you agree with all of the classifications? If not, why do you think it appears in that category? Where

would you have put the reading, and why? As you're considering this, think about what this tells us about the integration of the various components of our media system. Also consider what this tells us about the nature of any classification system; reflect on how such systems can be helpful even though they're flawed.

4. *Intersectionality* is presented as a major recurring theme in the chapters that follow. To what extent do you think it's important to acknowledge the variety of influences on our cultural identity? To what extent do you think it's possible to isolate just one element (say, gender or race) for study—what is lost, and what is gained, by doing so?

REFERENCES

Aufderheide, P. (1993). *Media literacy: A report of the national leadership conference on media literacy.* Queenstown, MD: The Aspen Institute.

Berger, P. L. & Luckmann, T. (1966). *The social construction of reality: A treatise in the sociology of knowledge.* NY: Doubleday.

Center for Media Literacy. (n.d.). Frequently asked questions. Retrieved May 15, 2008, from: www .medialit.org/faq/html

Facione, P. A. (1990). *Critical thinking: A statement of expert consensus for purposes of educational assessment and instruction.* ERIC Document Reproduction Service No. ED 315423.

Gamson, W. A. (1989). News as framing: Comments on Graber. *American Behavioral Scientist, 33*(2), 157–161.

Gerbner, G. (1972). Violence in television drama: Trends and symbolic functions. In G. A. Comstock & E. A. Rubenstein (Eds.), *Media content and control*, Television and social behavior (Vol. 1, pp. 28–127). Washington, DC: U.S. Government Printing Office.

Gerbner, G., & Gross, L. (1976). Living with television. *Journal of Communication, 26*(2), 172–199.

Gitlin, T. (1980). *The whole world is watching: Mass media in the making and unmaking of the New Left.* Berkeley: University of California Press.

Goffman, E. (1974). *Frame analysis.* Philadelphia: University of Pennsylvania Press.

Healey, J. (1995). *Race, ethnicity, gender, and class: The sociology of group conflict and change.* Thousand Oaks, CA: Pine Forge Press.

Lasswell, H. D. (1948). The structure and function of communication in society. In B. Lyman (Ed.). *The communication of ideas* (pp. 37–51). New York: Harper & Row.

National Communication Association. (1998). *The speaking, listening, and media literacy standards and competency statements for K–12 education.* Retrieved July 18, 2002, from: www.natcom.org/ Instruction/K-12/standards.pdf

Shannon, C., & Weaver, W. (1949). *The mathematical theory of communication.* Urbana: University of Illinois Press.

Stark, J. S., & Lowther, M. A. (1988). *Strengthening the ties that bind: Integrating undergraduate liberal and professional study.* Ann Arbor: University of Michigan.

Tuchman, G. (1978). The symbolic annihilation of women by the mass media. In G. Tuchman, A. K. Daniels, & J. W. Benet (Eds.), *Hearth and home: Images of women in the mass media* (pp. 5–38). New York: Oxford University Press.

Wulff, S. (1997). Media literacy. In W. G. Christ (Ed), *Media education assessment handbook* (pp. 123–142). Mahwah, NJ: Lawrence Erlbaum Associates.

PART I

AUDIENCES

Some people might argue that the audience is the most important element in our complex media system. We are, after all, the commodity that is bought and sold—bought for the price of the content provided by the media outlets, and sold by the media outlets to advertisers. Because the U.S. media system operates under the marketplace model, economic factors are paramount; and because a larger audience means greater advertising revenues, most media outlets strive to generate the largest possible audiences. If any given media text fails to bring in a large enough audience, it probably won't continue to be offered. It's not so much an "if we build it, they will come" perspective as an "if they don't come, we'll take it away." Because of the importance of knowing how many people are listening/watching/reading/and so on, each medium has its own mechanism for measuring audience size. Television programs, for example, live and die by the Nielsen ratings; the Audit Bureau of Circulations measures both magazine and newspaper circulation, and Arbitron is the key provider of radio ratings.

Yet the consideration of audience size is just one of several important attributes of media audiences. Size definitely does matter, but there's more to it than that; more even than size coupled with demographics. These aspects of the audience might seem the most important to media outlets, but perhaps that's just because they're the easiest things to measure and to quantify. Here, we'll ignore these traditional favorites of media organizations in favor of more scholarly considerations of audiences.

Before presenting the two chapters that make up the Audience section of the book, we should think about the nature of media audiences. We traditionally think of audience members as the receivers of the messages sent by the media (although of course the Internet and other new media allow the process of creating media to come full circle, when an audience member becomes a producer). Media audiences tend to be very large, heterogeneous (varied or diverse), and dispersed (spread over a wide area). We're also relatively anonymous; although when we're using new communications technologies such as the Internet we can sometimes be identified, usually the message sender doesn't really know who we are. Providing feedback to a content producer or media outlet is difficult, or at least involves greater effort than in other communication situations. Finally, there is debate over whether the media audience is active or passive. Some people argue we're nothing more than "couch potatoes," although if some of us are so involved that we actually begin to create content then we can be very active indeed.

At the very least, we are active enough so that we are the ones who initiate the communication process. We are invited to the communication event by virtue of the fact that media have produced content designed to appeal to us, but it is we who decide whether, when, and how we will partake. This book operates from the perspective that members of the media audience are active participants in the communication process. Excluding unintentional media exposure (such as when we're shopping in a store that has the radio on), we are the ones who approach the media. We decide which medium to use (TV or book?) and what specific content (a romance novel or a textbook?). We are not media victims, swayed to whatever perspectives we encounter. We use, interpret, and make sense of the media texts we consume as we go about our daily lives.

However, even though we're not passive dupes of the media, we have to remember that the media does matter. The media, taken as a whole, represents one of several social institutions that help us understand what it means to be a member of our society. These social institutions present to us and help instill in us the values, attitudes, and beliefs shared within our culture. In other words, much of the content produced by the media reflects society's dominant ideologies. And when we're exposed to so much material reproducing certain values and ignoring or denigrating others, we can't help but be affected in some way.

The chapters in this part of the book investigate the people who read, watch, listen, or otherwise engage with mediated messages. How do people interpret what they see and hear? Why and how do people use certain media or certain types of content? How are people affected by what they see and hear?

The 12 readings in these two Audience chapters represent two main emphases of media audience researchers. Chapter 2, *Considerations of Media Effects*, offers five readings reflecting both traditional social–scientific studies of media effects and critical cultural analyses that try to understand media effects more broadly. As mentioned in the preface and introduction, the readings represent a diverse array of viewpoints and voices (you'll agree with some authors more than others and prefer some authors' writing styles over others).

In Reading 2.1, Bradley Gorham reviews the social–scientific evidence demonstrating the effects that stereotypical images have on audiences—even on people who reject stereotypes. Travis Dixon, in Reading 2.2, reports on an experimental study investigating whether seeing stereotypical crime portrayals shapes perceptions of African Americans and crime. His findings suggest that participants tend to think of criminals as Black unless provided with overwhelming information that a suspect is White. Reading 2.3 presents another experiment. Cory Armstrong and Mindy McAdams examined how author gender influences the perceived credibility of Weblogs. Their findings suggest that gender stereotypes persist for credibility, especially for novice blog readers; experienced blog readers seemed to evaluate credibility by using indicators other than gender cues. Susannah Stern, in Reading 2.4, uses cultivation analysis to show that young girls (5–6 years old) who watch a lot of TV buy into what they see. Stern studied these girls' perceptions of beauty and found that heavy TV viewers—even at that young age—already believe that beauty is something to be purchased, that beauty is a feminine rather than a masculine attribute, and that being beautiful is easier when one is thin. Reading 2.5, by Michelle Wolf, Sandra Nichols, and Dave Decelle, presents the results of focus group interviews investigating media's influence on women's feelings about their body image. The authors extend traditional body image research to include not only straight women but also lesbians and bisexuals.

Chapter 3 addresses *Audience Reception, Use, and Interpretation of Media Content*. The first three readings in this chapter reflect on audience identity, considering identity as a social and cultural construction. To conduct her ethnographic study, Pamela Tracy (Reading 3.1) spent 10 months observing and talking with preteen girls at their school. She studied how the girls use popular music to understand and negotiate who they are in their social and cultural worlds (these negotiations included arguments featuring charges such as "Why don't you act your color?"). Gwendolyn Osborne (Reading 3.2) interviewed numerous Black women who read romance novels, looking at why it's important that these women find characters to whom they can relate; characters the interviewees described as "women who look like me." In Reading 3.3, Sheena Malhotra considers issues of ethnic, gender, and class identities as she reflects on how Bollywood films can evoke "home" for members of the South Asian diaspora (displaced or dispersed people).

The next four readings in this chapter move from looking at how audiences use the media to understand and negotiate their identities, to investigations of how audiences understand and make sense of specific examples of media content. Each shows—in different ways—how people's discussions and interpretations of media content can provide an understanding of contemporary race/gender relations. Debbie Owens (Reading 3.4) explores audience reactions to the Academy Award–winning film *Crash*. The film allows for sustained audience discourse about culture and ethnicity, gender, and race and racism. Similarly, Reading 3.5, by Dwight Brooks and George Daniels, explores audience reactions to Spike Lee's film *Bamboozled* and argues that how people interpreted this film had everything to do with who those people were. Richard King (Reading 3.6) analyzed audience response to and understanding of Native American mascots by looking at what *USA Weekend* readers had to say about whether sports teams should continue to use such mascots. King claims that these audience discussions are actually arguments about race. In Reading 3.7, Rebecca Lind found that to White viewers, a TV news story about housing discrimination was essentially irrelevant—reflecting what she calls "passive racism."

Taken as a whole, the readings in this section of the book illustrate the range of audience research that can be conducted. They also highlight the need to go far beyond merely counting how many people are consuming media texts. Remember, the average American household has the TV on for more than 8 hours a day—and although TV is our dominant medium, it's not the only one we use. We should understand how people are affected by the media, how and why people use media in their daily lives, and how people make sense of or interpret what they see/read/hear.

CHAPTER 2

CONSIDERATIONS OF MEDIA EFFECTS

2.1 THE SOCIAL PSYCHOLOGY OF STEREOTYPES: IMPLICATIONS FOR MEDIA AUDIENCES

Bradley W. Gorham

The author reviews the social scientific evidence demonstrating how stereotypical images affect media audiences. Don't be too quick to say, "The media don't affect me!"

On September 25, 1996, as part of a series on race relations in America, ABC's *Nightline* featured a short video clip that I often use in my classes on media effects. The video shows a large, stern-faced Black man in a white T-shirt in a classic mug-shot pose: The man is seen in profile, and then the camera slowly turns to face the man head-on. As the camera turns toward the classic head-on mug shot, the following words are slowly revealed: "Armed robbery . . . Battery . . . Drug Possession . . . Concealed weapon . . . Apprehended . . . March 1994 by . . . Police Officer . . . Robert Williams . . . shown here." Ted Koppel then comes on and asks viewers if they "fell for the premise of that video" and confides that he and much of the *Nightline* staff did. So did I the first time I saw it. So do most of my students.

The trick, of course, is that we are led to believe that the person shown in the video is the perpetrator of these crimes, a belief that's proven wrong by the last set of words. The Black man in the "mug shot" is the police officer, but a few seconds before, most people naturally assumed that he was the criminal. Do we think this because the man is Black? At this point, a small ruckus usually ensues, as my students bristle at the notion that the race of the man might have affected their interpretation of the video. They inevitably point out that if you did the same thing with a White guy, they'd think the same thing. After all, they argue, it's the format of the video—the mug shot, the crimes listed next to it, and so on—that tricks the viewer, not the man's race. They'd think *exactly* the same thing no matter what the race of the man pictured.

Well, not quite.

Although the format of the video clearly plays an important role in steering people toward the belief that the man pictured is the criminal, research in social psychology and media effects suggests a man's race also plays a role. In fact, experiments altering the race of suspects shown in TV news stories have found that people do *not* make exactly the same interpretations; this is true even for people who don't endorse any type of prejudice or bigotry.

In other words, race really does seem to affect how we interpret media, especially in subtle ways. My purpose here is to help explain why this is so and what it means for media audiences.

THE SOCIAL PSYCHOLOGY OF STEREOTYPES

It's important to realize at the outset that stereotypes aren't simply something that only bigots have experience with. We all know about stereotypes, and we're all pretty familiar with the stereotypes of various social groups circulating in our culture. In fact, research has shown that when asked to list the traits defining the cultural stereotype of Blacks, both high- and low-prejudiced people come up with essentially the same list (Devine & Elliot, 1995), including traits such as poor, hostile, uneducated, athletic, and rhythmic. It's only when asked to list their personal beliefs about Blacks that we see a difference: High-prejudiced people tend to list the same traits they listed for the cultural stereotype, while low-prejudiced respondents tend to list other, more positive traits. However, the cultural stereotype seems to play an important role in how we process information about people from various groups regardless of whether we endorse it. To understand this, we need to examine what a stereotype is more generally.

Psychologists Hamilton & Trolier (1986) defined a stereotype as "a cognitive structure that contains the perceiver's knowledge, beliefs, and expectancies about some human group" (p. 133). This definition highlights an important characteristic of stereotypes: They are structures in our minds, and as such, they function in much the same way as other structures in our minds do. Psychologists call these cognitive structures *schema* and believe that schema help simplify a complex social environment by quickly and efficiently processing incoming stimuli based on the presence of a few relevant characteristics. We have schema about objects (chairs, bicycles), events (what happens when we go to a restaurant), and people. Schemas help us categorize the world by telling us the basic characteristics of the things we encounter. This allows us to make judgments about our environment without having to expend much mental effort. Our dog schema, for example, says that dogs bark and have fur, four legs, and a tail. So when we see a creature with these basic characteristics, we don't have to examine it much further to know it's a dog and how we will act or respond. *A stereotype, then, is a schema for people we perceive as belonging to a social group.*

Schemas help structure not only our knowledge of things but also our expectations. Because they tell us what characteristics the category usually contains, schemas lead us to expect certain things once other traits of a category have been encountered. Thus, when we encounter someone of a particular social group, whether based on gender, race, ethnicity, sexual orientation, occupation, or something else, the schema we have for that group tells us what features or traits we should expect to encounter. Using the information stored in our schema for Latinos, for example, we can quickly make judgments about a Latina and our potential interaction with her without having to expend much mental energy to evaluate the person in great detail.

This expectation that we should see additional features associated with a schema once any features of the schema are encountered is called *priming*. Once we see or hear something in the environment that activates a schema, related concepts tend to be primed, or triggered, and we're more likely to expect them and respond to them than to unrelated concepts. This should especially be true when the schema is something we encounter often through repeated and consistent exposure. A primed concept is thought to be more accessible to our consciousness (and our cognitive processing). Furthermore, because we expect them, primed concepts can influence how we perceive subsequent information. That is, because we're looking for the primed concepts, we're more likely to perceive incoming stimuli as containing the traits and features our schema have taught us to expect. *In this way, priming tends to alter our interpretations of things toward what fits (is congruent with) our schema.*

Stereotypes, then, are schema that help organize our knowledge and beliefs about social groups. They also structure our expectations and influence how we perceive incoming messages. A landmark study in social psychology can help make all these concepts more concrete. Devine (1989) thought that because stereotypes are so pervasive in the media and in our everyday interactions with others, they become very well learned. Stereotypes become so well learned, she argued, that when we encounter someone of a particular social group, the stereotype for that group is primed and automatically activated and influences subsequent cognitive processing (the interpretation of the situation).

To test her hypothesis, Devine (1989) first primed research participants (all of whom were White) by showing them a set of words flashed on a screen so quickly that they couldn't consciously identify or recall them. Some people saw words that were consistent with stereotypes of Blacks, while others saw words that were not consistent with those stereotypes. People then read a paragraph about a person of unspecified race doing things that could be interpreted either as an aggressive shove or a playful push and evaluated that person.

What Devine found was that when subconsciously primed with words reflecting racial stereotypes, almost everybody (both prejudiced and non-prejudiced people) evaluated the racially unspecified target person in a fashion congruent with the stereotype. That is, people were more likely to think the person in the story was aggressive and hostile if they'd been primed with the Black stereotype. This was true regardless of whether the person endorsed the Black stereotype. Furthermore, although the prime words avoided references to hostility (part of the stereotype of Black men), people still activated that portion of the stereotype. As a result, Devine concluded that stereotypes are so well learned that they become automatically triggered in individuals whenever a person from that particular group is encountered.

Devine (1989) also found that there were important differences between knowledge of the stereotype and endorsement of it, and between high- and low-prejudiced individuals. She gave a different group of people 1 minute to list as many terms as they could think of, both socially acceptable and not, for the group "Black Americans." Shortly afterward, participants wrote down all of their thoughts and reactions to the term "Black Americans" and the labels they had just generated. While both low- and high-prejudiced people came up with similar numbers of pejorative and non-pejorative terms in the first task (reflecting the automatic and pervasive nature of the stereotype), there were significant differences in the second. Highly prejudiced people were much more likely to include stereotypical thoughts than less-prejudiced people were—despite the fact that the stereotype had been primed in all of them and that their label-listing task showed no significant differences. Devine concluded that low-prejudiced people used some type of controlled cognitive processing to suppress the automatically activated stereotype. They also seemed reluctant to try to describe the group as a whole. Thus, both high- and low-prejudiced people have the schema for the stereotype of Blacks, but it appears that only highly prejudiced individuals endorse it. Low-prejudiced individuals actively try to suppress it.

Since Devine's study was published, research has blossomed about how stereotypes can be triggered without us even being aware of it. The results are pretty clear: Stereotypes of various social groups can be activated automatically, and they can influence how we interpret incoming information (Blair & Banaji, 1996). What is even more disconcerting is that stereotypes can activate and influence processing even when people don't endorse them. Fortunately, research suggests that people can inhibit these tendencies if they know about them (Monteith, 1993) and if they have the cognitive capacity to work against them (Blair & Banaji, 1996). At the very least, people can try to work around stereotypes once they've been activated (Devine, 1989).

It's important to keep in mind that stereotypes often offer explanations about the groups they categorize. This is an especially nasty characteristic of many stereotypes: Not only can they tell us what people of a social group are like, but they also tell us *why* the people are like that. For example, Devine and Elliot (1995) showed that many people chose "poor" and "lazy" as traits describing the social stereotype of Blacks. It doesn't take much effort to link these and say that the stereotype is "Blacks are poor because they are lazy." In a broader sense, one can say that a stereotype asserts that people of a group simply *are* a certain way, and these "natural tendencies" lead to particular behaviors more often for that group than for others.

There's a lot of research about how people explain the behaviors of people belonging to various social groups. The theory of the *ultimate attribution error* (Pettigrew, 1979), for example, explains the behaviors of "ingroups" and "outgroups" as functions of either "internal" or "external" causes. Ingroups are the groups of people we identify with or feel we belong to (males, or Blacks, or Irish, or Chevy truck owners), while outgroups are people who are "not like us." Pettigrew argued that when we see a person doing something, we make an inference about why the person behaved that way. Maybe we think the person is simply responding to the situation, in a sense being pushed by external forces to act that way. On the other hand, we might infer the behavior is the result of the individual's personality or some other internal characteristic of the person and has nothing to do with the situation.

Pettigrew (1979) argued that the inferences we make about people's behaviors are biased in favor of our ingroups—we make the ingroups we identify with look good and the outgroups we don't identify with look bad. In Pettigrew's theory, ingroup members seeing someone doing something bad will be more likely to attribute that behavior to internal causes if the person is from an outgroup. But if it's an ingroup member doing it, they'll attribute the same bad behavior to external factors. At the same time, if we see a man do something good, we're more likely to infer that he had to do it under the circumstances (an external cause) if he's from an outgroup. But we'll think it represents "just how that guy is" if he is from a group we identify with. The relevance of this for racial stereotypes should be clear: White people could be more likely to think a Black person committing a crime did so because "that's what those people are like" (an internal characteristic of Black people), whereas a White person could be driven to the crime by bad parenting, alcohol addiction, or some other external factor. Likewise, positive behaviors will likely be attributed to external causes when performed by outgroup members and internal causes when performed by members of the ingroup. Thus, the ingroup is always held in higher esteem, because good behaviors are seen as internal to the group, whereas bad behaviors are the result of negative external influences.

It's important to keep in mind that, even though these cognitive mechanisms operate outside of our conscious awareness, they appear to support positive views of ourselves. This implies that, even if people don't endorse stereotypes, members of dominant social groups interpret information in ways that support their superiority and, by extension, reinforce the subordinate position of minority groups. Stereotypes are rarely neutral, and so they not only attempt to describe and explain the behavior of groups, but they also evaluate those groups based on the norms of the majority. For example, Peffley, Hurwitz, and Sniderman (1997) found that racial stereotypes played an important role in people's opinions about welfare mothers and criminals, but only when those welfare mothers and criminals were Black. Furthermore, people's opinions about welfare mothers were closely related to beliefs about Blacks' commitment to the work ethic, suggesting that the explanation that "Black welfare mothers do not want to work because they are inherently lazy" was more salient than a similar belief about White welfare mothers. This is hardly a neutral belief in a society brought up to believe in the value of hard work and merit-based rewards, and thus the stereotype of Blacks as lazy and uneducated may make it harder for many Whites to accept that the Black community should receive "extra" help or economic aid.

Stereotypes clearly don't give us the "whole picture" of a group, as if such a thing is even possible, and they aren't neutral in their evaluations. Instead, stereotypes give us highly edited and distorted images of groups that tend to support the way groups are treated in society. Cultural stereotypes of minority groups, especially, tend to reflect the biases and the histories of the majority, such that the people being stereotyped are reduced to a few characteristics that are socially relevant for understanding that group's place in society. The important thing to realize about this is that stereotypes often perform this function without our conscious awareness or control. We may not endorse these stereotypes at all, nor have any intention of seeing the world through prejudicial lenses. But unfortunately, *a stereotype, as just another schema that helps us process the world around us, helps maintain a view of that world that works in favor of the majority.*

STEREOTYPES AND THEIR EFFECTS ON MEDIA AUDIENCES

All of this research by social psychologists has not gone unnoticed by media researchers. Although relatively small compared to the body of work studying the stereotypes present in media content, a growing area of media studies uses psychological research to examine the effects of such images on audiences. For example, Peffley, Shields, and Williams (1996) investigated how manipulating the race of a suspect in a television news story affected viewers' interpretation of that story. In a sense, they tested the assertion my students make after viewing the *Nightline* segment described earlier—the race of the suspect doesn't matter because the story's format makes the suspect seem guilty. The researchers asked a sample of White students to fill out a survey about a variety of social issues (including questions measuring prejudice toward African Americans). A week later, the students watched a brief television news story about the murder of a prostitute. The story contained a 7-second video clip of the suspect, which the researchers had "manipulated." Half the students saw the news story with a Black suspect, and the other half saw a White suspect. Otherwise, the stories were identical. Students were asked about their reactions to the news story and the suspect in particular.

Peffley et al. (1996) found that the race of the suspect did indeed make a difference, but so did the level of prejudice of the viewer. People with negative stereotypes of Blacks judged the Black suspect more likely to be guilty and deserving more jail time than the White suspect, thus employing a "racially discriminatory double standard" (p. 316). People with positive stereotypes of Blacks, on the other hand, judged the White suspect as more guilty and deserving more jail time than the Black suspect. The only people who judged the suspects more or less equally were those who held neutral stereotypes toward Blacks. *Even a 7-second visual of a Black man in handcuffs was enough to trigger the Black stereotype, and the stereotype then affected the way the news story was interpreted.*

Power, Murphy, and Coover (1996) also believed priming played a role in the effects of race-related images. Of particular interest was how the causal attributions (primed by stereotypes) varied based on the race of the people involved. The researchers suspected that when negative racial stereotypes are primed, people's subsequent evaluations of a Black person in a news story would suggest that the bad behaviors discussed in the story were caused by the internal characteristics of Black people. On the other hand, people might be less willing to make such internal attributions of behavior if they were first exposed to a Black person who countered the stereotype. To test this, Power et al. (1996) asked students to evaluate a new campus newsletter featuring an autobiography of an African American student named Chris Miller (his race was indicated by the use of a photograph). The autobiographical information was manipulated such that in one version of the newsletter (the stereotypical condition), Miller was described using information relevant to four traits prominent in the stereotype of Blacks: lazy, unintelligent, aggressive, and engaging in socially destructive behavior. In a different version of the newsletter (the counter-stereotypical condition), Miller was described using the opposite of these four traits: hardworking, intelligent, gentle, and engaged in socially constructive behaviors.

In what they thought was an unrelated study, participants then evaluated two media events—the beating of Rodney King and Magic Johnson's disclosure of his HIV status—and rated the degree to which the two were victims of circumstance or had brought their fate upon themselves. The results showed that people who read the stereotyped version of the campus newsletter were more likely to blame King and Johnson for their circumstances and thus attribute the problems to the men's own failings. People who had seen the counter-stereotypical newsletter were less likely to make these internal attributions, instead believing that King and Johnson were victims of circumstance. Thus, the Power et al. (1996) study suggested that *stereotypes in media can lead to message processing that supports the ultimate attribution error.*

Domke, McCoy, and Torres (1999) wondered whether stories about race-related issues such as immigration could prime racial perceptions of relevant groups even if race was not specifically mentioned. Given that beliefs about race are relatively accessible schema, Domke et al. suggested that discussions of issues such as immigration, which are usually framed with a particular racial group in mind, might activate relevant racial stereotypes just because the issue is so frequently linked with race. The researchers asked subjects their positions on issues and their impressions of how common certain qualities are among members of racial and ethnic groups; they found that when people read news stories linking immigration with economics, their position on immigration was significantly related to their perceptions of Hispanics as violent, nurturing, and lazy. Furthermore, perceptions of Hispanics as violent or intelligent—both of which could make Hispanics seem a threat to U.S. communities or jobs—were related to anti-immigration attitudes and the view that immigration hurts the U.S. economy in general. Other research participants read news stories about immigration that stressed the principles governing admitting the "huddled masses yearning to breathe free" into the nation. For this group, positions on immigration weren't correlated with even one stereotypical characteristic of Hispanics.

Thus, the way immigration was framed in the news stories activated people's racial cognitions differently, and these cognitions subsequently affected people's broader interpretations of the issue. Domke et al. (1999) concluded that news frames can significantly affect the linkages people make between their perceptions of racial groups and race-relevant political issues. This is a concern because it suggests that *how the media talk about an issue can influence whether people use stereotypes to understand that issue, even when people don't endorse the stereotypes.* If people use stereotypes to understand a political issue, then the decisions they make in their civic life may have negative consequences for the groups being stereotyped—whether we intend it or not. In this way, portrayals in the media might help perpetuate discrimination and negativity toward some groups.

IMPLICATIONS FOR MEDIA AUDIENCES

Perhaps the most important implication to arise from this discussion of research about stereotypes is that stereotypes can influence our processing and understanding of media messages even when we're not aware of it. As the *Nightline* clip demonstrated, we may be led down one path by our processing of stereotypical information only to discover that we went down a path of stereotypes and prejudice that we wouldn't normally endorse and that violates our own ideals and morals. *The way our brains process information may lead us to think things we don't even agree with.* That is, we may automatically make stereotype-congruent interpretations of news stories or film snippets even though we reject the stereotype in question. This is especially troublesome given that stereotypes tend to be negative for all minority groups in society and that the application of stereotypes to political issues tends to hurt minority groups and keep members of majority groups looking good. If crime in Black neighborhoods is seen simply as the result of inherently aggressive Black people who don't want to work, then there's no incentive for people to tackle the economic causes of crime or implement solutions that might prevent crime in those neighborhoods. When performed by White kids in the suburbs, however, crime may instead be seen as preventable if the external forces acting on these kids can be alleviated. Thus lawmakers may provide resources for these kids but not kids in troubled Black neighborhoods.

Given the number of mass-media messages we consume on a daily basis, the potential for negative cumulative effects seems great. Each representation of a member of a social group could potentially trigger the stereotype of that group, giving viewers an example that helps reinforce the majority's dominance. There is much evidence that the media perpetuate stereotypical images, so if audiences interpret those images in ways that subtly support the stereotypes, then a lot of prejudice-congruent messages are being digested. Local television news, for example, often contains images of Blacks that reinforce the dominant cultural stereotype of Blacks as dangerous (Entman, 1990; see also Josey et al's piece in this book). If news is seen as an objective and accurate description of "the way it is," then those stereotypical images will help reinforce the truthfulness of the stereotype and the "explanation" that violence in Black neighborhoods is the result of the natural tendencies of Blacks themselves. Such an explanation excuses the majority from intervening, thus helping keep the majority in control.

Our own cognitive processing system may inadvertently reinforce the dominant positions some social groups enjoy, despite our conscious intentions to the contrary. As I've argued elsewhere (Gorham, 1999), this may help explain why prejudice and racism is such an entrenched problem. If the unconscious processing of information tends to push even low-prejudiced people toward making stereotype-congruent interpretations, no wonder we have such a hard time trying to put an end to prejudice. Furthermore, if the images and portrayals of groups in mass media enhance or reinforce our tendency to interpret information in stereotypical ways, then the media are inadvertently helping make the problem of prejudice and discrimination worse. The calls for change in media images are justified, but real progress will only be made when we also understand our role in the perpetuation of prejudice.

IT'S YOUR TURN: WHAT DO YOU THINK? WHAT WILL YOU FIND?

1. Discuss a news story you've recently encountered in terms of how it might prime stereotypes. What sorts of interpretations would you expect people to make based on those stereotypes?

2. What can news organizations do to try to limit the extent to which news stories automatically activate stereotypes?

3. Examine a magazine ad. How and to what extent might it prime our stereotypes to its advantage? How would you change the ad content so that it gets the desired message across without triggering people's stereotypes?

4. What can audience members do to try to counteract the effects of the automatic activation of stereotypes?

REFERENCES

Blair, I.V., & Banaji, M. R. (1996). Automatic and controlled processes in stereotype priming. *Journal of Personality and Social Psychology, 70*(6), 1142–1163.

Devine, P. G. (1989). Stereotypes and prejudice: Their automatic and controlled components. *Journal of Personality and Social Psychology, 56*, 5–18.

Devine, P. G., & Elliot, A. J. (1995). Are racial stereotypes really fading? The Princeton trilogy revisited. *Personality and Social Psychology Bulletin, 21*(11), 1139–1150.

Domke, D., McCoy, K., & Torres, M. (1999). News media, racial perceptions and political cognition. *Communication Research, 26*(5), 570–607.

Entman, R. M. (1990). Modern racism and the images of Blacks in local television news. *Critical Studies in Mass Communication, 7*, 332–345.

Gorham, B. W. (1999). Stereotypes in the media: So what? *Howard Journal of Communications, 10*, 229–247.

Hamilton, D. L., & Trolier, T. K. (1986). Stereotypes and stereotyping: An overview of the cognitive approach. In J. F. Dovidio & S. L. Gaertner (Eds.), *Prejudice, discrimination, and racism* (pp. 127–163). New York: Academic Press.

Monteith, M. (1993). Self-regulation of prejudiced responses: Implications for progress in prejudice-reduction efforts. *Journal of Personality and Social Psychology, 65,* 469–485.

Peffley, M., Hurwitz, J., & Sniderman, P. M. (1997). Racial stereotypes and Whites' political views of Blacks in the context of welfare and crime. *American Journal of Political Science, 41*(1), 30–60.

Peffley, M., Shields, T., & Williams, B. (1996). The intersection of race and crime in television news stories: An experimental study. *Political Communication, 13,* 309–327.

Pettigrew, T. F. (1979). The ultimate attribution error: Extending Allport's cognitive analysis of prejudice. *Personality and Social Psychology Bulletin, 5*(4), 461–476.

Power, J. G., Murphy, S. T., & Coover, G. (1996). Priming prejudice: How stereotypes and counter-stereotypes influence attribution or responsibility and credibility among ingroups and outgroups. *Human Communication Research, 23,* 36–58.

2.2 "HE WAS A BLACK GUY": HOW NEWS'S MISREPRESENTATION OF CRIME CREATES FEAR OF BLACKS

Travis L. Dixon

This experimental study investigates whether seeing stereotypical crime portrayals shapes perceptions of African Americans and crime. It builds on prior research that revealed that news tends to associate Blacks with negative stereotypical behavior. This association might then influence viewers' conceptions of both Blacks and crime—sometimes without the viewer being fully aware of this.

In my contribution to an earlier edition of this book, I recounted a story of how many of my friends and family felt a tenseness in their throat when they watched the news and some horrible crime had occurred. Their tense reaction was because they feared that if the news revealed the perpetrator was Black, it would reinforce the stereotype that many Blacks are criminals. Others, particularly those outside of the Black community, would then use that stereotype to unfairly judge other African Americans, the vast majority of whom are not criminals.

Knowing for sure whether the news over-associates Blacks with crime is the first step in establishing that news viewing influences whether people stereotype Blacks as criminals. The chapter that I wrote in the earlier edition, and some of my other work, documented how the news indeed appears to depict a world in which African Americans are overrepresented as criminals. There is a growing amount of research that establishes support for this first step.

The next step requires that we provide evidence that the news actually influences people's perceptions. This means that we must go beyond content assessments. We need to learn whether seeing these portrayals affects viewer's beliefs and attitudes. This chapter discusses a study that does just this. I report on an experiment where I exposed viewers to a news program that contained a majority of White criminals, a majority of Black criminals, a number of unidentified criminals, or non-crime stories. Afterward, I asked them about the race of the perpetrators in the stories and their views about the police and danger. Before I provide more description of what I did, I will give you some background so you can understand why I approached the topic this way.

BACKGROUND: STUDIES OF CONTENT AND EFFECTS

A number of research studies have concluded that local news programs often misrepresent African Americans as the primary perpetrators responsible for crime (Dixon & Linz, 2000a; Entman, 1992; 1994). For example, in some of my prior work, I found that Blacks were twice as likely as Whites to be portrayed as perpetrators of crime on local television news (Dixon & Linz, 2000a). In addition, African Americans were six times more likely to be depicted as perpetrators than as police officers on news programs. Furthermore, Blacks were overrepresented as criminals on the news, representing 37% of the perpetrators shown while composing only 21% of those arrested according to crime reports.

These findings are in stark contrast to the ways in which Whites typically appear on local news programs (Dixon & Linz, 2000a, 2000b). Whites appear as police officers twice as often as they appear as criminals, and they are overrepresented as officers (69%) on news programs compared to employment records (59%). In addition, Whites are more than twice as likely to appear as victims compared to Blacks, and they are overrepresented as victims in news stories (43%) compared to crime reports (13%). These studies, as well as a number of others, indicate that African Americans are much more often associated with criminality on television news in comparison to Whites.

Many scholars interested in the effects of distorted racial portrayals have used two theories to guide their investigations: cognitive accessibility theory and spreading activation theory. *Cognitive accessibility* theory suggests that people use mental shortcuts to make social judgments. So if you encounter something or someone related to the stereotype you might make a judgment about the person or thing based on repeated exposure to the stereotype.

Under certain circumstances, television news imagery of a majority of African American rather than White criminals might prime or activate a "Black criminal stereotype" when making social reality judgments regarding race and crime. If frequently activated due to media exposure, it may become chronically or easily accessible. This means that after exposure to a majority of Black rather than White criminals in the news, the Black criminal stereotype becomes activated (usually without the perceiver even being aware) and influences judgments related to race and crime (Bargh, Chen, & Burrows, 1996; Devine, 1989; Shrum, 2002). Even exposure to crime news devoid of racial identifiers may be enough to trigger the Black criminal stereotype (Devine, 1989; Shrum, 2002).

The other theory of interest, *spreading activation*, says that stereotypes form an associative network of related ideas or schemas linked in memory, and activating one idea spreads to other linked notions. In other words, we understand, remember, and evaluate the world based on the associations that are linked in our brain. So the link between two things (e.g., Black people and crime) can also influence the association between other things (e.g., fear of Blacks and support for the police). In short, people may make judgments about race-related issues based on their racial perceptions.

Thus exposure to a majority of Black rather than White perpetrators or race-unidentified suspects may activate other notions such as "fear of crime" and "protection from criminal activity." Such exposure may conjure notions of crime as a largely Black phenomenon that requires police intervention due to a Black predisposition toward criminal activity (Hewstone, 1990; Pettigrew, 1979). Prior research has found that exposure to Black criminality in the news encourages the endorsement of punitive crime policy and politicians (Gilliam & Iyengar, 2000; Valentino, 1999).

In addition, exposure to a majority of Black rather than White suspects or unidentified suspects in the news may cause viewers to misremember a non-Black suspect as Black (Gilliam & Iyengar, 2000; Oliver & Fonash, 2002). The Black criminal stereotype may influence encoding and memory such that stimuli may be recalled in a manner congruent with the schema (Fiske & Taylor, 1991). Once the Black criminal stereotype is activated, it also activates a generalized schema of African Americans (Ford, 1997). The mismemory effect described above results directly from "ambiguous" targets being processed and remembered in congruence with the activated schema (Devine, 1989; Fiske & Taylor, 1991). This occurs partly because under high-stress conditions or when decisions have to be made quickly, perceivers utilize what is most available to them in order to make decisions. Once the African American schema is activated, it is available for use and requires fewer cognitive resources than other decision-making processes.

Thus far I have described a two-part process. First, exposure to either a majority of Black rather than White suspects or a majority of unidentified suspects may prime the Black criminal stereotype. Second, after this stereotype is primed, schematic processing and spreading activation lead to various perceptual effects. Below, I provide an overview and the hypotheses or predictions of the current study.

HYPOTHESES AND METHOD

This study was designed to assess whether exposure to a majority of Black rather than White suspects or unidentified suspects increased support for the police. This study was also designed to determine the extent to which participants tended to cognitively associate unidentified suspects with Black suspects. Based on the priming paradigm and theories of stereotyping described above, I propose the following hypotheses:

Hypothesis 1: Exposure to a majority of Black rather than White suspects in the news will lead to mismemory of a non-Black suspect as Black and more support for the police.

Hypothesis 2: Exposure to race-unidentified suspects will activate the Black criminal stereotype and lead to mismemory of a non-Black suspect as Black and increased support for the police.

I wanted to be sure that people would tell me their real views and not what they thought I wanted to hear. Therefore, I used an experiment. Experiments are powerful because if done properly, they can provide good evidence for whether one thing (e.g., watching the news) causes something else (e.g., racialized perception of Blacks). Participants came into a laboratory and watched a news program and then completed some questionnaires. I did not tell them that I was actually interested in their views about race and crime policy.

The 20-minute news program they viewed contained seven crime stories about murder and eight "fluff" or distracter stories (i.e., human interest stories that contained no violence, crime, or disasters). Photographs of suspects in the murder stories were manipulated so that the experiment had three conditions: a) a majority of Black suspects, b) a majority of White suspects, and c) race of the suspects was not identified. I pretested the photographs to ensure that any potential outcomes were not due to differences in how the suspects were depicted. There were no differences between the Black and White photos on how menacing or dangerous they looked.

After viewing the news program, participants responded to a number of bogus memory items. At the end of this questionnaire the first murder story that participants had viewed during the manipulation was re-described to them. They were then asked to recount the race of the suspected murderer presented in that one news story. The crime story was the same in every condition, and except in the condition where all perpetrators were race unidentified, the murder suspect was always an identical White male. I was interested in the extent to which participants correctly remembered the race of the suspect as being non-Black.

At this point, a "second experimenter" entered the room. Participants were told that because they had signed up for a 1-hour experiment, they would complete the hour by assisting the second experimenter with another task. The second experimenter explained to them that they were pretesting a questionnaire to determine how long it takes to complete. However, the real purpose was to have participants complete the police-support measure along with a number of distracter/pretend questions. Once they completed the "second study," participants were debriefed and told the true purpose of the experiment. One hundred and forty-seven White male and female undergraduate students enrolled in an introductory communication studies course at a large Midwestern university were randomly assigned to one of the three conditions.

Two dependent measures (or sets of questions) were used in this study. Each consisted of several Likert scale items ranging from 1 (not very likely, definitely not, disagree) to 7 (very likely, definitely, agree). The first measure asked the extent to which participants supported the police force. The items tap the extent to which participants believe that police officers are a positive force in society. Police officers have received scrutiny regarding whether they contribute to or alleviate crime problems (Sunnafrank & Fontes, 1983). In fact, one could argue that citizens hold complex and often contradictory views of officers. However, once people feel threatened by crime, they most likely invoke positive thoughts about those (e.g., the police) who are charged with their protection (Valentino, 1999). In the current study, participants were asked to agree or disagree with a number of items designed to assess whether they held a positive view of the police, including "Police officers should get more respect," "Most police officers are good people," and "People exaggerate when they say that most police are corrupt." Exposure to a majority of Black suspects or race-unidentified criminality should increase feelings/thoughts regarding crime protection and this in turn should lead to positive thoughts about the police.

The second dependent variable was a two-item measure that assessed the extent to which participants misremembered as Black a non-Black suspect re-described at the end of the bogus memory questionnaire (e.g., "The suspect was definitely Black"). This measure assessed the extent to which participants were confident that they saw a Black suspect during the newscast even though we asked them to recount the race of a White suspect (or unidentified suspect in the race-unidentified condition). The higher participants score on this measure, the more they have incorrectly recalled the race of the suspect as Black.

RESULTS

All statistical tests were conducted at the $p < .05$ significance level, using Analyses of Variance (ANOVAs). ANOVA is a statistic that allows us to compare on average whether any differences exist for those who saw a majority of Black suspects, a majority of White suspects, or race-unidentified suspects.

Hypotheses 1 and 2 predicted that exposure to a majority of Black rather than White suspects or race-unidentified suspects in the news will lead to increased support for the police. The ANOVA for police support appears to provide support for these hypotheses. It revealed a significant main effect for exposure condition, $F(2, 145) = 5.62, p < .01, \eta_p^2 = .07$. Those who were either exposed to a majority of Black suspects (M [mean] = 4.61, SD [standard deviation] = .12) or race-unidentified suspects (M = 4.94, SD = .17) were significantly more likely than those exposed to a majority of White suspects (M = 4.25, SD = .12) to support the police. There were no statistically significant differences between those exposed to a majority of Black suspects and those exposed to race-unidentified suspects in terms of their support for the police.

The ANOVA for mismemory revealed results practically identical to the police-support measure. It revealed a significant main effect for exposure condition, $F(2, 145) = 7.71, p < .001, \eta_p^2 = .09$. Those who were either exposed to a majority of Black suspects (M = 4.11, SD = .22) or race-unidentified suspects (M = 4.04, SD = .32) were more likely than those exposed to a majority of White suspects (M = 3.04, SD = .21) to misremember a non-Black suspect as being Black. Most notably, there were no significant differences between those exposed to a majority of Black suspects and those exposed to race-unidentified suspects in terms of their mismemory.

DISCUSSION

In this study, two significant findings appear to have emerged that provide some support for Hypotheses 1 and 2. First, participants exposed to a majority of African American suspects or to a number of race-unidentified suspects showed increased support for the police. This provides evidence that racialized crime news invokes the Black criminality stereotype that in turn activates a cognitive linkage between Black suspects and perceived threat level. The increased sense of threat manifests in support for the authorities responsible for protection. Moreover, the Black criminal stereotype appears to be invoked whether participants are exposed to a majority of Black suspects or whether they simply encounter race-unidentified suspects.

Second, this study provides some evidence that complements prior research suggesting that viewers tend to think of unidentified suspects as Black suspects (Gilliam & Iyengar, 2000; Oliver & Fonash, 2002). When exposed to a number of unidentified suspects, participants were more likely to "guess" that the suspects were African American rather than White. This suggests that participants tend to think of criminals as Black unless provided with overwhelming information that a suspect is White. This finding offers support for the notion that a cognitive link has been formed between criminality and African Americans, which is reinforced by news programming.

Moderators and Fighting the Stereotype

One question that I did not examine in the current study is this: What kinds of things moderate (make weaker or stronger) these effects? We know from prior research that people who are already prejudiced against Blacks tend to be even more likely to use the stereotype in judgment after watching racialized news (Dixon, 2006a; Gilliam & Iyengar, 2000). There is also some evidence that suggests that people of color are less likely to use the stereotype when exposed to biased media coverage (Dixon, 2006a; Gilliam & Iyengar, 2000). However, there is also research that says that being a heavy news viewer makes you more likely to use the stereotype in judgment (Dixon, 2006a, 2006b).

So what are our options if we want to resist the effects of negative media coverage? The first step, of course, is to make a conscious decision to resist prejudice and stereotyping. The more we can resist thinking of people in a stereotypical ways, the less potent the media message. Many scholars have uncovered evidence that reflective thinking before making a judgment deflates the use of the stereotype (Devine, 1989; Livingston & Brewer, 2002).

The second step is to actually be very careful of what you watch. You should definitely expose yourself to the news, but you should consider what kind of news you consume. Be very careful of crime news, and approach it with a critical eye.

Third, as citizens, you should consider becoming involved in actually writing media outlets and advocating for more balanced coverage of topics. In theory, broadcast television operates with a license from the government, and they have a duty to be responsive to people from the community to retain that license. However, no matter what you decide, you should know that the media do have an effect and that we all play a part in dealing with it.

IT'S YOUR TURN: WHAT DO YOU THINK? WHAT WILL YOU FIND?

1. If you wanted to counter the negative effects of the news as a journalist or editor, how would you change the coverage?

2. Have you ever thought about an issue in the news, and a racial group just came to your mind even if they were not shown? If so, what group(s)? Why do you think this is, and do you think there is any way to stop it? Would it be helpful to stop it?

3. Watch politicians in the news. Do you see any subtle racial cues when they talk about certain issues? If so, what are the issues? What are the subtle cues?

REFERENCES

Bargh, J. A., Chen, M., & Burrows, L. (1996). Automaticity of social behavior: Direct effects of trait construct and stereotype activation on action. *Journal of Personality & Social Psychology, 71*, 230–244.

Devine, P. G. (1989). Stereotypes and prejudice: Their automatic and controlled components. *Journal of Personality & Social Psychology, 56*, 5–18.

Dixon, T. L. (2006a). Psychological reactions to crime news portrayals of Black criminals: Understanding the moderating roles of prior news viewing and stereotype endorsement. *Communication Monographs, 73*, 162–187.

Dixon, T. L. (2006b). Schemas as average conceptions: Skin tone, television news exposure, and culpability judgments. *Journalism and Mass Communication Quarterly, 83*, 131–149.

Dixon, T. L., & Linz, D. G. (2000a). Overrepresentation and underrepresentation of African Americans and Latinos as lawbreakers on television news. *Journal of Communication, 50*(2), 131–154.

Dixon, T. L., & Linz, D. G. (2000b). Race and the misrepresentation of victimization on local television news. *Communication Research, 27*, 547–573.

Entman, R. (1992). Blacks in the news: Television, modern racism, and cultural change. *Journalism Quarterly, 69*, 341–361.

Entman, R. (1994). Representation and reality in the portrayal of Blacks on network television news. *Journalism Quarterly, 71*, 509–520.

Fiske, S. T., & Taylor, S. E. (1991). *Social cognition* (2nd ed.). New York: McGraw-Hill.

Ford, T. E. (1997). Effects of stereotypical television portrayals of African-Americans on person perception. *Social Psychology Quarterly, 60*, 266–275.

Gilliam, F. D., & Iyengar, S. (2000). Prime suspects: The influence of local television news on the viewing public. *American Journal of Political Science, 44*, 560–573.

Hewstone, M. (1990). The "ultimate attribution error"? A review of the literature on intergroup causal attri-

bution. *European Journal of Social Psychology, 20*, 311–335.

Livingston, R. W., & Brewer, M. B. (2002). What are we really priming? Cue-based versus category-based processing of facial stimuli. *Journal of Personality & Social Psychology, 82*(1), 5–18.

Oliver, M. B., & Fonash, D. (2002). Race and crime in the news: Whites' identification and misidentification of violent and nonviolent criminal suspects. *Media Psychology, 4*, 137–156.

Pettigrew, T. F. (1979). The ultimate attribution error: Extending Allport's cognitive analysis of prejudice. *Personality & Social Psychology Bulletin, 5*, 461–476.

Shrum, L. J. (2002). Media consumption and perceptions of social reality: Effects and underlying processes. In J. Bryant & D. Zillmann (Eds.), *Media effects: Advances in theory and research* (2nd ed., pp. 69–96). Mahwah, NJ: Lawrence Erlbaum Associates.

Sunnafrank, M., & Fontes, N. E. (1983). General and crime related racial stereotypes and influence on juridic decisions. *Cornell Journal of Social Relations, 17*(1), 1–15.

Valentino, N. (1999). Crime news and the priming of racial attitudes during evaluations of the president. *Public Opinion Quarterly, 63*, 293–320.

2.3 BELIEVING BLOGS: DOES A BLOGGER'S GENDER INFLUENCE CREDIBILITY?

Cory L. Armstrong & Mindy McAdams

This study examines how gender and occupational cues influence Weblog credibility. Participants rated the overall credibility of a blog entry for which male and female descriptors of the author were manipulated. Findings suggest that while gender stereotypes persist for credibility, perhaps traditional cues used to discern media credibility may be less effective for blogs.

One of the newer terms in the public vernacular is *blog*. It can serve as a noun or a verb: "I saw your blog," "I blogged about my trip to Alaska last week," or "She's a blogger." The number of Internet users who maintain a blog is rising dramatically, and experts predict the "blogosphere" will double every 6 months. Blogs, or Weblogs, are widely varied presentations of an enormous range of content—from personal diaries to supplemental article information posted by news reporters.

Given this variety, researchers are still learning about blogs and blogger demographics and how they compare to other mass media. This type of information source is particularly compelling given that the vast majority of bloggers is under 30, and more than half are female.

This gender diversity leads to the question of the role of gender in gauging blog credibility. Generally, the overall credibility of Web sites is mixed, depending on the author of the site; government and media Web sites have often been deemed more trustworthy than those created by private individuals (Center for the Digital Future, 2005). It is unclear whether those credibility ratings are determined in part by the gender of the blog author. Are gender stereotypes employed by blog readers in determining the credibility of a blog?

So far, few studies have focused on blog users and how much they trust this content. Because Weblogs are becoming a significant source of information among U.S. Internet users, examining their credibility for the general public is important for communication research. Weblogs are a virtually untested medium, so learning more about how they are perceived will provide valuable insight. This study attempted to isolate the credibility of male and female Weblog authors. In particular, we used an experimental design to examine how gender cues might influence Weblog credibility.

CREDIBILITY IN NEWS CONTENT

In news stories, the source of the news story is responsible for conveying information about a story, so who is quoted may determine how the story is interpreted by readers. Most studies of source credibility within mass communication research were conducted in the late 1960s and early 1970s and targeted four dimensions of credibility: knowledge, trustworthiness, attractiveness, and dynamism. More recent studies have focused on key source credibility determinants, such as believability, topical interest, and source-selection evaluations. This line of research has also examined credibility from other venues, such as news medium credibility and message credibility.

More recent trends in journalism scholarship have been to examine relationships and predictors of credibility. For example, a 2003 study found that students attending universities in the northwestern United States rated political columnists as more credible than did students in the Southeast (Andsager & Mastin, 2003). A multimedia presentation of Internet news has been found to positively influence source credibility (Kiousis, 2006). Reliance on Weblogs was found to be a strong predictor of Weblog credibility, but reliance on traditional media and political involvement/knowledge and trust in government are weak predictors (Johnson & Kaye, 2004a). In other work examining overall Web site credibility, the authors found that amount of online activity and years spent online were not good predictors of Web credibility (Johnson & Kaye, 2004b). The results are inconclusive at best.

The linkage between credibility and gender has been mixed, depending on medium. White and Andsager (1991) found that gender was not related to the credibility of newspaper columnists. However, their results indicated that readers preferred columns written by authors of the same sex. A 1988 study found that college-age men viewed males as having more expertise, while women of the same age group found no difference between genders (Carocci, 1988). Later work found that female newspaper columnists—in particular African American women—were ascribed with higher credibility than men (Andsager & Mastin, 2003). Armstrong and Nelson (2005) found a relationship between credibility and source descriptors (official/nonofficial), suggesting that as credibility for a source decreased, readers processed information within a news story more thoughtfully. However, the results of that study only held true for the respondents who thought the source was male. Flanagin and Metzger (2003) found that men and women had different views of Web site credibility and that each tended to rate opposite-sex Web pages as more credible than same-sex Web sites.

Extending these ideas to Weblogs, the term *source* takes on different meanings. In traditional news coverage, the source is the person to whom information is attributed and, in some instances, the journalist who is conveying the story. However, as noted above, Weblogs are a bit different. Weblogs are generally written by an individual who shares his or her opinions and usually provides additional Internet links for more information. Those links are often to mainstream media or informational Web sites, which may lend credibility to the overall Weblog post, but the links themselves aren't generally examined for source credibility. The human sources quoted in a news story speak to the reader. Rather than speaking *to* the blog user, the links in a blog post speak *for* the blog author.

Generally, the blog author establishes a relationship based on trust with his or her audience. This relationship is intentionally personal, in contrast to the professional objective detachment of a journalist, who must rely on quoted sources to speak to the reader. Bloggers, however, speak directly to their readers. As a result, the blog author is the "source" within a Weblog. It is the author who is being judged for accuracy, newsworthiness, and believability, not others who might be quoted (or linked) in a post.

Gender Stereotypes

Credibility of Weblogs may also be influenced by the use of heuristics such as gender stereotypes. Readers may gauge credibility and trust of information based on the individual descriptors (including gendered words such as *he* and *she*) of sources within the text. Armstrong and Nelson (2005) found that when readers encountered official sources providing information, they were less likely to process the story thoughtfully, but when an unofficial source was quoted, individuals read the story more thoroughly. Further, when official or "expert" sources were used, most respondents tapped into their stereotyping heuristics, assuming that the source was male. Because gender is one of the most commonly accessed stereotypes, whether the author of a Weblog is male or female may influence the blog's perceived credibility. Herring and Paolillo (2006) found that diary-focused blogs tend to present female-oriented characteristics, while "filter" blogs—often political blogs that provide commentary and link to other content—seem to contain more male-oriented language and cues.

With the proliferation of blogs, questions arise as to how the credibility of these posts appears to readers. That is, how are these new media being perceived, and what types of cues are readers using to determine the authenticity of content? Given prior credibility scholarship, it seems likely that gender cues can influence the credibility of Weblogs. Individuals may perceive some topics as "belonging" to female or male bloggers or as requiring a particular expertise. Those cues may trigger stereotypes in readers, who may base credibility more on the source descriptors than on the information presented.

Blog Usage

Although mass media studies have found that credibility of a medium is often positively associated with how much an individual uses the medium (Wanta & Hu, 1994), that has not always been true with Internet use. In fact, studies have found conflicting information about whether more frequent Internet use predicted credibility (Flanagin & Metzger, 2000; Johnson & Kaye, 2004b; Kiousis, 2001). Johnson and Kaye (2002) found that traditional media use was a strong predictor of online credibility but that reliance on the Web was not. In a study of 3,747 blog users, Kaye (2005) found that for some motivations, blog usage (measured in hours used per week) was a predictor but Internet experience (measured in years of use) was not. This suggests that effects of blog usage may not be parallel to that of other media.

A Pew study in 2003 found that "about 11% of Internet users at that time had read blogs," (cited in Rainie, 2005, p. 2). Subsequent Pew studies showed that the percentage had increased to 27% by November 2004 but had not changed by September 2005 (Rainie, 2005). Rainie concluded that "[b]log readers are somewhat more of a mainstream group than bloggers themselves" (p. 2) and noted recent growth in blog readership among women and minorities. Blog readers, therefore, are not rare, but the amount of experience with blogs can be expected to vary widely across the population of U.S. Internet users.

Clearly, differences may exist between those who have had little or no exposure to blogs and those who use blogs on a regular basis. In a recent study of Internet users, 12% of blog users surveyed said they trusted information received in Weblogs, while 23% reported they trust most blog content they receive (Consumer Reports WebWatch, 2005). These differences may influence credibility of blogs. Experienced blog users may have more skill in judging the expertise of a blogger, even on the first encounter with a given blog. Lacking the branding of a well-known journalistic organization, an individual's blog exhibits other cues that encourage or inhibit a reader's willingness to trust the blogger. These include links to archives (how long has the blog existed?), comments (does the blog have a participating audience?), syndication (is the blogger sophisticated enough to provide an RSS feed link?), and a "blogroll" (what other blogs are linked to the blog?). Less experienced blog users may not recognize these features and thus may be more likely than experienced uses to trust a blog that lacks those conventions.

If those features are missing from a blog by an unknown author, then experienced users might be skeptical about the information provided, regardless of traditional cues such as gender or occupation of the blog author. This study suggests that perhaps gender cues—which are typically used to process information quickly—may be tempered by an individual's familiarity with blogs.

OUR EXPERIMENT: MANIPULATING GENDER OF BLOG AUTHORS

In this research, we addressed two specific questions: (1) Are individual credibility ratings different when the blog is perceived to have been written by a man or a woman? And (2) What is the role of blog usage in determining credibility?

To examine these questions, we wanted the views of students, among the largest audiences for blogs. We embedded an experiment within a Web-based survey conducted in

November 2005 and had 586 students at a southeastern university participate in the study (58% were female). Respondents read identical versions of a Weblog entry about rebuilding homes in New Orleans in the aftermath of Hurricane Katrina, written by James Fitzgerald, Ann Fitzgerald, or the gender-neutral pseudonym "Urbanite." The text was seven paragraphs (about 570 words) long and included six external links to other actual Web sites with additional information about topics discussed in the Weblog. We chose a blog post that we expected would be "fresh" to most of our study participants without being obscure. We also chose a topic that had no overt references to gender or politics.

Among other questions, we asked participants to rate the blog post on a 1 ("not at all") to 7 ("extremely") Likert scale for each of the following six dimensions: interesting, accurate, credible, trustworthy, believable, and held the respondent's attention.

OUR FINDINGS: BOTH GENDER AND BLOG USAGE AFFECT CREDIBILITY RATINGS

First, we examined how author gender affected respondents' credibility ratings of the post. In all six dimensions, participants reading the male author condition found the blog post more credible than those reading the female author condition and the gender-neutral author condition. Table 2.1 demonstrates those findings. Certain dimensions demonstrated little difference, whereas there appeared to be great differences in other elements of credibility, including level of trustworthiness and attention. The largest mean difference (–.51) occurred between male and female writers on the dimension of ability to hold the student's attention, and, in terms of statistical significance, the dimension of trustworthiness was also found to have a large disparity among conditions. To explore this result, we ran separate analysis of variance (ANOVA) tests on each dimension. ANOVAs allow us to compare whether differences exist across the gender manipulations. Our results indicate that there was a great difference between how students viewed the trustworthiness and the level of engagement (ability to hold attention) of the blog post, depending on whether man or women was perceived as writing it.

TABLE 2.1   Means* of Credibility Dimensions by Gender of Blog Writer

CREDIBILITY DIMENSIONS	MALE WRITER	FEMALE WRITER	GENDER-NEUTRAL
Interesting	4.49	4.16	4.26
Accurate	4.30	4.17	4.24
Credible	4.34	4.09	4.13
Trustworthy	3.99[a]	3.64[a]	3.77
Held attention	3.95[b]	3.44[b]	3.78
Believable	4.72	4.50	4.49

*Based on responses to a 1–7 Likert Scale.

[a]Means with like superscripts indicate the condition means for high and low credibility were significantly different from each other at $p < .05$. (Univariate ANOVA; a Scheffe post hoc test of each condition by dimension.)

TABLE 2.2   **Credibility Ratings by Blog Users and Nonusers**

CONDITIONS	NONUSERS	USERS
Female writer	26.1% (42[*])	25.7% (35)
Male writer	29.8% (48)	32.4% (44)
Gender-neutral	44.1% (71)	41.9% (57)
Total	161	136

[*]Number of subjects per condition given in parentheses.

Blog Users: x^2 (2, $N = 253$) = 2.19, p = .33.

Non-Blog Users : x^2 (2, $N = 289$) = 7.87, p = .02.

This result was interesting, because the text was identical across all conditions, except for the manipulation of the authors' gender. These findings suggest that respondents are using source descriptors—in this case, gender—to develop their credibility levels. These various dimensions of credibility that we examined may tell a bit more about the difference. Essentially, no gender difference existed in four of the dimensions—accuracy, believability, interest, and credibility. But, along the dimensions of trustworthiness and attention keeping, the post by a female author ranked much lower than posts by both the male and gender-neutral authors.

We also looked at whether blog users would rate the credibility of a blog higher than nonusers would. In particular, we were attempting to flesh out whether experienced blog users would use gender as a criterion for determining blog use in the same manner as non–blog users. To explore this idea, we combined all of the credibility dimensions by adding the scores together to come up with an overall rating. Then, we classified a person's rating of the blog as "credible" if the credibility score was above the mean and compared the scores across the three gender manipulations through a Chi-square test. The Chi-square statistic allows us to compare for significant differences across conditions or among groups, so here we ran two separate Chi-square tests, one each for blog users and nonusers. As noted in Table 2.2, we found that among users, there were no statistically significant differences in credibility. However, among nonusers, more students found the non-gender condition more credible than either of the gendered conditions. Both tests indicated the respondents found the non-gendered condition credible, but among nonusers the non-gender condition was significantly more credible than either male or female writers. This finding suggested to us that perhaps in the blogosphere, non-gendered pseudonyms (such as our "Urbanite") may connote more credibility than actual names.

WHAT DOES IT MEAN?

In terms of gender equality, the findings aren't good. We found that one criterion used to determine the credibility of blogs is gender. That is, when students read a blog post perceived to be written by a male author, they give it more credibility than a post perceived to be written by a woman. The findings demonstrate what many people—primarily women—have alleged for years: There is a perceived gender difference. Men are generally given more credibility than women. More specifically, our findings suggest that men are seen as more trustworthy, interesting, and engaging, at least when they write a blog post.

What is it about those specific dimensions that bring out these gender differences? It may not be surprising that trust is associated with males more than females, as traditionally men have been placed in more positions of authority, such as law enforcement personnel, national political figures, and even network newscasters. Perhaps more surprising is the idea that the post commands a greater level of attention when perceived as being written by a male author. Does that air of authority automatically awarded to men permit them to espouse information and commentary in a way that women cannot, in this society?

The study also illustrates the proliferation of gender stereotypes within our lives. Stereotypes are automatic shortcuts that our mind seeks to help speed up the interpretation of information and make quicker decisions. When confronted with information, people often rely on these heuristics to make choices or evaluations fast. In this case, it appears that part of the decision making on credibility was related to the gender of the writer, which makes sense, as research has found that gender is a common shortcut used to evaluate information (Armstrong & Nelson, 2005). In this case, despite identical material, the post was rated as more credible when it was supposedly written by a man. Perhaps most surprising, the question "held my attention" illustrated the greatest disparity, with a 17.5% difference between those posts written by men and women.

However, our results do offer some positive news, as it appears that students find higher credibility in blog posts when pseudonyms are employed—in this case, one that is nongendered. Among nonusers, we found that students engaged in gender stereotyping, but more students favored the nongendered condition. However, among blog users, there was no meaningful difference among the three conditions. As blog users become more savvy at reading and interacting with blogs, they may be developing a different way of evaluating blogs—looking at indicators other than gender cues. Although research has found that gender stereotyping is often used as a heuristic when evaluating information, it happened here only among non-blog users. In effect, blog use may lead to more gender-blind evaluations among individuals, while non–blog users may be using the same shortcuts we have seen in older media, such as newspapers.

The connection between gender and blog usage should provide some optimism for those interested in gender-related media issues. Overall, individual use and reliance on the Internet is growing; therefore, the possibility that it may help to mitigate some of the existing gender stereotypes is a positive outcome of this research. Perhaps the growing trend of gender-neutral screen names may help lessen gender stereotyping within the online world.

Those who pursue this line of research may want to try to isolate the indicators by which blog users are determining credibility. These could be based on links to external information, comments, links to other blogs (including the blogroll), or design components. Another cue may be related to the content of the blog. Much of the extant research about blogs relates to political blogs; however, the number of blog topics is large and hardly limited to politics. In this study, we looked at only one blog topic and one post—certainly more study is needed for other types of blogs before we can make a definitive conclusion. But whatever these factors are—and how they vary across topics—they appear to be more important in determining credibility than the gender of the author.

In a classroom setting that focuses on gender in media, the results of this study are provocative, if not puzzling. While the study is exploratory in nature, it seems encouraging to think that gender is becoming less important as a criterion for credibility. On the other hand, why is this still an issue at all? Many journalism schools in the United States now have more female than male graduates, so it isn't as if media work is a predominantly male field. Why does stereotyping happen? Perhaps our findings suggest that blogging may help to lessen the use of gender cues as a factor in credibility. Only time, and more research, will tell.

IT'S YOUR TURN: WHAT DO YOU THINK? WHAT WILL YOU FIND?

1. Use technorati.com to find five blogs about the same topic. Which ones do you find credible? What are your criteria for credibility? What factors do you examine to determine whether you believe the information you're reading? Make a list. What does your list say about you as a media consumer?

2. Share your list of the criteria and factors with your classmates. To what extent were these evaluative criteria gender based? Can you iden-

tify any patterns of difference among your classmates? Why or why not?

3. What makes someone an expert? Would you trust a male doctor to treat a woman during her pregnancy? Would you trust a female doctor to treat a man for prostate cancer? In what areas does gender *really* play a role in one's expertise? What about blogging? Is there a topic that only women, or only men, should blog about?

REFERENCES

Andsager, J. L., & Mastin, T. (2003). Racial and regional differences in readers' evaluations of the credibility of political columnists by race and sex. *Journalism & Mass Communication Quarterly, 80*(1), 57–72.

Armstrong, C. L., & Nelson, M. R. (2005). How newspaper sources trigger gender stereotypes. *Journalism & Mass Communication Quarterly, 82*(4), 820–837.

Carocci, N. M. (1988). Trust and gender ten years later: The more things change. *Women's Studies in Communication, 11*, 63–89.

Center for the Digital Future. (2005). *Digital future project: Year 5*. Retrieved March 21, 2006, from http://www.digitalcenter.org/pdf/Center-for-the-Digital-Future-2005-Highlights.pdf

Consumer Reports WebWatch. (2005, October 26). *Leap of faith: Using the Internet despite the dangers*. Retrieved March 30, 2006, from http://www.consumerWebwatch.org/pdfs/princeton.pdf

Flanagin, A. J. & Metzger, M. J. (2000). Perceptions of Internet media credibility, *Journalism & Mass Communication Quarterly, 77*, 515–540.

Flanagin, A. J., & Metzger, M. J. (2003). The perceived credibility of personal Web page information as

influenced by the sex of the source. *Computers in Human Behaviors, 19*, 683–701.

Herring, S. C., & Paolillo, J. C. (2006). Gender and genre variation in Weblogs. *Journal of Sociolinguistics, 10*(4): 439–459.

Johnson, T. J., & Kaye, B. K. (2002). Webelievability: A path model examining how convenience and reliance predict online credibility. *Journalism & Mass Communication Quarterly, 79*(3), 619–642.

Johnson, T. J., & Kaye, B. K. (2004a). Wag the blog: How reliance on traditional media and the Internet influence credibility perceptions of Weblogs among blog users. *Journalism & Mass Communication Quarterly, 81*(3), 622–642.

Johnson, T. J., & Kaye, B. K. (2004b). For whom the Web tolls: How Internet experience predicts Web reliance and credibility. *Atlantic Journal of Communication, 12*(1), 19–45.

Kaye, B. K. (2005). It's a blog, blog, blog, blog world. *Atlantic Journal of Communication, 13*(2), 73–95.

Kiousis, S. (2001). Public trust or mistrust? Perceptions of media credibility in the information age. *Mass Communication and Society, 4*(4), 381–403.

Kiousis, S. (2006). Exploring the impact of modality on perceptions of credibility for online news stories. *Journalism Studies, 7*(2), 348–359.

Rainie, L. (2005, January). *The state of blogging* [data memo]. Retrieved April 25, 2008, from http://www.pewinternet.org/pdfs/PIP_blogging_data.pdf

Wanta, W., & Hu, Y.-W. (1994). The effects of credibility, reliance and exposure on media agenda-setting: A path-analysis model. *Journalism Quarterly, 71*(1), 90–98.

White, H. A., & Andsager, J. L. (1991). Newspaper column readers' gender bias: Perceived interest and credibility. *Journalism Quarterly, 68*(4), 709–718.

2.4 ALL I REALLY NEEDED TO KNOW (ABOUT BEAUTY) I LEARNED BY KINDERGARTEN: A CULTIVATION ANALYSIS

Susannah R. Stern

This reading shows that even by the time they are 5 and 6 years old, girls who are heavy television viewers have already "bought into" the restricted mainstream ideals of beauty.

In recent decades, the magnitude of physical self-dissatisfaction in American girls and women has prompted widespread concern. Studies have demonstrated that more than half of 13-year-old girls and three quarters of 17-year old girls are unhappy with their bodies, only 45% of American college women report they feel good about their looks, and over 75% of American women think they're "too fat" (Field, et al., 1999; Garner, Garfinkle, Schwartz, & Thompson, 1980; Maine, 2000; Seligman, Joseph, Donovan, & Gosnell, 1987.) Not only are these women dissatisfied with their physical appearance, but many also take measures—sometimes drastic—to improve their looks. For example, more than $8 billion is spent on cosmetics every year in the United States (Hoovers.com). In 2007, nearly 11.7 million cosmetic surgeries were performed, the most of common of which for women was breast augmentation. For those age 18 and under, the most common procedures were laser hair removal, microdermabrasion, chemical peel, ear reshaping, and rhinoplasty (American Society for Aesthetic Plastic Surgery, 2008). And, perhaps most sadly, approximately 8% of American women suffer from an eating disorder (American Psychiatric Association Work Group on Eating Disorders, 2000). Overall, these statistics suggest that many girls and women are trying to obtain certain—and arguably similar—standards of beauty.

But where do beauty standards come from? How do we learn them? And why are they so dominant? Questions such as these have preoccupied me for several years, especially when I was in college, where I was surrounded by young women who constantly lamented the way they looked. Later, in graduate school, I began to study how electronic media affect children and recognized that girls' conceptions of beauty were likely associated, to some extent, with their life-long media consumption. After all, although many people are concerned about adolescents and women who are uncomfortable with their physical appearance, these attitudes don't suddenly develop when girls reach puberty or high school. Rather, they are shaped by many childhood years of learning about beauty and its apparent importance in American society. Television (in addition to parents, peers, and siblings) is a dominant part of many children's learning environment. Furthermore, TV is a well-documented disseminator of messages concerning physical attractiveness and its importance (Kunkel, Cope, & Biely, 1999). The overall implication, it seemed, was that girls' childhood perceptions of beauty should be studied in relation to their TV consumption to understand more about why adolescent and adult females might maintain certain feelings about their own appearance and self-worth. Very young girls are especially important to address, because they are just forming their impressions of cultural preferences and are among the most vulnerable to socialization messages due to their limited real-world experiences.

The study I describe here explored the relationship between the amount of television kindergarten girls view and their thoughts about beauty. I begin by summarizing TV portrayals of women and messages about beauty. Next, I describe a theoretical/methodological orientation, known as cultivation analysis, which guided the study. Finally, after explaining how I collected the data, I summarize some of the most important results and draw conclusions about their significance.

PORTRAYAL OF WOMEN AND BEAUTY ON TELEVISION

Many studies have examined TV's portrayal of women. In general, these analyses of both advertisements and programming have concluded that women on television are overwhelmingly young and thin. Indeed, youth and slenderness appear to be the chief qualifications for women in the news, commercials, and entertainment programming. If the dieting and cosmetics statistics mentioned earlier are any indication, youth and slenderness also compose the current standards of ideal female beauty in American society. Many scholars argue that the media's constant yet narrow depiction of female beauty both mirrors and perpetuates contemporary standards of physical beauty (Davis, 1990; van Zoonen, 1994).

Media messages emphasize the importance of physical appearance, especially for women. Significantly more advertisements geared toward females than males promote products to enhance appearance (Craig, 1992; Signorelli, McLeod, & Healy, 1994). The women in these ads not only are young and thin, but they also urge audiences to buy products and follow specified techniques to look as young and thin as they do. Even commercials not directly selling beauty products often emphasize appearance as important. Indeed, one study concluded that viewers are exposed to over 5,000 attractiveness messages in ads alone each year (Downs & Harrison, 1985).

Also, the plot of many TV programs frequently revolves around a woman's appearance or her efforts to achieve a certain look, and dialogue often reveals both women's and men's preoccupation with female appearance (Fouts & Burggraf, 1999; Ward, 1995).

Women on TV who are characterized as successful at work, at home, and in love are almost exclusively attractive, reinforcing the importance of beauty to a woman's achievements and happiness. Editing techniques often emphasize the importance of women's appearance by focusing on specific body parts via close-ups, and costuming choices accentuate women's bodies (Caputi, 1999; Hall & Crum, 1994; Signorelli, McLeod, & Healy, 1994).

Altogether, most scholars agree that TV emphasizes narrow standards of beauty and stresses the importance of beauty, especially for women, across all types of TV content. Because children consume an assorted diet of media fare (McGill, 1994), the likelihood that young girls will encounter implicit and explicit beauty messages from multiple television sources is high.

ASSESSING THE RELATIONSHIP BETWEEN TV AND BELIEFS: CULTIVATION ANALYSIS

One approach to understanding how television viewing may influence girls' attitudes about appearance is *cultivation analysis*. Cultivation analysts propose that people who watch a lot of television begin to construct a view of the world that's much more like the one they see on TV than the real world. Television thus cultivates a distorted social reality for those who watch a lot of TV (heavy viewers), compelling them to extend characteristics of the televised world to the real world. Cultivation analysis presumes that those who watch little TV (lighter viewers) tend to be exposed to more varied and diverse information sources (both mediated and interpersonal), while heavy viewers, by definition, tend to rely more on TV (Signorelli & Morgan, 1990). Cultivation analysis also posits that heavy viewers who are otherwise diverse often share a set of conceptions and expectations about reality. This phenomenon has been dubbed "mainstreaming."

A great deal of mass communication research has demonstrated that cultivation does take place among heavy viewers. Gerbner, Gross, Morgan, and Signorelli (1986) found that heavier viewers believed the world to be a more mean and dangerous place than did lighter viewers. Heavy soap opera viewers overestimated the number of abortions that occur in reality (Buerkel-Rothfuss & Mayes, 1981). In a study of over 3,000 high school seniors, Signorelli (1991) found that television cultivates ideas about marriage, interpersonal relationships, and family.

These are just a few of many studies that demonstrate TV's power to cultivate ideas and beliefs. Cultivation analysis also proves to be a useful way to address the relationship between television viewing and young girls' beliefs about beauty and its importance. Television may cultivate expectations about what beauty "looks" like and how significant it is in everyday life. With this possibility in mind, I communicated with kindergarten girls and their parents to better understand the relationship between how much television girls watch and how they think about beauty. I hypothesized that heavier viewers would share more common definitions of beauty than lighter viewers would, and that heavier viewers' ideas about beauty would more closely match those that are repeatedly shown on TV. I also hypothesized that girls who are heavier TV viewers would be more likely to believe that physical attractiveness was especially important for women.

To test these hypotheses, I collected two types of data. First, the parents of 63 kindergarten girls (ages 5 and 6) completed a survey assessing basic demographic information, household attitudes about appearance, and the amount of their daughter's TV viewing. Specifically, I inquired how much TV, on average, their daughter watched, and I used this information to classify each of the girls into one of two categories: lighter viewer (zero to 14 hours a week) and heavier viewer (over 14 hours a week.)

Next, I interviewed each of the 63 girls to learn more about their perceptions of and attitudes toward beauty. In general, the semistructured interviews were designed to identify how the girls defined beauty, to whom they thought it applied, and how important they thought it was.

Finally, I cross-tabulated the data gathered from the interviews and surveys to assess the differences in thoughts about beauty between the girls who watched less TV (lighter viewers) and those who watched substantially more (heavier viewers).

SUPPORT FOR CULTIVATION OF THOUGHTS ABOUT BEAUTY

Overall, I found mild evidence of a cultivation effect. Generally speaking, girls who were heavier viewers were fairly different from lighter viewers in terms of how they defined beauty, the amount of consistency among their definitions of beauty, and their attitudes about beauty.

Beauty Definitions: Differences Between Lighter and Heavier Viewers

Girls who were heavier viewers mentioned certain aspects of beauty much more than lighter viewers did. Most noticeably, heavier viewers were much more likely to consider beauty an explicitly female trait, whereas girls who watched less TV perceived beauty as gender neutral and applicable to both men and women. In light of television's propensity for linking beauty and appearance issues predominantly to women, cultivation analysis would have predicted these results.

Girls who watched more TV were also much more likely to define beauty as being young and thin. Specifically, heavier viewers were significantly less likely to agree that people with wrinkles and people who were overweight could be pretty. Lighter viewers believed that anyone had the potential to be pretty. Heavier viewers also expressed more uncertainty than lighter viewers about the possibility that people who were overweight could be pretty even "sometimes." No lighter viewers expressed such uncertainty.

It's interesting to note that many of the girls, regardless of how much television they watched, frequently qualified their responses to questions about weight. For example, when asked if overweight people could be pretty, girls typically responded, "Yes, they can still be pretty." The qualifier *still* was virtually absent from responses to questions about whether people who were thin could be pretty. Moreover, several subjects replied that people who were overweight should try to lose weight. One subject explained. "A fat person can be pretty. My mom is fat. But she is going on a diet. She is going to look like a beach girl." Another common response was that overweight people could be attractive, "But not as much as a thin person."

Consistency Among Beauty Definitions: Differences Between Lighter and Heavier Viewers

Girls who were heavier viewers also shared slightly more common perceptions of beauty than lighter viewers. This mainstreaming phenomenon is based on the idea that viewers who frequently share similar experiences (such as TV viewing) begin to share common perceptions. In this study, heavier viewers' definitions of beauty centered mainly on women, and they tended to conceive of beauty as an accessory (such as clothes, jewelry, makeup). In contrast, lighter viewers offered a wider and more diverse set of responses that reflected a conception of beauty as more gender neutral. Moreover, they thought of beauty not only in terms of accessories but also in terms of personality traits and natural physical qualities (such as blue eyes). Overall, heavier viewers had a more narrow vision of beauty, similar to that promoted by television.

Importance of Beauty for Women

The finding that heavier viewers thought about beauty more in terms of female qualities lent some support to the notion that heavier viewers placed more importance on beauty for women than did lighter viewers. However, other measures of beauty importance revealed little support for a cultivation effect in this area. Perhaps this can be explained by the fact that for most of the girls, regardless of how much TV they watched, beauty was important. Thus, if nearly all the girls already thought beauty was important, especially for women, the possibility of finding any cultivation effect was precluded.

The actual responses given by the girls regarding the importance of beauty were particularly interesting. Both light and heavy viewers were eager to identify the social advantages of being attractive. For example, when asked about the importance of beauty and whether they cared if they were pretty, the following responses were typical:

- "Yes. Because sometimes kids think you're not pretty and they won't play with you."
- "Yes, it matters because of boys. When girls dress up pretty than boys think they're pretty and want to marry them."
- "I'd rather be pretty than not pretty. It makes me nice. People will like me. If other people are pretty, than the whole class will get together."
- "Boys like prettier girls."
- "I'd like to be pretty because people make fun of you if you're not pretty."
- "I'd like to be pretty because when I'm pretty, I don't get in trouble as much."

Responses such as these indicated that kindergarten girls already recognize the rewards and advantages of beauty in our society, a message that is consistently reinforced by television and many other aspects of our culture.

Beauty as a Consumer Project

Despite the differences between each viewing group's definitions of beauty, the most frequent definition of what made someone beautiful, offered by light and heavy viewers alike, was feminine accessories (such as clothing, jewelry, purses, makeup, and nail polish.) This seems illustrative of the consumer culture with which children are currently confronted. Several girls mentioned that in order to be pretty, one must buy something pretty. Adorning oneself with clothes, jewelry, or makeup seemed the primary way to attain beauty. For example, one girl, when asked why she didn't think a man was pretty, replied, "They can't wear makeup"—it seems that makeup itself is the defining aspect of beauty.

While it's likely that girls encounter beauty accessories via their mothers, siblings, and friends, TV also promotes beauty as a consumer product that can be bought. Indeed, when asked to name who she thought was pretty, one girl said, "A princess. She is rich, so she can buy lots of things. Then she can be as pretty as she wants."

THE IMPORTANCE OF CULTIVATION FINDINGS

The findings of this study suggest that the recurring images of and messages about beauty presented on television may be cultivating similar ideas about beauty in young girls who view a lot of television. The overwhelming number of young and thin women portrayed in the media, at the expense of other types of women, may foreshadow heavier viewers' beliefs that to be pretty, one must not have wrinkles or be overweight. Furthermore, television's consistent emphasis on the link between women and beauty may well set the stage for girls who watch a lot of television to think about beauty solely in female terms.

It is important to note the significance of finding any cultivation effect at all, particularly in light of the fact that my interviewees lived in such overall appearance-oriented environments. Over 90% of the subjects lived in families in which at least one member exercised to improve appearance and 70% lived in families where at least one member dieted to improve appearance. Although not measured, it's also likely that many of the girls' family members attempted to improve their appearance through other means, such as wearing makeup or dying their hair—actions that might add to girls' perceptions of the importance of appearance. Indeed, more than half of the parents who completed the study indicated that beauty was at least "pretty important" to them. Comments about appearance from family members and friends might further heighten the salience of beauty issues in the minds of young girls. Thus, the finding that the amount of TV viewing made any impact in the way these girls thought about beauty is remarkable.

This study validates the myriad concerns voiced by media critics, parents, and educators across the country regarding the relationship between beauty messages in the media and girls' thoughts about beauty. Literally hundreds of books and articles have discussed the presumed link between the media and beauty perceptions, but so far, very little empirical evidence has been gathered to test this assumption. This study, however, provides some support for this idea. The media present distinct images of and messages about beauty, and children who watch more TV appear to bear similar beliefs about beauty. Among kindergarten girls, heavier viewers see beauty predominantly as a female quality and one that necessitates adornment. Furthermore, beauty is seen by almost all of the girls in this study as a commodity that can be bought and modified as needed.

Such notions about beauty among kindergarten girls are particularly striking. Cultivation analysis addresses the importance of cumulative exposure to certain and recurring media patterns. It is noteworthy that I observed cultivation effects in girls as young as 5 and 6 years of age. Indeed, the already significant effect television has had regarding beauty messages and imagery is likely to intensify. As the girls grow older and their physical appearance doesn't match that which they repeatedly see validated on TV, they may become disheartened.

Additionally, if girls are told throughout their childhoods that they can fix their physical imperfections merely by buying something or adding something to themselves, it makes sense that early adolescence is when we begin to see drastic effects such as excessive dieting, cosmetic surgery, and requests for plastic surgery. After all, it is usually during the early teenage years when girls' bodies begin to develop. This is also when many girls develop greater decision-making power, and when many begin to acquire discretionary income to purchase products to improve their looks. When the results of these products don't meet with girls' expectations to turn them into "perfectly" beautiful women (as seen on TV), dissatisfaction seems inevitable. This dissatisfaction may play out in the form of low self-esteem, poor body image, dieting, and fasting.

Given television's propensity to teach children, we should begin to explore its potential to cultivate more positive, diverse, and healthy perceptions of beauty. Perhaps the portrayal of more varied types of women (young, old, thin, overweight, Asian, Latino, Indian, African American, etc.) and a decreased emphasis on the importance of beauty may encourage girls to think of beauty in less specific and compulsory terms, and ultimately, help them to accept their own idiosyncrasies as they grow older.

IT'S YOUR TURN: WHAT DO YOU THINK? WHAT WILL YOU FIND?

1. What other gendered ideas or beliefs might be cultivated by TV? How might you test your hypothesis?

2. Which medium do you consider most influential in shaping beauty standards? Are the media more, less, or equally influential compared to parents, siblings, and peers?

3. Watch TV for an hour. Tally the number of references characters make about physical appearance. (For example, "I'm having a bad hair day," "Your skin will look ten years younger.") Pay attention to who says what, and to whom. How much emphasis was placed on appearance? Who was appearance most connected to? What overall message did the hour of television send to viewers about the importance of appearance?

4. Working in teams, create a TV comedy that you think would promote healthy attitudes about appearance. Who would the characters be? What would the situation be, and the plot? How would you enforce positive and diverse messages about physical appearance?

REFERENCES

American Psychiatric Association Work Group on Eating Disorders. (2000). Practice guideline for the treatment of patients with eating disorders (revision). *American Journal of Psychiatry*, 157 (1 Suppl.), 1–39.

American Society for Aesthetic Plastic Surgery. (2008). *Cosmetic plastic surgery research: Statistics and trends for 2001–2006*. Retrieved on October 26, 2008, from: http://www.cosmeticplasticsurgery-statistics.com/statistics.html#2007-news

Buerkel-Rothfuss, N., & Mayes, S. (1981). Soap opera viewing: The cultivation effect. *Journal of Communication, 31*(3), 108–315.

Caputi, J. (1999). The pornography of everyday life. In M. Myers (Ed.), *Mediated women* (pp. 57–79). Cresskill, NJ: Hampton Press.

Craig, R. S. (1992). The effect of television day part on gender portrayals in television commercials: A content analysis. *Sex Roles, 26*(5), 197–212.

Davis, D. (1990). Portrayals of women in prime-time network television: Some demographic characteristics. *Sex Roles, 23*(5/6), 325–332.

Downs, C., & Harrison, S. (1985). Embarrassing age spots or just plain ugly: Physical attractiveness stereotyping as an instrument of sexism on American television commercials. *Sex Roles, 13*(1–2), 9–19.

Field A. E., Cheung L., Wolf A. M., Herzog, D. B., Gortmaker, S. L., & Colditz, G. A. (1999). Exposure to the mass media and weight concerns among girls. *Pediatrics, 103*(3), E36.

Fouts, G., & Burggraf, K. (1999). Television situation comedies: Female body images and verbal reinforcements. *Sex Roles, 40*(5), 473–481.

Garner, D., Garfinkle, P., Schwartz, D., & Thompson, H. (1980). Cultural expectations of thinness in women. *Psychological Reports, 47,* 483–491.

Gerbner, G., Gross, L., Morgan, M., & Signorelli, N. (1986). Living with television: The dynamics of the cultivation process. In J. Bryant & D. Zillmann (Eds.), *Perspectives on media effects* (pp. 17–40). Hillsdale, NJ: Lawrence Erlbaum Associates.

Hall, C., & Crum, M. (1994). Women and "body-isms" in television beer commercials. *Sex Roles, 31*(5–6), 329–337.

Hoovers.com. *Cosmetics, beauty supply and perfume stores industry overview.* Retrieved on October 26, 2008, from: http://www.hoovers.com/cosmetics,-beauty-supply,-and-perfume-stores/—ID_294—/free-ind-fr-profile-basic.xhtml

Kunkel, D., Cope, K., & Biely, E. (1999). Sexual messages on television: Comparing findings from three studies. *Journal of Sex Research, 36*(3), 230–236.

Maine, M. (2000). *Body wars: Making peace with women's bodies.* Carlsbad, CA: Gurze Books.

McGill, L. (1994). By the numbers: What kids watch. *Media Studies Journal, 8*(4), 95–104.

Seligman, J., Joseph, N., Donovan, J., & Gosnell, M. (1987, July 27). The littlest dieters. *Newsweek,* 48.

Serdula, M. K., Collins, M. E., Williamson, D. F., Anda, R. F., Pamuk, E., & Byers, T. E. (1993). Weight control practices of U.S. adolescents and adults. *Annals of Internal Medicine, 7*(2), 667–671.

Signorelli, N. (1991). Adolescents and ambivalence toward marriage: A cultivation analysis. *Youth and Society, 23*(1), 121–149.

Signorelli, N., McLeod, D., & Healy, E. (1994). Gender stereotypes in MTV commercials: The beat goes on. *Journal of Broadcasting and Electronic Media, 38*(1), 91–102.

Signorelli, N., & Morgan, M. (Eds.). (1990). *Cultivation analysis.* Newbury Park: CA: Sage.

van Zoonen, L. (1994). *Feminist media studies.* London: Sage.

Ward, M. (1995). Talking about sex: Common themes about sexuality in the prime-time TV programs. *Journal of Youth and Adolescence, 24*(5), 595–615.

2.5 BODY IMAGE, MASS MEDIA, SELF-CONCEPT

Michelle A. Wolf, Sandra L. Nichols, and Dave Decelle

The authors explore the concept of body image and the role of the media in influencing women's feelings about their body image. Arguing that lesbian and bisexual women are too often ignored by media researchers, the authors compare the perceptions of body images among groups of straight, lesbian, and bisexual women.

Our culture abounds with evidence of great interest in our bodies, especially how we appear to ourselves and others. Reports of eating disorders, the popularity of cosmetic surgery, and our obsession with physical fitness are just a few examples. Many critics focus on media images as sources of body obsession, claiming, for example, that sexy women in advertisements and "perfect" bodies on television leave viewers feeling inadequate. However, the contributions of mass media to these behaviors and feelings remain unclear.

Here, we explore how women of different sexual orientations feel about their bodies, their attitudes toward mass-mediated images of women's bodies, and, ultimately, how messages from media and other people contribute to their developing sense of body image and self-conception.[1]

FORMATION OF BODY IMAGE

Body image is a subtle and complex phenomenon that represents the byproduct of the mind's subjective translation of the experience of the *physical body* into a *mental image* of it. The degree to which we are satisfied or dissatisfied with the mental image of our body is influenced by our self-appraisal of the image (Hutchinson, 1982). This evaluative process shapes our self-image in general and our feelings and attitudes about our bodies in particular.

Much of our self-image is formed by way of social comparison, whereby people compare themselves with others (including media people) to develop their self-image (Festinger, 1954; Kalodner, 1997). We begin the process of perceiving ourselves from the perspective of another person, a viewpoint that "gradually becomes disassociated from any specific person" and becomes that of society at large (Brim, 1968, p. 190). We eventually come to see ourselves partly in terms *how we think* other people see us, a concept known as *self-conception through other*.

This generalized, societal viewpoint is developed via our exposure to social norms and cues of the ideal body, which we internalize and use in our self evaluation. Eighty years ago Walter Lippmann (1922) wrote that much of what we do and how we feel is based more on the "pictures" of the world we have inside our heads than on our actual, direct experiences of the world itself. He argued that members of a society create unique realities through the stories we tell each other. This is especially interesting today because many of the ideas and images we get about the world and ourselves, what Lippmann called the "pictures in our heads," come from mass-mediated experiences provided by popular culture. As such, media are implicated in our self-conception.

So what stories do we tell each other as a society about the ideal body image? Researchers began to argue years ago that there is a steadily thinning cultural ideal for the female body from a voluptuous and curvaceous figure to a thin and angular shape (Garner, Garfinkel, Schwartz, & Thompson, 1980; Silverstein, Perdue, Peterson, & Kelly, 1986). This trend continues today, with an added emphasis on fit, lean bodies. Scholars also claim that "media are likely to be among the most influential promoters of such thin standards" due to the popularity of TV, film, and magazines. (Silverstein et al., 1986, p. 531). In their classic body image study, Myers and Biocca (1992) found that a woman's body image fluctuates when she is exposed to images of the cultural ideal body shape. In fact, "body shape perception can be changed by watching less than 30 minutes of television" (p. 126).

WHY IS THIS IMPORTANT?

A perceived disparity between our body image and the culturally ideal body creates body image dissatisfaction. Researchers have found that most women experience perceptual distortions of and negative feelings toward their own bodies and are generally dissatisfied with their weight and body shape (Gettleman & Thompson, 1993; Herzog, Newman, Yeh, & Warshaw, 1992; Myers & Biocca, 1992). Women who perceive their bodies as overweight are more likely to experience reductions in self-esteem and sense of well-being (Cash & Hicks, 1990). Moreover, women preoccupied with dieting to achieve the dominant cultural ideal of a thin body are susceptible to eating disorders such as anorexia and bulimia (Cash & Brown, 1987; Thompson, 1990).

In addition to exploring how young women feel about themselves in the face of mass media, our work is important because lesbian and bisexual women's concerns are virtually ignored by media researchers. Here we call attention to this oversight and acknowledge that lesbian, bisexual, and heterosexual women make use of and are affected by media messages in different ways.

WOMEN, BODY IMAGE, SEXUAL ORIENTATION, AND MASS MEDIA

Eleven heterosexual, seven bisexual, and nine lesbian women of different ethnic backgrounds between the ages of 18 and 33 years participated in our research. The three groups met for 2-hour discussions to explore four areas of media and self-evaluation. They talked about *common media images* of women's bodies, identifying their own and culturally defined "perfect" bodies. Next they examined media *representation* and *exclusion* of their body types. They then discussed *how they felt about their own bodies* and how these feelings affected their behaviors and life choices. The discussions concluded after the women considered the *sources* of their body image feelings.

Several recurring themes emerged that point to fundamental differences across the groups. Here we present two of the most intriguing themes. One centers on the women's willingness to *fragment* their own and media bodies, and the other concerns how they *evaluated* and felt about their own bodies.

Common Media Images: Body Fragmentation

The groups were asked to discuss common media images by referring only to bodies. To emphasize this focus, they were asked to consider bodies from the neck down.

The Heterosexual Women.   The heterosexual women readily accepted this request and quickly carved the body into parts. They spoke, for example, of Tina Turner's legs, Elizabeth Hurley's boobs, Isabella Rossellini's curves, and Angela Bassett's back. One woman said "showing the midriff" was very popular: "Like on *90210* [and] a Saturday morning show . . . that has all the girls wearing skimpy clothes. I think the costume designer was using Barbie as a model." For another woman, *Baywatch* portrayed the cultural ideal: "big boobs . . . everywhere I look it's flat stomach." The women also speculated on which performers had liposuction or other cosmetic surgeries to enhance their body parts.

The Lesbian Women.   The lesbian women refused to discuss their own and media bodies in terms of body parts. This isn't surprising; much of lesbian subculture suggests a focus on the entire person. They experienced the body in a holistic way that included outward appearance but stressed inner qualities—for example, attitudes and confidence. One participant incorrectly assumed that all women did this: "Most women are like that. Women don't see just one little thing. Women see everything. It's a complete package."

Considering body parts was painfully difficult for an African American participant who expressed concern over the "collagen lips" trend of White women. She was annoyed by the "racism behind the whole look in the first place," complaining that media were "going to, once again, appropriate this one little piece of you." Body fragmentation and what she called "whitified" media images of African American body types clearly offended her.

Dismissing body parts, lesbian women preferred healthy, fit bodies and paid acute attention to the few female athletic media women they perceived as having integrated, conventional masculine and feminine body types. For them, Jennifer Azzi, a professional basketball player in a Reebok ad, was a "walking muscle." They characterized images of the strong female body type they appreciated as recent and rare media phenomena. As one woman suggested, even televised Olympic games[2] limit women's softball coverage because "they don't have those bodies . . . We look different when we play softball than women who play volleyball. That's not what the media like to show off."

The Bisexual Women.   The bisexual women also had trouble with fragmentation, but in a different way. If you conceive of the range of perceptions across the three groups as moving from holistic concerns of body–mind to fragmented attention to body parts, the bisexual women fell somewhere in between. They spoke primarily of body states and types (e.g., "thin") rather than body parts or states of mind and healthy, fit bodies.

They identified the thin, pale, gaunt body type as the most common media woman. Terms like "heroin chic," "anorexic," and "sickly" were frequently used. Especially disturbing was one comparison of this image to the bodies of concentration camp prisoners: "I was looking at these pictures of people in concentration camps and the faces are so similar . . . [to] the faces of models now." Although this body type was perceived as most prevalent, the only example offered was Kate Moss, an "emaciated" model whom they discussed as an icon rather than an individual. Thus, the gaunt body type was effaced into a single mass image without individuality.

When addressing appealing media bodies, the women focused on individuals and body shapes. They had to dig into the past to find examples, describing media women like Marilyn Monroe and Judy Garland as "womanly," "fuller," "real" and "Rubenesque." Significantly, they also detailed the accomplishments and personalities of two less glamorous personalities, Rosie O'Donnell and Ellen DeGeneres. Unlike anonymous "thin" women, media women with "real" body types were perceived as admirable and accomplished.

Common Media Images and Representation
of Participants' Body Types

When asked if their bodies were represented in media, all three groups overwhelmingly said no. Again, their explanations differently reflected their willingness to fragment.

The Heterosexual Women.   Comparing themselves to media women was difficult for the heterosexuals, who continued to emphasize body fragments. One woman was very concerned with her feet: "My feet I never see. I have huge feet." Thighs also emerged as a topic of exclusion: "I definitely don't see my thighs for sure, they're big." Another mentioned hair: "It's naturally curly, but on TV everyone I see has straight hair." Droopy upper arms, which the women found typical in real life, were also perceived as absent from media.

The Lesbian Women.   The lesbians again rejected fragmentation and spoke instead of roles associated with their ethnic groups. Linking their exclusion to a lack of role models for their sexual identity, they felt personally invalidated. Exclusion was especially distressing for women of color, as an Asian American woman explained: "Asians in general, we get weird roles. We're like the math wizards or the foreign student. . . . To find a role model, or even just an image to identify in the media, for me is difficult."

The Bisexual Women.   Saying they couldn't possibly be reflected by the unattainable, unreal media images, the bisexual women denied representation even as they identified examples of their bodies. There was a tension between finding some recognition and feeling excluded because the media women they saw as similar to themselves were cast in negative, stereotypical roles.

They continued to discuss body types, as when a participant mentioned and then abruptly dismissed Roseanne Barr as an example of identification. A woman who liked her own body was offended by images that reflected her; they were objectified and portrayed as arm pieces for men. Even the two women who most closely resembled the cultural ideal found reflective media images to be shallow and silent. Ironically, shallowness and silence were also associated with fat female characters.

Regardless of the degree of fragmentation, the general consensus in all three groups was that media women were different not only from themselves but also from the real women these participants knew. Our participants did offer some examples of reflection in media imagery, but the experience of exclusion was profound.

Body Evaluation and Self-Conception

As we explained earlier, how we evaluate and feel about our bodies can be explained in part by the process of *self-conception through other*, during which we might find dissatisfactory disparities between our body image and that of the internalized cultural ideal. As such, body image construction can be seen as a constant struggle between perceptions of the self and others.

Body evaluation is also influenced by the attention we pay to distinctive attributes of mediated images. A psychological concept known as the *distinctiveness postulate* is useful for explaining the power of media to shape our self-conceptions. This postulate suggests that the more we perceive a stimulus as different from its environment, the more likely we are to attend to it. Kielwasser and Wolf (1991; 1993/94) extended this to human interaction and media usage, arguing that we attend more specifically to aspects of other people and media that reflect the qualities we believe make us unique or different. Thus, women with particular body image concerns (for example, "my breasts are too small" or "my waist is too big") will pay extra attention to media and real images of breasts and waists.

Women in our study saw themselves in part as they thought others saw them and paid special attention to qualities they believed made them distinctive. The discussions again evolved differently as the groups variously used inner and outer frames of reference for evaluating bodies. There seems to be a range of susceptibility to the socialization process in which, as adults, the heterosexual women were most vulnerable and the lesbian women were least vulnerable to external socializing forces.

The Heterosexual Women.   Overwhelmingly, the heterosexual women relied on outer frames of reference such as their reflections in the mirror. They were extremely concerned with and distressed by how they thought they appeared to others, and they focused on body parts they thought made them distinctive.

Many comments suggested refracted, external frames of reference. This is powerfully illustrated by the women's mirror images of themselves and how they evaluated these images in the face of mass media. Their self-concepts, in a sense, became distorted when placed in a context of both mirrors and mass media imagery: "I don't think of myself negatively until I see myself in the mirror . . . or until I see [a particular actor/woman] on television." A woman who compared herself to heavy women in media felt "okay" until she looked in a mirror: "The minute I look in the mirror I'm like, 'Oh God, there's no clothes I can wear. I am fat. Why was I feeling that I wasn't fat?'"

The discussion of mirrors continued for some time, as different impressions emerged: "I feel like the mirror lies to me. 'Cause when I look down at my body I see a lot of fat, but when I look in the mirror I don't see as much fat as when I look down. I hate the mirror." In another woman's words: "I'll look at my roommate's mirror and I'll look taller and skinnier. I'll look at my mirror and I'll look closer to how I perceive myself. Then the mirror's different at the gym . . . mirrors do vary on how they represent you."

These women didn't trust their own body impressions and found discrepancies between what they saw, the assumed perceptions of others, their reflections in mirrors, and images of media women. This was depressing to some: "I feel disappointed about my body. I feel it can be a lot more trim and fit. But I just can't reach that ideal that I want to reach." Echoing a common sense of dissatisfaction, sadness, and frustration about her body, another woman said eating made her feel guilty.

Positive evaluations of personal growth were typically accompanied by dissonance. One woman confessed that although she had partly come to terms with the body she had hated during adolescence, she was still dissatisfied and preoccupied with eating and exercising. Such feelings had a deep body–sexuality link, an experience that was its own topic of discussion: "My body is desexualized . . . if I were in a different body I would feel differently about my sexual persona, and people would perceive me differently. I hate my body." Another woman expanded this point, confessing that she hid her body from her boyfriend: "Okay, turn out the lights. Close the blinds. Don't let any light in." Again, assumed perceptions of others came into play.

These women were left wanting. With self-conceptions filtered through external influences and body parts they believed made them "stand out," the bodies they yearned for were elusive and seemingly just out of reach. If they could just fix specific body parts by working out a little more or eating a little less, maybe they could feel better. Failing to achieve the perceived images and expectations of others left the women feeling guilty. Overcoming negative feelings and low self-esteem was seen as a lifelong struggle. In short, the heterosexual women couldn't resist common, external influences on self-conception.

The Lesbian Women.   Two distinct themes emerged as the lesbians evaluated their bodies. First, they agreed that a healthy, fit body was much more important and attractive than the thin media ideal. One woman who was unhappy because a recent weight gain caused her to lose fitness explained that she felt better before because she "worked out every day" and "ate right." While she did appreciate hearing she "looked good" (as self-conception through other suggests), she emphasized very strongly that she took care of her body for herself, not for others. Another participant was very much at ease with her body, even though she was happier when she exercised. Despite her "flab," she was quite comfortable living in her body.

This expression of comfort shed some light on the second theme that emerged as the women discussed body image from a "self" versus "other" perspective: They evaluated their bodies based on how they felt inside, not on how they thought others perceived them. One participant explained a life-changing shift in her self-conception: "So now, as far as focusing on a mission instead of being wrapped up in 'Okay, what does my body look like, is everything looking okay? Do I feel good about this? Now I can go out and face the world.' It's not like that. It's more feeling good inside."

Again, the lesbians had an acute sense of what it felt like to be *in* their bodies. Rejecting culturally prescribed notions of how women should look, they focused on integral aspects of their lives. One woman provided persuasive insight into a consequence of membership in a lesbian subculture that supports women who seek more positive self-perceptions. To her surprise, after abandoning her body focus she met more women, experienced more satisfying relationships, developed a better attitude, and had more confidence.

The Bisexual Women.   Body evaluation and self-conception among the bisexual women emerged through discussions of both inner and outer influences. They had trouble accepting positive evaluations from others, yet they also rebelled against negative messages. Some expressed frustration with having to compensate for their "nonideal" body image by proving the desirability of inner qualities—for example, "you just have this sparkling, amazing personality." One woman described an interesting conflict. She felt bad that she didn't see her body type in media—she felt excluded—but she didn't want to see her body in media because to her it was unappealing.

Even those who were somewhat satisfied with their bodies shared internalized feelings of guilt about how others perceived them; this lowered their self-esteem. Two thin women even blamed themselves for other women's feelings of body inadequacy. The frustration of having to prove themselves and the distress of having a "desirable" body were exacerbated by a contradiction. There was a tension between recognizing both the appeal *and* the unhealthiness of the ideal media body, as one woman explained: "Like Kate Moss . . . I do think she's too thin, but I think she's attractive. And I don't feel like I'm allowed to think that she's attractive." There was a sense that an emaciated woman in real life was considered "sick," yet the same image in media was perceived as "sexual fantasy."

Such contradictions were not always so explicitly expressed. Despite their awareness that the media's ideal body type was excruciating to achieve, most of the women engaged in some form of body image fantasy. Desires to look like certain media characters surfaced frequently but less obtrusively than the longings of the heterosexual women. By the end of the meeting, one bisexual participant identified three media women she wanted to look like.

BODY IMAGE INFLUENCES

In the end, all of the women were asked to rate interpersonal and media influences on their body image feelings. Everyone agreed that the most direct messages and influences came from family members. The bisexual and heterosexual women shared painful stories of confrontational family comments about their weight—for example: "When my best friend started going through anorexia, my mother would say, 'It's a shame that can't happen to you until you reach your goal weight, so that you can lose all of that weight.'" The lesbians dealt with similar messages from family members and also contended with efforts to socialize them into traditional, heterosexist feminine orientations.

Everyone rated the power of messages from peers as second. While the heterosexual women focused on negative peer commentary, the bisexual women made clear distinctions between messages they received from homosexual peers and partners, men, and heterosexual women. They experienced homosexual peers and partners as supportive, men as negative, and heterosexual women as competitive.

The lesbian women also appreciated supportive communication from lesbian peers and partners. Describing her first sexual experience with a woman, one participant explained, "She made me feel more beautiful than a man would." Personal relationships within the lesbian community provided the most positive messages to these women.

The heterosexual women didn't mention sources of positive commentary to counterbalance negative messages they received. The most troubled group, they couldn't resist common, external forces of socialization. As members of more socially accepted demographic, they lacked the history of life experiences that the lesbian and bisexual women had long been using to resist dissonant and negative information from people and media.

It is worth noting that even the negative comments received from other women might ultimately be attributable to men. These other women were also socialized in a male-dominated world; they, too, were inundated with communication regarding how they "should" look that originated from a traditionally masculine, heterosexist frame of reference.

All three groups agreed that messages from media were ubiquitous and consistent and that they operated at an often imperceptible level. The bisexual and lesbian women especially recognized the influence of media on others, as friends and family directly and indirectly compared them to media images. The bisexual women were very concerned about the impact of traditional media body imagery on teenage girls. For some, this stemmed from the belief that they were more affected by the media as teens than as young adults. The lesbian women agreed that media stereotypes of lesbians exacerbate the influence of narrowly conceived body types. The heterosexual women recognized that any and all negative messages—mediated, interpersonal, and intrapersonal—far outweighed any positive messages they received.

As for what to do about what several participants called the "body image crisis," the heterosexual women were left wondering. The lesbian and bisexual women displayed the capacity to take personal responsibility for counterbalancing the media's impact on their lives. The bisexual women expanded this into a call for more affirmative media literacy efforts for teens.

NOTES

1. The authors thank Alfred P. Kielwasser for his assistance with data analysis and revisions of this manuscript.

2. The very future of Olympic softball is dim; unless the International Olympic Committee reinstates the sport, 2008 represented the final Olympic softball competition.

IT'S YOUR TURN: WHAT DO YOU THINK? WHAT WILL YOU FIND?

1. Have you seen your body represented in mass media? If so, where and in what ways? How is your body included in or excluded from media content?

2. How do you feel about your body? How have your feelings about your body evolved over time? How have these feelings directed your behaviors, such as what you wear, how you relate to both men and women, how you feel about food, and what you eat?

3. Media sexism is usually addressed in terms of women and the female identity, but we shouldn't ignore male imagery and its contribution to the development of male identity. What mediated images of men have you have seen in the past year? How might these images influence men's self-concepts?

4. Go to www.bodyimagesite.com and (a) using the Information link, visit the Web sites of two organizations supporting body image diversity, (b) go to the end of the Documentary link and reflect upon the additional body image discussion questions, group work, and individual projects, and (c) use the Share your Stories link if you want to participate in the ongoing discussion of body image and self-conception.

REFERENCES

Brim, O. G. (1968). Adult socialization. In J. A. Clausen (Ed.), *Socialization and society* (pp. 183–226). Boston: Little, Brown.

Cash, T. F., & Brown, T. A. (1987). A body image in anorexia nervosa and bulimia nervosa: A review of the literature. *Behavior Modification, 11*, 487–521.

Cash, T. F., & Hicks, K. L. (1990). Being fat, versus thinking fat: Relationships with body image, eating behaviors, and well-being. *Cognitive Therapy and Research, 14*, 327–341.

Festinger, L. (1954). A theory of social comparison processes. *Human Relations, 7*, 117–140.

Garner, D. M., Garfinkel, P. E., Schwartz, D., & Thompson, M. (1980). Cultural expectations of thinness in women. *Psychological Reports, 47*, 483–491.

Gettelman, T. E., & Thompson, J. K. (1993). Actual differences and stereotypical perceptions in body image and eating disturbance: A comparison of male and female heterosexual and homosexual samples. *Sex Roles, 29*(7/8), 545–562.

Herzog, D. B., Newman, K. L., Yeh, C. J., & Warshaw, M. (1992). Body image satisfaction in homosexual and heterosexual women. *International Journal of Eating Disorders, 11*(4), 391–396.

Hutchinson, M. G. (1982). Transforming body image: Your body, friend or foe. *Women and Therapy, 1*(3), 59–67.

Kalodner, C. R. (1997). Media influences on male and female non-eating-disordered college students: A significant issue. *Eating Disorders, 5*(1), 47–57.

Kielwasser, A. P., & Wolf, M. A. (1991, February). *The sound (and sight) of silence: Notes on television and the communication ecology of adolescent homosexuality.* Paper presented at the annual meeting of the Western States Communication Association, Phoenix, AZ. (ERIC Document Reproduction Service No. ED 332 242).

Kielwasser, A. P., & Wolf, M. A. (1993/1994). Silence, differentiation, and annihilation: Understanding the impact of mediated heterosexism on high school students [Special issue: *The gay teenager*]. *The High School Journal, 77*(1 & 2), 58–79.

Lippmann W. (1922). *Public opinion.* New York: Macmillan.

Myers, P. N., & Biocca, F. A. (1992). The elastic body image: The effect of television advertising and programming on body image distortions in young women. *Journal of Communication, 42*(3), 108–133.

Silverstein, B., Perdue, L., Peterson, B., & Kelly, E. (1986). The role of the mass media in promoting a thin standard of bodily attractiveness for women. *Sex Roles, 14*(9/10), 519–534.

Thompson, J. K. (1990). *Body image disturbance: Assessment and treatment.* Elmsford, NY: Pergamon Press.

CHAPTER 3

AUDIENCE RECEPTION, USE, AND INTERPRETATION OF MEDIA CONTENT

3.1 "WHY DON'T YOU ACT YOUR COLOR?": PRETEEN GIRLS, IDENTITY, AND POPULAR MUSIC

Pamela J. Tracy

This reading presents part of a larger qualitative study concentrating on social and cultural dimensions of preteen girls' popular music experiences. One dimension of the study was the ways that racial and gendered identities as well as friendship histories affect and are affected by the girls' uses of popular music. The reading focuses specifically on one phenomenon the author calls "why don't you act your color?" Explore with the author the relationships among identity, race, being a girl/boy, popular music use, and what these categories mean in terms of social interaction and constructions of difference.

Emily: They, like, listen to this kind of music [R&B, hip-hop, rap], and we listen to it sometimes. Once I was singing a song and I was singing "The Thong Song" and Vanecia and Teresa were like, "Emily, you're not Black, why do you act like a Black person?"

Vanecia: When we do this [pretend to be TLC] and stuff, we do dance clubs and all of that other junk and then Emily, she goes, "Okay, like you know," and she be acting all Black and all hard like this [Vanecia is snapping her fingers and moving her head back and forth] . . . and I be like, "Emily, don't be acting our color. Act your color." And, she's like, "Okay, then whatever." And, then on the next day she be acting our color and I tell her again and she gets real smart with me and we get into fights . . . what I'm trying to say is I can't see why White people don't act White. Black people act Black.

After spending several months with Emily and Vanecia and their fourth-grade classmates—I'll call them the Central girls—it became apparent that popular music was omnipresent and integral to their everyday lives. More specifically, as illustrated in previous quotes, listening, dancing, and singing to music meant more than entertainment. When they talked about popular music, sang and danced in the school lunchroom and on the playground, and acted out Destiny's Child and TLC in their bedrooms and basements, these girls communicated not only pleasure but also their racial and gendered identities. The type of music they listened to, how they listened to this music, and who they listened with mattered in terms of how they organized their friendships, how they expressed their identities, and how they negotiated their place in their social and cultural worlds. The girls' frustrations with each other and their struggles to understand what it means to "act your color" are an important part of their experience with popular music.

I argue that when they engaged with music, the Central girls constructed a sense of self and other that was tied to contextual conditions (e.g., where they were and who they were with), their understandings of social and cultural relations, and their interpretation of what it means to be "me" and "you." Of course, this reading doesn't tell the whole story. While the girls negotiated their own identities when engaging with music in the lunchroom and/or in their dance groups, dominant racial and gendered belief systems continued to affect their ways of seeing and being with others in other school- and home-based contexts.

I conducted research with the Central girls at their urban elementary school in a large Midwestern city. The participants were fourth-grade girls ranging in age from 9 to 11 years old. In terms of race and ethnicity, five girls, including Emily and April, described themselves as White/Caucasian; five girls including, Tracey, named themselves African American/Black; Teresa said that she was African American/American Indian/White; one girl described herself as American Indian/White; one said that she was Malaysian; and Maria named herself Hawaiian. I spent approximately 10 months and on average 3 to 4 days a week with the girls in their school. In addition to individual and peer group interviewing, administering questionnaires, and asking the girls to keep a media journal, I observed and participated regularly during recess, lunch, free time, literature, dance, and art classes. I also participated in a school-wide roller-skating party, cleanup event, read-a-thon, and spring concert. During all of these events, I took notes, asked the girls questions, and participated in their activities.

Before I begin, I want to briefly highlight the theoretical assumptions that guide my interpretations of the Central girls' popular music experiences. Cultural studies audience scholars are interested in understanding how people make sense of media and how media experiences affect everyday life. This scholarship is grounded in the assumption that media and popular culture experiences are important socialization practices that both negatively and positively influence how we construct a sense of self and others. While media and popular culture texts (e.g., movies, TV shows, songs, and fashion) are understood as potentially powerful influences, these scholars argue that audiences actively construct meaning when they interpret media images, sounds, and forms. In fact, sometimes people use media products to construct identities, to resist authority, and to build knowledge.

Nevertheless, meaning construction is understood to be a social process influenced by a variety of contextual conditions including audiences' day-to-day interactions with others, societal belief systems, economic relations, cultural experiences, other media texts, and familial practices. Some of these social practices, such as working, schooling, and advertising, function ideologically. That is, they work to create belief systems that are taken for granted as "the way things are." These belief systems, more often than not, serve to privilege some people and ways of being over others. For example, the Central girls frequently made connections between their everyday experiences with boys and the music lyrics about heterosexual dating. As they interpreted the texts they reflected on their direct knowledge about relationships. At the same time, many of the lyrics referenced sexual relations that the girls described as "about older girls" and "stuff we don't know about." Despite the fact that they had no direct experience, they accepted the lyrical messages—messages privileging heterosexuality and warning them about boys/men—as valid and important for future reference. In doing so, they relied on social and cultural belief systems about heterosexual relationships and particular gender behaviors to interpret media content.

In terms of research, a variety of scholars emphasize the value of ethnographic study for investigating how audiences engage with media (see, for example, Ang, 1996, and Bennett, 2000). Ethnographic research allows us to understand how the construction of meaning depends on a variety of social relations, practices, and situations. Through observation, participation, and interviewing, we can gain a better understanding of how day-to-day interactions and different contexts affect media experiences. In reference to the Central girls' study, the ethnographic methods I used enabled a closer investigation into their popular music experiences particularly in terms of understanding more fully how they enacted their identities. By spending more time with them and expressing my interest in their lives, we were able to create some space for discussing difficult and seemingly taboo topics.

In addition to valuing context and the social aspect of media use, cultural studies scholars also focus on the process of identity construction. Feminist scholars argue that identity (or how we understand and enact a sense of self and other) is "communicated" and "practiced" rather than predetermined by race, gender, class, age, sexuality, ability, and ethnicity. For example, Vanecia, one of the Central girls, defines herself as an African American/Black and "half White" girl. She explained that "when I am with my mom's family, they are White. I feel different than when I am with my dad's family." As you will read later, Vanecia identified quite strongly with other African American/Black girls when they talked about Whites listening to hip-hop and "acting Black," and, at other moments, she danced to this music with her White friends. How she understands her place in her social and cultural world is complicated and enriched by her many multiple and layered identities. Vanecia's interpretations of her immediate experiences, what might be required of her at any given moment, and her readings of larger social and ideological systems such as media influence the ways she communicates her identities. If we were to judge Vanecia based on her skin color or gender alone, we would most likely make assumptions that don't fully represent her day-to-day experiences.

In reference to their popular music experiences, the Central girls communicated their identities in a variety of ways. For example, the girls listened to particular types of music because they identified with certain lyrics, rhythms, and related fashion and dance styles—their lived experiences were reflected in the music form and content. Some girls listened to learn more about what "will happen in the future"—projecting ahead to a particular way of being a woman. Heather listened to Macy Gray because she liked the music but also because she wanted to communicate that she had different tastes than her classmates and, more important, that she was different than others. Maria listened to TLC because she felt that the song *UnPretty* and its message about "being yourself and not listening to others" verified her beliefs. And, some of the girls sang and danced to certain genres during lunchtime because this communicated that they knew the music, which helped them achieve a certain social status.

In addition, as the girls and boys listened, danced, and sang to particular songs, others around them were constructing perceptions about them. Because Kathleen, a White girl, didn't like rap or hip-hop, she was described as being "all that" or thinking that she was better than others. Conversely, when Marcus, an African American boy, listened to rap music with "cussing" in it, he was constructed as a potential troublemaker. The Central girls' experiences illustrate the relationship between music and identity and highlight that identity is simultaneously how we communicate a sense of self to others and how we are constructed by the world around us.

"WHY DON'T YOU ACT YOUR COLOR?"

Emily, April, and Maria on "Acting Black"

During their peer group interview, this group of girls discussed why they felt that African American girls might connect to Destiny's Child music more than non-Black girls did. This discussion slowly evolved into several stories about their experiences with being told to "act their own color."

Emily: They [African American/Black girls], like, listen to this kind of music [R&B, hip-hop], and we [non-Black girls] listen to it sometimes. Once I was singing a song and I was singing "The Thong Song" and Vanecia and Teresa were like, "Emily, you're not Black. Why do you act like a Black person?"

April: Like a lot of Black people like White things and White people never say anything bad about Black people . . .

Emily: Yeah. We all like Britney Spears . . .

Maria: Like at my birthday party . . . Remember at my birthday party, Chelsea just started dancing and Shaquilla and Vanecia were playing together and they just went, "Oh no, you're White, Chelsea. Listen to something else."

Pam: Does this affect your friendships?

Maria: Kind of.

Maria: Me, Emily, and April don't even listen to some of the music around them when we want to because we are their friends.

Emily: We know what they are going to say . . .

Maria: Yeah.

Pam: What kind of music? Like Destiny's Child?

Maria: Like even Destiny's Child, they go, like, Shaquilla goes, "Oh no, don't do that."

Emily: Me and April were singing it once and she's like "No, Emily; no, April."

Maria: And Tiffany, remember when they said that about Tiffany? They're not Tiffany's friend even though last year Shaquilla and them were Tiffany's friend. They're not her friend this year because they think she acts like she's Black.

Tracey, Vanecia, and Teresa on "Acting Black"

While they were discussing how they came to know poppin' (a dance move), Teresa, Tracey, and Vanecia started making fun of the boys in their class who have tried to make this move. In doing so, they told stories about one White boy, Kyle, who tried to "act Black." This conversation led to a more serious discussion about their frustrations with White girls who sang and danced in particular ways that, according to this trio, mirrored Black dance and communication styles. First, they explained that they liked to form dance groups during recess to act out their favorite singers, particularly TLC.

Pam: Okay, the other girls that you do this with, Shaquilla, Emily, April, Maria . . . you do the same thing. They say who they are [which singer they are] . . .

Vanecia: They say who they are. When we do this and stuff, we do clubs and all of that other junk and then Emily, she goes, "Okay like you know," and she be acting all Black and all hard like [Vanecia is snapping her fingers and moving her head back and forth]—this no offense, Tracey [I think she said this because she knows they are Tracey's friends]—but she acting all Black and hard and other things like that. And I be like, "Emily, no," and she be like, "Oh no," and sometimes I be playing with her and I be acting like I'm a different color . . .

Tracey: And then she go out and get a attitude.

Vanecia: I say, "Emily, don't be acting our color. Act your color." And she's like, "Okay then, whatever." And then on the next day she be acting our color and I tell her again and she gets real smart with me and we get into fights . . . I end up punching her and she end up running off crying and they end up coming back punching me back and I end up . . .

Pam: What bothers you about Emily acting your color?

Teresa: Cause it's like . . .

Tracey: It's annoying . . .

Vanecia: Well, what I'm trying to say is I can't see why White people act White, Black people act Black, it would be fine.

Teresa: I know. When White people try to act like Black people, it seems like they're not happy with their own color. Or when they try to be like Black . . .

Vanecia: So people will let them fit in.

Pam: So you do listen to this song with other girls. What happens when you are listening to it and Emily is trying to act Black, do you still keep on listening to it? Do you stop?

Vanecia: I listen to it and I tell her to stop.

Teresa: I know, because it gets on my nerves when she tries to act like Black people. Because it's like, why can't they just be happy with their color? Don't try to be like other people. If you don't fit into something, just let somebody know . . .

Friendship Histories

During the interviews, both groups of girls were very passionate about how they each conceptualized the relationship between music and identities. At those moments when they wanted to communicate racial unity, Vanecia, Teresa, and Tracey established a firm connection between skin color and who can listen to particular musical genres. However, the concepts of "acting Black" or, more broadly, "acting your color" continued to be more complex when enacted in everyday life. In this case, cross-cultural friendship histories and gendered relationships significantly affected how girls performed and thought about racial identities. For example, Kyle, a middle-class White boy who doesn't "act his color," represented for these girls (Teresa, Vanecia, Tracey, and Maria) the most visible "acting Black" case. They spoke frequently about Kyle's attempts to act like his Black friend, Nate. According to Teresa, "Kyle tries to be a Black boy . . . listening to our music and saying 'Hey, what's up, my homie'. . . this is annoying, and I tell him to stop." While it "annoyed" Teresa, she also explained that she doesn't think it bothered Nate because he and Kyle have been friends for a long time. Maria and Emily also made the same assessment. Tracey made the comment that "Yo, those are my sisters," indicating that while she didn't like them "acting Black," Emily, April, and Maria were her friends. Emily's comment that it was hard to talk about "acting your own color" because "one of her best friends is African American" may also indicate the ways in which friendship histories complicate these identity conflicts. Friendship histories in relationship to racial identities were important in terms of understanding how both girls and boys negotiated their differences.

Gendered Allegiances

Girls' accusations about "acting your color" only reveal part of their musical story. While racial alliances were forged at these moments, on other occasions, girls publicly relied on each other in their journey to "get the boys out of their face." Their gendered allegiance in this quest was evident in their collaborative attempts to make sure "their music" (not the boy's music) was played during lunch and free time in the classroom. In their mutual attempts to unite, Tracey, Vanecia, Teresa, Maria, Emily, and April formed a dancing/singing group.

> We do it outside on the playground. We can't find no hangout, but the one hangout is over here in a small corner we really like, when we get over there if it's cold or when we get over there, like, anyone will bring snacks for our group . . . the teachers don't know about the group . . . we make up our own songs . . . and, we only let boys who are nice to us be in the group.

While they occasionally let boys in, they did so only if the boys would let them be the leaders. According to Tracey,

> Like Mark. He's the boy you have to watch out for. Like all the girls, we're controlling him . . . we have to work hard to keep him away from the girls. We got him in check.

This girl-dominated group provided an opportunity for them to act out their favorite singers and bands and "to teach other girls who don't know how to dance our moves that we learned . . . so that others won't make fun of them." In addition, they often engaged in public scrutiny of boys who made fun of their music, especially when these same boys sang and danced to TLC and N'Sync at other times. Their connections to each other through their shared gendered experiences with boys reveals the necessarily unfixed nature of identity.

The Central girls also used their music to build and maintain their friendships. Tracey described the ways in which popular music helped her to "make up" with other girls after a playground fight. She explained,

> like, we were mad because we were outside and everything went wrong. Then during lunch, someone will go up and ask Isabella and Pete [teachers] to turn on Destiny's Child. So they play it and all the girls [who have been fighting] they, like, get back together once they get back in the class . . . because right when they say the words . . . you can picture your group together . . . when you get together, it makes you end up happy and makes you want to dance and stuff like that."

In this context, after a fight and in the lunchroom—a space that they associated with listening to "their music"—the meaning of Destiny's Child music and the relationship once established between genre and identity changed. For these girls, their relationships and the context of their interactions and engagement with music mattered in terms of how they expressed who they were and how they perceived others. While their racial and gendered identities were always present, these girls shifted their identification with others, at times, based on the exigency of the moment. The girls' experiences illustrate that identities are enacted, that we actively communicate who we are and use media to do so, and that our media consumption is always tied to social and cultural issues.

IT'S YOUR TURN: WHAT DO YOU THINK? WHAT WILL YOU FIND?

1. In reference to the concept of "acting Black," Williams (2000) argued that

   > it is sad to see rap music eviscerated of its passion and pathos and appropriated by the mainstream. . . . [E]ven though I have never enjoyed rap as an art form, I could always at least appreciate it as an authentic outlet of expression for poor, inner city Black youths. Madison Avenue has gotten into the act, with ads like William Shatner's ("Star Trek's" Capt. Kirk) on behalf of Priceline.com. To the beat of Young MC's hit tune "Bust a Move," Shatner raps his way through an ebonics-laced pitch for airline tickets. . . . Why is African Americana always fair game for such appropriation and ridicule? Is nothing Black sacred? Why is Black dialect considered comical in the mouths of whites? . . ." (p. A6)

   What do you think are the key elements of Williams's statement? What do you think about it? How does this relate to the Central girls' popular music experiences?

2. While conducting research, I witnessed several moments when students and teachers made assumptions about people based on their music preferences. What kinds of connections have you made or witnessed between identity and music taste? What are the potential social implications?

3. Interview a friend about a song he/she likes. Listen to the song together, and try to understand how she/he interprets and experiences this song. Consider what practices, people, and/or beliefs influence your friend's musical

experiences. What did you learn about this person? About music?

Possible questions you could ask include these: Why did you choose this song to bring in today? What is it about it that you like? Dislike? What does this song make you think and feel? What do the lyrics mean to you? Are they connected to your life? When, where, and with whom do you usually listen/sing/dance to this song? Is there any time, place, or person that

you would not listen/sing/dance to this song? Is there any music that you do not listen to?

4. Search the Internet for the phrase "acting Black" or the term "wannabe." What claims are made? By whom? What is being said about identity, race, culture, politics, media, etc? Do you agree or disagree with what is being said? Why? How is this connected to your experiences?

REFERENCES

Ang, I. (1996). Ethnography and radical contextualism in audience studies. In J. Hay, L. Grossberg, & E. Wartella (Eds.), *The audience and its landscape* (pp. 247–264). Boulder, CO: Westview Press.

Bennett, A. (2000). *Popular music and youth culture: Music, identity, place.* New York: St. Martin's.

Williams, L. (2000). Commentary: Whites' entertainment is Black's irritainment. *New Pittsburgh Courier, 91*(76), A6.

3.2 "WOMEN WHO LOOK LIKE ME": CULTURAL IDENTITY AND READER RESPONSES TO AFRICAN AMERICAN ROMANCE NOVELS

Gwendolyn E. Osborne

> *The author says, "I'd held a number of preconceived notions about romance fiction before I ever read it. Most of my ideas about 'those books' involved Harlequin romances, terms such as 'bodice rippers' or 'purple prose,' and book covers with Fabio embracing a blond, blue-eyed ingénue deep in the throes of passion. I thought romance fiction only appealed to the type of women one* Washington Post *reporter called 'the bored and the brain-dead'" (Parker, 1999, p. C1).*
>
> *What about you? What images or phrases do you associate with romance novels? The author attempts to challenge some of your notions about romance fiction—and the women who read it—through a look at the African American romance and its relevance for the cultural identity of its readers.*

The sale of romance novels accounts for nearly half of all paperback book sales in the United States—more than mysteries, science fiction, and Westerns combined. Industry estimates say African American romance readers contribute 10% to 30% of the more than $1 billion spent each year on romance novels. A significant number of college-educated Black women are among these readers—women such as feminist author bell hooks, who reportedly has read romances for two decades (Parker, 1999), and Portland engineer Wendy Davis, an avid reader whose friends often disparage her passion for romance novels (Osborne, 1999).

As I began to study the African American romance novel, I discovered very little scholarship was available. Modleski (1982), Radway (1991), and Krentz (1992), the most-cited works on romance readers, predate the major influx of Black readers into the genre. These works paid no attention to issues of race within the context of the romance novel or of African American readership. Likewise, anthologies of evocative works that explored Black male–female relationships in literature by African American authors such as Golden (1993) and Robotham (1999), and critical works such as that by Wade-Gayles (1984), excluded the growing body of romances by African American women.

I wanted to know what it is about Black romances that draws so many African American book buyers to the romance sections of the nation's bookstores. I interviewed many first- and second-generation African American romance readers. I define first-generation readers as those who read romance novels prior to the availability of romances featuring African American characters. Second-generation readers are those who began to read romance fiction after the inception of African American romance imprints.[1]

The readers I spoke with were Black women who regularly read romance fiction. They ranged in age from early-20s to mid-50s, were college-educated and worked outside the home. They read 1 to 25 romances a month and had attended at least one romance-related event or conference within 12 months of the interview. And, although they held varying definitions of the term, each woman considered herself a "feminist" or "womanist" and saw no philosophical contradiction posed by her enjoyment of romance fiction. At some point in the interview, each woman told me she read African American romances because she was drawn to stories about positive relationships between Black men and women (seen as missing in other forms of mediated communication) and that she liked stories about "women who look like me." Without exception, everyone highlighted the importance of her cultural identity as a Black woman when selecting romance novels.

According to Lusting and Koester (2000), *cultural identity* is "one's sense of belonging to a particular culture or ethnic group" (p. 3) and is pivotal to human experience and understanding. Tajfel (1978) presented a similar construct, *social identity*, as part of our self-concept, something we get from the knowledge that we belong to a particular social group, combined "with the value and emotional significance attached" (p. 63) to being part of that group. The interviews I conducted underscored the relevance of cultural/social identity and the importance of being able to see oneself reflected in the content of mass media—in this case, the romance novel.

THE COLOR OF LOVE

Because the essence of romance novels deals with love, courtship, and marriage, let's begin by looking at how readers' romantic perceptions have been shaped. Wexman (1993) described the role of Hollywood cinema in structuring American concepts of romantic love, courtship, and marriage. She noted that 85% of all American films produced before 1960 had romance as their main plot and relied on the classic cinematic scenario of "boy meets girl, boy loses girl, boy gets girl." As courtship rituals evolved, movies taught audiences about changing mores governing romantic love, reinforced social taboos, and created ideals of physical beauty and romantic desirability. The White Anglo-Saxon Protestant (WASP) model defined not only who was loved but also who was loveable.

"Love stories mean that people are human. If you want to keep people thinking they are not human, you don't see them kissing gently, rollicking, laughing through the streets. You [don't see them] in love and making love," said poet Sonia Sanchez in a story about Black love stories on film (Holmes, 1997, p. D-1).

The WASP model was fostered in other media—including the romance novel. African American women were most often depicted as docile servants, confidantes, victims, simpletons, schemers, tragic mulattos, and whores. These are not women with whom Black readers identify. For the most part, images of African American women in mainstream media perpetuated racial and sexual stereotypes that bell hooks (1981) argued devalues Black womanhood.

In the years following Harlequin's 1949 introduction of the romance genre to mass North American audiences, story themes and cover art kept pace with the lives and loves of White America. Although the genre continued to evolve, few novels by or about African American women were available. Aspiring African American writers were discouraged from publishing romances. According to an industry executive, Black romances were rejected because "the perception was that they wouldn't sell as well. There are all kinds of stereotypes at play—that [Blacks] aren't educated enough, don't read, or they don't go into malls to buy these books" (Hickey, 1991, p. 1).

AIN'T I A WOMAN?

As a result of such thinking, choices were limited for the first wave of African American romance readers. These readers seem to have had a conflicted relationship with romance novels—on the one hand, the books by White authors were enjoyable, but because they didn't adequately reflect the Black readers' cultural identities they left these readers wanting something more.

As historical romance author Beverly Jenkins (2000) recalled

> Not a one featured women who looked like us, but as we read them we longed for stories that did feature us, stories that reflected the love our parents shared or our grandparents shared; the love that we saw in that married couple at church who was always holding hands; or the love we see every time we look into our partner's eyes.

Shereen Jones of Kingston, Jamaica, is another first-generation romance reader. Two decades ago, she began reading English romances, but for the past few years she's been able to purchase African American romances during business trips to the United States and via the Internet. She now limits her romance reading to African American romances because she enjoys the depictions of Black women as beautiful and loveable—as people she can identify with:

> For many years I only read stories of slim, tall, and petite, Caucasian women with various shades of blue or green eyes and long, flowing blond hair. If you read that kind of

thing too often, and read nothing else, your idea of beauty begins to be formed by what you read. If you live in a country where 90% of the population is Black, you assume there are no beautiful women in your country because they sure don't have blue eyes and blond hair!

It wasn't until 1980 that Rosalind Welles' *Entwined Destinies*, the first romance novel by an African American writer, was acquired for the Dell Candlelight imprint by Vivian Stephens, an African American editor who created the "ethnic romance" (Walters, 1980). Later, as an editor with Harlequin, Stephens created an American line. (Prior to this, English language romance novels were written by Canadian, British, Australian and New Zealand authors.) In addition to purchasing early works by White romance authors who now grace bestsellers' lists, she bought Harlequin's first book by an African American: Sandra Kitt's *Adam and Eva*. However, the creation of a regular Black presence in the genre and the establishment of an imprint of romances by and about African Americans were still more than a decade away.

In 1992, the success of Terry McMillan's *Waiting to Exhale* and its definition of a solid Black book-buying market with mass crossover appeal is credited with opening publishing doors for African American writers in other genres—including romance. Within 2 years, Kensington Publishing, one of the nation's largest romance publishers, launched an African American imprint, Arabesque. (Arabesque was sold to Black Entertainment Television in 1999.)

First-generation readers such as Texas author Evelyn Palfrey, who read her mother's romance novels in the 1950s, were ecstatic about the new line.

> I was in heaven when the black romances came out. You no longer had to pretend that you were the character with long, flowing, blonde tresses or steamy blue eyes. We had to read that because it was all that was available. When I discovered the Arabesque romances, I just went stone crazy behind that stuff." (Moore, 2000, p. L6)

Other publishers quickly followed. That same year, both Avon Books and Fawcett released books by African American authors. In 1995, Mississippi attorney Wil Colon established Genesis Press in response to his wife's complaints about her inability to find romance novels that featured African American lead characters.

THE APPEAL OF THE AFRICAN AMERICAN ROMANCE TO BLACK WOMEN

Black readers of early African American romance fiction were drawn to the stories about middle-class Blacks involved in committed relationships with whom they were able to identify. Psychologist Renee A. Redd, director of Northwestern University's Women's Center, said the benefits for readers were often more than cosmetic.

> Romance novels offer women the chance to live the romantic lives we have been socialized from birth to believe is the province of beautiful, deserving women. Romance novels often

communicate the idea that if we are long suffering, if we just have persistence, some day Prince Charming will come along." (Osborne, 1999, p. 42)

Redd added that romance fiction also provides an escape from the statistical social reality many African American women face.

> They also offer a substitute for those who have resigned to never really being able to find a fulfilling love in their actual lives. The reality of a dearth of available straight black men for straight black women is a disconcerting and painful issue before us. For a long time we have lived with the idea of the strong black woman, who by implication can do without a romantic relationship if she must, but the truth is that she would rather not." (Osborne, 1999, p. 42)

It is the difference, said second-generation reader Jean Dalton of New York City, between sister–girl fiction and romance fiction.

> In *Waiting to Exhale*, four educated and successful Black women sat around complaining about Black men who were unable to commit, preferred White women, unemployed, incarcerated, gay, adulterous or sexually inadequate, and so on. African-American romance heroines are more in charge of their futures. They aren't sitting around waiting to exhale."

Author Gay Gunn agreed. "None of us could be found in black literature at that time. If novels gave us black women who were about something, they still gave us jerks for mates" (Osborne, 1999, p. 43).

Many feminist scholars and literary critics have berated the entire romance genre for its steamy sexual content, with some African American scholars arguing that the open sexual expression in romance novels reinforces negative stereotypes about Black women's sexuality. According to Redd,

> I think most black women still believe that the sexual expressiveness allowed the women in romance novels and to women of other races is not equally extended to black women. This is profoundly brought to our attention by the continued images of black women that are universally put forth." (Osborne, 1999, p. 42)

But as Rosemarie Robotham (1999) wrote, fears of such negative stereotypes are the product

> of a centuries-old need to protect against stereotypes that made Black women the object of tawdry fantasies, bringing rape and worse. In the face of this particular social danger, Black women learned to suppress their sexual natures, learned to silence expressions of love and longing that would reveal, and put at risk, the multiple dimensions of our lives." (pp. 2–3)

And although scholars and detractors have equated romance fiction with soft-core pornography, devoted romance readers understand the differences among romance, erotica, and pornography. Shareta Caldwell of Los Angeles, a second-generation reader, said, "Romances portray love, romance, and sensuality in an positive adult manner. In romance novels, a man puts a woman's pleasure first. This is not the case in pornography."

Jennifer Coates of Chicago enjoys the committed relationships depicted in African American romances. "In other media, we see intimate relationships being treated casually—like a handshake, but not that personal. The romance, the courting, the mystery seems to have disappeared from contemporary literature." This second-generation reader cites Beverly Jenkins's *Night Song* among her favorites because the interaction between the hero and heroine "demonstrates their appreciation and love for one another and solidified their relationship for me, elevating their sharing and mutual respect from a by-product, to the backbone of their intimate exchanges."

WOMEN WHO LOOK (AND READ) LIKE ME

As the debate over the social and literary merits of romance novels continues, the number of Black romances and readers is growing. African American romances are rarely reviewed by mainstream literary or romance media, but readers are undeterred. Readers get information about the latest releases from the Romance in Color Web site and from romance-friendly bookstores such as Emma Rodgers's Black Images Book Bazaar in Dallas.

The bookstore provides a venue for Romance Noir Book Club, one of several such clubs throughout the country. In addition to book signings and other special events, Rodgers also established Romance Slam Jam (RSJ) to connect romance readers and authors. Since its inception in 1995, it has evolved into a 4-day annual celebration of African American romance that draws hundreds of women from the United States, Canada, and the Caribbean. Second-generation reader Phyllis Redus of Huntsville, Alabama, said she attended RSJ 2001 in Orlando because she enjoys the camaraderie of other Black women she met via the Internet—women who like her read, understand, and appreciate African American romances.

Book clubs, message boards, and chat rooms on the Internet also give readers an opportunity to talk to authors and each other. Wilma Wilkerson of Houston parlayed her love for romance novels into a popular weekly chat room on America Online. "We meet on Thursday night for an hour to chat about books. We are occasionally visited by some of the authors. It's so exciting to read a book and then chat with the authors about it." Other popular online venues where romance readers gather are the Color of Love Chat Forum, Romance Watercooler, and the Black Literary Cafe.

CULTURAL/SOCIAL IDENTITY AND "WOMEN WHO LOOK LIKE ME"

African American romance readers are not a monolithic group and enjoy story lines that illustrate the depth and breadth of African American culture, that depict their history, and that dispel stereotypes. As Emma Rodgers of Dallas said,

African American romance novels are so popular because they reflect the values of the majority of the Black community [better] than most other types of media. The men and women are educated professionals, gainfully employed . . . or are entrepreneurs, upwardly mobile. The women are independent, career minded with goals. Both are law-abiding citizens. Readers seldom see these images reflected on the evening news or in the daily paper.

According to sociologist and romance novelist Gwynne Forster (1998),

> What makes characters uniquely African American is their perspective of the world around them; their optimism and tenacious pursuit of dreams and goals in the presence of towering social impediments; and their ability to laugh at awesome obstacles, or to ignore them and, often, climb over them. (p. 3)

The novels further reinforce African American cultural identities by including Afrocentric elements such as historically Black colleges and universities, Kwanzaa, and Black Greek organizations and religious denominations. The importance of music is often reflected in these stories and frequently provides a backdrop and context for the plot. Unlike novels by White authors, 35% to 40% of African American romances share titles with "old school" R&B songs or lyrics.

Generally, romance readers are drawn to the genre because—besides being devoid of gratuitous sex and profanity—the stories provide an escape. As Forster (1998) put it,

> The life and times of the less fortunate are not preferred as themes for the African American romance novel. People read romances for relaxation, to enjoy stories that are constructive and lift the spirit, not to grapple with the vicissitudes of someone else's life. (p. 3)

Well, if romance novels are escapist literature, African American authors have given their readers the ultimate fantasy: a world in which racism is virtually nonexistent. Plantation romances such as Kyle Onstett's *Mandingo*, which were part of the dominant (White) culture's bodice-ripping tradition, are nonexistent in Black romance. African American writers and readers agree that slavery is incompatible with the "happily ever after" world of romance. Interracial romances do occur (mostly African American women with White men) but are generally found in contemporary rather than historical stories.

Beyond issues of race, African American authors have begun to change the look of romance. Love comes in all sizes, shapes, and skin tones. There are romances among Blacks throughout the African diaspora. Full-figured women have been showcased as primary love interests. And, as baby boomers mature, many storylines have begun to reflect the changing demographic. In other words, African American readers can now enjoy romance novels that are relevant to various aspects of their cultural identities.

As you might expect, these changes don't satisfy everyone. Some people complain that the characters of African American romances "aren't Black enough." Others complain that the characters (or at least their depiction on the books' covers) "are too Black." In an *Arlington Morning News* story about crossover marketing of African American romances, a magazine publisher indicated that covers showing Blacks in Afrocentric styles might make White readers uncomfortable. "There are many people who might see the covers of the books, which often feature women with braids or short kinky cuts and men with clean-shaven heads and dark skin, as being too black and in-your-face" (Price, 1999, p. 1B). The publisher and others suggested covers without people.

African American romance readers chafe at the mere suggestion of removing Black characters from the covers. First-generation reader LaShaunda Hoffman of St. Louis said, "White romances have always had covers with White people on them. I didn't have a problem buying them. I bought them because I loved romances, not because there were White people on the cover." Shareta Caldwell said,

> I like it when there are Black faces on the books, especially if the cover is an accurate portrait of the character in the book. That is the reason I picked up Beverly Jenkins's *Indigo*. I loved the picture. And I don't like the idea of fooling people by not having real Black people on the front. If White readers can't get past the braids, locks, bald heads, and Black skin on the cover, then how are they going to get through the book?

Caldwell's statement (besides being a telling reflection of the state of race relations in our society) underscores the relevance of cultural identity to Black readers of African American romance novels. Each time a woman I interviewed expressed the desire for stories about "women who look like me," they emphasized the importance of at least one aspect of their cultural or social identities. This includes but is not limited to racial or ethnic identity. African American romance readers enjoy stories about women who look like them—not just physically, but politically, socially, economically, and emotionally as well. We deserve no less.

NOTE

1. Some interviews were conducted for a *Black Issues Book Review* article (Osborne, 1999); others were done for this reading. Unless I specifically cite another source, the quotes I provide come from those interviews.

IT'S YOUR TURN: WHAT DO YOU THINK? WHAT WILL YOU FIND?

1. Read a book on the suggested reading list on the next page. How do you describe the characters and themes? How do these compare to romance novels by White authors? How do they compare with non-romance fiction by African American women?

2. Select one of the couples profiled in Stovall's *A Love Supreme: Real Life Black Love Stories*. Discuss how the couple's story includes or differs from the basic elements of a romance novel.

3. Examine cover art from a variety of African American romance novels. Look at each cover and discuss whether the artwork reinforces stereotypes about romance novels. What led you to believe that these books are romances? The titles? The pictures? What does the pose indicate about the story or the relationship between the two main characters? What ideas do you take away from each? Can you judge a book by its cover? If so, what is your assessment of these books?

4. Examine cover art from a variety of White romance novels, addressing the same type of items as previously. How do these compare to the covers from African American romance novels?

REFERENCES

Forster, G. (1998, February). Culture and ethnicity in the African-American romance novel. Oakland: *Affaire de Coeur*, p. 3.

Golden, M. (1993). *Wild women don't wear no blues: Black women writers on love, men and sex*. New York: Doubleday.

Hickey, E. (1991, October 21). Buppy love rampant? Black urban professionals get their own romance novels. *The Washington Times*, p. D1.

Holmes, K. E. (1997, March 26). Black couples in Bohemian setting spark interest in the film *Love Jones. The Philadelphia Inquirer*, p. D-1.

hooks, b. (1981). *Ain't I a woman? Black women and feminism*. Boston: South End Press.

Jenkins, B. (2000, March 18). *Keynote address*. Romance Slam Jam 2000, Dallas, TX.

Krentz, J. A. (1992). (Ed.). *Dangerous men and adventurous women: Romance writers on the appeal of the romance*. New York: Harper Paperbacks.

Lustig, M. W., & Loester, J. (Eds.). (2000). *Among us: Essays on identity, belonging, and intercultural competence*. NY: Longman.

Modleski, T. (1982). *Loving with a vengeance: Mass-produced fantasies for women*. Hamden, CT: Archon.

Moore, C. (2000, October 8). How's this for a happy ending? Evelyn Palfrey succeeds as a romance writer by reaching out to overlooked readers. *Austin-American Statesman*, p. L6.

Osborne, G. E. (1999). Our love affair with romance. *Black Issues Book Review*, *1*, 40–45.

Parker, L. O. (1999, May 23). Fantasy aisle: Harlequin romance novels steam through 40 years of changing mores. *The Washington Post*, p. C1.

Price, L. (1999, May 23). Love lessons: Publishers are learning African-Americans are looking for romance on the bookshelves. *Arlington Morning News*, p. 1B.

Radway, J. (1991) *Reading the romance: Women, patriarchy and popular literature*. Chapel Hill: University of North Carolina Press.

Robotham, R. (1999). (Ed.) *The bluelight corner: Black women writing on passion, sex and romantic love*. New York: Three Rivers Press.

Tajfel, H. (1978). Social categorization, social identity, and social comparison. In H. Tajfel (Ed.), *Differentiation between social groups* (pp. 61–76). London: Academic Press.

Wade-Gayles, G. (1984). *No crystal stair: Visions of race and sex in black women's fiction*. New York: Pilgrim Press.

Walters, R. (1980, July 13). Paperback talk. *The New York Times*, p. 35.

Wexman, V. (1993). *Creating the couple: Love, marriage and Hollywood performance*. Princeton, NJ: Princeton University Press.

SUGGESTED READING

Alers, Rochelle: *All My Tomorrows* (2005, Kimani Press); *No Compromise* (2007, Kimani Press); *Just Before Dawn* (2000, Kimani Press).

Byrd, Adrianne: *Comfort of a Man* (2003, Kimani Press); *My Destiny* (2003, Kimani Press).

Gunn, Gay G.: *Pride & Joi* (2007, Genesis Press).

Jackson, Brenda: *A Family Reunion* (2001, Kimani Press); *Eternally Yours* (2008, Kimani Press); *Tonight and Forever* (2007, Kimani Press); *Whispered Promises* (2008, Kimani Press).

Jeffries, J. M.: *Southern Comfort* (2002, Genesis Press).

Jenkins, Beverly: *Topaz* (2007, Avon); *Edge of Midnight* (2004, Harper Torch); *Wild Sweet Love* (2007, Avon).

Mason, Felicia: *Seductive Hearts* (2005, Kimani Press).

Palfrey, Evelyn: *Three Perfect Men* (1996, Moon Child Books); *Everything in its Place* (2006, Simon & Schuster); *Dangerous Dilemmas* (2007, Simon & Schuster); *The Price of Passion* (2006, Simon & Schuster).

Ray, Francis: *Trouble Don't Last Always* (2004, St. Martin's Griffin).

Sims, Janice: *Desert Heat* (2003, Kimani Press).

3.3 FINDING HOME IN A SONG AND A DANCE: NATION, CULTURE, BOLLYWOOD

Sheena Malhotra

> *In this piece, the author considers issues of ethnic, gender, and class identities as she reflects on how Bollywood films can evoke "home" for members of the South Asian diaspora (displaced or dispersed people). Bollywood (a contraction of "Bombay" and "Hollywood") produces commercial Hindi films. It is the largest film industry in the world, producing more than twice the number of films that Hollywood produces annually.*

A diasporic community consists of people displaced from their homeland through voluntary or forced migrations. The struggles of diasporic populations center on two ongoing issues: the transmission of cultural values/norms to future generations and coming to terms with multiple home spaces. But what is home? And how do cultural values get transmitted? Chandra Mohanty (1993) reminds us that home is not necessarily a physical space but rather can be a space where we create a sense of belonging emotionally, politically, and through our ideas and beliefs. This sense of belonging is actually created through various sites of influence—our families, friends, school, media, power structures in society, and all the various communities in which we are involved. In this essay,[1] I focus on one of these sites (media) for one particular community (South Asian diaspora) and their negotiations with "home." I write from the perspective of a participant observer, someone who is both a participant and researcher within a community. I am a first-generation Indian woman, currently living in Los Angeles. First coming to the United States at 18, I have gone back and forth between India and the United States, looking for home in different spaces. My family lives in India, and I work and live in the United States. Like Mohanty, the more I traverse the globe, the more I too believe that home really is an ideological space. Or as they might say in the movies, "Home is where the heart is."

In this chapter, I unpack how Hindi films and the Bollywood dream machine come to symbolize home and occupy an increasingly powerful role of transmitting cultural norms within the South Asian community, particularly for first-generation immigrants. Yet, there are many different negotiations of home depending on one's subjectivity, or how one is positioned within society. For example, Gayathri Gopinath (2003) has written about the complicated relationships queer subjects have with "home" and "nation" because of their outsider status to "home" within a social system where men dominate and that assumes and enforces heterosexuality as the norm (heteropatriarchy).

So when diasporic populations evoke "home," it is important to ask how exactly home is construed and how it gets conflated with nation. What notions of the nation get reproduced in our imaginary? What are the omissions of class in these reproductions? What equations of gender do these films champion? What notions of "home" are reproduced, by and for different diasporic subjects? Can we complicate those readings?

Some crucial information to our discussion is that India opened up its economy in 1991 and global flows of people, culture, and capital became vital to its accomplishments

(Joshi, 1998). Additionally, the success of Bollywood films in the overseas markets post-1990 translated into efforts to be more inclusive of the diasporic experience, which was imagined (and portrayed) as primarily wealthy and educated in Bollywood. Framed through the *mediascapes*, which refer to the images of the world created by the media and their global distribution (Appadurai, 1996/2000), the diasporic Indian was increasingly represented as crucial to the Indian economy and nation-state (Mankekar, 1999). The effort to appeal to this group has produced representations in many Bollywood films of Indian identity that are no longer necessarily tied to the homeland. Post-1990 Bollywood notions of identity are based on cultural values, religious customs, even celebrations of wealth that are associated with the diaspora (Malhotra & Alagh, 2004). So increasingly, "home" is located in values, practices, and customs, which can be anywhere physically or literally (although we mostly see it being located in the United States or Western Europe). Bollywood speaks to and draws in the diaspora, and increasingly, the diaspora looks to Bollywood to find "home."

This chapter focuses on two instances of diasporic audiences using Bollywood in various ways to construct home. First, I read the documentary film *Bollywood Crossings* as an ethnographic study of diasporic audiences who engage (and struggle) with Bollywood films in their quest for home. Second, I write about an eventful evening with a queer diasporic community and its use of a particular film to reimagine home. Both instances focus on audiences of Bollywood films in global contexts and show us the power of Bollywood to insert itself into their imaginaries. I find that Hindi films are a powerful vehicle for evoking "home" for diasporic populations. Additionally, they are utilized by otherwise potentially disenfranchised populations to imagine themselves into the nation, even as the nation gets increasingly narrowly reimagined by Bollywood films.

BOLLYWOOD CROSSINGS: CULTURE IN THE MOVIES

When heterosexual, upper-middle-class, diasporic audiences use Bollywood films to cultivate relationships with home, those relationships often become an uncontested acceptance of the nation and its norms. But what aspects of the nation get erased in this easy acceptance? I come to these questions and discussion through *Bollywood Crossings*, a documentary directed by Tavishi Alagh that follows several diasporic subjects as they make sense of their lives and search for cultural roots in Bollywood-style filmic representations. The film is an ethnographic study filmed over 3 years. (I worked on *Bollywood Crossings* as a consultant; I viewed and worked with the approximately 90 hours of raw footage shot for the film.) The film interweaves dialogues with over 150 audience members, organizers, and performers involved with, and excited about, Bollywood shows and films touring the United States. It charts diasporic audiences' close relationships with Bollywood films and music by focusing on the lives of five central characters. Three of the main protagonists are friends living in New York. Each has a different and complicated relationship with Bollywood, India's dream industry. The three men, Sanjay, Ashwini, and Zulfi, come to represent three viewpoints of diasporic use of media to connect with home.

The first of the friends is Sanjay. For Sanjay, Bollywood *is* India. He is a working-class boy who has "made it" in the technology industry in America and now lives in a large suburban house. He argues that he has the best of both worlds, dancing with his wife

Bollywood-style for the viewer. He spends upwards of $200 per ticket on the Bollywood star shows he attends with his friends and is very impressed with himself for being in the second or third row, so close to the stars he loves and admires. Ironically for him, it is by being in the United States that he can "almost touch" the Indian stars. He is earnest in his embodiment of the Bollywood dream. It is a recreated nostalgic space that, in effect, exists only in his head and eclipses his lack of access back home. But it is powerful enough to sustain him. In fact, it is a home where he has affluence, control, and access. He no longer wants to make the distinctions between Bollywood and India.

The second friend is Ashwini. For Ashwini, Bollywood is a bridge, an educational tool. It is a bridge to connect him back to his roots, through the songs he shares with other diasporic friends. Bollywood is considered "cool" and hip these days, and so it makes him feel valued in mixed (American and Indian) social spaces. And it is an educational tool for his future children. He is a second-generation immigrant, having spent much of his formative years in Africa and Europe, being an outsider, constantly trying to "blend in." Now a proud New Yorker, Ashwini's voiceover is intercut between shots of him driving the streets, taking a ferry ride with the backdrop of New York City's skyline and prepping for a party at his house. As he reveals stories about learning Swahili as a boy, and then finding himself in Paris with no French language skills as a teenager, we see visuals of Ashwini in multiple intercuts of the spaces he inhabits in the present day. Form begins to mirror content as we realize that his grounding is never in one physical space. It is found instead through the imaginary bridge of Bollywood films. In fact, he no longer needs to return "home" to the physical space of India, partially because India is bridged for him culturally in the media products he consumes. Overlaid on visuals of a Thanksgiving feast at Ashwini's home where wine glasses clink to cheers of "Happy Thanksgiving," we hear him say, "I enjoy a fusion lifestyle. I enjoy being an Indian and being a New Yorker at the same time." Another cut shows him walking in an Indian Independence Day parade, waving an Indian flag on the streets of New York. He concludes, "I would even go so far as to say I'm *more* comfortable being an Indian in New York than being an Indian in India." For Ashwani, fusing the two worlds through the easy appeal of the love stories and songs, the mix of high fashion, Bollywood style, and designer rituals creates an accessible way for him to participate in nostalgia for a home, a culture, an India that he never knew, except through films. Perhaps, is it partially the bridge of Bollywood that has made that hybrid world possible for him?

And then there is Zulfi, born to Hindu–Muslim parents, who occupies a third diasporic relationship with Bollywood. For Zulfi, Bollywood remains a contested space, one that struggles to represent "India" through a certain lens, and one that he continually struggles with. He loves the old classic Bollywood films of bygone eras that evoke nostalgia for a time when his family had the elite lifestyle of the colonial Raj. His nostalgia for India and a lost world, a different era, is so palpable it coats his voice as he sings about a land he can never quite return to. He wrestles with the cultural loss he fears is inevitable for his daughter and argues that Bollywood cannot recreate India: "It's one thing to be nostalgic about films and film music, but what troubles me is the fact that Indian culture and Bollywood culture have become synonymous. And that, in a sense, is tragic."

As the film progresses, Zulfi journeys back to India, visiting old haunts and relatives, searching for home in different ways. But at his core, he continues to be a traveler torn between worlds. At the end of the film, Zulfi, probably with the most privileged heritage of the three friends, returns to India to work. In the last few sequences, Zulfi talks about the reasons people come to America, how this way of life becomes a part of who you are and yet you are confronted with the constant dilemma of whether to return home or not. We see Zulfi in the foreground; New York City lights in the distance. As we leave him sitting on a park bench watching the lights, there is a loneliness that seeps through his quintessential immigrant's dilemma. We end with him driving toward the airport. A poignant overlay of his voice singing an old Hindi song translates as, "These strangers are kind enough, I know. But they are still strangers in the end. Today, in a land of strangers, I'm craving the land that is home."

All three diasporic audience positions—the first, which conflates Bollywood with India, the second, which uses Bollywood as a bridge to create a hybrid world, and the third, which sees Bollywood as a contested space that can never quite capture India—give us insights into how powerful the engagement with media can be for a diasporic audience looking for home. These deterritorialized subjects seem to find home in the mediated worlds of their imagination. In fact that link is so powerful that even though they are outside the nation, they do not have the crucial distance to critique the Bollywood-produced discourses of the nation. Instead, they continually reproduce and glorify these discourses. The sexist gender portrayals in Bollywood films, and the disappearance of the working and poor classes, goes without interrogation. What gets foregrounded is a search for home, which is squarely equated with nation and brought that much closer in their imaginaries through the mediation of Bollywood.

QUEERING THE NATION, CREATING HOME THROUGH BOLLYWOOD

In this section I write about an evening spent with a queer diasporic group reclaiming Bollywood in ways that might open up the exclusions inherent in its representations. Gayatri Gopinath (2003) has written convincingly about how the desire to belong to a home or nation is framed through our particular lens of gender and sexuality. She argues that a traditionally invisible queer subjectivity within the nation might be able to negotiate alternative modes of belonging to the nation. My evening with Satrang illustrates her point.

It's a chilly Los Angeles night when I make my way to the home where I'm told that Satrang, the Southern California–based South Asian queer group, is hosting a *Sholay* night. It is my first time meeting the folks at Satrang. I am awkward. But they are welcoming. Hindi and English with varying accents fill the room as I enter its warmth. The latest Bollywood hit songs play in the background and at first, everyone mills about, eating, drinking, and reminiscing about their relationship with the film *Sholay* (which roughly translates as "Embers" or Flames"). *Sholay* is a film released in 1975 and became one of the highest grossing and longest running films in India. Many people watched the film repeatedly, and it became an instant cult classic of sorts. I overhear conversations comparing notes on how many times they'd seen the film "back home." The invitation had encouraged attendees to come dressed as their favorite *Sholay* character, and as I look around the room I see various characters from the film, some of whom are in drag. I watch a beautiful "woman" twirl with her many-layered skirt and ask, "How do you like my Basanti?" (Basanti is the film's heroine.) Most exclaim that the twirler, Salim (I have not used people's real names in this section), makes a beautiful Bollywood heroine. Someone teases him about the hours he must have spent on his stunning makeup. Soon, the hardwood floor in the living room is cleared as the call goes out to start the film. The gigantic television takes center stage. The film begins. Some are viewing it casually, popping in and out of the room during their favorite scenes, socializing in the next room when not watching. There are a select few, though, who are fully committed to the viewing experience and interacting with it.

Roshini has donned the garb of the bandit in the film, Gabbar Singh, and is thoroughly enjoying saying his lines a split second before the actor. "Kitne aadmi the woh log?" ("How many men were there?") she bellows, complete with gestures, almost drowning out the on-screen bandit. Some of the other audience members shush her; others join her in the dialogue. Almost everyone in the room knows these lines by heart. In fact, most of the dialogue is lip-synced by the entire audience. Entire decades and continents are spanned in their sing-along to one of the film's popular songs, "Yeh Dosti," or "This Friendship." There is particular pleasure taken in this song and the bond between the two male protagonists, because it is one that has been subversively read by critics (Ghosh, 2002) as signifying a possibly gay relationship. When done by this audience, performing the various characters and the speaking aloud of the lines take on an embodied intensity because they are inserting themselves into a heterosexually normative script, reading against the grain, finding pleasure in their subversive readings and side comments about what might "actually" be going on between the on-screen friends.

As the film approaches its climax, the heroine, Basanti, begins singing her last song on-screen. Salim, who has spent painstaking hours practicing this song in his twirly skirts, begins to mirror her every move in the center of the living room. Her song declares that she will dance as long as she breathes, dancing on broken glass to save the life of her lover (over-the-top drama being essential to the Bollywood formula). Salim puts all the tragedy, the angst, and the grace into his strangely mirrorlike dance. She twirls with a flourish. He twirls with a flourish. She glares down the villain bandit. He glares down the world that would judge him by staring down the bright, life-size screen image. In the spinning of his skirts, he embodies her. And in his embodiment of the classic film heroine, he produces a space where the queer South Asian diasporic community finally gets to go home. To a home where they are seen in their fullness, both South Asian and queer, where they are viewed as desirable subjects and are not relegated to the shadows or the sidelines. They return to a home where their queer embodiments of characters reclaim and reimagine films that evoke the nostalgia of their teenage years. It is a home that exists only in the interstices of fantasy and reality, of here and there, of queer and straight. Yet it is an important home. "For those who live on the borders," Hegde (2002) argues, "home is an imaginary construct that shifts between all these (geographical, historical, emotional, sensory) spaces" (p. 264).

Salim, Roshni, and other members of Satrang have formulated alternative modes of belonging to a nation that is not able to embrace their subjectivities in all their fullness. Their gender-queer performances have subverted and rewritten conventional gender norms within these films. There was obviously nostalgia for a film that represented their childhood. But they opened up new interpretations and new spaces for themselves in how they interacted with the film. Nostalgia, Gopinath (2003) reminds us, is a powerful mode strategically deployed to imagine new belongings even as queer South Asian subjects balance a complicated and sometimes contested relationship with their national identities and home. And so it was on that chilly Los Angeles night. Nostalgia met embodied performance to bring the Satrang folks home on their own terms.

IMAGINARY HOMES, LOST AND FOUND

By looking at the diasporic audiences in two ways, both as presented in *Bollywood Crossings* and as evoked by the *Sholay* night with Satrang, I have argued that when diasporic audiences engage with Bollywood, it can be a powerful way to evoke "home." However, one's relationship with that home is dependent on one's subject position. If one is from a more dominant group, the relationship with home and nation is one of acceptance and even celebration, where Bollywood is seen as equivalent to India, or as a bridge to the culture. However, there are many questions one can ask about the home that gets re-created through Bollywood films. When Bollywood becomes the medium through which one gets to "go home," it is crucial to ask about the "homes" that get erased or are no longer portrayed. I have previously argued (Malhotra & Alagh, 2004) that one of the trends in post-1990 Hindi cinema is a move away from films that deal with poverty and the "common" person to films that often glorify wealth. There are numerous gender critiques of Bollywood as well. Therefore, conflating Bollywood with the nation reproduces a nationalist, sexist, and classist discourse. When Bollywood becomes the primary framework through which one connects to India, the potential disconnects are many.

However, there may be ways to reclaim Bollywood, to subvert its dominant discourses and recuperate a sense of home and belonging. If one's subject position is marginalized, the relationships among home, nation, and Bollywood films can be a complicated and contested one. First, from a marginal position, the conflation of Bollywood and India is contested as hegemonic discourses about gender and sexuality are performed. Furthermore, in their embodied engagement with Bollywood, the marginalized find spaces not only to rewrite themselves but perhaps to rescript the imaginary discourses of the nation.

NOTE

1. I want to acknowledge and thank Tavishi Alagh for permitting me to use her film and footage for this paper. I also thank Kathryn Sorrells and Aimee Carrillo Rowe for their dialogue and editing help.

IT'S YOUR TURN: WHAT DO YOU THINK? WHAT WILL YOU FIND?

1. This chapter focused on diasporic audiences and their negotiations of home. Diasporic populations are people living away from their homeland. We encountered examples of how they might occupy more than one cultural space in their imagination. Think about how you negotiate moving between different cultural spaces to which you belong (perhaps between your family home and your college room). What are the tools you utilize to create a sense of home where you are? What are the tools you use to bridge these different spaces?

2. Think of a media text or music genre that evokes a sense of "home" for you. What aspect of home does it evoke, and why? Is there a sense of nostalgia for a past, or is it a new construction of home that is born in your imagination through this text? Is this "pull" stronger when traveling away from home?

3. Of all the "characters" you met in this chapter, is there one whose use of media and home you can identify with? What are the parallels you might draw with Sanjay, Ashwini, or Zulfi and

your own relationship with certain films or songs? Have you ever found yourself reading "against the grain" when watching popular films or television series?

4. The queer reading of Bollywood was an alternative reading of mainstream texts. It was a reading that created a more inclusive space for queer subject positions. Working in small groups with your classmates, chose a film you like, and try to create an alternative reading of that text. Rework its storyline in a way that it is more inclusive of your own subject positions, so you can see yourselves in the film. Or, rework the film to construct an alternative reading that disrupts mainstream ideas about gender, sexuality, race, or class. Be creative. Share your reworked story ideas so the class can discuss how it imagined an alternative, inclusive reality.

REFERENCES

Alagh, T. (Director). (2008). *Bollywood crossings* [Motion picture]. (Available from A Drink With Jam & Bread Productions, India).

Appadurai, A. (1996/2000). *Modernity at large. Cultural dimensions of globalization.* Minneapolis: University of Minnesota.

Ghosh, S. (2002). Queer pleasures for queer people: Film, television and sexuality in India. In R. Vanita (Ed.), *Queering India: Same sex love and eroticism in Indian culture and society* (pp. 207–221). New York and London: Routledge.

Gopinath, G. (2003). Nostalgia, desire, diaspora: South Asian sexualities in motion. In J. E. Braziel & A. Mannur (Eds.), *Theorizing diaspora* (pp. 261–279). Malden, MA: Blackwell.

Hegde, R. S. (1998/2002). Translated enactments: The relational configurations of the Asian Indian immigrant experience. In J. N. Martin, T. K. Nakayama,

& L. A. Flores (Eds.), *Readings in intercultural communication: Experiences and contexts* (pp. 259–266). Boston: McGraw-Hill.

Joshi, V. (1998). India's economic reforms: Progress, problems, prospects. *Oxford Development Studies, 26*(3), 333–350.

Malhotra, S., & Alagh, T. (2004). Dreaming the nation: Domestic dramas in Hindi films post-1990. *South Asian Popular Culture, 2*(1), 19–37.

Mankekar, P. (1999). Brides who travel: Gender, transnationalism, and nationalism in Hindi Film. *Positions: East Asia Cultures Critique, 7*(3), 731–761.

Mohanty, C. T. (1993). Defining genealogies: Feminist reflections on being South Asian in North America. In Women of South Asian Decent Collective (Ed.), *Our feet walk the sky: Women of the South Asian diaspora* (pp. 351–358). San Francisco: Aunt Lute.

3.4 AUDIENCE INTERPRETATIONS OF *CRASH*

Debbie A. Owens

> As audience members make sense of media texts, they construct interpretations based on their individual perspectives. The film Crash portrays many instances that allow for sustained audience discourse about culture and ethnicity, gender, and race and racism. Here, the author analyzes audiences' reactions to and interpretations of the film Crash.

One way to examine how people respond to media texts such as the film *Crash* is to employ an audience reception study. A reception study examines the audience or "reader" of a media text to uncover how people make sense of the text. Whereas the person who creates the text is its encoder, the person who reads the text engages in the act of decoding.

Reception study supports the notion of a "polysemic" or open media text, where messages, though encoded by the text's producer in one way, may be decoded in another—and different people can decode the same message in different ways. Ultimately, meaning is constructed by the audience and is not fixed within the text (Means-Coleman, 2002, p. 13).

For example, Jacqueline Bobo (1995) relied on an "encoding/decoding" model to help understand how a cultural product such as a film (*The Color Purple*) can evoke strongly different viewer reactions. According to Bobo, viewers read and interpret the text in a particular manner, based on their own unique perspective.

In this project, I focus on the film *Crash*, which directly addresses issues of ethnicity, culture, gender, and race. In my approach to audiences' interpretive analyses of *Crash*, I was interested in exploring how individual audiences members really interpret what they see in a film. How do individuals create meaning from a film? How do viewers interpret the film as being relevant to their identities or to their cultural, ethnic, racial, social, or gender groups? What themes emerged from viewers' interpretations of the film?

I conducted this study, using a combination of questionnaires and group discussions, from February to March 2008. A total of 27 people participated in three sessions. Sessions began with participants completing a demographic questionnaire, after which they viewed the film *Crash*. Next, participants completed a questionnaire asking about how much they enjoyed *Crash* and how much the film influenced their understanding of gender, race, or racism. They also responded to several open-ended questions about their initial reactions to the film and the character portrayals. Finally, participants engaged in a 20- to 30-minute group discussion, during which they expanded on their thoughts about these items. Nearly all participants were students and employees at a small Southern university. All of them had some connection with the university; 52% were women, 48% men; 67% described their race as either "White" or "European," and 26% described their race as either "African American" or "Black." The majority (59%) was aged 18 to 24. Overall, participants responded positively to *Crash*. Equal numbers of respondents (37%) said they enjoyed the film either "extremely" or "very much." All others (26%) said they "enjoyed" the film, except for one who did not enjoy the film.

AN OVERVIEW OF *CRASH*

Dubbed an intense urban drama, *Crash* premiered at the Toronto Film Festival in September 2004 and was released in the United States in May 2005. The film's synopsis describes *Crash* as "A provocative, unflinching look at the complexities of racial conflict in America," "a film that challenges audiences to question their own prejudices," and an examination of "fear and bigotry from multiple perspectives" (www.crashfilm.com).

The film presents various racially charged, riveting scenarios involving multiple sets of characters: A White district attorney and his White wife, a Black film director and his light-skinned Black wife, two Black carjackers, two White police officers, a Black detective and his Latina girlfriend, a Mexican American locksmith and his family, an Iranian storeowner and his assimilated daughter, a middle-aged Korean man and his wife, and a group of Thai immigrants. Class issues also emerge in several of the scenes. In the film, the scenarios converge as characters' situations collide on different levels.

RESULTS: READING *CRASH*

All of the participants responded positively to *Crash* in both their surveys and discussions. When I compared responses by race, the overwhelming majority (86%) of African Americans responding positively to the film said that they enjoyed it either "extremely" or "very much" and 14% said they "enjoyed" it. In comparison, 76% of European Americans said they enjoyed it either "extremely" or "very much" and 24% said they "enjoyed" it. There could be several explanations for the apparent differences in respondents' level of enjoyment of the film based on their race. Because the R-rated *Crash* often depicted violent conflicts among racially or ethnically different groups, certain viewers might have perceived this as a "race" film; so, their enjoyment levels may have reflected an aversion to a certain genre of film. In fact, the film so intensely challenged their beliefs about race that some viewers may have reverted to employing selective perceptions about incidents portrayed in the film. Under selective perception, an individual tends to interpret a message in terms of his or her prior attitudes and experiences (Rogers & Storey, 1987). In this case, an individual's perceptions lie in his or her attitudes and experiences regarding the racial issues addressed in the film. In other words, if Blacks or people of color repeatedly experience ethnic stereotyping and racism, they may more readily identify with *Crash* and thus may be more apt to "extremely" enjoy portrayals that lend voice to an otherwise muted population. This was the case for a Black respondent who said, "The storeowner, others [were] mistreated because of accents, racial identity . . . each race was interconnected and each set of people had problems; the film gives diverse audiences a glimpse into lives of people [who are] not understood." Conversely, Whites, who are often less familiar with the experiences of racism or ethnic stereotyping, might feel particularly uncomfortable about a film that exposes them to such situations. We see this in the case of a White respondent who considered the continuous issue of race and misunderstandings that cut across cultures in the film a "turnoff."

In terms of gender, more men (46%) than women (29%) said they "extremely" enjoyed the film; men (15%) were about half as likely as women (36%) to say they "enjoyed" the film. About equal numbers of men (38%) and women (36%) said they "very much" enjoyed the film.

How *Crash* Influenced Respondents' Understanding of Gender

In our patriarchal society, the social construct of gender is exhibited in terms of "gendered" roles assigned to either males or females. Gender labels are based on how individuals function within their respective roles. Whereas males are ascribed masculine attributes such as being aggressive or a provider, females are ascribed feminine attributes such as being passive or nurturing. Males, considered the dominant gender, are frequently able to exert control over females, subordinating them through economic, physical, psychological, or social means. The male gender is the cultural norm in our society; therefore, the female is characterized as being non-normative ("other") in comparison.

With a few exceptions, respondents indicated that the film contributed to their understanding of gender or gendered issues. The majority (56%) said the film either "very significantly," "significantly," or "somewhat significantly" influenced their understanding of gender. The other 44% said the film had either "minor" (26%) or "no" (18%) influence on their understanding of gender. Men (77%) were twice as likely as women (36%) to say the film either "very significantly" or "somewhat significantly" influenced their understanding of gender. Women (64%) were nearly three times as likely as men (23%) to say the film had either "minor" or "no" influence on their understanding of gender.

However, upon reviewing of the respondents' comments, I realized that these viewers generally honed in on issues relating to women rather than issues relating to men. And, though they expressed a variety of impressions about such portrayals, both female and male respondents reacted most strongly to key incidents in which men had violated women. Similarly, no matter what their race, both Black and White respondents generally sympathized more with the Black director's wife, who endured an invasive body search by police, than with the White district attorney's wife, who was carjacked at gunpoint. Thematically, their comments situated women as being vulnerable and requiring, if not deserving, the protection of men, usually from *other* men. As one participant put it,

> The woman [Christine] was not only humiliated by the cop but also hurt by her husband; I don't agree with the humiliated husband's [Cameron] behavior although [he had] no choice, it's not what a husband should do . . . The humiliated woman provoked my sympathy; in her struggle to accept [the cop's] help.

According to another, "I sympathize with the woman who was assaulted by the police . . . I can see that happen[ing] to any woman, not depending on race."

To some degree, female respondents even challenged character portrayals of masculinity. In essence, they situated men as being the stronger entity, thus, the protector of women. These comments further referenced women's subordination within a patriarchal society. One woman's comments exemplified this:

> My least favorite was the young police officer [Hansen]; he still pulled the trigger . . . a complete coward, where his partner was inappropriately touching the woman. During the scene where he was helping out the director, I think he was doing it to gain something for himself to make up for cowardice.

Another theme that emerged from female responses was that of the classic woman as nurturer or peacekeeper, such as in this statement: "My favorite character was the store owner's daughter . . . her character was well played . . . very understanding and compassionate both toward her family and even those who were unkind to her loved ones."

Male participants also addressed the film's portrayals of masculinity. In focusing on the locksmith's relationship with his family, several respondents emphasized the masculine attribute of provider. One man's comment epitomized this: "The locksmith was my favorite character because he was a working man . . . doing his best to take care of his family and lead a good life." In focusing on male aggression and dominance, male respondents interpreted one scene as showing conflict between *men*, making no mention of the woman who was violated by a man. We see this in one man's statement responding to the scenes in which police pulled over the director and his wife, and when he later confronted police, "The cop took the man's dignity, although, he took it back by standing up and gaining it back."

How *Crash* Influenced Respondents' Understanding of Race or Racism

Undoubtedly, participants read the racial motif of the film. More than a few said that it made them think about race conditions in our society. An overwhelming majority (93%) said the film either "very significantly," "significantly," or "somewhat significantly" influenced their understanding of race. The other 7% said the film had either "minor" or "no" influence on their understanding of race. Among African American respondents, 86% said it "somewhat significantly" to "very significantly" influenced their understanding of race versus 14% who said that the film had "minor" influence. Among European American respondents, 94% said it "somewhat significantly" to "very significantly" influenced their understanding of race versus 6% who said that it had "no" influence.

In our society, the construct of race is predicated upon the belief that one race is superior to another. As a condition of racism, "Whiteness" is the cultural norm in our society; thus, people of color are characterized as being non-normative ("other") in comparison to Whites. Non-Whites are labeled as inferior to Whites, who seek to maintain their dominant position in society by subordinating others with either physical threat or by exerting economic or social control over them. Both systemic and systematic racism are outgrowths of this concept. Often, because of systemic or institutional racism, members of groups labeled "inferior" experience negative conditions throughout society. For instance, in the film, a White police officer (Ryan) leveled racist comments against a Black female health claims supervisor (Shaniqua), first in reference to her name and then about how she held a job that belonged to a White male. Furthermore, social psychologists believe that racism adversely affects subordinate group members' interpersonal relations, their intrapersonal existence, or both. We see this in the acerbic argument between the Black director and his Black, light-skinned wife following their altercation with White police. The couple clashed over whether it was their race or her combative behavior that inflamed the cops. As individuals, they attacked one another's cultural representation of "Blackness" in a White society as well.

Both Black and White respondents read the blatant stereotypes and bigoted language that permeated *Crash*. But some appeared to distance themselves with comments such as this: "People get [so] caught up with race that they forget that everyone is human and people need to help each other."

Neither Black nor White viewers in my study discussed how pervasive racism was throughout the police department. In their reactions to the film's storyline, some of the Black respondents alluded to the negative social–psychological effects of racism on the Black community. They did not sympathize with the carjacker (Anthony) who, although considered "colorful, had no motivation and only helped further stereotypes of Black men." They referenced the scene in which the Black director resorted to aggressive behavior as he challenged police officers and afterward regained his composure, telling the carjacker, "you embarrass me as a Black man." In a way, both Black and White respondents attempted to make sense of depictions of the racial divide in America, how racism affects a community, and, more important, how far along our country really is(n't) in abolishing racism.

INTERPRETING FILM AS CULTURAL DISCOURSE

Researchers consider film a popular cultural forum in which some manner of structured discourse occurs. The film *Crash* has prompted sustained audience discourse about culture and ethnicity, gender, and race and racism. Generally, just as the filmmakers emphasized cultural and racial conflicts and gendered situations, the audience members in my study also focused on themes based on race and gender issues.

It is my concern, however, that some respondents in this particular study might have missed the impact of particularly gendered scenarios because they were overwhelmed by the overt characterizations of race and racism. For instance, that many respondents did not recognize certain instances of gender bias was somewhat surprising since several character portrayals hinged on specifically gendered issues. For instance, Christine (the director's wife) and Jean (the DA's wife) both are victimized by men. Additionally, we see other situations in which men leveled sexist comments at women as with the gun shop owner and the Iranian store owner's daughter, and with Detective Waters, his colleague/lover, Ria, and even his mother. Additionally, the district attorney's assistant, Karen, hears his disparaging remark about his wife's girlfriend. Furthermore, as was the case with some respondents, one could read as being male gendered the predicaments faced by the director, the locksmith, the detective, rookie cop Hansen, and Officer Ryan and his father as well. Each man deals with some sort of challenge to his masculinity, whether it is in Cameron's being bullied and having to watch helplessly while his wife is molested by police or in Hansen's refusing to intervene as his partner Ryan performs the dastardly act. Although Hansen later argues Cameron down and saves his life, the macho cop ultimately responds with deadly force to what he thinks is an aggressive move from the unarmed carjacker, Peter. We also see the male depicted as nurturer and protector in the locksmith's relationship with his daughter and, although more humiliating than nurturing, in Ryan's relationship with his emasculated father.

Another explanation, although even more speculative, could be that respondents were mostly young college students and may not have lived through such experiences. Thus, their limited experiences may account for their attitudes and opinions about what constitutes gender as well as their inabilities to recognize gender issues as such in the film.

When reviewing differences in responses based on race, I note that of the respondents who indicated that the film made "no" contribution to their understanding of race or racism all were European American. Due to the starkly intense nature of *Crash*, one could say that these respondents were in denial and chose not to underscore the primacy of race in the film text. As with gender issues, due to their limited experiences, perhaps these respondents could neither comprehend the hierarchy of racism nor recognize how the construct of race operates within our society. However, one can not rule out entirely the notion that such responses might also reflect another fundamental assumption, which is that those particular White respondents interpreted the film through the lens of what Jhally and Lewis (2005) term "enlightened racism" in cultural discourse in which they have "disentangled physical representations of race from the character representations" (p. 85). Under enlightened racism, images in popular media work, through their representations of race, to reinforce Whiteness as the cultural norm and subordinate non-White "others." In this case, respondents would view every "other" character in the film as existing on an even plane, thus, secondary to the White storyline. For such audience members, Whiteness represents the cultural norm, which implies that people belonging to all other groups deviate from that norm. As a result, to these viewers, the film's storyline might reflect the antics of a White district attorney and his wife, who are carjacked. He assuages his bigoted wife's anxieties about ethnically and racially different service workers in their home. The politically ambitious DA searches for a convenient Black "hero" to enhance his reelection campaign while he also conspires to force a Black detective to lie about the validity of a White cop's shooting of another Black cop. The DA's spokesperson even suggests that the problems that befall African Americans are a condition of their "tainted" race. In considering Jhally and Lewis's analysis of White viewers' responses to a television comedy (*The Cosby Show*), I would argue that the ability of certain White respondents to disentangle the physical from the cultural is a prerequisite for their apparently enlightened failures to identify the film *Crash* as having any influence on their impressions about race and racism in America.

From a critical cultural standpoint, one might argue that *Crash* promotes the perspectives of predominantly middle-class, particularly White, American males. Yet many, if not most, researchers and media industry workers do not believe that producers of mainstream media products are involved in a "conspiracy" against the audience. When they create an artistic piece, they draw upon their own background, experience, and social and cultural milieu. They are therefore under the "ideological pressure" to reproduce the familiar (Bobo, citing Grossberg, 1995). The director and writers of *Crash* do just that. The screenwriters' professional commitment to the film production process supersedes any presumed attempts to attain a deeper understanding of issues of gender, culture, race, or class. This aspect of film making does not answer completely why the aforementioned 6% of respondents said *Crash* had "no" influence on their understanding of race. However, it suggests that when Hollywood addresses such issues, the industry cannot be expected to serve as a vehicle for critical enlightenment of every audience member. Yet, it is through their constructed scenarios of perpetual conflicts that we experience other people's lives as they navigate the streets of Los Angeles. It is unclear whether the film's producers genuinely are familiar with how these individuals live on a daily basis.

This study of audience response to the film *Crash* adds to the understanding of how people interpret what they view from the standpoint of their unique cognitions, cultural experiences, and social groups. Responding to *Crash*, participants in this study engaged in a discourse about gender, culture, and ethnic identities. They explored the current state of race relations as well. I hope that audiences continue to view films of this nature and use these texts as flashpoints from which to cultivate significant dialogue about how such issues functions within our society.

IT'S YOUR TURN: WHAT DO YOU THINK? WHAT WILL YOU FIND?

1. View one scene from *Crash*. As individuals, write down what you think that particular scene says about (a) race, (b) gender, (c) culture, and (d) class. Compare your interpretations with those of your classmates. How do they differ, and how are they similar? What particular read-

ings were produced? Why do you think the lists differed or were similar?

2. Identify and discuss any other films or TV shows that deal overtly with (a) race, (b) gender, and (c) both race and gender. How are these

issues addressed in the shows? What are the differences and similarities in the shows focusing on race, gender, or both, and why do you think those differences and similarities appear?

3. Discuss any other films or TV shows that deal specifically with class. How do race and gender play in these media messages about class? Are issues of race, gender, and class presented as separate issues, or are they presented as interrelated? Why do you think that is the case?

4. *Crash* garnered many positive reviews, as might be expected of a film that later won the Academy Award for Best Picture, but not everyone praised the film. Roger Ebert liked it (calling it the best film of 2005). Robert Jensen and Robert Wosnitzer did not. Check out Ebert's review at http://rogerebert.suntimes.com/apps/pbcs.dll/rticle?AID=/20050505/REVIEWS/50502001/1023. Compare it to Jensen and Wosnitzer's review, titled "'Crash' and the Self-Indulgence of White America," at http://www.dissidentvoice.org/Mar06/Jensen-Wosnitzer21.htm. What do you agree with, and disagree with, in each review? Taken together, what do these two reviews demonstrate about the notion of polysemic, or open, texts, as presented in the first paragraph of this reading?

REFERENCES

Bobo, J. (1995). *The Color Purple*: Black women as cultural readers. In G. Dines & J. M. Humez (Eds.), *Gender, race, and class in media* (pp. 52–60). Thousand Oaks, CA: Sage.

Jhally, S., & Lewis, J. (2005). White responses: The emergence of "enlightened racism." In D. M. Hunt (Ed.), *Channeling Blackness: Studies on television and race in America* (pp. 74–88). New York: Oxford University Press.

Means-Coleman, R. (Ed). (2002). *Say it loud: African-American audiences, media, and identity*. New York: Routledge.

Rogers, E. M., & Storey, J. D. (1987). Communication campaigns. In C. R. Berger & S. H. Chaffee (Eds.), *Handbook of communication science* (pp. 817–846). Beverly Hills, CA: Sage.

3.5 *BAMBOOZLED*: AUDIENCE REACTIONS TO A SPIKE LEE FILM

Dwight E. Brooks and George L. Daniels

> *Spike Lee is a controversial figure, making purposely controversial films. In Bamboozled, Lee tries to motivate viewers to think about and discuss race relations, racial identity, and media images of racial groups—but what do audiences take away from the film? The authors found varying responses, reflecting the polysemic nature of the text—different people interpret it in different ways.*

You're a member of a large audience in a huge auditorium. You join them in their chants, "I'm a nigga, too!" as you watch various onstage performances—minstrel shows—comedians who sing and dance wearing white gloves with faces covered with burnt cork.

A string of well-known characters take the stage—Aunt Jemima, Rastus, Sambo, Uncle Tom, and little pickaninnies—and perform commonly held stereotypes of African Americans. The question is, are you in the 18th or 21st century?

You are in the 21st century, and you're watching Spike Lee's *Bamboozled*, a satire that asks you not to forget the offensive and disturbing images that are a part of our country's history. In fact, the film wants you to believe that racist images continue today on your TV screen—in prime-time network television, on commercials, and music videos. Are you being bamboozled?

Bamboozled opened in select American theaters in October 2000 to less than large audiences.[1] With a limited domestic release schedule in only large cities, the film grossed more than $2 million and received mixed reviews. However, before the film even opened, it received extensive media coverage. Besides the attention surrounding the film's premise—a 21st-century minstrel show—and many uses of the "N-word," controversy swirled around publicity material. The ad campaign for *Bamboozled* emphasized the film's minstrel theme an according to New Line Cinema, was refused by the *New York Times* (Goldstein, 2000). One poster, allegedly designed by Lee, featured a grinning, red-lipped "tar baby" standing in a field of cotton. The other prominent film poster depicted two of the film's stars (Savion Glover and Tommy Davidson) in their minstrel attire complete with blackface.

Critics appeared either to love or hate the film. There seemed no middle ground opinion on this dark, and at times humorous, look at how racial identity, television ratings, and the drive for success led to a TV writer's rise and fall. *Bamboozled* works from the assumption that audiences are getting a bad deal in our media-driven society. In fact, Lee claims to have made this film to do something about the images of Black people and to motivate people to think and converse about race relations, racial identity, and media images of racial groups ("Spike's Minstrel Show," 2000).

Here, we examine what some viewers of *Bamboozled* thought about its message and whether the film influenced people's understanding of race, gender, and the media. In 2001, *Bamboozled* was shown at a university theater stint several months after its initial release. Based on a survey of viewers, we address the following issues: how much the audience enjoyed the film; what people enjoyed most and least about it; how the film contributed to people's understanding of race and gender as well as to their understanding of the media/television; and what people thought about the film's director, Spike Lee.

Most of our participants were students, employees, and faculty at a large Southeastern university. About 80% had some connection to the university; 60% were women; 54% described their race as either "African American" or "Black" and 32% as "White" or "European." Following a short overview of the film, we discuss audience reactions to the film and its producer/director, Spike Lee.

We work from the premise that audiences have some power to resist demeaning media messages because all media texts are to some degree open to interpretation and that viewers of the film could create varied and different interpretations. In this vein, *Bamboozled*, like many media texts, has different layers of meaning. Texts that can generate multiple meanings are considered "polysemic"; interpretations are shaped by various factors such as gender, race, class, and so on. In our analysis, reactions to *Bamboozled* varied according to who the viewer was.

Bamboozled

Damon Wayans stars as Pierre Delacroix, a young Harvard-educated man and the only African American writer at an upstart network (CNS) with floundering ratings. Despite repeated attempts, Delacroix has yet to get any of his concepts onto the network schedule. His "ratings-hungry, culture-vulture" boss, Dunwitty (Michael Rapaport) issues "Dela" an ultimatum: Come up with a hot, trendsetting, headline-making, urban hit, or get fired.

Delacroix recruits a pair of New York City street entertainers, Manray (Savion Glover) and Womak (Tommy Davidson), to perform in blackface as Mantan and Sleep 'n' Eat, respectively, in *Mantan: The New Millennium Minstrel Show*. Blackface was an important aspect of 18th- and 19th-century minstrel shows in which White and Black performers applied burnt cork and bright lipstick to their faces and entertained audiences with racist routines. In spite of warnings from Dela's assistant, Sloan Hopkins (Jada Pinkett-Smith), about the dangers this show will cause, Dela creates a show so offensive that he hopes he will be fired.

However, despite some moderate public demonstrations led by Johnnie Cochran and Rev. Al Sharpton against the TV show, it becomes an instant phenomenon. Mantan and Sleep 'n' Eat become cultural icons. This angers Sloan's militant brother, Julius, aka Big Black African (Mos Def). His rap group, the Mau Maus, decides to do something dramatic to put an end to the demeaning representations of Blacks in the show. The film also features an assortment of subplots such as "Who is Black?" (Dunwitty claims to be "Blacker" than Dela because he's married to a Black woman) and Dela's conscious effort to distance himself from Black culture. There are parodies of the way certain products are marketed to young African Americans and, in turn, Black buying practices: "Timmi Hilnigger" clothing and Da Bomb malt liquor. *Bamboozled* also brings attention to media violence and police use of deadly force against African Americans.

Yet at the heart of *Bamboozled* is the *Mantan* minstrel show; in one sense it pays homage to yesterday's Black performers who paved the way for today's African American entertainers. Yet the film also is critical of the slow progress made in terms of the diversity of images Blacks represent in the new millennium. Instead of comforting the audience with the belief that all this belongs to the past, *Bamboozled* works from the premise that a minstrel show could exist on TV today. In spite of the range of audience reactions to the film and Spike Lee, we contend that the film can serve as both a history lesson and a call for action through media literacy. In the end, you will see the polysemic nature of *Bamboozled* as a film text.

LEVEL OF ENJOYMENT

In general, most people go to the movies for entertainment. However, when one sees a film with strong themes or messages such as *Bamboozled*, the emotions evoked by the film can affect one's level of enjoyment. Most of the people we surveyed seemed to enjoy *Bamboozled*. Two in five respondents "extremely" enjoyed the film, compared to a third who enjoyed it "very much." However, while some viewers read the movie in such a way that it could be "enjoyed," others took it quite differently.[2] One respondent said, "I couldn't say that the movie was enjoyed. It was rather deep and stirred up many emotions in me that I hadn't previously touched upon." Another explained, "it wasn't easy to see all the stereotypes, so I don't think 'enjoy' is appropriate." In terms of race, considerably more people calling themselves African American enjoyed *Bamboozled* than did people calling themselves White.[3] Interestingly enough, almost half the White respondents said they enjoyed *Bamboozled* "somewhat," compared to less than less than 5% of the African American respondents.

WHAT RESPONDENTS ENJOYED MOST ABOUT *BAMBOOZLED*

Responding to the open-ended question, "Describe what you enjoyed most about *Bamboozled*," about one-quarter of the respondents said the film was thought provoking and affected their personal ideas about race. One person said, "It addressed a lot of issues that as a White person I don't have a chance to explore very much. It really opened my eyes to the extent that Black stereotypes pervade American culture, and now I see it everywhere." Similarly, another respondent called the film "intelligent and thought provoking." One-fifth of respondents said the movie's depiction of the truth and its authenticity was what they enjoyed most.[4] In the words of one White female viewer: "It has a definite, lasting effect on me. It was very poignant and thought-provoking. At the end of the movie, I hardly felt like I could stand up and leave." An African American female wrote, "The thing I loved about the movie is the one thing most people hated . . . the movie tackled so many issues." A White male liked the way the movie challenged him to think about issues of race and media: "I thought this was a powerful movie that any thoughtful American should see." Yet he ended his response to the question by adding, "I didn't *enjoy* it."

WHAT RESPONDENTS ENJOYED LEAST ABOUT *BAMBOOZLED*

Clearly, the thing respondents disliked the most were the violent concluding scenes of the movie.[5] One person said, "I enjoyed least the dramatic ending as well as the conclusion surrounding the deaths of the characters." Another person took it a bit further in offering a reason for the ending, saying, "The ending seemed to come out of nowhere and seemed to suggest that Blacks are violent and irrational." Other things people listed as their greatest dislikes were the fact that the movie offered no solutions to problems related to race, the characters' use of offensive language, and Spike Lee's attempt to address too many issues in one film. Some respondents disliked certain characters. For instance, one person said, "I didn't fully enjoy Pierre Delacroix. I felt . . . that character was one-dimensional and apathetic."

UNDERSTANDING GENDER, RACE, AND MEDIA

Among the many themes addressed by *Bamboozled* are male–female relationships, race relations, and the media. Thus, our survey assessed respondents' reactions to each of these themes. First, we asked people how much the film contributed to their understanding of gender. The largest percentage of respondents (39% of females and 36% of males) said the movie made only a "minor" contribution to their understanding of gender. In all, few people thought the movie made a "significant" contribution to their understanding of gender. This is understandable given the fact that there was only one major female character in the film and her relationship with Dela and romantic involvement with Manray serve as the film's major representation of gender relations. One respondent said, "It looked like a soap opera—and ended like a soap opera! Characters were not believable, especially the lead female."

On the other hand, *Bamboozled* did make a significant contribution to the respondents' understanding of race. Nearly half of the people we surveyed said the movie made a "significant" contribution to their understanding of race or racism. In one person's words, "I appreciate Lee's layered approach to the complexities of racial stereotyping, and how both Blacks and Whites, liberals and conservatives are implicated." Another person said, "I loved the fact that the movie tackled so many issues. Spike Lee himself said the purpose of the film was to foster discussion. I think he achieved that goal." In fact, it was race that respondents talked about the most in their comments. For example, "I appreciated these questions raised: What is Blackness? Who owns Black identity?" Another respondent wrote, "I wonder whether Lee really believes that Whites can understand Blacks. I guess they can't . . . at least Whites can't completely understand what it's like to be Black in the United States." Yet another person read the images quite differently, saying the *Bamboozled* "accurately depicts the disturbingly accepting attitude of White society when it's faced with the most harmful and long-lasting stereotypes and notions in America." These differing and (at times) contrasting perspectives on the film's treatment of race illustrate the polysemic nature of the film.

A little more than a third of respondents said the film made a "medium" contribution to their understanding of race or racism. Of the respondents who said *Bamboozled* made a "significant" influence on their understanding of race, 50% were Black and 37% were White.

Because *Bamboozled* focused on popular culture images in general and TV in particular, respondents were asked if *Bamboozled* contributed to their understanding of the media/television. One person responded, "The honest portrayal of the TV industry—it was dead-on!" Another person made reference to what happens in the creation of a prime-time TV program and "appreciated the notion that talented Blacks are sometimes incorporated in these processes via the main character's creation of the series." Exactly half of the respondents thought the film contributed "significantly" to their understanding of media/television. Nearly one-third (31%) said the film made a "medium" contribution, and a small fraction (6%) indicated that *Bamboozled* made "no contribution" to their understanding of the media/television.[6]

IDEAS ABOUT SPIKE LEE

Bamboozled was Spike Lee's 15th cinematic venture.[7] At least one scholar has criticized film critics for being quick to pay accolades to Spike Lee's controversial flicks without carefully examining his ideas about race (Lubiano, 1991). Other academic–cultural critics such as bell hooks have challenged Lee on his representations of gender (hooks, 1990). Even some writers in popular journals have questioned his ability to sustain success as a filmmaker (Croal, 1996). In other words, Spike Lee has generated considerable discussion both about his films and his role as a filmmaker. Consequently, we asked our respondents about their views of Spike Lee as director, after they had viewed *Bamboozled*.

TABLE 3.1   Blacks' and Whites' Views of Spike Lee

AFRICAN AMERICANS	WHITES
"An excellent filmmaker and should be commended for his attempts to enlighten society in general."	"He needs a good editor . . . His works are sometimes overindulgent in length and story development."
"He presented facts that many people did not want to see."	"I am slightly biased, for I've always liked Spike Lee's films."
"Sometimes his anger clouds his vision."	"No change; I always find his films interesting."
"Great cinematographic ability, but a tendency to get sidetracked in his storytelling."	"I've always enjoyed Lee's work, and this film is no exception."
"Awesome, daring to put his feeling in boldly in front of moviegoers."	"I think Spike Lee is arguably a genius, but his 'act' is getting tiresome."
"Spike Lee makes movies that are hard to watch."	"One of the few visionaries left. *Bamboozled* was flawed, but at least Lee tries."
"I think Spike Lee made his best film with *Bamboozled*."	"He has an understanding of the complex layers of the current race situation in America."
"I appreciate his ability and strength to make this film."	He's very bright, perceptive—good use of images and of satire. However I don't think he's optimistic about race relations—and I think artists can offer solutions."
"Spike Lee is a dynamic and profound director who is not intimidated by facing issues that cause controversy."	"I admire the director for taking on issues without preaching about them—the way he challenges his viewers to form their own opinion."

Responses from Black and White viewers to the question, "Based on your viewing of *Bamboozled*, what opinions do you have of the film's director?"

Respondents were both critical and complimentary of Lee, although there were more positive reactions to him as a filmmaker—especially among Black respondents. For instance, according to one Black male respondent, Lee is "Da bomb, as always. . . Spike's movies make people think." A White female said that she "admires the director for taking on issues without preaching." Another African American simply wrote "very controversial." Table 3.1 lists some of the comments from our respondents.

CAN WE TALK?

Bamboozled can provide important history lessons in American popular culture and society. The film serves as a reminder of the dehumanizing images of non-White people that have permeated our culture's history. The film shows how some of yesterday's media stereotypes continue today in more subtle forms. Yet the film also can teach us about our contemporary media culture. *Bamboozled* takes viewers into the commercial-driven world of network television. The film satirizes network executives and writers, media consultants, advertisers, and, perhaps most important, audiences.

We hope that such a view of our media culture inspires you to be more media literate. Media literacy refers to the ability to understand how media images are produced and the commercial interests associated with those images. If you're media literate, you're also able to apply that understanding to your own consumption of those media images. Furthermore, media literacy allows you to develop the skills necessary to produce your own media images. Making a production is much easier today given the availability of affordable digital equipment. Thus, *Bamboozled* reminds us that *audiences* can play an important role in the *production* of media *content* and that we *can* do something about the content we receive. We do not have to be deceived, hoodwinked, or bamboozled!

Spike Lee expected and received a heated reaction to his film. Not everyone liked this film, and not everybody understood the film. These various reactions to the film are to be expected given the polysemic nature of media texts. Beyond the range of reactions to the film by the respondents in our survey, it appears that *Bamboozled* served at least one of its purposes—to move people to think about and discuss issues of race, gender, and the media. It is our hope that the film also contributes to more effective communication within and among various groups in society. We also hope that more media texts play a positive role in this dialogue.

NOTES

1. During the opening weekend, *Bamboozled*'s gross was $190,720 on 17 screens. The largest number of screens that the film appeared on was 244 (October 22–28). By the end of the *Bamboozled*'s theatrical run (week of November 19), the film's gross (U.S.) box office revenues were $2.185 million (IMDB, 2001).

2. The survey also showed that on the whole men enjoyed the movie more than women did—none of the male respondents said they enjoyed it "very little" or "not at all," although some of the women did. When responses were compared across genders, about the same percentage of women and men enjoyed *Bamboozled* "extremely," "very much," or "somewhat."

3. Fifty-seven percent of the Blacks said they "extremely" enjoyed the film and 36% said they enjoyed it "very much." Of Whites, 29% "extremely" enjoyed the film and 24% enjoyed it "very much."

4. One in ten people liked the old images of blackface and found the minstrel show the most enjoyable, while an equal percentage found the portrayals of Black stereotypes and great acting most enjoyable.

5. Forty-five percent of the respondents listed the "ending of the movie" as one of the things they liked least. Another 9% disliked what this violent ending said about African Americans—that "Blacks were violent." Fourteen percent didn't like the Damon Wayans character as the network executive whose personality and appearance offered a different media depiction of Black men.

6. In terms of the race of our respondents, considerably more African Americans (61%) indicated that the film contributed to their understanding of media/television than did Whites (29%). Whites were the only racial group to indicate the film made "no contribution" (14%) to their understanding of the media/television.

7. This figure was obtained from *Bamboozled*'s promotional material supplied by New Line Cinema. Among Spike Lee's other films are *She's Gotta Have It, School Daze, Jungle Fever, Mo Better Blues, Do the Right Thing, Malcolm X, Crooklyn, Girl 6, Get on the Bus, 4 Little Girls, He Got Game, Summer of Sam, The Original Kings of Comedy*, and the Peabody Award–winning film, *A Huey P. Newton Story*.

IT'S YOUR TURN: WHAT DO YOU THINK? WHAT WILL YOU FIND?

1. Divide the class into groups of those who have seen the film and those who haven't. If you've seen the film, discuss your general and specific reactions to it. Frame your discussion around the survey questions presented here. If you haven't seen the film, discuss why not, and whether this reading has made you more or less likely to see the film.

2. Discuss any other films or TV shows that deal overtly with race. Next, discuss any films and TV shows that deal specifically with the media. Third, discuss any films or TV shows that deal specifically with race and the media. Why do you think there are so few of these types of films?

3. In satire, things tend to be exaggerated and overblown for effect. Do you think a TV show like the *Mantan: The New Millennium Minstrel Show* would have any chance of becoming a national hit or critical success?

4. In class, view one scene (any scene that seems of particular importance to the film) from *Bamboozled*. As individuals write down what you think that particular scene says about (a) race, (b) gender, and (c) the media. Now get back together and compare your interpretations of what that one scene means. Do your lists demonstrate the polysemic nature of *Bamboozled*? If so, how? Why are so many meanings possible?

REFERENCES

Croal, N. (1996, April 22). Bouncing off the rim. *Newsweek*, 175.

Goldstein, P. (2000, September 29). Doing the right thing? Not yet. *The Los Angeles Times*, pp. A5, 104.

Hooks, B. (1995). Counter-hegemonic art: *Do the Right Thing*. In *Yearning: Race, gender, and cultural politics* (pp. 173–184). Boston: South End Press.

Internet Movie Database. (2001). Business data for *Bamboozled* (2001). Retrieved February 24, 2001, from: http://us.imdb.com/Business?0215545

Lubiano, W. (1991). But compared to what? Reading realism, representation, and essentialism in *School Daze, Do the Right Thing*, and the Spike Lee discourse. *Black American Literature Forum*, 25(2), 253–282.

Spike's minstrel show. (2000, October 2). *Newsweek*, 75.

3.6 ARGUING OVER IMAGES: NATIVE AMERICAN MASCOTS AND RACE

C. Richard King

> *The author claims that arguments about Native American mascots (such as the Cleveland Indians' Chief Wahoo) are actually arguments about race and hence a barometer of race relations in our society. To see these arguments in action, he analyzed statements USA Weekend audiences posted in response to a Web poll asking, "What is your opinion about changing a sports team's mascot because it offends Native Americans?"*
>
> *Before reading this essay, see the first "It's Your Turn" activity.*

Native American mascots, once accepted icons, have become controversial symbols over the past quarter century. Increasingly, they raise troubling questions. Does the continued use of American Indian symbols and nicknames in sports honor or insult Native Americans? Do mascots like Chief Wahoo of the Cleveland Indians and Chief Illiniwek at the University of Illinois perpetuate racist stereotypes? Does it matter whether the Washington Redskins' team name is intentionally offensive or merely that happens to offend many Native Americans? Answers to these queries have much to tell us about race. Indeed, arguments over Native American mascots are ultimately arguments about race. In obvious and invisible ways, critics and defenders invariably speak about race relations and ethnic identity when they speak about the use of Indian nicknames and images in sports.

An impressive literature has emerged discussing the racial politics of Native American mascots (see Churchill, 1994, especially pp. 65–72; Connolly, 2000; Davis, 1993; King & Springwood, 2001; Pewewardy, 1991; Spindel, 2000; Vanderford, 1996). It directs our attention to the ways individuals understand and construct race: *identity*, or how they imagine themselves; *imagination*, or how they perceive others; and *representation*, or how they give life to social categories (such as bravery, physicality, and masculinity) through cultural difference. Scholars and activists have contended that the creation and more recent contentiousness of mascots illuminates the stereotypical images central to Whites' interpretations of Native Americans, the centrality of "Indianness" to the formulation of Whiteness in the United States, and the changing place of Native Americans in American society.

In what follows, building on these discussions, I will not trace the evolution of specific mascots, nor unpack the meaning of Indian imagery. Rather, after a brief overview of some of the common stereotypes, I propose to make sense of mascots by listening to the unfolding dialogues about these sports symbols in an effort to grasp the place of race in popular interpretations of them. Moreover, to hear the positions advanced in these debates most clearly, I avoid rehearsed defenses, press releases, and official accounts orchestrated by institutions; instead, I concentrate on the ways in which citizens, consumers, and fans interpret Native American nicknames and symbols. Throughout, I make sense of how media consumers talk about Indians images in sports, asking what arguments do they advance to defend and criticize mascots.

Although elsewhere I have openly criticized mascots (see Springwood & King, 2001), here I want to step back and analyze the positions of supporters and opponents. I focus my attention on one representative case, an electronic forum hosted by *USA Weekend* in 1997. After briefly reviewing the historical uses of Indian symbols and nicknames in American athletics, I detail the various arguments. On this foundation, I touch on the implications of the mascot controversy for our understanding of race and the media.

BACKGROUND

For much of the past century, Indian symbols and nicknames have been a common, if increasingly contested, part of American sports. Today, numerous secondary schools across the country, more than 80 colleges and universities, and dozens of professional and semi-professional sports teams have Native American mascots. The origins, popularity, and problems posed by these athletic icons offers a useful foundation for a fuller consideration of ongoing arguments about them.

Euro-Americans have selected and supported Native American mascots for a number of reasons. Some schools, such as Dartmouth College, have historically defined themselves through a specific relationship with American Indians. More often, especially at public universities, regional history and local pride have inspired students, coaches, and administrators to adopt Indian mascots. The University of Utah Running

Utes and the University of Illinois Fighting Illini are two prominent examples of this tradition. Elsewhere, historical accident, coincidence, or circumstance gave rise to mascots. For instance, St. John's University was known as the Redmen initially because their uniforms were all red, and only later did fans and alumni create fuller traditions of "playing Indian."

Whatever the specific origins of individual icons, Euro-Americans were able to fabricate Native Americans as mascots precisely because of prevailing sociohistorical conditions. That is, a set of social relations and cultural categories made it possible, pleasurable, and powerful for Euro-Americans to elaborate images of Indians in athletic contexts. First, Euro-Americans have always fashioned individual and collective identities for themselves by playing Indian. Native American mascots were an extension of this long tradition (Deloria, 1998). Second, the conquest of Native America simultaneously empowered Euro-Americans to appropriate, invent, and otherwise represent Native Americans and to long for aspects of indigenous cultures destroyed by conquest. Third, with the rise of public culture, the production of Indianness in spectacles, exhibitions, and other sundry entertainments proliferated, offering templates for elaborations in sporting contexts.

Given this history it is not surprising that Native American mascots have relied on stereotypical images of Indians. Accentuating physical features (nose, skin color, or hair), material culture (buckskin, feathers, headdress), expressive forms (dance, face painting), or other attributes (stoicism or bravery) associated with the native nations of North America, they reduce past and present Native Americans to well-worn clichés derived from dime novels, Wild West shows, movies, scouting, and advertising. More often than not, such renderings have more to do with Euro-American interpretations and preoccupations than with indigenous cultures. Indian imagery in sport tends to be frozen in the past (romanticized representatives from a golden age), cluster around the peoples of Plains (the Lakota and other nomadic horse cultures principally), and elude to, if not emphasize, cultural conflicts between Euro- and Native Americans. In the process, generic Indians emerge that cannot be faithful to native histories and tradition, precisely because their invention depends on decontextualization. These invented Indians that dance at halftime, mark the stationery of educational institutions, and appear on baseball caps and T-shirts are of two types: the warrior and the clown, mirroring the historic bifurcation of indigenous people into two types of savages—noble and ignoble. The *warrior* aspires to honor. Stressing bravery and bellicosity, the warrior exudes character traits Euro-Americans have long prized: individuality, perseverance, pride, fidelity, and excellence. Numerous high schools, colleges, and professional teams have seized upon the warrior, real (Chief Osecola at Florida State University) and imagined (Chief Illiniwek at the University of Illinois). In contrast, the less common *clown* mocks, making Indians a joke, a sideshow burlesque. The Cleveland Indians' Chief Wahoo is perhaps the most recognizable clown. (For a fuller discussion of the portrayal of Native Americans, see King & Springwood, 2001; Pewewardy, 1991; Spindel, 2000.)

Despite, or perhaps because, of the imagery associated with them, Native American mascots increasingly have become contentious. More than three decades ago, amidst the civil rights movement and a cultural resurgence throughout Native America, Indians began questioning mascots, forcing both Dartmouth College and Stanford

University to change their mascots. More recently, while some institutions, including St. John's University and the University of Miami (Ohio), have *retired* their mascots, a smaller number, including the University of Utah and Bradley University, have *revised* their use of imagery. Other schools without Native American mascots, such as the University of Wisconsin and the University of Minnesota, have instituted policies prohibiting their athletic departments from scheduling games against institutions with Indian mascots. At the same time, countless communities and boards of education have confronted the issue. Many have deemed such mascots to be discriminatory, requiring (as did the Minnesota and New York State Boards of Education and the Los Angeles and Dallas School Districts) that schools change them. In the wake of these events, numerous individuals and organizations have challenged the persistence of such icons. Nationally, numerous organizations, ranging from the National Congress of American Indians and the National Education Association to the United Methodist Church and the National Association for the Advancement of Colored People, have taken positions against the continued use of Indian images in sports. Finally, the media have taken a leading role in modifying public perceptions of mascots, as when the *Portland Oregonian* changed its editorial policy and refused to print derogatory team names.

ARGUMENTS

In July 1997, the *USA Weekend* Web site (http://www.usaweekend.com/quick/results/chief_wahoo_qp_results.html) asked its visitors "What is your opinion about changing a sports team's mascot because it offends Native Americans?" Visitors could vote in support of changing or keeping such mascots and submit a reaction to the ongoing controversy. Of those who came to the site, 2,419 participated in the quick poll, with 42% voting to change and 58% voting to retain mascots. In turn, 299 visitors (124 opponents and 175 supporters) offered a fuller opinion. These opinions form the basis of my analysis. The comments will be reproduced exactly as they were written, typos and all, and people are identified here the same way they identified themselves online.

In Defense of Mascots

Supporters of mascots offer a number of interconnected arguments that collectively labor to make such images acceptable and to defuse the controversy. They stress respect, intention, fairness, and common sense notions of symbols, play, and politics.

To many who support mascots, the use of Native American symbols and nicknames honors Indians. Michelle from College Station, Texas, gave clear voice to this perspective: "Team masots are adopted to reflect positively on a team, to symbolize an image of bravery, agility, tenacity, and strength. Native Americans should view this as a compliment rather than an insult." Likewise, A. McClung suggests, "The naming of teams . . . whether it be Braves, Warriors, Indians, Cherokees, etc. have been a thing of honor, prestige and recognition . . . [It] conjures up images that are in my opinion, positive and wholesome to our Native Americans." And, Bob Dunwoody asserted that "Native Americans or American Indians whatever they wish to be know as today should be PROUD that they have been selected as a name because it honors their ancestors Pride, Honor, Bravery, and Physical Prowess and Endurance." More hypothetically, Rick Bartholomew, a staunch Cleveland fan, remarks, "If I was an Indian, I would be as proud as pie to have a team named after my heritage." And, Bee from Maine exclaims, "YOU PEOPLE SHOULD LIGHTEN UP!!!!!!!!!!!!!!! IT'S JUST THE NAME OF A BASEBALL TEAM. IT'S NOT EVEN MAKING FUN OF NATIVE AMERICANS. THEY SHOULD TAKE IT AS A COMPLIMENT." Finally, Jimmy Conn overtly mixes insult and honor: "I feel that native americans should take it as a compliment and have better things to complain about like america being stolen from them, but I guess alcohol does bad things to your train of thought."

Supporters often couple arguments about honor and respect with discussions of intentionality. Scott from Port Huron, Michigan, succinctly presents this position: "I DON'T THINK THE NAMES WERE MEANT TO HURT ANYONE. THEY WERE PICKED OUT RESPECT IF ANYTHING." Similarly, Hector Cadena notes, "If the team nicknames were meant to intentionally be derogatory, then I could understand someone taking umbridge with them. But in reality, the names are meant as a salute to the fierceness and bravery." And according to Terri McDowell, "PEOPLE NEED TO FIND BETTER THINGS TO DO WITH THEIR TIME! THESE NAMES WEREN'T MEANT TO BE OBJECTIONABLE."

Arguments in support of mascots on occasion speak about race through analogies between Native Americans and other ethnic groups. Many, like Betty from Albert Lea, Minnesota, are proud to see "their heritage" displayed in an athletic context: "I am Norwegian. I am happy to have the Vikings use this Scandinavian heritage as their team name." Jon from Apple Creek, Ohio, wonders, "Why isn't someone complaining about Notre Dame?" Similarly, Jenni from South Dakota asks, " My husband's family is of Norwegian heritage. Does this mean we should start a campaign to dump the Vikings?" Perhaps, she continues, those offended "should consider the advantages of the perpetual mass marketing campaign that rides along with these mascots . . . It isn't all bad!" Kim Stevens encourages critics "to lighten up. Don't take things so personal. Scandanvian people aren't up in arms about Minnesota using the name 'Vikings' . . . Take it with a grain of salt."

Many defenders of mascots like Terri McDowell and Bee from Maine cannot grasp the importance of mascots and resort to dismissive comments. They dub it "silliness" or "a waste of time" because other problems (usually unnamed) deserve attention. They encourage detractors to "lighten up," "to get over it," "to grow up," "to get a life," "to get a grip," or "to get real." In part, this derives from a collective sense of sport as playful, frivolous diversion. As Ralph W. Sullivan asserts, "Sports is entertainment, anybody who takes it seriously enough to get upset over a name, a score, or whose on first needs help. How about putting first things first. There are other priorities." Moreover, this refusal to take mascot seriously arises from a folk understanding of symbols. Richard from Salem, Oregon, argues against changing the nicknames because "After all it is just a name!" And Brookie from Birmingham, Alabama, does not understand "what the big deal is . . . A name is just a name, nothing else."

Not all arguments in support of mascots lean on honor, intention, or analogy. In fact, some proudly flaunt their intolerance, overtly advancing racist claims. Rick from Las Vegas opined, "The native Americans are mostly peaceable. Some need to be reminded who won the wars." And Bill Smith from El Paso added, "I tend to think that all of this noise about mascots offending certain groups of peoples is taking up valuable time and effort that could be directed at solving important issues. And besides the Indians lost the war and therefore it is our right to make fun of them (at least we give them welfare and a place to live)."

Taken together, arguments in defense of mascots take five key positions. First, they refuse to engage or take seriously the concerns of living Native Americans in their defenses of "their" imagined Indians. Second, they exhibit a propensity to tell Native Americans how it is or how they should feel (namely, respected and honored). Third, their arguments question the grounding of critics, enjoining them to "get real" or " get a life," precisely as they infantilize them through demands that opponents "grow up." Fourth, supporters display an inability and unwillingness to see or talk about race. When race does enter into their discussions, moreover, they qualify and constrain it. One the one hand, they suggest that racism is meaningful only when it is intentional, guided by ill will, and truly significant (that is, in the real world). On the other hand, many supporters claim parity between their ethnic heritage and racial condition and that of Native Americans, arguing that Irishness, for instance, is equivalent to Indianness in terms of the privileges, possibilities, and histories.

In Opposition to Mascots

Opponents of mascots advance a set of overlapping arguments. Throughout, they foreground race, history, and power.

Not surprisingly, opponents of mascots devote great energy to challenging the arguments advanced in defense of such symbols and nicknames. In the *USA Weekend* forum, opponents frequently underscored the ignorance of supporters. In playful and pejorative terms, they questioned supporters' familiarity with Native American cultures and their knowledge of American history and the English language. With almost equal frequency, opponents dispute assertions that mascots honor Native Americans. Jay Rosenstein asks, "Why do people continue to insist these nicknames honor American Indians when the people you claim to be honoring tell you that it's not? You honor and respect someone by listening to them." Jim Northrup, an Anishinaabe, has never felt honored by mascots; and more, he continues, "Someone telling me I should feel honored does not feel the same as being honored." As Arek Dreyer suggests, "It is pretty arrogant to dictate what someone else should be honored by."

Arguments against mascots pivot around race. Some note with sadness that Native Americans still lack parity with other ethnic groups. Elaine Flattery remarks, "Other races simply aren't subjected to this sort of racial stereotype propaganda. Native American images and names should not be the 'property' of corporate American exploit and merchandize." Similarly, Beth from Alstead, New Hampshire, argues,

> The fact that caricatures of American Indian people exist with the consent from white people means that the race isn't take seriously in this country and they are being "used" for the entertainment and contrived message that white people get from them. You don't see these kinds of mascots of other races . . . Because American Indian Nations have been stuffed

into third world roles for the past three centuries, they are being denied the voice to have white America listen to them.

Others question the racial content of names and symbols. "Using Native Americans as mascots," Danielle N'Dhighe asserts, "is racist and should be stopped immediately. After all we don't see teams like the Washington Blackskins . . . or the San Francisco Slant Eyes. Almost everyone would agree that such things would be racist and denigrating. Why then do we allow Redskins and Chief Wahoo?" And John Whalen asks, "How can 'redskins' be interpretted as anything other than blatant racism? How can any ridiculous charicature such as Chief Wahoo be seen as anything other than demeaning?"

Opponents of mascots do not simply highlight racism; they also actively strive to make the racial content of mascots tangible, linking them to more palpable and familiar version of race. For some, the historic tradition of blackface is a striking parallel. Nota Bell, for instance, finds mascots "no less distasteful than shuck & jive antics in black face is to Black Americans." More commonly, opponents offer racial analogies, comparing Native Americans with other racial groups. Frequently, they invent new and intentionally provocative team names. These include "New York Niggers," "Jersey Jewboys," "Washington Wops," "Mississippi Blackies," "Atlanta Rednecks," "Washington Palefaces," "Los Angeles Spics," "Chicago Pollacks," and "Cleveland Honkies."

In contrast with supporters, opponents of mascots stress history and power, situating nicknames and symbols in a broader context of oppression. Dolores Jones, for instance, suggests that "Native Americans have always been oppressed peoples . . . They DESERVE some RESPECT!!! What is being done by sports teams is mockery." Eric Anderson, in turn, asserts,

> This whole deal is a "controversy" only because non-Natives with power continue to show disrespect for Native peoples and cultures. You might think that five hundred years of genocide has been enough, but corporate greed and the longstanding tradition of racism in America just won't let go. If Native peoples are offended by these mascots—and they are— then the mascots should be changed. It is a matter of courtesy and respect.

Likewise, Bolaji from Pasadena, California, laments "the past of the USA continues to haunt it." Despite heartfelt claims to honor or respect indigenous peoples through mascots, he continues, "the bloodiness and hate of the country's history inevitably taints whatever good intentions there might be in [these] positive gestures." A. T. Lang pushes this thinking even further:

> The problem with this country now and in the past is they want to sweep 'THE INDIAN ISSUE' UNDER THE RUG! Over 60 million Indians were slaughtered, raped, enslaved, and [had] their land stolen. The "Indian Holocaust" was one of the cornerstones behind Hitler's slaughter of 6 million Jews. It is long past due for this country to show respect for the rights of the FIRST AMERICANS. That includes not using them for 'mascots' AND NOT sweeping Indian issues under the rug any longer!!!!

Undoing this history and respecting Native Americans as equals, Andrew Jackson demands not only that mascots be retired but also that "THIS COUNTRY HONOR THE TREATIES THAT WERE SIGNED WITH THE NATIVE PEOPLES."

Arguments advanced against Native American mascots display four key features. First, they overtly engage with and challenge supporters' knowledge and understanding. Second, they direct attention to race and its effects. Third, they actively racialize the debate over mascots, making analogies between the experience and condition of Native Americans and those of other racial groups, particularly African Americans. Fourth, they historicize the use of American Indian nicknames and symbols, connecting them with broader patterns of discrimination and oppression.

INTERPRETATION OF THE ARGUMENTS

The arguments over the continued use of American Indian nicknames and symbols have much to teach us about race and the media. They remind us of the creativity and situated agency of media consumers. Texts, images, and performances do not have fixed meanings but rather audiences actively interpret them, negotiating and literally creating their significance. The critique and defense of mascots, along with the efforts (successful or not) to retire and retain them, underscore, moreover, that these processes are not singular. Rather, audiences struggle with one another, and often with social institutions, including the media, to give meaning to signs (mascots), their worlds of experience and collective heritage (identity), and their positions, perspectives, and possibilities.

Supporters and opponents of mascots clearly disagree about the significance of mascots. Whereas supporters insist that mascots foster respect and are meant to honor Native Americans, opponents assert that they denigrate Native Americans, perpetuating historical patterns of discrimination and dispossession. The distinct positions advanced in the unfolding debates point to deeper differences: Supporters stress text (honor, intention), while opponents emphasize context (history and racism). Supporters isolate; opponents make connections. Supporters argue for intent; opponents argue for effect. Supporters consider symbols and names flat and more or less unimportant; opponents think of symbols as powerful cultural forms that reflect social relations and reinforce historical inequalities. Supporters deflect and deny the import of race; opponents highlight the centrality of race.

In effect, supporters and opponents occupy what Prochaska (2001) dubbed "mutually exclusive communicative communities" (p. 175) informed by distinct interpretive frameworks. To my mind, something fundamental is discernible in the arguments advanced and their "communities" of origin. That is, they advance competing visions of race. Supporters, who might be described as advocates of a more-or-less dominant, if not reactionary, notion, hold that "we are all more or less equal," that the ill intentions of prejudiced individuals produce racism and that discussions of discrimination should be confined to "real" and "important" social domains. In contrast, opponents advance an emergent, counter-hegemonic perspective—that is, an interpretation reading the social relations and cultural categories against the grain, exposing the power and meaning embedded within accepted norms, ideologies, and behaviors. Opponents argue that race and racism are central to the American experience, that the effects of racial hierarchy cannot be ignored, and that symbols such as mascots—ar from being frivolous—are significant measures of race relations. In this light, the ongoing controversy over mascots is as much about conflicting interpretations of race as it is a series of arguments over the appropriateness of Native American images in popular culture.

IT'S YOUR TURN: WHAT DO YOU THINK? WHAT WILL YOU FIND?

1. Before reading this essay, write down every word, image, or sentiment that comes to mind when thinking about Native American mascots (e.g., the Cleveland Indians' Chief Wahoo, the University of Illinois's Chief Illiniwek, or the Washington Redskins). Then, after reading the essay, individually analyze your earlier responses. As a class, identify and interpret themes and patterns that emerged from this exercise.

2. Compare and contrast mascots that represent ethnic groups. How is using names such as the Vikings or Fighting Irish (un)like using names such as the Redskins, Savages, and Fighting Illini? What do these differences suggest about how Americans have understood race and ethnicity? What do they tell us about racial identity, privilege, and relations in the contemporary United States?

3. Why are there no African American mascots? What does the prevalence of Indian symbols and nicknames paired with the absence of Black symbols and nicknames suggest about ethnic identity, racial stereotyping, and respect?

4. Visit one of the following Web sites. Study the tone, presentation, arguments, content, and effectiveness. Think critically about how the authors talk about mascots, Native Americans, race, symbols, and history. Consider, moreover, how they use the electronic medium and what the Web site suggests about audience involvement in cultural politics. To foster greater insight, visit a site in support of (www.honorthechief.com) and a site in opposition to (www.iwchildren.org/500yearhatecrime.htm) mascots.

REFERENCES

Churchill, W. (1994). *Indians are us? Culture and genocide in Native North America*. Monroe, ME: Common Courage Press.

Connolly, M. R. (2000). "What is in a name? A historical look at Native American related nicknames and symbols at three U.S. universities." *Journal of Higher Education 71*(5), 515–547.

Davis, L. (1993). Protest against the use of Native American mascots: A challenge to traditional, American identity. *Journal of Sport and Social Issues, 17*(1), 9–22.

Deloria, P. (1998). *Playing Indian*. New Haven, CT: Yale University Press.

King, C. R., & Springwood, C. F. (Eds.). (2001). *Team spirits: Essays on the history and significance of Native American mascots*. Lincoln: University of Nebraska Press.

Pewewardy, C. D. (1991). Native American mascots and imagery: The struggle of unlearning Indian stereotypes. *Journal of Navaho Education, 9*(1), 19–23.

Prochaska, D. (2001). At home in Illinois: Presence of Chief Illiniwek, absence of Native Americans. In C. R. King & C. F. Springwood (Eds.), *Team spirits: Essays on the history and significance of Native American mascots* (pp. 157–185). Lincoln: University of Nebraska Press.

Spindel, C. (2000). *Dancing at halftime: Sports and the controversy over American Indian mascots*. New York: New York University Press.

Springwood, C. F., & King, C. R. (2001, November 9). "Playing Indian": Why mascots must end. *Chronicle of Higher Education*, B13–B14.

Vanderford, H. (1996). What's in a name? Heritage or hatred: The school mascot controversy. *Journal of Law and Education, 25*, 381–388.

3.7 THE RELEVANCE OF RACE IN INTERPRETING A TV NEWS STORY

Rebecca Ann Lind

This reading presents the results of group interviews in which people evaluated a TV news story about discrimination by real estate agents. The author concludes that comments by Whites indicate the struggle for equal rights doesn't really seem to matter. Because of this, "passive racism" operates at a fundamental level. And if racism and racist practices are essentially irrelevant, we're unlikely to see much done to improve the situation.

The idea that media audiences' interpretation and use of texts is substantially due to the relevance the text holds is not particularly new, but very few studies have actually investigated how relevance relates to people's understanding of media content. For example, Cohen (1991) studied straight and gay men who viewed Harvey Fierstein's teleplay *Tidy Endings*. She found that relevancy of gay media content, oppression, AIDS, and gay identity were key to the homosexual participants' understanding of the program, but not to the heterosexuals.

Cooper (1999) analyzed essays describing personal reactions to the film *Thelma & Louise* and found that women enacted relevancies of friendship, role reversals, and sexism. Males were much less likely to do so. Earlier, Cooper (1998) analyzed similar essays providing reactions to Spike Lee's *Do the Right Thing* and found that "White and Hispanic spectators minimize the issues of racism and oppression underlying the film's narratives, while Blacks identify with this depiction and relate it to their life experiences" (p. 211).

Thus, relevance is a vital element in understanding how viewers make meaning from a text. Because I'm highlighting relevancies of race, some elements of van Dijk's critical theory of racism are useful. Van Dijk (1993) argued that racism is an intergroup phenomenon, because "Categorization, stereotyping, prejudice, and discrimination affect Other People primarily because they are thought to belong to another group, that is, as group members and not as individuals" (p. 20). Van Dijk said that the members of outgroups are "seen as essentially alike and interchangeable" (p. 20). To the degree that a particular segment of society (e.g., a particular racial or ethnic group) is perceived as "other people," that group and the social realities in which it exists will probably not be relevant to members of the dominant group. "Other people" means "not one of us," perhaps not important or not relevant.

This study is part of a larger effort based on 17 focus groups divided by race and gender. There were nine European American groups (four male; five female) and eight African American groups (four male; four female). Participants discussed their general attitudes toward television news, and then they viewed and discussed three news stories. Here, I focus on a story about discrimination.

From "Diverse Interpretations: The 'Relevance' of Race in the Construction of Meaning in, and the Evaluation of, a Television News Story," by Rebecca Ann Lind, 1996, *Howard Journal of Communications, 7*(1). Adapted by author and reproduced by permission of Taylor & Francis, Inc., www.informaworld.com.

"Steering You Wrong" is a three-part investigative piece by KSTP-TV, St. Paul–Minneapolis. Groups watched part two, in which a Black and a White couple posed as home buyers at 10 Twin Cities real estate agencies. The report focused on two agents. One described a neighborhood to the Whites in this way: "If you don't mind minorities, like Negroes, I'd say, 'beautiful.' If it kind of bothers you, I would say, 'stay away from it.'" He also told a White couple, " I would prefer to be in an all White neighborhood, myself. That doesn't mean I'm prejudiced, though." But he tells the Blacks a different story: "I would feel comfortable living in this neighborhood." Meanwhile, a community group is trying to save the neighborhood, and a former Minnesota Human Rights Commissioner says the agents' behavior is illegal.

RELEVANCE OF THE STORY FOR BLACK AND WHITE VIEWERS

There is no doubt that the relevance of racial identity was a major factor in both the Black and White viewers' interpretations of the story about discrimination by real estate agents. I found four main relevancies of race in the discussions: (1) the relevancy of oppression, (2) the relevancy of the problem of racism, (3) the relevancy of the characters in the news story, and (4) the relevancy of home ownership.

The Relevancy of Oppression

The relevancy of oppression for the African Americans became clear even before the story was shown. The sessions began with a discussion of what is well and poorly done in TV news, and in every group of African Americans but one, the negative portrayal of minorities (particularly Blacks) was spontaneously discussed as poorly done. Not only did most groups of Blacks raise this issue, but they raised it immediately. For example, consider the following excerpt from a group of African American women, who were disturbed by the images of Black interviewees on TV news.[1]

> (4) Okay, say for instance, if it's like something on a Black community. They always pick the people to interview, like on TV, they have rollers in their hair, they always pick those people. They never come into like, like for instance, my neighborhood. They never come into my neighborhood. They never come into my neighborhood and ask me questions. They always go into the street and pick the worst-looking person.
> (. . .)
> (1) I agree with that totally.
> (?) I do, too.
> (4) And then people think that that's how all these people are.
> (1) It perpetuates . . .
> (4) Yeah.
> (1) . . . negative images of—obviously—because they'll surpass any women that's standing there looking like she's able to speak coherently. I know they pass her . . .
> (4) Uh-huh.
> (1) . . . and they go to that guy with that plastic bag on his head to talk to him, and they do it all the time.

(2) They pick the most inarticulate people they can find.

(4) Yes.

(1) And they look and they scout these people out. Because sometimes you have to pick an articulate person. Just by, just random, just walking up to people, you have to pick some Black person that speaks well or, you, you can understand.

(2) Even last night I was watching the Channel 5 news and they actually found some Black people that portrayed, like, a positive image that sounded educated. And that's something they haven't done in a while, so I was surprised with that.

(1) I have yet to see it, and I watch a lot of news, too.

Many African American males took this point even further, addressing the alienation such practices perpetuate. For example, one Black man said this:

> It's, you know, "This is news and this is the people who's making the news," and, and, when you see all this negative on the TV, and say a person like myself ventures off somewhere, say out in a northwest suburb, and, I mean, people, Caucasian, what have you, they actually are afraid to really, you know, inquire, or just to even acknowledge seeing each other. They'll, they'll look, and "he's just like the guy we saw with the plastic cap on."

Negative portrayal of Blacks is perceived as a tool of oppression, because such images were seen to create fear in the hearts of Whites. As van Dijk's theory of racism points out, these images don't allow for the prospect of African Americans—particularly males—being fully integrated into society. As long as Blacks are portrayed as the causes of harm (gangbangers or drug dealers) or as incapable of filling useful roles in society (inarticulate simpletons) or as a subculture that merely sponges off the taxpayers (welfare mothers), they will not be able to gain a full and positive voice in our society.

White viewers never considered the negative portrayal of Blacks. Further, when asked if this story affected them personally, most Whites said it did not. The concept of oppression was irrelevant to White groups. Some Whites admitted not knowing much about fair housing laws and said how "nice" it was to learn about them—showing just how far removed from oppression they were.

> (1) It's, like, it's nice to know it does happen. It's nice to be aware of the fact that there is a law against that, which I had no, you know . . .
>
> (5) Yeah, I didn't know.
>
> (1) You never even think about it. And then you relate it to the whole social problem . . . segregation and everything and . . .
>
> (5) Mm-hm.
>
> (1) . . . it is pretty interesting.

The Relevancy of the Problem of Racism

The relevancy of racism is complex and contains several major themes. Again I found differences between Black and White groups; race was relevant to all of the Black groups. Race was also relevant to most of the White groups, but in a remarkably different way.

The Definition of the Problem Portrayed in the Story.   This theme is linked with other discussions of racism but is considered separately because it underscores how different groups interpret the problem portrayed in the story differently. Most Whites saw the problem as limited: racism in housing in Minneapolis.

> The only reason that it didn't hit me as hard is because it's set in Minnesota, so it's not close to home to me. I mean, I don't know anybody who lives in Minnesota, really. So, it was an interesting topic. I didn't mind watching it, but since it wasn't anywhere close to me, it didn't matter as much as the little girl getting hit in the Chicago area.

African Americans tended to frame the problem as being larger and more significant than the Whites did. Blacks stressed this problem isn't limited to Minneapolis.

> They presented it in a way to let you know that it is not just an isolated situation. And they also should have let you know that this doesn't just occur in Minneapolis; it happens other places. And I think that the way they presented it was . . . it couldn't have been presented effectively any other way.

The Perceived Seriousness of the Problem of Racism.   Again, different groups read the problem of racism in general and the agents' behavior in particular as having different levels of importance. As one White woman put it, this story just didn't belong on the air:

> It's not important. It's not a life-threatening situation. It'd be a lot—there's more important things to discuss on TV besides racial discrimination. I mean, there's so many people who are discriminating like this, it's not the end of the world.

This woman also compared the "crime" of racism to crimes that she considered really important, arguing that revealing the agents' names was unfair because they hadn't done anything "really serious." When I asked what might be "really serious," she thought for a moment and said, "stealing."

The Need to Expose Racism.   Another theme in the relevancy of the problem of racism is the need to expose racism in general. Again, this theme illustrates differences between Black and White groups' interpretations. For example, some Whites saw no need to expose these agents, while others found the agents' behavior commendable; racism may have no relevance, but the issue of race certainly does.

> (2) Well, I can see where a lot of people would be like, "That, that's wrong." But I don't think he did anything wrong. They saw him stating his opinion like that, but I don't know what the rules are, or, of the, you know, when you're in that business, you know. But I would say "Hey, thank you for telling me." Really, you know, that is what I would say to him.
> (1) That's the job. They know, they know, um, real estate, and that's their job. To inform you about the areas.
> (2) Exactly.
> (1) Because you don't know if you don't know.
> (Moderator) What, um . . .
> (1) You know, they, should they, I think it should be against the law for them to keep things like that from you. They should tell you everything.
> (2) Exactly.

(. . .)

(1) You know, they should be informed of everything, you, and you know, this guy did his job well.

(2) Exactly.

(1) He should be commended. [laugh]

Not all Whites expressed such opinions. Many thought it would be useful to expose racist practices and increase public awareness of the problem. This represents a different relationship with the problem of racism than the intimate involvement communicated by the Blacks. For example, one group of White women said:

(2) Whether it was one agency or a hundred, the fact is that we're letting, they were letting, the public know that this exists.

(1) Uh-huh . . .

(2) It's like a public awareness thing.

(1) Uh-huh . . .

(2) They're not saying that all of them do it, but watch out because they do exist out there.

Such interpretations that exposing racism is merely "useful" (or, to some, unnecessary) stand in sharp contrast with African American interpretations:

(5) . . . But it raised your consciousness.

(1) It was opening the eyes of Blacks and Whites and everybody.

(5) Oh, everybody. Yeah. It's opening everybody's . . .

(1) I mean if you didn't already know that.

(5) Letting them know that, yeah, we made, we made strides, we made accomplishments, but this is still here with us.

(1) Yeah.

The Relevancy of the Characters in the News Story

White groups empathized with the players in the news story much more than the African American groups did. Blacks seemed to look beyond this particular story and the individuals portrayed in it. Perhaps because of the relevance of racism and oppression, this story seemed to be part of a larger frame including all experiences with discrimination and racism.

Some groups responded to the spokesperson for the neighborhood community group. Whites tended to feel sorry for the grandmotherly figure, describing her as a "poor old woman sitting there by herself forever in this neighborhood," implying that only White neighbors are appropriate company.

Some Black responses to the spokesperson were quite different, however, and questioned her motivation:

The property value has gone down. So if that's the only reason the group exists, is because their property value has gone down and business has closed and economic opportunities have fallen. That's the only reason why that, that group exists. If that area was doing just fine, that group wouldn't even exist. . . . If that place was booming you wouldn't see her on there talking about "come on in here." Only because the stores are closing and property is empty and that neighborhood has really went down, you know, and the property values are so low. Of course you'll take anybody at this point. I mean come on now.

Many more groups, especially Whites, responded to the real estate agents. Again, the interpretations of the agents and their behavior differed for Blacks and Whites. Many Whites felt sorry for the agent:

(3) So they wrecked his life now.
(4) I don't know, if just because that guy did that, I don't know if they have the right to do that, the right to say that.
(3) Why did they pick him?
(4) They didn't say as far as—they actually said his name, as far as I recall. They said his name, unless—I have no problem if they bring up people's name if they are going to the gas chamber, or death row. John Wayne Gacey, I don't care if they mention his name. I mean, he is never coming out of jail again, what are they going to do, slander him? There are people you really can't slander, but it is nice and all to be the news but you should be a nonbiased and not be judge, jury, and executioner. That is what they did here.

A few White groups disagreed with such arguments, saying the agent did break the law, and his name should be aired. Still, the arguments were rooted in legalities, rather than any particular relevance of racism:

(4) Yeah. I would, I would air his name and everything. Because like, um, number 1, it was illegal, and number 2, I mean he should be doing his job, and it's against laws of the state, and federal, and whatever else they said . . .
(Moderator) Local, I think.
(4) Yeah, I mean, it's against the law. And by his name being aired, it just makes more people, like couples that are trying to buy houses, are more aware of, "ok, well, he's just trying to— look what he's doing, he's not doing his job the way he's supposed to be doing it."

The real estate agents weren't relevant to the Black groups; no Black group specifically addressed them. Because the problem of racism was framed in a larger social context than merely these individuals' actions, these particular players weren't of much significance to the Black viewers.

The Relevancy of Home Ownership

The idea of home ownership was far more relevant to the European American groups than to the African American groups. Very few Blacks mentioned this issue, and if they did, it was in the sense that they have been reminded what to expect. Every White group said the story didn't affect them personally because they weren't in the market for a home (but it might become relevant if they were). For White viewers, this story is deemed relevant to current or potential homeowners—which implies it isn't relevant to anyone else.

Thus, through the discussions it became obvious that even the most self-consciously liberal Whites failed to acknowledge the seriousness of the problem of racism, the extent to which it permeates our society, or the degree of oppression that continues. By framing the problem as one relevant to home buyers, these groups refused to see the larger extent and effects of racism. When asked why the story didn't affect them personally, many comments such as this were made:

> Well, because I'm not in, like, a situation where, I'm not a homeowner. I don't plan to be a homeowner. And I, you know, so I mean, I think that's more for, you know, if you're going to have to deal with a real estate person for you to be aware of certain things. I'm not in that category.

None of the African American groups considered this an issue pertinent *only* to home buyers, although many acknowledged this points up the need to scrutinize real estate agents when purchasing a home:

> It is good to know what your rights are and the laws, so you can be better able to detect when one is being unfair. And then you can search around for one that you feel is not being biased.

PASSIVE RACISM

This analysis of Blacks' and Whites' evaluations of an investigative report showed how viewers' differing social positions can lead to different interpretations of a text. To the African American groups, this story was incredibly relevant. It seemed to speak to the entire Black experience in the United States. It allowed Black viewers to consider and respond to the oppression of their race. It allowed Blacks to acknowledge that there is still a long way to go before equality is achieved. It allowed Blacks to reframe the story from being "a story about housing discrimination in Minneapolis" into "a story about racism and discrimination that operates at all levels of society." As a result, individual actors and situations faded into the background.

The White audiences, on the other hand, seized onto the story's characters, because there was little else they could relate to. White viewers consistently demonstrated that issues of racism and discrimination were beyond their experience, at times even beyond their comprehension. The White audiences' social, cultural, and historical positions made racism and discrimination irrelevant. Thus, many Whites empathized with the players rather than the issues. This story didn't resonate with their cultural experiences, and White viewers took it to mean more or less what the reporters said it meant: There was racial discrimination in housing in Minneapolis.

However, even though the issue of racism was not relevant for most Whites, the issue of race certainly was. For example, several groups applauded the agents and said they would want to know an area's racial makeup. To many White groups, the degree to which the story (and the racism it portrayed) became relevant was affected by their position in the housing market. Some viewers could find the story becoming temporarily relevant if they became home buyers.

This seems an important extension of the concept of enlightened racism Jhally and Lewis (1992) found in viewer interpretations of *The Cosby Show*. Enlightened racism assumes that minorities' struggles for equality are a thing of the past. Because the presence of minorities in positions of prestige and power proves "they can make it," programs such as affirmative action are no longer necessary. Further, because minorities enjoy full and equal opportunities, those who haven't "made it" have failed due to their own laziness or inability. This is not unlike modern or symbolic racism. Like enlightened racism, modern or symbolic racism (McConahay & Hough, 1976) assumes discrimination no longer exists. In addition, minorities are seen as making unfair demands and using unfair tactics to get into places where they are not wanted. Many gains by minorities are seen as undeserved, with minorities receiving more attention and status than they deserve.

However, while modern and enlightened racism are based on the assumption that the struggle for equal rights is over, I believe another form of racism operates at a much deeper level. *Passive racism* assumes the struggle for equal rights doesn't matter. At least for the individual, if not society as a whole, the continued existence of racist practices is irrelevant. Racism, ultimately, has little relevance for these people because it doesn't intrude into their social reality. The existence of passive racism can undermine even the most vociferous outcries against racism; people can decry racism all they want, but if it remains essentially irrelevant to them, they're unlikely to do anything about it.

For example, as liberal Whites reacted to the news story, they seemed aware—at least generally, and often with much conviction—that racism does occur and is harmful. Some said they were "appalled" at what they saw; however, by investigating the *relevancies* of race shown in people's discussions of the story, I found that even the most energetic protestations of disgust at racist practices can coexist with a contradictory lethargy about racism. For even the most concerned White viewer, the problem of racism can remain, at the core, irrelevant.

NOTE

1. Numbers in parentheses identify individuals, labeled in each group according to seating position. Speaker 1 within an excerpt is always the same person, but it isn't the same person as Speaker 1 in a different group.

IT'S YOUR TURN: WHAT DO YOU THINK? WHAT WILL YOU FIND?

1. Why do you think race is less relevant for Whites than Blacks? What does the finding that Whites can ignore race tell us about race relations in our society?

2. What could journalists do to try to encourage Whites to take issues such as this more seriously (and personally) than they currently do? Is it the journalists' responsibility to do this? Why or why not?

3. Talk with some friends about TV news. Ask them what they think TV news does especially well, and especially poorly. Listen carefully to the responses for cues as to the relevance of race as people interpret the news. What differences do you find in people of different racial groups? (Feel free to ask about TV entertainment content if you prefer.)

4. Do the same thing, but this time focus on comparing men's and women's responses. If you can, try to interview gays, lesbians, bisexual, or transgendered people as well as heterosexuals. For whom is cultural identity most relevant when evaluating media performance?

REFERENCES

Cohen, J. (1991). The "relevance" of cultural identity in audiences' interpretations of mass media. *Critical Studies in Mass Communication, 8,* 442–454.

Cooper, B. (1998). "The White–Black fault line": Relevancy of race and racism in spectators' experiences of Spike Lee's *Do the Right Thing. Howard Journal of Communications, 9,* 202–228.

Cooper, B. (1999). The relevancy and gender identity of spectators' interpretations of *Thelma & Louise.* *Critical Studies in Mass Communication, 16,* 20–41.

Jhally, S., & Lewis, J. (1992). *Enlightened racism: The Cosby Show, audiences, and the myth of the American Dream.* Boulder, CO: Westview Press.

McConahay, J. B., & Hough, Jr., J. C. (1976). Symbolic racism. *Journal of Social Issues, 32*(2), 23–45.

van Dijk, T. A. (1993). *Elite discourse and racism.* Newbury Park, CA: Sage.

PART II

CONTENT

When most people think about the media, they think about media content—a particular film or magazine, a treasured book, their must-see sitcoms, a helpful Web site, favorite songs, video games, or music videos, and so forth. Unfortunately, however, many people don't think critically about media texts. What do these mediated messages say about our social world? Some people may quickly respond "nothing!"—but that's not so. The media content we use is part of our popular culture, and it says a great deal about our world.

And what that media content says about our world matters a great deal to audiences, even if we don't know it. If we don't have firsthand experience with certain aspects of our world, and if we don't know certain types of people, then what we know about that part of the world and those types of people comes from the mass media. Sometimes the media actively and even overtly try to teach us something, as when the Count on *Sesame Street* starts doing his thing or when *The Young and the Restless* features a story line designed to combat AIDS or illiteracy. Many of us can sing "Conjunction Junction" from *School House Rock*. It's easy to see that audiences can indeed learn from the media. But the fact is, we learn even when the media don't intentionally set out to teach us—the content of media consistently (if implicitly) demonstrates who matters and who doesn't, who is taken seriously and who isn't, who is feared and who is trusted, and who is best suited to perform certain roles or functions in our society. If you have any doubts as to whether we're affected by the media content we consume, turn to Bradley Gorham's piece (Reading 2.1) at the start of the Audience section. He reviews the social–scientific evidence demonstrating how stereotypical images in the media affect audiences.

The readings in the Content section critically examine the texts presented by the mass media for our consumption—everything from Disney films to video games and beyond. There are 23 readings, divided into three chapters.

Chapter 4 presents *Journalism, Advertising, and Public Relations*. Some of its seven readings use content analyses, a method rooted in the social sciences that involves carefully counting each occurrence of whatever is being studied (the number of Blacks in crime stories, how many women are cited as experts, etc.). Other readings use more qualitative methods such as textual analysis or rhetorical analysis, which highlight and interpret the dominant themes found in media content but don't necessarily involve counting. The first four readings are rooted in news media. In Reading 4.1, Jaideep Singh claims that the intersection of White and Christian supremacy in the media leads to certain patterns of representation (linking Islam and terrorism, for example) that have resulted in significant harms for social groups that don't fit the White Christian norm, in particular the Sikh American community. Patti Brown (Reading 4.2) discusses how media have framed the coverage of people who have either entered the United States without the permission of the government or who have stayed in the country after their visas have expired. Different terms have different connotative meanings, and their use can influence how we think about and make judgments regarding the issue. Reading 4.3 presents Cynthia Lont and M. Junior Bridge's analysis of the front pages of newspapers. The authors studied how gender is represented in terms of who writes the stories, who is cited as an expert, and who is included in photographs. In Reading 4.4, Christopher Josey, Ryan Hurley, Veronica Hefner, and Travis Dixon collaborated on a study of how race is represented in online news to see whether different groups are systematically shown in a positive or negative light.

The next three readings focus on advertising and public relations. Jean Kilbourne, in Reading 4.5, addresses the representation of women in advertising. She argues that women and girls are "cut down to size" in a variety of ways, having significant ramifications for our society. In Reading 4.6, Susan Dente Ross and David Cuillier examine how American Indian tribes represent themselves on their own official Web sites, comparing tribes that operate casinos to those that do not. They found that tribes with casinos tend to play up Indian stereotypes. The chapter ends with Reading 4.7, in which Minjeong Kim and Angie Chung analyze three multicultural ad campaigns and demonstrate how the campaigns merely repackage racial stereotypes in their efforts to promote multicultural, globalized settings.

Chapter 5, *Film and Entertainment Television*, contains eight readings, investigating how specific films and TV shows represent race and gender. The first four readings focus on film. In Reading 5.1, Naomi Rockler-Gladen examines media content often deemed above reproach—Disney films. She looks at how *The Lion King* encourages and justifies racial separatism and hierarchy. Lea Popielinski (Reading 5.2) argues that *The Devil Wears Prada* and *The Nanny Diaries* represent the evolution of a familiar type of fairy tale: a maiden overcomes subjugation by a more powerful older woman to gain freedom and happiness.

Leslie Grinner (Reading 5.3) presents a tool that can help identify whether media content reinforces dominant ideologies by favoring certain social groups. Her *SCWAMP* framework (straight, Christian, White, able-bodied, male, property-holding) can be used to indicate which groups have power and hold privilege—even in media texts that might initially seem to be informed by alternative perspectives (such as the multicultural perspective that seems to exist in *Save the Last Dance*). In Reading 5.4, Gail Dines argues that a key to understanding how pornography works as a discourse is to analyze the role of racial representations in pornography. Doing so helps make clear the taken-for-granted assumptions about what makes pornography "pornographic." Turning to television, Laura Portwood-Stacer (Reading 5.5) analyzes reality makeover shows as products of a post-feminist culture. She argues that shows such as *The Swan* and *Extreme Makeover* perpetuate the ideology that consumption is an important means of feminine empowerment. In Reading 5.6, Emily Berg analyzes two prime-time programs featuring female U.S. presidents. Although both shows push the limits of the glass ceiling, ultimately both of the representations are stereotypical and simplified. They present a feminist façade. Janice Peck (Reading 5.7) analyzes the year-long series of shows called "Racism in 1992" airing on *The Oprah Winfrey Show*. She claims that the series framed the problem of racism as rooted more in individual attitudes and behavior than in the larger social context. Ultimately, the show didn't raise the difficult questions about how racism is imbedded in our social institutions. Ending this chapter (Reading 5.8), Laura Stempel discusses the representation of lesbians, gays, bisexual, and transgender people on television, focusing most closely on the shows *Queer Eye for the Straight Guy* and *Queer as Folk*. She argues that queer life has been "commodified" for the straight audience.

Chapter 6 presents eight readings addressing *Music and New Media*. The chapter begins with Jody Roy's study of racist Oi! music and the Oi! music scene (Reading 6.1). Roy considers how the Oi! music scene facilitates the maintenance and expansion of violent skinhead gangs. Reading 6.2 presents an analysis of rapper Eminem by Jon Martin and Gust Yep. Martin and Yep consider how the controversial White rapper managed to achieve unparalleled success despite what is commonly considered a foul mouth, offensive presence, and disturbing lyrics. In Reading 6.3, Marjorie Kibby studies online fandom, focusing mainly on fans of the Australian band Augie March. She shows how women and girls in online spaces have a breadth of experience of fandom that was much harder to achieve without online communication.

Katie Blevins and Adrienne Biddings (Reading 6.4) analyze the work of top-selling female rap artists. Male rappers are frequently criticized for how they talk about women. Taking a different approach, Blevins and Biddings investigate how female rappers talk about women.

The next four readings consider new media. In Reading 6.5, Nina Huntemann investigates how women have been represented in video games; although "damsels in distress" and "buxom babes" have predominated, other types of female characters can be found. Jody Morrison (Reading 6.6) looks at the PostSecret blog—a site where people's secrets are publicly posted. She investigates the role of blogging in identity and relationship maintenance and argues that blogging can provide a unique forum for the potential resolution of issues pertinent to men, women, and their relationships.

In Reading 6.7, Rob Baum examines how lesbians choose to identify online and what lesbians claim to want. She finds that the characteristics that generate ad interest for lesbians are different from the attributes given by heterosexual women and men, as well as gay men. However, what the lesbians claim to want is somewhat at odds with what they actually desire. Reading 6.8, by Cynthia Cooper, also addresses LGBT issues, but this time in the context of anti-gay speech on the Internet. Cooper analyzed the themes of this particular form of hate speech, finding, among other things, that the sites focused on sexual themes to such an extent that political and social issues involving gay rights and the gay community were ignored.

CHAPTER 4

JOURNALISM, ADVERTISING, AND PUBLIC RELATIONS

4.1 INTERPRETING MEDIA REPRESENTATION AT THE INTERSECTIONS OF WHITE AND CHRISTIAN SUPREMACY

Jaideep Singh

> *In the wake of the terrorist attacks on the World Trade Center on September 11, 2001, this essay notes how Muslims have been depicted in the media and then focuses on Sikh Americans—who, with their turbans and beards, are frequently mistaken for Muslims and labelled terrorists.*

INTRODUCTION: THE PUBLIC DISCOURSE OF RACE AND RELIGION

Although there cannot, by law, be an official state religion in the United States, Christianity has historically been given unofficial sanction and privilege in virtually every sphere of American life. This long tradition of Christian dominance has created a strong sense of entitlement and xenophobic entrenchment in significant and powerful sections of the population.

In an illustration of this broad trend, in 1997, Henry Jordan of the South Carolina Board of Education retorted to those who objected to a prominent display of the Ten Commandments in the state's public schools thusly: "Screw the Buddhists and kill the Muslims." Jordan later explained his response: "I was expressing frustration. . . . [Schools] can teach any kind of cult. Buddhism is a cult. So is Islam. I'm getting a little tired of it." Meanwhile, undeterred by the opposition of these "cultists," Nebraska governor Benjamin Nelson proclaimed May 17 of the same year "March for Jesus Day" ("News of," 1997).

The unconstitutional elevation of Christianity to a position of privilege in American society has frequently worked in tandem with the White supremacist strains of thought prevalent in significant segments of the population. An example of this widely held—if not publicly stated—system of beliefs occurred in August 2001, when Rep. Don

Davis, a White, Republican legislator in North Carolina, forwarded via e-mail a letter to every member of the state House and Senate that stated:

> Two things made this country great: White men & Christianity. . . . Every problem that has arrisen [*sic*] can be directly traced back to our departure from God's Law and the disenfranchisement of White men (Thompson, 2001).

While he later distanced himself from the remarks, Davis initially explained his reason for forwarding the e-mail as this: "There's a lot of it that's truth, the way I see it. Who came to this country first—the White man, didn't he? That's who made this country great." In forwarding the letter, Davis conveyed sentiments felt strongly among significant numbers of Euro-Americans, given new support in the wake of recent claims of "reverse discrimination."

Nonetheless, despite the recent spate of lawsuits from Whites claiming unfair treatment in favor of people of color, White males continue to maintain a stranglehold upon much of the real power in American society. From the presidency to the Senate, from the CEOs of Fortune 500 companies to the owners of professional sports franchises, from the tenured faculty at our institutions of higher education to the publishers and editors of major newspapers across the country, White males continue to exercise overwhelming control over the most powerful institutions that shape the daily lives of the citizens of this country.

Now, religion has joined race as a powerful and prominent channel through which to identify the "enemy," or "other," in America's national life. This disturbing tendency affects primarily non-Christian people of color. As a result, the intersection of White supremacy with Christian supremacy—the intermingling of racial and religious bigotry—has become an increasingly prevalent and influential trend in the United States, both in the media and among the general population.

DEMONIZING MUSLIMS AND OTHER RACIALIZED NON-CHRISTIANS

The United States has a lengthy history of targeting the sacred practices of peoples of color for persecution, dating back to the state-sanctioned assaults on the religious activities of Native Americans and African American slaves. More recently, as the nation continues to diversify, fearful White Christians have increasingly debased non-White members of non-Christian religious faiths, through the deployment of racialized terminology. The treatment accorded Muslim Americans provides an excellent example of this phenomenon of generalized denigration, based on racial background and religious beliefs.

As a result of international events and domestic actions by a miniscule handful of individuals, Muslims have become among the most demonized members of the American polity. Their religion has repeatedly been characterized in an inaccurate, misleading, and blatantly racist fashion; their property and religious sites have been vandalized; and their bodies have been targeted for hate crimes in alarming numbers. As Edward Said has noted, the last *sanctioned* racism in the United States is that directed at followers of the religion of Islam (Husseini, 1995).

The notion of the "Muslim terrorist" is one powerfully etched in the minds of most Americans. The racism behind this characterization, which goes unquestioned even by intellectuals in American society, can be gleaned from the depictions of the perpetrators of the Oklahoma City Federal Building bombing, bombers of medical clinics that provide abortion services, murderers of doctors who provide abortions, and members of various White militia groups. They weren't called "Christian terrorists." When violent acts designed to intimidate and instill fear—terrorism—are perpetrated by White Americans, their religious affiliation is neither a matter of newsworthiness nor comment.

When a White Christian commits acts of terror, if a reference to Christianity is made, it is only in the context of the person's actions being aberrant and abhorrent to Christians. However, no such contextualization occurs when Islam is the topic of discussion, because exoticizing Orientalism pervades Western coverage of issues related to Islam and Muslims. The Western media, due to willful ignorance of the faith of Islam, has consistently failed to mention what a grave crime it is for a Muslim to commit acts of aggression or to harm innocent people. The media continue to associate terrorists who violate Islamic law with this peaceful faith.

The continued and unquestioned utilization of the illogical term "Muslim terrorist" signifies how the norm in our society is *still* White and Christian. This is illustrated through media coverage emphasizing the stark contrast between dark-skinned, turbaned, and bearded Muslims—portrayed as antithetical to everything "American" and opposed to "freedom"—and "real Americans," who look a certain way and cherish their freedoms. No one points out that there is something obscenely racist about thinking that people of a certain race or national origin do not want to be free. While the circumstances of their lives and governments may prevent the majority of the world from realizing the freedom that Americans enjoy, to believe that they take pleasure in being repressed is tantamount to seeing them as subhuman.

CASE STUDY: SIKH AMERICANS

While Muslim Americans have been among the most affected by the aforementioned trend of two-headed bigotry, as their population has grown exponentially in recent years, other Asian Americans have increasingly faced the wrath of the White, Christian majority. The manner in which religious and racial bias combine to harm a community in the United States is clearly reflected in the experiences of Sikh Americans. They are among the religious communities of color who have suffered greatly from the commingling of racial and religious bigotry: sometimes mistaken for Muslims and other times singled out for abuse because of their conspicuous appearance, accents, or skin color.

The conflation of Sikh and Muslim Americans in the minds of their fellow citizens has resulted in numerous instances of mistaken identity, with sometimes terrible consequences. In the wake of such incidents as the Iran Hostage Crisis, the Gulf War, the Oklahoma City bombing, and most recently the attacks on the World Trade Center and Pentagon, Sikh Americans have been targeted for hate crimes by misguided racists who found them convenient scapegoats for the actions of the dehumanized, non-White "others" at whom they wanted to strike. The religious background of Sikh Americans provided an additional axis of visible difference for Americans whose racially informed logic prevented their recognition of followers of the Sikh faith as fellow Americans.

The stereotypical characterizations that proliferate about followers of Islam offer excellent points of comparison with Sikh Americans, whom most Americans find indistinguishable from Muslims because of their ostensible "racial uniform"—a turban and beard in the case of male Sikhs—which to Sikhs is actually a *religious* uniform. Over the past two decades, the international image of the Sikh community has suffered greatly. It has been tarnished considerably, as with Muslim Americans, by the involvement of an insignificantly small number of Sikhs in isolated violent incidents, primarily in India. Sikhs have also suffered from official efforts by the Indian state to generally depict them as violent terrorists in the wake of the militant Sikh independence movement of the 1980s and early 1990s, which India brutally repressed through massive human rights violations.

The Western media have tended to focus upon these exceptional, sensationalist events when covering Sikhs. This is due both to the obvious racial and religious difference of the highly visible, exoticized "others" involved, as well as the relatively unsophisticated manner in which the primarily immigrant Sikh American community has dealt with the U.S. media. As is so often the case in this country when dealing with members of racial minorities, the actions of this minute minority of Sikhs have been transposed onto the entire group through the production and deployment of simplistic stereotypes. The effect of this reductionist logic—a stereotypical classification subordinating the sum of a group's identity, history, and culture to the misguided actions of a few—has been magnified by the media's fascination with religious violence, particularly as it relates to non-Christian non-Whites. As a result, the media have not only been inaccurate in coverage of the Sikh American community but have also generated and proliferated fallacious, flattening impressions of the diverse individuals contained therein.

Sikh Americans have repeatedly found themselves the target of racist scapegoating and media misrepresentations. The ruinous and srecurring depiction of the "Sikh terrorist" was revived in December 1999, when major media outlets mistakenly reported that a plane hijacked in India had been seized by Sikhs. Although many later apologized and printed corrections in the wake of this erroneous attribution (but never explained why the hijackers' religious background was even mentioned), the hurtful initial reports only confirmed the validity of the siege mentality Sikh Americans feel on many levels. Many Americans[1] believe Sikh Americans are second-class citizens not only because of their racial background and lack of English proficiency, but also because of the religion they practice. This is an especially disquieting notion to Sikhs, because a number of them came to the United States to escape religious persecution in Hindu-dominated India.

One of the primary reasons the actions of so few Sikhs have affected so many has to do with the manner in which Western media focus on sensational events, particularly when committed by a member of a group other than the prevailing norm. In the Western world, this norm is White, Christian, and male. Sikhs deviate from this norm as a result of both their race and religion. In the case of Sikh women, gender is added to the equation of deviation. This reality has manifold ramifications.

Observant Sikh Americans of South Asian origin are about as far from this "norm" as one can imagine. The obviously visible differences of the swarthy-skinned, dark-bearded, turban-wearing, sword-carrying Sikhs present a protuberant obstacle to many Americans imagining them as conjoined citizens of the American polity, instead of potentially fear-inspiring foreigners. Consequently, the intersections of White and Christian supremacy have made the integration of Sikh Americans into the polity a formidable a task.

MEDIA COVERAGE AND ITS RAMIFICATIONS, IN THE WAKE OF THE "ATTACK ON AMERICA"

The United States media, in the wake of the tragic September 11, 2001, assault on our nation, demonstrated the same failings it has shown in the past when discussing Americans who are neither White nor Christian. Although reporters generally did appear more sensitive to the representations they created of Muslim and Arab Americans, and people who were mistaken for them (including Sikh Americans), this occurred primarily in the wake of the epidemic of hate crimes against people of color throughout the nation.

By failing immediately to investigate seriously and condemn forcefully the national epidemic of hate crimes—which began for at least one Sikh American as he was fleeing for his life from one of the collapsing towers of the World Trade Center—the media miserably failed in its duty. Like most of us, the media were entranced by the images of mass destruction. However, the free press also had a sacred duty to report that Americans were attacking other Americans in the wake of the terrorist assault on our nation and use the immense power it has to help their fellow Americans.

Instead, the media followed the erroneous lead of New York City mayor Rudolph Giuliani, who downplayed initial reports of hate crimes directed at dark-skinned and turban-wearing people throughout New York City. While Giuliani spoke about how few hate crimes were actually occurring, terrified immigrant cab drivers around the city were rushing to place American flag stickers on their cars, to deflect the violence and hatred with which they were suddenly confronted. The media never addressed this glaring error and only began to focus on the national hate crime epidemic days later, after it could no longer be ignored or downplayed.

It is a shame how little the American media learned from our nation's sordid recent history. The same outpourings of racial hatred occurred during the Iran Hostage Crisis and the Gulf War, and after the Oklahoma City bombing. There was every reason to believe it would happen again. Nonetheless, the media were far too late in reporting the nationwide surge in hate crimes, initially reporting they had scattered, unconfirmed reports of a "backlash" against innocent Americans from the terrorist attacks. The implication was that they didn't believe the many people of color decrying these incidents.

The Sikh American community has been particularly hard hit by the media's errors in the wake of the September 11 attacks. While Sikh Americans number far fewer than one-tenth the number of Muslims in the United States, the number of hate crimes reported against Sikh Americans is about half that reported for all Arab and Muslim Americans. Thus, proportionately, Sikh Americans were singled out for harassment far more than any other group during the hate crime epidemic, due to their appearance. You wouldn't know this from the media.

While Sikh Americans were among the main targets of the hate crime epidemic, the media often failed to mention them in the headlines of news stories examining the issue. Headlines usually mentioned only Muslim and Arab Americans, although the articles themselves often began with or referred to the murder of Sikh American Balbir Singh Sodhi (the first person murdered by domestic terrorists in the wake of the attacks) and numerous other attacks directed at members of the Sikh faith. Examples of this trend include the following headlines, none of which mention Sikh Americans despite the prominent detailing of hate crimes against Sikhs within the actual article: "Anti-Arab Acts Reported," "Arab-Americans Fear Backlash," "Arabs and Muslims Steer Through an Unsettling Scrutiny," "Assaults Against Muslims, Arabs Escalating," and "Attacks and Harassment of Middle-Eastern Americans Rising."[2]

The repeated failure to include Sikh Americans in the headlines of newspaper and magazine articles, as well as television news reports about the hate crime epidemic (see www.sikhcoalition.org/ListReports.asp), hid the breadth and depth of the community's frightening experiences with a double-pronged terrorism—the initial attacks, coupled with attacks by domestic terrorists using the airplane hijackings and crashes as justification to act out their bigotry.

The wave of hate crimes affecting Sikh Americans was certainly exacerbated by the irresponsibility of the American media. Within minutes of the first plane hitting the World Trade Center, images of Osama bin Laden proliferated, despite the fact that no possible connection could be shown at the time, nor for quite some time afterward. Later in the day, a press conference from Afghanistan was telecast, showing a Taliban leader denying any involvement in the attacks. Both bin Laden and the leaders of the Taliban sport turbans and beards, as well as dark complexions—the prototypical terrorist in the picture painted by the Western press.

The salience, weight, and lasting power of those first images has had a devastating effect on the lives of the 450,000 Sikh Americans. This fact became all the more poignant in the following days, as pictures of the hijackers and their suspected accomplices revealed that not one wore a turban. Still the attacks against Sikh Americans did not abate.

Sikh Americans continued to receive verbal and nonverbal threats. They were spat upon, had garbage thrown at them, were run off the road and tailgated. They were shot at with guns, suffered numerous cases of arson, firebombings, beatings, and at least one murder. It was not until weeks later that scattered reports began to appear (due to hard work and outreach by Sikh American community activists) that the vast majority of people wearing turbans in the United States were indeed Sikh, not Muslim. Mainstream sources were predictably late in picking up this vital and readily available information.

The failures of the media are well encapsulated in a comparison of the stories of two Sikh Americans: Sher Singh and Balbir Singh Sodhi. Balbir Singh Sodhi, a Sikh American who wore a turban and an uncut beard and worked in Mesa, Arizona, was the first person murdered in the post-attack hate crimes. Despite the national significance of his murder, almost none of the national television reports or print media articles about his death included Mr. Sodhi's photograph—a fact made even more appalling by the fact that he was killed because of his appearance. Because his face was almost never shown, he was never truly humanized, thus preventing Americans from actually imagining him as a person, tragically murdered because of the way he looked. In fact, the murder has generally been considered a minor story by the press—certainly considered far less newsworthy by the media than if Mr. Sodhi had been a White man murdered for similar reasons.

The one image of a Sikh American that was transmitted across the country by nearly every major media outlet was of Sher Singh, who was pulled off a train by authorities in Providence, Rhode Island, for looking "suspicious." The news that a possible terrorist had been arrested spread like wildfire, and national media outlets quickly picked up the story. Almost immediately, video clips of a young man with a green turban and a long, flowing beard being led away in handcuffs flooded the airwaves. CNN, Fox, and the Associated Press carried video and photos of Sher Singh, who was subsequently released and charged only with a misdemeanor for carrying a *kirpan*—a small, ceremonial sword that is a Sikh religious article of faith that baptized Sikhs must carry at all times. The charge was later dropped because of the obvious religious nature of the *kirpan*. Nonetheless, his image flooded the airwaves and Internet over the next few days—long after it had been established that he had nothing to do with the terrorist attacks—adding to the hysteria created by the bombardment of images of bin Laden and the Taliban leadership.

The televised images neatly fit the American media's stereotype of a terrorist. By showing Sher Singh being led away in handcuffs, and mentioning that the train was stopped because of the presence of "suspicious" individuals, the media firmly associated Sher Singh—and those who looked like him—with the terrorist attacks. The bias evident in this revolting episode is blatant, an example of clearly illegal racial profiling. Still, the media never apologized, nor did they seek to correct the misleading and dangerous impressions they created by repeatedly showing images of Sher Singh in close juxtaposition with those of bin Laden and the Taliban. In fact, they ignored the real story, that of racial profiling by authorities in arresting and harassing an innocent American. It is unimaginable that a story about a man arrested on a minor weapons charge could have risen to this level of national prominence if the accused had not been wearing a turban. Yet this important issue has, not surprisingly, been ignored.

While the president, religious leaders, and members of the media reiterated that Muslim, Arab, and Sikh Americans are part of our national mosaic, the rhetoric didn't match reality. Non-Christian Asian Americans have been repeatedly singled out because of their religious affiliation as well as their race, demonstrating that they still aren't part of the "mainstream." Almost without exception, media stories dealing with the post-attack hate crime epidemic were tokenistic in their positioning. Unlike other stories that detailed the "American Experience," these stories were reported as outside the purview of the mainstream of society. The direct implication was that people in these stories were marginal figures in American society. Their problems were "minority" issues, not something for all Americans to ponder.

RACIALIZED REPRESENTATION IN THE AMERICAN MEDIA

The United States remains a racist, race-obsessed society, and members of the media reflect the racism that stains our national psyche. As a result, mainstream media coverage of peoples of color in the United States is inevitably tainted by the nation's views toward race and its foundation of White supremacy.

The American media continue to employ simplistic racial stereotypes to convey meaning and information, particularly when the subject is a person other than the defined "norm" in our society—a White, Christian male. In media coverage relating to followers of non-Christian faiths such as Sikhism or Islam, the majority of coverage by mainstream sources is characterized by an exoticizing Orientalism. As detailed on the previous page, media coverage focuses more on the "strange" appearance and beliefs of the people involved than on the fact that they are Americans who have suffered doubly in the wake of the tragedy that struck our nation. This inaccurate representation has grave effects for the communities mischaracterized by such reporting.

Without a doubt, the media have tremendous power in our society. The images, views, and ideas disseminated via the mass media go a long way toward shaping and molding the manner in which individuals and entire groups are viewed. Media bias must be earnestly confronted and addressed by reporters and editors, and not only through overdue efforts at diversifying the newsrooms. The upper echelons of media organizations, where the real decisions are made, must also begin to reflect the racial and gender makeup of our nation. Most important, members of the media must begin to critically assess the bias that repeatedly seeps into their work and reassess the manner in which they engage in their vocation. They must ascertain why reporters across the nation continue to depict people of color and members of non-Christian faiths with stereotypical formulas that have long been discredited. Without such honest and painful introspection, the American media will never be able to play the critical role demanded of it in a democratic society.

NOTES

1. See, for example, Singh (2002, 2003a, 2003b), and also see reports of hate crimes, and in particular the utterances of those who committed them, at www.saldef.org.

2. The sources of these headlines are Goodstein, L., & Niebuhr, G. (2001, September 14). Attacks and harassment of Middle-Eastern Americans rising. *The New York Times*; Kong, D. (2001, September 12). Arab-Americans fear backlash. Story distributed by the *Associated Press Newswire*; Mangaliman, J., Nhu, T. T., & Wronge, Y. S. (2001, September 13). Anti-Arab acts reported. *San Jose Mercury News*; Sengupta, S. (2001, September 13). Arabs and Muslims steer through an unsettling scrutiny. *The New York Times*; Serrano, R. A. (2001, September 28). Assaults against Muslims, Arabs escalating. *The Los Angeles Times*.

IT'S YOUR TURN: WHAT DO YOU THINK? WHAT WILL YOU FIND?

1. Examine major newspapers and magazines in the two weeks after September 11, 2001, to determine when the media began to discuss the nationwide epidemic of hate crimes. Critically examine the manner in which the media framed coverage of this story. Was it portrayed as an aberration that would quickly go away, a major problem that reflected the deep-seated racism in American society, or a justifiable reaction to what happened?

2. How did the media portray Muslims and the religion of Islam immediately after the terrorist attacks? Was Muslim theology explained? Was it mentioned that Islam considers it a crime to murder innocent people?

3. Did the media attempt to abate the hate crime epidemic? How? Could they have done a better job? How, or why not?

4. How was the impact of hate crimes upon the Sikh American community portrayed? Visit www.sikhcoalition.org/ListReports.asp. Also consider the information presented in this reading. Do you think the media cover these hate crimes adequately? Why or why not?

REFERENCES

Husseini, S. (1995, July/August). Islam, fundamental misunderstandings about a growing faith. *EXTRA!*, p. 15.

News of the weak in review. (1997, June 16). *The Nation*, p. 7.

Singh, J. (2002, Spring). No Sikh Jose: Sikh American community mobilization and inter-racial coalition building in the construction of a sacred site. *UCLA Asian Pacific American Law Journal,* 8(1), 173–201.

Singh, J. (2003). The racialization of minoritized religious identity: Constructing sacred sites at the intersection of White and Christian supremacy. In J. Naomi Iwamura & P. Spickard (Eds.), *Revealing the sacred in Asian and Pacific America* (pp. 87–106). New York: Routledge.

Singh, J. (2003, Spring). Confronting racial violence. *ColorLines,* 6(1), 23–26.

Thompson, E. (2001, August 22). N.C. lawmaker apologizes for e-mail. Story distributed by the *Associated Press Newswire.*

4.2 WHAT'S IN A NAME?: FRAMING THE IMMIGRATION STORY

Patti Brown

> *This reading explores how media have framed the immigration story and, in the process, how the media have shaped both the story and public opinion.*

Immigration is among the most important media stories of our day. Actually, there are two different immigration stories. One deals with the nearly 1.3 million people who enter the United States through official immigration channels seeking permanent residence. The other concerns an estimated 1 million people per year who enter by crossing the U.S. border without government permission or who remain here after their visas have expired.

Both are important stories, and often the stories get intertwined, but the media's spotlight has been focused primarily on the conflict surrounding what is called "illegal immigration."

The *Dallas Morning News* ("The Illegal Immigrant," 2007) named the illegal immigrant its Texan of the Year. "He is at the heart of a great culture war in Texas—and the nation—credited with bringing us prosperity and blamed for abusing our resources. How should we deal with this stranger among us?" The Associated Press survey of U.S. editors and news directors selected immigration one of the top 10 U.S. news stories of both 2006 and 2007. The Tyndall Report, which tracks television evening news on the three major networks, placed immigration in the top 10 stories covered by broadcast news. The Pew Research Center's U.S. News Interest Index ranked immigration among not only the top most reported but also the most followed media stories.

Why does this matter? Because there is a strong correlation between the amount of coverage the media give to stories such as immigration and the salience or importance the public ascribes to those issues (McCombs & Shaw, 1972). Newspapers, television, radio, blogs, and news services tell us not just *what* to think about (called agenda setting), but they also can influence *how* we think about these issues (known as priming). By leading a news broadcast with a story on illegal immigration, or placing the story on the front page, the media let us know that immigration is an important issue. The way the media report on immigration—from the frequency, quantity, and angle of coverage to the selection of sources quoted—influences how we think about and make judgments regarding the issue.

A ROSE BY ANY OTHER NAME

Shakespeare's Juliet lamented the conflict between her family and Romeo's that served as the barrier to their romance. If only her last name wasn't Capulet, she surmised, there would be no obstacles. If only it were that simple.

What does the label we give something impose on the object? What do you call someone who comes into your home and moves into your spare bedroom? Some might call the person a new housemate, or a guest, or even an uninvited guest. Others might say the person is an intruder or a squatter. No matter how you describe this person, your choice of words frames the situation in a positive, negative, or neutral light and says as much about you as it does about the person who has taken up residence in your home.

The media are faced with a similar challenge in describing the nearly 12 million people who have either entered the United States without the permission of the government or who have stayed in the country after their visas have expired. How do the media frame the stories they present about these people? Are these people presented as "illegal aliens" or "undocumented migrants"?

Key stakeholders in the immigration issue (such as advocacy organizations or the U.S. Citizenship and Immigration Service) rely on different terms to describe the people who are in the country without permission. For example, the government uses certain official terms such as *illegal alien, nonresident alien, asylee, citizen, immigrant, migrant, refugee*, and *temporary worker*. Immigrant advocacy groups, on the other hand, often refer to undocumented individuals as "out of status." *The Associated Press Stylebook*, which guides many reporters, recommends "illegal immigrant" over "illegal alien" or "undocumented worker." The different terms have different connotative meanings. Some are positive, some negative, some neutral.

KEYWORDS

Print and broadcast media have struggled to choose the right words to use, both unbiased and accurate, when covering the immigration story. For example, the newspaper of the University of Minnesota, the *Minnesota Daily*, made a conscious decision to use "undocumented immigrant." After hearing opposition from readers about the use of "illegal immigrant." Editor in chief Anna Weggel (2006) wrote, "We wanted to find a phrase that in part names the people being referred to, but also describes the action that is making them the subject of a story" (p. A7). Many of the paper's readers saw the term "illegal immigrant" as "dehumanizing," and the paper acknowledged that the term "could have negative connotations that sway the way readers think about an entire group of people." "Hearing a group of people referred to over and over as 'illegal' can drill into readers' minds that these are bad, reckless individuals that do not deserve to be in our country." Recognizing that "undocumented immigrant" is not perfect, Weggel wrote, "Our goal is to create a level of understanding and fairness for all of our readers" (p. A7).

Things weren't always this way. Language is organic; it evolves over time with culture and use. What may have once been common usage may later become unacceptable. For example, in the mid-1950s the U.S. Immigration and Naturalization Services launched Operation Wetback, a repatriation program that removed more than 1 million illegal immigrants living in the Southwest. Referring to the Mexican nationals as "wetbacks" was considered acceptable. The *Washington Post* published a headline "'Wetback' Tide Overflowing Rio Grande Again," on June 7, 1953, and reported

> The annual spring tide of wetback labor reached record proportions last month, when 87,416 were picked up at the border. An influx sustained at this rate for a year could conceivably add up to more than two million in 1953, as immigration authorities estimate that for every wetback caught, one to three others escape. (Wilhelm, 1953, p. 3B)

Today racial slurs are understood to be derogatory, insulting, and inflammatory. Fifty years from now, people will look back at how the keywords, metaphors, concepts, symbols, and visual images used today—such as *illegal, amnesty, undocumented*, or *aliens*—not only shaped how audiences viewed the policies and the people who were at the center of the debate but how the words themselves shaped the very tenor of the discourse in the public square.

FRAMES

Frames are central organizing themes used in the narrative of a story. Entman (1991) says frames "are constructed from and embodied in the keywords, metaphors, concepts, symbols, and visual images emphasized in the news narrative" (p. 7). Frames present a certain view of a story in much the same way a picture frame or a window frame limits what a viewer sees. Media frames focus on certain themes and, in so doing, leave others out.

For a reporter, frames serve as tools to organize multiple story lines within a single news account. For a reader or viewer, frames focus attention to specific themes or details within a story. Frames provide a perspective to a story, and by their very nature they do not necessarily provide the entire story any more than a picture frame allows a viewer to see what lies beyond its perimeter. Frames can be constructed by either the media or by individuals or groups that have an interest in the way a story is told.

Some of the dominant frames in the immigration story include the national security frame, the population frame, the crime frame, the amnesty and guest worker frame, the sanctuary city frame, the documentation and credentialing frame, the language frame, the economic frame, the educational and health frame, and the diversity frame.

The National Security and Border Control Frames

The national security frame deals with the government's role in protecting the people, the borders, and the sovereignty of the United States from either a foreign or domestic threat.

The border control frame is intrinsically linked to national security but deals more precisely with the 1.2 million people who enter and leave the United States every single day.

Since the September 11 terrorist attacks by foreign nationals, stories about immigration have been tied to coverage of homeland security and the "war on terror." In the aftermath of the attacks, serious questions were raised about how the terrorists were allowed into the United States in the first place. When *The 911 Commission Report* was issued, the *New York Times* (Shenon, Jehl, & Johnston, 2004) covered its release, "Correcting the Record on Sept. 11, in Great Detail" and reported, "The commission's report found that the hijackers had repeatedly broken the law in entering the United States" (p. 1A).

In a story, "Are We Safer?" the *Miami Herald* (Gordon, Taylor, & Hutcheson, 2006), reported, "A close examination of the federal government's homeland security effort shows there have been major accomplishments since the attacks on Sept. 11, 2001. But it also reveals how vulnerable to a catastrophe the nation remains" (p. 1A). Pointing to stories that address the national security frame, many Americans ask if stricter immigration and border controls could prevent future attacks.

The September 20, 2004, *Time* magazine cover dramatically showed a photo of red and white stripes from the American flag being ripped apart at the seams by two hands with the headline "American's border: Even after 9/11, it's outrageously easy to sneak in." The news magazine's feature article, "Who left the door open?" tells readers "Despite all the talk of homeland security . . . millions of illegal aliens will pour across the U.S.–Mexican border this year, many from countries hostile to America" (Barlett, Steele, Karmatz, & Levinstein, 2004, p. 51).

Under the headline "America must secure its borders now," the *Erie Times-News* ran an opinion editorial by a Pennsylvania congressional representative (Peterson, 2007) reinforcing the concern about how "vulnerable we still are as a nation" 6 years after September 11 and how important border security is to prevent "terrorists, drug traffickers and violent gang members from entering our country and harming America."

Syndicated columnist and former White House director of communications Patrick Buchanan writes that a nation with an influx of millions of people who have crossed its borders and unlawfully taken up residence without the express permission of the government has been "invaded" (Buchanan, 2006). The *Washington Times* covered Buchanan's book *State of Emergency: The Third World Invasion and Conquest of America*" in a story "The threat of uncontrolled immigration to America" (Lefever, 2006), saying "he is determined to keep America and its unique culture from being corrupted or subverted by uncontrolled immigration" (p. 8BO).

One of the leading media voices in the immigration debate is CNN news anchor Lou Dobbs. "Broken Borders" is an almost daily segment on his program, *Lou Dobbs Tonight*, focusing on the government's failure to enforce its own immigration laws. Dobbs pulls no punches in referring to those here illegally as "illegal aliens" or chastising the government's "outright support of ethnocentric support of special interest groups" (Dobbs, 2008).

Some voices in the media claim that the way the United States controls the flow of immigrants has more to do with racial prejudice, ethnic bigotry, or xenophobia (a fear of people from somewhere else) than national security. *Los Angeles Times* columnist Gregory Rodriguez (2008) wrote an opinion editorial, "A 670-mile-long shrine to American insecurity," in which he expressed frustration with "ongoing strains of xenophobia and racism in U.S. society" (p. 1O).

In September, 2005, the *Arizona Republic* reported on an immigration bill that U.S. Representative J. D. Hayworth was working on, "Hayworth bill tackles 'invasion'" (Coomes, 2005). The article quoted one of the congressman's constituents, a contractor, who often is outbid on building projects because his competitors hire illegal immigrants and underpay them. Defending his position, Hayworth said, "This is not xenophobia. This is not racism. This is national security."

A frame, such as national security, can be used to report a story in either a positive or in a negative way, and over time, the frame can change in tone. Whereas public support of airport travel security measures was high right after the 2001 terrorist attacks, over time people have grown weary of the hassles and view the precautions as discriminatory to certain groups. In 2003, the *Oakland Tribune* published "How air travel has changed forever" in a special series, "9-11: Are we safer now?," and reported "the flying public has learned to live with National Guard troops in airports, shoe inspections, tweezer confiscations, 'no-fly' lists, longer waits in security lines and federal screeners" (Holstege, 2003). Near the sixth anniversary of the September 11 attacks, the *Pittsburg Post-Gazette* ran an article commenting on how many of the changes that have occurred in the name of national security are burdensome to travelers. Example included the Automatic Targeting System, an assessment system designed to calculate the security risks travelers pose:

> Foreign visitors are harassed at U.S. borders, sometimes for arbitrary reasons . . . Foreigners are often detained, cross-examined, fingerprinted, even sent straight back from where they came, all in the name of domestic security concerns . . . Even on domestic flights, foreign-looking travelers, whatever that may mean, are subject to special scrutiny simply because someone believes they look suspicious or are acting out of the ordinary. Congress recently passed a "good faith" law to protect people who raise concerns about suspicious-looking travelers from potential lawsuits for false accusations or overactive xenophobia. (Bear, 2007)

The (Over) Population Frame

The population frame is concerned with numbers of people. The frame focuses on the number of people who presently live in the country (more than 303 million) and the number of people (more than 1.3 million) who immigrate through official channels each year. It also includes the millions of people who apply each year in the hopes of immigrating but who are not granted visas to enter the United States and those who arrive without visas.

One of the many challenges with reporting the immigration story today is that it involves millions of people who are here both legally and illegally. The sheer number of people involved, larger than any previous wave of immigrants to North America, makes the immigration story very important. The U.S. population has increased 50% since 1970, due in large measure to immigration.

The crux of what the media call the "immigration debate" is about how many people are allowed to immigrate to the United States during any given year, from which countries, with what education, job skills, or family ties to those already in the country, and how those decisions are made. Countless numbers of individuals and special interest groups hold vastly differing views on U.S. immigration laws and on proposed reforms.

The tenor of this "debate" has become particularly contentious during the past decade as the number of people entering the United States, both legally and illegally, has increased dramatically.

When the media use certain terms to describe the number of immigrants, such as *flood* or *invasion*, readers are influenced to think about immigration as a serious problem needing a drastic solution. The *Houston Chronicle* used the headline "'Border baby' boom strains S. Texas, more illegal immigrants are pouring into the state to give birth" (Pinkerton, 2004). Readers are also likely to see the immigrants themselves as the problem instead of looking at other angles, such as the employers who eagerly hire undocumented workers for lower wages than they'd pay a citizen. The *Salt Lake Tribune* quoted a source who said Arizona would not be a "sanctuary state for illegal employers or illegal aliens" (Carlisle, 2008). If the media refer to businesses who hire undocumented workers as "illegal employers" there may be a shift in the public's focus from the immigrant to corporations that drive down wages among the working class and create a voiceless underclass of immigrants who number in the millions.

The Human Rights Frame

The human rights frame concerns the fundamental rights of every human being to dignity, freedom, justice and peace. The human rights frame is one of the most compelling because immigrants are frequently a disadvantaged and vulnerable population who may lack language skills, financial security, and employment opportunities.

In August 2005, governors Bill Richardson of New Mexico and Janet Napolitano of Arizona declared states of emergency on their states' Mexican borders. In a press release, Richardson declared that his state's southern border had been "devastated by the ravages and terror of human smuggling, drug smuggling, kidnapping, murder, destruction of property and the death of livestock."

Immigrants who cross into the United States illegally often do so with the aid of human smugglers called "coyotes" who charge as much as $2,500 or more to walk people across the border, and then hook them up with transportation, drop houses, and employment. The *Chicago Tribune* (Spagat, 2006) reported that "while most smugglers walk their customers several nights across the deserts that dominate the frontier's nearly 2,000 miles, others take frightening risks." The *Arizona Republic* reported that human trafficking was a vicious $2 billion business run by an "organized crime syndicate" (Wagner, 2006). In addition to paying money, people crossing the border are frequently forced to act as human mules by carrying backpacks filled with illegal drugs for their smugglers. Those who risk the difficult desert crossing are often physically abused, detained in miserable and unsanitary conditions, and if they cannot keep up with the mule train while making the arduous journey may be left for dead. In a story about *National Geographic*'s coverage of the "Border Wars," the (Louisville, KY) *Courier-Journal* wrote, "Lots of them are found dead in the desert, where temperatures soar well above 100 degrees. Their sun-bleached bones are discovered after the buzzards are through with them" (Dorsey, 2008, p. 5E). The *Christian Science Monitor* detailed some of the grim statistics: "As illegal immigrants have channeled into rural areas, one result has been the rising numbers of deaths in the desert. Arizona saw a record 473 deaths last year—and human rights groups say that statistic is probably a fraction of the actual number, because many deaths go unreported" (Wood, 2006, p. 1USA).

Open-border advocates who view U.S. immigration policy as biased against people of color point to news stories about those who are literally dying to come to America and question the moral compass of a nation that could let such a thing occur along its borders. Mike King, an editorial writer for the *Atlanta Journal-Constitution*, addressed conflicts between the national security and human rights frames:

> A true test of our feelings about race, the economy and the role low-wage earners play in it awaits. Indeed, the conversation will reflect the core values that move our moral compass as a nation. . . . There are the nativists who want to round up and deport 11 million to 12 million Latinos who have come into the country illegally, contending that the porous borders are an invitation to potential terrorists. . . . And then there are the bleeding hearts who contend that those here illegally are hard workers being targeted because of the color of their skin. . . . Not all illegal border crossers are members of terrorist cells. . . . Neither are they all hard workers just seeking the American dream. (King, 2006, p. 15A)

The Immigration Reform Frame

The immigration reform frame deals with the attempt to retool federal legislation that governs U.S. immigration policy. This is a political frame that includes the positions and opinions of lawmakers, political candidates, policy advisors, lobbyists, commentators, and citizens.

A bipartisan immigration reform bill came before Congress in 2006–2007 that would have provided a path to citizenship for millions of people who reside in the United States without documentation. The Comprehensive Immigration Reform Act of 2007 included provisions for increased border security, including the building of a fence along the nearly 2,000 miles of the U.S.–Mexican border and an expanded guest worker program. The bill was controversial to many groups for many reasons. Restrictions on family reunification were decried by immigrant advocacy groups. Labor unions and others saw the guest worker provision as creating an economic underclass. A significant factor in the defeat of the bill was conservative talk radio, which the *Washington Post* credited with mobilizing listeners across the country to put pressure on their legislators to squash the bill (Weisman & Murray, 2007). The article quoted Mississippi senator Trent Lott's comment to the *New York Times*: "Talk radio is running America. We have to deal with that problem" (p. 1C).

In the November 28, 2007, YouTube presidential debate carried live on CNN, Republican candidates were questioned by citizens about their positions on many issues, including immigrations. More than 5,000 questions were submitted via youtube.com; the first question selected was for former New York mayor Rudolph Giuliani: "Under your administration, as well as others, New York City was operated as a sanctuary city, aiding and abetting illegal aliens. I would like to know, if you become president of the United States, will you continue to aid and abet the flight of illegal aliens into this country?" After Giuliani's response, the debate's moderator asked Arizona senator John McCain if he would be willing to "veto any immigration bill that involved amnesty for those who have come here illegally."

Sanctuary city and *amnesty* are highly charged keywords in the national dialogue and serve to place people on opposite ends of the immigration reform frame.

REFRAMING, REFOCUSING, AND REPORTING

The way the media select and report stories is driven largely by factors attributed to dominant class biases inherent within the media. The mainstream media in the United States are largely owned by corporate conglomerates and run almost exclusively by educated, upper-income White men. Newsrooms are staffed overwhelmingly by people who are part of the dominant class, and they share certain class biases that influence the way stories are selected and edited.

The dominant class has a vested interest in maintaining the status quo to ensure its position of hegemonic power. Researchers studying how journalists report stories about minorities have shown that the media often perpetuate racial stereotypes and increase racial conflict, which serves to further the status quo.

The media have an enormous challenge to report well complex and controversial stories, such as the contemporary immigration story. The *Dallas Morning News* was highly criticized by readers for their choice of the illegal immigrant as the 2007 Texan of the Year. Some readers interpreted that the paper was bestowing an honor on the illegal immigrant. Far from it, the paper was acknowledging the reality of a phenomenon that is part of the public discourse. The paper concluded its editorial by saying, "What you think of the illegal immigrant says a lot about what you think of America, and what vision of her you are willing to defend. How we deal with the stranger among us says not only who we Americans are today but determines who we will become tomorrow."

IT'S YOUR TURN: WHAT DO YOU THINK? WHAT WILL YOU FIND?

1. Review a few editions of your local newspaper or a national newspaper, or go to library and find newspapers from Texas, New Mexico, Arizona, or California. Look for stories about immigration and count how many times you find the frames listed above. What other frames do you find? What do these frames tell you about the people who are here without permission? What do these frames tell you about the reporters and newspapers who published these stories?

2. Look for two sets of stories: one about immigrants from Central America and one about immigrants from Asia, Africa, and Europe. Try to find at least three articles for each set. What keywords and frames are used by the media in reporting on different immigrant populations? Are the stories about certain immigrants framed more positively, or more sympathetically, than the stories about others?

3. Compare how mainstream and alternative media cover immigration. Find a conservative paper, a liberal paper, a conservative news blog, and a liberal news blog. What differences do you see?

REFERENCES

Barlett, D., Steele, B., Karmatz, L., & Levinstein, J. (2004, September 20). Who left the door open? *Time*, 51–66.

Bear, D. (2007, September 9). Travelers bear brunt of post 9/11 sacrifices. *Pittsburgh Post-Gazette*, F1.

Buchanan, P. J. (2006). *State of emergency: The third world invasion and conquest of America*. New York: Macmillan.

Carlisle, N. (2008, February 18). Arizona crackdown could add to Utah's illegal immigration woes. *The Salt Lake Tribune*, 1A.

Coomes, J. (2005, September 1). Hayworth bill tackles "invasion." *Arizona Republic*, SRN1.

Dobbs, L. (Host/Producer). (2008, April 10). L.A. mayor demands federal government stop enforcing immigration laws. *CNN: Lou Dobbs Tonight* [Television series]. Transcript retrieved October 26, 2008, from: http://transcripts.cnn.com/TRANSCRIPTS/0804/10/ldt.01.html

Dorsey, T. (2008, March 26). *National Geographic* gives a view of "Border Wars." *The Courier-Journal*, 5E.

Entman, R. M. (1991). Framing U.S. coverage of international news: Contrasts of the KAL and Iran air incidents. *Journal of Communication, 41*(4), 6–27.

Gordon, G., Taylor, M., & Hutcheson, R. (2006, September 10). Are we safer? *The Miami Herald*, 1A.

Holstege, S. (2003, September 11). How air travel has changed forever. *The Oakland Tribune*, 1N.

King, M. (2006, March 30). Finally U.S. tackles illegal immigration. *The Atlanta Journal-Constitution*, 15A.

Lefever, E. (2006, September 17). The threat of uncontrolled immigration to America. *The Washington Times*, 8BO.

McCombs, M., & Shaw, D. (1972). The agenda-setting function of the mass media. *Public Opinion Quarterly, 73*(2), 176–187.

Peterson, J. (2007, June 29). America must secure its borders now. *Erie Times-News*, 1F.

Pinkerton, J. (2004, September 24). "Border baby" boom strains S. Texas: More illegal immigrants are pouring into the state to give birth. *The Houston Chronicle*, 1A.

Richardson, B. (2005, August 12). Press release.

Rodriguez, G. (2008, April 6). A 670-mile-long shrine to American insecurity. *Los Angeles Times*, 1O.

Shenon, P. Jehl, D., & Johnston, D. (2004, July 24). Correcting the record on Sept. 11, in great detail. *The New York Times*, 1A.

Spagat, E. (2006, December 31). Border smugglers in demand: Heightened security creates a boom. *Chicago Tribune*, 4B.

The illegal immigrant. (2007, December 30). *Dallas Morning News*, 1P.

Wagner, D. (2006, July 23). Phoenix's hidden $2 billion industry: Human smuggling's vicious organizations move thousands of immigrants through valley every day. *Arizona Republic*, A1.

Weggel, A. (2006, Nov. 13). An evolving language. *The Minnesota Daily*, A7.

Weisman, J., & Murray, S. (2007, June 20). Republicans hearing static from conservative radio hosts. *The Washington Post*, 1C.

Wilhelm, M. (1953, June 7). "Wetback" tide overflowing Rio Grande again. *The Washington Post*, 3B.

Wood, D. (2006, July 27). New troops at U.S. border, but the task is vast. *Christian Science Monitor*, 1USA.

4.3 CONFRONTING THE FRONT PAGES: A CONTENT ANALYSIS OF U.S. NEWSPAPERS

Cynthia M. Lont and M. Junior Bridge

The authors analyzed newspaper content over time to investigate the extent to which women are included as sources of news and as reporters of news. Before you read this, what does your "gut instinct" tell you—do you think the roles assigned to women and men are less stereotypical now than in the 1970s and 1980s?

A newspaper's front page is the window to the news within. Headlines and photos exposing political scandals, declaring wars, and focusing our attention on international affairs are printed on the front page because the front page sells newspapers. The front page catches our attention as we walk by the newsstand or check out at the grocery store. The front page tells the world who is important and, by their absence, who is not.

Whose faces do we see on the newspaper front page? Who writes the articles? Who are the experts we read about in the stories, and who headlines the news? These are some of the questions we answer in this chapter.

For the past two decades, we have examined the portrayals of women in radio (Lont, 1990, 1995), music (Lont, 1992), television news (Bridge, 1994, 1995a), and newspapers (Bridge, 1989, 1992, 1994, 1995a, 1995b, 1996, 2000). What we mean by "portrayals" are the roles assigned to women and men in popular media. Are women shown in the same nonstereotypical and diverse roles (something other than spouse, parent, sibling, child, or victim) as men?

One of the first things students assert in our Women and Media classes is that the roles assigned to females are more diverse and less stereotypical than in the 1970s, 1980s, or even the 1990s. Students give examples of women who break the stereotypes, such as Hillary Rodham Clinton, Oprah Winfrey, and Katie Couric.

Because people's perceptions of the media aren't always accurate, we ask students to back up their claims with numbers. Each student chooses her or his favorite medium (a women's magazine, a prime-time television program, their favorite film, or a radio station program) and then conducts a content analysis of the portrayal of females and males.

A content analysis is a method many scholars use to analyze media content. It gives hard numbers to discuss and compare. Very simply, a content analysis is the identification and counting of the number of times something occurs. It includes as well a close examination of language, topics, placement of news stories, negative and positive slants, and the like.

In the class exercise, students record a television or radio program, purchase a copy of the latest issue of a magazine or newspaper, or rent a film. Then they carefully examine the media content and begin counting. Are there more women or more men? What are the roles to which women and men are assigned? On the radio station, who are the DJs? Who are the fans? In the television program, who goes to work and who stays home? Who takes care of the household and the children? If women and men are portrayed at work, who is more concerned with their work and who is more concerned with their relationships or how they look? Who writes or presents the stories and on what do the stories focus? Clothes? Self-esteem? Accomplishments? Victimization? In terms of age, race, class, disabilities, and sexual orientation, who is portrayed and who is left out?

In most of their analyses, students find that men largely outnumber women. Also, women are usually younger, more attractive, more likely to be concerned with appearance, relationships, and the home. In general, if you are not young, White, thin, able bodied, and heterosexual, then you are underrepresented or not represented at all in the media. Gaye Tuchman (1978) referred to this lack of representation as "symbolic annihilation."

THE FRONT PAGE OF NEWS

Bridge has conducted content analyses of the front pages of newspapers since 1989. Although this chapter focuses on the latest study (2007), we discuss past studies as a comparison. First, let's look at the framework for the 2007 study. Five newspapers were analyzed from October 18 through November 17, 2007: the *Atlanta Journal Constitution*, the *Chicago Tribune*, the *Los Angeles Times*, the *New York Times*, and *USA TODAY*. We analyzed the front page; the first page of the local, business, and sports sections; and the opinion/editorial page. We determined the percentage of females and males referenced (references) in the articles, the percentage of times females and males appeared in the photographs on these key pages, and the percentage of males and females who wrote the articles (bylines).

Analysis of the newspaper front pages in 2007 showed that men overwhelmingly dominated the references (79%). Males appeared in 69% of the front-page photographs, while females appeared in only 31% of the pictures. Only 34% of the bylines were female. In addition, when stories written about, by, and with photographs of women were published, they were generally located on the bottom of the page, rather than in the prominent location above the fold. Given that women are the majority of the U.S. population, the majority of voters, and the strong majority of consumer decision makers, the news findings are surprising. Despite the gains in stature and recognition of women and their accomplishments in the past few decades, media coverage continues to underrepresent, underreport, and undermine the contributions and talents of the female population.

OK, but over time things must be getting better, right? How do these 2007 numbers compare to earlier studies? Bridge has studied the front pages of U.S. newspapers since 1989.

In 1989, women were 11% of the references, appeared in 24% of the photographs, and wrote 27% of the articles on the newspapers' front pages. As Table 4.1 indicates, the numbers rose to an all-time high in 1994 in two categories: references (25%) and photographs (39%). In that same year, bylines remained consistent at 33%. Then the numbers drop. By 1996, female references had dropped 10% to 15%. Photographs of women on the front page dropped to 33% in 1996. Bylines stayed much the same at 34%. By 2000, the percentage of female references went up from 15% to 17%. In 2007, the references for women rose to 21%, still below 1994's high point of 25%. Photographs of women on the front pages dropped consistently over time—from 39% in 1994, to 33% in 1996, 32% in 2000, and 31% in 2007. Female bylines dropped from 33% in 1994, to 28% in 2000, but rose to 34% (one point higher than in 1994, but the same as 1992 and 1996) in 2007.

Over the years, there was a small increase in media coverage of women up to 1994, then a sharp decrease in 1996. In the 2007 study, women as references and in photographs were still not at the same level as they were 13 years prior in 1994.

Women are 52% of the population in the United States, earn more money than in the past (although still not equivalent to their male counterparts), constitute about half of the paid workforce, predominate on major purchase decisions (whether they provide part of the household income or not), are the majority of the college students, are the majority of the voters, live longer than men, and are the heads of more households than ever before in U.S. history. One would expect that in 2007, women reporting the news, women as part of the news, women as references in news, and women in news photos should be comparable

TABLE 4.1   Front Page Analysis

	1989	1992	1994	1996	2000[*]	2007[*]
References	11%	13%	25%	15%	17%	21%
Photographs	24%	32%	39%	33%	32%	31%
Bylines	27%	34%	33%	34%	28%	34%

[*]The 2000 and 2007 studies did not include all the newspapers used in earlier studies.

TABLE 4.2   **Local News, Business , Op-Ed, and Sports Front Pages**

	1994	1996	2000	2007
Local References	26%	24%	23%	26%
Local Photographs	38%	37%	40%	38%
Local Bylines	42%	39%	38%	37%
Business References	. . .	13%	15%	15%
Business Photographs	. . .	24%	20%	24%
Business Bylines	. . .	33%	35%	33%
Op-Ed Bylines	28%	24%	26%	23%
Sports References	. . .	. . .	14%	5%
Sports Photographs	. . .	. . .	18%	6%
Sports Bylines	. . .	. . .	14%	11%

". . . " indicates data for a given variable was not collected during that year.

to their percentage in the population and their relevance in the rich fabric of American culture, yet in none of the areas we studied (photos, bylines, or references) are women even close to their representation in the population or their contributions to society. Coverage of females was and remains marginal.

That's the front page of the newspaper. What about the front pages of other key sections of the newspaper? Data for Local News, Business, Opinion-Editorial (Op-Ed), and Sports sections for 1994, 1996, 2000, and 2007 are presented in Table 4.2.

Women are more prominent in local positions ranging from top jobs to volunteering than on the national front, so we'd expect more coverage of women in the Business pages. The data show more women represented in all three categories in the front pages of the Local News than we saw on the front pages of the newspaper in 2007. Over the years, women in the Local News were referred to about one-quarter of the time. They are depicted in photographs more than one-third of the time and write between 38% and 44% of the stories. Because there are more women writing the stories, does that explain the increase in the number of references? Unfortunately, no. The data show female reporters are no more likely to use women as references in their stories than male reporters are.

What about the front page of the Business section? According to the Center for Women's Business Research (2008), women own about 10.1 million firms in this country, employ more than 13 million people, and generate $1.9 trillion in sales. For the last 20 years, women-owned firms have grown at about twice the rate of all firms (42% versus 24%). Forty-one percent of all privately held firms are owned by women. Wouldn't we expect the front page of the Business section to reflect this?

For the 3 years of Business section data available, we find the front page of the Business section has fewer women in all three categories than found on the front page of the Local News in any of the years for which Local News data are available. When compared to the national front page data of the same years, we find the same number, or fewer, women in the Business section with one exception. In 2000, women wrote more of the stories (35%) in the Business section than seen in the bylines of the national front pages

(28%). This means more women wrote stories on the Business front page than on the national front page but does not mean more women were seen in photographs or, in general, were included as references in Business front pages. In 2007, this trend changed and, once again, more women wrote front-page stories (34%) than in the Business section (33%).

If women are not in the news as much as men, perhaps we read their views in the Op-Ed page. Only bylines were coded on these pages because there are no photos or references. Less than a quarter of the Op-Ed pieces were written by women in the 2007 study. If women are the "talkative" sex, why are there not more opinion pieces authored by women? On average, men wrote 77% of the opinion pieces (85% in the *Chicago Tribune*, 81% in the *New York Times*). The Op-Ed content purportedly represents both the important opinion makers and the most critical topics, yet women's views are seen little more than 25% of the time.

In the 2000 and 2007 studies, we reviewed the front page of the Sports section. The data show that women haven't come close to parity in terms of coverage on the front page of the Sports section, and, in fact, have dropped significantly in the past 7 years. The 2000 and 2007 studies found that mostly men were covered in the Sports section. What is devastating is the drop is much larger than any other category we have seen between 2000 and 2007. Sports references dropped from 14% to 5%. Photographs dropped from 18% to 6%, and bylines dropped from 14% to 11% in a mere 7 years.

BEYOND THE NUMBERS

Overall, men heavily dominated in references, bylines, and photo appearances across the front pages studied. Women were more frequently found on the front pages of the Local News section, if they were covered at all. Large companies and their male leaders dominated the business stories. Opinion page writers were predominantly male. The front page of the Sports section carried little coverage or mention of female athletes, coaches, or fans. We also looked beyond the numbers, to see how women were covered in 2007. Four main themes emerged:

First, we found males who are not very successful are more likely to be covered than females who are very successful. This is especially apparent in the Sports section. The key sports pages focused on male sports, primarily football, basketball, and baseball. Male losses, poor performing male teams, and male athletes were covered extensively, while stories about high-achieving female athletes were either not carried at all, were covered by a mere photo within the section, or were treated to a few paragraphs within the Sports sections (not the front page). It was not uncommon during the 2007 study to find whole Sports sections (one was 19 pages long) wherein there were no stories of female athletes, negative or positive, or their sports. The number of women who participate in sports has increased over the past 20 years, yet the coverage would make readers believe few women athletes exist.

Stories about female accomplishments were frequently located within lesser spots in the newspaper. An example of tucking away successful females was a major story in *USA TODAY* entitled, "Missions Mark Giant Leaps for Womankind." The article, written by a female, concerned women's leadership in the space field. The story was buried on page 10A.

Second, we noticed that minority women were poorly covered, even in markets with large minority populations. Minority women were not included in political stories and were ignored in articles about leadership or opinion makers. Usually, minority women were featured as victims or perpetrators of crime or other mishaps.

Additionally, our examination of the front page showed that women, in general, were represented as victims far more often than as leaders, role models, heroes, or business successes. Women who did succeed in business, when covered in newspapers, were most often found as the subject of "fluff" or feature articles in less important parts of the publications.

Finally, we noticed that in many key pages, there was minimal to no female presence; the opposite (meaning a lack of male presence) was not found. In our analyses, it is common to find key pages, including front pages of major newspapers, in which there is NO female presence: no female bylines, no references to females, and no females in photos. The reverse has never been found in these studies starting in 1989. Can you imagine the uproar that would occur if the front page of the *New York Times* included not one reference to a male, not one male byline, and not one male in a photo? Yet, this happens to women and no one notices. What is the implication of this?

WHY IS THIS IMPORTANT?

Many students in our Women and Media classes ask why it matters that women and men are not represented equally in the newspaper. That's a good question, generating several important responses. If women are the majority of the population, one would think that they should be represented in the newspaper the majority of the time and be the majority of the references, write the majority of the articles and be portrayed in the majority of the photographs. However, if they are not the leaders or opinion makers or the breakthrough scientists, the counter argument goes, they don't deserve the dominant coverage. The fact is that there are female leaders and role models on every front, even though their numbers may not match that of males. However, how much does media and societal inattention and belittling of female accomplishments affect females' sense of self worth and ability to soar to the same heights that males have achieved?

Media coverage or lack thereof does affect females and males in multiple ways. Cultivation theory, for example, says if you're a heavy viewer of television, you have a skewed sense of reality. You think the real world is or should be more like the television world (Gerbner & Gross, 1976). Many theories about media effects focus on how media affects our perceptions of ourselves, our world, and our role(s) in that world. If you read in the newspaper that most experts are men, even in stories that concern primarily women, then you might believe men are the authorities on most subjects and women have little to contribute. If you see few female bylines, you might believe it is rare for women to be reporters, and, therefore, reporting is an occupation unsuitable for a woman. If you see women portrayed only as victims, or siblings, parents, or lovers, then you may perceive women's roles in society as only supportive of men.

Most of us decide what we want to be and can be based on the role models we see. The more we see women and men in diverse and nonstereotypical roles, the more possibilities open up for all.

IT'S YOUR TURN: WHAT DO YOU THINK? WHAT WILL YOU FIND?

1. Many students believe the roles assigned to women are less stereotypical and more diverse than they were 20 years ago. If you believe this is true, what examples can you give to demonstrate the changes? If you believe this is not true, what examples might you give to demonstrate things have not changed?

2. Why do you think that although there are more female journalists than there were 20 years ago, the front page stories continue to represent males far more often then females?

3. Conduct a content analysis. Randomly choose four editions of your newspaper (your school newspaper or local paper or your favorite Internet news site) from the past month. Choose different days of the week. Stay away from holidays.

   a. Take a marker (one color for males, one color for females, and a third for when you can't tell) and mark the bylines, references, and the times one or more females/males appear in front-page photographs. What percentage are female and what percentage are male? Do these percentages compare to the population of the community served by the paper?

   b. Do the same with other parts of the newspaper or Internet site, such as the Sports or Style section. How (and if so, why) do you think they differ from the front page?

   c. Next, write a list of what males are identified as doing and what females are identified as doing. What percentage of the female and males are references? What percentage of female and males are identified by their relationships to others (wife, husband, son, daughter, sister, brother, mother, father)? Do these percentages shift depending on whether it is the front page, the Sports section, or the Style section? What might that say about the status of females and males in our culture?

   d. Analyze stories you think concern either women (women's health issues, women's fashion, etc.) or men (men's health issues, men's fashion, etc.). Who wrote the women's stories and men's stories? Who are the experts cited in each? How many women experts are cited in men's stories, and vice versa? What does that say about men and women in our culture?

REFERENCES

Bridge, M. J. (1989). *Women, men and media: Women remain window dressing on the set.* Alexandria, VA: Unabridged Communication.

Bridge, M. J. (1992). *The news, as if all people mattered.* Alexandria, VA: Unabridged Communication.

Bridge, M. J. (1994). *Arriving on the scene: Women's growing presence in the newsroom.* Alexandria, VA: Unabridged Communication.

Bridge, M. J. (1995a). *Slipping from the scene: News coverage of females drops.* Alexandria, VA: Unabridged Communication.

Bridge, M. J. (1995b). What's next? In C. M. Lont (Ed.), *Women in the media: Content, careers, and criticism* (pp. 15–28). Belmont, CA: Wadsworth Press.

Bridge, M. J. (1996). *Marginalizing women: Front-page news coverage of females declines in 1996.* Alexandria, VA: Unabridged Communications.

Bridge, M. J. (2000). *Sidelining women: A fact sheet.* Unpublished paper.

Center for Women's Business Research. (2008). National numbers. Retrieved October 21, 2008, from: http://www.nfwbo.org/facts/index.php

Gerbner, G., & Gross, L. (1976). Living with television: The violence profile. *Journal of Communication, 26*, 173–179.

Lont, C. M. (1990). Roles assigned females and males in non-music radio programming. *Sex Roles, 22*, 661–668.

Lont, C. M. (1995). *Non-music radio programming targeting adolescents: An update.* Unpublished paper.

Lont, C. M. (1992). Women's music: No longer a private party. In R. Garafolo (Ed.), *Rockin' the boat: Mass music and mass movements.* (pp. 241–254). Boston, MA: South End Press.

Tuchman, G. (1978). The symbolic annihilation of women by the mass media. In G. Tuchman, A. Daniels, & S. Benet (Eds.), *Hearth and home: Images of women in the mass media.* (pp. 5–38). New York: Oxford University Press.

4.4 ONLINE NEWS AND RACE: A CONTENT ANALYSIS OF THE PORTRAYAL OF RACIAL STEREOTYPES IN A NEW MEDIA ENVIRONMENT

Christopher S. Josey, Ryan J. Hurley, Veronica Hefner, and Travis L. Dixon

The authors examined the nature of online news content to see how race is portrayed in headlines, images, and stories. The analysis was informed by Clark's (1972) stages of representation: nonrecognition, ridicule, regulation, and respect. Content analysis revealed that Asians are in the nonrecognition stage, Blacks and Hispanics are in the ridicule stage, none of the groups is in the regulation stage, and Whites are in the respect stage.

Growing up in rural southern Indiana, the first author of this reading distinctly remembers how awestruck he was the day that a man came to his parents' home and installed cable television. It was like nothing he had ever seen, and he found himself wondering exactly how all of those extra channels could fit into that small black wire and into his television. Through cable, he was able to explore worlds that he had little to no direct contact with. He and others living in less diverse communities could see many examples of people of color that they may have never personally encountered. When he grew up and eventually encountered people from different religions and races, he found that the notions he held of these individuals were often flat and one-dimensional, and at times altogether incorrect!

Years ago, television served to introduce many in the United States to racial and ethnic minorities. Today, the deepening penetration of the Internet into homes across America is having similar effects. Researchers have noted the importance of news programming in influencing people's world views (Dixon & Linz, 2000a; 2000b; Entman, 1992; Iyengar, 1991). News programming can help people having limited contact with diverse cultural groups peer though the looking glass and see what these groups are like in "real life." Although news is often considered an accurate representation of the world around us (Iyengar, 1991), for people to gain an accurate picture of the world, the portrayals of diverse groups must themselves be accurate.

Scholars have shown for years that traditional media (newspapers, TV newscasts) do a poor job in accurately showing the multifaceted nature of racial and ethnic groups (Dixon & Linz, 2000a; Entman, 1992). Racial minority groups, in particular, have been shown to be more criminal and more likely to be associated with race-specific stereotypes. Over and over again, research has demonstrated that stereotypes presented by traditional media play an important role in the development and maintenance of stereotypical beliefs. But what about new media, such as the Internet?

Although researchers have begun to broadly consider online media content, nuanced investigations are few. Yet, with over 1.4 billion Internet users in over 171 countries worldwide, the need for research on Internet content should be apparent (Internet World Statistics, 2008; Flanagin & Metzger, 2000). One study by the Pew Internet & American Life Project (2000) found that as the Internet has achieved a deeper penetration into more homes, people are turning less to traditional media outlets such as newspapers and television for their news and are relying on Internet-based news sources as their primary source of information.

But how is race portrayed in online media? We examined the nature of online news content and how race is portrayed in headlines, images, and stories. Whereas other investigations into the portrayal of race in traditional media have focused on specific content areas such as crime stories (Dixon, 2000), we took a more holistic approach by surveying the news presented on a diverse set of Web sites. Before we get into the specifics of how we did this, we explain the general framework for our analysis.

FOUR STAGES OF REPRESENTATION OF RACE IN THE MEDIA

Many early studies involving portrayals of race in television and in the movies focused on the substance and number of portrayals of various racialized groups, which eventually led to the development of four stages of representation (Clark, 1972): nonrecognition, ridicule, regulation, and respect. Clark specifically had television and movies in mind; however, these stages can be applied to news content as well, as we will soon discuss.

The first of Clark's stages of representation is *nonrecognition*. Groups that are in this stage will not be seen in substantial numbers in various media. Here, group members are extremely underrepresented relative to their presence in the actual population. This is not to say that groups in the nonrecognition stage are never seen. Rather, such groups are "mostly" invisible in the media as a result of minimal presence. Asian Americans are a clear example of a racial group in the stage of nonrecognition. It is unlikely that one would see an Asian individual portrayed as a primary character in a television program during any time of day or night. It is also important to note that groups in the nonrecognition stage are often shown for novelty's sake (e.g., coverage of the cultural traditions of Asians in China as a lead into the Olympics). In our analysis, for a group to be in the nonrecognition phase, they would have to occupy a very small portion of our sample.

The next stage advanced by Clark is that of *ridicule*. In this stage a group is still underrepresented but not to the extent of virtual invisibility. Ridiculed groups are often portrayed in extremely stereotypic manners, such as being ignorant or lazy. In news media, it can be thought that a racial group is in the ridicule stage of representation if they occupy a smaller than expected proportion of the overall racial landscape and have negative portrayals associated with them.

Clark said that the third stage of representation is that of *regulation*. A regulated racial representation happens when a minority group achieves a more accurate frequency of representation, in combination with a one-dimensional portrayal. Here a group has largely escaped the images of ignorance and laziness but is still portrayed in an unbalanced manner. Examples of this abound in police drama shows that portray Blacks as strong, silent, and physical men. The idea is that although diversity of character roles may have been improved, the depth with which each character is portrayed is lacking.

The final stage of representation noted by Clark is *respect*. Groups that are in the respect stage occupy an accurate proportion of the overall number of characters. They also have a diverse set of roles with an appropriate level of nuance to their portrayal. Clark and others have noted that only Whites are currently recognized as being in the respect stage. In a news media framework, respect would be indicated by accurate representations in number, depth, and lack of stigmatization.

ASSESSING STAGES OF REPRESENTATION IN NEWS CONTENT

Our intent was to assess the level, and if possible, stage of representation of racial groups in online news content. We used the Alexa Media Research rankings to identify the 11 most-visited news Web sites of 2006. (These were, in rank order: Yahoo! News, BBC News, CNN, the New York Times, Google News, Reuters, Fox News, the Washington Post, ABC News, USA Today, the Los Angeles Times.) We created a sample week of news content by downloading content from each site randomly over a 3-month period. Through this process we obtained a total of 35 news stories for each Web site representing 385 stories in all. Our research staff investigated representation across images associated with the story and story headlines. Images and headlines are important because of the nature of online news. Unlike television newscasts and newspapers, online news Web sites use images and headlines to gain a reader's attention in efforts to get them to link to the full story (Knobloch, Hastall, Zillmann, & Callision, 2003). From these links, an individual chooses which content to consume. This is an important distinction in that the consumer drives the ultimate order and amount of content consumed. Further, research has also shown that individuals often use headlines and images as primary resources in information gathering when using online media (Knobloch et al., 2003). Thus, the portrayal of race in images and headlines may be among the most influential representations online.

To investigate the stages of representation for Blacks, Whites, Hispanics, and Asians, we used two main strategies. First, we employed a chi-square statistic to look for the relative frequency of representation for each race in images and headlines. A chi-square statistic compares the actual frequency of characters in our sample to the frequency that would be expected by chance. It will allow us to see if the number of characters in our sample is significantly different that what we would expect, thus telling us if a particular race is over- or underrepresented in online news content. The second strategy we used compared the proportion of our sample of each race to the actual proportion of that race in the United States as measured by census data. This is useful because it allowed us to directly assess whether a particular race was over- or underrepresented relative to the general population. We followed these tests with more chi-squares examining the frequency of races connected to a negatively valenced stereotype: poverty. Finally, we went one step further to investigate whether any race is over- or under represented in the most popular (i.e., most frequently viewed) stories.

PORTRAYING RACE IN ONLINE NEWS

We begin our results by discussing the general nature of our sample of headlines. After deleting any images or headlines that did not feature a person, we were left with 81 total headlines and 82 total images. We included only headlines that explicitly mentioned race or where race was clearly inferable (e.g., the race of well-known individuals). Similarly, we included only images with at least one person (some stories had pictures of cars or buildings, but no people). Adhering to this strict standard helps ensure the validity of our results, but it also resulted in a sample that was smaller than we would have liked.

Representing Race in Images and Headlines

Images represent powerful means of conveying information. Thus, we examined how race was portrayed in images in online news. Of the 82 total images, there were 57 Whites, 18 Blacks, 6 Hispanics, and 1 Asian. We begin our investigation comparing the appearance of various races using a chi-square statistic. This statistic allows researchers to compare the observed numbers of persons of a particular race to the numbers that one would expect by chance. It makes no direct comparison to population data, but rather, the likelihood that we would obtain the observed frequencies by chance alone if all groups are fairly represented (e.g., all groups having an equal chance to be pictured in news stories). As a result, it allows us to see if particular races are more or less likely to be portrayed than others. When considering Black persons, a chi-square statistic revealed a statistically significant difference: X^2 (3, $N = 82$) = 94.1, $p < .001$. Specifically, Blacks were less likely to be shown in images than equal proportions would predict. This was even more pronounced with Hispanics and Asians. Whites were seen significantly more than one would expect. Together, this demonstrates that online news Web sites paint an unbalanced representation of race through their use of images. Since there were often multiple individuals pictured per image, a direct comparison to U.S. Census data here would be problematic at best, so we made no such comparisons. However, one can still see that when comparing the frequency of portrayals of race in images online, minority groups are underrepresented when based on equal chance probability comparisons to the majority group (e.g., Whites).

Our next step was to investigate whether online news headlines accurately portray racial groups. We began by comparing the observed number of races to that we would expect by chance, again using a chi-square statistic. Much like the case with images of persons of color, we found significant differences in the way race was represented in headlines: X^2 (3, $N = 81$) = 157.37, $p < .001$. Specifically, we found that Blacks were not likely to be mentioned in headlines (see the "sample frequency" column in Table 4.3). We also found this to be the case with Hispanics and Asians. Asians were almost nonexistent at the headline level, only appearing once in our entire sample. Similar to the portrayal of Whites through images, we found that Whites were mentioned with disproportionate frequency as a racial group.

Having compared the actual frequency of people of various races to that we would expect by chance, we needed to determine if each racial group was represented in a manner that was different than U.S. Census data. We did this by constructing confidence intervals. Confidence intervals are a statistical method used to determine whether an observed

TABLE 4.3   **Comparing Headline Characters to 2006 Population Data**

RACE/ETHNICITY	SAMPLE FREQUENCY	SAMPLE PROPORTION	US CENSUS PROPORTION	DIFFERENCE
Black	4	4.9%	12.3%	−7.4[*]
White	69	85.2%	66.4%	+18.8%[*]
Hispanic	7	8.6%	14.8%	−6.2%[**]
Asian	1	1.2%	4.3%	−3.10%

[*]Significant at $p < .05$, 1-tailed using a 95% Confidence Interval.

[**]Approaches significance at $p < .07$.

value (e.g., the number of Blacks mentioned in headlines) falls within an acceptable distance from a known value (e.g., the actual number of Blacks in the United States). If our number falls far enough from the known population value, we can be 95% confident that our sample value is different from the U.S. Census population value. We began by computing proportions for each racial group relative to our sample size (see Table 4.3). Then we use the confidence interval to compare our sample proportion to the actual proportion of U.S. residents of each racial group. When compared to U.S. Census data, Blacks were significantly underrepresented as headline characters. Specifically, we observed a −7.4% difference. This means that in our sample, Blacks accounted for significantly fewer appearances than should be expected if one is looking for a balanced portrayal. Similarly, Hispanics represented only 8.6% of our sample, a full 6.2% below what we would expect in the population at large. Asians were neither under- nor overrepresented when compared to population data. Whites, on the other hand, were significantly overrepresented, accounting for 85.2% of our sample. This is over 18% more than would be expected when compared to U.S. Census data.

On the whole, at the headline level, we find that Blacks and Hispanics are underrepresented both more than would be predicted by chance and when comparing our sample data to U.S. Census data. Asians were represented to a lesser degree than would be predicted by chance, but not when compared to Census data. Whites are overrepresented vis-á-vis chance alone and in comparison to U.S. Census data. Clearly, online news outlets are not advancing a balanced portrayal of race online.

Representation in Popular and Top News

To take our analysis one step further, we investigated differences that might emerge for popular or top news stories. For many Web sites, the most prominently featured stories are listed in a section called Top News. All of the Web sites we sampled had a Top News section. Differences in the portrayal of race in these stories are especially important given their overall prominence and the likelihood that viewers will pay special attention to them. We used a chi-square statistic to investigate any differences in representation. Like the image and story levels, we found significant differences: $X^2 (2, N = 22) = 19.7$, $p < .001$. Asians were completely absent from top news, meaning they were seriously underrepresented. Blacks and Hispanics were featured less frequently than we would expect. Whites were featured more than twice what one would expect by chance alone. We now turn our attention to stories that were ranked as popular news.

Looking at popular news is important given that it provides insight into what readers are self-selecting as their news. Thus, although one could argue that on the Internet, individuals could circumvent unbalanced portrayals by choosing news from their own set of balanced beliefs, seeing differences in the portrayal of race among stories that readers view most would give a clearer picture of the state of representation readers are consuming. To investigate this, we performed a chi-square test. Again, we found results consistent with our previous findings: $X^2 (2, N = 24) = 16.7, p < .001$. Among the stories readers are consuming most, Blacks and Hispanics are seen less frequently than should be expected. Asians are completely absent from popular news in our sample. Whites are featured more than twice what would be expected by chance. Taken together, these results demonstrate that among the stories deemed most worthy (e.g., top news) and those most frequently consumed (e.g., popular), readers of online news are getting an unbalanced portrayal of race.

Representing Minorities and Poverty

Poverty represents one of the most strongly associated negative stereotypes tied to racial minorities (Gilens, 1996; Iyengar, 1990). One way to move beyond merely reporting whether groups of color are over- or underrepresented is to investigate whether any group is portrayed more frequently as being poverty stricken than others. Here again we use a chi-square statistic to compare groups to each other based on expected frequencies and not to actual poverty statistics. We would expect that minority groups would be positively associated with poverty such that, compared with expected numbers of poor minorities, our sample may have more portrayals of poor persons of color. A chi-square statistic reveals that this is indeed the case: $X^2 (3, N = 20) = 9.47, p < .05$. In our sample, Blacks are more than twice as likely than expected to be portrayed as poor (thus associated with a negative stereotype). Hispanics follow the same pattern and are also positively associated with poverty. Asians are neither under- nor overrepresented as poor. Whites are negatively associated with poverty (they are not portrayed as being poor as often as would be expected). Taken together, these results demonstrate that minorities are more likely to be presented in a state of poverty than Whites, furthering a social stigma that reinforces stereotyped beliefs.

PORTRAYALS OF RACE ONLINE AND CLARK'S STAGES OF REPRESENTATION

Returning to Clark's (1972) four stages of race representation in media, some clear patterns emerge from our data. Asians are in the nonrecognition stage, Blacks and Hispanics are in the ridicule stage, none of our four groups is in the regulation stage, and Whites are in the respect stage.

Asians fall into the *nonrecognition* stage of representation largely due to the pervasive invisibility across levels. Asians were underrepresented in the image and headline levels. Further, Asians were completely absent from any top news or popular news. When comparing the number of Asians observed in our sample ($N = 1$) to actual population data, we could not safely categorize this group as underrepresented, yet the sheer low number itself shows the relative invisibility of Asians in online news content. These findings put Asians clearly in the stage of nonrecognition, where this group may not have negative stereotypes associated with them, but they are not seen.

We found that Blacks were underrepresented in images and headline mentions. Simply put, when race was discernable or mentioned, Blacks were not likely to be seen with the same frequency one would expect based on chance alone for images or population data from the U.S. Census for headlines. Further, Blacks are not likely to be featured in the most frequently read stories or stories categorized as top news. Lastly, Blacks were more than twice as likely to be portrayed as poor than expected. Together, these findings suggest that Blacks are within Clark's *ridicule* stage of representation. Implications of this are clear, given that Blacks are underrepresented in the stories consumers read most. Going beyond the most popular stories based on readership, the data also revealed that the stories selected by news gatherers as top news followed a similar pattern of representation. Online news readers are seeing an extremely distorted representation of African Americans.

Hispanics follow patterns similar to that of Blacks in our sample. At both the image and headline levels, Hispanics were underrepresented. When race was able to be determined, Hispanics were not seen with the same frequency, as would be expected by chance. Furthermore, when comparing these proportions to actual U.S. Census data, we see that Hispanics are also underrepresented. Hispanics were also not likely to be featured in either top news or popular news. More troubling is that Hispanics were portrayed as being poor more often than would be expected. As a group, Hispanics also fall into the Clark's *ridicule* stage, being seldom seen and often poor.

We previously noted scholars' claims that Whites are the only racial group to achieve relatively balanced portrayals in traditional media. Whites clearly fit into Clark's *respect* stage in online news content. They are overrepresented at both the image and headline levels. When compared to U.S. Census data, Whites at the headline level are overrepresented by a margin of nearly 19%. Looking into the portrayal of Whites as poor, the opposite pattern emerges: Whites are underrepresented. It seems as though Whites have the benefit of overrepresentation without the burden of negative traits (i.e., poverty). This pattern is troublesome for a number of reasons, which are discussed below.

CULTIVATING ATTITUDES ON RACE IN AN ONLINE ENVIRONMENT

Looking at the patterns of portrayals in online news content shows some interesting outcomes. We found consistently across all levels of analysis that Blacks and Hispanics are in a stage of ridicule, while Asians are in a state of nonrecognition. Investigation of these portrayals is important for many reasons. Unbalanced and stereotypic portrayals can ultimately influence the way media consumers think about, feel about, and behave toward racial minority groups.

Although the first author remembers relishing his opportunity to ultimately be exposed to a more diverse groups, friends, and schoolmates, many do not. Further, research has shown that once these opinions have been formed, they are likely to influence decisions regarding everything from crime policy to elections (Dixon, 2006; Valentino, Hutchings, & White, 2002). Opinions formed from contact with an unbalanced portrayal in news content ultimately cultivate a distorted worldview for many people. These people may see race and racial issues in a very narrow and inaccurate manner, which in turn can lead to the development of ineffective or even harmful policies meant to address some of our most serious problems. As a result, it is important to understand the ways the media portray race and the impact it may have on consumers of that media.

IT'S YOUR TURN: WHAT DO YOU THINK? WHAT WILL YOU FIND?

1. Conduct an informal analysis of your own. Go to your favorite news Web site and look at the individuals featured in the photos with each story. Count up totals for each race that appears in the photos and compare the frequencies you observe to our census data. Do any groups seem to be over- or underrepresented when compared to the census data in this chapter? What does this tell you about the potential message that readers are receiving?

2. Think back to the last few stories you have read online. Did they have images associated with them? What about the images motivated you to read the story? Ask several of your classmates to do the same. Are your reasons for reading these stories similar? What does this tell you about how images drive us to read news stories?

3. Journalistic convention is that the race of a character in a story should only be mentioned if the race of the individual is key to the core of a story. In an online environment, many of the traditional news conventions may be hard to apply because the most popular news sites do not write the stories that they publish. Should news aggregations services such as Google and Yahoo! News be held to the same traditional news standards as print newspapers? Why or why not? How should they go about determining which news sites to get their news stories from?

4. The Internet is a worldwide information system. Imagine that you wish to ensure a balanced portrayal of all races in news stories. Who would you have enact the regulations necessary for this balance? What problems do you imagine resulting from trying to adopt such a policy?

REFERENCES

Clark, C. (1972). Race, identification, and television violence. In G. A. Comstock, E. A. Rubinstein, & J. P. Murray (Eds.), *Television and social behavior, Vol. 5: Television's effects: Further explorations* (pp. 120–184). Washington, DC: U.S. Government Printing Office.

Dixon, T. L. (2000). A social cognitive approach to studying racial stereotyping in the mass media. *African American Research Perspectives, 6*(1), 60–68.

Dixon, T. L. (2006). Psychological reactions to crime news portrayals of Black criminals: Understanding the moderating roles of prior news viewing and stereotype endorsement. *Communication Monographs, 73*, 162–187.

Dixon, T. L., & Linz, D. (2000a). Overrepresentation and underrepresentation of African Americans and Latinos as lawbreakers on television news. *Journal of Communication, 50*(2), 131–155.

Dixon, T. L., & Linz, D. (2000b). Race and the misrepresentation of victimization on local television news. *Communication Research, 27*(5), 547–554.

Entman, R. A. (1992). Blacks in the news: Television, modern racism and cultural change. *Journalism Quarterly, 69*(2), 341–361.

Flanagin, A. J., & Metzger, M. J. (2000). Perceptions of Internet credibility. *Journalism & Mass Communication Quarterly, 77*(3), 515–540.

Gilens, M. (1996). Race and poverty in America: Public misperceptions and the American news media. *Public Opinion Quarterly, 60*, 515–541.

Internet World Statistics. (2008). Internet growth statistics, *Internet World Stats: Usage & Population Statistics.* Retrieved October 8, 2008, from: http://www.internetworldstats.com/emarketing.htm

Iyengar, S. (1990). Framing responsibility for political issues: The case of poverty. *Political Behavior, 12,* 19–40.

Iyengar, S. (1991). *Is anyone responsible?: How television frames political issues.* Chicago: University of Chicago Press.

Knobloch, S., Hastall, M., Zillmann, D., & Callison, C. (2003). Imagery effects on selective reading of Internet newsmagazines. *Communication Research, 30,* 3–29.

Pew Internet & American Life Project. (2000). *Internet election news audience seek convience, familiar names.* Retrieved June 22, 2007, from: http://www.pewinternet.org/ppf/r/27/report_display.asp

Valentino, N. A., Hutchings, V. L., & White, I. K. (2002). Cues that matter: How political ads prime racial attitudes during campaigns. *American Political Science Review, 96*(1), 75–90.

4.5 "THE MORE YOU SUBTRACT, THE MORE YOU ADD": CUTTING GIRLS DOWN TO SIZE IN ADVERTISING

Jean Kilbourne

> *The author discusses how girls and women are portrayed in advertising. She argues that we are relentlessly exposed to unattainable ideals of physical perfection and that women are portrayed as less powerful than men. She also considers the ramifications of such representations.*

"The more you subtract, the more you add," says an ad that ran in several women's and teen magazines in 1997. Surprisingly, it is an ad for clothing, not for a diet product. Perhaps it is overtly a statement about minimalism in fashion. However, the fact that the girl in the ad is very young and very thin reinforces another message, a message that an adolescent girl constantly gets from advertising and throughout the popular culture, the message that she should diminish herself, she should be *less* than she is.

On the most obvious and familiar level, this refers to her body. However, the loss, the subtraction, the cutting down to size also refers to her sense of her self, her sexuality, her need for authentic connection, and her longing for power and freedom. I certainly don't think that the creators of this particular ad had all this in mind. And it wouldn't be important at all were there not so many other ads that reinforce this message and did it not coincide with the current cultural crisis for adolescent girls.

When a girl enters adolescence, she faces a series of losses—loss of self-confidence, loss of a sense of efficacy and ambition, and the loss of her "voice," the sense of being a unique and powerful self that she had in childhood. Girls who were active, confident, feisty at the ages of eight and nine and ten often become hesitant, insecure, self-doubting at eleven. Their self-esteem plummets. As Carol Gilligan, Mary Pipher, and other social critics have pointed out in recent years, adolescent girls in America are afflicted with a range of problems, including low self-esteem, eating disorders, binge drinking, date rape and other dating violence, teen pregnancy, and a rise in cigarette smoking. Teenage women today are engaging in far riskier health behaviors and in greater numbers than any prior generation.

It is important to understand that these problems go way beyond individual psychological development. Even girls who are raised in loving homes by supportive parents grow up in a culture—both reflected and reinforced by advertising—that urges girls to adopt a false self, to become "feminine," which means to be nice and kind and sweet, to compete with other girls for the attention of boys, and to value romantic relationships with boys above all else. Girls are put into a terrible double bind. They are supposed to repress their power, their anger, their exuberance and be simply "nice," although they also eventually must compete with men in the business world and be successful. They must be overtly sexy and attractive but essentially passive and virginal. How can we resist these destructive messages and images? The first step, as always, is to become as conscious of them as possible, to deconstruct them.

Regardless of the intent of the advertisers, what messages are girls getting? What are they told? Primarily girls are told by advertisers that what is most important about them is their perfume, their clothing, their bodies, their beauty. Their "essence" is their underwear. "He says the first thing he noticed about you is your great personality," says an ad featuring a very young woman in tight jeans. The copy continues, "He lies." "If this is your idea of a great catch," says an ad for a cosmetic kit from a teen magazine featuring a cute boy, "this is your tackle box." Even very little girls are offered makeup and toys like Special Night Barbie, which shows them how to dress up for a night out. Girls of all ages get the message that they must be flawlessly beautiful and, above all these days, they must be thin.

Adolescent girls are especially vulnerable to the obsession with thinness, for many reasons. One is the ominous peer pressure on young people. Adolescence is a time of self-consciousness and terror of shame and humiliation. Boys are shamed for being too small, too weak, too soft, too sensitive. And girls are shamed for being too sexual, too loud, too boisterous, too big (in any sense of the word), having too hearty an appetite. Many young women have told me that their boyfriends wanted them to lose weight. One said that her boyfriend had threatened to leave her if she didn't lose five pounds. "Why don't you leave him," I asked, "and lose 160?"

The situation is very different for men. The double standard is reflected in an ad for a low-fat pizza: "He eats a brownie . . . you eat a rice cake. He eats a juicy burger . . . you eat a low-fat entree. He eats pizza . . . you eat pizza. Finally, life is fair." Although some men develop eating problems, the predominant cultural message remains that a hearty appetite and a large size is desirable in a man, but not so in a woman.

The obsession starts early. Today at least one-third of 12- to 13-year-old girls are actively trying to lose weight, by dieting, vomiting, and/or taking pills. Some studies have found that nearly 80% of fourth-grade girls are dieting. And a survey in Massachusetts found that the single largest group of high school students considering or attempting suicide is girls who feel they are overweight. Imagine. Girls made to feel so terrible about themselves that they would rather be dead than fat.

No wonder it is hard to find a woman, especially a young woman, in America today who has a truly healthy attitude towards her body and towards food. Bulimia and anorexia are the extreme results of an obsession with eating and weight control that grips many young women with serious and potentially very dangerous results. Although eating problems are often thought to result from vanity, the truth is that they, like other addictions and compulsive behavior, usually have deeper roots.

Advertising doesn't cause eating problems, of course. However, these images certainly contribute to the body-hatred so many young women feel and to some of the resulting eating problems, which range from bulimia to compulsive overeating to simply being obsessed with controlling one's appetite. Advertising does promote abusive and abnormal attitudes about eating, drinking, and thinness.

Being obsessed about one's weight is made to seem normal and even appealing in ads for unrelated products, such as the British watch ad featuring an extremely thin young woman and proclaiming "Put some weight on." The additional weight is the watch. The woman is so thin she can wear the watch on her upper arm.

The magazines and the ads deliberately *create* and *intensify* anxiety about weight because it is so profitable. On a deeper level, however, they *reflect* cultural concerns and conflicts about women's power. Real freedom for women would change the very basis of our male-dominated society. It is not surprising that many men (and women) fear this.

"We cut Judy down to size," says an ad for a health club. "Soon, you'll both be taking up less space," says an ad for a collapsible treadmill, referring both to the product and the young woman exercising on it. *The obsession with thinness is most deeply about cutting girls and women down to size.* Some argue that it is men's awareness of just how powerful women can be that has created the attempts to keep women small. Indeed, thinness as an ideal has always accompanied periods of greater freedom for women—as soon as we got the vote, boyish flapper bodies came into vogue. No wonder there is such pressure on young women today to be thin, to shrink, to be like little girls, not to take up too much space, literally or figuratively.

At the same time there is relentless pressure on women to be small, there is also pressure on us to succeed, to achieve, to "have it all." We can be successful as long as we stay "feminine" (i.e., powerless enough not to be truly threatening). One way to do this is to present an image of fragility, to look like a waif. This demonstrates that one is both in control and still very "feminine."

The changing roles and greater opportunities for women promised by the women's movement are trivialized, reduced to the private search for the slimmest body. In one commercial, three skinny young women dance and sing about the "taste of freedom." They are feeling free because they can now eat bread, thanks to a low-calorie version. A commercial for a fast-food chain features a very slim young woman who announces, "I have a license to eat." The salad bar and lighter fare have given her freedom to eat (as if eating for women were a privilege rather than a need).

Most of us know by now about the damage done to girls by the tyranny of the ideal image and the obsession with thinness. But girls get other messages too that "cut them down to size" more subtly. In ad after ad girls are urged to be "barely there"—beautiful but silent.

"Make a statement without saying a word," says an ad for perfume. And indeed this is one of the primary messages of the culture to adolescent girls. "The silence of a look can reveal more than words," says another perfume ad. "More than words can say," says another. A lipstick ad says "Watch your mouth, young lady," while one for nail polish says, "Let your fingers do the talking" and one for hairspray promises "hair that speaks volumes."

An Italian ad features a very thin young woman in an elegant coat sitting on a window seat. The copy says, "This woman is silent. This coat talks." Girls, seeing these images of women, are encouraged to be silent, mysterious, not to talk too much or too loudly. In so many different ways, they are told "the more you subtract, the more you add."

It is impossible to know how much of this message is intended by the advertisers. Is it harmless wordplay or is it a sophisticated and clever marketing ploy based on research about the silencing of girls, deliberately designed to attract them with the promise of at least some form of self-expression? I don't know. Advertisers certainly spend a lot of money on psychological research and focus groups. They usually know what they are doing. But sometimes they are just reflecting common cultural beliefs and concerns. It doesn't matter whether it is intended or not. What matters is the effect. And I contend that the cumulative effect of these images and words urging girls to express themselves through their bodies and through products is serious and harmful.

As Erving Goffman (1978) pointed out in *Gender Advertisements*, we learn a great deal about the disparate power of males and females simply through the body language and poses of advertising. Women, especially young women, are generally subservient to men in ads, both through size and position. Sometimes it is as blatant as a woman serving as a footrest in an ad for Think Skateboards.

Other times, it is more subtle but quite striking (once one becomes aware of it). A double-paged spread for Calvin Klein's clothing for kids conveys a world of information about the relative power of boys and girls. One of the boys seems to be in the act of speaking, expressing himself, while the girl has her hand over her mouth.

Girls are often shown as playful clowns in these ads, perpetuating the attitude that girls and women are childish and cannot be taken seriously, whereas even very young men are generally portrayed as secure, powerful, and serious. People in control of their lives stand upright, alert, and ready to meet the world. In contrast, females often appear off-balance, insecure, and weak. Often our body parts are bent, conveying unpreparedness, submissiveness, and appeasement.

We cover our faces with our hair or our hands, conveying shame or embarrassment. And, no matter what happens, we keep on smiling. "Just smiling the bothers away," as one ad says.

An ad for vodka features a woman in the water and the copy, "In a past life I was a mermaid who fell in love with an ancient mariner. I pulled him into the sea to be my husband. I didn't know he couldn't breathe underwater." Of course, she can't breathe underwater either.

Breathe underwater. As girls come of age sexually, the culture gives them impossibly contradictory messages. Advertising slogans such as "because innocence is sexier than you think" and "nothing so sensual was ever so innocent" place them in a double bind. "Only something so pure could inspire such unspeakable passion, " declares an ad for Jovan musk. And a very sexy ad features a couple making love while the woman is wearing a bra called "Pure." Somehow girls are supposed to be both innocent and seductive, virginal and experienced, all at the same time. As they quickly learn, this is tricky.

Females have long been divided into virgins and whores, of course. What is new is that girls are now supposed to embody both within themselves.

This is symbolic of the central contradiction of the culture—we must work hard and produce and achieve success and yet, at the same time, we are encouraged to live impulsively, spend a lot of money, and be constantly and immediately gratified. This tension is reflected in our attitudes towards many things, including sex and eating. Girls are promised fulfillment both through being thin and through eating rich foods, just as they are promised fulfillment through being innocent and virginal and through wild and impulsive sex.

Advertisers are aware of their role and do not hesitate to take advantage of the insecurities and anxieties of young people, usually in the guise of offering solutions. A cigarette provides a symbol of independence. A pair of designer jeans or sneakers conveys status. The right perfume or beer resolves doubts about femininity or masculinity. Because so many anxieties have to do with sexuality and intimacy and because advertising so often offers products as the answers and uses sex to sell, it is perhaps the concept of sexuality that is most deeply affected.

"You can learn more about anatomy after school," says an ad for jeans, which manages to trivialize sex, relationships, and education all in one sentence. Magazines targeting girls and young women are filled with ads and articles on how to be beautiful and sexy and appealing to boys—all in service of the advertisers, of course, who sell their wares on almost every page. "How Smart Girls Flirt," "Sex to Write Home About," "15 Ways Sex Makes You Prettier," and "Are You Good in Bed?" are some of the recent cover stories for *Jane* magazine.

The emphasis for girls and women is always on being desirable, not on experiencing desire. Girls who want to be sexually *active* instead of simply being the objects of male desire are given only one model to follow, that of exploitive male sexuality. It seems that advertisers can't conceive of a kind of power that isn't manipulative and exploitive or a way that women can be actively sexual without being like traditional men.

Women who are "powerful" in advertising are uncommitted. They treat men like sex objects: "If I want a man to see my bra, I take him home," says an androgynous young woman. They are elusive and distant: "She's the first woman who refused to take your phone calls," says one ad. As if it were a good thing to be rude and inconsiderate.

Mostly though, girls are not supposed to have sexual agency. They are supposed to be passive, swept away, overpowered. "See where it takes you," says a perfume ad featuring a couple passionately embracing. "Unleash your fantasies," says another. "A force of nature." This contributes to the strange and damaging concept of the "good girl" as the one who is swept away, unprepared for sex, versus the "bad girl" as the one who plans for sex, uses contraception, and is generally responsible. A young woman can manage to have sex and yet in some sense maintain her virginity by being "out of control," drunk, and/or deep in denial about the entire experience.

In adolescence girls are told that they have to give up so much of what they *know* about relationships and intimacy if they want to attract men. Most tragically, they are told they have to give up each other. The truth is that one of the most powerful antidotes to destructive cultural messages is close and supportive female friendships. But girls are often encouraged by the culture to sacrifice their relationships with each other and to enter into hostile competition for the attention of boys and men. "What the bitch who's about to steal your man wears," says one ad.

Of course, some girls do resist and rebel. Some are encouraged (by someone—a loving parent, a supportive teacher) to see the cultural contradictions clearly and to break free in a healthy and positive way. Others rebel in ways that damage themselves. A young woman seems to have only two choices: she can bury her sexual self, be a "good girl," give in to what Carol Gilligan (Brown & Gilligan, 1992, p. 53) terms "the tyranny of kind and nice" (and numb the pain by overeating or starving or cutting herself or drinking herself into a stupor). Or she can become a rebel—flout her sexuality, seduce inappropriate partners, seduce everyone, smoke, drink flamboyantly, use other drugs. Both of these responses are self-destructive, but they begin as an attempt to survive, not to self-destruct.

Many girls become women who split themselves in two and do both—have a double life, a secret life—a good girl in public, out of control in private. A feminist in public, involved in an abusive relationship or lost in sadomasochistic fantasies in private. A lawyer by day, a barfly by night. Raiding the refrigerator or drinking themselves into a stupor alone in their kitchens at night, after the children are in bed, the laundry done. Doing well in school, but smoking in order to have a sexier, cooler image. Being sexual only when drunk.

There are few healthy alternatives for girls who want to truly rebel against restrictive gender roles and stereotypes. What they are offered by the popular culture is a superficial toughness, an "attitude," exemplified by smoking, drinking, and engaging in casual sex— all harmful behaviors. In 1990 Virginia Slims offered girls a T-shirt that said, "Sugar and spice and everything nice? Get real."

In 1997 Winston used the same theme in an ad featuring a tough young woman shooting pool and saying, "I'm not all sugar & spice. And neither are my smokes." As if the alternative to the feminine stereotype was sarcasm and toughness, and as if smoking was somehow an expression of one's authentic self ("get real").

Of course, the readers and viewers of these ads don't take them literally. But we do take them in—each is another grain of sand in a slowly accumulating and vast sandpile. If we entirely enter the world of ads, imagine them to be real for a moment, we find that the sandpile has entirely closed us in, and there's only one escape route—buy something. "Get the power," says an ad featuring a woman showing off her bicep. "The power to clean anything," the ad continues. "Hey girls, you've got the power of control" says an ad for . . . hairspray. "You never had this much control when you were on your own" (hair gel). "Exceptional character" (a watch). "An enlightening experience" (face powder). "Inner strength" (vitamins). "Stronger longer" (shampoo). Of course, the empowerment, the enlightenment, is as impossible to get through products as is anything else—love, security, romance, passion. On one level, we know this. On another, we keep buying and hoping.

Other ads go further and offer products as a way to rebel, to be a real individual. "Live outside the lines," says a clothing ad featuring a young woman walking out of a men's room. This kind of rebellion isn't going to rock the world. And, no surprise, the young woman is very thin and conventionally pretty.

"Think for yourself," says yet another hollow-cheeked young woman, demonstrating her individuality via an expensive and fashionable sweater. "Be amazing" (cosmetics). "If you're going to create electricity, use it" (watches).

"Break the rules," says a perfume ad. It goes on to give the confusing advice, "Stand apart, keep your head, go with your heart." The thin and pretty young woman featured with her boyfriend is a perfect example of conventional "femininity." As is the young woman in the Halston perfume ad that says, "And when she was bad she wore Halston." What kind of "bad" is this?

"Nude with attitude" features a Black woman in a powerful pose, completely undercut by the brevity of her dress and the focus on her long legs. Her "attitude" is nothing to fear—she's just another sex object. Good thing, because a lot of people are especially scared of powerful Black women.

The British ad "For girls with plenty of balls" is insulting in ways too numerous to count, beginning with the equation of strength and courage and fiery passion with testicles. What the ad offers these girls is body lotion.

Some ads do feature women who seem really angry and rebellious, but the final message always is the same. "Today, I indulge my dark side," says an ad featuring a fierce young woman tearing at what seems to be a net. "Got a problem with that?" The slogan is "be extraordinary not ordinary." The product which promises to free this girl from the net that imprisons her? Black nail polish.

Nail polish. Such a trivial solution to such an enormous dilemma. But such triviality and superficiality is common in advertising. How could it be otherwise? The solution to any problem always has to be a product. Change, transformation, is thus inevitably shallow and moronic, rather than meaningful and transcendent. These days self-improvement seems to have more to do with calories than with character, with abdomens rather than absolutes, with nail polish than with ethics.

This relentless trivialization of her hopes and dreams, her expectations for herself, cuts to the quick of a young girl's soul. Just as she is entering womanhood, eager to spread her wings, to become more sexual, more empowered, more independent—the culture moves in to *cut her down to size.*

Black nail polish isn't going to help. But it probably won't hurt either. What hurts are some of the other products offered to girls as a way to rebel and to cope—especially our deadliest drugs, alcohol and nicotine. These drugs are cynically and deliberately offered by advertisers to girls as a way to numb the pain of disconnection, to maintain the illusion of some kind of relationship, to be more appealing to men, to be both "liberated" and "feminine," and, perhaps most tragically, to subvert their rebellious spirits, the very spark within that could, if not coopted, empower them to change their lives.

IT'S YOUR TURN: WHAT DO YOU THINK? WHAT WILL YOU FIND?

1. Look through the advertisements in a magazines catering to a diverse range of female readers (*Cosmopolitan; Ladies' Home Journal; O, The Oprah Magazine; Marie Claire;* etc.) To what extent do the ads reflect the types of images discussed here? Do the different magazines represent women and girls differently? How?

2. Work together in small groups to conceptualize a magazine ad for a new line called "Vocal" jeans. Be sure the copy and artwork make the product appealing to consumers, but take care not to "cut girls down to size."

3. If you were the producer of a teen-oriented TV program and an advertiser submitted a commercial demeaning overweight girls (and threatening their already fragile self-esteem), would you air it? Why or why not? Whose responsibility is it to make sure that ads are appropriate for the audiences?

4. Although the representation of men was mentioned, the focus of this chapter is on women. Look through popular magazines to see how men are represented in advertising. What do these images tell us about what it means to be a man in today's society?

REFERENCES

Brown, L. M., & Gilligan, C. (1992). *Meeting at the crossroads: Women's psychology and girls' development*. New York: Ballantine.

Goffman, E. (1978). *Gender advertisements*. Cambridge, MA: Harvard University Press.

4.6 GAMBLING WITH IDENTITY: AMERICAN INDIAN SELF-REPRESENTATIONS ON TRIBAL WEB SITES

Susan Dente Ross and David Cuillier

The authors examine how American Indian tribes represent themselves on their own official Web sites, comparing tribes that operate casinos to those that do not. They find that tribes with casinos tend to play up Indian stereotypes, such as teepees, demure maidens, connection with nature, feather headdresses, and savage braves. This might attract more non-Indian tourists, but at what price?

What if you went online to gather information for a research paper on American Indians and ran across a Web page displaying teepees, feathered headdresses, and savage braves with chopping tomahawks yelling "whoo-whoo-whoo-whoo!" Did you stumble across the homepage for the Cleveland Indians or Atlanta Braves? Or maybe you came upon a promo for a new stereotype-laden Disney movie, *Pocahontas and Sacajawea Weave Baskets*? Or maybe you accidentally typed in "Aryan Nation" in your Google search?

Or you might simply have landed on the official Web site of an American Indian tribe. What? How can that be? How could an American Indian tribe represent itself on its own official Web site in ways that would surely offend some people or, at minimum, perpetuate stereotypes? Well, the results—and implications—of our study might surprise you. When we delved into the self-representation of American Indians on official tribal Web sites, we discovered a world of familiar stereotypes.

IDENTITY AND REPRESENTATION

Before discussing the findings of our study, we should talk a little about identity and self-representation, something we all do individually and as members of the different groups to which we belong. Social scientists argue that identity is a process, not a fixed thing. Identity is the solidarity that arises from recognition of a common origin or shared characteristic with another person, group, or ideal (Weaver, 2001). In this sense, identity is constructed in and through interactions with others.

Power also plays a role in identity formation because those with power have greater influence over social and communication processes and, therefore, greater ability to shape the situations in which identities are formed and re-formed. The media, which dominate so much social communication, play a significant role in the social construction of identity. Media stories and images provide handy and salient information, which we sort through and organize to help categorize people and things. Particularly when we have little or no direct knowledge, media content provides the building blocks with which we form our perception of others' identity. All of this is important because the ability to construct identities can be a tool for power and prejudice.

Native American Identity

In the United States, historical representation of the Indian as "other," outside the mainstream, has established cultural boundaries of difference to justify occupation of Indian land and annihilation of tribes (Hanson & Rouse, 1987). The dominant Anglo culture has represented American Indian identity as non-human and savage (Said, 1979). Several scholars have called this destructive identity the "White man's Indian," built upon a number of stereotypes, including the stoic chief adorned in a headdress, the noble savage, the demure Indian maiden, and the spiritual soul connected to nature.

Whereas some of these images appear benign or even benevolent, the White man's Indian perpetuates "acceptable racism" and objectification of the American Indian throughout Euro-American popular culture—sports and school mascots like the Atlanta Braves, films including Disney's *Pocahontas*, advertising such as Land O'Lakes butter, and a stream of popular images, Web sites, and even news reports (Miller & Ross, 2004).

Yet identities are not constructed solely by the media or the powerful. Even the most disenfranchised members of society participate in their identity construction and may engage in practices of resistance to exert influence over their social identity. Many scholars have examined how identity is contested, negotiated, and adapted to resist those in power or to gain power by those who are subjugated. Vulnerable members of society may adopt explicit political and social positions to oppose dominant messages that manipulate or marginalize them.

Far from being seen as negative incidents to be avoided, moments of tension thus may provide opportunities to challenge dominant truth claims and to reshape information and images perceived as relevant and significant (Fairclough, 1992). For example, to diffuse the negative connotation of the term "queer" as used in the dominant culture, gays and lesbians have re-appropriated the term to affirm their self-identity (Henderson, 2001).

Similarly, indigenous peoples can negotiate Anglo-imposed identity to their own advantage. American Indians may adapt the White man's Indian identity to attract non-Indian patrons and increase economic gain. Navajo and Pueblo artists, for example, learned tourists purchased more wares that conformed to the non-Indians' stereotyped image of what Indian art *should* look like, an artifact of the past (Sorrells, 2003).

The identity adaptation central to such ethnic tourism also has been noted in the Indian gaming world. To promote and foster the success of tribal casinos, the facilities often appeal to non-Indian tourists by adapting the image of the White man's image of the exotic Indian "other" (Cooks, 1998). The décor and advertising of successful casinos represent a one-size-fits-all pan-tribal identity for the Indian that represents a horse-culture plains tribe, even though many Indian nations do not share the dress or traditions of this culture. Some tribes have even patterned their casino decorations after tips from Disney marketing specialists.

The financial outcome can be positive for indigenous peoples. By attracting more tourists, tribes increase economic power and, therefore, are better positioned to break cycles of poverty and subjugation. Indian gaming revenues, which increased from $500 million in 1988 to $25 billion in 2006, have provided a variety of benefits for tribes, including the building of roads, schools, utilities, and housing, a drop in mortality rates, and the ability to provide college scholarships for their members.

Framing Identity

Scholars have long studied texts to examine identity. Framing scholars, for example, examine the overt images, language, and structure of messages to identify the imbedded, culturally resonant, covert meanings that influence audience understanding of reality, including issues of race and self-identity (Goffman, 1974). Frames are unconsciously embedded in visual and verbal messages, and they call upon familiar and durable cultural values, ideologies, and narratives to establish relatively stable connections between familiar signifiers— even stereotypes—and new information.

In framing theory, meaning is socially constructed through a reciprocal, interactive cycle of communication. Framing theory acknowledges the creative ability of communicators to generate original meanings, their desire for efficiency, and their tendency to use shortcuts. It also recognizes the ability of audience members to reshape and recode the messages they receive. The key to understanding frames is to recognize that they can communicate only those meanings that the receivers already recognize, regardless of the intent of the senders.

Framing theory also recognizes that dominant messages in a given society tend to be the products of elite individuals and social institutions and to project the views and values of these elites. Accordingly, frames tend to reinforce the status quo and to be ethnocentric and pro-establishment. Thus, the use of old frames (such as the White man's Indian) in new ways (such as to attract tourism) may be fraught with the potential for misinterpretation by receivers who misconstrue the distinct or resistive intent.

At the same time, communicators may strategically adopt non-dominant frames. Therefore, tribes targeting the dominant society (non-Indians) through their Web sites might be expected to employ dominant cultural frames that reinforce the status quo. Tribes directing their Web sites toward their own community might employ frames that diverge from the elite consensus to challenge the status quo of negative stereotypes.

Studies have identified a variety of frames of American Indians communicated through the media. The frame of Indians as "historic relics" describes what scholars call the White man's Indian identity, encompassing elements of the three dominant media frames: the generic Indian, the Indian as the other, and good–bad Indian frames. The historic relic frame presents Indians as remnants of a mythical, colonial era. Historic relic Indians can display good traits, such as nobility and stoicism, or bad traits, such as savagery.

Either way, the frame situates Indians in the past, fixed in the world of the Pilgrims and up to the end of the 1800s. Historic relic Indians are obsolete in the contemporary world and therefore easier for the dominant society to ignore or subjugate.

In contrast, the frame of "voiced participant" Indian emerged from a recent study (Miller & Ross, 2004). Voiced participants are whole people who function fully within modern mainstream society either with or without embracing traditional aspects of Indian culture. Voiced participants are self-actualized individuals who speak for themselves with credibility on issues of significance if and when they adopt the perspective of the mainstream.

EXAMINING INDIAN IDENTITY ON TRIBAL WEB SITES

While many tribes appropriate the White man's Indian identity for casino marketing as an effective strategy to attract tourists and maximize profit, this represented identity may spread (intentionally or not) beyond the casinos themselves into other realms of tribal communications with non-Indians. In recent years, Indian nations throughout North America have expanded their online presence, with official tribal Web sites surging from about a dozen in 1995 to literally hundreds by 2003 (Mitten, 2003). These Web sites provide Indian nations the opportunity to communicate to millions of people in their own words and images.

This reading reports the results of our study of 224 official American Indian Web sites. Did Indian nations with the incentive to attract tourists to casino gambling challenge or perpetuate negative stereotypes?

We employed both framing and critical discourse analysis (CDA) to analyze how American Indians used their online spaces strategically to adopt, adapt, or resist the dominant Euro-American representation of American Indian identity. We coded each homepage as evoking one of three frames: the Informational frame, the Historic Relic (White man's Indian) frame, and the Voiced Participant frame.

Informational sites provided primarily text and graphics such as lists of tribal officers or programs, or basic tribal demographics. These data-driven pages typically presented very few, if any, graphic images. *Historic relic* (*White man's Indian*) sites relied predominantly on "conventional images" of the noble savage existing in a romantic natural state and embodying stoic, chiefly virtue. Images of teepees, warbonnets, fierce braves, demure Indian maidens, and other stereotypical images dominated, and text described tribal peoples as fixtures of another time, with little or no sovereignty or autonomy. *Voiced Participant* sites included portrayals of modern life in the tribe and described a community that had emerged from any mythical past to function within mainstream society (Miller & Ross, 2004). The tribes speak for themselves and participate in Anglo-European systems. The sites provide a complex set of both traditional and modern images, such as photos from powwows alongside images of tribal members dressed in Western shirts or suits, engaged in sports and community activities. The text might include assertions of sovereignty, challenges to the dominant culture, and discussion about contemporary tribal issues.

Besides coding the homepages of these sites, we also used critical discourse analysis to capture nuance and meaning that would be missed by our broad-based frame analysis. A primary goal of CDA is to make visible how a variety of players deliberately employ symbolic practices (images as well as words) to advance their own agendas within the complex societal play of differences of power and reach, and with both intended and unexpected results.

RESULTS

We found that most of the tribal Web sites provided genealogy, history, language, tribal government information, and community events. Overall, the informational frame was the most common on the Web sites, accounting for 57% (127) of all sites. The second most prevalent frame was historic relic at 26% (59). Voiced participant frames accounted for 17% (38).

Nearly two-thirds of the Web sites were produced by nations that have casinos. A few clusters of tribes shared similar informational homepage templates, usually provided by a coordinating regional agency. As shown in Table 4.4, more than a third of the casino-tribe Web sites represented their identity within the historic relic frame. In contrast, only about one in 10 non-casino tribes represented the historic relic frame. Therefore, casino tribes were nearly four times more likely than non-casino tribes to represent their identities within a historic relic frame.

The voiced participant frame was employed by 20% of the non-casino tribes but only 15% of the casino-tribe Web sites. Therefore, casino tribes are both more likely to represent themselves on their Web sites as historic relics and somewhat less likely to represent themselves as voiced participants than non-casino tribes.

Casino Tribes' Historic Relics

Many of the photographs on casino-tribe Web sites were dominated by feathers, war paint, young braves, eagles, and other stereotypical images. The Warm Springs Web site (www. warmsprings.com), which prominently displayed the image of a stoic Indian brave in a traditional headdress, was typical of casino tribes that represented the historic relic frame. Secondary images included an Indian mask, Indian blanket, eagle, teepees, Indians on horses, and three Indian women in traditional dress. No images depicted modern scenes of the reservation or members performing everyday activities.

TABLE 4.4   Frames for Casino- and Non-Casino Tribe Sites

FRAME	CASINO TRIBES		NON-CASINO TRIBES	
	n	%	n	%
Historic relic	50	36	9	10
Informational	67	49	60	70
Voiced participant	21	15	17	20
Total (total $N = 224$)	138		86	

The text on the homepage included a description of the reservation as a place where "time turns to the pace of a culture that has been thousands of years in the making." The text also focuses on connection to nature, reminding viewers that Indians are different and have a mystical connection to nature, land "stretching from the snowcapped summit of the Cascade Mountains to the palisaded cliffs of the Deschutes River in Central Oregon." The paragraph ends by differentiating the Warm Springs tribe from the dominant culture by inviting readers to "escape to another nation." This text delivers the message that non-Indians should view tribal enterprises as an escape to the exotic, the pastoral, carefree, natural world of the noble savage.

The Mashantucket Pequots of Connecticut, operators of the largest casino in the country, also have a homepage that represents the tribe as a historic relic (http://www.foxwoods.com/TheMashantucketPequots/Home). The page begins with this text: "The symbol of the Mashantucket Pequot Tribal Nation is a reflection of the past. The tree, perched on a rocky knoll and framed against a clear sky, represents Mashantucket, the 'much wooded land' where the people hunted and prospered." This statement embodies the tribe's expressed connection with nature (trees, rocky knolls, and clear skies), traditional cultural practices (hunting), and an idyllic peaceful life in the past (reflection of the past and "prospered"). Further, the background is a picture of a forest, and the Web site displays no modern images. The focus is on the past, of Indians hunting and being one with nature. Pictures on the site focus on Indian warriors with painted faces.

Yet the Web page speaks from the White man's position. The language is self-distancing; the authors are not, evidently, "the people." This symbolic displacement and identification with the reader recurs across Web pages that adopt the historic relic frame, where the tribe is often described as "they" rather than "we." For example, the Lac Vieux Desert Tribe of Michigan represented its noble identity on its homepage: "They are a nation of wise and intelligent leaders, non-obtrusive, talkative and happy people" (http://www.lvdtribal.com/). Within the historic relic frame, there is no discussion about discrimination, oppression, or problems on the reservation.

Nearly two-thirds of the casino tribes, however, did not represent their identity as the White man's Indian. Nearly half of these sites (49%) were informational and some 15% included a variety of images from the past and present that demonstrated a voiced participant frame. In the latter group, the Cabazon Band of Mission Indians in southern California included photographs of tribal members in modern clothes working on federal issues to identify and protect sacred sites as well as stories and photographs of tribal leaders discussing legislation with members of Congress (http://www.cabazonIndians-nsn.gov/). The Hoopa Valley Indian Tribe, also of California (http://www.hoopa-nsn.gov/), demonstrated some of the most voiced language and images of all tribes, including a photo of tribal members protesting dams.

Non-Casino Tribal Identity: Voiced Participants

Web sites for non-casino tribes were less likely to adopt the White man's Indian frame. Instead, these sites employed a greater proportion of modern images, focused on individual tribal attributes rather than a generic pan-tribal identity, explained the context and meaning of historical photos, and asserted tribal sovereignty. A significant proportion of the non-casino Web sites served as little more than online placeholders for the tribe, comprised mainly of generic text. Given the general economic disparity between casino and non-casino tribes (National Gambling Impact Study Commission, 1999), perhaps these tribes could not afford the more elaborate Web designs of casino-tribe Web sites that conveyed the stereotypical Indian symbols.

Despite reliance on text-heavy designs, non-casino tribes tended to picture local Indians in everyday life. For example, the Alabama-Coushatta Tribe of Texas pictured members in street clothes and baseball hats accompanying text that emphasized current tribal issues (www.alabama-coushatta.com). The Quinault tribe in Washington state pictured its leaders in modern dress as well as canoeing tribal members wearing orange life jackets—a mix of the old and new (www.quinaultIndiannation.com).

Sometimes non-casino tribes included historical photos, but they generally did so differently than casino tribes. Whereas casino tribes typically provided photos of chiefs and teepees without contextual explanation, non-casino tribes tended to explain the photos and provide less stereotypical images. For example, the Delaware Tribe of Eastern Oklahoma (www.delawaretribeofIndians.nsn.us) included images of their specific tribal heritage and decorated the page with a pattern described as a traditional Delaware ribbon pattern, but the text emphasized current affairs and events.

Textual assertions of sovereignty and resistance were strong on voiced participant non-casino tribal sites. The Delaware tribal homepage is comprised mainly of an essay written by the chief describing the history of the tribe, including how the tribe was subjugated and persecuted by European-Americans. The essay states, "Nevertheless, through war and peace, our ancestors had to continue to give up their lands and move westward." The site uses such words as "trickery" to describe Anglo-Americans.

The Skull Valley Goshutes tribe in Grantsville, Utah, also expressed resistance by focusing its Web site (www.skullvalleygoshutes.org, which has since been removed) on the nuclear waste and chemical weapons stored on and near the reservation. The homepage described the pollution and problems brought to the area, including a coal-fired power plant and the world's largest nerve gas incinerator. This site offered no images of braves or eagles. Instead, the tribe's homepage was dominated by a photo-collage of nuclear power plants, newspaper articles, a scientist, a pencil, and the planet Earth. The collage bore this quote from scientist Marie Curie: "Nothing in life is to be feared. It is only to be understood."

MAKING SENSE OF IT ALL

So what does all this mean? This analysis of tribal Web sites suggests that casino tribes are more likely to adopt the historic relic frame to strategically represent their identity as the White man's Indian than non-casino tribes. In line with prior research and theories, Web sites of casino tribes appear to seek to maximize their appeal to non-Indian audiences by relying on stereotypical images of the noble and ignoble savage and failing to assert sovereignty or to challenge oppression in other ways. We cannot identify intent, but it is possible casino tribes appropriate the dominant group's identity as a branding strategy to increase their own economic power.

Another explanation may be simply that tribes with casinos may have more financial resources to produce more elaborate, image-heavy Web sites. Such sites may use more stereotypical images in part because they emphasize colorful, striking visuals. In contrast, many non-casino tribal Web sites were outdated and of poor technical quality, lacking graphic art and timely information. Or, it is possible that non-Indian consultants or Web designers hired by the more affluent casino tribes may have influenced the design and content toward greater reliance on frames that resonated with the dominant Anglo culture.

Regardless of *why* casino tribes—and some non-casino tribes—adopted the historic relic frame on their Web sites, the fact that they do has important ramifications for American Indian identity and positioning in relationship to the dominant culture of Euro-Americans. New technologies such as the Internet have been heralded as a way for oppressed groups to voice resistance, but our study suggests tribal Web pages instead may reinforce existing power inequities. Although casino gambling has allowed many tribes to increase economic power, the images portrayed for tourists online could perpetuate stereotypes. The White man's Indian, created through language and visuals, exemplifies an ideology of exclusion, difference, and racism.

Any short-term increases in casino revenues stimulated by the adoption of the historic relic frame should be weighed against the harm such continued stereotyping inflicts upon all American Indians. While entrenched stereotypes are evident in the media, the impact of these stereotypes is magnified through their adoption in official tribal communications. When non-Indians see American Indians represent themselves as historic relics, that identity may be more readily and less critically adopted and reinforced among non-Indians.

If American Indians are to achieve equality in U.S. society, then the entrenched stereotypes and Anglo-imposed identity of Indians must be shed from discourse, popular culture, and from official tribal Web sites. Some tribes might benefit financially in the short term by displaying for the world an exotic representation of themselves as the other, but in the long term such gambling with identity likely perpetuates injustices against American Indians.

IT'S YOUR TURN: WHAT DO YOU THINK? WHAT WILL YOU FIND?

1. Go online and check out official Native American Web sites. You can find a list at www.indiancircle.com or at www.nativeculturelinks.com/nations.html. Look at the pictures they have on their Web. How many represent stereotypes? How many depict modern images of everyday life?

2. Read the text of Native American Web sites. How many integrate "nature" and tradition, as if they tribe is locked in the past? In contrast, look for examples of resistance, challenging the non-Indian establishment.

3. Go online and find Native American tribe casino Web sites. Are the images different from the official tribal Web sites? Who are they targeting?

4. Get into discussion groups and search online for examples of Web sites created by subjugated people in society. How do those groups represent themselves to the rest of the world?

5. Visit or talk with members of a Native American student club on campus and ask them what they think about tribal Web sites and the images you find on them. What are their feelings about it?

REFERENCES

Cooks, L. M. (1998). *Warriors, wampum, gaming, and glitter: Foxwoods Casino and the re-representation of (post) modern Native identity.* Mountain View, CA: Mayfield.

Fairclough, N. (1992). *Discourse and social change.* Cambridge: Polity Press.

Goffman, E. (1974). *Frame analysis: An essay on the organization of experiences.* New York: Harper & Row.

Hanson, J., & Rouse, L. (1987). Dimensions of Native American stereotyping. *American Indian Culture and Research Journal, 11*(4), 33–58.

Henderson, L. (2001). Queer communication studies. *Communication Yearbook, 24,* 465–484.

Miller, A., & Ross, S. D. (2004). They are not us: Framing of American Indians by the *Boston Globe. The Howard Journal of Communication, 15,* 245–259.

Mitten, L. (2003). Indians on the Internet—Selected Native American Web sites. *The Electronic Library, 21,* 443–449.

National Gambling Impact Study Commission. (1999). *Final report on national gambling impact.* Retrieved June 8, 2006, from http://govinfo.library.unt.edu/ngisc/

Said, E. W. (1979). *Orientalism.* New York: Vintage.

Sorrells, K. (2003). Embodied negotiation: Commodification and cultural representation in the U.S. Southwest. In M. J. Collier (Ed.), *Intercultural alliances: Critical transformation* (pp. 17–47). Thousand Oaks, CA: Sage.

Weaver, H. N. (2001). Indigenous identity: What is it, and who really has it? *American Indian Quarterly, 25,* 240–255.

4.7 CONSUMING ORIENTALISM: IMAGES OF ASIAN/AMERICAN WOMEN IN MULTICULTURAL ADVERTISING

Minjeong Kim and Angie Y. Chung

Based on an analysis of three advertisement campaigns, the authors argue that the emerging global culture has been packaged, commodified, and marketed by multinational corporations in a manner that widens their range of cultural repertoires but reinforces the racialized and gendered representations of Asian/American women as the Others, sustaining traditional hierarchies of American Orientalism.

Research studies have long challenged the ways in which advertising and marketing campaigns employ gendered imagery that objectify women and reinforce power differences between the sexes in order to sell their products (Cortese, 1999; Williamson, 1986). Among other things, print advertising has been shown to promote images that distort women's bodies for male pleasure, condone violence against women, or belittle the women's movement itself as a playful prank. From a historical perspective, however, women of color rarely figured into the marketing campaigns of these companies—partly because of their small numbers and their invisibility to mainstream American society. As a result, aside from research

From "Consuming Orientalism: Images of Asian/American Women in Multicultural Advertising," by Minjeong Kim and Angie Y. Chung, 2005, *Qualitative Sociology, 28*(1), pp. 67–91. Adapted by author. Reprinted with permission from Springer Science + Business Media.

on racial stereotypes in the TV and films (Gee, 1988; Hamamoto, 1994; Lee, 1999), few scholars have fully examined the commodified images of Asian/American women[1] that have come to play an integral role in today's consumer culture.

In recent years, advertising campaigns have sought to diversify their cultural repertoire through the greater inclusion of Asian and Latino/American characters and the invocation of global imageries. However, we will argue that representations of ethnic minority groups in such advertising campaigns are usually based on gendered and racialized reflections of global culture that draw on resurrected themes of colonialism and American Orientalism.

THE HISTORY OF AMERICAN ORIENTALISM

In his influential book, *Orientalism*, Edward W. Said (1979) argues that "the essence of Orientalism is the ineradicable distinction between Western superiority and Oriental inferiority" (p. 42). Westerners' knowledge imagines the East in a way that polarizes the Orient from the Occident and places the Occident higher than the Orient in the world hierarchy. The West is depicted as developed, articulate, and superior, while the East is seen as undeveloped, mysterious, and inferior. While European Orientalism was purported to justify the colonization and domination of Third World people, early American Orientalism was first invented to exclude Asian immigrants from entering or settling on American soil.

To this end, the mass media began its long history of cultivating insidious stereotypes of Asian/Americans for the visual consumption of the White American public— everything from the aggressive, ominous images of Japanese and Chinese immigrants during the "yellow peril" to modern depictions of Asian/Americans as the passive "model minority" (Lee, 1999). In all these stereotypes, the assimilability of Asian/ Americans has always been at question (Palumbo-Liu, 1999). For example, in movies such as *The Bitter Tea of General Yen* (1933) and Fu Manchu films, the image of emasculated, asexual Asians co-existed with the image of Orientals as licentious beasts that threatened to undermine the economic and moral stability of the U.S. nation and the American family. Such cultural representations help set the ideological backdrop for anti-Chinese fervor, which led to the outbreak of anti-Chinese rioting and the implementation of the first Chinese Exclusion Act in 1882.

Within this context, the practice of "consuming Orientalism" evolved long before the advent of the post-industrial era. In the early twentieth century, Americans supported Orientalism in their day-to-day consumption practices. Advertising cards for various products drew on Sino-phobic themes, such as Chinese queues, porcelain doll-like Chinese women, and hyper-feminized Asian men (Chan, 2003). These cultural representations reinforced White America's moral and masculine superiority over the foreign elements of the East and allowed them to lay both physical and sexual claim to the bodies of Orientals at home and abroad.

Throughout the evolution of American Orientalism, the notion of the Orient as the culturally inferior Other has converged with the concept of women as the gender-inferior Other. Orientalist romanticism in the West synchronized White men's heterosexual desire for (Oriental) women and for Eastern territories through the feminization of the Orient (Marchetti, 1993). Aside from such stereotypes as the yellow peril, the model minority, and the gook, typical representations of Asian/American women in the media have centered on "the Lotus Blossom Baby (e.g., China Doll, Geisha Girl, and the shy Polynesian beauty), and the Dragon Lady (e.g. prostitutes and devious madams)" (Tajima, 1989, p. 309). American Orientalism also depended on the masculine, superior image of White men juxtaposed with the emasculation of Asian/American men. By portraying Asian/American men as sexually excessive or asexually feminine, such cultural themes reaffirmed Orientals' deviance from heterosexual gender norms implicit in White middle-class families (Lee, 1999). Although distinctive in many ways, both images have served to stimulate the sexual voyeurism of White American males and the objectification of Oriental women as their rightful property (Gee, 1988; Lee, 1996; Marchetti, 1993). Another prevailing image of Asian/American women which is illustrated in movies such as *The World of Suzie Wong* (1960) embodies the conflation of the two images, fixating on their shameless sexual desire, their aggressive and manipulative traits, and their inability to resist White men. The storylines of more contemporary movies (e.g., *Year of the Dragon,* 1985; and *Heaven and Earth,* 1993) continue to focus on Asian/American female characters who are betrayed or exploited by men of their own race but are later saved by White male heroes. Thus, Orientalism in all its guises has been an underlying feature of American culture.

ADVERTISING MULTICULTURALISM

Asian Americans were never targeted as a significant consumer base for many of these marketing campaigns until the 1980s and 1990s when ethnic minorities rapidly grew in numbers (Cortese, 1999; Cui, 1997). As one of the fastest-growing racial groups in the United States, Asian Americans have offered a very attractive market to advertisers because of their high levels of income and education. Furthermore, the steady global expansion of corporate branches into modernizing economies in Asia and the growing sector of Asian professionals within the U.S. and abroad have also increased the need to re-conceptualize advertisement campaigns in a multicultural fashion.

Some pundits argue that multicultural marketing is more sensitive to the needs of minority consumers and helps to update or abandon traditional stereotypical representations of these populations (Cui, 1997). However, we will demonstrate how such campaigns merely re-package racial stereotypes in their efforts to promote multicultural, globalized settings. Images of Asian/Americans in multicultural ad series often employ traditional themes of American Orientalism with a new global twist. In the words of Williamson (1986), "capitalism's constant search for new areas to colonize" (p. 116) has permeated the realms of advertisement in terms of the way they portray social movements, feminism, the gay and lesbian movement (Cagan, 1978; Cortese, 1999), and now multiculturalism. Under the guise of multiculturalism, Orientalism has evolved into an object to consume and a vehicle to stimulate consumption.

To this end, we highlight three advertising campaigns chosen from six different magazines, including *Newsweek, Business Week, Cosmopolitan, In Style, Premiere,* and *Entertainment Weekly*. We looked at all issues of these six magazines from September 1999 to December 2000. The three ad campaigns (Virginia Slims, Hennessey, and Ofoto) were mainly selected because they are part of a larger multicultural ad series. The multicultural ad series feature models in various ad copies, poses, or appearances within a series of thematic frames. The campaigns try to include diverse racial groups and have thus generated an increase in Asian/American representations in advertising.

Virginia Slims

The first series of multicultural advertisements comes from the "Find Your Voice" campaign, which depicts different images of women from diverse racial backgrounds expressing ways to "find your voice" in life. The ads were featured in *Business Week, Cosmopolitan, In Style, Premiere*, and *Entertainment Weekly*. Virginia Slims is a brand of cigarettes specifically targeting racially diverse females. Established in 1968, Virginia Slims first played on themes of female empowerment through campaign slogans such as "You've Come a Long Way Baby," which elicited angry responses because of how it distorted and trivialized feminist issues in order to profit on women's addictions (Cagan, 1978). The Virginia Slims multicultural ad series, introduced in 1999–2000, again promoted themes of female liberation, but this time with attention to a broader multicultural and global consumer base.

The ads from the "Find Your Voice" campaign featured individual models of different races, such as a blonde White woman next to the words "I look temptation right in the eye and then make my own decisions"; an African woman proclaiming "No single institution owns the copyright for BEAUTY"; a Latino woman stating "Dance around naked with a rose between your teeth if you want . . . but do it like you mean it"; and an Asian woman with the words "My voice reveals the hidden power within." In another ad, the same Asian woman is juxtaposed next to the words "In silence I see. With WISDOM, I speak."

Focusing on the Asian model, we can see blatant references to time-old themes of Oriental feminine exoticism perpetuated by numerous Hollywood films, as well as Western literature and musicals in the past century. Stepping away from the feminist undertones of Virginia Slim campaigns, the posture of the Asian woman in two different ads is of femininity and sexual invitation. She is looking down and sideways, and her head is tilted as well, with a cryptic smile. Her hands are curled in front of her in an "Oriental-like" gesture as if she is dancing. She appears as an entertainer, a Madam Butterfly, a courtesan, a geisha, and "a Lotus Blossom baby." Historically, Lotus Blossom images represented Asian women as exotic, subservient, pampering, self-sacrificing and sensual. In a similar manner as this ad, Asian women in Lotus Blossom images throw sexually suggestive smiles and gazes but hesitate to speak. References to "Hidden power" and "In silence I see" again reaffirm the "non-language" embodiment of Asian women. Furthermore, although the ads make no explicit references to men, it is important to note that Lotus Blossom images were traditionally used to obliterate Asian women's subjectivity by validating their role as the objects of White men's sexual fantasy.

What is more interesting about this ad series is the way the "exotic," "feminine," and "mysterious" allure of the Orientalized character becomes accentuated by the projected normalcy of the White characters. In the case of the Asian woman, this aura of foreignness is highlighted by the antediluvian attire and posture. The Asian woman in both ads is wearing dresses and makeup that are modified renditions of traditional Chinese dresses and hairdos that are no longer worn today. This theme derives from Orientalist depictions of Asia—that is, the unchangeable and undeveloped portrayal of a colonized Orient

(Said, 1979). Furthermore, this series invokes feminine and hyper-sexualized stereotypes of Asian women (as well as Latino women) in stark contrast to the themes of liberation and empowerment associated with the White and African American characters.

At the same time, the Westernized version of Orientalism reified by the ad serves to commodify Asian culture. Westerners' indulgence in Asian culture has been often understood as a signifier of their wealth and ability to consume (Marchetti, 1993). The consumption of Asian culture has never required an accurate comprehension of Asian cultures and histories and empathy with Third World experiences of colonialism, imperialism, and economic exploitation. In the ad, the costume of the Asian woman looks Chinese but is pseudo-authentic at best. Her hairdo is not done in a traditional Chinese style. Her makeup is modern. Furthermore, her posture is pan-Asian, drawing on gestures, expressions, and stances that stem from various Asian cultures. One of the ads even features messages written in Chinese that make no sense in interpretation. The Orientalist depiction of Chinese customs and written characters were there not to be understood but to be objectified by viewers in their visual consumption of the Asian female model.

Hennessey

The second ad campaign comes from cognac-producer Hennessey. The Hennessey ads seem to downplay the more blatant kinds of cultural differences we saw in the Virginia Slims campaign but are still able to connote racial difference through the sexual interplays of its multi-racial cast. The typical design of this advertisement series (seen in *In Style, Premiere*, and *Entertainment Weekly*) features two to three models in a set background with one or two words placed strategically next to each figure in order to convey the identities, personalities, or thoughts of each model. Usually, the labels have opposite meanings meant to highlight differences among the models. For instance, one ad focuses on two White men and one White woman. The copy indicates that the two male models are a "designer" and a "demolition expert," while the woman is shown to be an "architect." The advertisement seeks to challenge social norms and gendered expectations by associating the female with a semi-intellectual profession (architect) as opposed to a feminized, aesthetic-oriented profession (designer). However, she is also set in contrast to the masculinized "demolition expert" seated next to her.

Furthermore, the Hennessey campaign is most notable for its invocation of what can be called "gay window advertising" that "speak[s] to the homosexual consumer in a way that the straight consumer will not notice" (Stabiner, 1982, p. 81). The strategy of this type of advertising is to feature one person or a group of same-sex people in a sexually ambiguous or androgynous style that does not explicitly speak to homosexuality but can potentially hint to either sexuality or homosexuality. This may explain the inclusion of a male designer. A second photo shows an African American and a White woman, a matchmaker, and a divorce attorney respectively, wearing fancy dresses and locking arms as they come out of a car while an unidentified White male holds an umbrella for them in the background. Another advertisement shows a pair of women's legs with the label "tomboy." This type of dual marketing strategy allows companies to attract both homosexual and heterosexual consumers (Stabiner, 1982), but as we shall see, subtle references to cross-racial lesbianism may also be used as a ploy to gain the attention of White men.

Two photos, in particular, juxtapose Asian American women with White women and inject a racial component to sex, sexuality, and sexual competition. The first features an Asian American woman and a White woman in the intimate back seat of a car. The White woman's arm and widespread hand is loosely draped on the bare legs of the Asian American woman, which hints of both lesbianism and domination over the Asian American woman. Interestingly, they are given the same labels, "loves oliver." Interestingly, this particular ad does not provide explicitly opposite labels for its characters, thus pushing the viewers to find hidden oppositional meanings. The White woman leans back and looks outside while the Asian American woman sits up and looks directly at us. Although the ad hints at lesbianism, her orientation towards the viewers and her thoughts about "oliver" can insinuate that she is looking at/longing for somebody else—presumably "oliver." Furthermore, the fact that both the White and Asian American woman "like oliver" can imply either that their lesbianism is directed towards this unseen third male party or that they are competing sexually for the White man.

The other photo continues this theme of sexual competitiveness and lesbianism in its portrayal of Asian American women. The ad shows a White and Asian American women both looking into an unseen mirror. The Asian American woman dressed in black is applying lipstick, presumably prepping for something, and the blonde woman is simply half-sitting on the counter in her white feminine dress. The copy labels the White woman as a "vegetarian" and the Asian American woman as a "man-eater"—a play on the word "meat-eater." The label "man-eater" may be making subtle references to the fact that the White woman may be a lesbian since she does not "eat man" and the Asian American woman is not.

More importantly, the term "man-eater" conjures up images of an aggressive sexual predator. This is played up by the black dress, the lipstick gesture indicating preparation for fierce competition, and the general facial structure and glaring expression on the Asian American woman's face. "Man-eater" also captures the impure intentions of Asian American women's desire for White men. Whereas Lotus Blossom stereotypes tend to emphasize Asian women's sexual submission to White men, Suzie Wong–like images of Asian/American women also depict them as desiring White men as "a ticket to be accepted" and succeed in life. Suzie Wong characters are portrayed in such a mysterious and manipulative manner that viewers (and the White men) cannot be certain whether her avowal of love is sincere. The licentiousness and moral depravity suggested in this ad separates the Asian American female character from the virginal purity of her White counterpart in a way that prevents her from truly assimilating into American society despite her exterior appearance of acculturation.

Ofoto

A subsidiary of Eastman Kodak Company, Ofoto is an online photography service that gives consumers a virtual space to store and edit their pictures. This ad campaign, launched in late 1999, was featured in *Newsweek* and *In Style*. The general concept of the Ofoto advertisement series features an individual sitting on a chair, looking at an unseen picture of himself/herself with someone else. A caption describes what the person is looking at.

We found four different types of messages, each featuring models of different races: The White man is supposedly looking at a photo labeled "Tom Gilmartin with the star of the kindergarten play, Hannah Gilmartin, the purple rabbit princess"—a father and daughter scenario. The photo held by an older African American man is captioned "Daryl Lamar Edwards II with Daryl Lamar Edwards IV"—or grandfather with grandson. The White woman is looking at "A rare nose-to-nose meeting between Carol McBride's cat, Manny, and her dog, Marley"—a picture of family pets. Lastly, in the Asian/American version of the series, a woman is holding a picture of herself—"Tia Fong with a 'friend' on her hotel room balcony in Prague."

Several points stand out when analyzing these ads. Whereas both the White and African American men have a connection to their families and lineage, the female characters do not. Although Carol McBride's wide-legged posture in the ad manifests her power and confidence, her beloved family is her pets, not her family or child. The picture of Tia Fong, the Asian American woman, is even more problematic, because first, Tia's "friend," unlike Carol's pets, does not even have a name, and second, she is seeing herself in a hotel room situated in the distant, exotic land of Prague. In essence, Tia Fong is not to be associated with the comforts of home and family but rather, the erotic setting of foreign lands and forbidden pleasures. The fact that Tia's photo includes a mysterious "friend" and that she is located in Prague evokes mystic images of the Orient. This aspect of positionality has racial implications because it symbolizes not only Asian Americans' detachment from both home and lineage but also their dislocation from American society itself. In essence, these advertisements once again hint to the unassimilability of Asians in America.

The illustration of Tia Fong is imbued with other gendered meanings as well—the most obvious of which is the sexual connotation behind the faceless "friend" and the hotel room where she is staying with this friend. Unlike the other two ads that conjure up feelings of familial belonging (albeit a surrogate family in the case of Carol), the Asian/American ad is replete with references to sexual liaisons within a Prague hotel room—perhaps the modern equivalent of a geisha teahouse. The quotations around the word "friend" and the mysterious smile of the Asian American character are meant to imply the forbidden pleasures associated with this trip. Furthermore, her legs are crossed in a demure, intimate manner that evokes images of Orientalized sitting postures, while her fingers delicately hold the photo in a gesture that strongly resembles the dancing hand movements of the Virginia Slims Asian model. Again, Ofoto's advertising campaign draws on traditional representations of Asian/American women as exotic and erotic objects of White men's sexual adventure.

CONSUMING ORIENTALISM

These three ad campaigns exemplify the diverse ways in which Asian/American women are sexually objectified, culturally misrepresented and visually consumed in contemporary American Orientalism. By highlighting the ascribed "foreign" nature of Asian/American women, these three corporations aim to profit off the sense of identity and place they provide for White males in the U.S. through their products, while simultaneously targeting an increasingly diverse global audience. In this way, the perception of multiculturalist advertisements as the symbolic site for cultural diversity and equality overlooks the subtle complexities with which Asian/American bodies are presented and represented to White America.

NOTE

1. The slash in the word "Asian/American" represents "a choice between two terms, their simultaneous and equal status, and an element of indecidability, that is, as it at once implies both exclusion and inclusion" (Palumbo-Liu, 1999, p. 1). This element of "indecidability" is an important factor in this word choice, because Asian Americans are still considered to be "foreigners," or Asians. In this paper, we use "Asian American" only for specific situations related to Asian Americans.

IT'S YOUR TURN: WHAT DO YOU THINK? WHAT WILL YOU FIND?

1. As we note, at times we use the term "Asian/American" here on purpose. Do you agree or disagree with our doing so? Why? Do you think it matters? Why?

2. Look at recent issues of the magazines we analyzed. Can you find ads with Asian/Americans? Are they part of multicultural ads? Do you see any patterns? What companies or businesses are the ads are for?

3. What about editorial (non-advertising) photographs in the magazines? To what extent are Asian models included? How are they presented? What does that mean?

4. Look at recent issues of ethnic magazines or commercial publications distributed by ethnic communities. Compare the ads in these magazines to mainstream magazines.

REFERENCES

Cagan, E. (1978, May/June). The selling of the women's movement. *Social Policy*, 4–12.

Chan, J. (2003) "Rough on rats": Racism and advertising in the latter half of the nineteenth century. Retrieved March 10, 2008, from http://www.chsa.org/research/ching_conference_excerpt.php

Cortese, A. J. (1999). *Provocateur: Images of women and minorities in advertising*. Lanham: Rowman & Littlefield.

Cui, G. (1997). Marketing strategies in a multi-ethnic environment. *Journal of Marketing Theory and Practice*, 5, 122–134.

Gee, D. (Director). (1988). *Slaying the dragon* [Film]. San Francisco: Cross Current Media and National Asian American Telecommunication Association.

Hamamoto, D. Y. (1994). *Monitored peril: Asian Americans and the politics of TV representation*. Minneapolis: University of Minnesota Press.

Lee, J. (1996). Why Suzie Wong is not a lesbian: Asian and Asian American lesbian and bisexual women and femme/butch/gender identities. In B. Beemyn & M. Eliason (Eds.), *Queer studies: A lesbian, gay, bisexual & transgender anthology* (pp. 115–132). New York: New York University Press.

Lee, R. G. (1999). *Orientals: Asian Americans in popular culture*. Philadelphia: Temple University Press.

Marchetti, G. (1993). *Romance and the "yellow peril": Race, sex, and discursive strategies in Hollywood fiction*. Berkeley: University of California Press.

Palumbo-Liu, D. (1999). *Asian/American: Historical crossings of a racial frontier*. Stanford: Stanford University Press.

Said, E. W. (1979). *Orientalism*. New York: Vintage.

Stabiner, K. (1982, May 2). Tapping the homosexual market. *The New York Times Magazine*, pp. 35–36, 75–76, 79–81, and 83–85.

Tajima, R. E. (1989). Lotus blossoms don't bleed: Images of Asian women. In Asian Women United of California (Ed.), *Making waves: An anthology of writings by and about Asian American women* (pp. 308–317). Boston: Beacon Press.

Williamson, J. (1986). Woman is an island: Femininity and colonization. In T. Modleski (Ed.), *Studies in entertainment: Critical approaches to mass culture* (pp. 99–118). Bloomington: Indiana University Press.

CHAPTER 5

FILM AND ENTERTAINMENT TELEVISION

5.1 RACE, HIERARCHY, AND HYENAPHOBIA IN *THE LION KING*

Naomi Rockler-Gladen

> *The author presents a textual analysis of Disney's* The Lion King. *She argues that the film reinforces the concept of a hierarchical society—a segregated society—in which it is "only natural" that one social group (in this case the hyenas, whose portrayal echoes stereotypes of African Americans) is outcast and doesn't receive adequate resources.*

If you're like many of my students, you might be puzzled by the title of this chapter. Race and hierarchy in *The Lion King*? Why would anyone think about a children's movie in such a manner? After all, if you're like my students, you love *The Lion King*. In my public speaking classes, I ask my students to give an introductory speech about three objects that represent their past, present, and future. One semester, three different students brought in a copy of *The Lion King* as the object to represent their past. People love this film. According to the Internet Movie Database, *The Lion King* is the seventh highest grossing film in the United States of all time (IMDB, 2001a) and the sixth highest grossing film worldwide of all time (IMDB, 2001b)—which means that by far, *The Lion King* is the world's most popular animated film. So why take such a lovable, popular film and think about what it has to say about race?

Many people are quite reticent to analyze Disney films critically. In 1995, several professors edited a collection of critical essays about Disney films. They gave some of the essays to their students, and this is what they found:

> Even our own students, occupying a halfway house between film critic and mass audience, are extremely resistant to the critique of Disney film . . . [O]ur students commonly complained, "You're reading too much into this film!" and "You can't say that about Walt Disney!" These students consistently cite four easy pardons for their pleasurable participation in Disney films and its apolitical agendas: it's only for children, it's only fantasy, it's only a cartoon, and it's just good business. These four naturalizations create a Disney text exempt from material, historical, and political influences. . . . Our students' attitudes suggest that Disney successfully invites mass audiences to set aside critical faculties (Bells, Haas, & Sells, p. 4).

You may feel the same way, or perhaps you've never given much thought to what the "messages" of a Disney film might be. I invite you to put your skepticism on hold for a few pages and think critically with me about *The Lion King*. Here, I argue that *The Lion King* makes the concept of societal hierarchies seem natural and desirable, especially in relationship to race.

This is a textual analysis of *The Lion King*. As with all textual analyses, it's important that you understand that I'm not looking for "hidden" or "subliminal" meanings in *The Lion King*, nor am I arguing that I am telling you the "correct" meaning of the film. Rather, I am offering my interpretation of what I think this film says about race and hierarchy. I doubt very much that Disney intended the film to be interpreted in this way, and I doubt your average 4-year-old viewer even knows what a racial hierarchy is. However, when a critic analyzes a film textually, it doesn't matter whether the producer intended the film to mean something in particular, or whether a viewer interprets the film in a similar way. Textual critics operate under the assumption that films are one of the places where members of a culture learn implicitly about the rules, norm, and power structures of their cultures. In other words, the media is one of the places where people learn about their culture's *ideology*—just as we also learn about a culture's ideological rules, norms, and power structures from our parents, peers, teachers, and clergy.

The Lion King is one of many places where a child might learn implicitly about how race and hierarchy function in his or her culture. For this reason, I believe it's important for us to think critically about what we're watching.

HIERARCHY AND *THE LION KING*

A hierarchy is a system in which some members of a culture have more privilege, economic resources, status, or other form of power than other members of a culture. Your classroom is a hierarchy. The instructor has more power than you and the other students. He or she decides what you will do in class every day and has the power to assign you a grade. You are expected to sit in your desk and do as the instructor asks.

Hierarchies usually are shaped like triangles. In a hierarchical system, usually only a few people have power, while many people have little power. In your school, the students outnumber the instructors, and yet the instructors have all the power. There are even fewer deans and administrators in your school, and yet they have even more power than the instructors.

Most important, hierarchies are *naturalized*. That is, they seem normal and typical to many or most members of the hierarchy, even to the people without the power. You have spent many years of your life in a classroom, and it seems normal and typical to you that the instructor has more power. You've probably never seriously questioned this. Because hierarchies often remain unchallenged, the powerful people stay in power.

There are many hierarchies within societies. In U.S. culture, for example, we have a gender hierarchy. Although there are many individual exceptions to this statement, in general men have more power than women. According to the U.S. Census Bureau (2001), in 1999 women made about 72 cents for every dollar men made. In heterosexual marriages, women often are expected to do the majority of the domestic work and are commonly expected to take their husbands' last names.

Similarly, although there are many individual exceptions to this statement, we also have a racial hierarchy in the United States There has never been a minority president, and in 2001 there was only one minority Senator. According to the U.S. Census Bureau (2001), while the average 1999 White family income was $40,816, the average African American family income was $27,910, and the average Hispanic family income was $30,715. As sociologist George Lipsitz (1998) argued, minorities in the United States disproportionately live in toxically polluted environments, are more likely to receive longer prison terms than Whites for the same crimes, and receive inferior health care. Unlike many minorities in the United States, most Whites have never been pulled over unfairly by police officers, followed around a store, or otherwise experienced "racial profiling." Unlike minorities, Whites can turn on a television set and see many people who look like them.

In case you haven't seen *The Lion King*, the film is about a lion cub named Simba who is heir to the throne of the Pridelands, a fictitious animal jungle society. Scar, the brother of King Mufasa, longs to become king himself. He enlists the help of the hyenas, a group of outcast animals who live outside the Pridelands, to help him kill the king and usurp the throne. After murdering Mufasa, Scar persuades Simba that he's to blame for his father's death. Simba goes into exile, and Scar assumes the throne, telling the other lions that Simba is dead. In exile, Simba is befriended by a warthog and meerkat who teach him to live the carefree life of "hakuna matata." Meanwhile, the Pridelands fall apart under Scar's rule, largely because the hyenas have been allowed to move in and have depleted all the resources. Simba's childhood friend Nala finds Simba, now grown, and urges him to dispense with his "hakuna matata" lifestyle and claim responsibility for the throne. After seeing an image of his father from the heavens, Simba goes home, defeats Scar, and becomes the rightful king. Order and beauty is restored to the Pridelands.

The Lion King contains a society in which power is in the hands of a few, and in which this hierarchy is naturalized and deemed desirable to all. In the Pridelands, the lions are the most powerful members of society, while all the other animals are hierarchically inferior. This is demonstrated visibly at the beginning of the film, when the newborn cub Simba is presented to the Pridelands as the future king. All of the animals of the kingdom gather around Pride Rock, the lions' den which, physically, is high above them, to watch Simba's presentation. As Rafiki, a monkey and spiritual figure, presents the cub to the Pridelands, a beam of light illuminates the cub, a Christian allusion suggesting divine sanction of the cub's predestination to power. As Simba is presented, the other animals in the kingdom bow and applaud wildly.

In an early scene, King Mufasa justifies the hierarchical society to young Simba, referring to the hierarchy as the "circle of life," which he claims must not be violated for fear of chaos:

> **Mufasa:** Everything you see exists together in a delicate balance. As king, you need to understand that balance and respect all the creatures, from the crawling ant to the leaping antelope.
>
> **Simba:** But, Dad, don't we eat the antelope?
>
> **Mufasa:** Yes, Simba, but let me explain. When we die, our bodies become the grass. And the antelope eat the grass. And so we are all connected in the great circle of life.

Here, Mufasa fails to problematize the power relationships in the "circle of life" that operates clearly in the interests of the lions, who thrive at the top of the hierarchy as the dominant elite. Instead, he justifies the inequality of the hierarchy by arguing that it's beneficial to all. None of the other animals in the Pridelands question their inferior status, despite the fact that sometimes the lions eat them. No revolutionary antelope group is shown plotting to demand more equitable conditions. Even Zazu, a dodo who is the king's servant, doesn't question the hierarchy, although he is humiliated repeatedly by Simba and by Mufasa, who uses Zazu as a subject of a "pouncing lesson" for Simba. In fact, the only resident of the Pridelands who questions the societal hierarchy is Scar, the film's villain. Thus, the hierarchy is *naturalized*; it's made to look normal, desirable, and necessary for the good of all.

RACE AND HYENAPHOBIA IN *THE LION KING*

The Lion King contains a number of hierarchies. For example, *The Lion King* naturalizes a gender hierarchy. The lions clearly have more power than the lionesses. Although Nala is shown to be physically stronger than Simba, it is Simba who is predestined to be the leader. Power is passed in the kingdom from male to male, even though in the case of Scar, the kingdom falls apart under male leadership, and the Pridelands would have been better off with a female leader such as Nala. But here, I'll focus specifically on the topic of race, and what I believe *The Lion King* says about race and hierarchy.

Historically, racial hierarchies often involve segregation of hierarchically "inferior" groups, who are separated from the rest of society and forced to live with inadequate resources and few opportunities. In Nazi-occupied Poland, for example, Jews were removed from society and forced to live in desolate ghettos, where they eventually were murdered. In South Africa, through the system of apartheid, the indigenous African population was segregated from the more affluent White population and forced into inadequate living conditions with inadequate schooling. Similarly, in the Southern United States until the 1960s, "Jim Crow" laws legally separated African Americans from Whites and forced them into inadequate housing, schools, and economic situations. In the United States today, de facto segregation and "White flight" make segregation a continuing reality; as of 1993, 70% of all Latino and African American children attended predominantly minority schools (Lipsitz, 1998, p. 38). In California and Texas, angry public sentiment struggles to keep "illegal" immigrants out and to make English the official U.S. language, and throughout the Midwest, Native Americans for years have lived on reservations where they suffer some of the highest poverty rates in the country.

In *The Lion King*, the segregated group is the hyenas. The hyenas don't necessarily represent any *particular* group (although as I argue below, their portrayal echoes derogatory stereotypes of African Americans) but rather might represent any hated group of outsiders throughout history—Native Americans, Mexican Americans, immigrants, and so forth. They represent the *concept* of the feared and hatred outsider whom the mainstream culture fights to keep out. The order of the circle of life depends on the hyenas staying outside the lush Pridelands. When hyenas wander into the Pridelands, King Mufasa chases them out. When hyenas are integrated into the Pridelands, the Pridelands disintegrate.

Similar to other segregated groups throughout history, the hyenas live in a poverty-stricken land. Unlike the lush Pridelands, the hyenas' land is barren. They don't have enough food. Unlike beautiful Pride Rock, where the lions live, the hyenas live in caves and amongst elephant skeletons that are the *Lion King* housing equivalent of dilapidated projects in the inner cities. Although they're wealthy, the lions feel no obligation to help the hyenas overcome their poverty. In fact, when the hungry hyenas venture into the Pridelands in search of food, Mufasa chases them out.

At no time in *The Lion King* do we learn that segregation is not a good thing and that lions ought to learn to overcome their "hyenaphobia" and create a more multicultural society. Quite the opposite is true. Hyenaphobia is never proven irrational. When King Scar invites the hyenas to move into the Pridelands, all of the lions' worst fears are realized. After a period of time, the Pridelands are as barren as the hyena lands, and the food supply has run out. In response to the decay of the Pridelands, the lionesses encourage Scar to desert the Pridelands and move on. It is the story of White America's flight to the suburbs. As the old unspoken fear goes, if minorities are integrated into mainstream culture, everything will fall apart. *The Lion King* creates a situation where these fears are justified and naturalized. Some creatures, *The Lion King* tells us, really do deserve to live in poverty and be segregated.

The Lion King does contain some positive nods to African Americans. Two well-known African Americans provide the voices of prominent characters: James Earl Jones as Mufasa and Whoopi Goldberg as one of the hyenas. Many African Americans and Africans were involved in the production of the film, and the film contains a good deal of African music (both of these trends continue to an even larger degree in the theatrical version of *The Lion King*). However, although these inclusions shouldn't be dismissed, they don't mask the negative stereotypes of African Americans that surface in *The Lion King*.

The hyenas signify the stereotypical caricature of the African American welfare recipient. Popularized by President Ronald Reagan in the 1980s, the legendary "welfare queen," who "poached" the taxpayers' money by having babies out of wedlock, became the scapegoat for the nation's economic problems. Like the "welfare queen," the hyenas are the villains in this individualistic tale because they are "scavengers" taking resources they haven't earned. They aren't self-sufficient; they sneak into the Pridelands and poach food. No explanation is ever given as to why the hyenas aren't entitled to share the resources of the Pridelands, just as no clear explanation is given as to why the Pridelands disintegrate when the hyenas are integrated. The needy hyenas simply are assumed to be unworthy scavengers.

Physically, the hyenas resemble the post-slavery "Black Sambo" stereotype that was prevalent in U.S. popular culture for many years, including in the popular radio and television series *Amos 'n' Andy*. This stereotype emerged from the traditional minstrel show, in which African American or White men would mock African Americans by covering their faces with unnaturally dark blackface, exaggerating common African American physical features, and acting comically inarticulate and insipid. The hyenas resemble this stereotype. They have bulging eyes, protruding lips, and as Scar describes them, "vacant expressions." They laugh hysterically and loudly all the time. Two of the main character hyenas show some intelligence, but the hyena, Ed, is the ultimate Sambo. He never speaks; he just laughs and laughs, and wags his protruding tongue like a rabid dog.

The hyenas represent an odd, contradictory mix of racial phobias. They are violent, and the lions' stereotypes of the violent hyenas are justified throughout the hyenas' actions. At the same time, the hyenas who are feared for their violence are helplessly buffoon-like—especially Ed. They are at the bottom of the food chain and scarcely can find enough food to eat to stay alive. When Scar instructs the hyenas to kill young Simba, they fail miserably, instead falling into a pile of thorns as they run after the cub. In accordance with their dishonest nature, they lie to Scar and claim they have killed Simba. This is similar to stereotypes of minorities throughout history, including African Americans, who contradictorily are considered by many to be ignorant, yet somehow frighteningly violent. In addition, the hyenas roam together like gang members, representing stereotypical fears and of minority gangs.

Scar's use of the hyenas to usurp the throne reflects the fear that minorities might be mobilized to overthrow the powers that be, reminiscent of *Birth of a Nation* (Griffin, 1915), the epic Ku Klux Klan propaganda film in which Northern outsiders mobilize evil, stereotypical former slaves to wreak havoc upon the South. In addition, "Be Prepared," the musical sequence in which Scar invites the hyenas to support his coup, alludes visually to Hitler's propaganda film *Triumph of the Will* (Riefenstahl, 1935). The hyenas march in perfect procession, their forms emphasized by tall, looming shadows, a scene that echoes the high-stepping, redundant marching scenes from *Triumph of the Will*. Scar, through this analogy, is like Hitler. "Stick with me and you'll never go hungry again!" he roars throughout the canyon, a promise similar to Hitler's promise in the skeletal remains of post–World War I Germany. The analogy between the hyenas and the Nazis is evidence of the film's justification of the race hierarchy. The Nazis, after all, are widely understood as racial *oppressors*, not as victims of an unjust racial hierarchy, and by comparing the hyenas to Nazis, the film shows no sympathy for the hyenas' plight.

The hyenas, as it turns out, fight miserably in the final race battle between the lions and hyenas. The race hierarchy is restored at the conclusion of *The Lion King*. The surviving hyenas presumably are sent back to the shadowy place, and the Pridelands are once again idyllic. The circle of life is restored—and part of that circle of life includes the exclusion of the outsider hyenas.

RECONSIDERING THE CIRCLE OF LIFE

We live in an unjust, hierarchical world. A relatively small number of people have access to wealth, privilege, and opportunity, while millions and even billions of others live in poverty and have little access to resources. In the United States, we live in a nation where equality and justice are valued highly, and yet our nation is filled with economic, gender, and racial hierarchies.

One might say that this is just the way the world works. Some people will always have more money, status, freedom, and resources than other people. However, the fact that hierarchies *do* seem like "the way the world works" is evidence that hierarchies have become naturalized to us. It seems natural, normal, and perhaps even desirable that some people are more powerful than other people.

But it's just a children's film, you might say. How can a children's film have such impact? It is precisely because *The Lion King* is seen as "just entertainment" and "just a children's film" that it does have impact. Viewers don't take it seriously. People assume that as a popular, lovable Disney film, its message must be positive. The film's larger ideological implications remain unchallenged.

The Lion King is by no means the only example of media content that teaches us about concepts such as race, segregation, and hierarchy. As you read this book, you'll find other discussions of media texts that reinforce similar lessons. As I noted earlier, an assumption of textual media analysis is that through the media, members of a culture learn implicitly what the rules, norms, and power structure of their culture ought to be—the *ideology* of their culture. Certainly *The Lion King* does not turn children into racists. However, when members of a culture view many messages such as *The Lion King*, the ways in which we as a culture view ideological concepts such as race, segregation, and hierarchy are shaped.

IT'S YOUR TURN: WHAT DO YOU THINK? WHAT WILL YOU FIND?

1. I believe that media texts are one of the places where members of a culture learn about the rules, norms, and power structures of our culture—that is, our *ideology*. Think about other Disney films that you seen. What do you think are the ideological lessons of these Disney films? Are there other Disney films that you feel have an ideological message about race, hierarchy, or segregation?

2. I've found that many people don't think Disney films ought to be analyzed critically. Do you agree that many people feel that way? Why or why not? If people don't think that Disney films ought to be analyzed critically, what (if any) might be some negative consequences of this?

3. Sometimes, the ideological nature of a media text can be made more visible if viewers try to understand the text from a different point of view. To do this, conduct a mock *Lion King* debate on this topic: "Should the hyenas be integrated into the Pridelands?"

Divide the classroom into four groups: Hyenas; Lions, the "Circle of Life Party" (a political party of Pridelands animals who firmly believe every animal should behave in accordance with their place in the "circle of life," and that the lions are benevolent rulers), and the "Progressive Jungle Democratic Alliance" (a political party consisting of Pridelands animals who want to create a more democratic system where all animals govern the Pridelands equally). Each group should create a statement and debate each other on the topic. Afterward, discuss the exercise and the film. Has your perspective on *The Lion King* changed after this activity? Do you agree with me that *The Lion King* promotes segregation?

4. Imagine you wanted to create a film like *The Lion King* but that didn't promote segregation. Could you tell the same story in a different (more inclusive) way? How? Using the same characters, what other stories could you tell that would be compelling but not exclusionary?

REFERENCES

Bell, E., Haas, L., & Sells, L. (Eds.). (1995). *From mouse to mermaid: The politics of film, gender, and culture.* Bloomington: University of Indiana Press.

Griffin, D. W. (Director). (1915). *Birth of a nation* [Motion picture].

Internet Movie Database. (2001a). *The top grossing movies of all time at the USA box office.* Re-

trieved June 13, 2001, from: us.imdb.com/charts/usatopmovies.

Internet Movie Database. (2001b). *The top grossing movies of all time at the worldwide box office.* Retrieved June 13, 2001, from: us.imdb.com/charts/worldtopmovies

Lipsitz, G. (1998). *The possessive investment in Whiteness: How White people profit from iden-*

tity politics. Philadelphia: Temple University Press.

Riefenstahl, L. (Director). (1935). *Triumph of the will* [Motion picture].

U.S. Census Bureau. (2001). *Frequently asked questions about income statistics.* Retrieved June 13, 2001, from: www.census.gov/hhes/income/incfaq.html

5.2 WICKED STEPMOTHERS WEAR DIOR: HOLLYWOOD'S MODERN FAIRY TALES

Lea M. Popielinski

The author argues that The Devil Wears Prada *and* The Nanny Diaries *represent the evolution of a familiar type of fairy tale: a maiden overcomes subjugation by a more powerful older woman to gain freedom and happiness.*

A young woman gazes up from the foot of a Manhattan skyscraper, awed by its power to dwarf her and excited by the challenge it represents. She's just finished college and is about to enter another world that promises to transform her and deliver her into the professional life of her dreams. She's no Rapunzel, waiting inside a tower for a dashing hero to whisk her away, but an adventurer in her own right, prepared to scale the tower herself. With an ambitiousness as inspired as it is naïve, our young woman is about to become the heroine of the modern-day fairy tale.

Recent films *The Devil Wears Prada* (2006) and *The Nanny Diaries* (2007) follow protagonists much like this young lady as they begin jobs they consider transitional but necessary trials toward their ultimate aspirations. The only obstacles confronting *Devil's* Andrea "Andy" Sachs and *Diaries'* Annie Braddock in attaining their career goals, ironically, are their employers. This chapter will discuss the evolution of a familiar subset of fairy tales: the story of a maiden overcoming subjugation by a more powerful older woman to gain freedom and happiness. Once upon a time, this antagonist was often a witch or a wicked stepmother motivated by jealousy, greed, or fear of being dethroned, but in contemporary films targeting an adult audience, she appears as a wealthy woman whose status affords her the ability to make the rules. I will address how Miranda Priestly and Mrs. X, the characters who take on this role in these movies, carry on the wicked stepmother model in updated variations. Andy and Annie, meanwhile, are hardly Snow White and Cinderella, but the spirit of the character type is maintained in a form relatable to young 21st-century women.

This chapter deals with archetypes, classic models of a person or concept that take a consistent form by appearing repeatedly within a cultural genre. The wicked stepmother and the innocent, persecuted heroine are major fairy-tale archetypes. Psychoanalysts have interpreted the use of archetypes in storytelling as symbolic of the beliefs of a culture's collective unconscious (Franz, 1973). Other authors focus on the archetypes' social context to examine how they reflect their cultures (Zipes, 1993). I use a combination of the two methods, in using *Devil* and *Diaries*, to explore how the two archetypes have changed in some ways but are still recognizable in others, in relation to women's changing roles and concerns. I suggest that North American culture is conflicted about how contemporary women's roles diverge from fairy-tale ideals, proud of the independence and ambition of young women with no real influence yet more ambivalent about women who are aged and/or successful enough to wield social and economic power, and that the race, sexuality, and class status of the women in these films are significant to the reproduction of these archetypes.

THE MOVIES

In *Devil*, Andy Sachs has moved to New York seeking work in her dream profession of journalism. She procures a position that "a million girls would kill for," as junior assistant to *Runway* fashion magazine's notoriously patronizing editor in chief, Miranda Priestly. Although her frumpy style indicates to Miranda a lack of credibility, Andy is determined to persevere because the experience will open all the doors in Manhattan's journalistic offices to her. Eventually, with help from coworker Nigel, she adapts to her circumstances and the workplace's standards of appearance while developing the business contacts and self-confidence that boost her job performance and Miranda's approval. As she grows devoted to her job, however, she loses touch with her boyfriend and friends. When she becomes party to politics and back-stabbing, she finally wants out, unwilling to sacrifice her ethics. As the movie ends, Andy's boyfriend is moving away, and she goes to work at a more modestly run newspaper, on Miranda's favorable recommendation.

Meanwhile, *The Nanny Diaries*' Annie Braddock is less certain about her ambitions. After failing a job interview, she saves a child named Grayer from an accident and is invited by his wealthy mother, Mrs. X, to become his nanny. Believing that the work will be a good source of income while she figures out her life, Annie accepts. She finds herself performing all the parental duties for a socialite mother and philandering father. She finds support from her friends and from a studly neighbor in the Xes' building, whom she calls "Harvard Hottie." Annie's affection for Grayer balances her growing frustration until Mr. X makes an unwanted pass at her, which Mrs. X uses as an excuse to fire her. She vents her anger on a teddy bear outfitted with a "nannycam"; the resulting video, in which Annie pleads that the Xes become more active parents, shames Mrs. X in front of a seminar, though Annie later learns that Mrs. X has taken her advice. Meanwhile, she applies to graduate programs in anthropology, and her romance with Harvard Hottie appears to be underway.

THE INNOCENT, PERSECUTED HEROINE

The phrase "innocent, persecuted heroine" is a standard way of describing this character type among fairy-tale theorists (see *Western Folklore 52*[1], 1993). It should be immediately apparent that in the present-day fairy tale, this figure has undergone dramatic transformations, not least of which is the fact that Andy and Annie are not persecuted in any traditional sense, having freely accepted their jobs. Although surface details have changed quite substantially, the changes are consistent with the innocent, persecuted heroine's (hereafter, IPH's) history as an archetype and the core elements to the narrative structure and positioning of the IPH tale. Andy and Annie are not actual IPHs, but their films belong to a related subgenre.

It's essential to see the development of archetypes within their historical contexts. Many European fairy tales began as products of oral folklore before being published (Franz, 1973; Tatar, 2002), often existing in multiple forms in different periods and locales. Publication and distribution, however, caused particular versions, such as the Grimm brothers' adaptations, to become more widely accepted. These privileged versions obscure the diversity of the previous contexts in which the stories appeared.

Even within the IPH subgenre, the heroines have not always been innocent and persecuted but often became so when their stories were adapted for wide appeal. "Little Red Riding Hood" gives us one fascinating example: In

> an oral version of the tale recorded in France at the end of the nineteenth century, Little Red Riding Hood performs a striptease before the wolf, then ends the litany of questions about the wolf's body parts by asking if she can go outside to relieve herself (Tatar, 2002, p. 17)

Thus she outwitted the wolf and escaped, rather than being saved by a hunter. Other heroines are innocent throughout the story but allow brutal violence to occur once they've attained higher status: The Grimms' Cinderella invites her stepsisters to her wedding, where birds peck out their eyes, and Snow White allows her stepmother to be placed in red-hot iron shoes that cause her to dance herself to death. The idealistically innocent heroine did appear in earlier eras, but she was not as monolithic as she gradually became.

Since the 1930s, probably the most influential transcriber of fairy tales has been Disney. Their animated feature film versions of IPH tales are so iconic that many in recent generations regard them as the gold standard and may not be familiar with earlier versions. It may be worth considering why the IPH archetype proliferated at this time. The construction of morality and femininity in 20th-century North America may have demanded less ambiguity than Europeans of earlier periods were comfortable with.

Things became more complicated with the emergence of the women's movement, beginning in the 1960s. The first feminist engagements with fairy tales appeared in the early 1970s (Lieberman, 1972; Lurie, 1970; Rowe, 1979), and even non-feminists in the present day recognize feminist objections to the archetypes. Some latter-day Disney films feature noticeably more active or intelligent heroines, and parodies such as *Shrek* defy the archetype altogether. Likely because of feminist influence and the sense that the archetype has become cliché, it has become difficult to produce straightforward IPHs. A fairy tale meant to be relevant to contemporary women must be more complex. Thus, the fact that the goals and concerns of the heroines of *Devil* and *Diaries* diverge dramatically from those of Disney's midcentury prototypes does not necessarily exclude them from being kin to the IPH subgenre. In some ways, the stories and their protagonists conform to the conventions of standard IPH narratives, such as in the heroines' solitude and in their search for identity.

Michael Mendelson (1997) observes that while male heroes and wicked women in Grimms' fairy tales occasionally collaborate with one another, young, virtuous women seldom work together in a similar fashion. Although Andy and Annie have friends and boyfriends outside of their workplaces, their social lives conflict with their jobs. While Annie has no peer coworkers at all, Andy begins her job as an outcast among her colleagues. The nearest that women in the Grimms' tales come to a collaborative relationship, Mendelson suggests, is when a fairy godmother or similar figure arrives to offer brief and temporary assistance to a heroine. Andy has a helper of this sort in Nigel: The scene in which he brings her to *Runway*'s castoffs closet and dresses her, Cinderella-like, in designer garments, marks the turning point in the film, after which she becomes a model employee and eventually impresses Miranda.

Mendelson (1997) also focuses on "the coming into selfhood" and how in "this singular process of psychological individuation, the solitary figure takes center stage" (p. 120). Andy has chosen her future identity, and her time at *Runway* is her journey toward self-realization. In *Diaries*, this process is even more transparent. In an early scene, a job interviewer asks our heroine, "Who is Annie Braddock?" Annie's inability to answer this question leads her to take the job she believes will help her find herself. That she expects to find self-discovery through nannying makes most sense with respect to her relationship with Mrs. X: Having one's very own wicked stepmother becomes a rite of passage toward adulthood.

THE WICKED STEPMOTHER

The stepmother is so important to the Western coming-of-age story that now that she is no longer a domestic terrorist infiltrating the heroine's home, the young women must seek her out on her own territory. Andy would not have the credentials, the recommendation, or the first-rate experience to compete for her dream job, and Annie might still be taking ill-fated interviews at business offices, if they had not first passed through gauntlets conceived by Miranda and Mrs. X. Besides the workplace taking on a familial quality in both films, both films include the motif of parental replacement. In *Devil*, Andy's father visits, but she is continually interrupted by telephone calls from Miranda and her impossibly urgent demands. The evening grows increasingly frustrating, peaking when the distracted Andy shuts a taxi door on her father, literally and painfully. In *Diaries*, the mother substitution is more overt. Annie has been raised by a single mother and nurse, whom she doesn't want to disappoint. When she takes the nanny job, she lies to her mother and says she was offered a financial position. The ruse falls apart in a tense confrontation between Mrs. X and Mrs. Braddock, in which the former says to Annie, "I didn't know you had a mother."

Compared to Andy and Annie as IPHs, Miranda and Mrs. X retain more traditional characteristics relating to the wicked stepmother, most visibly in their dictatorial styles. Steven Swann Jones (1993) regards the "jealous stepmother who favors her own daughter and forces the heroine to perform disagreeable, dangerous, or impossible chores" (p. 28) to be a staple of the IPH genre. Miranda reduces Andy to running errands and performing menial tasks, culminating in an ultimatum for Andy to find an unpublished *Harry Potter* manuscript; Mrs. X's to-do list for Annie is less demanding but more degrading, frequently designed to emphasize their difference in status. Although danger is not a theme in either movie, disagreeable and impossible chores certainly are.

IN A LAND NOT SO FAR AWAY

The release of two very similar films that reinvent these archetypes in more familiar guises suggests that there's a social need or desire for such images to be reproduced in this way. The critical questions are, what do *Devil* and *Diaries* say about their social context, and why are the symbols packaged the way they are?

We must view these symbols in terms of how we understand race, gender, class, and sexuality in our cultural context. In some respects, the archetypes are still strongly bound to the correct combination of these four dimensions. More marginal archetypes, like the fairy godmother, may be flexible. Others, like Prince Charming, are optional. The heroine and the stepmother, however, might not be recognizable as such were they not both White, heterosexual women of the economic classes appropriate to their character types.

Archetypes must appear to represent the broadest range of subjectivity possible. The cultural separation of social categories into One and Other, in which One is not merely the dominant of the two but the standard, neutral, and default category, casts Othered categories as marked identities, seen in terms of their difference from the "norm." Using the example of sex/gender, Simone de Beauvoir (1949/1989) writes, "man represents both the positive and the neutral, as is indicated by the common use of *man* to designate human beings in general; whereas woman represents only the negative, defined by limiting criteria, without reciprocity" (p. xxi). Applying the concept to race, then, a Black heroine would be able to stand as an archetype for all Black women, but only a White heroine is constructed to stand for all women: Whiteness, unlike other(ed) races, does not need to be articulated. Only Whiteness, in de Beauvoir's terms, is neutral.

Similarly, a version of *Devil* with Andy as a lesbian would probably not allow her to "just happen to be" a lesbian. Rather, her inevitable tomboyishness might be used comically as she fumbles with feminine clothing, or she might grapple with homophobic parents. While there's nothing wrong with producing a film about a straight, White woman, we can't assume that her race and sexuality are therefore any less important to her character development than for those with more marked identities. Whiteness and heterosexuality are just as central to constructing these characters as class and gender.

The centrality of Andy and Annie's Whiteness is actively reinforced by the fact that each one's closest female friend is Black. Annie's friend Lynnette directly emphasizes that Annie's choice to enter domestic servitude is made from a position of racial privilege when she points out that generations of women in her own family have worked hard not to perform that labor again. Annie can *only* submit herself to it knowing that her racial privilege grants her other options. She herself acknowledges that her race, citizenship, and English language fluency make her "the Chanel bag of nannies." Andy and her best friend, Lily, never talk about race as overtly, but the absence of other White women in Andy's social circle highlights her dyadic relationship with the older White mother-substitute.

Andy and Annie's heterosexuality is also reinforced by those around them; Lynnette's roommate, Calvin, is openly gay, while Nigel is depicted using stereotypically gay mannerisms. The deflection of homosexuality away from the main characters renders gayness as a marked identity, so that any character not "read" as gay will appear to a heterosexist audience as straight. The heroines' heterosexuality is not incidental: It's necessary to maintain the characters as archetypes, not only because of heterosexuality's default status but also because it leaves open the possibility of a Prince Charming, necessary for the fairy-tale framework, even if that possibility does not come to fruition. Straight woman-hood must be opposed to straight manhood, without all of the complicated ambiguities that lesbian and bisexual identities and nonconformist gender expressions introduce.

Class advancement has always been a central theme of fairy tales, especially IPH tales (Panttaja, 1993). Andy and Annie frame their ambitions as paths to careers rather than wealth, but the economic disparity between the heroines and their employers underlines a direct correlation between money and power. Reading the films side by side illustrates that the differences between women who marry into money, like Mrs. X, and women who earn it themselves, like Miranda, are not necessarily significant to archetypal readings. Andy and Annie's seemingly humble approach to money is necessary to further contribute to their neo-IPH profile to the extent that standard IPHs are often rewarded specifically for not seeking a reward. The connections among power, money, and a lack of ethics demon-strate why the wicked stepmother archetype has been revived in this form at this time: Contemporary North American culture feels very differently about young women who work hard to achieve all the hallmarks of middle-class female success than it feels about older women who have actually attained positions of power.

"Women's liberation" of the 1970s gave way to "girl power" by the 1990s. Girls of the current generation are often taught they can do anything. North American culture is proud of young women earning college degrees and entering the job market because it ex-emplifies cultural progress and open-mindedness. Critically, this pride only lasts while these women have little social power. Our culture feels much more ambivalent toward older women who are succeeding, as is reflected empirically by research suggesting that workplace advancement grows increasingly more difficult for women than for men (and more difficult for Black men than for White men) over the course of their careers (Maume, 2004). The face of *new* employees is diverse in many fields, but our culture is still most comfortable with White men in the *most elite* positions. Although many claim to support the advancement of women and people of color to powerful positions, there may still be an unconscious cultural anxiety about this ideal's realization. Because it is inappropriate to admit this anxiety, it emerges in our cultural products through the use of archetypes em-bedded in the collective unconscious.

For example, Miranda acts as both Andy's challenger and her mentor. She considers Andy, on some level, a successor. But Miranda is not depicted as a strong executive who takes employees under her wing to groom them, a character type more strongly associated with men; she's depicted in a gendered manner, insofar as terms like *shrew, ice queen*, and *dragon lady* only exist at the intersection of femaleness and class power. Movies about this type of powerful woman give voice to otherwise suppressed cultural fears about giving women "too much" power. Andy's refusal to be seduced into this role is crucial to the archetype she continues to embody.

What's more, these fears are not restricted to the office setting. Mrs. X obtained her power by marrying a rich man. The differences and similarities to Miranda are notable. On the one hand, her power is much more limited, and working for her does not provide up-ward mobility. She restricts her nannies from dating out of concern that the nanny will be less devoted to her work, but when she learns of Annie's relationship with a young man in their own building, the offense is doubly threatening for the transgression of class bound-aries. Mrs. X thus exhibits more of the classic wicked stepmother's characteristics of jeal-ousy and fear of losing her privilege. The gulf between her and Annie is much smaller than the gulf between Miranda and Andy. The former is a question of whose wedding band lands on one's finger; the latter is a matter of years of experience and ladder-climbing.

On the other hand, all of the emblematic terms I listed on the previous page—*shrew*, etc.—are similarly applicable to Mrs. X. Bestowing economic power on a woman, according to these narratives, transforms her from naïf to harpy. Both films give their stepmothers a personal edge but do so through tumult in their marriages. The only person who has the power to hurt each of these women is her husband. The circumstances under which the divorces loom and the impact they have on the two women are very different, but it is intriguing how the same device is used in both to create chinks in the stepmothers' armor.

HAPPILY EVER AFTER?

This discussion of *Devil* and *Diaries* suggests that contemporary North American culture strongly values progressive gender politics to the extent that it results in young, educated, unmarried women joining the workforce with great ambition but modest goals. It also suggests, meanwhile, that this same culture is simultaneously ambivalent about women gaining a surplus of power within the same context. I call this "ambivalence" because there does not seem to be an outright objection to women holding positions of power so much as a sense that women who hold these positions fit a certain—and not always complimentary—category of womanhood. On this note, it is important to end by observing that neither film completely demonizes its wicked stepmother. In the transition from fairy-tale archetype to contemporary social construction, this character type has grown more complex, appropriately so, for her relevance in an increasingly complex society.

IT'S YOUR TURN: WHAT DO YOU THINK? WHAT WILL YOU FIND?

1. With a partner, choose a different film genre—action, romance, science fiction, and so on—and discuss the types of female characters who appear in it. What patterns can you recognize in their depiction? What cultural beliefs about womanhood or femininity seem to be illustrated in these character types? How do race, sexuality, age, and disability (even if they are unmarked) contribute to creating these character types?

2. Find a book containing fairy tales you've never read or heard before, perhaps from a non-European culture. Choose one and imagine what would change or remain the same if it were made into a movie. Which themes or characters seem to fit easily into contemporary scripts, and which don't? Thinking about elements like violence, morals, and characters' objectives, what aspects of 21st-century culture, possibly aspects we usually take for granted, make an adaptation of the story difficult?

3. Look for articles in news magazines about women and men in powerful positions, such as politicians and business leaders. Compare the way the authors describe their subjects. To what extent do they discuss their subjects' family lives, career histories, appearance, and professional success? How positive or negative do they sound? What similarities and differences are there in the articles and any accompanying photography? If you can, find news magazines from 10, 20, and 30 years ago to see if, and how, profiles of female and male professionals have changed.

REFERENCES

de Beauvoir, Simone. (1949/1989). *The second sex*. New York: Vintage Books.

Franz, M. L. (1973). *An introduction to the psychology of fairy tales*. Zurich: Spring Publications.

Jones, S. S. (1993). The innocent persecuted heroine genre: An analysis of its structure and themes. *Western Folklore, 52*(1), 13–41.

Lieberman, M. (1972). "Some day my prince will come": Female acculturation through the fairy tale. *College English, 34*, 383–395.

Lurie, A. (1970, December 17). Fairy tale liberation. *New York Review of Books*, 42–44.

Maume, D. (2004). Wage discrimination over the life course: A comparison of explanations. *Social Problems, 51*(4), 505–527.

Mendelson, M. (1997). Forever acting alone: The absence of female collaboration in Grimms' fairy tales. *Children's Literature in Education, 28*(3), 111–125.

Panttaja, E. (1993). Going up in the world: Class in "Cinderella." *Western Folklore, 52*(1), 85–104.

Rowe, K. E. (1979). Feminism and fairy tales. *Women's Studies, 6*, 237–257.

Panttaja, E. (1993). Going up in the world: Class in "Cinderella." *Western Folklore, 52*(1), 85–104.

Tatar, M. (2002). *The annotated classic fairy tales*. New York: W.W. Norton & Company.

Zipes, J. (1993). Spinning with fate: Rumpelstiltskin and the decline of female productivity. *Western Folklore, 52*(1), 43–60.

5.3 HIP-HOP SEES NO COLOR: AN EXPLORATION OF PRIVILEGE AND POWER IN *SAVE THE LAST DANCE*

Leslie A. Grinner

> *The author presents a framework—applicable to any text—that you can use to help determine the extent to which media content perpetuates dominant ideologies. Using the SCWAMP framework, the author concludes that even though* Save the Last Dance *is set in a discourse of multiculturalism, the film actually reinforces dominant ideologies.*

MTV had its genesis on August 1, 1981, and has since become a vital part of our cultural lexicon. The network has affected the ways in which the world experiences music, television, and, most recently, film. Now considered a site of multicultural media, this was not always the case. It took over a year for MTV to debut a music video by a Black[1] entertainer. Michael Jackson's "Billie Jean" video secured his place at the pinnacle of pop royalty and set MTV on a course from which it has yet to veer. With a bevy of Black "crossover" artists following Jackson's lead, MTV has become the place where people of all races learn what it means to be Black: how to talk, walk, speak, dance, and live as Black people. MTV reinforces (and often creates) words, signs, and symbols ("codes") that exist in our culture, codes that help the audience learn to "read" media texts in a particular way. Hence, we learn about Black women's sexuality or Black men's materialism through the representations presented to us in music videos. In short, this is a space where Blackness is performed before—and consumed by—the world.

It is fitting, then, that MTV would have a hand in the production of the interracial romance film *Save the Last Dance*. The film tells the story of Sara (Julia Stiles), a white female from the suburbs, and Derrick (Sean Patrick Thomas), a Black male from the "inner city." Sold to a youthful audience as a film uniting Blacks and whites, the promotional Web site explains "Yet against all the odds they overcome the obstacles to their dreams, and discover that ultimately the only person you have to be is . . . yourself."

Though *Save the Last Dance* attempts to stand on the premise that racism is wrong and that "love sees no color," the film actually promotes and reinforces the dominant ideologies at work in mainstream U.S. culture. That is, emphasis is placed on the superiority of whiteness, masculinity, heterosexuality, ability, Christian morality, and middle-class status. The film presents stereotypical images of Black men and women and supports the notion that, ultimately, women need men to be successful. It promotes the idea that Black men are predisposed to stupidity, violence, and criminal activity and that Black women are jealous, manipulative, or burdened by teenage pregnancy.

It may seem I'm "overanalyzing" this film, that it's less harmful than I'm making it out to be. Certainly, *Save the Last Dance* follows the same formula as have so many Hollywood movies before it, using an "order, disorder, and restoration of order" narrative structure. Furthermore, the pervasive cultural story of the "American Dream" stands as the foundation for this film. But there's something else—an invisible set of ideals that guides this film and others. We need to make these ideals visible, and in doing so we can become a more media-literate population. I refer to this set of ideals as *ideology*.

Ideology can be defined as a set of beliefs that guide a culture—the most commonly known and understood values and mores. However, the role of ideology is much more complex than this. Ideology tells us who or what is *most valued* in our culture (and by extension, what is *least valued*). It's so pervasive that it lies in the very foundation of our society. Media can reinforce or resist ideology. To analyze how *Save the Last Dance* reinforces the U.S. culture's dominant ideologies, we must first identify what they are. I've developed a framework to help assess the dominant ideological positions at work in media/popular culture texts and to explore what the material consequences of these may be. I call this tool SCWAMP.

SCWAMP, which stands for Straight, Christian, White, Able-bodied, Male, and Property holding, is an intersectional framework. Intersectional analysis explains that ideological positions are interconnected and relational. These relationships are shaped and affected by the society in which they're embedded. Being able to identify the dominant ideologies present in media, and the ways in which we buy into those ideologies, provides us with a way to either consciously conform to or actively resist them. We can become a culture that is more media literate, which will allow us to be more educated and informed consumers of media.

I'll use *Save the Last Dance* to demonstrate how the SCWAMP framework operates. The film is well suited for this type of analysis, because it reinforces dominant ideologies yet obscures this by placing them within a discourse of multiculturalism. Once you learn to use SCWAMP, you can apply it to any media text.

Save the Last Dance centers around a young, middle-class white woman who loses her mother and subsequently moves from a posh suburb to Chicago's mostly Black South Side to live with her father, a down-and-out jazz musician. A ballet dancer, Sara gave up her dream of attending Julliard because her mother was killed in a car accident en route to the audition. She believes that she is responsible, because her mother was rushing to support her. She begins her new life by sleeping in the living room of her father's run-down home and attending the local high school.

On her first day of school, Sara is introduced to the other key players in the film. After setting her backpack on the floor while opening her locker, she meets Chenille. A young Black woman who is a South Side native, Chenille warns Sara never to lay her things on the floor in school, lest they be stolen. Chenille will become Sara's first real friend. As one of very few white students, Sara is protected by Chenille against Black students who aren't as welcoming. Chenille provides Sara with an entrée into Black life. Indeed, she guarantees Sara a certain amount of street credibility just by being her friend. In an effort to aid Sara as she struggles to fit in, Chenille takes her to the local dance club where she's exposed to hip-hop culture for the first time. Most important, Chenille introduces Sara to her brother, Derrick, who will become Sara's love interest in the film.

Sara actually met Derrick before she met Chenille, but under unpleasant circumstances. Upon entering her first class, she encountered a room filled with students of color who hadn't read the assigned text for the course. Though the Black male instructor offered to give Sara extra reading time, there was no need; she had read the text before. This heavily implied that the education Sara received at her white, middle-class suburban high school is far superior to that received by these urban students of color. Sara eloquently explains the author's writing style and purpose, as the class looks on in awe. Derrick, who is represented as a pompous intellectual, counters her. The tension between them is palpable. As we are introduced to other (mostly Black) students, we discover that no other students of color can match Derrick intellectually. This is especially true for the women at the school, including Derrick's sister, Chenille. While Derrick speaks in "standard" or "proper" English, sometimes adding slang for emphasis, Chenille speaks using a much more stereotypically "Black" linguistic style. It is she who begins teaching Sara how to "perform" Blackness, starting with word choice. (Her reaction to Sara's use of the word *cool* is met with the retort, "It's *slammin.*")

Chenille is quickly replaced by Derrick as Sara's teacher. Not only can Derrick teach Sara how to dance, sit, and "act" Black (though he refers to this as an instruction in hip-hop culture), he can also match wits with her. Chenille, a teenage mother, cannot provide this same support. She is involved with a Black man (depicted as a "deadbeat dad") and leaves her young child with her grandmother while she goes dancing. Derrick, on the other hand, has plans to attend college and then medical school. He has begun a romantic relationship with Sara, in part because she is the only woman in the area with aspirations that match his own. Sara begins hanging out with Derrick and learning how to dance and "act" in the (Black/male) hip-hop style. While sharing their passion for dance, they fall in love, much to the chagrin of their classmates.

Nikki, Derrick's ex-girlfriend, is the person most opposed to their relationship. Nikki is depicted as a manipulative light-skinned beauty who uses her feminine wiles and sexual charms to try to seduce Derrick. She plays the role of antagonist to Sara's protagonist and is depicted as a conniving Black woman who cheated on Derrick but now wants him back. At one point, she and Sara engage in a "catfight" during which the film places the audience clearly on Sara's side.

A subtext of this film is the relationship between Derrick and his childhood friend Malachi. He symbolizes (or is coded as) the stereotypical "troubled Black male." Although he and Derrick once ran the streets together committing petty crimes, Derrick has changed his ways. Malachi, who has just returned from a stint in Juvenile Hall, has become a drug-dealing maniac. In comparison to Derrick's strong sense of moral responsibility, Malachi is depicted as inherently violent and amoral. Derrick is thus coded as the "good Black man" in contrast to Malachi and the other Black men in his neighborhood.

APPLYING THE SCWAMP FRAMEWORK

How can we discern whether the components of SCWAMP are at work in *Save the Last Dance*, and in society at large? The components can easily be tested by investigating the privileges and benefits connected to them, the ways in which they constitute societal norms, and the consequences associated with deviance from those norms.

Straightness/Heterosexuality

How do we know that *straightness/heterosexuality* is most valued in our culture? Evidence of this can be found in the treatment that gay, lesbian, bisexual, and transgendered people encounter on a daily basis, such as gay-bashing and other forms of discrimination. Same-sex couples are unable to marry legally in most states. In contrast, heterosexuality is taken for granted as a normal, natural part of humanity. When we meet people, we often assume that they're heterosexual and treat them accordingly.

Heterosexuality is the prevailing norm in *Save the Last Dance* (as in so many films), with the primary relational focus on Black and white women fighting over Black men. At one point, Nikki confronts Sara with the idea that white women are always "creepin' up and takin' our men." This point is later repeated by Chenille, who explains that there are very few "good" Black men around, and the one decent Black man—her brother, Derrick—has been taken by a white woman. This is one of the few scenes presenting an opportunity to deal with the issues of race and gender raised by the film; however, it ends with Chenille emerging as yet another antagonistic Black woman. Later Chenille redeems herself by blaming these rantings on her own dysfunctional (Black male/female) relationship.

Christianity

In a society founded in part on the premise of religious freedom, how is it that *Christianity* may be considered a dominant ideology? Certainly there are numerous ideological positions rooted in non-Christian religious beliefs. However, we continue to conduct life in the United States according to the Christian calendar, where even in public schools and government institutions breaks correspond to Christmas and Easter. Many of the legal and moral codes guiding our society, such as "an eye for an eye," are steeped in Christian ethos. In film, Christian-based moral tales pervade almost every narrative. The consequences for not conforming to a Christian ideology can include living with a poor reputation because of sexual practices or other choices involving individual morality. In most Hollywood films, people who don't prescribe to the dominant

Christian ethos are often punished in some way, such as experiencing illness, financial hardship, or unhappiness.

In *Save the Last Dance*, a Christian-based standard of morality is kept firmly in place by a "good/bad" (Madonna/whore) dichotomy wherein Sara is placed on a higher moral ground than both Chenille and Nikki. Initially, it seems that Chenille is morally situated next to Sara, but the revelation that she's a teen mother disrupts this. Nikki never has the opportunity to be Sara's moral equal, because she's depicted as jealous, manipulative, and hypersexual. (It's fitting that Nikki is light skinned, because this reinforces the idea that while the best woman for Derrick is white, the next best falls as closely to that standard as possible.)

Derrick proves himself to be Malachi's moral superior throughout the film. When Malachi admonishes Derrick with the remark that he's "not from this neighborhood anymore," the audience is expected to view this as a compliment. Indeed, Sara tells Derrick that he "seems so different from Malachi," which he denies. In the end, Derrick realizes he *is* different from Malachi. He embodies the spirit of rugged individualism and high moral virtue that is so highly valued in U.S. culture. In contrast, Malachi falls prey to a life of crime and ends up in jail; hence, Derrick succeeds while Malachi fails. Derrick becomes the exception (a Black male who is ambitious and triumphant), while Malachi is the rule (a deviant, criminal, pathological Black male).

Whiteness

How can we be sure that *whiteness* is most valued in our culture? There are numerous examples demonstrating this. People of color still hold very few positions of power in government, in media, and in the corporate world. Blacks and Latinos continue to be racially profiled and are often prevented from obtaining employment, housing, and other resources. Like all components of SCWAMP, whiteness is an attribute that is taken for granted such that it is almost invisible. In media, we refer to certain television shows, types of music, and films as "Black," while it is almost never heard that a film is "white"—even though many are written, directed, and produced by white people and contain an entirely white cast. There are also myriad images of whiteness in media, and very few depictions of other racial and ethnic groups.

Though it claims opposition to white supremacy, *Save the Last Dance* actually reinforces whiteness as a standard of superiority. While the cast of the film is predominantly Black, the ways in which Blacks and whites are coded indicate that whiteness is considered more valuable throughout the film. The film defines Blackness in a certain way, with poverty, drug abuse, and violence at its core. As a consequence of this, the most successful characters in the film are those that conform most closely to a hegemonic "white" norm (viz., Sara and Derrick). At one point in the film, Malachi accuses Derrick of "forgetting where he came from," particularly in regard to choosing a path of nonviolence in his life. Most notably, Malachi chooses to engage in a drive-by shooting. Instead of joining him, Derrick literally runs away from this criminal activity to support Sara during her audition. Malachi embodies "Blackness" in all of its infamy. Derrick's goodness is marked by his rejection of Blackness in the form of both Malachi and Nikki and his selection of whiteness in the form of Sara. His acceptance to Georgetown University reinforces the fact that he is more intelligent than his Black counterparts. Derrick is a Black man, but he values whiteness as the ideal.

Able-Bodiedness

How do we know that *able-bodiedness* is most valued in our culture? To be blind, deaf, to read/write/comprehend differently, to have autism or retardation, to be in a wheelchair or to walk differently . . . in short to be differently abled in our culture is to be devalued. Those who are differently abled continue to struggle against debilitating stereotypes and must fight to maintain basic rights to access, agency, and resources. Mainstream culture continues to covertly add more attributes to the "disabled" list; people who are overweight, don't speak English, or don't fit into the dominant beauty standard of our culture are often treated as if they are not capable—as if they are disabled. In media, differently abled people are often portrayed as villains (think of Darth Vader with his disfigured face) or as comic relief (Mary's brother Warren in the popular film *There's Something About Mary*). They are often placed in media to be pitied, laughed at, or despised.

We can see that physical ability is highly valued in a film dedicated (at least in part) to dance. In fact, this is the only area where Blackness is considered superior, because it is Sara's mastery of hip-hop that ultimately secures her acceptance to Julliard. In popular culture, Blacks are often depicted as skilled athletes, dancers, and entertainers, to the exclusion of other attributes such as intelligence and academic acuity. Intellectual ability is constructed as being strongly tied to either "good" suburban educational settings or to an individual's resolve to "escape from the ghetto." Exceptional intellectual ability is Derrick's ticket out of the "inner city." Sara's athletic ability in the form of dance provides her with a way out, too. Blackness itself is coded as a disability in this film, except when it is related to dance.

Male

Are *men* truly more valued than women in society? Examples of this can be found in everything from language to economics. When either women or men perform a courageous act, it is often said that they "have balls" (referring to testicles). People never said that someone "had ovaries" when they've taken a risk or shown bravery (even though ovaries are just as "ball-like" as testicles.) The common belief in U.S. culture is that anything associated with the feminine is weak, while masculine traits are deemed stronger and more valuable to society. A material consequence of this belief is that women are paid less than men for performing the same work, and work perceived as feminine—parenting, nursing, teaching, and so on—remains completely undervalued in our culture. In media, women are often relegated to inferior status.

Gender is written on this film in a variety of ways, including Sara's appropriation of a Black male standard for "performing" Blackness. Though Chenille first embraces Sara, Sara's acceptance into the Black community is clearly marked by her relationship to Derrick. In this film, the success of a woman is completely tied to her acquisition of a man. Chenille—who is at first presented as strong and streetwise—becomes weak and vapid when confronted with her ill-suited love interest. Nikki represents the jealousy, promiscuity, and depravity that U.S. culture has imputed upon Black women. Her body represents sex, as in one scene where she "steals" Derrick from Sara on the dance floor and begins dancing in a sexually explicit and provocative way in contrast to Sara's innocent movement. After this debacle, Derrick explains to Sara that he was "just dancing," and Sara invites him to her home, where they can be alone. There they begin kissing, and it is implied that they make love for the first time, as the song "True Colors" plays in the background. Their naked skin, black and white, is highlighted in this scene as Sara replaces Nikki's coarse sexuality with one that seems innocent and pure.

Property Holder

Finally, what does it mean to be a *property holder*, and how can we know that this is most valued in U.S. culture? The term *property holding* as I use it here refers not only to land as property but to capital in its many forms: economic, intellectual, and cultural. Economic capital includes cash, credit, and other material possessions. Intellectual capital consists of a level of education deemed most valuable by society. Cultural capital often includes both economic and intellectual capital but can also include athletics and other accepted forms of "coolness" or "street credibility." In media, material wealth and social status are presented repeatedly, which reinforces audience members' desire for them. Lower class or unpopular people are often presented as despicable characters, and the emphasis is often on either their transformation into more socially acceptable human beings or their demise.

The film is heavily inscribed with issues of class. Though Sara is forced to spend a year at this urban, lower class school, she is rewarded with acceptance to Julliard and the promise of a life more suited to her middle-class background. Her father, whose poverty was from the outset presented as proof of his inferiority and ineptitude, recreates himself as a "good father" by the film's end. His transformation is marked when he creates a bedroom for Sara, equipped with fake snowflakes on the bed (an allusion to whiteness and purity) and a picture of her mother. Similarly, Derrick is accepted to Georgetown University and will thus emerge from his lower class upbringing into a middle-class (or even upper-class) existence. In fact, when Derrick first learns of his acceptance to Georgetown, the next scene finds him escorting Sara to the ballet. This reinforces the notion that the educational capital he's about to receive will be accompanied by an exploration of so-called high culture. The most shocking marker of class (and race) difference is the fact that the death of Sara's mother is highlighted twice, both times in ways seemingly designed to move the audience to tears. In comparison, Derrick and Chenille's mother is mentioned only once, when Chenille describes her as being in jail for "drugs and things women do to get drugs." The fact that their mother is a drug-addicted prostitute isn't something the audience is encouraged to identify with or feel sad about. This shows us which lives are most valued in our culture. We've come to accept (and even expect) this image of the Black mother. Chenille and Derrick's father is neither seen nor mentioned, alluding to the stereotypical Black "absentee father."

MEDIA LITERACY: A STRATEGY TO END OPPRESSION

With SCWAMP as a supplemental framework, we can begin to understand the multiple and sometimes hidden messages that exist in media. They may not otherwise be obvious to us, for good reason. The more comfortable we are with our media experiences, the less we question them; we dutifully support existing structures that are oppressive to ourselves and others. We don't often think about ideology, because it has been normalized and naturalized to the point that it's no longer visible to us. It is the air that we breathe and the food that we eat. Identifying ideology is the first step in becoming a media-literate society. We must take this step in order to work on ending oppression in our culture.

NOTE

1. I capitalize the term "Black" because it is not only a racial designation, but a political location. I don't capitalize the term "white," because I use it merely a descriptor. By capitalizing "Black" and not "white," I wish to disrupt the relations of power within this binary construction.

IT'S YOUR TURN: WHAT DO YOU THINK? WHAT WILL YOU FIND?

1. Choose several different texts and apply SCWAMP to each of them. If one or more of the SCWAMP elements doesn't apply, explain why.

2. We all buy into the dominant ideologies of our culture (SCWAMP) at some level, even if we don't fit into one or all of the SCWAMP elements. With a partner, list some of the ways that your beliefs or actions might reflect the dominant ideology.

3. Identify some popular culture texts that have helped you buy into SCWAMP and some that have helped you resist it. Explain how the texts support each position.

4. If you were going to retell this story in such a way that the SCWAMP elements wouldn't apply, what would you change?

5.4 THE WHITE MAN'S BURDEN: GONZO PORNOGRAPHY AND THE CONSTRUCTION OF BLACK MASCULINITY

Gail Dines

> *The author argues that a key to understanding how pornography works as a discourse is to analyze the role of racial representations in pornography. Doing so helps make clear the taken-for-granted assumptions about what makes pornography "pornographic."*
>
> *As you read this, consider why you think the author included language and examples that people might find offensive. How might the impact of this essay be affected if she had not done so?*

Recent articles in *Adult Video News*, the major trade magazine of the porn industry, have called attention to the fact that the fastest growing and most bootlegged sub-genre in hard-core pornography is "Interracial." While these Web sites advertise a multicultural

Reprinted by permission of the Yale Journal of Law and Feminism, Inc. from *The Yale Journal of Law and Feminism, 18*(1), 2006. Adapted by author.

mix of males and females, by far the dominant performers are Black men and White women. With titles such as *Black Poles in White Holes, Huge Black Cock on White Pussy* and *Monster Black Penises and Tight White Holes*, the male viewer knows what to expect when he punches in his credit card numbers. Although there are sites that advertise Asian and Latina women, there are very few sites with Latino and Asian men and White women. Indeed, if the heterosexual male wants to gaze at Asian or Latino men, then he has to move into a truly forbidden world for straight pornography, namely gay pornography.

Analyzing the role of racial representations in pornography is, I argue, key to understanding how pornography works as a discourse, as it explicates taken-for-granted assumptions about what makes pornography pornographic. If, as radical feminists argue, pornography is pleasurable because it sexualizes inequality between women and men, then the more degraded and abused the woman, the greater the sexual tension and thrill for the male viewer. It is indeed hard to conceive of a better way to degrade White women, in a culture with a long and ugly history of racism, than having them penetrated again and again by a body that has been constructed, coded, and demonized as a carrier for all that is sexually debased, namely the Black male.

PORNOGRAPHY AND MASCULINITY

In order to explore the way that race functions in pornography, it is important to first examine the contemporary world of Internet pornography, since the explosion of electronic pornography has had enormous implications for content as well as form. Mainstream pornography today looks nothing like the scrubbed, sanitized world of *Playboy*. In place of the "girl next door" smiling suggestively at the camera with her legs spread is the girl pornography consumers wished lived next door. Mainstream porn movies today are populated with what the male performers call "cumbuckets," "sluts," and "cunts" who love pounding anal, oral, and vaginal sex, who enjoy being smeared with semen and see their life's goal as breaking the record for the greatest number of "gang bangs" within a 24-hour period. Threaded throughout all these movies is an overt hatred for women that is evidenced in the dialogue and the fascination with body-punishing sex, such as frequent references to how much the woman can take before she breaks. Paul Little, AKA Max Hardcore, became famous (and rich) for his particular style of pornography, which specializes in extremely violent and degrading sex. On his Web site, he boasts, "I audition a new model, but she's too fat, so I make her puke-up all the piss I pump down her throat, after fucking ass & fisting cunt!"

It is no accident that Max Hardcore has more hits on Google than nearly any other male pornography performer, as his particular brand of "sex" has helped to define the contours of hardcore pornography, called Gonzo in the industry. By far the biggest money-maker for the industry, this type of pornography makes no attempt at a story line but is just scene after scene of violent penetration, in which the woman's body is literally stretched to its limit. To argue that the pleasure of heterosexual pornography for men is not somehow wrapped up in the degradation of women is to ignore the multiple verbal and image-based cues that form the codes and conventions of mainstream pornography (Jensen, 2005).

Moreover, failure to see pornography as a text about the elevation of men and the degradation of women also misses the role that pornography plays in the production of masculinity as both a category of material existence, and an identity that is contested, negotiated, and in need of constant reproduction (Jensen, 2007).

It is now a given in much of academic feminism that masculinity and femininity are social constructs that work together to produce a gender system that is fused with inequality, hierarchy, and violence (Cornell, 2005; Carby, 1998). Until recently, much of the analysis of masculinity sought to explain how hegemonic masculinity is defined in opposition to femininity, where hegemonic masculinity is unproblematically coded as White. However, as many Black scholars have argued (McBride, 2005; Neal, 2004), White hegemonic masculinity is always in negotiation with Black masculinity as the two exist in what James Snead (1994) calls "a larger scheme of semiotic valuation" (p. 4), in that the elevation and mythification of White masculinity relies on the debasement of Black men as sexual savages, Uncle Toms, and half-wits such as Stepin Fetchit. Patricia Hill Collins (2004, p. 187) goes further by arguing that Black masculinity is so debased by White culture that it becomes a fluid category whereby any man of color can become marked as Black should he in any way fail to conform to the strict disciplinary practices of White masculinity.

However, what constitutes hegemonic White masculinity is itself a moving target depending on the socioeconomic dynamics of a given time and place. In the United States, and indeed most of the Western world, there is a general consensus that a real man (read: White) works hard, puts food on the table and an SUV in the driveway, shows some interest in his children's welfare, and exhibits a somewhat restrained set of sexual practices within state-sanctioned heterosexual marriage. On virtually every level, Black men are defined by White culture as failing to meet the standards of White hegemonic masculinity. They are portrayed as shiftless, they need welfare to get food for their families, they drive pimp cars (when they can afford cars), and they engage in what Cornel West (1993) mockingly refers to as "dirty, disgusting, and funky sex" (p. 83). And this is the problem for White men. While they would not swap their material privileges with Black men, many White men would indeed like "Black" sex as it is seen in the White racist imagination, as "more intriguing and interesting." I argue that this White racist construction of Black male sexuality is what drives interracial pornography (IP), and serves to heighten the sexual tension in the pornography while simultaneously making this country an increasingly hostile and dangerous place for people (especially Blacks) who fall outside the markers of Whiteness.

According to *Adult Video News*, IP is emerging as the biggest single growing category of pornography, with one in four new films fitting into this sub-genre. A recent article quotes a producer who says "right now interracial gonzo is probably the strongest genre. . . . The demand for interracial far outweighs all other forms of gonzo" (*AVN Monthly*, 2005). Most of the producers and directors of IP are White, and the articles in *Adult Video News* speak to a White male audience that is increasingly looking for more IP and, moreover, desires it to go increasingly hardcore. The obvious question here is why do White men want to gaze at and masturbate to Black penises penetrating White women's vaginas, mouths, and anuses, given the historical coding of the Black penis as defiler of White womanhood and emasculator of White masculinity?

INTERRACIAL PORNOGRAPHY: LOOKING
FOR THE PRIMITIVE (BLACK) MALE

The most startling fact that jumps out at anyone who surfs these sites is the absence of men of color who are not Black. A more precise term for interracial would be Black men and White women, but in a society where the color line is defined by the binary Black/White categorization, such precision would be redundant. This binary system has engaged many theorists who seek to interrogate how race has been constructed in American history against the backdrop of slavery. One insightful analysis is offered by Snead (1994) when he writes, following W. E. B. Du Bois, that the "negro" is "the metaphor . . . the major figure in which those power relationships of master/slave, civilized/primitive, enlightened/backward, good/evil, have been embodied in the American subconscious" (p. 2). This does not mean that other races don't exist in America, but that Blacks are the "idealized" other, and different racial groups float between the two poles of the color line, depending on their economic, social and cultural status.[1] And since pornography is not a genre known for its subtlety, when it deals with race, it deals with the clear, uncomplicated racial categories that define American society, ideologically if not materially.

Since the race of the performers is the key to marketing IP, it is not surprising that the Black male tends to be very dark skinned and the White woman very blond. While skin color can vary among Blacks, blond hair is a clear signifier of White womanhood. One of the most popular series of IP movies is called *Blacks on Blondes*, which features blond women with multiple Black males. As in most IP, the blond performer is "applauded" for being able to take a Black penis in her White mouth, vagina, and anus. In one particular movie with "Liv Wylder" we see an example of a theme running through IP, namely the emasculation of the White man by the big Black penis. The text on the *Blacks on Blondes* site reads:

> Bring out the cuckold mask again! Time for another white couple to live out their naughtiest fantasy, and thanks to *Blacks on Blondes* for making it happen! Liv and Hubby have been married for a few years, and she wears her ring proudly. But lately the spark has left the bedroom, if you know what I mean. A few e-mails later, and we've got Hubby in a cage while Boz and Mandingo work Liv over. And when I say they work her over, we mean it. She takes so much Black dick it amazed even us. The best part of this whole deal was the end: after Liv has about a gallon of cum all over her face and clothes, and grabs a plastic bowl—for Hubby to beat off in. He does, and his wad was weak, and Liv lets him know that.

The White man's body is literally and metaphorically contained in this movie by both his Whiteness and the physical cage in which he is locked during the sex scenes. References to his poor performance in bed ("the spark has left the bedroom") and his ineffectual semen ("his wad was weak") stand in sharp contrast to the size of the Black men's penises, the skill of their sexual performance ("they work her over, we mean it"), and the amount of semen they produce ("a gallon of cum"). And to illustrate where the White woman's allegiance lies, the last line lets us know that Liv is only too happy to ridicule the husband in front of the Black men. Indeed, in many such movies, regular reference is made to the White woman's distaste for White penises after she has sampled a "real man's" penis. It is thus apparent why one popular series of IP films is called *Once You Go Black . . . You Never Go Back.*

In straight heterosexual non-interracial pornography, it is the woman's body that is scrutinized, talked about, focused on, and visually interrogated. In IP it is the Black penis that becomes the star of the show and, in keeping with the racist narrative of the sites, is routinely described as "huge," "enormous," "monstrous," and "gigantic," and "unbelievable." The Black penis is a source of much interest for the porn users, and on one site where users post their reviews of movies, there is a debate going on about the apparent authenticity of the Black penis in the movie *White Meat on Black Street*. Some of the viewers are outraged at what they see as the fake quality of the penis, while others express a desire to have such a penis. While the race of the user is not clear from the name (most use "anonymous"), the tone of the posts suggests a White male reader. One particularly angry viewer wrote "the dick is clearly fake. Watch how he has to hold it on. It doesn't cum realistically either. Stupid niggers trying to fake big dicks." This "heterosexual" viewer seems more entranced by the Black penis than the White woman's body and his sense of betrayal at having paid to see a real Black penis, and getting what he sees as a fake one, is palpable.

The Black men in IP are often described as thugs, pimps, hustlers, hip-hoppers, mofos and bros who live in the "hood" and drive "pimp-mobiles." The class markers here make apparent that it is working-class Black men who are sexual savages, and the most esteemed is the "Black pimp," who keeps his girls in line and has taught them all they need to know about being a "ho." Pimp-themed movies abound in IP, where the Black pimp is defined as the "king of the hood" who uses the particular skill that Black men "innately" have of combining sex and violence to turn Black "bitches" into "hos."

The pimp, thug/hustler Black man of the "hood" with the out-of-control body is not only a favorite of White straight men, but also seems to be a popular object of desire for gay White men. Titles such as *Blacks on White Boys*, *Ebony Dicks in White Ass Holes*, and *Black Bros and White Twinks* make clear who does what to whom in Interracial gay porn. The "hood" once again figures largely on the Web sites, where users are encouraged to become site members by clicking the mouse, which will let them "join the hood." It seems that White gay men can buy their way into the hood for a short (and contained) time.

In his analysis of the visual and verbal clues that inform the fetishized and commodified Black male body in IP gay porn, McBride (2005) suggests that such images "presume a viewer who is other to the experience of the man represented in the films" (p. 103). Moreover, the racial ideologies that make these images intelligible and pleasurable are the very ideologies that underscore mainstream White racism. As McBride argues:

> [H]ere in the form of typical images of black men in the mediated context of black gay porn, the viewer can enjoy fantasies about his sexual relationship to blackness without having to account for the possibly troublesome dimensions of the brand of thinking about race that he must necessarily bring to these images for them to work their magic, so to speak. (p. 103)

These "troublesome dimensions" are what need to be explained, not only for gay IP but also straight IP, and indeed for many of the images that have circulated and continue to circulate in White-owned and White-consumed media. IP does not exist in a world of its own but rather draws from, and contributes to, the hegemonic ideologies of race in America that have justified, legitimized, and condoned the deeply rooted systems of racial oppression. However, the way that IP articulates and rearticulates these ideologies is linked to the particular form of pleasure that it offers its readers, namely (White) masculinized sexual pleasure.

INTERRACIAL PORNOGRAPHY AS THE NEW MINSTREL SHOW

The pleasure that White audiences receive from consuming images of Blacks is complex and rooted in the politics of Whiteness as an identity that affords status, privileges, and a sense of belonging to some mythical (glorified) racial group. The above mentioned argument articulated by Snead, that the debasement of Blacks is linked to the elevation of Whites, is not hard to grasp given the vicious stereotypes of Blacks as savages, coons, half-wits, mammies, and Jezebels. Whiteness as an identity is a meaningless concept outside of the constructed notions of Blackness that Whites have produced and circulated in popular culture. Thus, in this wholly mythical world, to be White is to be the opposite of Black: It is to be hardworking, law abiding, intellectual, rational, and sexually restrained and controlled. These are all traits that in the everyday world have very real currency, providing status to those who operate with a clear allegiance to the culture of Whiteness. However, the world of pornography is actually a parallel universe where, for at least the time it takes to get aroused and ejaculate, the currency is one that is in direct contradiction to Whiteness. In this world, the traits of Whiteness are indeed a burden for the White man, since restraint of any type threatens to undermine the full sexual pleasure that can be achieved with a bevy of "sluts," "whores," and "cum buckets" willing to do anything you want. In this world, the mythical Black man who is uncontrolled, unrestrained, animalistic, and savage will always trump the uptight, contained, and penis-challenged White guy. Why then do White men who do not, in the real world, take kindly to seeing themselves as demasculinized by Black men, buy IP porn?

To look for possible answers to this conundrum, I suggest that we go back in time and examine another genre that poses similar questions for historians of race, namely the blackface minstrel shows that swept through America in the 1830s and 1840s. Much has been written about the politics of these shows, the ways that they encoded Blackness, and the pleasures afforded the White, mainly male audiences through displays of White actors in blackface "performing Blackness" by singing and dancing (see, e.g., Butters, 1998; Lott, 1995; Rogin, 1998). Some scholars suggest that once given the mask of Blackness, White men could "sing, dance, speak, move, and act in ways that were considered inappropriate for White men" (Butters, p. 10). While there is general agreement that these shows were unapologetically racist, historians suggest that multiple and contradictory pleasures were afforded the audiences, in that they identified both with and against the White performers in blackface.

Part of the identification process was facilitated by the fact that these shows did not employ some unrecognizable songs or melodies; instead, the musical style and structure borrowed heavily from European patterns. What was different, however, according to Deane Root, was in the style of the performance of the songs, which was "much cruder. It was . . . foreign. Out of the culture. . . . They were trying to exaggerate and make [something] exotic." In IP, the "songs or melodies"[2] are indeed similar to White-on-White porn since the sex acts between Black men and White women are the recognizable anal, vaginal, and oral penetrations. However, the style is, in a sense, exaggerated and cruder in its focus on "big Black dicks" pounding away at "small White orifices" that are stretched to foreign proportions. The aim here, however, is not so much to make the performance *exotic* as it is to make it *erotic*, since the sexual pleasure of IP is intensified by the increased sexual abuse of the woman, and the (partial) identification of the viewer with the hypersexual Black male.

The fact that Black men perform Black pornography rather than White men in blackface speaks to the ways in which White ownership of media and pornography has defined and continues to define the contours of Blacks playing Blacks as Whites see them. When Black men were eventually allowed on to the stage, they had to cork their faces and behave as the Whites did in blackface. The reason for this, argues Mel Watkins, is that Whites assumed that the minstrel shows depicted something real and essential about Blacks, because the shows "Were advertised as the real thing. In fact, one group was called 'The Real Nigs' . . . they were advertised as 'Come to the theatre and get a real look into what plantation life was like.'. . . It was advertised as a peephole view of what Black people were really like."

Rather than a peephole, IP porn is a peepshow for Whites into what they see as the authentic Black life, not on the plantation but in the "hood" where all the conventions of White civilized society cease to exist. The "hood" in the White racist imagination is a place of pimps, hos, and generally uncontrolled Black bodies, and the White viewer is invited, for a fee, to slum in the world of debauchery. In the "hood," the White man can dispense with his Whiteness and become his true authentic self, just like the Black man, and this authentic White man is as sexually skilled and sexually out of control as the Black man. Here he does not have to worry about being big enough to satisfy the White woman (or man), he does not have to concern himself with fears about poor performance or "weak wads" or cages like poor hubby in *Blacks on Blondes*. Indeed, the "hood" represents liberation from the cage, and the payoff is a satiated White woman (or man) who has been completely and utterly feminized by being well and truly turned into a "fuckee."

But before we celebrate the IP text as subversive and liberatory, we need to put the text in the context of the material world of racist America. The body that is celebrated as uncontrolled in IP is the very same body that needs to be controlled and disciplined in the real world. Just as White suburban teenagers love to listen to hip-hop and White adult males gaze longingly at the athletic prowess of Black men, the White pornography consumer enjoys his identification with (and from) Black males through a safe peephole, in his own home and in mediated form. The real, breathing, living Black man, however, is to be kept as far away as possible from these living rooms, and every major institution in society marshals its forces in this defense of White society. The ideologies White men take to the pornography text to enhance sexual pleasure is the very ideology they use to legitimize the control of Black men, and while it may heighten arousal for the White porn user, it makes life intolerable for the real body that is (mis)represented in all forms of White controlled media.

To ignore the racist codings of Black men in pornography in favor of a simplistic, decontextualized reading of the pornographic text as subversive is to operate in a world of White privilege where being a "fucker" is a status symbol with no real world burden. This burden belongs instead to the Black male and, of course, the entire Black community, and as long as academic discourse continues to assume a de-racialized woman or man, then our work will have little meaning outside of the few who have access to elite academic institutions. Meanwhile, the pornography industry can continue, unencumbered by academic or cultural criticism, to produce images that make *Birth of a Nation* indeed look like the good old days.

NOTES

1. The study of how different racial and ethnic groups became "White" illustrates the fluid nature of "race" and identity in this country. For a particularly insightful analysis, see Ignatiev (1995).

2. For an analysis of how pornographic films can be likened to musicals, see Williams (1989).

IT'S YOUR TURN: WHAT DO YOU THINK? WHAT WILL YOU FIND?

1. In what ways are the images of Black men in pornography similar (or different) to images of Black men in pop culture?

2. Talk to men and women friends and ask about their experiences with pornography. How do the men's and women's experiences differ?

3. Why do you think White men make up the majority of viewers of interracial porn?

4. How would you explain the virtual absence of Asian men in straight IR pornography?

REFERENCES

AVN Monthly. (2005, September). Ethnic diversity in adult: Can't we all just fuck along? Retrieved on December 17, 2005, from: http://www. adultvideonews.com/cover/cover0905_01.html

Blacks on Blondes homepage. Retrieved on December 16, 2005, from: http://blacksonblondes. iwantanewgirlfriend.com

Butters, G. R. (1998). *Black manhood on the silent screen.* Lawrence: University Press of Kansas.

Carby, H. V. (1988). *Race men.* Cambridge, MA: Harvard University Press.

Collins, P. H. (2004). *Black sexual politics: African Americans, gender, and the new racism.* New York: Routledge.

West, C. (1993). *Race matters.* Boston, MA: Beacon Press.

Connell, R. W. (2005). *Masculinities.* Berkeley: University of California Press.

Ignatiev, N. (1995). *How the Irish became White.* New York: Routledge.

Jensen, R. (2005). Empathy and choices: Rethinking the debate on pornography. *American Sexuality.* Retrieved on February 17, 2008, from: http://nsrc.sfsu.edu/MagArticle.cfm?Article=465

Jensen, R. (2007). *Getting off: Pornography and the end of masculinity.* Cambridge, MA: South End Press.

Lott, E. (1995) *Love and theft: Black face minstrelsy and the American working class.* New York: Oxford University Press.

McBride, D. A. (2005). *Why I hate Abercrombie and Fitch: Essays on race and sexuality.* New York: New York University.

Neal, M. A. (2004). *New Black man.* New York: Routledge.

Rogin, M. P. (1998). *Black face, White noise: Jewish immigrants in the Hollywood melting pot.* Berkeley: University of California Press.

Root, D. (n.d.). Interview excerpt. Retrieved on February 15, 2008, from: http://www.pbs.org/wgbh/amex/foster/sfeature/sf_minstrelsy_3.html

Snead, J. A., MacCabe, C., & West, C. (1994). *White screen, Black images: Hollywood from the dark side.* New York: Routledge.

Watkins, M. (n.d.). Interview excerpt. Retrieved on February 15, 2008, from: http://www.pbs.org/wgbh/amex/foster/sfeature/sf_minstrelsy_5.html

Williams, L. (1989). *Hard core: Power, pleasure and the "frenzy of the visible."* Berkeley: University of California Press.

5.5 "ME, ONLY BETTER!": REALITY MAKEOVER TELEVISION AND POST-FEMINIST GENDER IDEOLOGY

Laura Portwood-Stacer

"We help women transform their lives. . . . We rebuild and enhance their bodies . . . help them overcome life-long obstacles . . . and drive them to reach beyond themselves" (The Swan). *"I am a different person. I'm healthier, I'm younger, I'm just a little more powerful. . . . I have the ability to pursue whatever I want to pursue. I can pretty much conquer whatever I want to"* (Extreme Makeover).

The author analyzes reality makeover shows as products of a post-feminist culture. She argues that the site of women's empowerment is often the commercial sphere (rather than representing more traditional women's rights), and that, as evidenced in the quotes above, shows such as The Swan *and* Extreme Makeover *perpetuate the ideology that individualist consumption is an important means of feminine empowerment.*

Our popular culture is rife with stories of personal transformation, where individuals who make positive changes in themselves are rewarded with good fortune and the admiration of their peers. The lesson is usually the same—those who are beautiful on the inside deserve to be beautiful on the outside, and the attainment of external beauty brings fulfillment and happiness. Television has certainly tapped into the pleasure that audiences derive from this kind of narrative, perhaps nowhere more clearly than in reality programs. The reality makeover show tells the quintessential ugly duckling story: Everyday people, with the right attitude, tools, and advisors, can become beautiful. In 2004, *The Swan* debuted on Fox. This show was different than many of its predecessors—the women of *The Swan* achieved their personal transformations by undergoing a battery of drastic medical procedures to alter their physiques. In this chapter, I argue that the emergence of programs like *The Swan* at this particular historical moment is no mere coincidence. On the contrary, reality television's graphic representations of women's personal "improvement" through physical transformation can be understood as timely media products of contemporary post-feminist culture.

The term "post-feminism" is often used to refer to the dominant mode of gender politics to be found in contemporary popular culture. Although various scholars have produced multiple and complex characterizations of post-feminism, Angela McRobbie (2004b) offers a useful and concise definition of post-feminism as feminism taken into account. Feminism is "taken into account" insofar as it is generally recognized that the feminist movements of the 20th century resulted in important social gains for women, yet there is broad consensus that such movements are no longer needed. Whereas traditional feminism is concerned with critiquing social systems in which women are routinely disempowered and devalued, post-feminism discards these critiques in favor of a celebration of the ways in which women are empowered. While more conventional women's rights (including pay equity and reproductive freedom) remain tenuous throughout the world, there is absolutely no question about women's right to be active consumers. Thus the site of women's empowerment is often the commercial sphere—through decisions about what and how to consume, women take charge of defining themselves and shaping their immediate environments. Reality makeover television both reflects and perpetuates the ideology that individualist consumption is an important means of feminine empowerment.

In addition to situating empowerment within the commercial sphere, post-feminism also encourages women to turn their attention inward to themselves, often in the form of an intense focus on physical appearance. Such attention to the self is positioned as empowering insofar as individual self-improvement is seen as the means to attaining personal fulfillment, social power, and the love and respect of others. In other words, if a woman is unhappy, poor, disrespected, or unloved, there is no use tracing this state of affairs to oppressive social structures or unreasonable cultural standards. A woman should instead work on herself; by becoming a "better" person, she will achieve whatever goals have been previously unattainable. Such work on the self of course involves many acts of consumption, from the purchase of clothing and beauty products, to gym memberships and dieting guides, to dental procedures and cosmetic surgery.

Obviously, the cultural demand that women cultivate and maintain an attractive physical appearance is nothing new. What is fairly new is the normalization of surgical procedures as part of the feminine beauty regimen. Some feminists have objected to the very idea of cosmetic surgery, viewing it as a dangerous practice which women are manipulated into undergoing by the pressure of unrealistic standards of feminine beauty (Morgan, 1991). It may be true that our cultural beauty standards are unrealistic for most women to achieve naturally, but it is too simplistic to say that women are somehow duped into going under the knife. Real social rewards accrue to those women who understand and engage in the "disciplinary practice of femininity" (Bartky, 1990). That is, social acceptance is often conditional upon a woman's willingness and ability to bring herself in line with dominant gender norms. Therefore we must understand the decision to surgically alter one's appearance as a strategic move in a woman's ongoing efforts to embody the norms of female identity. The point is that women generally do not undergo cosmetic surgery because they feel forced to become beauty queens; rather, they may elect cosmetic surgery in order to attain a feeling of normalcy which might be necessary for their overall sense of well-being and belonging in society (Davis, 1995).

One of the ways in which makeover-type procedures are normalized is their positioning as part of the post-feminist project of self-empowerment. Thanks to earlier feminist movements, common sense has shifted away from the notion that women should be beautiful objects in the service of others' pleasure. The attainment of physical beauty is now positioned as important for a woman's own feelings of self-confidence; work on one's appearance is an act of self-love and a celebration of one's own potential. Reality makeover shows are a key site for this rhetoric of personal empowerment through physical alteration. These shows offer personal narratives of individuals as they undergo extensive cosmetic surgery as a way to "make over" their lives—the physical alterations are positioned as effective means through which one can achieve a more general life transformation. Thus the programs contribute to the normalization of cosmetic surgery and to the post-feminist version of feminine empowerment as they conflate personal fulfillment and individual achievement with the attainment of a physically ideal body.

MAKEOVERS ON REALITY TELEVISION

Although women have been receiving surface-level makeovers on television for over half a century now, shows featuring cosmetic surgery are a phenomenon unique to this particular historical moment.

The first major series to take cosmetic surgery as its central focus was ABC's *Extreme Makeover*. Each episode features two individuals (usually women) who "need" radical physical transformation, often due to some major personal goal such as changing careers, entering a new romantic relationship, or getting over a traumatic past. Their appearance has long been holding the women back from achieving their dreams, but with the help of *Extreme Makeover*, they will receive the boost in self-esteem necessary to achieve the desired life changes. We accompany the subjects on consultations with doctors and other beauty experts and are told about the numerous procedures they will undergo. These may include liposuction, chin implants, botox injections, breast implants, dental reconstruction, teeth whitening, laser vision correction, a nose job, brow lift, and tummy tuck, in addition to fitness training, new clothes, and hair styling. We follow the individuals through weeks of surgery and recovery, and into the "reveal," where the subject shows off her new look to her friends and family (and us).

FOX's *The Swan* is like *Extreme Makeover*, although the subjects are always women and *The Swan* introduces competition by setting up the two subjects of each episode as opponents for a place in the Swan pageant, to be held at the end of the season. Episode structure is much the same as in *Extreme Makeover*. The surgical procedures are similar, although *The Swan* also emphases dieting, psychotherapy, and "life coaching." The circumstances of the reveal are slightly different as well: The subjects are deprived of mirrors throughout the entire process, so their new appearance is revealed to themselves and the audience simultaneously.

There are numerous ways in which these programs work to normalize their particular version of physical transformation and personal empowerment. One is by the selection of subjects. The women are quintessential "ugly ducklings"; their looks have caused them to be neglected by their lovers, teased by their families, and ridiculed by their peers. The feeling of social rejection and physical inadequacy is utterly relatable for the female audience, thus they are immediately invited to empathize with the subject of transformation. In addition, most of the subjects come from working or lower-middle-class backgrounds, which taps into the broadly accepted ideology of the American dream, where those of a lower socioeconomic class can succeed at becoming middle-class citizens if they put forth the effort to take advantage of all the opportunities they are given. This discourse of class mobility is implicitly reinforced by the settings in each series. In *Extreme Makeover*, the subjects are whisked away from their rural or suburban homes to glamourous Los Angeles where they meet celebrity doctors, trainers, designers, and stylists. *The Swan's* home base is "the Swan Mansion," where the makeover subject finally experiences her reveal amidst the luxurious surroundings of an affluent lifestyle. The subtle message is that personal transformation will open the door to a better social milieu.

A second way in which the programs work to normalize their ideology of transformation is through the use of legitimating cultural authority figures. Most prominent among these are the doctors and other medical experts who advise the subjects about how to realize their ideal selves. The experts of *The Swan* and *Extreme Makeover* are characterized as ultra-qualified to plan and execute the subjects' physical transformations. This faith in the capacity for medical experts to work miracles of tranformation is underpinned by the shows' use of pseudo-scientific, technological imagery in describing the changes that will be made to the womens' bodies. On *The Swan*, for example, the woman's body is graphically displayed in a boxed-in grid, complete with cross-hairs, digital sound effects, and an inexplicable running set of numbers in the bottom left-hand corner. Off to one side, the various procedures that will be conducted appear as futuristic-looking bullet points.

Perhaps the most significant technique through which reality television attempts to win the audience's belief in the benefits of personal tranformation is indeed the *realism* of the genre. Because everything we see on screen has *actually taken place* (or so we should believe), it is tough to dispute the effectiveness of the physical procedures in achieving the happiness and fulfillment so clearly expressed by the subjects.

For the ideology of the reality makeover program to be credible, two aspects of realism must be attained—audiences must be convinced first, that the physical tranformation is real, and second, that the personal changes and resulting empowerment experienced by the women are real. Makeover shows perform their physical realism by doing work on actual bodies and by documenting every step of the process in excruciatingly graphic detail. The camera follows the subject into the normally private setting of the medical examination room, where it zooms in on her naked flab being grabbed, measured, and marked up. We are also present for the surgery itself, where we witness the slicing of skin, the insertion of implants, and the suction of fat. During the healing process, we see and hear the painful expressions of the subject, which confirm the harsh reality of the physical transformation. And finally, we are there for the spectacular reveal, when we can gaze upon the remarkable finished product.

In addition to putting the physical proof of transformation before our eyes, reality makeover programs are masters of emotional realism. At every step of the way, the audience is privy to the emotional state of the subjects. In the "confessional" the audience comes face-to-face with the women as they verbalize their feelings about their bodies, their lives, and their transformations, often breaking down in tears of shame, sadness, and gratitude. We cannot help but to empathize and identify with the women's desire to feel better about their bodies and, thus, themselves. Beyond the confessional, we are shown the positive emotional and social rewards won by the subject during her reveal—she squeals with pleasure at her reflection in the mirror, the hosts gasp and grin, friends and family members cry and embrace her, co-workers applaud. This not only naturalizes a faith in the positive physical effects of plastic surgery, but also affirms the contemporary post-feminist ideology about individual transformation and the rewards that come from constructing the perfect feminine self.

THE POST-FEMINIST GENDER IDEOLOGY
OF THE REALITY MAKEOVER PROGRAM

Given the increasing normalization of cosmetic surgery in the United States, it is no surprise that the reality makeover genre is so successful. Personal transformation through surgery is consistent with the context of post-feminism and contemporary commodity culture. All makeover programs are about becoming a better "you" by making better purchases and adopting better lifestyle habits. One *Swan* contestant captures this with her plea of, "I just want to be me again," while another woman declares, after her *Extreme* makeover, "It still looks like me, only better!" Cosmetic surgery programs not only capitalize on this ideology of improving the self through consumption, but are also products of this ideological climate which normalizes the consumption of medical procedures rather than—or in addition to—a new haircut or a new pair of jeans.

One of the problems with consumption as the site of citizenship and identity formation is that the social pressure to conform to dominant standards is masked by the rhetoric of choice provided by the free market. This is typical of post-feminist culture, in which political concerns about sexist and racist norms are dismissed as old-school ignorance about the freedom we all supposedly have to determine our own circumstances through our individual choices. A perfect illustration of this is that, despite the supposed freedom of individual expression experienced by women today, the overwheming trend in the makeovers depicted on *Extreme Makeover* and *The Swan* is a kind of mainstreaming—the construction of new, improved selves who eagerly conform to dominant norms of femininity.

The emphasis on conventional femininity is at times belabored to the point of absurdity. In one episode of *Extreme Makeover*, for example, a voice-over introduces one of the subjects with, "This woman works a man's job, but secretly wishes she was Cinderella." In another episode, a woman is literally given a lesson on how to be more ladylike, and confirms the importance of this when she announces, "I feel so feminine. It's an amazing what a difference that really does make." Of course, this newfound femininity wins the women social rewards—often their male partners are blown away at how "hot" they are, and their children express awe at how beautiful their mothers have become. For example, one woman's adult daughter gushes to the camera, "For her to feel beautiful and to feel pretty, you know, to feel like a woman should, then that is one of the most wonderful gifts that could be given to her, I think."

In addition to being a feminine body, the ideal body is also implicitly a White one; this becomes especially clear when the makeover subjects are women of color. Kinky hair is relaxed and straightened, wide or humped noses are reshaped, dark facial and body hair is lasered away. This enthusiasm for attaining an ideal-by-dominant-cultural-standards body is consistent with the ideology of post-feminism, which holds that women have the right to celebrate themselves and their achievements. What goes unstated (but always assumed) is that this right must be deserved by the individuals who exercise it—by having the right *kind* of self and the right *kind* of achievements.

The women undergoing surgery to improve their appearance state repeatedly that they want to be beautiful as a *means* to achieving their life goals. The underlying assumption is that appearance *is* one's character and capacity for achievement in all aspects of life. Indeed, according to Gareth Palmer (2004), "[makeover] television is possible because it is now widely agreed and understood that 'appearance is everything'" (p. 184). Within the contemporary media environment, the meanings inscribed on the bodily surface come to be increasingly central to individual identity.

It goes unquestioned that a surgical makeover will repair the psychological damage of such traumas as parental abandonment, the death of a loved one, depression, and general low self-esteem. For example, one *Extreme Makeover* subject seeks a transformation to overcome a poor self-image dating back to her childhood. The narrative positions her as the classic liberal subject who has overcome many obstacles to become successful. However, as this woman states, "The one thing I haven't overcome is my image." Time after time in this episode, her "image" is privileged as the site of the most important transformation, the one that will finally complete her process of self-actualization. As the narrator says "Elisa's nose [has been] reshaped, along with her poor self-image," Elisa's self-image is unproblematically bound to the state of her body. There is no acknowledgement that self-image might be much more dependent upon cultural pressures and psychological issues than actual physical appearance.

This lack of critical discourse is troubling, not only in reality makeover programming, but also in post-feminist culture in general. When the presumption is that individuals are free to make their own choices and are responsible for their own failings, the possibilities for political critique are shut down. Power becomes something individuals win for themselves through personal struggle and self-improvement, rather than something which is systematically denied to or collectively fought for by social groups. In this context, unreasonably restrictive standards of appearance and gender expression are not the problem—the only problem is your failure to live up to those standards. Hence the only solution is your own personal project of self-improvement, not a radical shift in cultural norms. Indeed, the feminist critiques of unreal standards of appearance come to seem, as McRobbie (2004a) points out, cranky and reactionary (and certainly old-fashioned). The historical feminist insistence that disciplinary femininity is a symptom and effect of gender oppression is even seen as *disempowering*, in that it supposedly denies women's agency and the pleasures they can win through personal transformation.

The celebration of the self is the post-feminist version of "empowerment"; it is a logic that implies that loving one's own (surgically enhanced) female body is as much a promotion of (post-)feminist values as staging a political protest with one's revolutionary sisters was 40 years ago. Within this context, a woman's right to citizenship is passé and hardly worth talking about; post-feminism now seems to be about a woman's right to sculpt her body to more closely approximate a constructed ideal. The un-tempered enthusiasm with which the subjects of reality makeover programs embark upon a project of self-actualization almost wholly within the consumer market differentiates and marks the new genre as part of a post-feminist media culture. Building upon the traditional liberal trope of the disciplined self in search of fulfillment against all odds, the new feminine subject transcends even the limitations of her own body to participate in a discourse that encourages her to "'imagine the possibilities' and close [her] eyes to limits and consequences" (McRobbie, 2004, p. 39). The message of reality makeover programming is that nothing, and certainly not your own body, can stand between you and what you want to become.

IT'S YOUR TURN: WHAT DO YOU THINK? WHAT WILL YOU FIND?

1. Within post-feminism, women are encouraged to empower themselves through consumption. Pay attention to the advertising you are exposed to in the next few days. What kinds of messages about "empowerment" are you getting?

2. Look for examples of makeover television programs or magazine articles from the past. What differences do you notice, in how makeovers and women's bodies are thought about? Are there differences in what counts as beautiful or

attractive? In what way does the text reflect the dominant gender ideology of their time?

3. We usually think of femininity as something that comes naturally to women, yet the women on reality makeover shows seem to struggle to acquire it. What might this tell us about the constructed nature of gender roles in our culture?

4. Do you think it is important that the makeovers in these programs are performed on "real" women? How might audiences engage with makeover programs differently if the subjects were celebrities or professional models?

REFERENCES

Bartky, S. L. (1990). Foucault, femininity, and the modernization of patriarchal power. In *Femininity and domination: Studies in the phenomenology of oppression* (pp. 63–82). New York: Routledge.

Davis, K. (1995). *Reshaping the female body: The dilemma of cosmetic surgery.* New York: Routledge.

McRobbie, A. (2004a). Notes on postfeminism and popular culture: Bridget Jones and the new gender regime. In A. Harris (Ed.), *All about the girl: Culture, power, and identity* (pp. 3–14). New York: Routledge.

McRobbie, A. (2004b). Post-feminism and popular culture. *Feminist Media Studies, 4*(3), 255–264.

Morgan, K. P. (1991). Women and the knife: Cosmetic surgery and the colonization of women's bodies. *Hypatia, 6*(3), 25–53.

Palmer, G. (2004). "The new you": Class and transformation in lifestyle television. In S. Holmes & D. Jermyn (Eds.), *Understanding reality television* (pp. 173–190). London: Routledge.

5.6 THE FEMINIST FAÇADE: THE CONSTRUCTION OF THE FEMALE PRESIDENCY ON PRIME-TIME TELEVISION

Emily Berg

The author analyzes two television programs featuring female U.S. presidents. Commander in Chief *and* Prison Break *push the limits of the glass ceiling: A woman penetrates the traditionally male-dominated world of the executive branch of the government. However, this is as far as these texts go in that push. As ground-breaking as a female presidential character could be, the author concludes that both of these representations are stereotypical and simplified and that in a post-feminist prime-time world, the characterizations of these women contribute to a feminist façade.*

Depicting women in positions of power in commercial media content can be a precarious task. Even as a text portrays female authority and ascendancy, to maximize a program's appeal, it must also stay true to social norms and values. This tension has been true across several genres of television programming for several decades. Commercial networks must appeal to a relatively large audience, while at the same time respond to increased pressure to present something new and different. Depicting a female president could be the ultimate test. It is an opportunity to show a woman holding the most powerful position in the United States and to prove that she belongs there.

So how has television balanced pushing norms while still appealing to social expectations? Examining two recent portrayals of a female president can help answer that question. Vice Presidents MacKenzie Allen and Caroline Reynolds take over the presidency to become female presidents on *Commander in Chief* (ABC) and *Prison Break* (FOX), respectively. Both programs premiered in the 2005–2006 television season; *Commander in Chief* lasted one season, and as of this writing, *Prison Break* remains on the air.

Although the character of a female president has the potential to take advantage of her position and use it to dispel stereotypes, aspects of each television series negate this possibility. Because the shows represent women in a traditionally "masculine" space, and who exhibit traditionally "feminine" characteristics, the depictions suggest that women need to conform to stereotypes. As cultural critics, we must acknowledge these hidden stereotypes and recognize that even surface-level strength could be a cleverly veiled reinforcement of gendered social norms.

The idea for this project came as I was watching an episode of *Prison Break* during its second season and reflecting on how much I thought the character of President Caroline Reynolds looked like Hillary Clinton. I was convinced that this was purposeful. I then recalled my attempt to watch *Commander in Chief* a year earlier, and how frustrated I had been with Geena Davis's character MacKenzie Allen. I went back and watched the entire season of *Commander in Chief*, and I slowly began to posit why I had been so frustrated. After comparing and contrasting the two characters, I came to the conclusion that both of these representations of the female presidents are stereotypical and traditional. They simplify the roles that women play and how women act. While depicting a female president may seem, at the surface, to be a move away from traditional expectations, the characters themselves do not fit this mold. *Commander in Chief* presents a domesticated president, a "good girl" who is perfectly situated in feminine space. *Prison Break* represents a manipulative president, a "bad girl" who uses her power to control men and dominate all political discourse. These portrayals do more to harm than they do to help the image of women in power.

Traditionally, the field of television studies has focused on gender roles in terms of identity and representation. Society holds preconceived notions of what particular genders are supposed to look and act like (D'Acci, 2004), and because television producers often work within those norms they play an important role in constructing social ideas (Brunsdon, D'Acci, Spigel, 1997; Dow, 1996). Many studies have focused on portrayals of women on television (Ang, 1990; Moseley & Read, 2002). As the field has evolved, more attention has been paid to the portrayal of gender, the social norms or questions that it puts forth, and the effect such representations might have on the overriding forces guiding gender politics.

Women in positions of political power represent a breaking of the "glass ceiling," right? If stepping into the office is enough, then yes. But what about how women are expected to act once they attain that position? Many feminists believe that women in power are forced to conform to stereotypes more than ever before, and that society has reverted to a "pre-feminist" state. In post-feminist theory, many have determined that "feminism" as a movement is a thing of the past. Much of our popular culture represents a return to dichotomizing women's roles between the professional and the domestic worlds. Women have traditionally been pushed toward fulfilling the roles of wife and mother (Campbell, 1983). Being "feminine" by social standards often means acting domestic, family oriented, caring, and relying on the heroic nature of men. Women who are typically "feminine" do not step outside this world. These "good girls" are the opposite of "bad girls," women who take hold of power and use it to manipulate men. Traditionally, this has been the fear that society has had with feminism. Feminists are often seen as scary, power-hungry women who will trample men on their path to gaining social superiority. Our popular culture reflects this tension. A woman is accepted if she maintains her feminine image. If she breaks out of this mold, it is feared that she will turn into a powerful and greedy nemesis to men. So what happens when a woman steps into the "masculine" space of the presidency (on prime time)? Apparently, she must either maintain her "good girl" behavior, or she will resort to "bad girl" tendencies. These two portrayals of female presidents do not give us the non-stereotypical portrayal for which we might hope.

Commander in Chief and *Prison Break* do push the limits of feminism: A woman penetrates the traditionally male dominated world of the executive branch of the government. However, this is as far as these texts go in that push. As ground-breaking as a female presidential character could be, the two series tend to embrace the domestic–professional, good girl–bad girl, submissive–overbearing, sweet–nasty dichotomies. A critique of the full first season of each program leads to several conclusions about popular culture's construction of a potential female president.

COMMANDER IN CHIEF: PRESIDENTIAL FEMININITY

Commander in Chief follows the beginning stages of the first female presidential administration. MacKenzie Allen is vice president under President Richard Bridges. When Bridges dies after complications from brain surgery, Allen becomes the first female president of the United States. Allen moves into the White House with her husband, Rod, and her three children.

Commander in Chief has constructed the female president as a woman who considers her domestic and familial duties just as important as her political ones. Domesticity shines and is the most important quality in terms of her obligation to her family, her place in domestic spaces, her maternal instincts, and the gender issues she confronts in her marriage. She is a "good girl," the ultimate feminine woman, maintaining her poise while always concerned with her household.

Allen attempts to fulfill her familial obligations as president and as mother in a way that is complicated and stressful. At times her presidential obligations get in the way of her perceived family obligations. For instance, Allen stops discussions of her first major plan of action as president to say goodnight to her daughter. Allen refuses official phone calls so she can speak with her children and frequently drops all work obligations to fulfill the needs of her family. In one episode, Allen simultaneously speaks with the National Security Advisor and reprimands her daughter Rebecca for having a boy in her room.

In addition to finding time to deal with family problems, Allen clearly prioritizes family dinners. After returning from a trip to Florida, Allen emphasizes that "she wants everyone home for dinner tonight." During a flashback of her days as a member of the House of Representatives, Allen cuts short a meeting with the Speaker of the House and says, "If you'll excuse me, I'd like to go home and have dinner with my family." These family dinners highlight Allen's dedication to holding her family together as a tight-knit unit.

The safety of her family constantly worries Allen as well. In one episode, a terrorist attack on a school causes Allen to worry about her family extensively. While this is a typical reaction, the script privileges Allen's familial concern over any political one. The attack happens just days before Halloween, and Allen is shown brushing her daughter Amy's hair while explaining the situation. Furthermore, because her husband is out of town Allen must balance caring for her family and the country. On the phone, Allen asks him, "Why do you think I couldn't sleep? Amy thinks I ruined Halloween, Rebecca is entertaining boys in her room, and Horace got into a fight." During that same episode, Allen looks longingly after Amy as she drives away to trick-or-treat, sad that she couldn't go with her. Allen's political obligations also seem to put a toll on the people in her family. Her children become increasingly uncomfortable with her status as president. In one episode, Allen and her husband discuss the possibility of her running for reelection. She states, "Maybe I shouldn't run; we are parents first." This suggests that it might be impossible for Allen to be both a successful parent and president, and that she would choose the former over the latter.

In addition to her own familial obligations, much of the show focuses on Allen being framed as the nation's "mother." She has maternal instincts and a particular dedication to education. Allen's character illustrates the concerns a female (president or not) is expected to have. The show opens with Allen sitting in the front row of a children's concert in Paris. The first thing she notices her first time in the Oval Office is a picture of the late president and his son. We also see her reading to children at a disaster relief site. Finally, while negotiating with the Chinese to save submarine troops from death in North Korean waters, she calls the mission "Operation Homecoming," as if to suggest her only prerogative is to safely return the troops home, just as a mother should do.

Domestication continues by continually showing Allen in traditional "female" spaces and situations. For example, in a flashback sequence, Allen is hosting congressional leaders at her home and they ask her to run for Congress. She is shown bringing in a cheese plate and casually sitting on the couch with her feet up with her arms around her husband. A congressman then says to Rod Allen, "Amazing wife you've got there. She spends her days putting murderers away and then she comes home and whips up a mean cheese spread." In addition to cooking, her casual demeanor, dress, and position was neither professional nor appropriate for the type of meeting she was having.

Allen also seeks the comfort of a man during times of crisis. Allen consistently turns to a trusted male advisor, whether the Speaker of the House, her husband, her chief of staff, or the national security advisor. After a particularly long day, her husband sends her staff home and takes care of her once she makes her way up to the residence. It is in fact he who convinces her to take the job as president. He sits at the head of the dinner table and constantly calls her "kiddo." Allen states that "Rod is protecting me; that's what he does." Rod solves problems and calms MacKenzie down, often jumping into "hero" mode to save the day.

There are several gender-role-based tensions between MacKenzie Allen and her husband, which leads to another aspect of presidential domestication. Rod is clearly uncomfortable with fulfilling the traditional role of "first spouse." There is a constant suggestion that the "First Gentleman" be responsible for being a host and in charge of the household, the menu, and other hospitality issues. There is a discussion of designer suits, office design and decoration, and other household duties. The power struggle for masculine and feminine spaces is hard on their marriage, and the tension is evident in the bedroom and at the dinner table. Rod eventually seeks comfort elsewhere and accepts the position of the commissioner of baseball. He says, "I am uncomfortable with the [job] I have here. You are where you should be; I'm not." However, after saving his wife during a political crisis, Rod decides he does want to work for the administration after all, but not in the capacity of "First Gentleman." He demands of his wife, "Make me a part of this administration, Mac, or this isn't going to work, professionally or personally."

A final example of a feminine Allen is her physical look, appeal, and actions. Her constant need to take her high heels off suggests that her heels obviously add stress to her life, but because of the requirements of women's fashion, she is forced to wear them. She frequently sighs with relief when she takes off her shoes. Allen always wears fashionable suits, often in satin and soft colors. This costume design makes her seem gentle and calm. Camera angles also construct Allen as smaller (despite the fact that the actress herself is 6 feet tall). Most of the time when she is in conversation with a powerful man, such as the Speaker of the House, the camera looks up at him and down at her, making the man seem much taller.

It could be insinuated that *Commander in Chief* overcompensates for the gender of its president and attempts to make her more masculine. MacKenzie Allen is called "Mac." The show's title, *Commander in Chief*, suggests that a female president would have to emphasize her ability to take control of military situations. The title insinuates that the show is not about the presidency as a whole, but the military aspects of the presidency. The majority of the issues that Allen deals with are either international military crises or "feminine" social dilemmas. It seems as if the show might want to prove that a woman can handle international crises, while still upholding her obligation to femininity in politics and her personal life. This, in combination with the domestication of the office, contributes to the construction of this post-feminist female president.

PRISON BREAK: **PRESIDENTIAL MANIPULATION**

Whereas Allen is a president in domestic turmoil, President Caroline Reynolds on *Prison Break* is causing political turmoil. Reynolds is not caring or feminine but evil and manipulative. This image suggests the negative impact of a woman stepping into a traditional male role. The show suggests that a woman with too much power results in a "bad girl," a woman who uses her wiles to control the nation, manipulate men, and achieve her own personal agenda, regardless of cost.

Prison Break, rather than featuring the female president as the primary character, follows the creation and effect of a female presidential regime on several prisoners. The main plot of the show focuses on two imprisoned brothers, Michael Scofield and Lincoln Burrows, who are planning a large-scale prison break. Over the course of the first season, a massive government conspiracy is revealed, with Vice President Reynolds as the spearhead. The conspiracy involves the staged murder of Reynolds's brother, in order to gain financial support for her campaign. Her brother was in fact never killed, although a body and a crime scene were planted as a cover-up. The prisoner, Burrows, was framed and convicted of this "murder." Reynolds follows the two brothers' every move as they attempt to break out of prison, trying to guarantee that the truth about the "murder" is never revealed. To gain political power, she eventually kills the president and steps into the role herself. Reynolds is a secondary character who appears periodically throughout the season and did not become president until the last episode.

The actions Reynolds orders are villainous. To frame Burrows, a gun and bloody pants are planted, and a surveillance tape is tampered with and later destroyed. To get Scofield transferred to another prison (so as not to interfere with his brother's scheduled execution), Reynolds orders her Secret Service henchman to blackmail the prison warden. She has a bomb planted in Burrows' lawyer's apartment. Her Secret Service agents commit several murders to help Reynolds attain her goals. They kill Burrows' ex-wife and attempt to kill his teenage son. Reynolds has her brother's teeth extracted to put in the body planted at the staged murder scene. Ultimately, she murders the sitting president so she can become president herself. These are just some of the many examples of the malicious acts performed at Reynolds' command. This "bad girl" would stop at nothing to take control of the country. She is always angry, mean, condescending, and fearless in doing whatever she needs to gain power.

Furthermore, all of the malicious acts were performed for Reynolds by men, suggesting that a woman can manipulate and control the men who work for her. This control was accomplished mainly through her language and her threats. She issued death threats on more than one occasion and also was consistently in command of every conversation. She controlled her brother, the men who worked for her, and many of her political opponents. In addition, when her men failed in one of their missions, Reynolds is not hesitant to bring in other men who could, in her mind, get the job done.

On her quest, however, Reynolds still is portrayed in some ways as feminine. The feminization of her actions happens when, in several instances, Reynolds gives her evil orders from female spaces. The first time she is on screen, we only see her hands. She is wearing a large diamond ring, talking on the phone, and chopping tomatoes. Not only is this an image of a woman, on the phone, wearing a diamond, and cooking, but it is also an image of Reynolds planning a murder with a sharp kitchen knife in her hands. She is chopping furiously, linking the domestic space with her murder plot. Reynolds also takes the presidential oath of office in a kitchen. In another instance, Reynolds is shown making a vegetable smoothie for her brother in a house in rural Montana. Her womanly manipulation is linked to womanly spaces.

Reynolds is strong and persuasive, always using her power to manipulate men. Because hers is a secondary character, unlike that of MacKenzie Allen in *Commander in Chief*, there are fewer examples from which to draw. However, Reynolds's influence is as great, if not greater than Allen's. Her cunning ways drive the plot and enhance her influence as vice president and president. To her constituents, she appears a benevolent leader; she is shown often giving press conferences suggesting that she is the victim of familial grief. However, she secretly carries out malevolent plots to ruin the lives of others. She is a woman who wields power through her threats, creating a presidency built on manipulation and fake altruism. She is popular culture's example of a female presidency gone awry. The fear of women's ability to control men when not confined to feminine space is illustrated and shown to be formidable. Reynolds is a woman who takes advantage of her power and uses it for evil.

THE FEMINIST FAÇADE

Prime-time television has constructed female presidents with two very distinct personalities. One is caring, kind, and motherly; she is the ultimate feminine woman. The other is manipulative, controlling, and immoral; she is a woman to be feared. *Commander in Chief* and *Prison Break* are two prime-time dramas that encompass what might be popular culture's conception of what a female presidency should look like. One keeps a woman in her feminine space, and one uses feminine space to suggest corruption and hostile control.

Popular culture may influence the political happenings of the day. Media constructions of candidates in advertisements and debates can play an integral role in shaping how the candidates look to the public. It is safe to assume then, that even a fictional image of a female president (particularly one that resembles contemporary politicians such as Hillary Clinton, as does Reynolds in *Prison Break*) might affect what Americans expect or hope (or even fear) a female executive will be like. Whether this is a family-oriented woman who is in some ways subservient to the men in her life or a devious woman who manipulates the men surrounding her for her own nefarious purposes, female presidents on these two television dramas conform to typical female stereotypes. These two presidents represent a "good girl" and a "bad girl," an angel and a devil. The women have penetrated the male, professional space—but as ideally domestic or brazenly villainous figures. These representations of women in power, which may at first blush seem positive and edgy, are instead stereotypical and simplified. In a post-feminist prime-time world, the characteristics of these women contribute to a feminist façade. With female presidential characters, a boundary seems to have been breached. Beneath this feminist surface, however, the women still exhibit idealized and expected forms of female behavior.

IT'S YOUR TURN: WHAT DO YOU THINK? WHAT WILL YOU FIND?

1. Do television portrayals accurately reflect reality, or do they simply portray stereotypes that are not applicable to general society? Think of examples of other television shows that portray stereotypical characters.

2. Are the depictions described in this chapter positive or negative for society? Imagine a scenario that does not show women in traditional ways. Do you think it would be popular? Why or why not?

3. Are these stereotypes present in real life? How should a female president behave? What should be the role of a female president's husband?

4. Pick another television show that pushes limits and depicts characters in nontraditional spaces. What other social views are portrayed on prime-time television? Just how far can television go?

REFERENCES

Ang, I. (1990). Melodramatic identifications: Television fiction and women's fantasy. In M. E. Brown (Ed.), *Television and women's culture* (pp. 75–88). London: Sage.

Brunsdon, C., D'Acci, J., & Spigel, L. (1997). *Feminist television criticism: A reader*. Oxford, UK: Clarendon Press.

Campbell, K. K. (1983). Femininity and feminism: to be or not to be a woman. *Communication Quarterly, 31*(2), 101–107.

D'Acci, J. (2004). Television, representation, and gender. In R. Allen & A. Hill (Eds.), *The television studies reader* (pp. 373–388). London: Routledge.

Dow, B. J. (1996). *Prime-time feminism: Television, media culture, and the women's movement since 1970.* Philadelphia: University of Pennsylvania Press.

Moseley, R., & Read, J. (2002). Having it *"Ally"*: Popular television (post-)feminism. *Feminist Media Studies, 2*(2), 231–249.

5.7 TALKING ABOUT RACISM ON *THE OPRAH WINFREY SHOW*

Janice Peck

> *Oprah Winfrey addressed racism in a year-long series of shows called "Racism in 1992." The author argues that even though racism was presented as a "bad" thing, and overtly racist statements were criticized, the series was far less likely to challenge "inferential racism." As a result, many racist implications of what was said on the show were left unexplored. Further, the series treated the "problem" of racism as one rooted in individual attitudes and behavior, rather than in a historical, political, and institutional context.*

Applauding the impact of her talk show, book club, magazine, movies, and charitable activities, *Time* named Oprah Winfrey one of the 100 most influential Americans of the 20th century. Because, according to *Ebony*, Winfrey's popularity "transcends race," she can't afford to forget that a majority of her predominantly female fans are White, especially when her program addresses racial issues. On Martin Luther King Day in 1992, Winfrey introduced the first installment of "Racism in 1992," a year-long, 13-episode series on racism, including two shows taped in Los Angeles shortly after the Rodney King verdict uprising.

The series didn't take a neutral stance toward racism, which was depicted as "bad" even by participants who expressed racist sentiments. But because the show employs the media's preference for dramatic conflict, and given the conflict-ridden history of U.S. race relations, the series included expression of racist views by many of its 150 guests and more than 2,000 studio audience members. While overtly racist statements were usually criticized, less often challenged was "inferential racism"—ways of interpreting events and situations related to race that are based on unquestioned racist premises and assumptions. Inferential racism's relative invisibility lets speakers remain unaware of the racist implications of their utterances. For example, many Whites in the series identified "not being racist" with "not seeing color," oblivious to the impossibility of such myopia for people of color in the United States. As the norm against which others are judged, "Whiteness" is the "absence of color," so that "not seeing color" means seeing everyone as "White." For those

From "Talk About Racism: Framing a Popular Discourse of Race on *Oprah Winfrey*," by Janice Peck, 1994, *Cultural Critique* 27 (Spring), pages 89–126. Copyright 1994, the University of Minnesota Press. Reprinted and adapted by author with the permission of the University of Minnesota Press.

who don't identify themselves as "White," this erases a basic aspect of their existence. It also implies they can be seen as "equal" only if they're willing to accept this erasure.

Inferential racism's "invisibility" relies on ideologies of race that are part of the social conditions into which we're born, and through which we acquire racialized identities, understand others based on race, and interpret social relationships within racial categories. Ideologies are frameworks of meaning rooted in dominant societal values and embedded in key social institutions, such as the law, education, the media, and the family. Through these institutions, ideologies shape our understanding of the world and our conduct; through our conduct we participate in maintaining and perpetuating our society's ideologies. The media draw on and circulate these ideologies and, through a process of selection, emphasis, inclusion and exclusion, provide a "frame" for understanding race and racism.

In Winfrey's series, racism was organized within three interpretive frames—a liberal political philosophy, a therapeutic view of relationships, and a generic religiosity. These frameworks can also be considered as "discourses," or ways of conceptualizing and discussing racism that determine how people are expected to interact and what they can legitimately talk about. These three discourses or interpretive frameworks played a powerful role in defining the nature of the "problem" of racism by treating it almost exclusively as a result of individual attitudes and behavior. In failing to examine racism as a historical, political, and institutional phenomenon, the program necessarily envisioned solutions at an individual level, which allowed Winfrey to tackle a profoundly divisive issue in American society without alienating her majority White audience or jeopardizing her appeal.

LIBERALISM AND THE CODE OF INDIVIDUAL RIGHTS

Liberal political philosophy is based on the primacy and autonomy of the individual. It sees human beings as "owners" of themselves and fundamentally motivated by self-interest. Capitalism is understood as the natural outcome of self-interested individualism and society as a collection of individuals pursuing their interests. The ability to engage in this pursuit without constraint constitutes individuals' rights, and equality is the condition in which all individuals have equal access to the means to pursue their private ends.

In "My Parent Is a Racist," a young White woman who dates people of other races against her mother's wishes says race "doesn't matter" because "each person is an individual and you get to know them as an individual. . . . I don't look at their color or their sex or anything else. It's a person and you learn them as a person." In the first L.A. session, a White woman says she doesn't have problems with race "because I don't really see color. . . . I try not to because everybody's an individual. People are so different. Some of them are terrible and then some of them are really nice, of all colors." In "An Experiment in Racism," the audience was divided into blue-eyed and brown-eyed groups and the former was mistreated in the first half of the show. Several "blue-eyes" resented being judged by a physical trait rather than being seen "as individuals." Their indignation didn't subside even when other audience members and guest expert Jane Elliott explained that the exercise was designed to let them experience discrimination first-hand.

Because liberalism identifies freedom with people's right to choose their own beliefs and actions, it limits the way racism is discussed and the extent to which it can be criticized without violating individuals' freedom to think, feel, and believe as they choose. In "My

Parent Is a Racist," Ron opposes his daughter dating a Mexican American but doesn't consider it racism because "I don't see where it's causing a problem in my life or anyone else's life. . . . I'm the type of person that believes it's wrong." In the concluding episode, Winfrey asks a White guest if the show had changed his views about Blacks. His reply: "No. I don't think that my thoughts were incorrect. . . . unless we change the name of this country from America, I still believe I have the right to have the beliefs and thoughts I have." When opinions are seen as the property of individuals, the expression of one's opinion is a natural right and must be respected regardless of its content.

This "code of respect" (Carbaugh, 1988) threatened to break down in the volatile Los Angeles sessions and "Experiment in Racism." In these shows, Winfrey enforced the code by controlling the microphone and issuing verbal reminders (e.g., "Ladies and gentlemen, we made a vow to each other that we would be heard in this room"). Tolerance of different (including racist) views is buttressed by the assumption that all people speak only for themselves as individuals exercising their rights. When a White male guest calls Native American protests against derogatory sports team names "utterly ridiculous," an audience member retorts, "if he thinks he's representing White people, I don't want to have anything to do with him." The man replies, "I'm representing myself." This allows both speakers to claim validity for their positions within the code of individual rights and respect. In the series finale, a young White woman who had been criticized in the L.A. sessions for defending the jury's decision is dismayed that "everybody was just bashing each other and nobody would listen to every other opinion. Everybody is entitled to their own opinion." Winfrey replies: "Absolutely. This is America. You're absolutely right." In another episode, an African American woman says Black men are attracted to women who are "docile and White." When Winfrey challenges this generalization, the panelist replies, "I'm just saying that in my particular instance, that's just what I perceive." Winfrey responds, "which is good, to speak from your own personal experience." If our opinions arise from our own experience, then, to disagree with us is to trample on our rights as individuals.

It thus becomes difficult to justify liberalism's desire to correct racially based inequities among different social groups when the code of the individual can be used to criticize racial stereotyping (defined as a failure to recognize people as individuals) *and* to refute the argument that racism is practiced by and directed at social groups. This is apparent in "White Men Who Fear Black Men" when Winfrey asks the White panelists if they "feel a sense of historical guilt . . . because of what's happened to Black people?"

> **Joe:** Not in the least, because I did not commit these crimes. I don't feel that the White race—I mean, how long can we continue to be guilty?
>
> **Chuck:** Well, I have no control over what happened in the past. And I feel I didn't have anything to do with it, just as Joe feels the same way. . . . The Black race has no control of what individuals do. That's the way I feel. Just like the White race has no control over individual acts. So why should we feel anything against a race per se, just because of individual acts?

Several White guests denied that people of color have suffered collectively from racial oppression, citing their own or acquaintances' having overcome personal hardships as proof that Blacks or Native Americans are "not taking personal responsibility" or have "a chip on their shoulders." Although Winfrey counters, "We all tend to individualize what went on in our lives without looking at how racism is systematically carried out from year to year," she's undermined by her acceptance of the individual code that pervades the series. In "Japanese–Americans: The New Racism," a White guest accuses the Japanese of "infiltrating" the U.S. economy. Winfrey responds, "But isn't what you're saying dangerous? When you say 'they do'—when you start looking at individuals as a group—isn't that very dangerous? Isn't that racism itself?"

The liberal frame defines racism both as unequal rights among different social groups *and* as a violation of individual rights by placing people within those groups. In either case, solutions must not infringe on individuals' rights to believe and act as they choose. The consequence is to remove race relations from a historical, political context. Our race becomes an individual characteristic, as does our attitude toward the race of others. Because liberalism lacks a basis for asking some individuals to give up some of their rights (privileges) to benefit others, it's trapped in a contradiction that generates the need for another framework for talking about racism.

THERAPEUTIC DISCOURSE AND RACISM AS DISEASE

A therapeutic way of thinking about self and society, which pervades American culture, shapes the way we think about ourselves, relationships, institutions, and politics. The therapeutic perspective translates everything into individual, interpersonal terms; expects that any problem can be improved through communication; favors feeling over other modes of experience; makes individual experience the primary source of truth; and encourages "taking responsibility" for our own feelings and behavior based on the belief that we're powerless to change anything beyond our own lives.

Winfrey's fondness for this therapeutic perspective, which dominates talk shows generally, reinforces its use in the racism series (Peck, 1995). Racism becomes an individual psychological phenomenon by labeling it "prejudice," connoting a natural human tendency to mistrust the unfamiliar. It can then be separated from race (one can be prejudiced against men, or attorneys, or dogs) and universalized as an innate human tendency (everyone has some forms of prejudice). Prejudice can be corrected by educating people to new patterns of thinking (with better information, we'll reject stereotypes and discard prejudices). This way of conceptualizing racism occurs often. In "Too Little, Too Late," Winfrey calls racism "ignorance personified," which individuals have a responsibility to overcome. A Native American guest suggests that "maybe we don't have an issue of racism here" but a problem of lack of information. In "My Parent Is a Racist" (where all three guest parents deny they're "prejudiced" while uttering blatantly racist statements), one panelist blames their attitudes on ignorance: "When people are sitting here saying they can't know whether we're prejudiced or not, it's because we lack the understanding or the knowledge of it."

Racism is seen as an attitude driven by unconscious motives and hidden anxieties. Winfrey states that "the whole concept of racism is based in fear." We fear what we don't know or understand. Prejudice, she says, can be "passed from one generation to the next without even knowing it." A Black guest agrees: "White racism is learned and it is a condition. It's part of a social condition, and any circumstances can trigger it." Seeing racism as a "condition" fits with the therapeutic affinity for disease metaphors. Guest expert Elliott says that to judge people "by the amount of a chemical in their skin" is to "have a mental problem." The effects of racism are psychologized by a Native American guest who says stereotyping of Native people "contributes to the low self-esteem of our teenagers, and low self-esteem is the main cause of teenage suicide, and we have the highest teenage suicide rate of any population in this country."

In the therapeutic model, the first step in dealing with one's problem is to admit it exists. In "Are We All Racist?" Winfrey explains that "you can't begin to solve the problem unless you admit there is one." Elliott admonishes people to "learn about your own racism. First, admit that you have that problem. Then we've got to stop denying it." This therapeutic "breaking out of denial" is prominent in the premiere episode featuring a family of former Ku Klux Klan members. The parents acknowledge their problem and locate it in their childhood: "We were taught to hate and that's basically what we did. We hated everybody that was not White." They passed on the "disease" to their daughter, who says she was "taught to hate the niggers, as they were put, and the queers." They examine the psychological effects of their pathology: "I had so much hatred in my heart. . . . You get where you can't sleep, the things you do, the things you say. I got to drinking pretty heavy trying to sleep. . . . It destroys your whole family." As in therapy, this revelation is acknowledged sympathetically.

> **Winfrey:**   I have to believe that somebody filled with this much hatred [would] have to have a miserable life.
>
> **Guest expert Kesho Scott:**   This is an example of one of the ways that we have to understand racism in the '90s as something that does not just hurt people of color. . . . You're seeing how racism hurt them.

Confession is prerequisite to a "cure." Winfrey confesses to using the phrase "honest injun" in an interview and later feeling ashamed when confronted by a Native American viewer. Elliott tearfully admits to being "infected with racism at birth. I want to get over it. It is going to take me the rest of my life to get over it, but I can do it, but I have to choose to do it." The final episode is organized around confession as guests, audience members, and viewers testify how the series helped them stop denying their problem of racism and move toward recovery. Several White guests who had earlier expressed racist feelings offer as proof of their recovery that they no longer "see color" but now view everyone "as individuals." When racism is situated within therapeutic discourse, solutions are framed as "healing." In the second L.A. session, actor Lou Gossett empathizes with the audience's discontent but rejects angry solutions: "If it has to do with violence, I won't join you. I'll understand, but when you get to the healing, please call me." Winfrey joins in: "We are a country in need of healing."

Because it treats all problems at the level of the individual psyche, the therapeutic framework cannot formulate a vision of a non-racist society beyond one comprised of "healthy" individuals. Based on the view that healthy people have overcome unconscious constraints, are free to choose their attitudes and behavior, take responsibility for their thoughts and feelings and let go of the need to control others, the therapeutic frame lacks a basis for expressing a *social* ethic because the only grounds for moral judgment is one's personal experience. In fact, to take responsibility for others is to regress into pathology (to be "codependent"). The absence of a socially based morality creates a need for another approach to racism.

RELIGIOUS DISCOURSE: ALL WE NEED IS LOVE

Religious discourse draws on traditional religion to endow public issues with moral authority. It's strongly influenced by Protestantism, the dominant religious orientation in the United States, which is based on individual salvation. A redeemed society is a collection of redeemed individuals, but the obligation to be saved rests with the individual whose personal salvation isn't dependent on the actions or fates of others.

Religious discourse relies on the notions of "understanding" and the equality of people before God, stressing unity over division as the collective basis for moral behavior. The problem of racism is defined as a lack of understanding, failure to recognize others as divine creations, a violation of the "golden rule," and spiritual disharmony. Religious language appeals to authorities (God, spiritual leaders, religious teachings) and often employs imperative terms ("ought," "should"). In the premiere episode, a Black woman in the audience asserts, "God has made all of us equal, no matter what color our skin is." A White female audience member in "My Parent Is a Racist" proclaims, "We are all of different colors and different faiths, but we are all human beings and we should love each other just because we're human beings, not because of color." In "Experiment in Racism," Elliott tells a White man who says God created racial differences, "God created one race, the human race, and human beings created racism." A White male in the L.A. sessions whose brother was killed in the riots asserts, "I've been raised all my life that if this man here [points to a Black audience member] cuts himself shaving and I cut myself shaving, the blood in the cup's the same thing; if they lay him and me on a slab somewhere and peel our skin off, unless you're an expert, you don't know who we are, and that we all have a soul that comes from one God."

The emphasis on unity and love leads to rejecting anything that threatens these values, in particular *anger*. The series associates anger with psychological and spiritual illness, disharmony, violence, immorality, a breakdown in communication, and ultimately with racism itself. This view of anger is consistent throughout the series, as is the assumption that it can be eliminated through communication and understanding. The closing sequence of the L.A. sessions affirms this message by interspersing shots of angry South Central Los Angeles residents with clips of Martin Luther King rejecting violence and Rodney King saying, "We can get along here." This theme is reiterated elsewhere. During a heated exchange in "Are We All Racist?" Winfrey breaks in: "you can get a lot more said through . . . calmly expressing your feelings than through everybody being angry, because the idea behind this show is to promote understanding."

Winfrey says the L.A. sessions are intended to help viewers understand "why are Black people so angry?" But while South Central residents are expected to explain their anger, they're not supposed to *be* angry when they do it. In both sessions, when speakers' statements become too heated, Winfrey defuses them by switching to another speaker or cutting to commercial. Gossett asks participants to replace anger with "solutions"—"I don't want you to walk out of here angry." "Experiment in Racism," intended to educate Whites about the experience of racism and promote "understanding," backfired because so many White audience members took offense at being "discriminated against" by an "angry" Jane Elliott. Several people walked out during the show, leaving Winfrey visibly shaken.

Anger can be overcome through understanding and forgiveness, as expressed by a Black participant in the LA session: "We need to understand each other. OK. We can't point fingers at each other and say we're all wrong or we're all right," and by a White participant: "like Martin Luther King has stated, it's the renewing of the mind and the spirit, and we have to start a healing process and stop continuing to point a finger, but to look in the mirror and to forgive, start forgiving and loving one another as human beings." Those who are "prejudiced" are encouraged to forgive themselves for harboring anger and racist attitudes and seek forgiveness from those they've harmed; victims of racism are encouraged to release their anger and forgive their transgressors. A Black woman is asked if she's been able to forgive the White mob who murdered her husband in 1946. She replies that living "with all that hate" toward Whites had made her ill, so she decided to pray and "leave it in the hands of the Lord." In another episode, a White audience member says prayer will stop racial hatred: "We should pray more instead of arguing and fighting. If you want to stop racism, pray and ask God to make the change." The former Klan family testifies to finding salvation from racism in God and asks their Black neighbors' forgiveness.

In its quest for a common moral ground to overcome racism, religious discourse frames solutions in primarily individual terms: To end racism, individuals must change the way they think, feel, and behave. Winfrey states in the premiere program, "true racial harmony [begins] from the heart." The White wife of a Native American asserts, "We all have to understand that we have got to better our society, and in order to do that, we're going to have to change within ourselves." A Native American woman suggests that ending racism is an "individual choice" involving a willingness to "stop behaving badly to each other." In the first L.A. session, a White woman argues that racism won't subside "until we decide to look into our hearts" and "take responsibility for our own actions." A White audience member proposes that racism can't be solved "unless we start making a difference and everybody does their own part," to which Winfrey responds, "each individual is a part of the society. That's how you start to change it." Thus, the solution to racism comes from individuals choosing to understand, overcome ignorance, reject anger, be fair, seek healing, and love their fellow individuals—all of which are envisioned apart from questions of politics and institutionalized power.

THE LIMITS OF INDIVIDUALIZED SOLUTIONS TO THE PROBLEM OF RACISM

Liberal discourse defines racism as "unfair" and proposes solutions in terms of individuals choosing to extend rights to others to create a *fair society*. Therapeutic discourse diagnoses racism "unhealthy" and sees the solution in individual quests for personal recovery that will produce a *healthy society*. Religious discourse judges racism "wrong" and poses solutions in terms of individual changes of heart that will lead to a *redeemed society*. These interpretive frameworks assume racism will be solved if individuals will simply change their perceptions, feelings, and behavior. Sampson (1981) argues that emphasizing the "primacy of inner events and transformations over external events and transformations" implies that individuals can achieve "harmony" by "abandoning the hope of affecting material reality and learning rather to change themselves" (pp. 735–736). By framing racism as a purely personal problem, "Racism in 1992" enabled Winfrey, participants, and viewers to feel good about themselves without raising far more difficult questions about how racism is embedded in our social institutions and how those institutions have shaped us as social subjects in the first place.

IT'S YOUR TURN: WHAT DO YOU THINK? WHAT WILL YOU FIND?

1. If Winfrey's show were to emphasize the social, institutional dimensions of racism, what kinds of things might it have included? Given the dominant therapeutic orientation of talk shows, is it possible for these programs to tackle issues like racism other than as an individual "dysfunction"?

2. Compare the treatment of racism in Winfrey's series to its treatment in other media forms (e.g., newspaper and magazine articles, television and film documentaries, feature films, Web

sites). Do you see evidence of the interpretive frames discussed here? What are the strengths and weaknesses of these different treatments of racism?

3. Does the intended audience affect the way racism is or can be addressed? Might Winfrey's series have examined racism differently if most of her viewers were African American? If so, how?

4. Should we try to solve racism by "not seeing color"? Why or why not?

REFERENCES

Carbaugh, D. (1988). *Talking American*. Norwood, NJ: Ablex.

Peck, J. (1995). TV talk shows as therapeutic discourse. *Communication Theory, 5*(1), 58–81.

Sampson, E. E. (1981). Cognitive psychology as ideology. *American Psychologist 36*, 730–743.

5.8 QUEER LIFE FOR THE STRAIGHT EYE: TELEVISION'S COMMODIFICATION OF QUEERNESS

Laura Stempel

> *The author discusses the representation of lesbians, gays, and bisexual and transgender people on television, focusing most closely on the shows* Queer Eye for the Straight Guy *and* Queer as Folk. *She argues that queer life has been "commodified" for the straight audience.*

In many ways the 1990s and early 2000s have been a boom time in television's presentation of gay, lesbian, bisexual, and even transgender people. Major commercial networks and important cable services have devoted episodes of major series to the lesbian, gay, bisexual, and transgender (LGBT) "lifestyle," and many performers, both straight and queer, seem to have overcome the longstanding fear that taking on a gay role would typecast them forever. There's no question that this is good news: It's impossible to overestimate the value of giving LGBT viewers a chance to see people like themselves in the mass media and of providing non-LGBT viewers with a reminder that, as the bumper sticker says, we are everywhere. But it's also important to recognize that the queer world presented on TV is as much of a media construction as every other world in the television landscape, and that it is packaged specifically for sale to a mass audience. In fact, that's precisely what's new here: Queer life is no longer simply a subject of interest to those who live it, but has been newly commodified for straight eyes.

DEFINING THE TERMS

Commodification is a key idea in political and economic theory, particularly in explanations of the rise of capitalism or market economies. Commodification refers to a process by which objects become things for sale; usually items that were originally made in the home for personal use, such as clothing or food, are turned into or made specifically to be commodities, or objects to be bought and sold. Under late industrial capitalism, which is based on mass production and mass consumption, a successfully commodified object must appeal to a mass audience. The wider its appeal (e.g., brand-name jam for grocery store shoppers), the more money it makes, and to achieve that goal, it must be designed and produced in a form that most potential buyers will want. There are occasional flukes in which an item that is initially aimed at a narrow audience becomes a hit with a larger one—think of Hummers or Starbucks—but capitalist success isn't based on flukes. While some describe the practice of appealing to a mass audience as catering to the lowest common denominator, it's the "common" rather than the "lowest" that matters. It's not that there's no market for an object without a mass appeal. It's just that if a product doesn't appeal widely, it must move to a more specialized market where a smaller group of shoppers may be willing to pay a higher price for something more individualized (e.g., organic jam sold in gourmet food stores).

This process occurs whether the object is something tangible that can be sold directly (jam) or something intangible that must be "bought" in a more subtle way. An important feature of Marxist theory was the extension of the concept of the commodified object to political and cultural ideas, identities, beliefs, personal relations, and even to people themselves. For commodification of these intangibles and abstractions to work, however, something normally thought of as lying outside of financial relationships—for instance, love—must either be connected to something that can be sold, such as matchmaking Web sites, or somehow be assigned an economic value so that it can be put up for sale. While the appeal to a mass commercial audience is still necessary, it happens in a slightly different way than in the selling of jam or T-shirts. The commodification of ideas or relationships requires an act of simplification that usually draws on familiar definitions of the particular intangible and on received notions about how the world works. Love can happen "at first sight" but is best experienced in the context of a serious relationship—hence the TV ads for online dating services celebrating successful matches that somehow also involve the partners' instant recognition that they've met their perfect mate. The point of this process is to make the version that's for sale fit into the rest of the culture as it is presented in the society at large or through a particular cultural product such as television.

For example, while religion as an idea abroad in the world must somehow accommodate a huge variety of practices and beliefs, the commodified version presented on television tends to be reduced to a simple set of behaviors: going to church, synagogue, or temple, celebrating holidays or rites of passage, wearing specific kinds of clothes. If you think about weddings or holidays as they're presented on TV, you'll see that unless they're part of a "very special episode," the nuances we recognize as part of daily life are erased. This may even require a degree of misrepresentation—for instance, the elimination of great differences in practice among branches of, say, Judaism in favor of a monolithic version that is easier for viewers to recognize and understand. Similarly, and more to the point for this essay, while real-life sexuality may be experienced by some people as clear-cut and easily understood, but by others as fluid, changeable, or part of a process of transformation, commodification requires that it be represented in a form that allows potential "buyers" to identify clearly which "product" appeals to them. Thus, in nearly all mass-media representations, people are either straight or they're not, and any blurring of that distinction is a result of personal confusion (not yet coming out) or, more rarely, unique sexual adventurousness (Samantha on *Sex and the City*), rather than an embracing of, say, bisexuality.

The point here is that commodification does not take place in a cultural vacuum but usually operates to support and reinforce what many theorists call the dominant ideology—the concepts promoted as natural, inevitable, or "just common sense" within a particular social and cultural world. In the early 21st century United States, certain things are understood as typical or normal—Whiteness, Christianity, heterosexuality, middle-class status, speaking English, and so on—and these are reinforced by most cultural and social institutions, such as government, the public schools, mass media, and so on. Because of its prominence in U.S. culture, television, and especially commercial television, plays a central role here (note, for example, that the majority of TV families include straight White couples and their biological children).

At the same time, though, consumer capitalism of the sort practiced in the United States prides itself on allowing challenges from within, providing room for identities (African Americans, Jews) or behaviors (speaking Spanish, being wealthy) that aren't strictly "normal" in the sense of "average" but don't deviate enough from the typical to pose a serious threat. Those that present a more fundamental challenge (being queer, practicing Islam) are often identified as "not normal" in the sense of "deviant"—too far outside the mainstream to be fit in. Thus, gay characters, on the rare occasion of their pre-1980s appearance, tended to be confined to secondary roles, Muslims are even now essentially invisible on series TV, and most families of color differ from White ones mainly in appearance and pop culture references.

While the significance of commodification has remained fairly consistent, *queer* has been a highly contested term. Once avoided as a term that evoked shame because of its use as a slur, it was seized and redefined in the 1980s as activist groups like Queer Nation organized around the AIDS epidemic, and in the 1990s it began to be adopted more widely as a way to name a community that is inclusive rather than exclusive and to describe sexuality as fluid rather than rigid. Thus people might identify themselves individually as gay men, lesbians, and so on, and the larger community as queer, or they might identify themselves as queer regardless of whether they fit one of the traditional categories.

BEFORE *QUEER EYE*

Until the 1990s, few queer fictional characters or openly queer performers appeared on television, even on narrowcast or pay cable stations. Queer viewers often understood ostensibly "straight" programming on their own terms, watching TV obliquely and interpreting it through their own experience—focusing, say, on the relationships between women characters (Lucy and Ethel) and relegating their male partners to the background (Doty, 1993). But there were no ongoing queer protagonists on daytime soaps, nighttime dramas, or sitcoms, and only a handful of queer characters even appeared, usually on large ensemble shows (*SOAP, Dynasty, L.A. Law, One Life to Live*), in secondary roles (*Roseanne, My So-Called Life*), or as short-term characters (*Thirtysomething, All My Children*). Until a few series such as *Roseanne* began to introduce characters whose sexual identity was simply one trait among many, TV's glimpses of queer life tended to define it either in terms of a problem or as a source of humor, and even sympathetic portrayals often focused on the difficulties queer characters faced. Similarly, while local cable systems often carried community access programming such as *Dyke TV*, mainstream nonfiction programming only really began to change in 1992, when *In the Life*, a documentary series, premiered in public television stations.

The 1997 season of the ABC sitcom *Ellen* marked a dramatic change in the fictional landscape by identifying the first queer series protagonist on network TV. While the floodgates didn't exactly open to let through a wave of queer-centered—or even queer-friendly—programs, queer characters and performers gradually began to appear in increasing numbers. Especially important because of its critical and commercial success was the premiere of NBC's *Will and Grace* in 1998, whose central relationship was between a gay man and a straight woman. While many queers critiqued the series for Will's nearly total lack of a sex life and the caricature-like nature of his best friend, Jack, those very things explain at least partially why the show succeeded where *Ellen*, with its prominent coming-out storyline, had not. The reliance on familiar stereotypes about gay men, the marginalization of queer sexuality, the relegation of Will and Jack's coming out to the past, and its organization around a male–female "couple" kept the series from disrupting the status quo.

Still, *Will and Grace* marked a significant turning point, demonstrating not only that network viewers would happily watch a sitcom about someone gay but presenting a kind of primer on how queerness could be sold to a mass audience. Two cable series that ran during the early 2000s, both centering on groups of gay men, make it even more clear how TV's commodification of queerness works and, perhaps even more important, how a critique of that commodification can actually be contained within it.

Queer Eye for the Straight Guy

By the 1990s, reality makeover series were ubiquitous on U.S. television, particularly on cable services like HGTV and TLC, which featured large blocks of decorating and style programming. *Queer Eye for the Straight Guy*, running on NBC-owned BRAVO cable from 2003 to 2007, is typical of these series in its real-life transformation of someone in obvious need of style advice. But as its title suggests, the show's premise is new: Instead of the familiar straight or asexual host, *Queer Eye* presents five openly gay hosts transforming a straight man so that he can charm the woman of his dreams.

Each cast member has a specialty—hair, clothes, décor, cooking, pop culture—and together they do their best to change slobs with no dress sense or manners, living in horrid apartments and eating junk food, into the kind of man a straight woman might actually find attractive. The objects of these makeovers are often nominated for the show by a sister or other woman who has run out of patience; the two gay and one F-to-M transgender men who were eventually featured only serve as blips on the radar of the Fab Five's united power to work their transformative magic on the straight world.

The path to *Queer Eye* was paved less by *Will and Grace* than by shows such as TLC's *Trading Spaces*, which regularly feature openly or implicitly gay men as experts on remodeling and interior decorating, if not as hosts. But because they are part of a rotating cast of designers that includes straight women, the emphasis is less on their queerness than on their expertise. Similarly, HGTV's remodeling series have presented many renovations by or for gay (usually male) couples, but the "product" being "sold" here is the act of renovation rather than the renovators. In all of these programs, sexuality takes a back seat to remodeling, and even openly gay couples are presented entirely in terms of the project at hand.

In contrast, *Queer Eye* is all about queerness—or at least about the features of queerness that can be turned to the service of straight people. And while many other reality makeover series have turned their hosts or regulars into stars, only on *Queer Eye* has the commodification focused primarily on the cast members from the very beginning. From the opening montages to the individual segments, every episode reinforces the identification of each individual cast member with his special role in the transformation, and each one's personality is clearly defined: "Fashion Savant" Carson is flamboyant, "Food and Wine Connoisseur" Ted is serious, and so on. The familiar commercial offshoots (a book, videos) and the five's frequent appearances on talk shows underline their status as celebrities.

In a 2004 appearance on PBS's *Charlie Rose* show, the *Queer Eye* cast inadvertently revealed their own participation in the commodification of queerness when Rose asked them about charges that they simply embody stereotypes. They responded by insisting that the series' status as a reality show means that it merely presents, in the words of "Grooming Guru" Kyan Douglas, the five "being gay on our own terms." What was never mentioned is how these five men came to be cast as the makeover artists. Instead, the fact that their behavior corresponds to stereotypes is just the result of them "being who they are" (Carson Kressley). The idea that they may have been chosen precisely *because* they embody particular stereotypes remains unmentioned. In fact, they argue that the show actually turns the tables by presenting the "hopeless straight guy" as desperately in need of skills that have usually been seen as "too gay" (Ted Allen), and the fact that these skills are used to help straight men impress women somehow makes it even more transgressive.

Yet it's easy to recognize the ways in which this show supports a narrow and very particular view of queer experience, and it's equally easy to believe that this played a huge part in its success. (Queer-focused organizations such as GLAAD praised the series, but to some extent that is probably less a celebration of these particular characters than of the mere fact of their existence.) What could be more appealing to a mass audience that a show whose fundamental goal is to promote successful heterosexual dating? For what is most striking about *Queer Eye* is the fact that its entire premise is a stereotype that makes gay men not only nonthreatening but valuable members of straight society.

Queer as Folk

In contrast, *Queer as Folk* emphasizes gay men's marginality, their sexuality, and their inability and even refusal to support, much less promote, the values associated with straight life. The U.S. version of *Queer as Folk* (*QAF*) has been criticized for homogenizing the gritty sexuality of the British original (Channel 4, 1999–2000), but in the context of U.S. commercial TV, it appears as a sharp critique of the usual representations of queerness. As first aired on Showtime (2000–2005), a premium cable service, the series portrayed the lives of a group of gay men and to a lesser extent their two lesbian friends, focusing on Brian Kinney, whose sexual exploits were often presented in graphic scenes. (When *QAF* was rebroadcast on Logo beginning in 2005, the sexual scenes were highly censored or removed.) Overall, the series is undeniably consistent with dominant ideas about how gay men live: The main characters are White and live in a gay ghetto of Pittsburgh; most have comfortable lives even when they appear to have little money; and they are obsessed with partying and sex—in contrast to their lesbian friends, who are committed to family and home.

While *QAF* may not undermine stereotypes of gay men, though, it does explicitly identify queerness as a challenge to the dominant culture. The series returns several times to Pittsburgh city politics, depicting a mayoral election, the campaign around an anti-gay statute, bashing incidents, and gay parenting as sites for pitched battles between queer-friendly and anti-queer forces. Despite its focus on the personal realm of sex and relationships, the series positions that realm within a political context in which queers are at risk—from the law, from commercial interests, from AIDS, from violent homophobes. The characters live in a world full of danger, building a protective if in many ways isolated community out of an obvious need for self-defense.

Paradoxically, it is sex addict Brian who openly presents the most political arguments. He is repeatedly proven right in his contention that there are only two kinds of straight people: those who hate queers to their faces and those who hate them behind their backs. And even as he proclaims his total lack of interest in politics, we see him making financial and personal sacrifices in support of the queer community's continued existence. In fact, his bitterness about straight society's treatment is part of an overall pride in being queer, a constant struggle not to compromise that identity, and a rejection, until the last few episodes of the series, of straight institutions such as marriage. Throughout the series, Brian represents a consistent critique, not just of straight society, but of queers whose campaigns for inclusion seem to him like a vain attempt to curry favor with the very people who hate them the most.

THE *FOLK* MEET THE *EYE*

I bring this up in part to demonstrate that U.S. television occasionally has room for this kind of critique—if only on premium pay cable stations, and not coincidentally voiced by what for many people is the most negative character of the series. Brian is portrayed as selfish, self-centered, emotionally repressed, incapable of accepting or expressing love or support in socially recognizable ways. He's bitter, angry, often cold and mean, unwilling to pretend interest in the things even his dearest friends care about—and as sexually promiscuous as the most homophobic fantasy about gay men. Thus, while the program presents one of the sharpest and most sustained critiques of straight culture ever seen on U.S. TV, at the same time it contains that critique by attaching it to the most dislikeable character. *QAF* manages to have it both ways by offering two apparently conflicting "products" that appeal to at least two potential audiences, depending on their political opinions and their feelings about Brian as a character. Viewers who hate or, more likely, disapprove of him are free to dismiss his political comments, and may even understand what they dislike about his character as a critique of his opinions. Those who agree with his view of straight society may, if they dislike him, see his politics as existing separately from—or even redeeming—his negative traits; if they find his character appealing, they may see his politics as explaining or even justifying his behavior.

Yet among viewers who are drawn to *QAF*, even those who don't embrace his overall critique of straightness are likely to agree with Brian's primary targets: gay bashing, prohibitions on gay parenthood, and so on. In the final season, however, he takes on *Queer Eye* directly, and it's here that the contrast between the two series becomes particularly pointed.

Emmett, who has at various times worked as a clothing store clerk, a naked waiter, a party planner, and a porn star, gets a gig as the "Queer Guy" on a local TV news show. This brief spot features Emmett giving the same kind of advice the Fab Five provide: tips on appearance, clothes, housewares, and so on for the presumably straight audience. He becomes a local celebrity, with men at the bar and the store where he works recognizing him from TV as they once recognized him from his porn videos. His friends are proud of his fame and his contribution to queer visibility, but Brian is openly hostile, congratulating Emmett on becoming "television's latest gay eunuch," "nonsexual, nonthreatening, ball-less." Brian makes it clear that this is the reason for Emmett's popularity: "You do homage," he declares, "to the long line of lovable, laughable clowns who've come before you."

Emmett does eventually come to recognize his role as the TV news show's clown, but his presence at the TV station also helps his macho pro-football-player boyfriend to come out publicly and thus does increase queer visibility in a significant way. Yet Brian's critique of his spot, and vicariously of *Queer Eye*, is apt. Like the "Queer Guy," *Queer Eye* is created to entertain straight viewers by offering them gay men who fit familiar and safe stereotypes—interior decorator, hair dresser, culture maven—and whose self-presentations on TV never stray into the territory occupied by, say, Brian. Interestingly, Emmett is nearly as sexually active as Brian, but Emmett is generous and optimistic where Brian is self-absorbed and angry, a distinction that explains their very different roles in the "Queer Guy" storyline.

Despite Carson's campy remarks or the fact that three *Queer Eye* episodes feature queer men, and despite the fact that the entire series' reason for existence is sexuality, there is no room on the show for open expressions of any of the sexual aspects of queerness. In fact, there's not even any room for the suggestion that grooming straight people for romance may not be gay men's primary sex-related function.

Anna McCarthy (2001) has made a related point about the coming-out episode of *Ellen*:

> *Ellen*'s coming-out episode was momentous because it promised to make queer life something other than an interruptive force, something potentially *assimilated* . . . into the repertoire of romantic and personal situations replayed weekly on the prime-time sitcom. But the logic through which this occurred was a heteronormative one." (p. 599) (By "heteronormative," McCarthy refers to a context that reinforces heterosexuality as the norm.)

In other words, there's a paradox in television's presentation of queer life as "something other than an interruptive force," a cost to making queerness seem "normal" rather than "deviant," and the cost is that queer life is stripped of the very things that make it queer.

Queer Eye perfectly demonstrates this: The five hosts may see themselves as "just being who they are," but the show makes their queerness, including their belief in the possibility of transforming the self, subservient to straight romance. For *Queer as Folk*, though, queerness is its own justification. Straight life makes only rare appearances, usually as an antagonist rather than the raison d'être of the series. By linking its strongest criticisms of the straight world to its most contentious character, even *QAF* provides an easy out for viewers who might be uncomfortable questioning the dominant ideology too deeply. But by proving Brian right over and over again and supplying satisfying victories for the queer folk of Pittsburgh, *QAF* demonstrates the possibility that critique can coexist with commodification.

IT'S YOUR TURN: WHAT DO YOU THINK? WHAT WILL YOU FIND?

1. I argue that the way the Fab Five are represented in *Queer Eye* actually makes their queerness subservient to straight romance, and that queerness is being commodified so that a straight audience will "buy" it. Do you agree or disagree? Why?

2. I've concentrated on queer commodification on television. What about other media—can you identify gays or lesbians in magazine advertising, for example? Are there any differences between ads aimed at general audiences and those in queer magazines? If so, what kinds of differences do you see? If so, why do you think that has been done?

3. Find some TV programs that focus on African Americans and try to compare their portrayals to the ones I've described. Is "Blackness" commodified the same way as "queerness"? Can you think of reasons why or why not?

4. Talk with some of your LGBT classmates about how gays are represented in the media. How do they say they've been affected by this? If you know any older LGBT people, talk with them about how media presentations have changed over the years.

REFERENCES

Doty, A. (1993). *Making things perfectly queer: Interpreting mass culture.* Minneapolis: University of Minnesota Press.

McCarthy, A. (2001). *Ellen*: Making queer television history. *GLB: A Journal of Lesbian and Gay Studies, 7*(4), 593–620.

CHAPTER 6

MUSIC AND NEW MEDIA

6.1 "MUSIC TO RIOT BY": CALLS TO RACIAL VIOLENCE IN THE OI! MUSIC SCENE

Jody M. Roy

The Oi! music scene plays a pivotal role in maintaining and expanding the racist skinhead gang phenomenon. To help us better understand this role, the author surveys the roots of skinhead culture and the nature of skinhead gangs today. She then offers a summary of the primary themes of American Oi! music, derived from analyses of song lyrics, and shares some insights about how Oi! music and the Oi! music scene enable the existence and expansion of violent skinhead gangs.

> *Victims all around me*
> *I feel nothing but hate*
> *Bashing their brains in*
> *Is my only trade*
> *Line them up against the wall*
> *Shoot them, watch them die*
> *I love to hear the agony*
> *They vomit scream and cry*
> *(Dees & Fiffer, 1993, p. 187)*

Ken "Death" Mieske penned these graphic lyrics in the hope of someday forming his own musical group. Although Mieske never achieved his musical aspirations, he did live the life described in his hand-written lyrics. As a member of the gang East Side White Pride (ESWP), Mieske terrorized people on the streets of Portland, Oregon. On November 13, 1988, Mieske and fellow ESWP member Kyle Brewster fatally attacked an Ethiopian man named Mulugeta Seraw. Clad in brass-knuckles, Brewster led the attack by punching Seraw in the face. Mieske then took over, beating Seraw with a baseball bat. As Seraw lay helpless in the street, he suffered a final torrent of blows from Mieske's steel-reinforced combat boots (Dees & Fiffer, 1993).

Ken Mieske and his comrades in ESWP are "skinheads," the name commonly given to American youth who not only espouse White supremacist ideology but also violently express their prejudices through physical attacks on minorities. Originally a British working-class youth movement, significant skinhead activity first erupted in America in the 1980s. By 1993, researchers estimated that some 3,500 "hardcore" skinheads were known to exist in the United States (Moore, 1993). According to the Southern Poverty Law Center (2006, p. 55), fifty-six fully organized skinhead gangs, several with chapters in many cities, were active in 2005. Significantly, law enforcement officials recently reported "the reappearance of large numbers of skinheads in their communities."

I first became interested in skinhead culture as a graduate student when several violent incidents involving skinheads occurred on my campus. Because my research focused on the persuasive strategies of nationally organized adult hate groups, I was curious to learn how seemingly unorganized, local groups of young people could become so tightly committed to racist theories and so very predisposed to violence. In the decade I've since spent learning about skinhead culture, I've discovered that an underground music scene called Oi!, facilitated greatly in recent years by the expansion of the Internet, lies at the core of racist skinhead culture. Non-racist Oi! music exists, as do anti-racist, or SHARP, skinheads; however, my focus here will be on the Oi! bands deeply interwoven into the racist skinhead movement.

The racist Oi! music scene functions as a critical medium of communication for youth involved in or simply curious about skinhead culture. At the most obvious level, Oi! conveys themes of racism and rationales for racially motivated violence. More subtly, Oi! serves as a means for skinhead gangs and other organized hate groups to attract and recruit new members. The Oi! music scene thus invites youth to enter the relatively underground world of skinheads, informs youth of the racially based conspiracy theories skinheads accept, and, ultimately, encourages youth to ally with skinhead gangs or other organized hate groups that advocate varying degrees of violence as appropriate responses to life in a racially diverse world.

BOOTS, BRACES, AND BANDS: FOUR DECADES OF SKINHEAD CULTURE

The roots of the skinhead phenomenon can be traced to Britain in the mid-1960s when the popular "mod" subculture splintered. So-called smooth mods tended to be "older and better off, sharply dressed, moving in small groups and usually looking for a bird [woman]" (Cohen, 1980, p. 187). In contrast, "hard mods" closely cropped their hair and clad themselves in workers' attire—Ben Sherman shirts, cuffed jeans, suspenders, and heavy, black Dr. Marten boots. The relatively young hard mods traveled in large groups and quickly earned a reputation as hard-drinking brawlers. Although the hard mods espoused no set political agenda, they were "on the paranoic edge" (Cohen, p. 187), "given to imagining or actually seeing conspiracies ranged against" their prospects for the future (Moore, 1993, p. 28).

By 1977, the British hard mod style and reputation had become fixed; the moniker "skinheads" came into common use as a reference to the hard mods' nearly shaved haircuts. The hard mod skinheads had no defined hierarchy but did organize themselves into local "crews." The skinhead crews were territorial; boundaries appear to have been established around local football (soccer) districts and teams. In the late 1960s and early 1970s, instances of violence involving skinheads often erupted during or after football matches when the crews of the opposing teams would do battle in the stands or in the streets.

When not attending and disrupting football matches, hard mod skinheads spent much of their time in bars and clubs featuring the West Indian music genres of ska and reggae. Nick Knight (1982) argued that the hard mod skinheads found commonality with West Indian immigrants in the working-class themes of ska and reggae lyrics. However, Jack Moore (1993) cautioned against reading the shared musical tradition as evidence of "meaningful racial or ethnic harmonies" (p. 37). While the hard mods did incorporate a preference for ska into skinhead culture, in particular, almost all hard mod crews remained exclusively White.

Although hard mod skinhead crews continued to operate in the early to mid-1970s, they soon were overshadowed on the youth culture scene by the first wave of British punks. The fans and members of bands such as Sham 69, the Sex Pistols, the Clash, and Suicidal Tendencies ushered in a new and flamboyant style that conflicted with the working class look of the hard mod skinheads. But while the hard mod skinheads rejected the punk look, they tried to embrace punk music. For a time in the mid-1970s, they appear to have been welcomed by the punks; the aggressive skinheads seemed an obvious audience for the aggressive themes and thrashing beats of punk music. However, as Knight explained, the punk scene actually was characterized by aggressive posturing and ultimately could not tolerate the very real aggressive behavior that necessarily accompanied any significant skinhead presence. In the late 1970s, the band Sham 69, a favorite among skinheads because of the group's violent lyrics, publicly "disavowed the skins' support" (Knight, 1982, p. 24).

No longer welcome on the punk music scene, British skinheads banded around a newly emerging variation on punk called "Oi!" Musically, Oi! is a uniquely punk fusion of ska and heavy metal. Oi! has been described by one outside observer as "'a ritual purge on everything that doesn't sound like the voice of the [skinhead] Mob with its back against the wall'" (Knight, 1982, p. 29). A skinhead source describes Oi! as "music to riot by" and notes that "Oi! is for warriors" (Moore, 1993, p. 47).

Formed in 1977, the British band Skrewdriver generally is considered the original and quintessential Oi! band. Skrewdriver's founder and lead singer, Ian Stuart, who died in 1993, likewise is revered by contemporary skinheads worldwide. Although Skrewdriver maintained dominance of the Oi! scene for fully 20 years, other Oi! bands have arisen to share the stage: Last Resort, the Oppressed, 4-Skins, the Exploited, Combat 84, Cock Sparrer, and Blitz are among the more enduring and well-known British Oi! groups (www.skrewdriver.com).

While the British Oi! bands were forming in the late 1970s and early 1980s, building on what was already a decade of established hard mod style and skinhead crew structures, the first signs of a skinhead impulse appeared in America. Unlike the British skinhead pattern of development, American skinheads emerged from within the urban punk music scene, in time forming a mini-subculture of their own within the larger punk subculture. In sharp contrast to their British counterparts, the original American skinheads were not bound to crews but instead operated either individually or in very casually related social circles. Nevertheless, even disorganized, American skinheads quickly earned the reputation for heavy drinking and violence that long had been held by British skinhead crews.

By 1984, the first organized American skinhead group appeared in Chicago. Calling itself Romantic Violence, the group (which still exists) more closely resembles a traditional American inner-city street gang than a British hard mod skinhead crew. Like most American gangs, Romantic Violence uses graffiti to mark its territory. The gang's identifying "tag" is a swastika. Members of Romantic Violence have been arrested in a variety of incidents, many involving violence against racial and ethnic minorities (Anti-Defamation League of B'nai B'rith, 1987).

Since 1984, skinhead gangs have increased in number in America. In 2005, Romantic Violence was only one of 56 known skinhead gangs operating across the United States.

Contemporary American skinheads have adopted the British hard mod style as their uniform: Dr. Marten combat boots, Ben Sherman shirts, cuffed jeans, suspenders, and shaved or nearly shaved haircuts. The number 88, code for "Heil Hitler," is a common emblem for all American skinhead gangs and a shared rallying cry to riot. Although skinhead gang membership normally is open only to males, young women—referred to as "skinchicks"—cluster around the male gangs and share their devotion to the White power movement and, to some degree, their penchant for violence.

No national organization controls the various American skinhead gangs. Rather, their alliance seems to be informal, fostered by the sharing of information and ideas through the mail or, more recently, via Internet. The various skinhead groups' connections to larger, established White supremacy organizations—Ku Klux Klan, Aryan Nations, White Aryan Resistance—also provide opportunities for the local gangs to interact.

However, recordings and performances by Oi! bands, as well as a vast cyber network tied to Oi!, serve as perhaps the most important channel of communication for skinheads. In the mid-1980s, Romantic Violence leader Clark Reid Martell set up a post office box from which the gang could operate a distribution center for Oi! music and skinhead clothing and paraphernalia (Moore, 1993). As recently as August, 1997, mailing addresses for more than 40 distributors of Oi! music were listed on the Skrewdriver Internet homepage.

As access to and, correspondingly, demand for Oi! recordings has increased in America since the mid-1980s, American-based Oi! bands have formed. In 1988, White Aryan Resistance sponsored an "Aryan Woodstock," which featured such homegrown Oi! groups as the Tulsa Boot Boys, Haken Kreuz, and Hammer Heads (Anti-Defamation League of B'nai B'rith, 1987). Throughout the 1980s and 1990s, Aryan Nation's leader, Rev. Richard Butler, hosted an annual "Aryan Olympics" featuring performances by skinhead bands at his sprawling Idaho compound (Aryan Nations, 1994).

In the 1990s, Rahowa (skinhead slang for "Racial Holy War") and Bound for Glory emerged as two of the more dominant Oi! bands on the American skinhead music scene. Both Rahowa and Bound for Glory have produced several studio-quality collections of their songs (Bound for Glory discography, 1998; Rahowa discography, 1998); both groups' recordings regularly are offered for sale by virtually all distributors of Oi! music. Significantly, in 2000 Resistance Records, the primary producer/distributor of Oi! in North America, was purchased by the National Alliance, one of the older and more established organizations dedicated to racist causes in America (www.natall.com). The National Alliance is perhaps best known for serving as a clearing house for racist publications and recordings. In addition to publishing the periodical *National Vanguard* since 1975, the National Alliance's founder, William Pierce, authored *The Turner Diaries*, the book alleged to have guided Timothy McVeigh and Terry Nichols in plotting the Oklahoma City bombing (Cole, 1997). Clearly Pierce recognized the power and the potential of Oi! to spread White supremacist ideology when he brought Resistance Records into his influential fold.

THEMES OF RACISM AND VIOLENCE IN OI! MUSIC

So, what exactly does Oi! music say about race, racism, and racially motivated violence that inspires even leaders of established adult hate groups such as the National Alliance to realize its power to influence young people? In my studies of racist Oi! music (Roy, 1999;

Roy & Belling, 1998), I've found that a few key themes define the genre. American racist Oi! music centers on the theme of an alleged Jewish-controlled conspiracy against Whites, or "aryans,"[1] the racial designation preferred by most White supremacists. Because race is intrinsic to the line between "good" and "evil" in the conspiracy/counter-conspiracy battle that forms the plot of American Oi! songs, racism and calls for racially motivated violence are explicit in the lyrics of the genre. American Oi! thus constructs messages about the past, present, and future in terms of the alleged Jewish conspiracy and, significantly, advocates very specific, usually violent, responses to the conspiracy.

Oi! lyricists rely on two different but complementary tactics to construct and convey their unique vision of the past: glorification of martyrs and accounts of ancient aryan history. Oi! bands elevate to martyr status people they believe were loyal to the aryan cause who lost their lives fighting for the cause. Thus, fallen members of skinhead gangs as well as legendary adult White supremacists, such as Bob Matthews and Randy Weaver, are immortalized in Oi! songs. By glorifying those who died in violent racially motivated conflicts, Oi! songs subtly encourage the next generation of racist youth to be willing to give their life for the cause; those who die in battle live on as heroes within the culture.

Oi! music also creates its own vision of the past by recounting tales of ancient aryan history. These tales suggest aryan superiority to other races is innate because aryans always have been superior in all ways. Additionally, by embedding stories of the tension between aryans and Jews into the musical histories, Oi! writers are able to introduce listeners to the most elemental components of the theory of a Jewish conspiracy to destroy aryans, the theory at the heart of virtually all organized racism in America today.

While American Oi! bands do reconstruct the past in their lyrics to reflect their beliefs about aryan supremacy, they devote much more time to developing a musical analysis of the present as a showdown between aryans and all other races. Jews are conceived by American Oi! bands as the leaders of a conspiracy against Whites. According to Oi! writers, the Jewish conspirators influence the government, the economy, the media, the schools—in fact all aspects of society—to oppress White people by denying them what skinheads maintain is their destined supreme role in society. Oi! bands view any situation in which aryans have less than complete control to be proof of the progress the Jewish conspirators are making. Not surprisingly, extremely racist expressions dominate Oi! music when it turns to this theme. Jews are stereotyped as power hungry, sneaky, and evil. African Americans, and to a slightly lesser extent Hispanics, are portrayed as unintelligent, lazy dupes unwittingly carrying out Jewish-devised plots against aryans.

Of particular concern to Oi! writers is the notion of blood purity, or the supposed purity of the aryan bloodline, which is both the means and the end of theories of White supremacy. Oi! music often warns against racial "mixing" as the ultimate plot of the Jewish conspiracy—to eradicate the superior aryan race permanently by contaminating the bloodline via sexual encounters with people of other races.

While violence infuses Oi! tellings of the racial conflicts of both the past and the present, American Oi! bands paint their most vivid pictures of violence when they envision a full-scale race war in the future. Because they believe racial conflict to be inherent to human existence and because they believe people of all other races to be inherently evil, Oi! writers simply cannot conceive of compromise among the various races. Thus, within Oi! music, the only possible future outcome is continued racial violence ultimately culminating in a decisive war. Because they are committed wholly to the notion of aryan supremacy, they of course prophesy that aryan victory in the race war is inevitable. At the least, Oi! lyricists sing of a day following the war when America and Europe will be ruled and inhabited only by aryans. Some Oi! songs actually advocate genocide of all non-aryan races worldwide. Clearly, although Hitler's Third Reich fell more than 60 years ago, his so-called final solution still lingers in the minds of today's youngest but perhaps most ardent White supremacists.

THE IMPACT OF THE OI! MUSIC SCENE

Because racist Oi! music is tied so tightly to skinhead gangs, the Oi! music scene really has to operate at an underground level; put simply, law enforcement officials now realize that where there is Oi! there are gang members. From the early 1980s until the mid-1990s in America, the Oi! scene developed via small, local, usually unadvertised concerts and through the sharing of bootleg recordings and correspondence.

With the rise of the Internet since that time, skinheads have developed a vast Oi! cyber-scene. Of course, in doing so they have created an electronic "paper trail" of their ideology and activities that police and academic researchers can follow. But police and scholars aren't the only ones visiting the Oi! cyber-scene; skinheads themselves and young people curious about skinheads are the target market for the Oi! sites. The Internet allows skinheads worldwide to meet online and share ideas and plans; it also provides what we might call a "skinhead school" for young people who've never actually encountered skinhead culture.

Today, by visiting a couple of Web sites, anyone can learn the dress codes, slang, and visual symbolism (such as tattoos and gang tags) identifying members of particular skinhead gangs. More important, by including the lyrics of Oi! songs, as well as essays about skinhead thinking, the sites on the Oi! cyber-scene introduce visitors to the theories of a Jewish-controlled conspiracy against aryans that ground skinhead ideology. Oi! sites also provide links to the sites of other skinhead gangs as well as established adult hate groups, thus opening up the full array of White supremacist thinking to visitors with just a few clicks of a mouse. The Oi! cyber-scene has not replaced the "real" Oi! scene, but it has allowed it to reach new audiences, including potential recruits for skinhead gangs.

The Oi! music scene, both actual and virtual, also helps entrench the gang mentality of skinhead culture. Most basically, because virtually all racist Oi! band members are themselves members of formal skinhead gangs, they model gang membership as a norm for young fans. At a more subtle level, because Oi! songs "reveal" the secret conspiracy against Whites, Oi! singers and songwriters set themselves up as leaders based on their assumed access to special information, their seemingly limitless knowledge of aryan history and, of course, their prophetic vision of the future and prescriptions for how to enact that vision. The voices of the Oi! music scene thus fulfill all three hallmarks of successful social movement leadership: charisma, prophecy, and pragmatism (Stewart, Smith, & Denton, 1989). And, in doing so, Oi! bands reinforce their own gang allegiance and structures as the appropriate model of organization and behavior for any White youth willing to listen.

Although membership in skinhead gangs in America has been increasing steadily since Romantic Violence first organized in Chicago in 1984, racist skinheads remain a very small minority. But when instructed and inspired by Oi! music, even one skinhead can unleash a deadly rage against members of the various groups he believes are trying to hurt him. For skinheads such as Ken Mieske, Oi! is "music to riot by," but for victims such as Mulugeta Seraw, Oi! is music to die by.

A FINAL WORD OF CAUTION

As you've just learned, a vast Oi! network exists on the Internet. If you decide to explore the Oi! Cyber-scene, be advised that Oi! sites sponsored by skinhead gangs and other hate groups often are monitored by the groups themselves and/or law enforcement agencies. You may receive follow-up contacts after visiting an Oi! site. As such, carefully consider the possible ramifications of "site-seeing" on this subject before doing so.

NOTE

1. Although White supremacists capitalize the term *aryan* I don't because they use the term incorrectly. "Aryan" in proper usage refers to prehistoric peoples of the Indo-European language–cultures, a group much more inclusive than the "pure" Whites defined narrowly in biological terms by contemporary White supremacists.

IT'S YOUR TURN: WHAT DO YOU THINK? WHAT WILL YOU FIND?

1. Although no other genre of contemporary music approaches the same level of overt racism of Oi!, other genres do rely heavily on themes of conspiracy and, in turn, depict violent scenarios against alleged enemies. Consider the lyrics of some gangsta rap songs (examples by artists such as Tupac, Snoop Dogg, N.W.A., and Ice T can be found on the Internet). Who do these artists set up as the enemy? In what ways do they suggest the "enemy" is acting as part of a larger conspiracy? What responses—in particular, violence—are advocated? How do gangsta rap lyrics or even the artists themselves model the gang lifestyle for fans?

2. When people first learn about racist Oi!—in particular how easily young people can access it via the Internet—many initially believe Oi! should be banned or at least severely restricted. What can we do to protect young people from potentially dangerous media influences without compromising the Constitution's ability to protect the right of freedom of expression for all of us?

3. Is there an Oi! scene on or near your campus? Visit a local alternative music store. You're unlikely to find an Oi! category (look), but browse the sections for ska and punk. Look for the names of racist Oi! bands discussed here. Look for CDs on the Resistance Records label. Examine cover art for racist Oi! and skinhead gang identifiers—swastikas, 88, crossed hammers, spiderweb designs. *The purpose of this exercise is to raise your awareness of the level (if any) of skinhead activity in your area, not to bring you into contact with skinhead gang members. If you find evidence of an Oi! scene near your campus, don't make contact with gang members; some react violently to any outsiders they perceive to be too curious.*

4. This reading has looked at issues of race, but from the music and any other images of the scene you've come across, what can you tell about gender roles within the racist Oi! movement?

REFERENCES

Anti-Defamation League of B'nai B'rith. (1987). *Shaved for battle: Skinheads target America's youth.* New York: Author.

Aryan Nations. (1994). Adolf Hitler youth camp flyer. Hayden, ID: Author.

Bound for Glory Discography. (1998). www.whitepower. com/bfg/fight. Accessed February 7, 1998.

Cohen, S. (1980). *Folk devils and moral panics: The creation of mods and rockers.* New York: St. Martin's Press.

Cole, P. E. (1997, March 31). McVeigh: Diaries dearest. *Time, 149*(13), p. 26.

Dees, M., & Fiffer, S. (1993). *Hate on trial: The case against America's most dangerous neo-Nazi.* New York: Villard Books.

Knight, N. (1982). *Skinhead.* London: Omnibus Press.

Moore, J. (1993). *Skinheads shaved for battle: A cultural history of American skinheads.* Bowling Green, OH: Bowling Green State University Press.

Rahowa Discography. (1998). www.whitepower.com/ rahowa/cult. Accessed March 3, 1998.

Resistance Records. (1997, 1998). *Catalogues.* Detroit: Resistance Records.

Roy, J. (1999). Fragments of Hitler in contemporary Oi!: Skinhead music and the propensity for violence in skinhead gangs. *Journal of the Wisconsin Communication Association, 30,* 1–8.

Roy, J., & Belling, M. (1998, April). *"Back with a bang, back with the gang": A comparative analysis of British and American Oi!/skinhead music.* Paper presented to the Central States Communication Association Conference.

Skrewdriver history and discography. (1998). www. skrewdriver.com. Accessed July 21, 1998.

Southern Poverty Law Center. (2006, Spring). Hate groups active in the year 2005. *Klanwatch/ Intelligence Report, 121,* 53.

Stewart, C., Smith, C., & Denton, R. (1989). *Persuasion and social movements* (Rev. ed.). Prospect Heights, IL: Waveland Press.

6.2 EMINEM IN MAINSTREAM PUBLIC DISCOURSE: WHITENESS AND THE APPROPRIATION OF BLACK MASCULINITY

Jon B. Martin and Gust A. Yep

> How did a young White rap artist with a foul mouth, an offensive presence, controversial viewpoints, and disturbingly violent songs against women, gays, and lesbians manage to capture so many listeners and fans, not only within the world of hip-hop but also in the American musical landscape? How did Eminem accomplish a level of success unparalleled by other performance artists of his genre? The authors examine these questions by analyzing how Eminem has been presented in mainstream media.

Being a hip-hop head has always meant having to say you're sorry—to Jews for liking Public Enemy; to the police for liking N.W.A.; to Koreans for liking Ice Cube; to women for liking just about anybody. At this point, many fans blow off extra-musical moralizing, assuming that hip-hop's streety, volatile lyricism will always defy polite society and that that's sort of the point. With Eminem, that attitude has truly gone mainstream. (Norris, 2001, p. 64)

You know it's going to hell when the best rapper out there is white and the best golfer is black. (Charles Barkley, quoted in Norris, 2001, p. 60)

Marshall Mathers, more commonly known as Eminem, is "a pissy 24-year-old white welfare kid from inner-city Detroit" (Aaron, 1999, p. 80) who has risen to prominence in the music world. He has been compared to Bob Dylan, Allen Ginsberg, Jim Morrison, the Velvet Underground, Patti Smith, Johnny Rotten, Kurt Cobain, and nineteenth-century poet Arthur Rimbaud (Rafferty, 2001). In *Rolling Stone*'s Critics' Music Awards 2000 he was honored as Artist of the Year, Best Male Performer, and Best Hip-Hop Artist and was awarded Best Album. *Rolling Stone*'s readers awarded him Artist of the Year, Best Male Performer, Best Hip-Hop Artist, and Year's Biggest Hype. *The Marshall Mathers LP* has now sold over 7 million copies in the United States alone. This success culminated in his Grammy nomination as Artist of the Year, one of the highest honors for a performing artist in the United States.

To understand how Eminem became so successful, we analyze the way he bas been presented in mainstream media. We begin by examining Eminem's background and the striking features of his public persona. We then introduce the concept of Whiteness and the strategies that allow Eminem to go into the predominantly African American (male) world of hip-hop and appropriate this musical style for mainstream musical entertainment consumption. We conclude with a discussion of the implications of this analysis, from the perspective of both student and critical consumer of media, through the lens of race and gender.

EMINEM AS A POPULAR CULTURE PRODUCTION

According to a biography by Martin Huxley, Eminem was born Marshall Mathers III in Kansas City, Missouri, in October 1975. He claims to have had a difficult childhood, residing in economically disadvantaged areas and moving frequently. He formed his first rap group at the age of 15 and adopted the stage name Eminem. After repeatedly failing the ninth grade, he dropped out of school and began immersing himself in Detroit's local music scene. He won second place in the 1997 Rap Olympics in Los Angeles and came to the attention of Dr. Dre, one of hip-hop's most successful producers and rappers, eventually securing major-label distribution for his *Slim Shady EP* (Huxley, 2000). This was the beginning of his unprecedented rise to fame.

Eminem, the "celebrity," is a popular culture production due to the fact that the discourse of celebrities is, after all, merely a collection of media images that don't represent any "authentic" information about the subject (King, 2000). What we know of Eminem we know through consumption of media. Two striking features seem to characterize the public persona of Eminem. First, Eminem acts, sings, dresses, and talks like an African American. He favors popular hip-hop styles such as oversized athletic gear, baggy jeans worn low on the hips, backward baseball caps or bandanas, and oversized jewelry. He presents himself in ways typically associated with gangsta rap, such as wearing an orange prison jumpsuit on stage and including numerous references to weapons and crime in his lyrics. Both in his lyrics and in interviews he frequently uses slang and speech styles incorporated from African American Vernacular English. In short, Eminem "embodies Blackness."[1]

Second, his songs are violently misogynistic and homophobic. His lyrics vividly describe acts of violence, including physical abuse of women; rape; murder of gays, lesbians, and transgenders; and even fantasies of murdering the mother of his daughter. One of the songs that includes this last example even features vocal samples of his infant child as he comforts her after recounting a fantasy of killing her mother. In an album review, Touré (2000a) described Eminem's anger and violent nature as vital to his appeal and serving as "a boundary between his fans and outsiders" (p. 136). Most critics, as well as the Gay and Lesbian

Alliance Against Defamation, have criticized his angry, violent, and offensive material. Through media coverage, these are the images that have come to be associated with Eminem.

EMINEM AND THE RHETORICAL STRATEGIES OF WHITENESS

Great attention has been paid to Eminem's success as a White rapper in the predominantly Black hip-hop world. Whereas his talent has been widely credited, there has been little interrogation of the nature of Whiteness by the popular media. In this section we discuss the nature of Whiteness, public discourses about Eminem as "White trash," Eminem's appropriation of Black masculinity, and discourses about Eminem at the intersections of race, class, gender, and sexuality.

Whiteness

Whiteness refers to the "everyday, invisible, subtle, cultural, and social practices, ideas, and codes that discursively secure the power and privilege of White people, but that strategically remains unmarked, unnamed, and unmapped in contemporary society" (Shome, 1996, p. 503). Whiteness can be seen as a strategic rhetoric that influences White individuals and people of color with certain political (e.g., who gets to speak and who will listen) and material (e.g., who gets to have access to specific resources) effects on the entire social structure (Nakayama & Krizek, 1995/1999).

Whiteness studies have as their goal marking, naming, and mapping Whiteness as a social category and exposing White privilege. One feature of Whiteness is its universal character, which renders it seemingly race-less and culture-less (Shome, 1996). This gives the White subject, especially the White male, the ability to cross cultural borders and assume the identity of others. This also includes the ability to successfully appropriate cultural practices, language styles, and dress and appearance of "others."

Eminem as White Trash

Recently, research has begun addressing how Whiteness intersects with issues of social class, gender, and sexuality. The often pejorative notion of White trash, or economically disadvantaged Whites, engages on both the lines of race and class. According to Newitz and Wray, "white trash is, for whites, the most visible and clearly marked form of whiteness" and can therefore

> perhaps help to make all whites self-conscious of themselves as a racial and classed group among other such groups, bringing us one step closer to a world without racial division, or, at the very least, a world where racial difference does not mean racial, symbolic, and economic domination. (1997, p. 4)

Hartigan (1997, p. 50) described White trash as a "cultural figure and a rhetorical identity" that inscribes a "contempt-laden social divide, particularly (though not exclusively) between whites." Newitz and Wray (1997) argued that White trash is both a "classist slur" and a "racial epithet," marking poor Whites as a separate group, and suggested that from a Whiteness lens, White trash might resemble a separate racial minority group in that it doesn't see itself as being part of the "norm from which all other races and ethnicities deviate" (p. 5). However, this configuration of White trash, while potentially fruitful, should not obscure the fact that Whiteness, being (in)visibly (un)marked, retains certain privilege despite class or gender issues.

Eminem seems to be aware that by positioning himself as White trash he can gain credibility and identification with his audiences. He frequently refers to his disadvantaged background and unstable family situation. In Huxley's (2000) biography, Eminem is quoted as saying that his was a "stereotypical, trailer park, white trash upbringing" (p. 7). He has also referred to his mother's drug use during his childhood. These comments prompted a strong response from Debbie Mathers-Briggs, who is suing her son "for defamation, over his characterizations of her in interviews as an irresponsible, welfare dependent drug user" (Huxley, p. 95).

Images of his disadvantaged background also surface in Eminem's lyrics. "Rock Bottom," from the *Marshall Mathers LP*, describes his bleak, disadvantaged upbringing and lack of opportunity to better his situation. The media have aided in establishing this representation, with Touré's (2000a) review of *The Marshall Mathers LP*, referring to the rapper as a "very blond, white trash homeboy from Detroit" (p. 135).

Positioning himself as White trash serves two major functions. First, it helps establish Eminem's credibility within the hip-hop community. Wildman & Davis (1995) noted that members of privileged groups may identify with certain forms of oppression, and this identification may serve to mask their other privileges. Eminem focuses on the oppression of his poverty to win identification within hop-hop culture. Because he was poor, worked low-paying jobs, dropped out of high school, lived in predominantly African American neighborhoods, and so on, he claims to speak with an "authentic" voice. In hip-hop terms, he is "keepin' it real." Newitz and Wray (1997) noted that White people often feel the need to claim some form of social victimization in order to claim a place in the multicultural order. They described this as "victim chic" and discussed how "glamorously marginalized" (p. 5) Whites sometime emulate the authenticity of oppressed groups.

The second function of Eminem's White trash identification is its appeal to disenfranchised White youth. Dolan (1999), in a concert review in *Spin*, described one demographic of fans as

> "young, Midwestern hip-hop kids from the suburbs, for whom the uberwigga's chart domination is sweet vindication. The guy leaning over the balcony in a *White Trash Always* T-shirt had memorized every rhyme and revenge fantasy, and was high on . . . empowerment." (p. 63)

Voices of rebellion or those that speak to the (often-difficult) experiences of young people are common in popular music. Eminem's positioning as a victim of poverty and parental neglect provides a means of identification with a large body of White youths (Huxley, 2000).

EMINEM'S APPROPRIATION OF BLACK MASCULINITY

A central feature of Black hip-hop masculinity is the importance of "keepin' it real," or the desire to maintain credibility by staying true to the codes of conduct of urban settings and maintaining the proper masculine expressions (Ross, 1994). The desire to appear invincible, always ready to fight, and without weakness is one cause for the prominence of homophobic lyrics and attitudes in hip-hop (Rose, 1994). According to Touré (2000b), today's hip-hop homophobia is due to "the black male's effort to keep up with his legendary dick, and the resulting caricaturishly exaggerated manhood that emerged to quash even a hint of waffling" (p. 317). Pinn (1996) noted that in hip-hop, "Manhood is often defined in opposition to womanhood" resulting in the "blatant espousing of negative and destructive attitudes toward women" (p. 66). Control of women is sought through language and sex, a weapon of "damage, domination and control" (p. 64).

As discussed earlier, one privilege of Whiteness is the ability to appropriate aspects of other cultures. Eminem does this with Black masculinity. Although Black masculinity is not an essential, unified, and monolithic category, masculinity in the hip-hop community has several common features. In the United States, Black masculinity is often viewed as inherently angry (Orbe, Warren, & Cornwell, 2000), physically threatening (Orbe et al., 2000; Pinn, 1996; Touré, 2000b), and sexually aggressive (Orbe et al., 2000). Eminem clearly embodies these aspects of Black masculinity.

Orbe and associates (2000) describe Black males as possessing an anger "triggered by a past, present, and future of racism" (p. 114). In his biography, Eminem frequently describes how he has always been hated for his rebelliousness, his audacity, and as a White person in the hip-hop community. Eminem habitually raises his middle finger as a gesture of anger: Five out of nine photos of the rapper in his biography show him with his middle finger prominently raised. His anger can then be seen as a response similar to that of Black men suffering from racism.

One manifestation of Black masculinity is a claiming of physical and psychological space to call one's own in a world where such spaces are often not readily available or are even denied (Pinn, 1996). The physically threatening nature of Black masculinity can be seen as a response to any challenge to or infringement on this space. Similarly, Eminem repeatedly threatens physical violence in response to any perceived disrespect. Touré (2000a) even described him as "rage-filled, drug-addled [and] homicidal" (p. 136).

The sexual aggressiveness associated with Black masculinity "solidifies a clear justification for societal concern and fear" (Orbe et al., 2000, p. 116). This association often manifests itself with the image of the Black male as a potential rapist. Eminem encourages such an association with his own sexuality: "Kill You' [from *The Marshall Mathers LP*] finds him fantasizing about raping his mother. . . ." (Huxley, 2000, p. 120).

Eminem clearly manifests these aspects of Black hip-hop masculinity, as evidenced by both his lyrics and mainstream media representations. Touré (2000a), in a review of *The Marshall Mathers LP* (p. 135), described Eminem as "nearing the aesthetic zenith of the celebration of black maleness called hip-hop."

EMINEM AT THE INTERSECTIONS OF RACE, CLASS, GENDER, AND SEXUALITY

Thus far we have attempted to employ Whiteness to examine Eminem's public image and success. His Whiteness allows him to cross cultural borders and assume the identity of "others." By positioning himself as White trash he can disassociate from many of the privileges of Whiteness and claim oppression and hence a more authentic voice. And to further gain credibility he appropriates characteristics common to Black hip-hop masculinity, made possible through the universal character of the White (male) subject. Our analysis makes clear that Eminem's public persona is situated at the intersections of numerous social categories.

Eminem is presented in the media as being White, male, heterosexual, and from an economically disadvantaged background. Each of these social locations is vital to the representation of him as a celebrity. Identification with any other category would greatly alter the public perception and reception of Eminem. If he were Black would he receive the same mainstream media attention? If he were a woman would her skill as a rapper garner the same success? If he came from an economically privileged background would he be afforded the same credibility? If he were gay, how would this alter his public persona and identification with his fans? Because of his identification with these specific social locations Eminem has access to spaces that others do not. He can move into and out of those spaces freely, taking advantage of privileges his social location provides him, and claiming oppression and disenfranchisement when it's to his advantage.

IMPLICATIONS

Media images create, shape, and reinforce our view of the social world and our place within it. Therefore, it's critical for students of media to understand how media institutions and messages teach us how to be women and men, how to dress and look, how to react to individuals from different social groups, and how and what to think, feel, behave, believe, and desire. Media messages perpetuate current social arrangements and systems of inequality (e.g., Eurocentric superiority, male domination) through various rhetorical strategies. Whiteness, as an analytical framework, names, highlights, and examines the rhetorical strategies that create the conditions for the White (male) subject to travel freely and successfully across cultural spaces. Such travels have, in a number of instances, resulted in the appropriation of "other" cultural forms. Ledbetter (1992/1995) wrote,

> Whites have been riffing off—or ripping off—black cultural forms for more than a century and making a lot of money from them. Whether it's Al Jolson, Elvis, the Rolling Stones, Blues Brothers, Commitments, New Kids, or Beasties, it's impossible to deny that, as a rule, the market responds much better to a black sound with a white face." (p. 541)

Why is this the case? Although the answer is too complex to be considered here, we, as critical consumers, can have different ways of engaging, reading, and listening to popular cultural productions such as music.

As audience members, we can decode—engage with, read, listen to—media messages from a range of perspectives or positions (Hall, 1990/1999). For example, when we read or listen to stories about Eminem in the popular media, we might believe that the rapper's success is solely due to his artistic talents and dedication (the common belief) and not consider his social position. This is an example of what Hall called the *dominant hegemonic* position, and it reflects acceptance of the dominant ideology. We could also subscribe to the belief that Eminem's talent and hard work (the dominant belief), along with market conditions and musical trends (the current situation), determined his success in the hip-hop world. This is an example of the *negotiated* code interpretation, in which the dominant ideology tends to be accepted except in certain instances. We could also follow the *oppositional* code—in which the dominant ideology is rejected. In such cases the consumer interrogates and questions the dominant interpretation and provides an alternative decoding. In this instance, we might not only question the dominant belief that success depends solely on talent and hard work but consider Eminem's race, class, gender, and sexuality as interlocking factors that greatly contribute to his unparalleled success.

Both students and consumers of media have many options and choices about how to analyze and decode messages. We can enjoy the words, the sounds, and the performances; develop and challenge multiple meanings; and resist media manipulation. As active and critical consumers of hip-hop, we can perhaps have a deeper understanding that hip-hop "is African in its storytelling, jiving, jonesin' (mock insulting) and general carrying on" (Venable, 2001, p. 19). That the most popular hip-hop artist is White is no accident. As activist Shanté Smalls (2001) compellingly observed, "This is 'AmeriKKKa,' where white maleness is the default setting" (p. 26) and "anything is accessible to you, if you are white" (pp. 24–25).

NOTE

1. *Blackness* is used here to suggest a complex and amorphous social code associated with African American identity that cannot be simply reduced to skin color.

IT'S YOUR TURN: WHAT DO YOU THINK? WHAT WILL YOU FIND?

1. What is meant by the "universal character" of Whiteness? Do you agree or disagree with this way of looking at Whiteness? Why? Discuss the meaning and implications of "White trash" as a distinct social category.

2. Discuss the intersections of various social locations (e.g., race, gender, sexuality) in Eminem's public persona. How do they affect his reception and success? Discuss the differences that might be perceived if he occupied different social locations.

3. Examine lyrics from several of Eminem's songs, such as "Rock Bottom" or "Criminal." How do they reflect his ability to appropriate aspects of hip-hop culture? How are they affected by his social location?

4. Discuss the public persona of other celebrities, such as Tiger Woods, Madonna, or Elton John. How do media representations of their social locations affect their careers?

REFERENCES

Aaron, C. (1999). Nine for 1999. *Spin, 15*(2), 80.

Dolan, J. (1999). Just don't give a f%@#!. *Spin, 15*(8), 63.

Hall, S. (1990/1999). Encoding, decoding. In S. During (Ed.), *The cultural studies reader* (2nd ed., pp. 507–517). London: Routledge.

Hartigan, J. (1997). Name calling: Objectifying "poor whites" and "white trash" in Detroit. In A. Newitz & M. Wray (Eds.), *White trash: Race and class in America* (p. 41–56). New York: Routledge.

Huxley, M. (2000). *Eminem: Crossing the line*. New York: St. Martin's Griffin.

King, J. (2000). Any love: Silence, theft, and rumor in the work of Luther Vandross. In D. Constantine-Simms (Ed.), *The greatest taboo: Homosexuality in black communities* (pp. 290–315). New York: Alyson.

Ledbetter, J. (1992/1995). Imitation of life. In G. Dines & J. M. Humez (Eds.), *Gender, race, and class in media: A text-reader* (pp. 540–544). Thousand Oaks, CA: Sage.

Nakayama, T. K., & Krizek, R. L. (1995/1999). Whiteness as a strategic rhetoric. In T. K. Nakayama & J. N. Martin (Eds.), *Whiteness: The communication of social identity* (pp. 87–106). Thousand Oaks, CA: Sage.

Newitz, A., & Wray, M. (1997). Introduction. In M. Wray & A. Newitz (Eds.), *White trash: Race and class in America* (pp. 1–12). New York: Routledge.

Norris, C. (2001). Eminem: Artist of the year. *Spin, 17*(1), 64.

Orbe, M. P., Warren, K. T., & Cornwell, N. C. (2000). Negotiating societal stereotypes: Analyzing *The Real World* discourse by and about African American men. *International and Intercultural Communication Annual, XXIII*, 107–134.

Pinn, A. B. (1996). "Getting' grown": Notes on gangsta rap music and notions of manhood. *Journal of African American Men, 2*(1), 61–73.

Rafferty, T. (2001, April). Eminem: A fan's notes—Stop fuming and fussing. Chill out and enjoy the outrageous brilliance. *Gentleman's Quarterly, 123*, 124, 133.

Rose, T. (1994). Rap music and the demonization of young Black males. In T. Golden (Ed.), *Black rep-*resentations of masculinity in contemporary American art* (pp. 149–157). New York: Whitney Museum of American Art.

Ross, A. (1994). The gangsta and the diva. In T. Golden (Ed.), *Black representations of masculinity in contemporary American art* (pp. 159–166). New York: Whitney Museum of American Art.

Shome, R. (1996). Race and popular cinema: Rhetorical strategies of Whiteness in *City of Joy. Communication Quarterly, 44*, 502–518.

Smalls, S. (2001, Summer). Keeping it real: A conversation about race, sexuality and hip hop. *Images, 22*–27.

Touré. (2000a). [Review of *The Marshall Mathers LP*]. *Rolling Stone, 845*, 135–136.

Touré. (2000b). Hip-hop's closet: A fanzine article touches a nerve. In D. Constantine-Simms (Ed.), *The greatest taboo: Homosexuality in Black communities* (pp. 31–32). New York: Alyson.

Venable, M. J. (2001, Summer). Homiesexual hip hop. *Images*, 18–21.

Wildman S. M., & Davis, A. D. (1995). Language and silence: Making systems of privilege visible. In R. Delgado (Ed.), *Critical race theory: The cutting edge* (pp. 573–579). Philadelphia: Temple University Press.

6.3 THE GENDERED PRACTICE OF MUSIC FANDOM ONLINE

Marjorie Kibby

> *One of the early hopes for the Internet was that it would erase social differences of race, class, and gender, which were seemingly invisible in the online world. These utopian dreams have not been realized, but women are using the Internet to resist sexism and empower themselves by occupying spaces that are problematic in a face-to-face environment. This is evident in online fandom. Focusing mainly on fans of the Australian band Augie March, the author studies how women and girls in online spaces have a breadth of experience of fandom that was much harder to achieve without online communication.*

The popular image of the music fan is linked to media images such as those of the hysterical female teenagers greeting the Beatles on their first tour. Music performance and production has always been primarily a male domain with limited roles for women, and the role most publicized has been that of the "groupie"—a fan with more interest in the musician than the music. Music fandom in general "seems to be considered as a mainly female phenomenon which revolves around the person of the star rather than around the music" (Rhein, 2003, p. 56). The screaming fans that greeted the Beatles were unable to hear the music, let alone appreciate its finer points, and their response to their idols has influenced the way female music fans have been viewed. The female music fan's experience has been seen as a preteen idolization, rather than as a mature appreciation of the music culture.

Lisa Lewis (1992, p. 1) said,

> We all know who the fans are. They are the ones who wear the colors of their favorite team, the ones who record their soap opera . . . . to watch after their workday is over, who tell you every detail about a movie star's life and work, the ones who sit in line for hours for front row tickets to rock concerts.

Fans differ from ordinary audiences in the degree of interest in even minor details of the object of their fandom. Fans spend a significant portion of their leisure time and often a large portion of their energy and financial resources following their interest; the object of their fandom becomes a major focus of their lives. The female experience of fandom has always been different from the male and has been recorded differently. Females were absent from early studies of subculture, because while the males were on the streets as mods and "Teddy Boys," girls were in their bedrooms journaling, scrapbooking, and sharing elaborate fantasies over the phone.

One of the early hopes for the Internet was that it would erase social differences of race, class, and gender, which were seemingly invisible in the online world. While these utopian dreams have not been realized, and the online world has reproduced the sexual inequality of everyday life, women are using the Internet to resist sexism and empower themselves by occupying spaces that are problematic in a face-to-face environment. In doing so they are creating a sense of community that facilitates the involvement of other women. While gender is not invisible in the online environment, it is not as overt as in offline spaces.

One area where is this evident is online fandom. The Internet has changed the way that fans acquire and listen to music, exchange information, communicate with each other, and connect with the musicians. It facilitates a growing range of fan practices, including those that were traditionally female activities. Online fan forums provide a space that is somewhere between the bedroom and the street—it is open and public and yet feels private and secure. Women's journals and scrapbooks are still created in their own spaces, but as music blogs, fan Web sites and MySpace pages they are viewed in public arenas. Without the Internet it was difficult for women and girls to display their knowledge, and their musical connections were devalued as female fans were generally assumed to be sleeping with the drummer rather than acquiring expertise in the music or establishing musical bonds. Online fandom has involved a growth in new discursive spaces and systems that blur the boundary between public and private discourses, a trend toward disintermediation that facilitates connections between fan and performer, and a reconfigured experience of space and time that reduces the importance of the street and the night in the fan experience. Through the sharing of social chat, information, feelings, connections with the musician, and musical knowledge, women and girls in online spaces have a breadth of experience of fandom that was much harder to achieve without online communication.

In the following, I consider each of these areas, primarily focusing on Augie March fans. Augie March is an Australian group, formed in 1996 and based in Melbourne. Their music is labeled "indie" or "alternative" rock, although they are signed to the major label Sony/BMG. Although their fans are relatively small in number, they are active, and they are actively encouraged by the band. Augie March has a strong female following, with the live audience fairly gender balanced, and an even distribution of male and female identifiers in online fan sites.

ONLINE FAN PRACTICES

Social Chat

A large part of fandom is associating with other fans. This is particularly true for female fans who seem to place importance on the feelings of community that fandom brings. For Augie March fans this social dimension is evident in their Yahoo! Group (http://groups.yahoo.com/), which supports photograph and file sharing and has a searchable archive. Messages can be read and replied to on the Web site, however most subscribers receive messages as individual e-mail. The forum provides a discursive space that unbounded by geography, time, or other constraints of face-to-face discussion. It allows an online community to form around members' shared taste culture. Fans engage in a variety of activities, including exchanging information and opinion, making purchasing decisions, and producing new and adapted texts. The forum is 36% male, 35% female, and 29% gender unspecified. Much of the discussion from members who are perceived to be female is social in tone and content—for example, the discussion around March 20, 2008, on men's hair styles was simply small talk, communication to make social connections. On other fan forums this is also the case. For example a female fan posted to U2-talk on Yahoo! Groups, "I haven't written anything in a long while . . . well months really. lol. Missed you all" (January 6, 2008).

"The most primal instinct a fan has is to talk to other fans about this common interest" (Clerc, 2000, p. 74), and the Internet has provided new opportunities and new mechanisms for this discussion. Norms and patterns of communication on the Internet are fundamentally influenced by offline contexts, and influence them in return (Baym, 1995). However, the Internet, which offers "constant access to a fan identity and community" intersects "with fans' affective relationships in such a way as to alter fan practices" (Hills, 2002, p. 172). Within fandom a sense of individuality-in-community is articulated, and fan identity is dependent on a relationship with other fans. This relationship is always available online. Early studies of Internet use revealed that females were more likely to communicate online and males to search for information (Jackson, Ervin, Gardner, & Schmitt, 2001). However, social networking sites link communication and information gathering and dissolve some of these gendered distinctions.

Information

The Augie March Web site provides standard biography, discography, and tour schedules and has a page with links to fan sites. Most fan sites complement the official site, linking to biographical information and tour dates rather than repeating them. These fan sites exemplify textual production by music fans and contain reviews and photos, guitar tablature and song lyrics, background information on film clips and CD art, gossipy news, and guest books for visitor comments. Originally using print-based media, most fan groups now use the Internet to share information, from breaking news to archived facts. Christina Aguilera's Fanorama lists over 400 fan Web sites that mostly female fans maintained to publish information on Christina, her life, and her music.

The Augie March fansites are an online equivalent of the fan magazine. Anyone with an interest in the band can publish online, and amateur sites can happily coexist with the official publication. Online publication enables expanded use of graphics and multimedia and interactive elements. Online publication also enables a breadth of distribution, provides an immediacy of revision, enables a complexity of presentation, and permits a more inclusive production process. Online textual production therefore may be more available to a broader range of fans, and the online versions of traditionally female texts such as journals and scrapbooks are no longer personal texts viewed only by close friends but public documents available to the world. The personal home page in recent years has been replaced by social networking sites that include a range of textual possibilities; however, Augie March's official site still contains links to fan pages developed by female fans, including the information- and opinion-rich *A Bullet for a Diamond Ring* (www. geocities.com/jojo_girl7/augie.htm).

Online discussion forums also provide a place in which "listeners actively interpret and collectively construct their sense of music and its world" (Shepherd, 1986, p. 307). The characteristics of computer-mediated communication perhaps allow for a more in-depth, more highly reasoned, and more accurately researched exchange than some face-to-face discussions, where exchanges tend to focus on the immediate context. In online forums, information is authenticated, arguments extended to logical conclusions, and wide-ranging opinions presented. With gender often unknown or ambiguous, participants are accorded respect on the basis of the information shared, so female participants have more or less equal access to the knowledge of the musician and the associated cultural capital.

Amazon.com provides a number of spaces for fans to express their musical knowledge. Visitors to the Augie March listing can rate or review each CD, submit a "best-of" list, or provide a guide to a genre, movement, or artist. The fan involvement in commercial sites such as Amazon spans a wider range of discursive practices than is readily available offline. Rating performances, reviewing collections, documenting histories, establishing personal connections, and publishing guides to music genres are activities available to all fans regardless of gender. Female fans can publicly demonstrate a level of knowledge and expertise in a way that they might be too intimidated to do in a mixed-gender, face-to-face discussion of the band. Fans regularly review albums and post lists of favorite tracks justifying their choices and suggestion for additions to a collection. This provides a range of opportunities for textual production. The Amazon reviews and ratings are difficult to differentiate on the basis of gender. Listmania lists compiled by apparent females that feature Amy Winehouse have similar comments on technique, musicality, and genre as the lists featuring the Foo Fighters, compiled by apparent males.

The lists on the Augie March page include *My Favourite albums of 2000*, by saint 77; *So you'd like to . . . balance on an elephant in an obscure Melbourne café*, a guide by phaedrus 1; *Augie March—best tracks,* by statistic no 1; and *Staggering works of musical genius* by Kate. Lists vary in the detail and quality of the information presented, but the mere aligning of particular musicians may influence listening choices and potentially purchasing patterns. Again, lists associated with both male- and female-seeming names discuss the work in terms of both technical quality and emotional appeal.

Before recording what is one if the greatest albums ever made, they came up with a couple of EP's, including this one. Fantastic of course, rich in flavour and feel, mood and text, but all words fail on describing track #l 'Century Son.' Let's just say I haven't heard a kaining rock song so hard since 'Teen Spirit,' and before that 'Search and Destroy'" (Steph 11/8/07)

Whereas females have traditionally been more involved in the creative side of fandom, and males in the collecting aspect, many online sites dissolve the boundaries between collecting and creating, hence blurring gender divisions as well. Amazon's Listmania is an example of this, where compilers put together collections in personal ways, linking items creatively and presenting them as new texts. This combination of collection and creative text may account for the similarities between males' and females' lists.

Connections

People who subscribe to the Augie March e-mail list see themselves as "real" fans—"the site is meant for people who are passionate about Augie March more than the part-time fan" (Kris 8/03/06). It is a place where only mild criticism of particular gigs or songs is tolerated, and then only if the criticism is qualified or tempered with general praise: "with it being an Augie March mailing list do you really think this is the right place to be telling people about how your friends think Augie March is boring?" (Daniel, 23/01/06). The "fanatic" fandom usually ascribed to women is the norm for the group and consequently loses its gender associations. Being fanatical about the band is almost a prerequisite for membership, and the most fanatical are accorded a level of respect not generally given to "groupies." While Mel's comment below might seem reminiscent of the Beatles' hysterical girls, it was met with agreement by male members of the forum and respected as an appropriate response for a fan:

> I got to tick off everything on my list for these concerts. . . . I met and talked with all of the band, embarassed myself by asking for their autographs, I got setlists on both nights (Glenn's on Thursday and Kiernan's on friday), danced during every song and screamed up a lung during both shows, and got to meet a few more people from this list. (Mel, 24/12/07)

"The Christmas shows were everything I hoped they would be and more. Well worth the trip, and I'll be joining Mel in booking early for next year's" (James, 28/12/07).

MySpace is a social networking site that offers an interactive network of communication tools including an e-mail and messaging system, blog, and video and audio files. On the Augie March MySpace site, it is evident that posters are communicating directly with band members. "Hi AM. Thanks for that amazing show at the Cambridge" (Assia, 9/5/06). "You guys rocked @ newtown on friday night!! absolutely fantastic show . . . plus i loved the bible lesson :D" (Jo, 2/5/06). To post a message to Augie March, users must first be added to Augie March's friends list, so someone connected with the band must "accept" the user as a "friend." This sets up a very different dynamic from online groups or mailing lists. Although the messages are public—even available to nonmembers—most are personal in tone and appear as private one-on-one communications of a type that is rarely possible for fans offline. Fans can ignore the information that Augie March has 2,403 friends and believe they are members of a select group. This sense of connection with the musician is available to female fans without the risks that may be associated with forming face-to-face connections.

Feelings

Given that females are generally more intimate and emotional in their friendships than males and tend to place a higher value on these friendships than males do, and that females emphasize talking, emotional sharing, and discussing personal problems with their friends whereas men emphasize sharing activities and doing things with their friends (Aukett, Ritchie, & Mill, 1988), social networking sites that facilitate talking and the sharing of personal and emotional content can validate traditionally female ways of connecting with friends and of making friends with the objects of fandom. For example, on U2-talk, a poster said, "Just came in from a stressful day, and your message made me feel good. It is always nice to be amongst friends" (U2girl, 12/4/08) and received a number of responses offering sympathy and support. Even in a genre with a traditionally male fan base such as hip-hop, female fans leave messages of emotional support. On Kanye West's MySpace site, comments such as "Hey Sweetheart . . . just coming through to show some luv . . . stay blessed and gorgeous:)" (Nikole, 6/4/08) are common. Fans share personal information with Kanye: "Just lost my Grandmother & Uncle . . . He's calling his saints home . . . Continue to strive for excellence we need your inspiration to help light the world" (Angel Eyes, 6/4/08).

Space and Place

The growth of the Internet has facilitated a move from a "local" based merely on the accidents of geography to a "virtual local," experienced in ways unbounded by geography. Fandom has traditionally been organized within local boundaries, and the virtual local opens up new places for the construction of fan communities based on shared taste cultures that come together in a shared forum made possible by the new globalized media. Locality is constructed through the symbolic meanings attached to place (Appadurai, 1995), and online spaces are constructed as places by the meanings attached to them. Spaces in the face-to-face environment have traditionally been gendered, with some music spaces more available to males than females. Online spaces are not gender neutral, but they may not be as gender specific as their physical equivalents.

A key experience of fandom is the communal gathering to watch the musicians perform. Online fan practices extend and support this experience with pre- and post-gig meetings arranged, set lists posted, and reviews shared through the online forum. Venues and meeting places are experienced differently by males and females, and although online spaces are also gendered, the absence of physical constraints such as safety and propriety lessen the gender gap in the experience of online space.

GENDERED FANDOM

In this work, I have identified and categorized (where possible) fan practices along gender lines at a variety of sites and have then compared them to what I found to be fan practices described in the literature. The major differences I identified were (a) the use of new discursive spaces and practices that negated some of the traditional gender associations;

(b) a tendency for more direct contact with fewer intermediaries, which altered the relationships between fans and musicians; and (c) a redefinition of concepts of space and time, such as "local" and "now," which opened up new spaces in which female fans could participate. Female contributions could still be ignored or disparaged in online spaces, but gender seemed less obvious in the interactions. Female fans contributed significantly to the online fan activities of musicians such as Augie March who have cross-gender appeal. And the activities, texts, and communications were often not able to be coded as "gendered"—similar fan activities were identified with male and female personas.

Fandom requires a community and necessitates active participation in that community. Fandom also requires an engagement with the object of fandom, with the recorded music and the live performances, with the paraphernalia and memorabilia, with the information, and with the emotional associations. In addition, fandom generally involves creation of new texts, often the creation of personal texts from mass-mediated ones. Women have always used technology to bridge the divide between public and private, though the history of women's technological engagement has tended to be ignored. From phones and phonograms to mash-ups and MySpace sites, women have made use of the available technology to construct and represent their identities, to make connections, and to engage with others. The variety of production, communication, and distribution mechanisms known as the "Internet" facilitates this on a massive scale.

As Nancy Baym (1995) points out, discursive practices on the Internet do not exist in a vacuum, but are an extension of other norms and patterns of communication. Just as Baym's (2008) study of soap opera fans revealed that the face-to-face practices of fandom greatly influenced the communicative practices of the fans online, for the fans of musicians, online fan practices arise out of everyday music consumption habits. What the Internet provides is not a whole new experience of fandom for women and girls but rather enhanced opportunities, a greater variety of experiences, and increased returns for effort. The Internet makes it easier to be a fan, it changes the relationship between fans and between fans and musicians, and it makes it more rewarding to be a fan. While none of these characteristics are gender specific, together they facilitate female fans presentation of themselves as "music fanatics" rather than "groupies" and enable their contributions to fan communities to be assessed on their merits, deemphasizing the contributor's gender. Gender does not disappear online. However, in the absence of physical cues, contributors have a greater chance of being respected and responded to as contributors rather than female contributors, and in the absence of physical barriers contributors have a greater chance of being female contributors.

IT'S YOUR TURN: WHAT DO YOU THINK? WHAT WILL YOU FIND?

1. Interview a number of your friends about the music they like. Ask whether they consider themselves a fan of an artist or band. Find out what they think makes someone a "fan" rather than just someone who listens to the music. Do males and females describe differences in being a fan?

2. Create one issue of a fanzine for a musician or group that has a predominantly male or female fan base. You can do this as a print magazine, a wiki, or a blog. What information and activities would female fans want to read about, and what would appeal to male readers? Are there differences? Why or why not?

3. Do a content analysis of a music magazine such as *Rolling Stone*, *NME*, or *Under the Radar*, identifying each story, advertisement, and feature as "appeals to female fans," "appeals to male fans," or "appeals to everyone." Can you conclude that the magazine has an overall appeal to male or female music fans?

4. Analyze a fan discussion forum in Yahoo! Groups, MySpace, Facebook, or another social Web site. Label the contributors as "male," "female," and "unknown." Looking at the male and female messages, categorize them under headings such as social chat, information, shared feelings, musical knowledge. Are there any differences between the messages posted by males and females?

REFERENCES

Appadurai, A. (1995). The production of locality. In R. Fardon (Ed.), *Counterworks: Managing the diversity of knowledge* (pp. 204–226). London: Routledge.

Aukett, R., Ritchie, J., & Mill, K. (1988) Gender differences in friendship patterns. *Sex Roles, 19*(1/2), 57–66.

Baym, N. (1995). The emergence of community in computer mediated communication. In S. Jones (Ed.), *Cybersociety* (pp. 138–163). London: Sage.

Baym, N. (2008). *Online fandom blog.* www.onlinefandom. com/who-runs-this-site/

Clerc, S. (2000). Estrogen brigades and "big tits" threads: Media fandom online and off-line. In D. Bell & B. Kennedy (Eds.), *The cybercultures reader* (pp. 73–97). London: Routledge.

Hills, M. (2002). *Fan cultures.* London: Routledge.

Jackson, L. A., Ervin, K. S., Gardner. P. D., & Schmitt, N. (2001). Gender and the Internet: Women communicating and men searching. *Sex Roles, 44*(5/6), 363–379.

Lewis, L. (1992). (Ed.) *The adoring audience: Fan culture and popular media.* London: Routledge.

Rhein, S. (2003). Gender differences in teenage-fandom: A teenie-fan survey on musical interaction in fan cultural contexts. *Proceedings of the 5th Triennial ESCOM Conference, September 8–15* (pp. 56-60). Hanover University of Music and Drama, Germany.

Shepherd, J. (1986). Music consumption and cultural self-identities: Some theoretical and methodological reflections. *Media Culture and Society, 8*, 305–330.

6.4 WOMEN ON WOMEN: THE REPRESENTATION OF WOMEN BY FEMALE RAP ARTISTS

Katie Blevins and Adrienne Biddings

> *Rap is generally labelled misogynistic (women hating), but most studies look at how male rap artists portray women in their music. The authors of this reading examine the lyrics of top-selling female rap artists to see how women are being portrayed by other women.*

This chapter started on a courtyard bench. Adrienne and I (Katie) had decided to collaborate on a project and were trying to decide on a topic. The ideas started out wild and unfocused, but during the brainstorming session we decided that we wanted to talk about music and women. And we wanted to talk about something that mattered.

Adrienne suggested rap. I was interested, but I worried about rehashing old communication research. *Everyone* knows that rap, a music genre mostly dominated by men, presents music and images that degrade women. But suddenly we stopped and asked ourselves, if male artists talk negatively about women in their music, what do *women* artists do?

Even though rap began as an underground movement, media saturation has made it more and more popular in the mainstream. Rap is usually associated with male artists and has been referred to as an "all male sport" (Fleurant, 2006). Occasionally, female artists manage to become prominent, but overall the rap scene is dominated by men. According to Rhym (1996), one side effect of having such male dominance is that many of rap's themes tend to be anti-women. Black women especially are a target for disrespect (Davis, 2004). "Gangsta rap" in particular is said to be characterized by both self-centered and misogynistic (women-hating) ideas. Rhym presents three emphases common in gangsta rap: self-promotion, using sex to sell music, and appealing to sexist audience members by "selling" a stereotypical woman in their music.

In general, much of the literature suggests that the depiction of women in rap is negative. Sometimes women themselves reinforce this idea. Collins (2004) notes that women artists and women audience members sometimes claim to embrace their independence by expressing their sexuality when actually they have made themselves into the sexualized version of women that males rap about. Although some women artists and audience members might actually be becoming independent, the majority are more likely norming, or adapting to fit in, with the rest of rap in a self-fulfilling prophecy. Scholars such as Fleurant (2006) speak of a "vicious cycle" in rap, where male artists degrade women in their music, women artists and audience members accept this, and male audience members see this treatment of women as normal while growing up listening to rap.

The few women artists who succeed in rap face many challenges. Morgan (2005) writes that most women rappers take one of two paths: They either become the sexual stereotype put forth by gangsta rap, or they try to write progressive and educational lyrics while not promoting themselves as sexual. Many female artists who choose the more difficult route of not dressing and not acting in a sexually suggestive manner have to deal with vicious rumors and gossip about their sexuality and other personal topics.

However, because one of the accepted emphases of rap is self-promotion, women artists also have an important opportunity to talk about themselves and to create their own identities (Collins, 2004). Rappers are supposed to proclaim who they are and how great they are, so it isn't selfish, just natural, for women rap artists to do the same thing. This is very different from many opportunities that women have in other media genres because women rappers are encouraged instead of discouraged to have a strong individualistic voice.

Overall, most of the research on rap looks at how male artists talk about women in their music. A smaller segment of research looks at how female rap artists talk about themselves in their music. There is almost no research looking at how female rap artists talk about women in general in their music. In this chapter we will look at top female rap artists' lyrics and see how female rap artists talk about women in their music. In other words, women on women.

WHAT WE DID: SETTING UP THE CONTENT ANALYSIS

To see how female rap artists talk about women, we analyzed female rappers' lyrics. We decided the best approach was to examine mainstream rap, or what gets seen by the most people. *Billboard* is generally considered the music industry standard, so we used the *Billboard* charts and album sales in a two-stage sampling process. First, we identified the top-10-selling female rap artists during 11 years, 1996–2006. Then, we picked all of the songs by these 10 artists that appeared on the Top 20 rap charts during the 11-year period. One top-selling female artist had no songs that cracked the Top 20, so we narrowed the number and looked at nine. Our analysis focuses on the hits of these nine artists: Missy El-liot, Lil' Kim, Eve, Da Brat, Foxy Brown, Trina, Queen Latifah, Khia, and MC Lyte.

This yielded a total of 32 songs for our sample. Instead of listening to the songs or watching music videos we concentrated on the lyrics so that we could do a content analysis of written things. This made the study much more cohesive, because not all of the songs had music videos or easy to get unedited recordings, but it took out some of the contextualization since we couldn't consider the inflection the artists had during their performances or the visualizations that may have accompanied the music. Lyrics were gathered from online sources, and unedited lyrics were used for the content analysis.

Two coders originally conducted the content analysis. They used Holsti's formula to determine inter-coder reliability, or how accurate the two coders were in relation to each other's answers. Inter-coder reliability varied quite a bit due to coder error on a few variables, but generally there was 80%–90% reliability. Therefore, despite the overall high reliability, the counts were checked by two new coders. All differences were resolved by consensus. These are the final counts that are reported here.

The coders looked at two things during the content analysis: the words themselves and the language in the context of the lyrics. In the first step, the lyrics were examined for nouns that are usually identified as being related to being a woman. Coders were given a glossary with words and definitions to use as a reference that was cross-referenced with a hip-hop dictionary as well as a standard dictionary. This is because some words have a very set meaning, like, for instance, *daughter*. This word does not have any other meanings that are generally accepted, and while it may appear in rap, the meaning you will find is the same as what you would find in a regular dictionary. Variations of the words *mom* and *wife* are other examples. Some words, though, have deeper and more varied meaning in rap.

You might think that *wifey* would have the same meaning as *wife*, but in rap, *wifey* does not necessarily mean the wife of someone. Instead, it generally means a committed or preferred relationship between two people, where the man might refer to his partner as his "wifey" (Rap Dictionary, 2006). Some words only have a meaning that relates to women within rap. *Chickenhead*, for instance, would probably mean a chicken's (severed) head to most people, but in rap, it refers to a woman who either talks a lot or who performs oral sex on a man (the name coming from the bobbing motion of her head while she performs the act) (Rap Dictionary, 2006).

It was important for coders to understand the depth that some of these definitions entailed, which is why the detailed glossary was provided with words to look for, especially because they could only count words when they referred to women. If there was a song about cutting off a chicken's head and had the word *chickenhead* in it 30 times, none of them would have counted if they referred to chickens, not women, as the glossary defined. This might seem fairly straightforward, but other words like *bitch* (which can, in hip hop culture, be used with intended positive connotations) were more complicated. Despite *bitch* being a word that most people associated with women, it is in general a derogatory term that also can be used to demean men or comment about situations. Phrases like "he's a bitch" or "it's a bitch" would not have been counted in the totals.

The glossary listed and defined 25 words. Coders did not count pronouns such as *you* and *she* or anytime proper nouns were used. Parts of female anatomy such as *breast*, *vagina*, and so on were not counted. Coders read the lyrics, tallied the number of times each word appeared in each song, and then added those counts up for the total number of times each word appeared. This gave us the raw counts.

Second, after the raw counts, the *contextual usage* of each identified word was coded. Understanding contextual usage is important because a word that may typically be considered derogatory can be used in a positive way, and vice versa. To conduct their analysis of the contextual usage, coders went back and evaluated the use of each of the previously identified words in the context as positive, neutral, or negative. They looked at each word in the context of the verse, not the song as a whole. For example *bitch* might be used negatively at the beginning of a song but positively at the end. Most songs tell a story and have transitions that make such recognitions important. Even a single word can vary in meaning throughout a single song. A value of -1 was assigned when the word appeared in a negative context, 0 for neutral, and $+1$ for positive. These counts were totaled so we could see how many times a word, like *bitch*, was used positively, negatively, and neutrally in all of the songs. These were the scaled counts. After everything was coded, we compiled the data. We came up with the raw counts, or the total number of times each word appeared, and the scaled counts, or how the words were used in the context of the lyrics. These are presented in Table 6.1.

One song did not have any of the listed words at all, so only 31 of the songs were counted. For the raw counts, each coder looked at how many times the words provided appeared. *Bitch* and derivatives of *girl* were the two words that appeared the most by far, with *bitch* appearing 53 times and *girl* appearing 56 times. Almost all of the other counts were surprisingly low, as no other word showed up more than 13 times. Most of the words only showed up once or twice. Not even all of the words listed in the glossary appeared, and some words, mostly some slang we hadn't thought of, showed up while we were coding. *Block bender, female, gold digger, grandmother, homegirl, hoodrat, skank, skeezer,* and *slut* weren't in any of the songs, though coders were instructed to look for them. *Sista, queen, gal, ladies, groupay, fishes, birds, sleepin' beauties, dames, queen bee, dyke,* and *broads* were found, though they weren't on the list.

The scaled counts reveal some intriguing trends. It's interesting that nearly half of the appearances of *bitch* were positive, at 24 of 53 total occurrences. *Ho*, which is usually considered an extremely negative word as well, appeared 8 times in the lyrics and was used in a positive way 5 times! The single appearance each of *dyke* and *hoochie* were positive.

Most of the neutral counts are unremarkable, with a small percentage of a few words being neutral, but the negative counts are as interesting as the positive ones. Many words that are usually considered neutral, if not positive, have at least a few instances where they were used in a negative way. *Boo, broad, chick,* and *girl* all show up in the negative counts, as does *girlfriend, wife,* and *woman.*

TABLE 6.1   **Frequency and Contextual Use of Words about Women**

WORD	TOTAL RAW COUNT	TIMES POSITIVE	TIMES NEUTRAL	TIMES NEGATIVE
Girl	56	44	4	8
Bitch	53	24	6	23
Mom/Mother/Mama	13	9	3	1
Queen	10	9	1	0
Chick	9	7	0	2
Ho/Hoe	8	5	0	3
Lady(ies)	5	3	2	0
Woman	5	2	2	1
Wife/Misses	4	3	0	1
Queen Bee	3	3	0	0
Shorty/Shawty	3	2	1	0
Gal	2	2	0	0
Boo	2	1	0	1
Girlfriend	2	0	1	1
Barbie	1	1	0	0
Dykes	1	1	0	0
Hoochie/Hoochiemama	1	1	0	0
Sista	1	1	0	0
Sleepin' Beauties	1	1	0	0
Wifey	1	1	0	0
Daughter	1	0	1	0
Birds	1	0	0	1
Broads	1	0	0	1
Chickenhead	1	0	0	1
Dames	1	0	0	1
Fishes	1	0	0	1
Groupie/pay	1	0	0	1
Trick	1	0	0	1
Whore	1	0	0	1

WHAT IT MEANS: REDEFINING WORDS OF HATE

Most of the research done on rap discusses how anti-woman male rap artists are in their music. You would think that certain words would make an appearance in women's lyrics, too, especially because research suggests that a lot of women artists are just trying to fit in and play along by norming with the mostly male genre. However, by looking at the counts you can see that only *bitch* and *girl* appear in any large numbers. *Whore* only shows up once, and other negative words like *slut* and *skank* never even make an appearance. In fact, the numbers in general are fairly low. One of the songs didn't even have any of the words listed at all! This seems to suggest that though one might expect misogynistic messages in these songs, something else very different is going on with successful female rap artists.

The scaled counts suggest much the same thing. Some extremely negative words appear in relatively high numbers in the positive section. *Bitch* is the clearest example of this, with nearly half of its counts showing up as positive. How is this possible? Well, if you look at the glossary definition for *bitch* you find the usual negative definitions, like "prostitute, meaning literally a female dog" (Rap Dictionary, 2006). But you'll also find other definitions, like "an empowered woman," or even, "a strong, confident, secure woman" (Rap Dictionary, 2006; Westbrook, 2002). These definitions, which used to be sort of against the grain of what words like *bitch* usually mean, are gaining prominence and acceptance in these lyrics.

Likewise, presumptively neutral or positive words are being used in a negative context. *boo*, which means "one's girlfriend or boyfriend," is used negatively in the songs (Rap Dictionary, 2006). *Chick*, which merely means "a woman or girl," also shows up in the negative counts. The same applies to several of the other words, such as *wife* and *woman*. It is important to realize that there are no corresponding negative definitions for these words, even in rap. Unlike *bitch*, which can be grudgingly used in both the traditional negative way and a less accepted but still documented positive way, these words really only mean what they have always meant.

So what is going on overall? What this study seems to suggest is that these particular women rap artists are using words traditionally meant to degrade women as opportunities to be powerful and positive. Female rap artists have to survive and appeal to the current rap culture, which is heavily male dominated and usually very sexist. As a result, many female artists have to express themselves and write within the framework of the rap genre as a whole. These female artists are using certain words, like *bitch* and ho, in their music, but they're not using them as frequently, or with the same meaning, that male artists do.

On some level, top female rap artists seem to be redefining words that are generally considered negative. This might not be conscious on their part, but while certain misogynistic words are appearing in female artists' lyrics, they may not be appearing with the same meaning and connotation that they usually do. These women artists appear to be reworking the female image in rap by using rap's own anti-woman language in a positive way and making words such as *bitch* mean entirely different things, such as referring to a close friend as a *bitch* in a possessive way or congratulating a woman for showing strength by displaying characteristics that might get her called a bitch in male rap music, like dumping a boyfriend. On the other side, words that are traditionally less negative in nature are being used with negative context. This is not necessarily a bad thing. Songs are stories, and not everything in the stories these women are sharing is positive. But instead of referring to the woman who stole their boyfriend as a slut, or whore, artists are using words like *girl* or *chick* to talk about these "bad" women. There is still a movement toward a new version of rap that is perhaps on many levels, more true to the lives of the people who live and write it.

Given that this study relied on a small sample—even though it included all the top-20 songs by the 10 top-selling female rappers during an entire decade—it's difficult to draw complete conclusions based on this look at how women rap artists are singing about and representing women in their music. Yet it seems obvious that something important is going on in rap. That maybe some of the stereotypes about women are being rewritten and changed by the women who have struggled to the top of this genre. That maybe sometime in the future rap won't just be an "all male sport" but one where women have equal say, both about themselves and about the image portrayed of women in general.

IT'S YOUR TURN: WHAT DO YOU THINK? WHAT WILL YOU FIND?

1. Does it seem plausible that female rap artists portray women differently in their music than male rap artists? Look at the hits by the top 10 male rappers from 1996 to 2006 and see what you find.

2. How do rappers portray men? Look at the top male and female rappers for male-gendered language, then determine whether the use of each word is positive, negative, or neutral. Is this better or worse than how women are portrayed? Do male and female artists portray men differently?

3. Watch some rap music videos, by both male and female artists. Think critically about the stories being told both in the song and the video itself. How are women being talked about? How are they being visually portrayed? Do you see differences between the male and female artists? Why do these differences exist (or not)?

4. What about underground rap artists and their music? How do non-mainstream rappers portray women and men? Is it better or worse?

REFERENCES

Collins, P. H. (2004). *Black Sexual Politics*. New York: Routledge.

Davis, T. (2004, March). The height of disrespect: New study on hip-hop sexuality finds anti-women strain, even among young women. *The Village Voice* [Electronic edition]. Retrieved May 19, 2007, from www.villagevoice.com/news/0411, davis,51847,1.html

Fleurant, J. (2006). Hip hop sells sex to women. *Nobodysmiling.com: Hip hop street knowledge*. Retrieved May 19, 2007, from www.nobodysmiling.com/hiphop/editorial/86512.php

Morgan, M. (2005). Hip-hop women shredding the veil: Race and class in popular feminist identity. *South Atlantic Quarterly, 104*(3), 425–444.

Rap Dictionary [Electronic version]. (2006). Retrieved June 20, 2007, from www.rapdict.org

Rhym, D. (1996). Here's for the bitches: An analysis of gangsta rap and misogyny. *The Womanist: Theory and Research, 2*(1), 1–15.

Westbrook, A. (2002). *Hip hoptionary*. New York: Random House.

6.5 PIXEL PINUPS: IMAGES OF WOMEN IN VIDEO GAMES

Nina B. Huntemann

> *As with any popular art form, video games are a cultural expression of—among other things—how society thinks about gender and the relationships among men and women. This reading focuses specifically on the evolution of female video game characters from early portrayals of women as "damsels in distress" to contemporary depictions of strong, independent, but still hyper-sexualized characters.*

Often informed by a feminist perspective, media studies scholars have produced both critical analyses of and theoretical frameworks for understanding the social influence of mass mediated images of femininity and female sexuality. However, the images of women in video games hasn't been as widely explored as such images in advertising, film, television, and music. Compared to traditional forms of media, video and computer game[1] technology is relatively new and has played a minor economic and cultural role in the entertainment industries. However, this is changing—during the last two decades video games have moved into the mainstream of popular culture.

While competing segments of the entertainment industries have declined in recent years, video games continue to experience enviable growth. In 2007, with a boost from the launch of two new console systems, the industry celebrated a 34% increase in software sales and 54% increase in hardware sales over the previous year (Ault, 2008). When *Halo 3* was released for the Microsoft Xbox 360 in September of 2007, the game generated more retail revenues in its first day ($170 million) than the blockbuster film *Spiderman 3* earned at the box office during its opening weekend ($151 million) (Fritz, 2007). By the end of the year, *Halo 3* sold 4.82 million copies (Olson, 2008), while the top-selling album *Noel* by Josh Groban sold 3.7 million copies (Veiga, 2008).

According to the Entertainment Software Association (2007), the industry's trade organization, 69% of all American heads of households play video games. In 2007 computer and video game software sales topped $9.5 billion, selling over 268 million games, or 9 games a second every day of the year (ESA, 2008).

With growing numbers of Americans buying and playing video games, it is critical to examine the images of women and men such games present. As noted video games scholar Henry Jenkins (2000, p. 11B) wrote, "the time has come to take games seriously as an important new popular art."

DAMSELS IN DISTRESS

Similar to and often modeled on fairy-tale narratives, the most common role for female characters in video games is the "damsel in distress." A staple of early video games, this character is often central to a game's back story, which establishes the purpose and goal of a game. However, she usually fills a minor role during game play and often disappears from the game altogether until the final scene, when the hero eventually rescues and receives an obligatory display of affection from the damsel. Kisses and hugs are typical rewards for heroic rescue. But, as discussed below, some female characters also undress and use sexually suggestive language toward their saviors.

Perhaps the most famous distressed damsel is Pauline, the object of a plump male carpenter's affections in the 1981 Nintendo arcade hit *Donkey Kong*. Upon dropping a quarter into the arcade game, players watch a brief animation of a large gorilla carrying Pauline to the top of a scaffold-like structure. The hero/player's job is to reach the top of the scaffolding while avoiding barrels the gorilla rolls down from on high. Pauline's only action is a cry for help at the beginning of the game. During game play she simply stands at the perilous top, guarded by the menacing ape, awaiting her hero.

Donkey Kong, which is largely responsible for the early success of Nintendo, developed into a mega-hit series of video games. The carpenter became Mario, an Italian plumber, and Pauline was replaced by Princess Daisy in *Super Mario Land*. She later became Princess Peach Toadstool in *Super Mario World*. Although the back story changed slightly with each release, Mario's basic goal remained the same—rescue the girl.

Further incarnations of the Mario games did expand Peach's role. She was one of several characters players could choose from in *Super Mario Bros. 2, Mario Kart, Mario Golf*, and *Mario Tennis*. In her most fleshed-out performance, in *Super Mario RPG*, Peach was granted magical powers that relied on stereotypically feminine traits. She could heal her fellow characters' wounds, and a magical hug from Peach would cure the entire Mario gang.

The Legend of Zelda, a widely popular series launched in 1986 for the Nintendo console system, also relied upon the damsel in distress device to establish its premise. In the original game, Link, the male hero, must rescue the captured Princess Zelda and save the world by keeping ancient magical artifacts from falling into evil hands. In *Zelda II: The Adventure of Link*, the hero returns to the land of Hyrule to find Zelda in a deep, deadly sleep. To save the princess this time, Link must find six long-lost magical crystals and return them to their proper kingdoms. Princess Zelda is imprisoned again in the third game release, *The Legend of Zelda: A Link to the Past*. In this game, she contacts Link via telepathic power to come to her rescue.

The typical rewards for rescue—kisses and hugs—suggest affection with veiled overtones of sexuality between heroes and the damsels they rescue. But what is expressed as cartoonish affection in Mario and Zelda games becomes lascivious interaction in the *Duke Nukem* video game series popular in the 1990s. The protagonist, Duke Nukem, is a hyper-masculine character with exaggerated muscles, gigantic weapons, and chauvinistic attitudes. His favorite bar, where the games usually begin, is a strip club called Bootylicious. The general premise of the series involves an invasion by outer space pigs who attempt to imprison the Earth's women (referred to as "babes") and take over the planet. Duke's job is to rescue the women from slavery and save the world from the swine invaders. The barely clothed women Duke rescues are grateful for his heroism and often suggest that their gratitude includes sexual favors. In *Duke Nukem 3D* and *Duke Nukem Zero Hour* the hero enters strip clubs, porn shops, and bars to find women dancing in bikinis. A player can hand a stripper money, upon which the female character flashes her breasts while Duke says, "Shake it, baby."

The common element in the *Duke Nukem, Zelda, Mario,* and other damsel-in-distress games is the essential but passive role of the female character. Without her, the hero has no reason to embark on his (and the hero is typically male) adventure. However, once the goal is established she disappears from the action. If evoked during game play, she merely reminds the hero of his purpose. Solely an object to be located and returned, like lost treasure, the female character has no control over her destiny. She is not only a victim of violence and abuse (forcefully captured, locked away in prisons, and mortally threatened), she is robbed of agency with no means to save herself from danger. As players interact with these characters, the overwhelming message is that women are essentially powerless, fully dependent on men, and indebted to the heroes who rescue them.

FEMME FATALITIES

Although female characters are still greatly underrepresented, the option of playing a woman or girl has existed since the early history of video games. Most notably, *Ms. Pac-Man* (released as an arcade game in 1981 by Midway) became the first female video game celebrity. She was nearly identical to her predecessor, *Pac-Man*, but *Ms. Pac-Man*'s gender was signaled by a red bow, lipstick, eyelashes, and a beauty mark. A conspicuous but nonetheless hugely successful marketing stunt to attract girls to video games, *Ms. Pac-Man* was even more popular than *Pac-Man* and is generally considered a superior game.

In terms of human female characters, *Gauntlet* led the way in 1985 when it featured Thyra the Valkyrie, one of four character options in its role-playing arcade game. *Mortal Kombat* followed in 1992 with Sonya Blade, a member of a U.S. Special Forces unit whose lethal move (called a "fatality") was a "kiss of death" that, when blown toward an opponent, exploded his torso. Later releases of *Mortal Kombat* included additional female characters, each with similarly sexually suggestive fatal moves. For example, Tanya could jump on the shoulders of her enemy and, with her thighs tightly wrapped around the victim's neck, break it by spinning herself around.

Fighting games such as *Mortal Kombat, Street Fighter*, and *Virtua Fighter* have consistently offered female game characters who kick butt as skillfully as male characters do. In stark contrast to damsels in distress, these game characters take care of themselves and are indebted to no one for their freedom. However, in exchange for personal agency, most female protagonists are depicted with overtly sexualized bodies. Wearing variations of skintight leotards or plate-metal bikinis, female characters have exaggerated breasts and hips, tiny waists, and long legs. While 7% of the female population has the body type of women portrayed in advertising (Olds, 1999), perhaps no one has the dimensions of the virtual women in video games. Unlike the "real" women in *Elle, Cosmopolitan*, and *Vogue* magazine, video game characters are computer generated. Their body proportions do not have to be realistic. Like *Barbie*, if female video game characters were real, they would be too breast heavy to walk and would live less than a minute because their torsos are too small to hold their vital organs. Despite such grossly inaccurate proportions, these fantastic females can jump across rivers, flip backwards over fences and deliver roundhouse kicks, all while managing to stay in their tiny outfits.

Examining the attire of female characters reveals the purely decorative nature of their clothing, whereas male characters' apparel generally serves a functional purpose. Although some male characters face fire-breathing dragons and plasma guns wearing little but a loincloth, most often they are covered by metal armor or space-age suits. Notably, even the super-muscular torsos of male characters are protected by molded chest plates. The ridiculously exaggerated chests of female characters are usually exposed, with barely a piece of cloth covering their breasts. Julia Chan from Namco's *Tekkan 5* fights her enemies while donning a sports bra and denim miniskirt. Her colleague, Christie Monteiro, manages to pummel her opponents while dressed in a small bikini top and sequin-clad, low-rise bellbottoms. As with most female characters, Julia and Christie's pneumatic bodies and revealing clothing were created for the viewing pleasure of players—often assumed to be heterosexual boys and men. The strength, skill, and autonomy of these characters rarely exists without the grossly obvious sexual portrayal of the female body.

BUXOM BABES

The sexualization of women's bodies in video games has paralleled advances in game technology. As the graphics capability of computers and video game consoles have improved, game designers have increased the visual detail of backgrounds, objects, and characters. Part of the "ooh-aah" factor of a video game is its realistic portrayal of an environment, and adding animation not necessary for game play is one way to capture the fascination of players. Game designers spend precious time and production money perfecting the hair and clothing movement of characters in order to draw players into the realism of a game.

When Sega released the much-hyped 128-bit Dreamcast console in 1999, *Soul Calibur* was among its premiere games. The game utilized Dreamcast's enhanced 3D polygon graphics environment and was visually stunning for its time. A review of *Soul Calibur* stated, "no other machine or developer has ever come close to replicating human movement so realistically in a videogame" (Holden, n.d.). Among the human movements replicated was the bounce of its female game characters' massive breasts—a gratuitous use of cutting-edge graphics technology. The women boxers Lulu Valentine and Selene Strike in Midway's *Ready 2 Rumble*, also playable on Dreamcast, displayed a similar top-heavy swing as they strutted around the boxing ring.

As graphics technology advanced, so did the quality of "breast physics." Temco's *Dead or Alive Xtreme 2* on Xbox 360 features the female cast of the well-received fighting game series *Dead or Alive* vacationing on an island, playing volleyball, giggling with each other, sharing bikinis, and jiggling for a player-controlled camera. However, the modeling of mammaries in *Dead or Alive Xtreme 2* is far from realistic; breasts move independently, and the slightest shift of a character creates a full frontal wave. This constant motion made one video game reviewer feel "seasick" while playing (Brudvig, 2006). Although *Dead or Alive Xtreme 2* is certainly an excessive example of "breast physics" in action, the push for realistic body movement simulation continues to encourage game designers to exaggerate the upper body of female characters.

The most notorious well-endowed pixel pinup is Lara Croft of the *Tomb Raider* series. Much-hyped by her creators and publishers, Lara, whose persona developed an international celebrity following, is a female video game version of *Indiana Jones*, hunting ancient treasure and defending herself from treachery along the way.

Lara's introduction in 1996 paralleled a technological leap in 3D game play and marked the first lucrative heroine-centered video game since *Ms. Pac-Man*. Core Design, a British video game software developer, chose to deviate from the popular first-person perspective games of the time and make a 3D third-person perspective game. In first-person perspective games the player sees only the hands (or the gun held in the hands) of the character she or he controls. For the player, the camera angle of the monitor is the eyeball view of the character. In a third-person perspective game, the camera angle of the monitor floats above the character, so the entire body of the character is visible to the player. With this in mind Core Design set out to create a new action/adventure game to rival *Doom*. Adrian Smith, operations director for Core Design, said that the motivation for making the *Tomb Raider* star female was, in part, aesthetic. "[T]he explanation we like to give is that if you have to stare at someone's bum, it's far better to look at a nice female bum than a bloke's bum!" ("An Interview," 1996, p. 76).

Although Lara offered female game players an alternative to the mostly male-dominated video game world, she was specifically created to appeal to male gamers. Furthermore, given the way she was designed and promoted, Lara Croft reinforced the notion that a woman's ultimate value is in her appearance. Toby Gard, creator of Lara Croft, admitted that the *Tomb Raider* star was his idea of a perfect woman. According to *Tomb Raider* promotional material, the perfect woman is 5 feet, 9 inches tall, has a 36D bust, 24-inch waist, 34-inch hips, and weighs merely 110 pounds (most of which must be in her breasts). A tight tank top emphasized her upper figure, and high-cut shorts highlighted the back-end view players had while controlling Lara's movements.

Lara's sexuality was heavily promoted outside of the game as well. Calendars, posters, and screen savers featured her in bikinis and slip dresses and under bed sheets. Models were hired to play Lara at promotional events where *Tomb Raider* fans (mostly men) waited in long lines to put their arms around her for a picture. Early after its first release, rumors spread that a secret code used during the game would disrobe Lara. At first Core Design quietly denied the "nude raider" gossip but then threatened legal action against Web sites that offered doctored computer images of Lara in her birthday suit.

Far from being just another busty female character, Lara is a complex figure in the evolution of video games. Unlike females in the fighting games mentioned above, players were encouraged to get to know Lara. *Tomb Raider* publisher Eidos allocated huge marketing budgets to promote Ms. Croft, and much of the promotional material was devoted to developing her personality profile. Players learned from the game and supplemental material that Lara is English, highly intelligent, self-reliant, and confident. She went to prestigious elementary and secondary schools, attended Oxford University, and was about to marry an aristocrat when she gave him up to become a full-time renegade archeologist. She is resourceful and has sharp survival instincts, defeating her enemies with a combination of physical strength, gun power, and imaginative problem solving.

Creating a cult of personality for a video game character has become a standard marketing practice in the industry and will likely increase as the financial success of video game franchises grows. Standout characters are easy to market and lend themselves to transmedia ventures. *Tomb Raider* spawned two major motion pictures starring Angelina Jolie, which combined grossed over $430 million worldwide. Other game characters, such as Rayne from the *Blood Rayne* games, have followed in Lara's footsteps with films, comic books, and television series.

Along with the increased appearance of female protagonists in video games has come the peripheral media and fan attention that celebrity status often attracts. Web sites devoted to "game hotties" abound, and the October 2004 issue of *Playboy* featured a spread of virtual women, several in the buff. Likewise, *Play* magazine publishes "Girls of Gaming," an annual special issue dedicated to pinup versions of female game characters in the style of the *Sports Illustrated* swimsuit edition. The hype around female game characters still emphasizes sexuality at the expense of intelligence, agility, and ingenuity. This is unfortunate since a handful of recent games have attempted to break the hyper-sexualized stereotype and offer players strong, intriguing characters that just happen to be female. Games and characters among this group include Joanna Dark from *Perfect Dark*, Cate Archer from *No One Lives Forever*, Jade in *Beyond Good & Evil*, and Alyx Vance in *Half-Life 2*.

REDESIGNING WOMEN

The slow introduction of female characters such as the ones listed above is, in part, the result of a male-dominated industry. A handful of women are artists, but very few women are programmers or designers. The designer decides the mission and rules of play and develops the characters inhabiting a game. Roberta Williams, a pioneer in the industry, managed to negotiate a female character, Princess Rosella, into an adventure game in the late 1980s. She recalled in an interview with womengamers.com how the concept of a female protagonist was met with resistance from colleagues:

> I purposely 'greased the skids' of using Princess Rosella as a major character in *King's Quest IV* by including her at the end of *King's Quest III*. . . . Still, in spite of all of my careful preparations, there was still some doubt as to the wisdom of having her be the main character in *King's Quest IV*. Interestingly, though, the doubts were with people in the company, not with the computer gamers themselves. I never heard any problem with it from the players, but there were people at Sierra who thought that it was a bad idea, and that it would spell the end of *King's Quest*. . . . Not only did it work, but using a female protagonist actually increased the sales of *King's Quest* overall—obviously, by bringing in more female game players. (Wright & Marold, 2000)

Diversifying the workplace is one important element in changing the image of women in video games. Equally critical is recognizing that women and girls constitute a significant portion of the video game market. Although video games were once assumed to appeal only to teenage boys, now 38% of all players are women (ESA, 2007). Most female gamers play online trivia and card games, but more women are discovering action/adventure and role-playing genres. As they do, it is financially prudent for the industry to create games that appeal to female players. Anecdotal evidence suggests that women players, although attracted to games such as *Blood Rayne* because at least they can play a female character, are frustrated by the sexist stereotypes.

> I am bothered by the fact that decent models . . . are so limited for women. I don't understand why developers of games continually use standard female models that look like bimbos. Are they telling us that the only power a woman has is to distract the other players by looking sexy? (Gemstone, n.d.).

The future of video gaming lies in game designers' ability to create increasingly realistic virtual environments. No other form of media entertainment holds that potential. What remains to be seen is whether images of women, which in the past were nearly absent from virtual worlds, will evolve beyond what one game producer called "fantasy art wet dream material" ("Girl trouble," 1998, p. 99) and into strong, independent characters that are not trapped by sexist stereotypes.

NOTE

1. Technically, "video games" refers to games played on dedicated console systems, such as the Microsoft Xbox 360 or Sony PlayStation 3. Computer games are games played on computer systems that also operate various applications, from word processing to Internet browsing. For the sake of simplicity, I use "video games" in reference to either type of game system.

IT'S YOUR TURN: WHAT DO YOU THINK? WHAT WILL YOU FIND?

1. How do video games differ from other types of media? Think of a recent action movie and an action video game. In what ways are the two similar and different in terms of plots, characters, scenes, and sounds? How does the experience of playing a video game differ from watching a movie?

2. Why do you think more men and boys play video games than women and girls do? What other types of game play and recreation do males seem to engage in more than females do? How are these games similar to or different from video games? What might explain these differences?

3. How are images of women in recent video games different from those in older games? Do you think the images are better or worse? Explain. What do you think a "better image" of woman would look like? Women who don't need to be rescued (e.g., Lara Croft) are more independent and, some argue, more violent than earlier female video game characters. Is this an improvement? What are the pros and cons of the newer images of women in video games?

4. Investigate images of female and male characters from video game magazines such as *Play*, *PC Gamer*, and *Electronic Gaming Monthly*. See also *Spin* and *Rolling Stone*. Or, use the images provided on the Pixel Pinups Web site at www. mediacritica.net/research/pixelpinups/images. html. Compare and contrast the characters, focusing on clothing, armor, and body size. What are the differences in appearance between male and female characters? Are these significant? How (or why not)? Compare the male and female body sizes to images of real men and women, both in advertising and among your family and friends. What is exaggerated in the male bodies? The female bodies? What does body size convey about the characters? What is the apparent purpose of the characters' clothing and armor, and what does that convey about the characters?

REFERENCES

An interview with Core Design. (1996, October). *Next Generation*, 75–76.

Ault, S. (2008, January 17). Videogames lift 43% in 2007. *Video Business Online*. Retrieved on February 1, 2008, from: http://www.videobusiness.com/index.asp?layout=article&articleid=CA6523709

Brudvig, E. (2006, November 16). [Review of *Dead or Alive Xtreme 2*]. *IGN.com*. Retrieved on February 1, 2008, from: http://xbox360.ign.com/articles/745/745683p1.html

Entertainment Software Association. (2007). *Essential Facts, 2007*. Washington, DC: Author. Retrieved on February 1, 2008, from: http://www.theesa.com/archives/files/ESA-EF%202007.pdf

Entertainment Software Association. (2008, January 24). Computer and video game industry reaches $18.85 billion in 2007. Washington, DC: Author. Retrieved on February 1, 2008, from: http://www.theesa.com/archives/2008/01/computer_and_vi_1.php

Fritz, B. (2007, September 26). *Halo 3* nabs $170 million on first day. *Variety Online*. Retrieved on February 1, 2008, from: http://www.variety.com/article/VR1117972821.html?categoryid=20&cs=1

Gemstone. (n.d.). *Women in g-strings*. GameGirlz. Retrieved on July 29, 2001, from: http://www.gamegirlz.com/editor/gstrings.shtml

Girl trouble. (1998, January). *Next Generation*, 98–102.

Holden, G. (n.d.). *Top 20 Sega games*. Retrieved on July 29, 2001, from: http://www.consoledomain.com/articles/1156.html

Jenkins, H. (2000, October 14). Think tank: Zap! Rat-a-tat-tat! Ping! Ah, 'tis art aborning. *The New York Times*, p. B11.

Olds, T. (1999, July). *Barbie figure life-threatening*. Paper presented at the Body Culture Conference, conducted by VicHealth/Body Image & Health, Inc., Melbourne, Australia. Retrieved July 29, 1999, from: http://www.rch.unimelb.edu.au/BIHInc/m_releases/barbie%20media%20release.htm

Olson, D. (2008, January 17). 2007 game sales topped by Nintendo Wii, *Halo 3*. *SlipperyBrick*. Retrieved on February 1, 2008, from: http://www.slipperybrick.com/2008/01/halo-3-best-selling-games-2007

Veiga, A. (2008, January 3). U.S. album sales down, digital sales up. *Associated Press*. Retrieved on February 1, 2008 from http://biz.yahoo.com/ap/080103/music_sales.html?.v=3

Wright, K., & Marold, A. (2000). *Game goddess: Roberta Williams*. Retrieved on July 29, 2001, from: http://www.womengamers.com/interviews/roberta.html

6.6 COMMUNITY BLOGGING AS RELATIONAL AND IDENTITY RESOLUTION: GENDER, RACE, AND THE POSTSECRET PHENOMENON

Jody D. Morrison

> *This chapter looks at the PostSecret blog—a site where people's secrets are publicly posted. The author investigates the role of blogging in identity and relationship maintenance, and argues that blogging can provide a unique forum for the potential resolution of issues pertinent to men, women and their relationships.*

> *"When I fight with my Marine Corps father . . . I feel like describing all the gay sex I've had."*

This message was typed on white paper, cut into pieces, and glued to a postcard adhered with the image of the award-winning photograph "Raising the Flag on Iwo Jima." The postcard was anonymously sent to the home of Frank Warren in Germantown, Maryland, and then appeared on Warren's blog, postsecret.blogspot.com, on February 3, 2008. This postcard might also eventually appear in one of Warren's books, in a slideshow at one of his lectures, or as part of a national or international art gallery exhibit.

Why would this person choose to self-disclose by creating and mailing a postcard to a stranger? Why would people want to share a secret knowing it might appear in a public forum like a blog? This reading addresses a unique and popular community blog designed to showcase people's anonymous secrets artfully constructed on postcards and mailed to a stranger who requested them. After describing the history of Warren's project, an analysis of the PostSecret phenomenon will shed light on the role of blogging in identity and relationship maintenance. Blogging also provides a unique forum for the potential resolution of issues pertinent to men, women, and their relationships.

THE HISTORY OF POSTSECRET

While vacationing in Paris, France, in 2003, small businessman and "accidental artist" (Gammage, 2005, E6) Frank Warren bought three postcards of Antoine de Saint Exupery's *The Little Prince*. Before bed that night he put the cards in the nightstand drawer, went to sleep, and had a vivid dream about the cards. He dreamt that he opened that very drawer and found the cards with messages written on their backs. One of the cards read, "You will find your answers in the secrets of strangers." The next Sunday Warren began thinking about an art project involving postcards and secrets, which became PostSecret.

Starting in November 2004, Warren distributed 3,000 postcards inviting people to share anonymous secrets. One side of the postcard was his home address, as well as directions to transform the other side of the postcard from a blank canvas so it could become part of a community art project. Messages were to be legible, brief, creative, and to reveal anything truthful that had never been shared with anyone. Warren distributed the cards on the street, in the library, in metro stations, left them in art galleries—and people started mailing them back. The cards often address provocative topics like marriage, parenting, abortion, infidelity, repressed fantasies, coming out, office romances, and incest. He exhibited the cards in Washington, DC's annual Artomatic multimedia arts event. After the exhibit closed and he had stopped passing out the cards, people kept sending him cards, but not the ones he had distributed. People created their own cards and "somehow the idea of PostSecrets spread virally in the real world" (Warren, 2008).

Warren wanted to keep sharing the cards that came in, so he created a blog, now the largest advertisement-free blog on the Web, where he displays a selection of the cards and viewer responses, updating the blog every Sunday by replacing the old cards with the new (they are not archived). Every Saturday night, Warren selects cards for the blog from about 1,000 secrets he receives during the week. He thinks of himself "almost like a film editor, taking these little visions of people's lives and connecting them together to tell this narrative" (Warren, 2008).

Over 150,000 postcards later, the cards have been featured in a popular music video (*My Dirty Little Secret* by the All-American Rejects). Warren has published four books and appeared on most major news broadcasts. Selected cards are displayed in traveling art exhibits and numerous art gallery shows in the United States and abroad. In January 2005, when federal funds ended for the 1-800-SUICIDE hotline, Warren's plea for funds on his site resurrected it. Warren also recently started PostSecret blogs in France (postsecretfrance.blogspot.com) and Germany (postsecretdeutsch.blogspot.com).

WHY SELF-DISCLOSE ON A POSTCARD?

The choice to self-disclose, revealing information about yourself that is unknown to others, is a decision everyone faces in the course of relationships. As part of deciding whether to disclose, we weigh the perceived risks and rewards by considering the topic of the disclosure, characteristics of the intended recipient, the context, and most important, the perceived impact on the relationship. Although we certainly do self-disclose at times without giving it much thought (oftentimes with regret), we also approach disclosing as an important relational turning point. Sometimes though, as a result of considering the costs and benefits, we also choose not to self-disclose (Thibaut & Kelley, 1959).

Given the decision not to self-disclose, we are faced with the challenge of private rumination about the issue we once considered sharing. For some people, this is comforting, for others, it is quite painful.

Given these options, the choice to self-disclose by creating and mailing a postcard to a stranger is an interesting phenomenon. The fashioning of the secret on a small canvas like a card gives people the opportunity to visually represent what they may not be able to share with someone face-to-face. They can depict on the card what they cannot put into words. Perhaps through the creation of the card people are able to work through the issue represented in the secret.

The small size of the typical card, 4×6 inches, might matter as well. Maybe people feel like their secret is more manageable if it can fit on a postcard. The small size might also make it possible for people who are not generally creative to have confidence in some artistic ability. The visual elements are usually quite compelling and help portray the message. As you can see from the selection of cards if you check out the blog, some people spend a great deal of time selecting the images to complement what they write. Many of the visual elements are clipped or altered images from other sources. Some appear to be unique works of art and graphic design. Sometimes it's hard to tell what is unique and what is re-appropriated. Some cards are, indeed, just writing, but very few cards have no writing whatsoever.

WHY SELF-DISCLOSE ON A POSTCARD . . . AND SEND IT TO A STRANGER . . . ?

Creating a postcard is but one part of this process—self-disclosing on a card that you keep to yourself is not as beneficial as mailing it to a stranger. At least that is what my students tell me. For 2 years I engaged my interpersonal communication undergraduates in a classroom activity that involved students researching, creating, and exchanging anonymous postcard secrets and writing an essay about the process. My students revealed that creating the postcard is insufficient, and the real benefit comes from mailing it in so that it is shared. You get to self-disclose, but not to the involved recipient, thus eliminating any potential perceived relational fallout. In their essays, some students admitted to not participating in the exchange part of the activity (which intended to simulate the "mailing" of the cards) and some confessed to not putting a lot of effort into creating their cards. They admitted feeling left out, since after seeing the number and quality of other student cards, they believed they missed out on the benefits others had received. They felt that they had not fully self-disclosed. So what then is the benefit of mailing the postcard to Warren? It is the "unburdening of the secret to the world," one student wrote. "It doesn't feel as heavy inside knowing that someone else knows."

Warren is often asked why he thinks people mail in the postcards and confess their secrets. At a lecture he gave at my university, he said,

> If you look at the cards you know that some people just want to share a funny story or talk about a sexual taboo, but other people in other cards, they are so painstakingly made and they have such detail and the secrets are complex, and I think other people might be sharing secrets in order to search for grace or authenticity or maybe to understand their secret in a new way, maybe to redefine a part of their past in a more empowering way. (Warren, 2008)

. . . WHO POSTS IT ON HIS BLOG?

Students also report they like the idea of sending a card to Warren, not just because he is a stranger, but specifically because they know that it might appear on the blog. Students who submit postcards tell me that they get caught up in monitoring the site to see if their card is selected. Many report feelings of excitement, relief, and resolution about the shared issue when their card is posted on the blog—even if it is only displayed for a week. The blog is a unique forum, unlike the experience of, for example, writing a secret on a bathroom stall. If your card appears on the blog, it has a (perceived) large audience who can choose to give anonymous feedback. This is what in part makes the PostSecret blog unique—not only do people contribute to the blog by sending in cards, but they can also post comments. It truly is a "community" blog. So for the PostSecret artist who cannot discuss issues of sexuality with his/her Marine Corps father, one can imagine that perhaps he/she has gained some strength or clarity about his/her sexual identity knowing that blog viewers have read the secret. Perhaps the sender envisions compassion from this blog audience, maybe even a response submitted to the site, such that the problems apparent in this parent–child relationship will be assuaged.

Sharing a secret on the blog might also be a way to help others. Knowing the large viewership, perhaps submitting a secret is a way to "give back" to a community of like-minded people. Warren suggests that sharing secrets are "cathartic and therapeutic" and can "bring a sense of healing" not only to your own life but to the community (Warren, 2008).

In addition to facilitating identity-issue resolution or giving back to the community, my students have told me that the blog is a perfect forum for sharing things they otherwise cannot reveal in their relationships, especially their most intimate ones. Gammage (2005) suggests that people view the blog "as the Internet version of a confessional, a kind of virtual therapist's couch" (p. E6).

Communication scholars, especially Dr. Sandra Petronio (2000), argue that the viability of a relationship is dependent upon one's ability to manage disclosures in a relationship. Her theory of privacy management is centrally concerned with the inevitable tensions, or "relational dialectics" we face between privacy and openness, between being private and being public (Baxter & Montgomery, 1996). In relationships we are constantly managing these boundaries—navigating what we want to share and what we do not. Sometimes the boundary is permeable, and sometimes it's not. The permeability of a boundary will change over time and depending on the circumstance. A closed boundary can provide safety and autonomy, whereas an open boundary can promote intimacy, but with greater vulnerability. This theory suggests that the public self-disclosures on PostSecret postcards help people balance the tensions they experience in their relationships so that the relationships can be maintained.

The PostSecret blog is really then a conversation between strangers, with text and pictures instead of talk and nonverbal cues, about things we cannot share within our relationships. The individual secrets are not necessarily what draw people to the blog; rather, it is their desire to make connections. Although the first connection is between the postcard creator and Warren, Warren then has the choice to expand the connection to the online community worldwide. Warren helps people connect, as McLuhan (1964) posits, by providing the medium for a global village, extending our senses, bodies, and minds through the blog.

Warren also started a PostSecret chat room space on the U.S. blog (in English and French) called "PostSecret Community," which further facilitates these connections. The English "community" is divided into 10 different forums, including "ages 20 and over," "ages 35 and over," "the LGBT community," and "advice."

WHAT SECRETS ARE PEOPLE SHARING?

So now that we know a little about *why* people are disclosing on a postcard (to a stranger hoping it might appear on a blog), you might be wondering just *what* people are sharing. According to Warren, the most common secret submitted is not that lofty. Warren receives the secret, "I pee in the shower," artistically rendered in many different ways at least two times a week (Warren, 2008). However, other patterns and trends have also emerged. He reports receiving a "surprisingly large number of secrets" dealing with issues related to body image, eating disorders, self-harm, and suicide. Here are a few examples:

- Sometimes I wish that I was blind, just so I wouldn't have to look at myself every day in the mirror (Warren, 2005).
- I can't pee with someone next to me. . . . I fear someone will see my small penis (Warren, 2006).
- When I eat, I feel like a failure (Warren, 2005).
- For years I tried to hurt myself so that he'd notice me (Warren, 2005).
- I've stopped cutting myself but started plucking my pubic hair with tweezers instead (Warren, 2005).
- I was seven years old the first time I attempted suicide (Warren, 2005).
- Every time I approach an overpass, I think how easy it would be to simply turn the wheel ever so slightly to the left and find peace, at long last . . . (Warren, 2005).

Another common theme in the cards is "longing for intimacy—which can also be seen as frustrations with a boyfriend or girlfriend—not wanting to be alone" (Hiaasen, 2007, p. 3E). Here are some selections from the PostSecret blog on February 11, 2008 (just before St. Valentine's Day) that exemplify this theme:

- I wish you still loved me the way you did when we drove down this road in Montauk.
- If I could only fall out of love with you I would.
- I still don't believe you love me.
- The only thing worse than being single on St. Valentine's day is wishing you were single.

He has also received secrets on more than just 4 × 6 postcards, including on parking tickets, report cards, yearbook pages, maps, sonograms, photographs, napkins, CDs, hotel card keys, and even on a 1-pound bag of coffee. It appears as if people select a particular correspondence format to become part of the message. For example, the following secret was submitted on a cracked and damaged videotape: *I destroy videos of myself as a child because it pains me to see a time before I ruined my innocence* (Warren, 2007b). This message was typed on a part of a death certificate: *I never kissed my son after he was born because he was sick and I was scared. He died 2 hours later . . .* (Warren, 2007b*)*.

GENDER AND RACE ON POSTSECRET

Although Warren has identified some patterns and themes suggesting that many of us struggle with common problems, he also acknowledges noticing a subtle gender difference among postcard creators. "Even though men and women both keep secrets, women keep the best secrets. Women have these rich, creative, interior lives" exposed in these cards (Warren, 2008). He suggests that perhaps part of it has to do with social power, in that men still have more power than women and may feel more freedom to express emotions. Perhaps this is why postcard senders are mostly women (Zayas, 2005). Although women may be more emotionally expressive, they may not have as many outlets as men in which to share. PostSecret might thus be especially valuable to women. In addition, Warren said that a recent survey indicated that, "among college women, PostSecret is viewed more often than eBay, Amazon or Yahoo" (Hiassen, 2007, p. 3E).

According to Warren, of his four books, *The Secret Lives of Men and Women* (2007a) primarily represents issues relevant to both genders. He contrasts secrets from men and women but also shows their similarities. Key themes include issues related to choice of partner, sex (fantasies, sexual identity, promiscuity), parenting, infidelity, divorce, and pregnancy (birth control, miscarriage, abortion). Here are a few examples:

- I often wonder what it would have been like if I chose the "other man" instead of my husband.
- Sorry that I'm a horny bastard and wouldn't let you sleep last night. I suck, I know. Have a good day babe.
- To save time in the morning I always put my kids to bed with clothes, _shoes_ and socks on!
- My wife is having an affair with my neighbor's wife. They don't know that I know.
- I knew I was gay on my wedding day but wanted children and feared aids [sic]
- It's not his baby.
- I will never forgive myself for letting my girlfriend get an abortion.
- Sometimes I feel like I lied to you when I said I was ok with not having children . . .

It is important to note that the gender of the postcard creator in many of the cards is not always evident, unless as a specific part of the verbal message or visual element. My students told me that if the gender of the sender wasn't obvious, they tried to figure it out by analyzing handwriting style ("too puffy for a guy"), colors used ("no guy would own a sparkly marker"), and sometimes the amount of effort put into creating the card (the more effort, the more likely it was perceived to be created by a woman).

Although Warren doesn't seem to have explicitly referred to race on PostSecret, my review of the cards he's posted since the start of the blog suggests a couple of interesting findings. The books and the site seem to be a neutral, racially level playing field for those with secrets to share. Racial identity has all but vanished on the blog, or at least has been rendered invisible (by either postcard creators or by the selection process). When race is revealed, although not a common theme, it is only as part of an "issue" disclosed or as part of the visual on a card, and is usually about a mixed-race relationship, prejudice, or someone coming to terms with racial identity. Here are *all* the PostSecret messages in Warren's four books that I could easily identify as overtly dealing with race. Interestingly, in the first PostSecret book, called simply *PostSecret* (Warren, 2005), cards specifically dealing with race were placed together.

- I use the word nigger.
- I love black girls and I am white.

- I wish I was white.
- I feel ugly because I'm half-black, half-white.
- My boss is Black, I've dated Black men, I have friends of all ethnic backgrounds and I am a minority, too . . . but I'm still a racist.
- I'm extra nice to blacks to show them that I am nothing like my forefathers.

IF YOU SHARE A SECRET, IS IT STILL A SECRET?

My students thoroughly enjoyed discussing the PostSecret phenomenon, and I'd like to report one final question we pondered. We wondered whether this self-disclosure process changes the nature of secrets—is it no longer a secret if you share it, even if you don't know the recipient? The responses were mixed, but most believed that in sharing the secret, the secret and the person disclosing it are changed. Warren, however, has a different perspective. He says that his blog contains "living secrets," especially since he has more freedom to post offensive, obscene, violent, and sexual comments (Warren, 2008).

So what changes about the secret varies, perhaps depending on whether you are the postcard artist or the blog viewer. I believe the answer lies in the double meaning of PostSecret: It's not just a secret one posts in the mail, but in posting the secret, you are now beyond its hold.

IT'S YOUR TURN: WHAT DO YOU THINK? WHAT WILL YOU FIND?

1. Visit the PostSecret blog and read the cards and feedback submitted to the site for the week. What strikes you the most about what you see?

2. While viewing the cards on the blog, do you find that you are attempting to identify the race and/or gender of the postcard creator? How is race and gender signified? How is it meaningful to be able to identify race or gender?

3. Would you consider creating and sending a card to the site? What kinds of issues would you need to consider to make your decision?

4. How do you feel about self-disclosing via postcard to Warren, fully aware of the potential for the card to be published in a book for profit?

REFERENCES

Baxter, L. A., & Montgomery, B. M. (1996). *Relating: Dialogues and dialectics.* New York: Guilford.

Gammage, J. (2005, July 7). A secret service. *The Philadelphia Inquirer*, pp. E1, E6.

Hiaasen, R. (2007, December 30). Gathering and sharing secrets. *The Baltimore Sun*, p. 3E.

McLuhan, M. (1964). *Understanding media: The extensions of man.* New York: McGraw-Hill.

Petronio, S. (2000). *Balancing the secrets of private disclosures.* Mahwah, NJ: Lawrence Erlbaum Associates.

Thibaut, J., & Kelley, H. (1959). *The social psychology of groups.* New York: Wiley.

Warren, F. (2005). *PostSecret.* New York: HarperCollins.

Warren, F. (2006). *My secret.* New York: HarperCollins.

Warren, F. (2007a). *The secret lives of men and women.* New York: HarperCollins.

Warren, F. (2007b). *A lifetime of secrets.* New York: HarperCollins.

Warren, F. (2008, January 31). Lecture at Salisbury University.

Zayas, A. (2005, July 19). Artist's blog shares secrets with the world. *Chicago Tribune.* Retrieved July 27, 2005, from: http://www.chicagotribune.com

6.7 PINK SOFAS, PURPLE ROOFS: LESBIANS IN ONLINE CHAT

Rob K. Baum

The author examines how lesbians choose to identify online and what lesbians claim to want. She finds that the characteristics that generate ad interest for lesbians are different from the attributes given by heterosexual women and men, as well as gay men. However, what the lesbians claimed to want was somewhat at odds with what they actually desired.

Whether posting a response to Web-based articles, in discussion groups, or replying to a dating service, online chat often holds out one "real" site as its ultimate destination: the bedroom. This reading considers what lesbians seek in Internet meeting; to that end, I examine how lesbians choose to identify online and what lesbians claim to want. From empirical study, I believe that the characteristics that generate ad interest for lesbians are materially, if not radically, different from the attributes given by heterosexual women and men, as well as gay men. So I ask: Has anything really changed but the mode(m) of communication? Is the online meeting place a utopian site for identification, politics, or self-change? Or are lesbians online likely to be as entrapped in virtual reality as in quotidian existence? My overarching feeling is that what lesbians state as grounds for commonality is in conflict with the constraints upon lesbian desire, a matter of societal and family conditioning, persuasion, and coercion about which much has already been written, especially in feminist studies and queer commentary.

BACKGROUND

It's important to keep in mind that studying online media represents a relatively new field of research. Although there is a growing amount of material written about online communities, relatively little has appeared in conventionally "authoritative" sources, such as academic books or journals. And although the field is growing, among these authoritative sources, only a small fraction pertains to women or lesbians. Although in order to expand the literature I could extensively quote from blogs, it is a practice I discourage in my own students, unless authorship is known and credibility is (somewhat) ensured—for instance, through the practice of peer reference (academics reviewing each other's work). My reference material is drawn from third-wave feminism, a movement that in its concentration on "grrrl culture" and aspects of female and feminine beauty seems very distant from the militant social consciousness of the "second wave" of the feminist movement, in which women claimed ownership over their own bodies and resisted being identified with men's material property. (Remember that "suffrage"—the right to cast a vote in a federal election—was the original unifying issue for women.) For instance, Angela McRobbie and Jenny Garber (1976) wrote that girl culture had been neglected due to its existence in the private or domestic sphere, whereas Susan Hopkins

(2002), who sees third-wave feminism as shaped by teen commodification, noted how "girl-powered popstars have reached millions of girls in ways parents and teachers could not: through the virtual world of mass media images" (p. 12). While most of the literature about online communities addresses heterosexual females conditioned to attract males, I believe that the material generally extrapolates to practices of women hoping to attract other women. Within the larger context of hetero-normative society, in which a nuclear family is still defined as a procreating woman and man, and marriage usually proscribed for any other coupling, the heterosexual model remains oppressively dominant. According to Driscoll (2002),

> Commodified as both consumer and marketplace, the girl is produced as not only the space in which Woman will be delineated but also, because of this incompleteness, as full of diverse possibilities for self-production. This feminine adolescent identity is the ultimate commodity on sale to girls. (p. 247)

Reid-Walsh and Mitchell (2004) call the Internet is a "cultural space" in which a "girl's homepage appears to be a kind of contradictory space—a *private* space that exists openly in a *public* domain" (p. 181). With open access to online communities (such as pinksofa.com), I might have remained anonymous (or virtual) myself. Instead, I determined to conduct interviews with women who identify themselves as lesbians and have used online dating services in the past 3 years. The time period (of 3 years) was meant to discourage earlier waves of online and computerized company services that did not permit as much self-selection and that moderated contact between the participants, with each instant of contact (letter, telephone, photograph exchange) considered a point of sale. I have also eschewed the dating services advertised in newspapers, where an initial "personal assessment" (questionnaire) is conducted by a "trained professional" (trained by whom?) for the purpose of guiding the customer toward a successful meeting and, presumably, mating. Finally, and perhaps most important, I have not conducted a random or blind survey. While absence of such a survey might seem to skew my information considerably—I have made the personal, real-time acquaintance of each woman interviewed—I carefully chose this unorthodox method.

Our electronic Web matrix is, I believe, a kind of utopian vortex of communities, in which anyone can be anything, at any time, to different people, including simultaneously. In other words, within the same period a user might engage online self-identified as a lesbian, an adolescent boy, a male heterosexual sex worker, a transsexual computer genius, or a teenage mother of three—and these avatars are not necessarily exclusive. The Internet brings together a number of "private rooms or domains open to the public under certain conditions stipulated by the owners" (Reid-Walsh & Mitchell, 2004, p. 179), in this case, the online provider or chat room.

In successive sweeps of electronic (and print) media, I notice that age, class, and above all gender differences abound, and the most obvious disparities occur between gay men and straight women. (I cannot possibly cite them all, but I encourage you to look for yourself.) While these are not the only ads I see, I marvel at the number of straight men who write in the same three lines that "looks are no issue" yet require a woman who is "slim," "fit," or has "a Dolly Parton body." Similarly, I wonder at the straight women who are only seeking a "friend to go bowling with," a "dance partner," or someone to "meet for coffee." Is this really all women want? Gay men express the largest range, especially depending on the source (suburban broadsheet, gay newspaper); yet I note with some sadness how many gay men seek another who is "straight-acting," as well as "Asian." (Are these considered synonymous, or is this gay cultural language for "young looking" and "smooth skinned"?)

What generates ad interest for lesbians—apart from a hot photo—is largely centered on age, and younger women are still more likely to hook up in dance or sports clubs. For women over 30, terms like *professional, employed*, and *financially independent* are big hits, and *children* seems more palatable alongside the adjective *grown*. Knowing the risks of garnering falsified information by generating a randomized, "invisible" survey such as one I could conduct online, especially of receiving answers from males posing as lesbians, I determined to consult only with women willing to identify themselves as lesbians and to share their stories with me directly. This necessarily reduced the sampling stratum, but it also produced some honest, amusing, and self-reflective interviews—as well as some fun in the process. In accordance with customary ethnographic practice, the women whom I interviewed have been given pseudonyms.

Of particular importance here is the notion of *simulacrum*, in which the replication and imitation of things, objects, and events is perceived "as if" it were identical with the original phenomenon. As the philosopher Jean Baudrillard (2005) commented, simulacrum is so omnipresent that the virtual is the only reality remaining, a world "so real, hyper-real, operational and programmed that it no longer has any need to be true. Or rather, it is true, absolutely true, in the sense that nothing any longer stands opposed to it" (p. 34). The quest to write a "personal advertisement" that will provoke the desired response has been compared to writing a letter of reference, a personal memoir, and a curriculum vitae—usually, however, limited to between 25 and 100 words. Within these guidelines, the capacity for self-invention, personal transformation, and performance (Harris, 2004) is unbounded. A photograph may be attached—if the writer feels it will help clinch the deal. Physical attractiveness appears just as much a part of online dating as meeting in a club. In the Pink Sofa community, Australia's largest online lesbian community, a photograph may pop up only for members—people who pay to subscribe to the service. But "guests" can put a toe in the water, looking over the "merchandise" (I'm being a bit glib here) before subscribing in order to make contact.

DEPTH INTERVIEWS

I ended up speaking with dozens of women, and more closely interviewing six women who self-identified as lesbians and who had met other lesbians online and (as a result) offline. I did not interview curious straight women or bisexual women—especially as the latter include straight women attached to a man, who for various reasons seek a woman to fulfil *his*, rather than *her*, fantasy. Each in-depth interview addressed the language of the first ad, wording of successive ads if different, "success" rate, the ad category (chat, friendship, sexual encounter, relationship), what kinds of women were encountered, and, eventually, the integrity of what was claimed by all. I did not set out to select women of different nationalities or ages, but I nonetheless ended with an age range from 35 to 62, from five countries. I discovered that, like straight women, lesbians were often looking for other women to *do* things and *go* places—and, like many straight women, they longed to be in a place where they might fall in love (but wouldn't go alone). Despite the lodging of most initial ads under "friendship," the preferred destination was "relationship." Yet, two cases were already in relationships and felt a lack of stimulation or sexual interest; these women, also listing for "friends," sought sex. As long as the women found and made social contacts, they subscribed to the service. Once these women entered into a *partnership* (defined as a loving and sexual relationship), they usually "left the Sofa."

I will introduce the Pink Sofa setup alongside my first in-depth interview. Faye has responded to about 40 women online and has met at least 15 women from the Sofa; they will correspond for about 2 months before their first meeting. (Women seeking "casual encounters" are obviously not spending as long in conversation.) Although she swears that she no longer has time for reading all the online of ads and letters, she continues to subscribe. She searches within a 10-year age range of interest, telling me with certainty that she does not want to meet a woman "too young" for her. It is relevant that the Pink Sofa requires that users insert a birth date, that this is one of the first attributes addressed, and that the tag or user name then appears next to an age. While the age is not checked in any definitive way, it seems to me that women who do not wish to be identified by age may be turned off by this requirement or feel inclined to lie.

Each of Faye's physical meetings begins in a café at breakfast; successive meetings include going to dinner, theater, film, and dance parties. Faye is now a grandmother and has attracted responses from other women with grown children. Thus I note that the presence of family is also likely is inhibit the commitment women may make. Faye commented that she is more likely to respond when a photograph is attached to a word ad and pointed out to me that the Pink Sofa was just then running an online poll asking if other members felt the same way. She directed me to some of the language of the sofa, such as "sending a smile" (letting a user, including a non-member, know of one's interest, but without the ability to directly message). A question such as "What is your star sign?" is usually filled in, as is the category of "Habits"—where one learns whether another member smokes, drinks, or exercises (and how regularly). The "Type" category presents no fewer than 16 boxes for people to select, including identifiers or labels such as "pagan," "sports fan," "vegetarian/vegan," and "expatriate." "Employment" has a large number of possible (but fixed) choices, as does the category "Children," which has nine possibilities. What does this say about what contemporary women want?

Like two of the others interviewed, Remi had been married for many years and, like one of the others, began looking while still living with her husband and their children. Initially Remi seemed to defy the picture I built on my empirical data: She was somewhat younger than the others, had four "casual encounters" (pink sofa speak for "one-night stands"), and changed her ad often as she began to come out. She was the only one who did not have or remember her original ad. And she did not appear to be looking for a relationship but was rather looking for confirmation of her identity. I had to include these "new data," precisely because they contradicted what was now my working hypothesis about what women seek. I was concerned about how I would integrate this new information into the context of the project as it had already taken shape, but to exclude it simply because it contested my theories would have felt unethical. I felt obliged to find a place for Remi and her "unique" needs in my research.

But upon further discussion, the contrast suddenly ended. Although she stated that she was seeking casual encounters only, she—unlike any of the others I interviewed—met or made a "partner" on the sofa. To top it off, Remi completely moved into the other woman's residence within 6 months of meeting. This behavior closely resembles lesbians *offline*, especially babydykes (newly identified lesbians). The relationship had quickly soured, and she was now looking for new housing—as well as friendships of any kind.

Frances and Sela met on the Sofa within 2 months of joining. My interviews with Frances and Sela were conducted together, with the two women interrupting, correcting, and adoring each other throughout, and for that reason I speak of them in the same context. I had known one of the two (Frances) longer and was aware that she had used the Pink Sofa as a means of helping her return to the uneasy world of lesbian dating. Her previous relationships had been of long duration, and she was wary of dating "exes of exes" (the lesbian world can be quite small) or losing her own sense of self. Frances had identified as a lesbian for her entire adult life and took great care as she entered into this relationship, maintaining her other friendships (and keeping them separate from this one), retaining her independence as she began to fall in love with Sela. Meanwhile, Sela's second lesbian relationship had just ended and she was, as she put it, "unwilling to lose the momentum" gained from her newfound lesbian identity: She was still married to and living with a man. For Sela the Pink Sofa offered a way to interact with more women in a shorter time frame, and the virtual nature of the world provided security as well as distance as she returned from work each day to her family. The two did not move in together for about a year and a half—until Sela's husband moved out—and then because of financial necessity rather than romantic imperative. The maturity with which they each approached this relationship became the foundation for a level of trust and respect I rarely see in romantic relationships of any kind.

Among my informants, Krystal was the most revealing—and direct. Her letter of introduction, which aired on Craigslist before moving to another site, ran over two pages and was full of personality, humor, and honesty. While she claimed to be already involved with a long-term lover whom she loved and had no intention of leaving, and was simply looking online "to make some friends" in the region to which she'd recently moved, in her first ad Krystal boldly cited sexual proclivities and desires: butch, top, and sexually adept. She says she trawled for about 3 months and hauled in four regular "friends"—including one who wrote from a distant province but with whom she entered into deep, regular correspondence and photograph exchange. Of the locals, all of whom she met within 2 months, two were fearful at what they perceived as sexual aggressiveness. The third local rapidly transitioned from friend to lover, and thereafter presented a problem—by falling in love with Krystal. This story is, of course, classic in traditional (offline) circles, where a woman meeting a married man (or vice versa) becomes convinced that once Ms. or Mr. Right appears the spouse will vanish. In this case, the Internet served to bring together lesbians who might otherwise not have met, but—because of its disembodied nature—may also have enhanced the impression that divorce was imminent. As I edited this article, that relationship took a sudden turn—one I did not then feel was final: Krystal informed me that her (Internet) lover had decided to return to being "just friends—and stick to it" (for her own emotional protection). I predicted more changes to their relationship in the coming months, and, indeed, there were more, as Krystal became anxious, angry, and protective toward her former lover. And what would Krystal do now, I asked, to fill the gap in her sexual life? She claimed that she was relieved (and I am certain she was). But how long would relief suffice, when fresh sex had been available? At this writing, Krystal is back on the prowl.

MORE THOUGHTS

The trend toward televised "reality shows" echoed a similar trend in computer technology, away from the already visible reality of simultaneity and into a "virtual reality"—"as if" it were true. Into this wedge leapt "cam girls," sex blogs, and online sex chat. While Barbara Creed (2002) argued that these are "new forms of reality" (p. 6) permitting temporary release from typical boundaries on time and space, they might also be considered one of the oldest professions appearing at higher speed, for different durations. I feel therefore, that electronic mail, online chat, and even listservs, blogs, and cam girls, are not revolutionary or even novel forms of communication, but older ones ramped up and with much larger audiences—though logging on individually and often invisibly. What appears online is, after all, still primarily *written*, in a spoken language, sometimes with a photograph or video clip thrown in. I suggest that, for most women, our social conditioning is still too strong to escape, and therefore what we claim to want and what we actually desire are somewhat at odds. The online "meeting" service is thus a bright simulacrum of the smoky, mood-lit club, in which mating, not dating, is the ultimate goal.

IT'S YOUR TURN: WHAT DO YOU THINK? WHAT WILL YOU FIND?

1. What do you think of the questions asked of "members" by the Pink Sofa, as revealed by this reading? What would you ask, in order to satisfy a broad range of users?

2. The author suggests that the Internet may be a utopian location. What does this mean to you? If you participated in an online meeting space, to what degree would self-invention enter into your own description?

3. What are the implications of meeting a person online? Is such a relationship likely to be any different from one conducted completely offline, and if so, how?

4. The author makes a number of inferences about what lesbians might actually seek, constructed from in-person samples including in-depth interviews. Given the title of the article, what kinds of assumptions did you begin with, and, as you continued to read, how did they change? Do you feel that you have learned something about lesbian culture, or about relationships in general?

REFERENCES

Baudrillard, J. (2005). *The intelligence of evil or those lucidity past.* New York: Berg.

Creed, B. (2003). *Media matrix.* Sydney: Allen and Unwin.

Driscoll, C. (2002). *Girls.* New York: Columbia University Press.

Harris, A. (2004). *Future girl.* New York: Routledge.

Hopkins, S. (2002). *Girl heroes: The new force in popular culture.* Annandale, NSW: Pluto Press Australia.

McRobbie, A., & Garber, J. (2000). Girls and subcultures. In A. McRobbie (Ed.), *Feminism and youth culture* (pp. 2–25). London: Macmillan.

Reid-Walsh, J., & Mitchell, C. (2004). A room of one's own. In A. Harris, (Ed.), *All about the girl* (pp. 173–184). New York: Routledge.

6.8 CYBER-HATE AND THE DISINHIBITING EFFECTS OF ANTI-GAY SPEECH ON THE INTERNET

Cynthia A. Cooper

> *If you go to a certain Web site, you'll encounter a cute little cartoon puppy named Sherman wagging his tail and barking playfully. A commentator explains that this dog is barking as nature intended, in stark contrast with a hypothetical dog that moos like a cow. The Web site further explains that "Dogs aren't born mooing, and people aren't born gay." Log onto another site and you'll see Matthew Shepard enshrined in flames alongside a counter indicating how many days he's "spent in hell" since his 1998 murder. Click below the flames and you'll hear Matthew's screams and his pleas for you to repent, before it's too late for you, too.*
>
> *Welcome to the world of cyber-hate: content on Internet sites run by hate groups and individuals seeking to spread their ideology to the masses and recruit like-minded people. This reading discusses the main themes of anti-gay hate speech on the Internet.*

The two sites described above are among the most anti-gay sites on the Web, but they certainly are not alone. Internet sites advocating hate against gays, Jews, African Americans, immigrants, and women have grown so fast in recent years that getting an accurate count of their number is nearly impossible. A 2007 report by the Southern Poverty Law Center reported 844 hate groups in the United States, most with active Internet sites or links to sites of a national organizing group (Beirich, 2007). The Simon Wiesenthal Center (2007), another group that monitors Internet sites, identified 7,000 different Web sites, blogs, and newsgroups devoted to the activities of hate groups worldwide. That is almost five times greater than the Center's 2004 identification of 1,400-plus hate Web sites worldwide. The growth of hate group Web sites also coincides with an increase in reported hate crimes. A 2006 FBI study reported a 7.8% increase in personal and property crimes based on bias against a specific race, religion, ethnicity, or sexual orientation (Beirich, p. 1). Although no explicit link can be identified between Internet hate group sites and bias crimes, it is clear that both are on the rise.

Most hate group sites offer information about the organization's ideology but may also sell merchandise such as books, T-shirts, and even music. Many also solicit memberships and donations. Don Black, former KKK Grand Dragon and creator of the Web site Stormfront, claims that his site is the first contact most new members have with the Klan, as nearly 2,000 people log onto the site each day (Marriott, 1999, p. 4). Similarly, Matthew Hale, leader of the World Church of the Creator, says his site is his primary means of recruiting his target demographic of young adults and children (Borow, 2000, p. 100). Traditional print media such as newsletters, newspapers, and brochures are expensive to produce and distribute, as are television and radio shows. In addition, hate groups don't always have open access to traditional communication channels. Consequently the Internet has become the most powerful and economical tool in the hatemonger's arsenal of communication devices. The anonymous access, sophisticated Web design with video and audio capabilities, and relative lack of regulation make it the perfect medium to reach the masses.

Of course, anti-gay rhetoric is nothing new, and Internet hate speech directed at gays and lesbians is simply an outgrowth of hate against other identifiable groups. For example, the Christian Identity Movement and Aryan Nation traditionally have promoted the belief that Whites are the Bible's chosen people with their primary enemies being Jews—often dubbed the "Agents of Satan." In recent years, however, as mainstream media and legislative initiatives have lent more exposure to the gay community, many of these groups have expanded their focus to include hate against gays and lesbians. Each instance of *Will & Grace*, *Brokeback Mountain*, Domestic Partnership, and Don't Ask Don't Tell is met with an equally prominent anti-gay voice, even if that voice doesn't address specific issues but just spews generalized hate. For many years most of these extremist organizations were dismissed as disorganized fanatical fringe groups preaching to a relatively small and geographically dispersed congregation. However, the Internet has provided a centralized information center uniting followers of the Christian Identity, Aryan Nation, and KKK movements across economic and geographic boundaries, and increased numbers of followers can link to such causes via the Net.

I became interested in this increase in Internet hate speech and began a series of studies accounting for much of what I discuss here. Over a 10-year period I've studied Web sites of hate groups for form and content. By coding the content of these sites (content analysis) and exploring the texts and messages on these sites (textual analysis) I gained greater understanding of the meanings behind the messages and the motivations of anti-gay groups. While there are some differences among sites in content and presentation, most anti-gay Web sites share some basic characteristics. First, the major theme is to speak out against the gay lifestyle, although discussion of other groups (Jews and African Americans) or social concerns (abortion, affirmative action) may also occur. Little attention is given to bisexuals, transgender individuals, or people with other sexual orientations; the focus is mostly on gay men and lesbians. Second, the sponsoring organization identifies itself with Christian, family-oriented values. Groups including Watchmen on the Wall, the Christian Gallery, and Focus of the Family all rely heavily on Bible scripture to justify their anti-gay views. In fact, a report by the Southern Poverty Law Center also noted that

> anti-gay sentiment is exploited by Christian white supremacists to organize the bigoted. Neo-Nazis, Skinheads, Christian Identity followers, white robed cross burners and talk show circuit "racialists" may be divided over tactics, but they agree on who their enemies are. And gays, like Blacks and Jews, are categorically hated. (Berrill, 1992, p. 31)

One note of warning: Many of the sites discussed here track visitors and post the comments and email addresses of anyone who criticizes their organizations. You should consider this before deciding whether you want to view any Internet sites of hate groups.

THE ANATOMY AND COMMUNICATION OF HATE

Explaining why people hate others is a monumental, if not impossible, task. It is hard to find any person who is completely without prejudice or dislike of some person or group. But hate, repulsion, and justification of violence or oppression against those different from us is a completely different level of behavior altogether. Hate has been the subject of research and examination for years, most of which focuses on describing its genetic and psychological underpinnings. Biologists often describe hate as a biological mechanism of adaptation, a natural outgrowth of the fight-or-flight reflex. Psychologists study manifestations of hate as societally created attitudes, especially in the form of prejudice against certain groups that are seen as threats to one's own identity. Social scientist Zillah Eisenstein (2000) succinctly stated that hate is a learned trait: It "seeks safety and self-protection on one hand, destruction and annihilation on the next" (p. 93). This involves not merely disliking others but supporting (through words or actions) attempts to cause them harm. Such attitudes often result from complex interaction among societal, political, and religious institutions.

Politically, hate defines communities exclusively by race, religion, ethnicity, or sexual orientation. This results in the isolation of those groups and continues the cycle of prejudice, discrimination, and even violence. Socially, people who aren't members of the targeted group are often willing to turn a blind eye to hate and discrimination. Though they may not participate themselves, their unwillingness to speak out against those who exhibit hateful speech and action allows the hate to flourish nonetheless.

Hate also often has a religious component. Virtually all identifiable hate groups root their beliefs in the Bible, which they believe justifies their actions against others. The use of Christian ideology and dogma can be a powerful ally when trying to convince others of the validity of a viewpoint.

The most extreme manifestation of hate is the hate crime. Groups tracking hate crimes report a marked increase of such crimes in the United States against Jews, African Americans, and gays and lesbians since the early 1990s. The Columbine shootings, Matthew Shepard's murder, the dragging death of James Byrd Jr., and shootings at various religious institutions are all hate crimes that captured national media attention and precipitated increased calls for stronger hate crimes legislation.

A far more common form of expressing bigotry is through hate speech, although these incidents rarely garner as much media attention. Hate speech denounces whole groups of people solely because of their race, ethnicity, religion, or sexual orientation. It can be delivered through a variety of communication channels, whether printed in brochures or newsletters, recorded on audio- or videotape, or delivered interpersonally through intimate conversations or to larger audiences at rallies, revivals, and meetings. While hate crimes are illegal, hate speech is not; it is generally protected by the First Amendment.

To understand anti-gay hate speech on the Internet is to consider the union of basic human instincts with advancing technologies, the clash of protected rights with concerns for social responsibility, and the evolving distinctions between traditional and changing meanings of community. There is little doubt that the development of the Internet has changed the way in which people communicate and form communities. Some have envisioned the Internet as the ultimate public sphere where individuals define themselves by choosing which communities to join. Thus the potential for individual empowerment is deemed a major benefit of Internet communities. Indeed, gay and lesbian advocates have long argued against Internet filtering systems that block community health and education sites because this deprives users, particularly gay youth, of essential resources. Linking to PFLAG (Parents and Friends of Lesbians and Gays), PlanetOut, or gay.com may be the only source of information and belonging for an isolated youth struggling with his or her sexuality.

But the Internet's empowering force can't be harnessed only for so-called positive purposes. If the Internet has the potential to bring together people to enlighten, educate, and form communities, it may also be used by groups who intend to defame, misinform, or even harm others. This equal-opportunity communication medium can't make a distinction between *good* and *bad* communities. In fact the special qualities of the Internet make it a perfect meeting hall for hate groups whose beliefs are not readily given voice in traditional media.

Likewise, the anonymity provided by the Internet can fuel more aggressive behavior than people would be comfortable expressing in traditional social situations, especially if they are not immediately criticized for their beliefs. These disinhibiting effects of the Internet can easily turn aggression into cyber-violence, causing Internet users to feel free to express anger and hatred they'd censor in a more public, and accountable, setting. Imagine in your own life a situation in which you felt comfortable giving someone a real piece of your mind via email, IM, or text. Could you have been as candid in person or on the phone? The same may be true of the hatemonger who proudly spouts hate in the relative anonymity of an Internet chat room but would think twice before walking down Main Street displaying a white hood or a swastika.

ANTI-GAY SPEECH ON THE INTERNET

As stated before, the anti-gay Web sites I studied certainly have some differences in content and format, but there are many shared themes and tactics. One notable feature of all anti-gay Web sites is the focus on the sexual behaviors of gay men almost to the exclusion of all other aspects of gay life. Most narratives and visuals highlight male sexual activities, including crude and explicit depictions of oral and anal sex. American Guardian has explicit text and visual descriptions of scatology, bestiality, and S&M as the norms in gay sex, accompanied by statistics including these: "68% of all mass murderers are gay men; 92% of all homosexuals ingest feces at one time or another; and child sexual molestation is a defining characteristic of the homosexual lifestyle . . . sex with kids is at the foundation of homosexuality." This misrepresentation of the gay lifestyle easily becomes a basis for hatred as well as implicit and explicit calls to action against gays.

In recent years many of the anti-gay groups have expanded their focus to include commentary on political and social issues involving the gay community. For instance, the American Guardian site is devoted entirely to what it identifies as the growing and evolving threat of child molestation, which it concludes is perpetrated solely by gay men. Ignoring government statistics proving otherwise, gays are shown to prey on young boys as a way to recruit and perpetuate the "species." When hate groups do address the political issue of gay rights, it too is typically reduced to terms of sexuality and disease. For example, gay rights protection "laws" are defined on the American Guardian Web site as a transparent attempt to spread AIDS, including "blatant attempts to force sodomite immorality down the throats of the public." Similarly, the Web site of conservative talk-show host Bob Enyart labels any AIDS advocate as someone who "does everything in his power to spread AIDS" and encourages citizens to fight for the re-criminalization of homosexual behavior. Similarly, the Family Research Council, a conservative Christian organization, wrote in one of its posted publications that a goal of the gay rights movement is to "abolish all age of consent laws and to eventually recognize pedophiles as the 'prophets' of a new sexual order."

Most disturbing is the recent rise of the Christian organization named Watchmen of the Wall, whose Web site declares that they are particularly "focused against homosexuality because those who practice this self-destructive vice . . . are the chief enemies of the natural family." Watchmen describes itself as a global coalition of believers, but its U.S. membership is primarily Russian and Ukrainian immigrants in northwestern states. Scott Lively, a leader in the Watchmen movement, is also the author of a book titled *The Pink Swastika*, which claims that Hitler was gay and that fascist gays were the masterminds behind the rise of Nazism and the systematic murder of millions of Jews, gays, and gypsies during the Holocaust. Lively's book has been dismissed by Holocaust scholars as completely false and full of inaccurate, revisionist history, although it remains a fixture of the Watchmen's Web site. Despite the group's declaration that it does not promote or condone violence, Lively himself was ordered in civil court to compensate a lesbian for assault, and Watchmen members are linked to assaults at gay-pride events and gay rights rallies throughout the western United States. In 2007 several men linked with the Slavic Christian group were charged in the death of Satender Singh, a 26-year-old man who was picnicking with friends when self-identified church members attacked him because they thought he was gay (Sanchez, 2007, p. 1). Singh was not gay, and he later died from his injuries.

Although the representation of gays on these sites is disturbing, the techniques employed are rather commonplace. Reducing individuals to a singular trait, particularly an undesirable one, lays the groundwork for hate against them. So it follows that anti-gay Web sites paint a picture of gay life as one-dimensional, revolving around an insatiable need for "bizarre" sex. Representing any individual as a single-dimension being, especially through a representation as contentious as "deviant," "predator," or "pedophile," begins the process of dehumanizing that individual. And once a person is seen as less than human, targeting him or her for verbal or physical violence becomes much more acceptable.

Another shared characteristic of anti-gay Web sites is the encouragement of some type of call to action or advocacy. While all anti-gay sites are steeped in Christian dogma, some also encourage proactivity in the "fight" to stop gays and lesbians. The Westboro Church, through its site Godhatesfags.com, promotes pickets against community, business, and civic leaders who support gay rights initiatives. Rather than commenting on specific gay rights issues, the group believes that generalized protests of gays or lesbians are better because to acknowledge specific political issues would only serve to legitimize the gay community. Until recently, the church was most infamous for its pickets at funerals of AIDS patients, and its Web site includes photos and press releases regarding future protests. But in the past few years the church has catapulted itself into the worldwide spotlight by expanding its anti-gay protests to the funerals of fallen service men and women. The group now shows up at funerals with sign reading "God Hates America" and "Thanks God for Dead Soldiers." Westboro's message is that God is punishing America for its acceptance of gays and lesbians by killing soldiers in Iraq and Afghanistan. The church's efforts have resulted in a federal law and several state laws banning protests within certain distances of cemeteries. Still, the group protests nearly every day and features hundreds of photos on its Web site to memorialize its efforts.

Other groups advocate action in a much less confrontational manner. The American Family Association site and Reagan.com both advocated protests over Ellen DeGeneres's appearance on *Sesame Street*, claiming that PBS was pushing a homosexual agenda on unsuspecting children by having DeGeneres appear on the popular show. Concerned citizens were encouraged to complain to their congressional leaders. In even bolder terms, the Christian Gallery encourages citizen's arrest of all gays and lesbians, while the Family Research Council endorsed a "war" against the so-called destructive homosexuals.

Finally, it is worth noting that all anti-gay Web sites share two other common elements: justification of their hatred rooted in biblical teachings and use of American patriotism to promote the virtues of hating gays and lesbians. The use of the Bible as authority is a staple throughout, reinforcing the divine justification for hatred and bigotry against gays and lesbians. Absent any scientific, legal, or statistical evidence to support their claims, these groups rely on their interpretation and enforcement of God's word as their sole authority. After all, there's no need to defend one's position when it has been ordained by God.

A second characteristic is the representation of anti-gay imagery in terms of American patriotism and symbols. Many sites include American flags, songs, and strong patriotic images such as the bald eagle to imply that homosexuality is un-America, and that it is a citizen's responsibility to combat homosexuality. One cartoon features Uncle Sam in his typical finger-pointing stance proclaiming "I WANT YOU—TO HATE FAGS."

COMBATING ANTI-GAY SPEECH ON THE INTERNET

When the polarizing and disinhibiting effects of cyber-communities lead to the spread of hate, questions often arise as to whether these expressions are protected speech under the First Amendment. Throughout our nation's history the concept of free speech has been valued and is typically questioned only when it conflicts with other universally acknowledged values such as national security and public safety. Supreme Court rulings historically have extended constitutional protection to all speech unless such speech encourages imminent incitement to violence or serves as *fighting words*—words that by their very utterance inflict injury or tend to incite violence.

So what's to be done to combat the hatred and violence advocated on anti-gay Internet sites? Until such speech crosses the line into advocacy of imminent criminal behavior against gays and lesbians, it's protected by the very same laws that prohibit censorship of Web sites providing useful resources to gay and lesbian youth.

The answer is more speech, not less. Undesirable (even bad) ideas are best countered not by censorship but by better, more enlightened speech. Although it may not be comforting to those who find themselves targets of hateful rhetoric, it is best when hate speech is out in the open. Without their protected right to expose themselves and their rhetoric, the messages of anti-gay groups would flourish in an underworld of hate never subjected to public scrutiny. Indeed, anti-gay groups often prove to be their own worst enemies when their messages are exposed as unsubstantiated claims and falsehoods that don't represent the world in a truthful manner. A statement by Logan Pearsall Smith, which served as the motto for the advocacy group hatewatch.org, sums it up best: "How it infuriates the bigot when he is forced to drag out his dark convictions."

IT'S YOUR TURN: WHAT DO YOU THINK? WHAT WILL YOU FIND?

1. The author claims that "the answer is more speech, not less." Divide into groups representing various sides of this issue (the number of groups depends on the size of the class, so you should pick the viewpoints you consider most significant). Debate the issue, using this as your topic: "Should hate speech on the Internet be allowed?"

2. What, if anything, do you think should be done about hate speech on the Internet? Should it be banned? Require that users be 18 years or older? Given a rating so that parents can block access from their children? What are some other options?

3. Imagine you're designing a system to prevent hate speech from being posted on the Internet. How might you accomplish this task? Who might determine what should or shouldn't be allowed? On what grounds might the decisions

be based? In other words, what would be okay, what wouldn't, and why?

4. Log on to a Web site of a group working to combat Internet hate. You can do a search to find one or look at those of these advocacy groups: the Southern Poverty Law Center (www.splcenter.org or www.tolerance.org,), the Anti-Defamation League (www.adl.org), or the Center for the Study of Hate and Extremism (www.hatemonitor.org).

What groups do these organizations identify as spreading hate on the Internet? How do they define hate speech and determine that a group should be identified as a hate group? Do you agree/disagree with these definitions? How do the organizations combat hate speech on the Internet? What approach or strategy do they take to counter those who spread hate? What can you do?

REFERENCES

Beirich, H. (2007, November 17). *FBI releases hate crime statistics*. Southern Poverty Law Center, pp. 1–7. Accessed November 3, 2008, at: www.splcenter.org/blog/2007/11/19/fbi-releases-hate-crime-statistics/9

Berrill, K. T. (1992). Anti-gay violence and victimization in the United States: An overview. In G. Herek & K. Berrill (Eds.), *Hate crimes: Confronting violence against lesbians and gay men* (p. 31). Newbury Park, CA: Sage.

Borow, Z. (2000, February). Marketing hate. *Spin*, 92–102.

Eisenstein, Z. (2000). The politics of hate. In R. Gottesman (Ed.), *Violence in America: An encyclopedia* (Vol. 2; pp. 93–94). New York: Charles Scribner's Sons.

Marriott, M. (1999, April 6). Extremists find open forum on the Internet. *The San Diego Union-Tribune*, pp. 3–7.

Sanchez, C. (2007, August 1–7). *The Latvian connection*. Southern Poverty Law Center. Accessed November 3, 2008, at: www.splcenter.org/intel/intelreport/article.jsp?aid=809

Simon Wiesenthal Center. (2007). *Digital terrorism and hate: Growing menace of digital terrorism and hate exposed in new interactive report* (p. 1). Los Angeles: Author.

PART III

PRODUCTION

Films, TV shows, newspapers, and Web sites don't appear out of thin air; they exist because people create them. While that statement may appear so obvious that it borders on the absurd, the fact remains that we often do forget about the constructed nature of all media messages. Someone decides on the topic and the goal of the message; someone writes it; someone prepares its audiovisual elements; someone distributes it. Who produces the content consumed by media audiences? What pressures do they face?

In this age of mergers and acquisitions, the majority of mainstream media content is produced by individuals or teams working for large corporations that are increasingly interested in the bottom line. But that doesn't mean everything is mainstream. New media and the Internet have made it possible for regular people such as you and me to produce and distribute our own mediated messages. Independent filmmakers still strive to realize their dreams and visions. And it doesn't mean that everything mainstream is profit driven, nor that profit is attainable only at the sacrifice of social responsibility.

If you've ever been involved in media production, you probably learned how to operate equipment (camera, audio recorder, computer, etc.), how to tell a story, and how various elements of sight, sound, and motion can help you convey your message. You've probably also considered your target audience, so that the media text you create will serve the audience's needs, desires, and interests. Even if you haven't been involved in media production, you may understand that the process of producing media texts is often complex and always involves a wide range of activities: conceptualizing, writing, revising, planning desired audio or visual elements, recording/creating raw materials, editing, adding audio or visual effects, and the like.

This section isn't going to address things such as whether female producers have a different working style than men do, or whether people of color employ various production aesthetics in an identifiable or unique style. We won't do much with the technical side of things, or in terms of making direct comparisons across types of people. Instead, these readings present glimpses into a variety of situations in which real people, creating real media content, have found themselves. They shed light on certain aspects of the production process—perhaps aspects you haven't yet considered.

Specifically, in this section, authors discuss race and gender in media production by addressing the reality of what it's like to create various types of content and by examining media professionals or media organizations to illuminate the (often political) environment in which these people work.

The eight readings in this section fall into two chapters. The first, *Producing Documentary and Entertainment Programming*, contains four readings looking at how media content is created in a variety of real-life contexts. In Reading 7.1, Ralina Joseph investigates the challenges a writer/director faced as she attempted to get a distributor for her first motion picture (*Mixing Nia*). Because the film didn't fit the industry's constricted vision of how to represent and market "race," the writer/director didn't have much luck. The creator of the TV show *Any Day Now*, on the other hand, did succeed in finding an outlet for her work. In Reading 7.2, Amanda Lotz offers an understanding of how the storylines were generated and the process by which *Any Day Now*'s producer and the Lifetime network negotiated plotlines and scripts. The producers wanted to create a show consistent with their vision, but the network wanted the show to be consistent with its image (and attract an audience). Cynthia Conti (Reading 7.3) presents a candid first-person look at some of the issues facing documentary filmmakers. As she produced her film *Out of Bounds*, she resolved some ethical issues by utilizing the technique of participatory cinema—a technique allowing a film's subjects to have input into how they are represented in the film. Turning to radio, George Daniels and Dwight Brooks round out this chapter in Reading 7.4 with a look at the *Tom Joyner Morning Show*. The authors show us how Joyner uses his syndicated radio program to accomplish his urban activist mission and investigate the show's success in light of several important trends in the radio industry.

Chapter 8, *Media and Related Organizations*, presents four readings. It begins with Donnalyn Pompper's analysis (Reading 8.1) of how Latina public relations practitioners think that gender–ethnicity plays a role in how others view them and how they respond to gender–ethnicity challenges at work. She also presents their recommendations for enhancing value of gender–ethnicity in organizations. Robert Papper, in Reading 8.2, provides an overview of some of the key findings he has uncovered during his many years researching race and gender in newsroom employment in the United States. This reading focuses on women journalists. Reading 8.3, by Rebecca Lind, crosses the Atlantic to study what British broadcasters think are the major factors serving as opportunities and constraints for women in the industry. The Production section ends with the book's final reading (8.4), in which Rodney Benson critiques the extent to which one of the largest and fastest-growing journalistic professional organizations, UNITY: Journalists of Color, truly is a voice of diversity. He argues that UNITY focuses on a narrow racial–ethnic definition of diversity and is closely allied with corporate media companies and advertisers; with such a myopic perspective, UNITY cannot be a genuine force for diversity in news.

If you're interested in becoming involved in any aspect of producing media messages—whether under the auspices of an established media organization or on your own using new media or the Internet—you should find these readings enlightening and informative. Even if you don't plan to be involved in message production, they should help you become informed of the social reality within which media content is created and as a result be a more critical audience member.

CHAPTER 7

PRODUCING DOCUMENTARY AND ENTERTAINMENT PROGRAMMING

7.1 "WHO IS THE MARKET FOR THIS FILM?": THE POLITICS OF DISTRIBUTING *MIXING NIA*

Ralina L. Joseph

> *Writer/director Alison Swan's first film,* Mixing Nia, *tells the tale of a 20-something Black/White mixed-race woman, Nia. Nia works as an advertising copywriter until her conscience prevents her from writing a malt liquor campaign targeting young Black males. While Nia proceeds to "find herself" racially and sexually, the film comically shows Nia trying on different "authentic" Black personae and imagining herself in various failed book plots. Nia's constantly changing racial and sexual personae assert that race and sexuality offer no singularly defining qualities. Note also how the author's exploration of why* Mixing Nia *never made it to movie theaters is linked to a broader political issue.*

We had a lot of trouble distributing the movie because the executives and the distributors said, "Who is the market for this film?" And when I told them that (a) the film is very universal, and (b) that it's not only biracial people, but that Black people, and White people would relate to it because there is so much of it in our families and in our lives and our friends. And it's just fun, you know what I mean? (*Alison Swan, writer/director of* Mixing Nia, *2001*)[1].

The controversy over a multiracial category on census forms shows that racial and ethnic advocacy groups aren't worried about fairness as much as they're worried about spoils. (*David Horowitz, conservative writer, 1997*).

Will we be able to identify black votes in terms of fair representation? (*Kweisi Mfume, president of the NAACP, 1997*).

The independent film *Mixing Nia* (1998) was never distributed in movie theaters. *Mixing Nia*'s unsuccessful theatrical marketing demonstrates that investigations of racial ambiguity remain outside of the Hollywood mold. Not only is the film's protagonist female and paradoxically African American (and yet not quite "authentically" Black), but she also questions the "natural" nature of identity categories and dates interracially. Hollywood executives' rejection of the film demonstrates how racial mixture and inquiries are anathema to Hollywood's images of "authentic" female characters.

Mixing Nia's $600,000 budget allowed for a cast and crew of over 150 along with professional features such as a split screen, 32 filming locations in New York City, an original music score, and a music supervisor (Roberts, 1998). These elements should make the film appealing to distributors, because it looks like a mainstream Hollywood film. Swan also scored talented actors, including Karyn Parsons, famous from playing Hilary on *The Fresh Prince of Bel-Air*, and Isaiah Washington, an acclaimed independent film actor. Therefore, it was not "amateur" filmmaking elements that prevented *Mixing Nia*'s theatrical distribution.

Swan searched for a distributor for the sole contemporary American film delving into mixed-race identity just as the biggest multiracial battle of the 1990s waged—the creation of a "multiracial" category on the 2000 census. The mid 1990s ignited already existing controversies about claiming and naming a "multiracial" identity. Discomfort about mixed-race,[2] or cultural fusion in general, comes about perhaps not because it is so foreign but in fact because it is so commonplace. In other words, accepting a multiracial category, or a multiracial film, means that it is not taboo.

Newspapers largely represented *the* White response from critics such as David Horowitz (1997), who belittled civil rights struggles as petty fights for "spoils"; his larger argument was that because race (and mixed-race) no longer "matters" in the United States' "colorblind" society, Americans should simply stop discussing it.[3] Meanwhile, also according to newspapers, *the* Black response came from equally vehement critics such as Kweisi Mfume (1997), who spoke out against mixed-race "defection" from the Black category and the subsequent decline of political power for all African Americans.

In this reading I unpack Swan's notions of universalism, the commonplace nature of mixed-race, and fun. I link these to critiques of *Mixing Nia* as an inauthentic, or non-appropriately representative, image of a Black and a "universal" independent film. I then discuss the arenas of film festivals and video and cable distribution where *Mixing Nia* was a success largely because it was marketed as an authentic, or appropriately representative, Black independent film. I end by describing how Swan's frustration with the distribution of *Mixing Nia* has led her to ignore race in future projects. *Mixing Nia*'s failure to receive a theatrical release appears to be related to the passionate newspaper rejections from both the "Black" side and the "White" side of the multiracial category on the 2000 census.

THE 2000 CENSUS AND MULTIRACIAL SELF-IDENTIFICATION

Questions of racial classification have been central to American identity since the founding of this nation. The latest manifestation of these debates came with the 2000 census, causing anxiety for both communities of color and White people. Self-proclaimed multiracial nationalists, or those who assert that "multiracial" is the only appropriate label for mixed-race people, actively promoted the issue of mixed-race self-definition. In 1997 this proposed census category was defeated in lieu of a "check all that apply" instruction, which extreme multiracial nationalists saw as a failure and others saw as a success. The spring 2001 release of the census results sparked off another media blitz, reproducing the newspaper sentiments of the Black community and the White voice.[4]

According to newspapers, some White neoliberals reject the idea of a separate multiracial category because race no longer matters. Some Whites lament the continuing focus on race, causing one writer, for example, to praise actress Whoopi Goldberg for saying, "I'm not African-American. I'm an American" (Thomas, 1997). These responses go hand-in-hand with those of neoconservatives such as David Horowitz, who fear that people of color are receiving yet another "unfair benefit," such as the creation of another separate racial category or affirmative action.

The papers also presented the idea that many African Americans fear mixed-race identification as multiracials may result in the "watering down" of or "defecting from" African American culture and political power. Mixed-race and Black identities are presented as polar opposites instead of constitutive elements. Thus, it is seen as troubling that "Blacks 17 and younger are four times as likely to identify themselves as belonging to more than one race than blacks 50 and over" (Morse, 2001) and that "nearly 2 million black Americans say they belong to more than one race, more than what many government demographers and civil rights officials had projected based on surveys in 1996 and 1998" (Schmitt, 2001). These singular White and Black points of view on mixed-race were what Swan was up against as she sought a distributor for *Mixing Nia*.

SWAN TRIES TO GET HER FILM DISTRIBUTED

As seen in the opening quote, writer/director Swan brought up three reasons her film should have found a distributor. Each reason describes *Mixing Nia* as a text encouraging a "color-blind" reading: universalism, where all viewers, regardless of race, relate to the film; the commonplace nature of mixed-race, where people readily admit to multiracial heritage; and "fun," where a film about a racial and sexual identity crisis is pleasurable. These three readings speak to Hollywood's sentiment that films by women of color must be "narrowcast" into "niche films." However, *Mixing Nia* was rejected as both "too Black" to be a "universal" independent film and "not Black enough" to be a Black independent film. Swan explains that "[Hollywood executives] don't understand Black film. And it's not even a Black film. This film was so out of the range it didn't fit into anything they had ever seen before."

"THE FILM IS VERY UNIVERSAL"

Critiquing *Mixing Nia* as "too Black," film executives who produce "universal" independent films told Swan that if she paired Nia with two White men the film would be more appealing to Hollywood sensibilities: "One producer called and was interested in the film, but he wanted me to change [Nia's African American love interest] to a White guy" (Palmer, 1998, p. 13). In order for the film to draw in White viewers (the real universal audience), the film apparently must feature Nia against multiple White male bodies so that White viewers might be able to identify with someone on the movie screen. But Hollywood distributors who carry Black independent films critiqued *Mixing Nia* for the opposite reason: It was not "Black enough." One producer told Swan he'd be interested if she made Nia's White love interest an African American character. Thus, an "authentic" Black film seemingly does not feature interracial relationships, especially when the protagonist questions her racial identifications.

Some studio executives told Swan that her film wasn't marketable as an independent film because it didn't fit into a "niche" marketing scheme (targeting a small, marginalized demographic group). *Mixing Nia* was not seen as Black enough, nor "urban" enough (a codeword for "authentically" African American). But *Mixing Nia* wasn't supposed to be solely a Black film. Swan's belief that "the film is universal" means that her target audience has no singular racial profile. As she told me, "I'd love to get everybody. I don't make films necessarily for the Black audience or necessarily for the White audience."

As a marketing label, Swan's classification of *Mixing Nia* as "universal" reflects a liberal modern notion that there are certain experiences, values, and narratives that transcend race; in other words, all people can relate to her images of dating, love, and sex. She implies that *Mixing Nia* is a text allowing spectators to rise above their own racial alliances. Swan argues that in *Mixing Nia* questions of race, or mixed-race, do not alienate mono-racial viewers; rather, elements of universalism, like the story and the characters, encourage audience members to identify with the characters on the movie screen despite our own racial identifications. However, we all experience "universal" events through our bodies, which are racialized or identified by race; this racialization affects how we date, fall in love, and have sex.

Racialization often prevents colorblindness, or the ability to see people as somehow "raceless," precisely because our society has been structured with, in the words of George Lipsitz (1998), "a possessive investment in whiteness" where "whiteness has a cash value" (p. vii). This is the force that would make it unheard of for a White male (clearly included in Swan's target audience) to identify with the multiracial woman he sees on the movie screen. This rejection of claimed mixed-race identity is echoed in a newspaper columnist's response to the 2000 census, deriding the desire of mixed-race people to claim all parts of their heritage. Paradoxically, the columnist sees ethnicity as a private, personal quality, and yet feels slighted because he cannot identify his Irish heritage on the census, which "only" lets him be White, while mixed-race people have the "privilege" of identifying all the facets of their heritage (Morse, 2001).

In addition, the distribution executives Swan approached could not imagine the audience as colorblind, not only because the film stars a mixed-race Black woman but also because Nia belies Hollywood stereotypes of African American women: She is articulate and college educated, has a White father, and dates interracially. Nia fluctuates from attempting to embody an "authentic" Black subjectivity to denying the importance of race; there is no easy label to put on her. Misunderstanding her hybrid identities, one reviewer critiqued Nia's lack of a singular racial and sexual identity by calling her "a blank page, too easily influenced by the others in her life to reveal a personality of her own" (Hunt, 1999, p. 79).

Swan's deployment of the term universal was rejected in part because a film about mixed-race recalls angry sentiments such as those of David Horowitz (1997): "Where will the present path lead—down a road to deeper and more bitter racial divisions, ugly struggles over diminishing racial spoils, increasing civil conflict and eventually a South African future?" Horowitz used the issue of claimed multiracial identity to predict a racial apocalypse. Similarly, other columnists tied mixed-race identity to the imagined destruction of "monitoring and enforcing civil rights, tracking poverty, ensuring racial balance in public schools and providing aid to minorities" (Schmitt, 2001). Scare tactics from *the* White side demean mixed-race identity as a burgeoning sign of "civil conflict" while *the* African American side denigrates mixed-race as the breakdown of hard-fought years of civil rights advances. These newspaper responses help describe a larger social context that wouldn't allow a film such as *Mixing Nia* to be deemed marketable.

"OUR FAMILIES . . . OUR LIVES AND OUR FRIENDS"

In addition to designating *Mixing Nia* as a universal film, Swan also argues that her film is marketable because it recalls an issue (mixed-race identity) that is a common American occurrence. The 2000 census illuminated the fact that almost 7 million Americans identify themselves as mixed-race people. Fifteen percent of births in California are to interracial couples (Beech, 2001). In addition, images of mixed-race people circulate frequently in all forms of media.

However, there is a big difference between featuring an isolated, undeveloped image of a multiracial woman in an advertisement and getting to know her in a film by delving into her identity questions. *Mixing Nia* questions the "natural" nature of identity categories and hence demonstrates that Nia need not identify solely with one race. Perhaps executives' decisions not to bite at Swan's lure of the "commonplace" nature of mixed race shows that Hollywood still derides mixed-race as an "ugly little secret" that must be swept under the carpet. Or, as one White columnist asserted, "maybe racial unity would come more easily if we *stopped* talking about race" (Blumner, 2000, p. 1).

"AND IT'S JUST FUN, YOU KNOW WHAT I MEAN?"

The third reason Swan provides for why her film should have a broad appeal is that it is "fun." Like "universalism," fun is understood through colorblindness. Swan hoped that the film's "fun" aspects would override the fact that even independent producers (operating in a realm defined by niche marketing) felt that the film was too marginal for any imagined audience. To Swan, the film is enjoyable because the funny dialogue, engaging narrative, and interesting characters transcend singular racial alliances. However, the issue of a racialized, gendered, and sexualized mixed-race identity crisis, even when portrayed in a largely comedic manner, couldn't be imagined as "fun" by Hollywood executives, their imagined "universal" (essentially White) audience, or the niche "urban" (essentially Black) audience. Focusing on the "fun" aspects of the film is also a way of implicitly racializing *Mixing Nia* as a Black film: Hollywood is more accustomed to and accepting of African American comedies than mixed-race dramedys (texts fusing comedy and drama).

MIXING NIA FINDS OTHER VENUES

Despite the fact that it was never released theatrically, *Mixing Nia* did achieve success in other arenas such as film festivals, cable airings, and a DVD/video release. However, various executives changed the marketing strategy of the film for it to achieve these successes: Here *Mixing Nia* was marketed as "just" Black, or with African American content that targets a Black audience. Nia's mixed-race and interracial dating and identity search were safely claimed as Black issues in order for it to receive some success.

Mixing Nia scored well at film festivals, venues for many films that never get a theatrical release; it was largely labeled as a "Black film" there. It played well with audiences at the Toronto Film Festival's Planet Africa Program, and Urbanworld's "Black College Tour." It also won the Magic Johnson Theater's Best of Festival award at the Acapulco Black Film Festival. However, paradoxically, Swan was later told by a film distributor, "we couldn't put this movie up at the Magic Johnson Theater [which is located in a working-class African American area]." The assumption of this distributor is that *Mixing Nia* wouldn't attract an urban audience because it's not "Black enough." This illustrates how racial politics differ in movie theaters, which desire more "standard" images, and film festivals, which embrace non-mainstream images. Without the worry of "appropriately" marketing to a niche audience, *Mixing Nia* received popular and critical support. The film won the Festival Grand Prize at World Fest Houston, the Entertainment Weekly Audience Award at the Bermuda Film Festival, and the Jean Renoir Award at the Huntington Film Festival.

Mixing Nia has also found an assumed African American audience on cable television. It was aired on Black Entertainment Television (BET), then Home Box Office (HBO), and then Lifetime Television. Implicitly understanding how *Mixing Nia*'s cable audiences are imagined to be primarily Black, Swan explains, "the cable companies like HBO and Showtime become so important because they're the only people who are showing them [Black films]. Because they know that a large segment of their audience is Black, they can cater to them." Here Swan identifies *Mixing Nia* as a Black film, or at least as a film that would attract a Black audience; this demonstrates how Swan also changes her description of the film to make it marketable.

For its video and DVD distribution, Swan sold *Mixing Nia* to Xenon Entertainment Group, a company marketing harder-to-find films attracting an African American audience. Xenon uses niche marketing techniques for the film, as is evident in the video case for *Mixing Nia*. The front cover features light-skinned Nia embracing her dark-skinned boyfriend, Lewis. The New York City skyline is barely visible behind them; the only colors are their skin and Nia's chocolate brown sweater. Both actors are smiling, but while Lewis appears to be watching something off in the distance, Nia's eyes are closed in rapture—she is entirely giving herself to this moment with Lewis, as she appears to entirely be giving herself to Blackness.

The back of the video case features a large picture of tank-top-clad Nia next to a description of her desire to write "the great African American novel," a label Nia herself never uses in describing her book. The Xenon Web site summary of the film adds, "a young biracial executive . . . has to learn a little about being black" (Xenon Pictures, 2001). The front of the video case implies that Lewis is the one who teaches her. There are also three small pictures on the back cover: The left one is a shadowy photo of Nia and her White love interest, the middle one is of her Black boyfriend, and the one on the right is of Nia alone. Her Latino love interest is visually absent, while Nia's White boyfriend is minimally featured. Successful niche marketing requires this "just Black" façade.

Swan is also in the process of translating *Mixing Nia* into an hour-long television show. Swan told me that stereotypical "Black" comedies are an easier sell and that "It's very hard right now to get a Black drama." To make her "dramedy" more marketable, Swan realized that she must eradicate Nia's racial confusion:

> So its latest incarnation, it doesn't really deal with the [mixed-race identity] theme. Because I learned my lesson with *Mixing Nia*, so I'm trying to come up with another overall theme for the

show whereas, yet she's still dealing with being biracial, but it's not the overall theme of the show. So basically now the show is like, young girl moves to New York with . . . her two friends.

To a contemporary television viewer, this plot sounds familiar. The difference is that this protagonist is mixed-race. Swan is therefore making Nia's identity fluctuations peripheral. Swan is also removing central supporting Black characters from her show. Nia will live with a White girlfriend, a Jewish man, and a Black ex-boyfriend. Instead of making her Black girlfriend a central character, as she was in the film, Swan has moved her to another apartment, explaining, "I feel like it would work better for television this way." "Working better for television" appears to mean including fewer people of color. Hoping to successfully market her television show, Swan pragmatically erases Black and Latino elements and fills in White ones.

SWAN CHANGES FOCUS: "SO THAT'S IT FOR AWHILE ON THE RACIALLY THEMED STUFF"

As she understands market forces, Swan is now following the dictate of the "White" newspaper response to the creation of a multiracial category on the census, which reflect the underlying cultural and political environment: She is staying away from the "racially themed stuff." Because movie theater distributors told Swan that *Mixing Nia* was not Black enough to fit in the niche of an African American independent film and too Black to work within the niche of a universal independent movie, she plans to ignore race in future film projects. Swan told me, "It's just too hard to do the racial stuff because it's too hard to get them sold. No one . . . wants to . . . deal with it. And they think that it's not going to sell tickets."

As Ed Guerrero pointed out in *Framing Blackness* (1993),

> If the situation for black male independent filmmakers has proven difficult, then it has been almost impossible for black women. Compared to black men there are few black women filmmakers and, in most cases, they must negotiate the "triple oppression" of their work predicated on independent vision, race, and gender. (p. 174)

Because of this "triple oppression," Swan has chosen to shift her focus to unquestionably "universal" projects: those featuring White actors and catering to a White audience.

NOTES

1. On March 2, 2001 I interviewed Swan in Los Angeles. Her comments here come from that interview.

2. I use "mixed-race" as both a noun and adjective here, following the lead of work in the emerging field of critical mixed-race studies (see Ali, 2003; Beltran & Fojas, 2008; Ifekwunigwe, 2004; and Zarembeka, 2007).

3. In their investigations of the census, many newspapers appeared to presume that Black and White communities each monolithically present one unified voice against claiming a mixed-race identity.

4. Although virtually all communities of color spoke out for or against the issue of a multiracial category on the census, as I examine the Black–White text *Mixing Nia*, I focus on what newspapers present as *the* Black and White responses.

IT'S YOUR TURN: WHAT DO YOU THINK? WHAT WILL YOU FIND?

1. List five films and/or TV shows starring actresses of color. Describe each protagonist's socioeconomic status, romantic and platonic relationships, family, and geographic area. Now do the same for five White actresses, White actors, and actors of color. Compare your observations. What does this tell you about how society views different groups of people?

2. Break into small groups, and have each person find the following information about one of the top 10 grossing films of the previous year (this should be easily accessible through newspapers and the Internet): Who are the distributors (and the head of each distribution company), producers, writers, directors, and actors? What are their racial or ethnic backgrounds? Summarize each film's plot. What does this tell you about who makes creative decisions in Hollywood today, and what types of films are deemed marketable?

3. Find a list of the top 10 "Black films" of the last decade. Summarize the plots. Describe the stars. What does this tell you about makes a "marketable" Black movie? Why do you think these films were picked up for theatrical distribution?

4. What do you think we as a society lose when artists don't create films saying what they really want to say but rather what they think will sell?

REFERENCES

Ali, S. (2003). *Mixed-race, post-race: Gender, new ethnicities, and cultural practices.* Oxford, UK: Berg.

Beech, H. (2001, April 19). Eurasian invasion. *TIME Asia.* Retrieved April 19, 2001, from: http://www.time.com/time/asia/news/printout/0,9788,106427,00.html

Beltran, M., & Fojas, C. (2008). *Mixed-race Hollywood.* New York: NYU Press.

Blumner, R. (2000, December 7). Here's a radical thought: If we stop obsessing on race, people might actually become colorblind. *Jewish World Review.* Retrieved April 30, 2001, from: http://www.jewishworldreview.com/cols/blumner120700.asp

Guerrero, E. (1993). *Framing Blackness: The African American image in film.* Philadelphia: Temple University Press.

Horowitz, D. (1997, July 18). American apartheid. Retrieved March 30, 2001 from: http://www.salonmagazine.com/july97/columnists/horowitz2970718.html

Hunt, R. (1999, March 17–23). [Review of the film *Mixing Nia*, written and directed by Alison Swan]. *The Riverfront Times,* 79.

Ifekwunigwe, J. O. (2004). *Mixed race studies: A reader.* London: Routledge.

Lipsitz, G. (1998). *The possessive investment in whiteness: How white people profit from identity politics.* Philadelphia: Temple University Press.

Mfume, K. (1997, January 6). NAACP weekly radio address. Retrieved March 30, 2001, from: http://www.multiracial.com/news/naacp1.html

Morse, R. (2001, March 14). Kiss me—I'm White. *San Francisco Chronicle.* Retrieved April 30, 2001, from: http://www.sfgate.com/cgibin/article.cgi?file=/chronicle/archive/2001/03/14/MN219094

Palmer, J. C. (1998, September 9). A diamond waiting to be discovered. *Chicago State University Tempo,* 13.

Roberts, T. (1998, September). Independents' day: Black women behind the camera are fighting to tell our stories. *Essence,* 105.

Schmitt, E. (2001, March 14). Multiracial identity might affect programs. *The New York Times.* Retrieved on March 30, 2001 from: http://www.nytimes.com/2001/03/14/national/14CENS.html

Thomas, C. (1997, December 9). America doesn't need racial labels. *The Holland Sentinel.* Retrieved March 30, 2001, from: http://www.hollandsentinel.com/stories/120997/opn_racial.html

Xenon Pictures. (2001). Retrieved March 30, 2001, from: http://xenonpictures.com/mixingniastory56.html

Zarembeka, J. M. (2007). *The pigment of your imagination: "Mixed-race" in a global society.* Washington, DC: Madera.

7.2 BARRICADED INTERSECTIONS: *ANY DAY NOW* AND THE STRUGGLE TO EXAMINE ETHNICITY AND GENDER

Amanda D. Lotz

> *The author spent time on the set of a TV show, observing and interviewing producers, writers, and others to understand how and why they put the show together as they did— including the negotiations between the network and the producers as the producers sought approval for plotlines and scripts.*

Perhaps one of the most valuable developments arising in understandings of feminism in the 1980s and 1990s was an emphasis on intersectionality, or how different aspects of identity combine or intersect. This shift toward recognizing that each woman experiences gender oppressions differently (for example, as a Black college professor, a working-class lesbian, a rural White housewife, or a college-educated Latina) deviates from some foundational beliefs of second-wave feminism, a type of feminism relying on notions of commonality among women. Feminists who emphasize intersectionality explore how aspects of identity such as ethnicity, class, gender, education, sexuality, and age combine to make it impossible ever to be only female, only middle class, or only biracial. Perceiving these identities as inextricably intertwined requires sophisticated understandings of how racism, sexism, classism, and so on affect how we experience interactions with others.

Unsurprisingly, this transition toward emphasizing women's different experiences of gender developed in the writings of women of color, many of whom felt excluded by the beliefs and tactics of second-wave feminism that stressed a common sisterhood or shared experience among women. Feminist legal scholar Kimberle Crenshaw (1991) applied the term *intersectionality* to a phenomenon that other Black women began articulating by the late 1970s. Crenshaw cited the title of one of the first Black women's studies books, *All the Women Are White, All the Blacks Are Men, But Some of Us Are Brave*, as one expression of the sense of perpetual marginalization encountered by Black women (Hull, Scott, & Smith, 1982). The exclusion Black women experienced from women's groups because they were Black, and from Black activist groups because they were women, may not immediately seem to be a foundation for an approach to feminist theory, but Crenshaw identified numerous occasions in both legal cases and cultural phenomena that illustrate the material consequences Black women face because of the intersection of their marginal status as women and Blacks. Although Crenshaw mainly used situations in which gender and ethnicity bisect as the basis for identifying the value of intersectionality as a foundational feminist tenet and approach to understanding injustice, she also acknowledged that intersectionality is useful for exploring other marginalized identities such as sexuality, class, age, and ability.

Some of the most powerful evidence of the need for intersectionality develops from the legal examples Crenshaw identified, cases in which the distinct experiences of Black women are not recognized or protected because their experience as women deviates from a supposed White middle-class norm, and their experiences as Blacks differ from that of

Black men. Crenshaw also adeptly moved into the popular sphere and explored cultural events such as the obscenity prosecution of 2 Live Crew, the Anita Hill/Clarence Thomas hearings, and the O. J. Simpson murder trial as examples in which underdeveloped understandings of the nexus between identities such as ethnicity and gender erased the position of Black women because it fell outside the dominant interpretations of feminism and antiracism (Crenshaw, 1991).

The work of Crenshaw, Patricia Hill Collins (1990, 1998), Chela Sandoval (1990, 1991), Bell Hooks (1981), and many others emphasized the connections among aspects of identity, acknowledged the diversity among women and their consequent experiences, and recognized that seeking justice for women is an incomplete act unless we also seek justice for those oppressed because of ethnicity, class, sexuality, age, education, or other identity-based attributes. As Crenshaw's acknowledgement of 1990s cultural events indicates, intersectionality informs contexts more ordinary than legal disputes. Here, I examine how the Lifetime series *Any Day Now* (1998–2002) developed stories that recognized the intersectionality of identity for its two lead characters and the challenges its staff faced in telling these unconventional stories. Series creator, writer, and executive producer Nancy Miller sought to write about the relationship between two women of different ethnicities; however, the centering of female characters and the series' examination of racism and ethnic difference made it unorthodox for U.S. television. Exploring how the series developed reveals both possibilities for and barriers to uncommon representations. The challenges Miller faced in finding an outlet for her series and the day-to-day struggles over story ideas encountered once she had a network contract indicate how American society tries to separate aspects of identity into discrete categories, barricading the intersections that offer more complex understandings of identity in contemporary U.S. culture.

In order to understand how this unusual series developed, I went to Los Angeles and spent a week on the set of the show and interviewed its executive producers, writers, and other series staff about how and why they constructed the show the way they did.[1] My goal was to understand the challenges and negotiations the executive producers faced in their attempt to tell compelling stories about female characters, while also trying to instigate "watercooler" conversation about the state of racism and relations among ethnic groups in contemporary America.

Any Day Now aired on the Lifetime cable network, which explicitly announces itself as "Television for Women." The series fit Lifetime's network brand by focusing on stories about the friendship of two women who were childhood companions in 1960s Birmingham, Alabama, and rekindled their friendship as adults. The series' use of identity-based differences to define each character provides a key component of the women's relationship, the aspect that makes it complex enough to tell compelling stories. Mary Elizabeth (Annie Potts) is a White working-class housewife with two teen children, who never went to college but aspires to be a writer; her friend Rene (Lorraine Toussaint) is African American, the daughter of civil rights activists. As a child, Mary Elizabeth contradicted her parents' racist beliefs by developing a friendship with Rene, although her family's beliefs, and the Catholic environment in which she is raised, contributed extensively to her sense of identity. Mary Elizabeth became pregnant her senior year of high school and married, while Rene left Birmingham for college, law school, and many years working in Washington, DC, as a lawyer. In opposition then, Rene is highly educated, upper class, unmarried, and strays from her Baptist religious background. The series examines the women's relationship in both the present and their 1960s childhood, consequently affording their identity differences even more focus, as episodes often intertwine the past and present stories through the depiction of a character trait that was either established in the girls' childhood or has changed with their maturation.

Miller and co-creator Deborah Joy LeVine originally sold the concept for *Any Day Now* to CBS in 1990. At that time the series was a half-hour comedy/drama blend akin to *The Wonder Years* and was set entirely in the 1960s. Days before the series was scheduled to begin shooting, Orion (the production company producing the series for CBS) cancelled production. Gary Randall, who headed Orion at the time (but later became Miller's partner and co-executive producer on *Any Day Now*) recalls feeling the time wasn't right for a series about children. More to the point, the series' focus on female characters and issues of racism resulting from the interracial friendship would have been unprecedented on network television in the early 1990s.

A 1990 debut substantially predates the explosion of female-centered series that occurred by the end of the decade and brought TV series such as *Living Single, Xena: Warrior Princess, Sabrina the Teenage Witch, Buffy the Vampire Slayer, Ally McBeal, Sex and the City, Felicity, Charmed, Providence, Judging Amy, Once and Again*, and *Gilmore Girls* into U.S. homes. The examination of racism Miller and LeVine planned, however, would have been comparable to that of critically acclaimed series such as *Homefront* and *I'll Fly Away*, which debuted in 1991. Neither series achieved ratings success, however, and both were cancelled in 1993.

Randall's decision was arguably a prudent one. The business of U.S. network television was particularly complicated in the early 1990s because of the transition instigated by an enormous rise in competition. Throughout most of U.S. television history three broadcast networks (NBC, CBS, ABC) competed for audiences. In order to be "successful," each network needed to draw a third of television viewers, which required shows with broad appeal. Consequently, networks sought series that attracted both men and women and targeted the majority White audience, although shows that also drew African American and other minority groups were particularly valuable.

In the late 1980s and 1990s, the competitive structure of the U.S. television industry changed drastically, as new networks (FOX in 1986; the WB and UPN in 1995) increased broadcast competition. Also during this time the number of U.S. homes subscribing to cable or satellite increased from just under 20% in 1980 to nearly 75% in 2000 (Stevens, 2000). Consequently, the audience size a series needed to be successful changed significantly between *Any Day Now*'s initial purchase by CBS and the time it began airing on Lifetime. During this time, Lifetime Television developed into a cable network strong enough to finance an original series with a budget close to that afforded to broadcast network series. The economics of a cable network such as Lifetime differ greatly from a broadcast network such as CBS. The audience necessary for Lifetime to consider *Any Day Now* a success (1–3 million viewers) is much smaller than that required by a broadcast network (13–15 million for ABC, CBS, and NBC; 10 million for FOX, 3–4 million for the WB and UPN) in the late 1990s and early 21st century.

Because of the changes in economics and competition that occurred between Miller's first sale of the series in 1990 to when Lifetime contacted her in 1997, she needed to adjust the vision of her show. Lifetime requested that the series be an hour-long drama and that it include a present dimension, so audiences could see what the characters were like as adults. Although this request significantly altered the series, Miller didn't consider it exorbitant. Adding a contemporary component to the series greatly expanded the stories she could tell, and the incorporation of past and present periods provided a vehicle through which she could create complex character development. As a result of the revision, the series examines the everyday racism of the 1960s and often connects it with everyday racism of the late 1990s; it compares the paths available to and taken by two women and how they reconcile their choices with the things they now desire, and it depicts the manifold challenges that develop as a result of maintaining a friendship despite formidable obstacles.

Miller still found challenges in telling the stories she intended once she had a series order from Lifetime. For many of the years prior to creating *Any Day Now*, Miller worked as writer on a variety of series, as a writer and executive producer on *The Profiler*, and as the creator of *Leaving L.A.* and *The Round Table*. Even before this work, Miller established her career writing for police dramas (*Houston Knights, Law & Order, Mann & Machine, Bodies of Evidence, The Marshal*), often as the only woman on the writing staff. By the time she was in a position to decide what projects to work on (such as *Any Day Now*), she acknowledged that she was "sick of writing female rape victims . . . sick of writing wives that are there to service their husband's story." This experience and a sense that compelling and complex stories about women's lives were missing from TV schedules led her to develop a series about the relationship between and struggles of two female characters.

Miller didn't necessarily set out to tell stories addressing the intersections of various aspects of identity in women's lives. At its most basic conception, *Any Day Now* is semiautobiographical, about a childhood friendship Miller shared. Miller (who is White) didn't have an African American best friend, nor did she grow up in Alabama. She did, however, recognize the narrative value of focusing on an interracial friendship and had vivid recollections of visiting relatives in the South as a child. Miller sought to construct stories that explored the paradox of many Southerners she had known, people she identified as racist, yet as having "good hearts." Although many complicated periods and moments in America's past (such as the Vietnam War) have been examined from different perspectives that illustrate the complex ways people experienced these human dramas, Miller considered the civil rights history and its repercussions in contemporary society relatively unexplored. Ongoing stories in which characters developed and changed over time, the type of story series television tells best, were notably missing. *Any Day Now* resulted from Miller's experiences and perceptions as a storyteller and retold the 1960s struggle for racial equality through characters the audience cared for and whose motives they understood.

Miller shared the vision for her show with a staff of writers. In hiring the writers, Miller put together a group well able to address complex issues of identity intersections due to its atypical diversity. At the time of my visit, the series employed six writers and one writer's assistant, in addition to Miller, who also wrote two or three scripts per season.[2] The *Any Day Now* writers brought a variety of demographic identities and subjectivities to the show; among them were three African Americans, one Asian American, a gay man, a lesbian, a father, and a mother. They were single, divorced, and married and embraced religious perspectives that included Christianity, Hinduism, and atheism. Such a range of perspectives helped constructed characters who also occupy diverse subjectivities. Miller told me she emphasized diversity in hiring because,

> The more people with different life experiences the better. It makes for a lively and passionate writers' room. And our stories come from personal experiences. How arrogant it would be to assume White (usually male) writers have all the interesting and exciting life experiences that go into writing a good script.

In their brainstorming process, the writers considered the different meanings audiences might take from their scripts as they composed episodes. For example, at one point a writer raised the possibility of constructing a plot in which Rene's boyfriend, Bill (a detective played by Richard Biggs), has an affair with his new female partner. The writer based the idea on the experiences of a friend who is a female police officer and began dating her partner. Another writer suggested that this might not be a good plot for the series to explore because female African American detectives occupy so few roles on TV in which they are represented strictly as professionals. This discussion revealed the writers' recognition that the choices they make contribute to the perceptions the audience may make about the world around them. Indeed, having such a diverse writing staff was significant in this regard because of the range of sensitivities each offered.[3]

The writers were also aware of the comments viewers posted on the Lifetime Lounge chat room for discussing *Any Day Now*. The writers felt differently about reading the viewers' comments; some found the critiques too harsh because viewers didn't understand the complex process of negotiation that the original idea must endure, while others logged in as soon as their episodes aired. Miller also read the Web postings, and the office staff forwarded some to the lead actors. Olivia Friedman, who played Mary Elizabeth's teenage daughter, Kelly, posted comments to the chat room directly. Although Miller said viewers' opinions on storylines and suggestions for future episodes didn't lead the writers to change anything, she did find the comments useful in understanding what viewers take from the series.

As the network distributing the series, Lifetime also had a voice in the series' production. Miller followed conventional practices and received approval for plot ideas from Lifetime, allowing the network some influence in the content and form of the series. Miller cleared script ideas with the network before developing them into outlines, and then again once the script was completed. Despite the requirements of constant approval, the writers were generally happy with the relationship with the network and the content permitted to air. Lifetime allowed the series to use the word *nigger* (71 times in an episode that examined what the word means in U.S. society in the 21st century) in order to accurately express the speech of Southern Whites in the 1960s. Lifetime also allowed other references generally considered unacceptable in public speech in an effort to maintain the realism of often awkward discussions of ethnic difference and racism. This freedom was particularly important to the explicit way the series explored the often unspoken significance of ethnicity in contemporary society and retold painful stories of racism from America's past.[4]

But creative freedom was not absolute. During my visit, Miller was debating with Lifetime over the line "you came over to get laid," a struggle she conceded Lifetime would probably win with its suggested change to "you came over to have sex." In this case, the suggested change in dialogue wouldn't significantly alter the meaning or intensity of the comment so much as revise the attitude Miller intended for her character. Miller was less deferential on objections with specific narrative importance, and Lifetime's feedback often targeted aspects of the script more crucial than changes in phrasing. A suggestion midway through writing the second season, for example, advised that the series' "past" plots were focusing too heavily on civil rights stories. This is not to suggest that the network was averse to these stories; rather, they sought more diversity in the events represented from the 1960s. Nonetheless, the shift away from stories focusing on racism was noticeable and prevented the series from continuing a successful defining feature of its first season. "Past" plots commenting on racism or race-related topics in the second season dropped from 56% of shows before the Lifetime recommendation to 17% of shows after.

Unfortunately, Lifetime doesn't brand itself as "Television for Women of Diverse Ethnicities" or, even better, as "Television for Women Who Share Interracial Friendships." As a result, Miller often faced challenges from the network in emphasizing the stories about ethnicity she identified as crucial to the overall story about the friendship between Mary Elizabeth and Rene. Many of the conflicts resulted from a fundamental difference in the network's and Miller's perceptions of the series and the stories it should tell. To Miller, the series primarily explored the differences in ethnic identity and how it shaped the characters, as well as the difference between the present and the past. Although Miller set out to write complex central female characters, her understanding of a "women's program" differed from that held by the network. Lifetime sought stories focusing more on the women and less on conflicts arising from ethnic differences or the discrepant ways the characters understand the environment of racism that defines their past.

BARRICADED INTERSECTIONS

This case study reveals a great deal about why series that use intersections of identity haven't found a central place in the stories dominating American culture. Until the mid 1980s, TV sought a broad and heterogeneous audience, often downplaying any kind of identity difference as programmers sought stories with universal appeal. When competition increased and niche broadcast and cable networks began addressing the specific desires of groups who weren't represented in this universal appeal (basically anyone other than White men), audience sizes decreased as underrepresented members turned to programs and networks that specifically hailed them. Niche networks such as Lifetime or Black Entertainment Television (BET) aid program diversity but don't ensure that subgroup needs are met, because even these niche providers seek relatively broad audiences. As opposed to the magazine industry, in which many different voices speak to similar audiences (consider the diverse magazines targeting women and girls: *Vogue, Essence, Cosmopolitan, HUES, Ladies Home Journal, Working Woman, Working Mother, Ms., Redbook, Shape, Latina Style, Jane, O: The Oprah Magazine, Seventeen,* etc.), the expanding range of broadcast and cable networks cannot offer such specificity. Consequently, voices such as Miller's may have difficulty receiving distribution because they recognize intersections more specific than those currently served by networks.

NOTES

1. For a more elaborate discussion of my method, see Newcomb and Lotz (2002). Generally, the method is derived from anthropology's ethnographic approach of fieldwork and utilizes both observation and interview techniques. Research on the television industry more generally, as made available through examination of trade publications, also informs my analysis of the processes I observed and responses to my inquiries. Also see Lindlof (1995).

2. Beginning in summer 1999, many grassroots activist organizations began staging protests about the lack of non-white TV characters and the corresponding lack of diversity behind the camera. A 1999 survey revealed that of 839 employed network prime-time writers, only 55 were African American, 11 Latino, and 3 Asian Ameri-

can, which together amounted to less than 7% of working writers. Many of these 69 non-White writers worked on shows airing on UPN and the WB—a major network such as NBC had only one African American writer on all its series, and CBS had only two (Braxton, 1999).

3. Although diversity aids in developing complex stories, be wary of essentialism—emphasizing biological difference as a predictor of behavior. In this example, a White male writer voiced concern about the plot, while the idea originated with a Black woman.

4. Cable networks more commonly offer this freedom, with premium cable providers such as HBO exercising the least regulation, network TV the most, and basic cable occupying a middle ground; this is a result of government regulation and industry standards.

IT'S YOUR TURN: WHAT DO YOU THINK? WHAT WILL YOU FIND?

1. Pick a favorite TV series and think of ways its writers could incorporate intersectionality into the stories it tells. If you were a writer, how would you tell stories that acknowledge intersectionality?

2. What other media texts (TV, film, books, etc.) have constructed characters with attention to the various ways different aspects of their identity intersect? Where did these texts appear? Did they appeal to broad or narrow audience tastes?

3. As a media consumer, what kinds of stories do you prefer? Do you only enjoy stories with characters that seem like you?

4. How frequently do you find characters like yourself in the media? What aspect of your identity do you have difficulty finding in media texts? What consequences might result from not seeing characters like yourself represented?

REFERENCES

Braxton, G. (1999, October 9). Survey cites low number of minority writers on series. *The Los Angeles Times*, p. F2.

Collins, P. H. (1990). *Black feminist thought: Knowledge, consciousness, and the politics of empowerment.* New York: Routledge.

Collins, P. H. (1998). *Fighting words: Black women and the search for justice.* Minneapolis: University of Minnesota Press.

Crenshaw, K. W. (1991). Mapping the margins: Intersectionality, identity politics, and violence against women of color. *Stanford Law Review, 43*(6), 1241–1299.

Hooks, Bell. (1981). *Ain't I a woman: Black women and feminism.* Boston: South End Press.

Hull, G. T., Scott, P. B., & Smith, B. (Eds.). (1982). *All the women are White, all the Blacks are men, but some of us are brave: Black women's studies.* Old Westbury, NY: Feminist Press.

Lindlof, T. R. (1995). *Qualitative communication research methods.* Thousand Oaks, CA: Sage.

Newcomb, H., & Lotz, A. D. (2002). The production of media fiction. In K. B. Jensen (Ed.). *A handbook of media and communications research: Qualitative and quantitative methodologies* (pp. 62–78). London: Routledge.

Sandoval, C. (1990). Feminism and racism: A report on the 1981 National Women's Studies Association conference. In G. Anzaldua (Ed.), *Making face/Making soul* (pp. 55–71). San Francisco: Aunt Lute Books.

Sandoval, C. (1991). U.S. Third World feminism: The theory and method of oppositional conscious-

ness in the postmodern world. *Genders, 10*, 1–24.

Stevens, T. (Ed.). (2000). *International television and video almanac* (45th ed.). La Jolla, CA: Quigley Publishing.

7.3 LOCATING BUTCH IN *OUT OF BOUNDS*: FEMALE FOOTBALL PLAYERS, EXPRESSIONS OF MASCULINITY, AND PARTICIPATORY CINEMA

Cynthia Conti

> *Here is a first-person account of a documentarian's use of participatory cinema to provide a voice for her subjects. Note also the consideration of gender identity as much broader, and reflecting more of a continuum, than the bipolar "masculine" and "feminine."*

In October 2000, I began work on a documentary about a women's flag football team in the Jamaica Plain Women's Flag Football League (JPWFFL) of Boston, Massachusetts. The league has 150 members in 10 teams. One of these, Team Nemesis, consists of about 15 players diversified in age, race, profession, sexual orientation, class, and gender identity. Every Sunday in the fall, the women of Nemesis gather as fierce athletes to engage in some of the most aggressive aspects of professional football, such as full-contact blocking, diving for passes, and rushing at the 1-yard line, notably without helmets and pads. Inspired to start attending games when my girlfriend joined Nemesis, at first sight I was struck by the intense physicality with which the teams play. I was even more surprised to find myself enjoying the game, considering I am not much of a sports fan. There was something about watching women playing a sport that has been culturally designated for men that intrigued me. I wanted to know more about the team members and why they played the game.

During this time, I entered my second year of graduate school in media studies. Feeling distanced from the theories of media, cultural, and queer studies that I was constantly immersed in, I was frustrated with the direction of my academic career. I rarely found any opportunities to apply this type of intellectual thought to my own life and my own surroundings. To deal with my feelings of unfulfillment, I decided to dedicate the next semester to a project that would allow me to bring theory into practice, one in which theories of gender and media would unfold as I went deeper into research. I believed I would find such a project in Nemesis—by making a documentary about the team, I would explore issues of gender identity among the members. Sensing it as a way to take an intellectual leap in my relationship to theory, I decided to use the medium of digital video to examine how gender manifests for these women on and off the football field.

This reading is a reflection on my experiences during the first 4 months of production for *Out of Bounds*. I detail the ways digital video was used to explore team members' notions of gender identity and how I applied Judith Halberstam's theory of female masculinity to help me better understand women's interest in football. Additionally, I discuss the ethical dilemma of representation that documentary filmmakers frequently confront, something that arose for me through exploring Halberstam's theory. Along the same lines, I discuss the techniques of participatory cinema that I implemented in an effort to treat my subjects fairly and filmmaker Jean Rouch's influence in this endeavor. Finally, I demonstrate how participatory cinema contributed to my original exploration by revealing important information about team members' attitudes about gender identity.

EXPLORING FEMALE MASCULINITY THROUGH DIGITAL VIDEO

I immediately saw the football field as a rich space for exploring gender identity. Whether they are conscious of it or not, every time the members of Nemesis play football, they subvert traditional beliefs that males are naturally masculine, not feminine, and females are naturally feminine, not masculine. In other words, they challenge the binary alignment of sex and gender by engaging in a masculine activity such as football. Halberstam's (1998) concept of "female masculinity" concerns this specific form of gender subversion, referring to the masculinity that many women feel and embody. Halberstrom calls for a separation of gender (masculinity) from sex (male) by presenting historical and cultural examples of females who refuse to conform to social expectations of femininity. These "alternative masculinities" range from tomboys to drag kings. By doing this, Halberstam makes an academic effort to remove the stigma from women who are not feminine, asserting that the masculine gender does not solely belong to men but is legitimately experienced by all sexes. She pointed out that this is something even the most liberal individuals fail to recognize, as demonstrated by the rejection of women who assumed the gender identity of "butch" by many members of the lesbian feminist movement during the 1970s (Halberstam, p. 121).

Although *butch* is a popular term to describe women "who are more comfortable with masculine gender codes, styles, or identities, than with feminine ones" (Rubin, 1992, p. 467), many have misunderstood it to mean a female who desires to be male, rather than a woman who possesses an organic sense of masculinity—which is independent from maleness. Additionally, butch–femme lesbian couples (in which one woman is masculine and the other feminine) have historically been frowned upon within the lesbian feminist movement, read as "a gross mimicry of heterosexuality" (Halberstam, 1998, p. 121). Halberstam challenges such outdated stigmas by applying a fresh perspective to interpreting expressions of masculinity in the lesbian community, one represented in the use of the term "female masculinity."

Through making *Out of Bounds*, I examine how Halberstam's notion of female masculinity manifests among one particular group of female athletes. To reveal team members' feelings toward masculinity, I use footage of games and interviews that I shot and edited using digital video production and postproduction equipment. Much of the footage consists of Nemesis playing football against other JPWFFL teams. During each game I captured a number of action shots, including attempts to run the ball down the field, quarterbacks passing to receivers, defensive blocks, and players grabbing others' flags, as well as sideline shots of players cheering, slapping hands, and strategizing with others. Each of these shots depicts the competitive edge surfacing in every player on the field, often manifesting as aggressive physical behavior. This is most evident during line blocks when two players come head to head, with one attempting to push the other out of the way to get to the quarterback and the other acting as guard for her team. I interpreted these actions as masculine, and after shooting a few games I was convinced that during interviews players would discuss the masculinity that is expressed on the field.

However, despite what I perceived as clear evidence of masculinity in the field footage, interviews revealed that most of the 10 players I spoke to didn't think about football in relation to gender. Mel, a player on the defensive team, said she didn't see "any of that [gender] stuff going on [while we're playing] because we're all women. . . . I think people might see it differently if it was coed flag football and we were playing with the guys, and we had to think about the gender." Speaking for other team members as well, Mel pointed out how sex and gender are seen as closely linked, and by not having to confront this binary difference—male and female—among players on the field, issues of gender are avoided. Instead of perceiving the game as an expression of gender identity, half the team members I spoke to said football is just something they want to play. As Laura explained: "It is sort of progressive in some ways, you know, women playing football, but . . . it's kind of like the way I was brought up playing sports. It's just . . . an extension of myself. For me, it's not a big deal."

Notably, with one exception, players such as Laura who see football as unrelated to their gender identity do not identify themselves as butch. Of these players, a couple took offense at the suggestion of a connection between football and masculinity. As Jenn explained, discussing the game as a masculine sport unjustly perpetuates a stereotype that all female football players identify as butch: "I don't really feel like I'm this . . . butch lesbian, at all. But I guess stereotypically people are like bad-ass bull-dykes on the field, but I mean, not everyone's a lesbian that plays football, so it's not fair." Kim echoed this sentiment when she said she likes the league because women do not have to be butch to play: "That's what I love about our team and most of the teams. People think that girls who are going to be playing football are just like really butch. You know but, we're not, and I'm not."

Although Jenn, Kim, and the majority of women I interviewed said they don't think about playing football in relation to their gender identity, the two members of Nemesis who identify themselves as butch lesbians understand football and gender as intricately connected. In fact, Kath directly locates the game in her butch coming-out process:

> Once I found that label [butch] and thought that it fit me and wanted to take that on, that was when I began to really feel like I could fill myself out. Like I felt like I had been holding parts of myself back, and that's when I began to research things that I really wanted to do, that I had *always* wanted to do, that didn't feel like that I really could because they were too . . . over on the male side of the spectrum. So I started doing things like . . . accepting the stuff that my father had taught me about plumbing, and carpentry, and all those sorts of things that he had taught me as a kid, but I was sort of pushing aside because I had thought that it was too outside of the ordinary, and football fit right into that.

Like Kath, Chris became interested in the game while developing her masculine gender identity. After a girlfriend gave her a football to show support for "what she considered my butchness," Chris casually played around with it, only to discover an affinity for the game. Eventually, she came to realize that football is indeed a part of her identity, something her girlfriend had a sense of when giving her the gift: "I think [she] was like, 'this is you.' [Later on] I was like, 'Yeah, this is me.'"

Unlike Chris and Kath, half the players I interviewed don't perceive football as a masculine act. Further, the vast majority doesn't see masculinity as part of their own gender—a point that I interpret as connected to Halberstam's (1998) notion of a masculinity continuum. In discussing a social tendency to narrowly define gender identities, Halberstam conceives of a continuum that showcases categories of queer females and their traditional meanings in relation to masculinity, with "androgyny" on the "not masculine" end, "female-to-male" (transgendered) on the other, and "butch" in the middle. Besides limiting how a person can define herself, such strictly outlined categories perpetuate the stigmatization of women who do identify as masculine, presenting it as something that is experienced by only a small amount of women. For this reason, it makes sense to me that most of the players don't see themselves as experiencing masculinity when they play football. If they did, they'd be vulnerable to criticism from both the straight and queer communities.

In my mind, the footage from the field strengthened this interpretation. With all players participating in what I perceived as masculine acts of aggression and competition, I found it hard to understand why most of the players I interviewed didn't see masculinity as an important component of their identity. While an interesting point of research, the perceived content disparity between the masculine messages of the field footage and most players' opinions that football is not gendered presented a challenge. It created an ethical dilemma for me as a filmmaker. During postproduction I realized that by juxtaposing scenes from the field and interviews, I potentially threatened the assertions of the subjects. To some viewers (including myself) images of aggressive behavior such as blocking, diving, and screaming may undermine the players' verbal denials of masculinity. This might portray them as out of touch with aspects of the game, or even their own self-identity. I wondered if these or other edits would leave players feeling misrepresented. Because the members of Nemesis trusted me to represent them fairly, I wanted to take steps to ensure that this unspoken agreement be respected.

TECHNIQUES OF PARTICIPATORY CINEMA

After some research into different methods of documentary filmmaking, I found that many filmmakers have attempted to achieve fair representation by giving their subjects some degree of editorial control, otherwise known as techniques of "participatory cinema." A special approach named by ethnographic filmmaker David MacDougall (1995), participatory cinema occurs when a film's subject actively contributes to the production process by taking on the role of filmmaker, editor, and/or critic at various times during filmmaking. In this way, the subject transcends her traditional role of passivity—as someone whom the filmmaker uses to convey a message—and ultimately exercises some degree of control over the final cut.

One of the first practitioners of this collaborative approach to filmmaking was the anthropologist-turned-ethnographic filmmaker Jean Rouch. In 1954 Rouch initiated what he called "shared cinema-anthropology" with the Songhay fisherman of Niger. Three years after shooting the fishermen hunting a hippopotamus, Rouch returned to them with a projector and a cut of a film about this event (an early version of *Bataille sur le grande fleuve* from 1951). To his surprise, the subjects had a great deal to say after viewing his film, a response he detailed in *Our Totemic Ancestors and Crazed Masters*: "They saw their own image in the film, they discovered film language, they looked at the film over and over again, and suddenly they started to offer criticisms, telling me what was wrong with it" (Rouch, 1995, p. 224). Based on their feedback, Rouch came to better understand the Songhay people and eventually changed the soundtrack to more accurately depict their culture.

In *Chronicle of a Summer*, made in 1961 with sociologist Edgar Morin, Rouch documented this technique of participatory cinema. The second-to-last scene depicts a group of his subjects watching images of themselves during a short cut compiled from the film's rushes. After the screening, the filmmakers listen to subjects' thoughts regarding how they and their peers were represented.

I was inspired by the honest discussion between filmmaker and subject that such a situation could evoke, so I organized a feedback session with the members of Nemesis. A few weeks after the season ended, 14 team members, several guests, and I gathered at one of the player's homes to watch and discuss a 30-minute rough cut of *Out of Bounds*. For research purposes, I recorded the discussion with two digital video cameras. One was designated to capture both video and audio from the perspective of one of the subjects, Kim, who some days earlier had expressed an interest in filmmaking. I used the other to record the audio of the discussion that followed the screening. Whereas players had become comfortable with the camera on the football field by the end of the season, they clearly felt uneasy around it in other settings, becoming silent in its presence at social events. Because it might have inhibited the discussion, I decided not to hold a camera in their faces when asking them to speak about such sensitive topics as their representation in the film and gender identity. Instead, I recorded players' voices by holding a shotgun microphone connected to a camera that sat behind a wall. This setup was a compromise between my desires to document the discussion and increase the subjects' comfort.

The technical setup proved successful and resulted in a full hour of discussion about the rough cut—a dialogue that helped me better understand my subjects, especially in relation to gender identity. Far from my expectations, none of the players directly voiced concerns about their representation in *Out of Bounds*. However, what many questioned was my decision to present equal amounts of interview segments containing discussions of gender identity and action shots from the field. These players thought it would be better to prioritize one type of footage over the other. Fran, who has played on Nemesis for 4 years, suggested choosing between the topics, a point echoed by a guest at the screening who considered football to be the more interesting subject of the two: "Women have struggled with labels [like butch] for decades now. . . . And I think what's new is football. So the newer explanation I think you can have in the video is about football." Team member Carolyn seconded this when she said, "The whole essence of the film is that these are women that are very physical, so you want to show that physicality more, and blend that in with what they're talking about." Through these comments, players encouraged me to reevaluate the emphasis of the film, suggesting that I make the action of football the focus. It is in these moments that the team members assumed the position of the filmmaker and the participatory cinema process was evident.

Continuing to think as the filmmakers of *Out of Bounds*, the players moved to a discussion of gender identity. When addressing team members' differing opinions about football's relation to gender identity, the players asked whether it's better to show each individual's perspective or leave some out for the sake of continuity. For example, they wondered if I should exclude a player's interview from the video because she suggests there is no such thing as butch identity, while the others that were interviewed all recognize its existence. One player suggested prioritizing continuity, only to have several teammates quickly disagree with her, saying this edit could conceivably make them all look the same. Ironically, a player received the concerns of misrepresentation that I had expected would be directed at me. Discussions such as this taught me a lot about Nemesis, specifically that the majority of players believe misrepresentation derives from absence of voices rather than inclusion. In other words, contradictory opinions are seen not as vulnerabilities, but strengths. This knowledge alleviated many of my worries about juxtaposing field footage with testimonies of non-masculinity because I recognized that players didn't find such discrepancies threatening; rather, they saw them as adding dimension to the team.

CONTINUING WITH PARTICIPATORY CINEMA

Because *Out of Bounds* is a documentary-in-progress I feel content in saying that I still don't entirely understand the place of female masculinity in relation to the members of Nemesis. However, although I don't yet have an answer to the initial question that sparked this project, the first 4 months of production uncovered information I never anticipated, as well as challenges I never expected to confront. By applying Halberstam's theory of masculinity to the footage I was collecting, I interpreted the disparity between the masculinity of the field footage and comments of non-masculinity as deriving from players' fear of stigmatization. This inspired me to consider how to fairly represent the perspective of each team member. In searching for ways to address this concern, I was inspired to incorporate techniques of participatory cinema into the production process. To my surprise, the feedback session yielded important information regarding gender identities, particularly that the members of Nemesis recognize they are varied and prefer showing everyone's identity, rather than leaving people out.

As I continue to work on *Out of Bounds*, I will use this information to guide the direction of the project. This experience has taught me to continue to embrace disparities in footage because they may contain compelling details. Additionally, I learned that participatory cinema is not only a way to respect my subjects but also a means of getting to know them. I believe that if I continue on this path of subject participation, I will move closer to understanding female masculinity in team Nemesis among the players of the team.

IT'S YOUR TURN: WHAT DO YOU THINK? WHAT WILL YOU FIND?

1. Describe the main point the author makes about academic theory. Do you think she succeeds in using theory to inform practice? Why or why not? To what extent might using theory to inform practice result in a better film?

2. Imagine you're a filmmaker making a documentary about a social group you belong to, and you want to incorporate techniques of participatory cinema into the production process. Knowing what you do about this community,

how would you go about achieving participatory cinema with them? List the ways you'd involve your subjects in the production process and why you chose these methods.

3. What might be some of the negative aspects of participatory cinema? In other words, what are some complications that might result from involving subjects in the production process? How may filmmakers resolve these issues?

4. Consider the gender identities of women and men represented in the media today. To what extent do these representations reflect traditional bipolar "masculine" and "feminine" identities? To what extent do they reflect gender identity as falling along more of a continuum? What do you think are the ramifications of these representations?

REFERENCES

Halberstam, J. (1998). *Female masculinity*. Durham, NC: Duke University Press.

MacDougall, D. (1995). Beyond observational cinema. In P. Hockings (Ed.), *Principles of visual anthropology* (2nd ed.; pp. 109–124). New York: Mouton de Gruyter.

Rouch, J. (1995). Our totemic ancestors and crazed masters. In P. Hockings (Ed.), *Principles of visual an-*thropology (2nd ed.; pp. 217–232). New York: Mouton de Gruyter.

Rubin, G. (1992). Of Catamites and kings: Reflections on butch, gender, and boundaries. In J. Nestle (Ed.), *The persistent desire: A femme–butch reader* (pp. 466–482). Boston: Alyson Publications.

7.4 *THE TOM JOYNER MORNING SHOW*: ACTIVIST URBAN RADIO IN THE AGE OF CONSOLIDATION

George L. Daniels & Dwight E. Brooks

> *This reading introduces you to* The Tom Joyner Morning Show (TJMS) *and its activist community-oriented programming in an era of consolidation that focuses on the bottom line. Although some fear that media consolidation has an adverse impact on racial minorities, the* TJMS, *its predominately African American audience, and the 100+ stations that carry the show have benefited from consolidation and other related industry trends. By examining the* TJMS *in this context, you'll understand how this syndicated morning show has combined entertainment and community service into a commercially successful formula. Following an overview of the* TJMS *and its unique brand of community service and activism, the authors examine the show in terms of six radio trends and issues.*

It's just after 6 a.m., and while many people are rolling over for a few more minutes of *z*'s, thousands awake to their radio and a funky riff: "Oh, Oh, Oh, it's *The Tom Joyner Morning Show*." This short musical theme is followed by an R&B song introduced by the "Fly Jock," Tom Joyner.

Tom Joyner, the self-proclaimed "hardest working man in radio," has become a household name within African American communities. Joyner's Dallas-based program, syndicated since 1994 by ABC Radio Networks, is one of the first nationally syndicated radio programs hosted and produced by an African American and distributed by a non-Black network. According to ABC, *The Tom Joyner Morning Show* is the #1 rated urban radio show and combines music, comedy, news, and commentary for more than 100 radio stations and over 5 million listeners. Together, Joyner and the *TJMS* are fixtures not only in the African American community but also in the radio industry. Joyner is the first African American elected to the National Association of Broadcasters Hall of Fame. In addition, Joyner has been featured in numerous publications and on television's *60 Minutes, The Today Show*, and C-SPAN.

THE TOM JOYNER MORNING SHOW

The *TJMS* debuted as a syndicated radio program in January 1994 on 28 stations. The program targets an older, more affluent African American audience for local and national advertisers. Monday through Friday from 6:00 to 10:00 a.m. EST, the *TJMS* presents "old-school" music, news and information, guests from politics and entertainment, and an assortment of segments including open telephone lines, humorous advice, and commentaries by Tavis Smiley. One of the show's most ambitious segments utilizes the theatrical talents of a Los Angeles ensemble for the soap opera *It's Your World*. Joyner sums up the strategic goal for his show in simple terms: "First we get people to listen, second we get 'em laughing, and then we get them involved. If I can reach people, then they begin to think, and that's when they start making a difference in their communities."[1] On one morning, the theme music for the *TJMS* is followed by the sounds of cheering crowds. No, that's no sound effect. Those are actual people—a crowd estimated at 3,000 gathered at the convention center in Indianapolis. Then the voice of the biggest name in urban radio, Tom Joyner, is heard: "We are here at the Indiana Black Expo. This is the Southwest Airlines Sky Show. We have landed."

Joyner then introduces his on-air crew as they come on stage to audience applause: Sybil Wilkes, J. Anthony Brown, Myra J, Miss Dupree, D' White Man, and Tavis Smiley. The "Sky Show" is just one of the things that makes this morning radio program unique. What other show draws thousands to an arena in the predawn hours? Joyner characterizes his Sky Shows and similar events, held several times a year, as a "Party With a Purpose," and it is that purpose that leads us to consider the *TJMS*'s activism.

TJMS: ACTIVISM ON THE AIR

During the Sky Show in Indianapolis, a performance by an old-school funk band was followed by the following exchange between Joyner and Tavis Smiley, the former Black Entertainment Television (BET) talk-show host who does commentary twice a week on the *TJMS*:

Joyner: We party for a purpose and always looking for a purpose to party with and always the purpose of the Sky Show from the time we started this thing has been to register people to vote. Yesterday, we tried to register Brian McKnight to vote. You know, Brian McKnight expressed a sentiment very common with people who were very frustrated with last year's election. People said "my vote doesn't count." You really can't argue with him. In the last election, a lot of votes didn't count. Our job is to persuade these people that voting DOES count and if we don't vote, there will be no change. If you want change, you have to make it change and in order to do that—

Smiley: We don't do a Sky Show without bringing the NAACP along with us [to register people to vote].

Joyner: We register people to vote here. We register to vote wherever you are. All you to do is call our 24-hour hotline number and you can register to vote over the phone.

Another regular component of the program that took place during the Sky Show in Indianapolis occurred when Joyner received corporate donations for two college scholarships to be given by the Tom Joyner Foundation. Each month the *TJMS* features a different historically Black college or university (HBCU) and awards scholarships to students attending that institution. On this particular program, a student from Talladega College in Alabama received a scholarship. In the foundation's first year (1997), contributions averaged about $25,000 per month, whereas in July 2000, $270,000 was raised for students at Alcorn State University.

Besides voter registration efforts and student scholarships, the *TJMS*'s community service programming is unique in its activist campaigns against racism in American society. One example was the 1997 movement sparked by the Manhattan auctioneer Christie's decision to sell 19th-century slavery documents and memorabilia. After the *TJMS* gave the telephone number of the auction house over the air, thousands phoned in their objections and Christie's president appeared on the *TJMS* to announce changes in the company's policy.

Another example of the *TJMS* activism is a 1999 campaign targeting CompUSA for not advertising to Black consumers. *TJMS* listeners mailed in sales receipts to CompUSA to demonstrate that African Americans shop at the computer store and affect the company's bottom line. Unlike the Christie's campaign, the listener response initially did not cause the company to change. ABC, the owner of *TJMS*, allegedly ordered Joyner and Smiley to back down on the CompUSA campaign and even threatened to cancel the program. Upon hearing of the threat, callers flooded the switchboards at both ABC and Comp USA. The CompUSA president appeared on the *TJMS*, apologized for the "misunderstanding," and agreed to hire a Black-owned advertising agency.

Talk radio is known for the political views of its hosts and listeners, but few entertainment-oriented programs are as politically active as the *TJMS*. This approach is consistent with a framework known as the "public sphere," a perspective highlighting social issues in considering the public interest role of the mass media. The public sphere model argues that society's needs cannot be met entirely through a market system emphasizing business success via profit. Thus, the media become central elements in a vibrant public sphere (Croteau & Hoynes, 2001). Because both the market model and the public sphere are important in understanding the media, we'll examine the *TJMS* in the context of the market model and, more specifically, some of the issues and trends that have emerged from this model—the dominant business model within media industries.

THE MARKET MODEL: DEREGULATION AND CONSOLIDATION

The market model suggests that society's needs are best met through a relatively unregulated process of exchange based on the dynamics of supply and demand. In broadcasting, this could best be achieved through deregulation. Deregulation relies on the marketplace, rather than government intervention, to establish priorities and standards of business conduct. Deregulation intensified in the 1980s when policymakers argued that most media regulation was not in the public interest (Croteau & Hoynes, 2001). By the 1990s, the rise of new digital technologies led to increasing expansion of media industries. As more media conglomerates emerged from a decade of market-oriented media policy, many argued for a wholesale rewriting of the laws and regulations that drive U.S. media policy.

The result was the Telecommunications Act of 1996, which has led to major changes in the media industries. For instance, it intensified consolidation—the rise of media conglomerates of unprecedented size. In terms of radio, the Act removed limits on the number of stations a company could own and sparked a wave of mergers among radio companies. Staff and other resources were consolidated. Stations are increasingly part of regional or national ownership "groups"; by 1999, some groups had more than 1,000 AM and FM stations under their control. Even within a single market, one owner could hold up to eight radio outlets. Many policymakers and media companies claimed that greater concentration of broadcast outlets meant good business: Media conglomerates create economies of scale that allow them to better compete with expanding information and entertainment distribution platforms such as satellite TV and the Internet.

By 2001, the nation's largest radio group (Clear Channel Communications) owned 19 of the 110 stations that carried the *TJMS*. Some feared such consolidation would hurt racial minorities, many of whom owned stations likely to carry an urban/Black radio program such as the *TJMS*. In one instance, two minority owners competed for the *TJMS* in Washington, DC. The owner of a larger station group won by offering to air the *TJMS* on stations the group owned in other markets. This shows how consolidation and minority ownership are connected. The larger station group would allow the *TJMS* to be heard by a wider audience in a greater number of places than could a single, independently owned station.

In many ways consolidation has been good for the Black/urban-oriented *TJMS* because it has resulted in placing a Black-oriented program on stations with stronger financial backing owned by companies with greater distribution potential. The battle between two minority-owned radio stations for the *TJMS* leads to a discussion of another industry issue: the minority ownership of broadcast stations.

MINORITY OWNERSHIP

It was not until 1949 and the purchase of WERD-AM in Atlanta that Blacks started owning radio stations. Over the years, the Federal Communications Commission (FCC), which awards broadcast licenses, has implemented programs to help racial minorities join the ranks of station owners. Although ABC Radio owns the *TJMS*, it's more useful to consider the ownership of stations that air the *TJMS*. In fact, only 17 of 110 *TJMS* affiliates in 2001 were minority owned. Data from the National Telecommunications and Information Administration (2001) showed a dip in the number of minority-owned radio stations from 314 in 1995 to 284 in 1996–1997 and a recovery to 426 by 1999–2000, the latest year for which ownership data were available. Joyner would like to see more Black station owners and believes consolidation has all but destroyed Black ownership.

DIVERSITY

The FCC's efforts to increase minority ownership were directed at increasing workforce diversity and, ultimately, greater content diversity. However, even if the owners of most *TJMS* affiliates are not African American, mostly racial minorities staff the 100+ stations that air the show. In addition, the *TJMS* represents workforce diversity because the majority of the show's staff is African American. Besides this type of workforce diversity, the show contributes to diversity in radio in other ways. Few shows regularly take on causes such as supporting African American fathers, raising funds for HBCUs, or recognizing trailblazers in Black history such as Rosa Parks. Thus, the *TJMS* contributes to content diversity in radio.

The *TJMS* is just one of the many choices listeners have during morning drive, traditionally the time period when listenership is highest and thus most lucrative for radio owners. The show's mix of music and talk results in a unique format for that hour of the day—most stations focus either on music or news–talk during morning drive. Joyner describes a major difference between his show and other radio stations: "They don't program . . . in a way that super-serves the community. We try to super-serve the community. We talkin' . . . we're not more music, less talk; we're more talk and less music." Therefore, the *TJMS* also contributes to diversity in radio formats, which in turn has seen a trend of developing specific formats for niche audiences known as microformatting.

MICROFORMATTING

ABC Radio's Web site lists the *TJMS* along with Doug Banks's morning program under its "Urban Programming" menu. As syndicated African American announcers, Joyner and Banks reach urban/Black audiences of different age groups and preferences. In other words, as a college student, you probably listen to different radio stations than your parents. Stations that target programming to different people's specific tastes represent the idea of microformatting.

Black/urban radio is comprised of various music formats including urban/R&B, R&B oldies, urban/AC (adult contemporary), and Black gospel. Other radio formats targeting Black listeners are Black talk and jazz. Within the Black/urban format, some stations choose the adult format or R&B hits and oldies (adult urban contemporary) because it appeals to advertisers marketing to African American adults. These are the stations that tend to carry the *TJMS*, whose listeners tend to be African American females with an average age of 40 ("Study Reveals," 2000). On the other hand, stations targeting a younger Black demographic tend to label their format as urban (or in some cases, hip-hop). These stations are more likely to carry ABC's *The Doug Banks Show*.

LOCALISM

Localism entails programming to meet the needs of the public in the area in which the station has been licensed to broadcast. For urban radio stations carrying the *TJMS*, localism isn't a problem because it's part of the show's formula for success. Despite being distributed to over 100 stations across the nation, Tom Joyner makes a concerted effort to allow affiliates to maintain a local flavor throughout the show. In fact, many listeners have said the show sounds like it's broadcast from a station in their local area. This is one of the major appeals of the show.

From his Dallas studio, Joyner uses four microphones to tape customized announcements and introductions of local air personalities daily for each of his affiliates. These elements go beyond traditional customized promotional "drop-ins" (5- to 10-second messages played between songs and announcements) provided by satellite radio announcers. In the case of the *TJMS*, local drop-ins are recorded and updated daily to give the show a live and local flavor. Besides these drop-ins, the show also allows ample time for local news, traffic, weather, and other information throughout the 4 hours. At one time Joyner put his show together as a "national show that sounded like it was local" (Farber, 2000, p. 136). Joyner now admits there is less of an effort to sound local, although he makes a point to regularly visit the cities in which his show airs. In cities where the *TJMS* is not available, people can listen on the Internet. Thus, the *TJMS* brings to light another trend in radio—webcasting.

WEBCASTING

When a radio station "streams" its broadcast signals over the Internet for individual reception on computers, we call that "webcasting." Don't confuse this with "Internet radio," in which programming is available *only* online. While many stations at the beginning of the 21st century were still examining the possibilities of extending their Web sites beyond static marketing pages to active places where consumers may hear the radio signal even as it is broadcast, the *TJMS* utilized this technology to reach African Americans—especially in areas where the show is unavailable.

In addition to live streaming audio, the *TJMS*'s Web site also allows visitors to download segments of previous shows. This utilization of computer technology by the *TJMS* and its audience provides the potential to narrow the so-called digital divide, a term describing the gap between White and non-White users of computers and the Internet. Beyond offering people a chance to listen to both live and previously aired shows, the *TJMS* Web site includes things such as news and information ("In the News"), Sky Show information, and links to other sites such as ABC Radio, the Tom Joyner Foundation, and various corporate sponsors.

THE BOTTOM LINE

We concluded our look at six radio trends and issues with webcasting because it's a technology that was still evolving as the 21st century began. The other five—consolidation, minority ownership, diversity, microformatting, and localism—are also areas where change is likely to continue. As the general trend of consolidation continues, its impact on minority ownership, the minority media workforce, and content diversity remains to be seen. What is more certain, the *TJMS*—even when affiliated stations are not minority owned—with its community service and activism on issues of race and social justice, will continue to be an attractive media product because of its commercial appeal. While hundreds of commercially successful radio stations use Black/urban formats to appeal to African American audiences, most don't include the level of activism that the *TJMS* promotes. Stations including community involvement or activism as part of their programming and promotional strategy may find they're able to serve the public interest while increasing their bottom line. (Such a commitment to community service is a traditional element of Black/urban radio.[2])

In conclusion, while the two models used here to evaluate media—the market and public sphere—are both necessary in understanding the media, we contend the market model has limitations. Businesses, especially media businesses, should not be judged solely by profitability. Not only do markets tend to produce inequities, but they also don't necessarily meet democratic needs. According to the public sphere model, the media are more than just profit-making components of large conglomerates. For a participatory democracy to function, citizens must have access to the resources necessary for meaningful participation. Because the media play a crucial role in preparing citizens for active participation in our democracy, the *TJMS* makes an important contribution to our society.

NOTES

1. Unless indicated otherwise, all quotations from Tom Joyner were obtained from an interview conducted by the authors on July 21, 2001.

2. For more information on the tradition of Black/urban radio, see Barlow (1999); Newman (1988); Williams (1998).

IT'S YOUR TURN: WHAT DO YOU THINK? WHAT WILL YOU FIND?

1. The *TJMS* has been mistakenly labeled a "talk show" even though it has considerable music and entertainment. Can you name other entertainment-oriented radio programs that also have an activist theme? What are those themes? Would you listen to those programs? Why or why not?

2. As we mentioned, most *TJMS* affiliates are not minority owned. What do you think this says about the relationship between who owns a station and the opportunities for minority-oriented media content? Some people claim that minority ownership is necessary for achieving a minority workforce and developing minority content.

What do you think? Discuss the importance of ownership of radio and TV stations by racial and gender minority groups.

3. Identify the closest station to you that carries the *TJMS*. List the station's call letters, location, and format. Listen to the show for an hour and compile a "log" of its program elements (song, commercial, news break, etc.). Use this log to analyze the show's content in terms of its combination of entertainment and community service programming. If no station in your area carries the show, you can listen to the show on the *TJMS* Web site (http://www.tomjoyner.com/).

4. Again, listen to the *TJMS* for an hour. How many references to "race," "African Americans," or "Whites" did you hear? Describe the way(s) race was referenced (jokes, serious commentary, news content, etc.). Did anything make you feel uncomfortable? If so, do you think the source of discomfort was because of your own racial background or identity? If not, do you think this suggests your comfort level is high in dealing with issues of race? Why or why not?

REFERENCES

Barlow, W. (1999). *Voice over: The making of Black radio*. Philadelphia: Temple University Press.

Croteau, D., & Hoynes, W. (2001). *The business of media: Corporate media and the public interest*. Thousand Oaks, CA: Pine Forge Press.

Farber, E. (2000, April 7). Publisher's profile: Tom Joyner. *Radio & Records*, p. 136.

National Telecommunication and Information Administration. (2001). *Changes, challenges and charting new courses: Minority commercial broadcast ownership in the United States*. Washington, DC: United States Department of Commerce.

Newman, M. (1988). *Entrepreneurs of profit and pride: From Black-appeal to radio soul*. New York: Praeger.

Study reveals brand leadership of ABC Radio Networks' personalities Tom Joyner and Doug Banks. *Yankelovich Report*. Retrieved February 24, 2001, from: http://www.abcradio.com

Williams, G. (1998). *Legendary pioneers of Black radio*. Westport, CT: Praeger.

CHAPTER 8

MEDIA AND RELATED ORGANIZATIONS

8.1 USING FEMINIST STANDPOINT THEORY TO DISCOVER LATINAS' REALITIES IN PUBLIC RELATIONS ORGANIZATIONS

Donnalyn Pompper

This study examines experiences of Latinas who work in public relations. In particular, it probes intersections among dimensions of gender and ethnicity in organizations and recommends further adaptation of the workplace as a site for embracing difference.

We know that organizations' policymakers tend to "play it safe" with management models that downplay sexuality, overlook class relations, and appear gender neutral. Yet, to do so negates female and multicultural perspectives—and means that Anglo-Eurocentric biases shape organizations, becoming normalized over time. Such effects may be worst for women of color, "because they disappear in the gap between 'women' (often considered White) and 'minorities' (often considered male)" (Reuther & Fairhurst, 2000, p. 237).

I concur with those who suggest that valuing both women *and* ethnic diversity is a prerequisite for organizational effectiveness. We know far too little about why Latinas[1] are so conspicuously absent from management ranks, and this exploratory study sought to gain insight into their experiences.

HISPANICS IN THE UNITED STATES

The U.S. Bureau of the Census originated the term "Hispanic" in 1980 to categorize people who originate from Spanish-speaking countries or regions (Flores-Hughes, 1996). The Census Bureau located 35.3 million self-described U.S. Hispanics in 2000 and predicts that they will achieve majority status by 2050. Only 1% of managers among Fortune 2000 industrial and service companies are Hispanic, even though they made up 8% of the working population. Among U.S. Hispanics (35.3 million), women are the largest subgroup—those of Mexican (5.7 million), Puerto Rican (1.1 million), and Cuban (485,000) origins (U.S. Department of Labor, Women's Bureau, 1997).

U.S. Hispanics battle racial stratification (Thompson, 1989), "Anglo-conformity" (Oboler, 1995, p. 28), reconciling multiple identities (Kong, 2001), and dealing with those who remind Hispanics of their "place" (Torres, 2003). Furthermore, popular culture trivializes and vilifies Hispanics as poor Catholics, uneducated, lazy, sexually promiscuous, violent, and unable to speak English (Holtzman, 2000).

CULTURE & ETHNICITY IN ORGANIZATIONS

Overall, researchers tend to view organizations as having *culture* and people as having *ethnicity*. *Ethnicity* has been socially defined, based on cultural, psychological, or biological traits (Jackson & Garner, 1997). *Culture* is a root metaphor for an organization and its historically transmitted system of valuing some members over others along demographic lines (Jost & Banaji, 1994). *Organizational cultures* are blamed for effects such as discrimination in employment, status, and resources among minorities.

Few minorities are represented at management levels when an organization's culture and its diversity strategy are out of sync. It is well documented that organizations fail to keep up with increased societal demographic complexity (Operario & Fiske, 2001). Workers situated on the margins of organizational power structures must negotiate their organizational positions and adopt unique ways to exist in mainstream organizational settings (Fox & Giles, 1997).

LEADERSHIP APPROACHES AMONG WOMEN OF COLOR

Contributions of women of color in management are unique and invaluable. Yet, many organizations still view leadership as a set of universal constructs that fail to generalize to women of color and conflict with ethnic stereotypes (Parker, 2001).

The workplace for a woman of color is a contested terrain. For example, Latinas and other women of color are subordinated in the workplace through rejection and exclusion (Hurtado, 1996) and Latinas may experience the worst effects of sexual harassment because they are acculturated to stay loyal to an employer since their earnings are essential to household income (Shupe, Cortina, Ramos, Fitzgerald, & Salisbury, 2002). African American women's leadership approach is steeped in interactivity, empowerment of others, openness, and boundary-spanning (Parker, 2001). In public relations they fulfill unique roles, such as pioneer, educator, mentor, and agenda builder (Pompper, 2004). Similarly, Chow (1994) posited that Asian American women possess qualities of inner strength, firmness, and resourcefulness.

LATINAS IN PUBLIC RELATIONS

Latina public relations practitioners are outnumbered, underpaid, and underrepresented in management. Hispanics comprise 5.5% of public relations specialists and only 4.2% of managers in marketing, advertising, and public relations (U.S. Bureau of the Census, 1995). The public relations profession is about 70% female (PRSA/IABC Salary Survey, 2000), with most women working at entry- and mid-levels. Among women employed in the "management and public relations industry," 39% are White[2]—as compared to 4.5% African American and 1.5% Hispanic (U.S. Department of Labor Bureau of Labor Statistics, 2001). In 1999, among 67,210 public relations managers, the mean annual wage was $56,770 (U.S. Department of Labor Bureau of Labor Statistics, 1999). White women's weekly earnings were 37.4% higher than those of Hispanic women—and women generally earn a little more than half (63%) as much as men (U.S. Department of Labor Bureau of Labor Statistics, 2001).

Valuable insights about Latinas' realities are embedded in studies of "minorities" and "multiculturalism." Findings suggest low practitioner numbers, salary differentials, low status, and stereotyping. Once hired, minority practitioners advance slowly (Len-Rios, 1998), are pigeonholed into servicing "ethnic" projects (Banks, 1995), and experience salary caps and salary inequities (Abeyta & Hackett, 2002). It is assumed that Latina practitioners can speak and write Spanish fluently—but this is not always the case (Abeyta & Hackett, 2002). They suffer high degrees of workplace stress, take on extra work to prove they can "do it all," and often leave the field frustrated (Kucera, 1994; Zerbinos & Clanton, 1993).

Some Latina practitioners choose to work among Hispanic audiences with whom they feel most comfortable—as reflected in a recent trend called Hispanic public relations (HPR). The Hispanic Public Relations Association (HPRA) defines it as "a new field within public relations; unique because it requires a communications professional who can work in at least two languages, Spanish and English" (Vendrell, 1994–1995, p. 34).

FEMINIST STANDPOINT THEORY

Feminist theory exposes gendered social, political, and economic inequities in organizations—where males tend to set policy and dominate certain fields. To make sense of women's experiences in context, many feminists of color embrace feminist standpoint theory (FST) as a methodology, a point of departure, or a critical framework (Bullis & Stout, 2000). FST exchanges the universal reference point (wealthy, White, heterosexual men as Western society's architects) for that of those traditionally defined by distance from the dominant social subject. FST suggests that all truths are rooted in some subjective standpoint and that not all group members occupy the same standpoint. Therefore, FST offers a means for promoting a "chain of linkages" (LaClau & Mouffe, 1985) for women to join together in opposition, resistance, and transformation.

Upon a foundation of research reviewed here, three research questions were posed to learn more about Latinas' experiences working in public relations.

METHOD

Focus group meetings with Latinas where hosted in Houston, New York, Miami, and Los Angeles, since these cities are geographically diverse, include the largest Hispanic populations in the United States, and represent major markets for public relations practice. A snowball sampling technique was used to recruit focus group participants—Latinas working in public relations at the time of data collection. The 2000 Public Relations Society of America (PRSA) Multicultural Membership Directory served as a starting point for the first telephone number used in each city to invite Latina practitioners. Attempts were made to assemble diverse focus groups according to age, self-ascribed ethnic heritage (Cuban, Mexican, Puerto Rican, other), public relations environment (agency, corporate, not-for-profit sectors), job level (executive to entry-level positions), and years of experience. I reimbursed participants for transportation costs (bus, taxi, parking) and provided light refreshments. No financial incentives were used.

A total of 25 Latinas participated in four focus group discussions which ranged in duration from $1\frac{1}{2}$ to $2\frac{1}{2}$ hours during September through December 2002. Meetings were held at centrally located, easily accessible, comfortable sites. Data were derived from 88 pages of verbatim transcribed audiotape recordings and arranged in patterns and themes by use of index cards that were categorized and reshuffled, as needed, with anomalies noted (Glaser & Strauss, 1967). The unit of analysis was Latinas' voices—experiences in their own words categorized and analyzed as data (Harding, 1987). To address potential researcher bias (I am an Anglo woman), I asked four Latinas (two academics and two practitioners) to also analyze transcripts, looking for patterns.

FINDINGS

Focus group respondents ranged in age from 23 to 59 with a mean of 9.95 years' public relations experience in industries like consumer packaged goods, fundraising, public affairs, real estate, telecommunications, and travel–tourism. All but six had an undergraduate college degree, four had earned a master's degree, and one had earned the accredited public relations (APR) distinction.

Research Question 1:   In what ways do Latina public relations practitioners perceive that gender–ethnicity plays a role in how others view them?

Three overlapping issues emerged among responses: 1) Sexism by Latinos, 2) Ethnic Discrimination by Anglos, and 3) Within-Culture Stress and Pressure.

> *Sexism by Latinos.*   Respondents in all cities shared stories of Latinos' gender discrimination. Respondents perceived sexism to be less rampant in the general market.[3] Those working in agencies lamented that non-White international clients focus more on their appearance than expertise. It would seem that machismo is "accepted" as "part of the culture" since some respondents said that some HPR firms have dress codes requiring female employees to show their legs. Even among Latino reporters, disrespect is a norm that Latina practitioners encounter daily.

Ethnic Discrimination by Anglos.   Respondents were most incensed by Anglos' attempts to "de-ethnitize" and exclude Latinas from social networks. They perceive that Anglo managers of both genders hold Hispanic employees to a different standard and "other" them routinely. Not all respondents were satisfied to exclusively work with Hispanic audiences but feel forced to do so. Some respondents also suggested that Anglo clients and bosses perceive Spanish language media as second-rate.

Within-Culture Stress and Pressure.   Finally, respondents reported feelings of betrayal—working hard at a career that limits their role as mother and wife. Like other stressed working women, Latinas work a "second shift" as caregivers. Hence, servicing international clients generally involves much travel. Working in public relations is not a 9–5 job, and respondents struggle to fit in family care, housekeeping chores, and caretaking for parents and grandparents. Becoming a workaholic and putting family life on hold was an effect reported by both married and unmarried respondents.

Research Question 2:   How do Latina practitioners respond to gender–ethnicity challenges at work?

Most respondents reported passively dealing with gender–ethnicity challenges for fear of losing their job. Coping mechanisms offer varying degrees of relief, such as crying, abandoning volatile situations, "developing a thick skin," "toughening it out," being patient, "just surviving," and "enduring." Perhaps in denial, some blamed career stasis and low pay on geographic location—in other words, they believe they would make more money if they lived in another city. Other passive reactions to work-related sexism included dressing in gray, black, or navy blue to "avoid standing out" and ignoring disrespectful advances. On the other hand, some respondents shared active responses to workplace racism and sexism, such as "standing your ground," "confronting them," and "demanding respect."

Latinas also have responded to challenges by adapting their views on gender roles and reaching out for family support. Latinas described a fervent work ethic and drive to build multiple skill sets to overcome economic conditions that their parents experienced. Finally, Latinas seek to improve their odds through networking, mentoring, continued education, and improved Spanish language fluency. Several regularly read Hispanic Business to stay on top of trends and read Spanish language books.

Research Question 3:   What recommendations do Latina public relations practitioners offer for enhancing value of gender–ethnicity in organizations?

Four themes emerged among recommendations: 1) Eliminate Gender–Ethnicity Discrimination, 2) Enlighten Clients and Supervisors, 3) Change Cultural Assumptions Within Hispanic Communities, and 4) Increase Numbers of Latina Practitioners and Business Owners.

Eliminate Gender–Ethnic Discrimination.   A New York Hispanic senior account executive, 28, seemed to speak for all respondents: "It's still a man's world," implying that little will change until women acquire greater power in organizations and EEOC legislation is enforced. Ethnic stereotyping hurts. New York practitioners said it is assumed that all Puerto Ricans are recent mainland immigrants who live in the South Bronx and know no English. Likewise, Cuban American Miami practitioners said they are regarded as "just having gotten off the boat," called "scrubs on rafts," or "spic." A Houston Mexican American practitioner, 36, told how clients facing an OSHA issue twice invited her to leave a factory meeting: "It was all White male . . . because I'm a Hispanic female, they would have preferred that I put on my little apron and go make the tacos." A Los Angeles Cuban American not-for-profit practitioner, 45, was told at a workshop that "All Latinas have bad tempers."

Enlighten Clients and Supervisors.   Respondents opined that ignorance and xenophobia damages workers' self-esteem and organizations' bottom lines. Importantly, supervisors' failure to stand up to Latino clients and colleagues for sexually harassing Latinas fuels job dissatisfaction. Some attributed Anglos' racism to lack of awareness, more so than malice.

Change Cultural Assumptions Within Hispanic Communities.   Respondents anticipate that altering assumptions among Hispanic communities will be the most difficult. Hispanics, too, engage in labeling behaviors. A New York Latina working in a not-for-profit setting, 27, bristles against accusations that she is "not being Latina enough." On the other hand, respondents loathe Latinas who deny their culture. Finally, respondents posited that now is the time to modify traditional Hispanic gender roles.

Increase Numbers of Latina Practitioners and Business Owners.   Overall, respondents anticipate that their status will increase with greater numbers of Hispanic practitioners. A Los Angeles Cuban American not-for-profit practitioner, 45, explained that greater numbers means power: "Eventually the message has to resonate."

DISCUSSION

Latinas' stories described layers of gender and ethnicity overlap in organizations negatively—in terms of discrimination. It is clear that Latinas perceive that they are neither fully valued nor trusted to offer the full range of abilities that male and Anglo public relations practitioners are assumed to have. Overall, discrimination barriers in organizations make ascending the management ladder next to impossible for Latinas and other women of color.

Moreover, few respondents overtly admitted it, but their tone, body language, and choice of anecdotes suggest that they also routinely navigate identity crises. Such a bicultural lifestyle for a woman of color in a management position means that she may feel forced to "sacrifice the racial/ethnic part of her identity" in order to conform to "what is normal" at work (Bell, Denton, & Nkomo, 1993, p. 18). Hegemony causes "between and among" conflict that provokes identity crisis (Clair, 1993). Latinas shared numerous difficulties associated with trying to negotiate gender–ethnicity barriers in organizations ("between" identity). Also, a Latina's "among" identity as wife, mother, sister, daughter, cousin, and friend conflicts with her work identity. Family support helps, but today's Latina puts a lot of pressure on herself to change, excel at work, judiciously plot a career, fulfill traditional gender roles, and fight the biological clock. Surprisingly, Latinas interviewed were positive and confident in the face of such steep challenges. Forever optimistic, Latinas interviewed believe that equity in the workplace is a real possibility, for *they* will be the force for change.

Discovering that complex social forces are at work in the intersection of ethnicity/race and gender in organizations is not news. However, findings underscore similarities (and unique differences) among realities of diverse women of color in organizations.

Consistent with my findings in an earlier study of African American women in public relations (Pompper, 2004), Latinas studied here also preferred to change jobs without trying to negotiate solutions with bosses and clients. Black feminists characterize this pattern as "out-spiraling career moves" (Bell & Nkomo, 2001, p. 161). Also, Latinas and Asian American women (Chow, 1994) may experience similar paradoxes that result from organizational control carrying over into family life, forcing a dependence on patriarchy.

I posit that a two-pronged approach for eradicating glass-ceiling outcomes is called for: inspiring women of color to find new ways to claim a professional identity in their organizations while also encouraging real, positive change in organizations in order to embrace *all aspects* of difference.

NOTES

1. Terms like "Hispanic," "Latino," "ethnic," "minority," "marginal," "alternative," and "Third World," are politically charged (Oboler, 1995). Yet, in the absence of a more enlightened terminology, researchers must use them—carefully. *Latina*, the feminine form of *Latino*, is used here, although I agree that "Latinos do not comprise even a relatively homogenous ethnicity" (Flores, 1993,

p. 199). It is important to recognize that individual human experiences are unique and defy categorization. No disrespect or insensitivity is intended.

2. White men (48.3%) hold most jobs at this level.

3. Latinas in all focus groups referred to public relations practice involving White target audiences as "general market."

IT'S YOUR TURN: WHAT DO YOU THINK? WHAT WILL YOU FIND?

1. How would you handle discrimination at work? Do you think it's better to just quit?

2. According to the Feminist Standpoint Theory (FST) framework, every woman has unique experiences—even if she shares certain demographic characteristics (like religion or skin color) with other women. What do you think?

3. In what ways do you think people will reconcile work and family demands in the future? For example, will women continue to be the primary caregivers to children? Who will take care of aging parents?

REFERENCES

Abeyta, N., & Hackett, M. (2002). Perspectives of Hispanic PR practitioners. *Public Relations Quarterly*, *47*(1), 27–30.

Banks, S. P. (1995). *Multicultural public relations: A social-interpretive approach*. Thousand Oaks, CA: Sage.

Bell, E. L. J. E., Denton, T. C., & Nkomo, S. M. (1993). Women of color in management: Toward an inclusive analysis. In E. A. Fagenson (Ed.), *Women in management: Trends, issues, and challenges in managerial diversity* (pp. 105–130). Newbury Park, CA: Sage.

Bell, E. L. J. E., & Nkomo, S. M. (2001). *Our separate ways: Black and White women and the struggle for professional identity*. Boston: Harvard Business School Press.

Bullis, C., & Stout, K. R. (2000). Organizational socialization: A feminist standpoint approach. In P. M. Buzzanell (Ed.). *Rethinking organizational & managerial communication from feminist perspectives* (pp. 47–75). Thousand Oaks, CA: Sage.

Chow, E. N-L. (1994). Asian American women at work. In M. B. Zinn & B. T. Dill (Eds.), *Women of color in U.S. society* (pp. 203–228). Philadelphia: Temple University Press.

Clair, R. P. (1993). The use of framing devices to sequester organizational narratives: Hegemony and harassment. *Communication Monographs, 6*(2), 113–136.

Flores, J. (1993). Divided borders: Essays on Puerto Rican identity. Houston, TX: Arte Publico Press.

Flores-Hughes, G. (1996, September). Why the term "Hispanic"? *Hispanic,* p. 64.

Fox, S. A., & Giles, H. (1997). "Let the wheelchair through!" In. W. P. Robinson (Ed.), *Social psychology and social identity: Festschrift in honor of Henri Tajfel* (pp. 215–248). Amsterdam: Elsevier.

Glaser, B. G., & Strauss, A. L. (1967). The discovery of grounded theory: *Strategies for qualitative research*. Chicago: Aldine.

Harding, S. (1987). Introduction: Is there a feminist method? In S. Harding (Ed.), *Feminism and methodology: Social science issues* (pp. 1–14). Bloomington: Indiana University Press.

Holtzman, L. (2000). *Media messages: What film, television, and popular music teach us about race, class, gender, and sexual orientation*. New York: M. E. Sharpe.

Hurtado, A. (1996). *The color of privilege: Three blasphemies on race and feminism*. Ann Arbor: University of Michigan Press.

Jackson, R. L., II, & Garner, T. (1997). Tracing the evolution of "race," "ethnicity," and "culture" in communication studies. *Howard Journal of Communications, 9*, 41–55.

Jost, J. T., & Banaji, M. R. (1994). The role of stereotyping in system justification and the production of false consciousness. *British Journal of Social Psychology, 33*, 1–27.

Kong, D. (2001, August 4). Voices unite in anti-Hispanic fervor. *Albuquerque Journal*, A4.

Kucera, M. (1994). *Doing it all: Why women public relations managers tend to fulfill both the managerial and technical roles*. Unpublished master's thesis, University of Maryland, College Park.

Len-Rios, M. E. (2002). Latino professionals in public relations. *Public Relations Quarterly, 47*(1), 22–26.

LaClau, E., & Mouffe, C. (1985). *Hegemony and socialist strategy*. London: Verso.

Oboler, S. (1995). *Ethnic labels, Latino lives: Identity and the politics of (re)presentation in the United States*. Minneapolis: University of Minnesota Press.

Operario, D., & Fiske, S. T. (2001). Causes and consequences of stereotypes in organizations. In M. London (Ed.), *How people evaluate others in organizations* (pp. 45–62). Mahwah, NJ: Lawrence Erlbaum Associates.

Parker, P. S. (2001). African American women executives' leadership communication within dominant-culture organizations: (Re)conceptualizing notions of collaboration and instrumentality. *Management Communication Quarterly, 15*(1), 42–82.

Pompper, D. (2004). Linking ethnic diversity & two-way symmetry: Modeling female African-American practitioners' roles. *Journal of Public Relations Research, 16*(3), 269–299.

Public Relations Society of America. (2000). *PRSA/IABC salary survey 2000*. Retrieved February 23, 2001, from: http://www.prsa.org./salser/secure/tempfile/index.html

Reuther, C., & Fairhurst, G. T. (2000). Chaos theory and the glass ceiling. In P. M. Buzzanell (Ed.), *Rethinking organizational and managerial communication from feminist perspectives* (pp. 236–256). Thousand Oaks, CA: Sage.

Shupe, E. I., Cortina, L. M., Ramos, A., Fitzgerald, L. F., & Salisbury, J. (2002). The incidence and outcomes of sexual harassment among Hispanic and non-Hispanic White women: A comparison across levels of cultural affiliation. *Psychology of Women Quarterly, 26*(4), 298–308.

Thompson, R. H. (1989). *Theories of ethnicity. A critical appraisal*. Westport, CT: Greenwood Press.

Torres, E. E. (2003). *Chicana without apology: The new Chicana cultural studies*. New York: Routledge.

U.S. Bureau of the Census. (1995). *Current population survey: Annual averages of persons detailed by occupation, sex, race, and Hispanic origin*. Retrieved October 14, 2002, from: http://ftp://ftp.bls.gov/pub/special.requests/lf/aat11.txt

U.S. Bureau of the Census. (2000). *Current population survey: Annual averages of persons detailed by occupation, sex, race, and Hispanic origin*. Retrieved October 14, 2002, from: http://ftp://ftp.bls.gov/pub/special.requests/lf/aat11.txt

U.S. Department of Labor, Bureau of Labor Statistics. (1999). *1999 national occupational employment and wage estimates*. Retrieved October 19, 2001, from: http://www.bls.gov/oes/1999/9es112031.htm

U.S. Department of Labor, Bureau of Labor Statistics. (2001). *Highlights of women's earnings in 2000* (Report 952). Washington, DC: Author.

U.S. Department of Labor, Women's Bureau. (1997). *Women of Hispanic origin in the labor force*. Retrieved November 29, 2001, from: http://www.dol.gov/dol/wb/public/wb_pubs/hisp97.htm

Vendrell, I. (1994–1995). What is Hispanic public relations and where is it going? *Public Relations Quarterly, 39*, 33–37.

Zerbinos, E., & Clanton, G. A. (1993). Minority practitioners: Career influences, job satisfaction, and discrimination. *Public Relations Review, 19*(1), 75–91.

8.2 WOMEN IN TV AND RADIO NEWS

Robert A. Papper

> *The author has been investigating race and gender in newsroom employment for 15 years and has conducted more than 20 studies of working journalists. This reading presents an overview of some of the most telling results of his and previous research into women's employment patterns, salaries, and obstacles to success.*

Change came quickly for women in radio and television news back in the 1970s; it has been slower and more complex in the years since. In fact, the percentage of women in television news has been largely unchanged in the past decade, but that's just the big picture. The details reveal a slow evolution in terms of women's roles in TV news. Radio is more complex still. Deregulation efforts—beginning with the Carter administration in the 1970s and continuing with the reforms of the Telecommunications Act in 1996—revolutionized radio and radio news, and everyone, including women, has been affected.

SOME HISTORY

Broadcasting was among the first fields to mandate equal employment opportunity. In 1969, the Federal Communications Commission installed Equal Employment Opportunity (EEO) rules that required radio and television stations to conduct, track, and report special efforts to recruit minorities. In 1971, the FCC extended that rule to include women.

The regulation was revolutionary. Stations which had no minorities and few, if any, women outside of secretaries suddenly found themselves on recruiting binges in search of women and minorities. At the time, the station where I worked, WCCO-TV in Minneapolis, one of the largest CBS stations in the country, had just one woman reporter on the air and no minorities at all. Under the new mandate, the percentage of women (and minorities) in radio and television news soared. Within a decade, you could find women in significant numbers in every position except top newsroom and station management. Growth has been slower ever since.

In 1973, Vernon Stone published the first of his studies of local radio and television news for the Radio Television News Directors Association. He found that about 10% of the news staffs in both radio and TV were women. By the end of the decade in 1979, both radio and TV news had grown to 26% women (Stone, 1987). The 1980s saw continuing—but much slower—growth. By the late 1980s, Stone (1988) found that women made up 33% of the TV news workforce and 31% of the radio news workforce.

Although the landmark 1971 EEO rules encouraged the hiring of women, three major legal and legislative changes since then have affected the gender landscape in broadcasting.

In 1979, toward the end of the Carter administration, the FCC began its deregulation move into what became known as "marketplace" regulation. The idea was that rather than have the government impose rules about station operation, the marketplace itself—

consumer demand—would take care of that. It was a concept that the succeeding Reagan administration embraced and pursued across much of government. Part of that deregulation included the elimination of the requirement that all radio stations run local news. Some might quibble with that wording because, technically, the FCC never required stations to run news. But everyone in the industry understood that the FCC had an unpublished quota for the percentage of news to be run on AM and FM stations. With that requirement gone, predictably, many radio stations cut back or even dropped local news completely. Prior to deregulation, every radio station in America had a news department, and even many small stations employed several newspeople. Radio news staffing—and the consequent opportunities for both genders—has generally gone downhill ever since.

The Telecommunications Act of 1996 (overhauling the Communications Act of 1934) further deregulated radio (among many other things). Perhaps most critically—at least as far as radio was concerned—it allowed for significant consolidation in the radio industry. Based on the Communications Act of 1934, a single company could own no more than seven AM stations and seven FM stations all told and no more than one AM and one FM in the same market. The FCC liberalized those restrictions in comparatively small ways in the 1980s and 1990s, but under the deregulated landscape of the 1996 Act, there was virtually no limit on the total number of stations a single company could acquire, and companies started collecting hundreds—and in the case of Clear Channel, over 1,000—of stations all across the country. And in the deregulated landscape after 1996, a single company could own as many as eight stations in a single market (depending on market conditions).

The result was a predictable consolidation of news departments. Why support eight separate news departments when a company could have one news department with two or three people handling news on four or five of the eight stations? The other stations in the group could drop news completely. This consolidation further eroded the opportunities for everyone in radio news—including women.

The last significant change came in 1998 as a result of a ruling by the U.S. court of appeals for the D.C. circuit. Long a critic of the FCC and what the court felt was the FCC's frequent lack of justification for the FCC's rules and regulations, the court used what was, at its core, a religious case to strike down those EEO rules from the 1960s and early 1970s. In *Lutheran Church-Missouri Synod v. FCC*, a radio station filed suit against the FCC saying that the FCC's rules against discriminatory hiring prevented it from hiring people whose religious convictions matched the radio station's religious orientation. The court of appeals basically struck down the FCC's EEO guidelines. The court said that preventing discrimination was acceptable but that the FCC's rules went beyond that to promote the hiring of certain groups.

The effect of that ruling was felt more by minorities in radio than any other segment of the population, but women were certainly also affected by the end of regulations.

In the 1990s, women continued to grow as a percentage of the TV news workforce, but slowly. By the end of the decade, women were 39% of the TV news workforce—up just 18% in the previous 10 years. However, in radio news, women dropped to 29% of the workforce—a 6% drop during the decade (Papper & Gerhard, 1999).

By the late 1990s, it's possible that market forces changed the broadcasting landscape more than the FCC's EEO rules had. When those EEO rules first came out, women suddenly had an advocate in the FCC—an advocate that was virtually nonexistent in any other field. Over time, as other fields opened up, women had more employment options than ever before. Now the marketplace largely determines employment. While there are jobs in radio, it's been many years since radio could be considered a "growth" industry. Most radio hiring today is replacement for people who have moved up or moved out. The lure of television remains high, however, despite punishingly low starting salaries.

Most of the rest of this chapter is based on surveys conducted on behalf of the Radio and Television News Directors Association (RTNDA). I took over the responsibility of the annual RTNDA Survey in 1994, and, starting in 1996, I began collecting data for women (and minorities) by specific position—every 3 years. For detailed results and statistics, visit www.rtnda.org/pages/research.php.

TELEVISION NEWS TODAY

As far as women in local broadcast news, the new century looks a lot like the end of the last one. In television news, the workforce has stabilized at just about 40% women, which is essentially where it ended the 1990s (Papper, 2007). According to the U.S. Department of Labor (www.dol.gov/wb/stats/main.htm), women make up 46% of the full-time U.S. workforce, so, overall, TV news isn't far behind.

There is a perception that the number of women in TV news is steadily increasing. That's not correct, but the roles women occupy within the newsroom have changed.

Women are nearly two-thirds (65.9%) of all TV news producers, but that's actually been true for a dozen years. The biggest change involves women reporters and anchors. Women ended the 1990s as a majority of both groups, but that majority position has edged up steadily. And while pairing women anchors on any show was virtually unthinkable as recently as the 1990s, it's more and more common among secondary news broadcasts: morning, noon, and 5 p.m. It's still rare to see two women co-anchors for main newscasts (weekdays at 6 p.m. and the late news), and there's an increasing trend toward solo anchors on the weekend (as a cost-cutting measure). Women have made some progress in the traditional male strongholds of sports and weather, but the numbers are still small. Women do better among writers, associate producers/news assistants, executive producers, and the assignment desk. Women have also made grudging progress as news directors.

If women have generally increased among so many of the positions in the newsroom, why are the overall numbers not higher? That's because of the decline in women photographers. The percentage of women photographers has dropped steadily over the last dozen years, and because the typical TV news department has more photographers than any other single position, a drop there has offset the gains elsewhere. The drop in women photographers is particularly interesting because it coincides with a drop in the size and weight of the equipment that a photographer has to carry around. Still, the photographer position is frequently considered the blue-collar bastion of the newsroom (along with tape editor) while virtually all other newsroom positions mandate a college degree.

According to Becker, Vlad, and McLean (2006), women continue to enter college in higher numbers than men (57% versus 43%), and they continue to major in various communication fields in even higher rates than overall college attendance (63.7%). Women graduate in even greater numbers (67.5% in communication).

Although the percentages vary from survey to survey, the general trends are fairly clear. Among managers, news directors, and executive producers are more likely to be women today than in the mid 1990s, but assistant news directors have changed little. Women assignment editors are a little more common (and nearly 50%), but women producers remain static near the two-thirds mark. Note that both news anchors, and especially news reporters, have seen women move steadily up. Sports anchor and sports reporter have both seen large percentage increases in women, but the numbers for both remain low. Women weathercasters have only edged up slightly. Women as photographers have dropped steadily. Other newsroom support positions, measured since 1999, have exhibited little trend, moving up and down from survey to survey.

RADIO NEWS TODAY

In radio, since 2000, the numbers have tended to bounce up and down, but the general trend is down. In 2007, the most recent year for which numbers are available, the radio workforce was just under 25% women.

During 2000 through 2002, women were in the low to mid-30th percentile range in the radio workforce. Since then, however, the number has slid into the mid-20s. While there is some evidence that women have been more affected than men by the consolidation of radio news discussed earlier, it is far from conclusive.

Even less clear is how many women in radio news are more "sidekick" than news people—part of a morning "zoo," where the woman provides less news then feature material and provides a different voice to contrast with a male announcer team. Some women at contemporary radio stations have argued that they get the title of "news director" instead of the same money received by the men on the air. There's no empirical evidence on that, one way or the other.

TV NEWS DIRECTORS

Even as women have made gains in a variety of TV news positions, those gains have been more grudging at the top than most other areas. Stone's first survey in 1972 found only two women television news directors—under 1% of the total. By 1976, that number had risen to 4%, but Stone found most of those to be at small, independent stations.

By 1986, the percentage of women news directors had grown to 14%. It went up again to 16% in 1990 and 21% in 1994 when I first conducted the survey (Papper & Sharma, 1995). But the number has only inched up since then, moving into the mid 20s in 2000, which is where it has remained ever since. The percentage actually peaked in 2003 at 26.5%, although 2007, the most recent year for which numbers are available, was just a shade behind at 26.3%.

Women are still more likely to be found as news directors in smaller markets and at smaller stations, but women are also increasingly heading large and major market news departments. At this writing, there are no women news directors at any of the big four network affiliates (ABC, CBS, FOX, and NBC) in New York City, the nation's number-one market. But there have been. Two out of four of the news directors at the network affiliates in Los Angeles (the number-two market) are women, and three out of four in third-ranked Chicago are women. Women are also news directors at some of the other, smaller stations in those markets as well. At this writing, women make up exactly 40% of the TV news directors at the four network affiliates in the country's 10 largest markets.

RADIO NEWS DIRECTORS

In Stone's first survey for RTNDA in 1972, he found just 4% of radio news directors were women. Those numbers jumped to 16% in 1981 and 27% in 1986. The percentage stayed in the mid to upper 20s through 1994 but generally hasn't been that high since. For the most part, women make up in the low to mid-20th-percentile range of radio news directors. The most recent RTNDA Survey in 2007 put women radio news directors at 23.5%.

GENERAL MANAGERS

I started asking about the gender (and ethnicity) of radio and television general managers in 2000, so there are no data before that available for comparison. In 2000, we found 14% of TV general managers were women. The number has held steady between 12 and 16% every year—sometimes up a little, sometimes down. In 2007, the latest year for which statistics are available, the percentage of women general managers was 15.8%.

In 2000, we found 12% of radio general managers were women. Through 2004, the radio figure generally held in the 11%–13% range. But in 2005, and for the next 2 years (through 2007), the percentage jumped to about 20%.

It's important to remember two things about those numbers. First, it's the news director who's filling out that data, not the general manager him- or herself. Second, the data only applies to radio and television stations that run news, because the survey is just among radio and television news directors. That doesn't mean that the numbers don't apply to the larger station universe (including the ones that do not run news), just that we don't know for sure.

SALARIES

There's little information available on this. We gather data for men and women in various positions, and we gather data on salaries, but don't combine them because of how difficult and time-consuming that would be. The only place to directly compare women versus men is in the position of news director, because that's the only position in a newsroom where there's only one.

When Stone (1993) looked at gender and salaries in the early 1990s, he found that age and experience accounted for any salary differences between men and women. When we analyzed salaries for men and women news directors in this century, we found that the only variables to determine the salary of a TV news director were market size (how big is the city where the station is located?) and staff size (how big is the station within that city?). No other factors came into play.

Does that mean there's no discrimination against women in TV news? No, it doesn't. First, women make up 40% of the TV workforce but only 25% of TV news directors. Second, women are still, overall, more likely to be news directors at smaller stations and in smaller markets. So, yes, there's still discrimination—it's just not directly based on salary.

When Stone (2004) looked at the data, primarily from the 1980s, he argued that there was some evidence of salary discrimination against women based on his examination of producers, a position even then dominated by women. Stone noted that while "their responsibilities are great . . . they are among the lowest paid staff, with the least to gain financially by taking another producer job in a larger market" (p. 337).

First, I'm not sure I accept the logic of the argument; in any case, it's certainly no longer true. First, news producer salaries have moved up noticeably. And if we look at which five positions (for instance) have the greatest percentage salary increase from smallest markets to the biggest markets, we find that women are a majority in three of the five positions (news anchor, news reporter and news assistant, along with male-dominated sports anchor and tape editor). And news assistants have the highest disparity in pay (up 225%) and the highest percentage of women (66.3%) of any TV news position.

THE FUTURE

The new century has not given us meaningful changes in the percentages of women in radio or television news.

In radio, women have moved up among general managers, but the general shrinkage of radio news and consolidation of companies controlling radio stations have left radio news a static business at best. Few stations make new hires in radio; almost all hiring involves replacement positions for people who have moved up or out. Even though we're seeing some early signs of backing away from consolidation (as this is written, Clear Channel has already sold hundreds of its stations), there's no evidence that the future of radio news is going to be noticeably different from its present.

More changes are taking place in television, and its future and opportunities are far less clear. First, we need to dispense with the myths. With a 1-year exception, more stations run local news each year than were running it the year before. The number increase each year is small, but the number continues to climb. Second, television newsrooms are not shrinking. Again, with a 1-year exception, the size of TV newsrooms has gone up every year. So has the amount of news that the average TV station runs. TV news remains a growth industry.

But it's also true that the increasing number of stations and the increasing number of video outlets (including news and information) have led to an increasing fragmentation of the audience. What that means is that while the total audience for video news and information has grown, the audience size for any given news program has generally been shrinking. And as media choices expand, media advertising choices do as well. More and more advertising dollars have been going into the Internet, mobile video and information, and other new technology areas, and it's clearly affecting advertising income for both radio and television. Those changes are not gender based; whatever the impact, it's likely to affect men and women in much the same way.

Women continue to enter college in higher numbers than men, and they continue to major in various communication fields in even higher rates than overall college attendance. So far, that has not led to a higher percentage of women in TV news because of a reshuffling within TV newsroom jobs. While more and more women are on the air as reporters and anchors, gains in sports, weather, and newsroom management positions have been slower. And, although TV news equipment is generally getting smaller and lighter, fewer and fewer women are becoming photographers.

As we look to the future, it's likely that women will increase in both sports and weather. That has the potential to raise the overall percentage of women in TV news. There is some evidence that we may see an increase in one-man (or, in this case, woman) bands—journalists who operate on their own, both shooting and reporting stories. Although many people assume that this is a growing trend, the evidence isn't there yet, but news directors are clearly looking in that direction. That could conceivably lead to an increase in the number of women photographers. Certainly it's ironic that as the equipment has gotten smaller and lighter that the number of women photographers has actually diminished. I suspect we'll see that leveling off and even increasing sometime in the foreseeable future.

Overall, I think that we're at a temporary plateau for women in TV news at 40% but that the percentage will start to go up again, slowly, by about 2010 and edge up to as much as 45% by 2020. No one area will account for the increase, I predict; rather, almost all areas will contribute to the growth.

IT'S YOUR TURN: WHAT DO YOU THINK? WHAT WILL YOU FIND?

1. Watch different local TV newscasts in your area. Compare the gender pairings from one station to the next and one newscast to the next. Compare the number of women as opposed to men in TV news who anchor the weather and sports. Do you see differences? Why?

2. Talk to women in your local TV news who are doing jobs that are mostly held by men. Ask what their experiences have been in getting where they are. Talk to women in radio news in your area. Ask them about their experiences in the male-dominated world of radio.

3. How have the obstacles and progress of women in broadcast journalism reflected the status of women in our society as a whole?

4. Are there ways in which you see or suspect discrimination against women in radio or TV news? Could you design a research project to determine the answers?

REFERENCES

Becker, L. B., Vlad, T., & McLean, J. D. (2006). Enrollments level off; Online instruction now routine. *Journalism & Mass Communication Educator, 62*(3), 263–288.

Papper, B. (2007, July/August). Women and minorities in the newsroom. *RTNDA Communicator*, 20–25.

Papper, B., & Sharma, A. (1995, October). Newsroom diversity remains elusive goal. *RTNDA Communicator*, 18–25.

Papper, B., & Gerhard, M. (1999, July). Making a difference. *RTNDA Communicator*, 26–37.

Stone, V. A. (1973, June). Radio-television news directors and operations. *RTNDA Communicator*, 5–12.

Stone, V. A. (1987). Changing profiles of news directors of radio and TV stations, 1972–1986. *Journalism Quarterly, 64*(4), 745–749.

Stone, V. A. (1988). Trends in the status of minorities and women in broadcast news. *Journalism Quarterly, 65*(2), 288–293.

Stone, V. A. (1993). *Let's talk pay in television and radio news.* Chicago: Bonus Books.

Stone, V. A. (2004). The changing status of women in television and radio news. In Lind, R. A. (Ed.), *Race/gender/media: Considering diversity across audiences, content, and producers* (pp. 331–338). Boston: Allyn & Bacon.

8.3 WOMEN IN BRITISH BROADCASTING: AN EXAMINATION OF PERCEIVED OPPORTUNITIES AND CONSTRAINTS

Rebecca Ann Lind

> *This reading complements the previous one and presents the results of open-ended, in-depth interviews with successful British broadcasting professionals. The interviews revealed the major factors that serve as opportunities and constraints for women in the industry.*

The British broadcasting industry has often been held up as a model to which other broadcasting systems might aspire. But how well are the BBC and the commercial broadcasters doing in the difficult process of integrating women into an industry that has traditionally been a male stronghold? What opportunities and constraints do women face?

To answer these questions, I conducted in-depth interviews with 21 British broadcasting professionals. These were people who had "made it" in the tough, competitive environment of professional broadcasting. They have unique vantage points due to their success and stature in the field. They represent broadcasting industry employees, broadcasting regulators, and trade unions. All told, I interviewed 19 women and 2 men; of these, 6 were employed by the BBC, 12 by independent (commercial) broadcasters, 2 by the Irish national broadcaster RTE, and 1 by the trade union ACTT. Five were radio workers, 7 were television workers, 7 worked at a corporate level, and 2 worked for the agency regulating broadcasting.

OPPORTUNITIES AND CONSTRAINTS: FIVE MAIN DIMENSIONS

After I transcribed the interviews, I read carefully what all of these media professionals had told me about their own experiences. It seemed clear that there were five general types of opportunities and constraints, and each type seemed to present both advantages and disadvantages for women. I'll discuss them in more detail below, but the five types can be defined as follows:

- *Societal:* The presence and effects of the women's movement on perceptions of appropriate gender roles versus the still–strong traditional perception of such roles.
- *Institutional:* The presence and effects of formal agencies designed to increase equality in the workplace, or social institutions such as educational programs that

encourage girls to study math and science versus those that steer girls away from such subjects.

- *Organizational:* The presence and effects of programs designed to improve the status and range of opportunities for women versus gender-based job classifications.
- *Physical:* The presence and effects of technological developments such as smaller and lighter cameras (and other equipment) versus the belief that women aren't capable of carrying and operating equipment, as well as medical developments facilitating women's ability to work.
- *Individual:* A woman's own assertiveness, career-mindedness, or goal-directedness versus the stereotypical "timid woman" or the woman who works "for pin money" rather than having a career.

Opening Doors: Perceived Opportunities for Women

1. *Societal Issues.* One of the most clear-cut factors that may help women enter and advance in British broadcasting is the fact that the birthrate in Britain is declining. A broadcasting regulator compared these circumstances to World War II:

> The most important thing is that there's going to be a big need for women's skills, certainly in the next decade, anyway, with the demographic shortage of young people coming into the workforce. And it's going to be just like the Wars, you know, in that 'get women on the buses and in the factories and in the offices,' and in places where men wouldn't usually wish to see them. Because there's going to be an economic need to get women in there.

So, if for no reason more lofty than that of basic staffing needs, there may soon be good opportunities for women in British broadcasting.

2. *Institutional Issues.* The British play a major role in the Commission of the European Communities' Steering Committee for Equal Opportunities in Broadcasting, which is concerned with equality for all underrepresented groups. The Steering Committee has three main functions:

> (1) Exchange of ideas and information on ways to overcome obstacles to equal opportunities, leading to a series of recommendations on basic mechanisms to promote equal opportunities, training and career development, working conditions, attitudes and awareness, recruitment and selection; (2) Establishment of projects, with the financial support of the European Commission, aimed at promoting equal opportunities; (3) Statistical monitoring of employment patterns in broadcasting." (Steering Committee, 1990, pp. 3–4)

The Steering Committee should be an important resource for research and recommendations to help gender equality in broadcasting across Europe.

3. *Organizational Issues.* One tactic to promote gender equality in an organization is to appoint an equality officer. Another is to create an organizational goal, action plan, or strategy to create a balanced gender mix. The best of these are both specific and realistic. For example, the BBC's 1990 strategy for reaching its goal of reflecting the gender composition of the UK concluded,

> To claim that we will do this by the year 2000—that is of 3,900 secretaries and clerks ensure that 2,400 are *men* (there are currently 11) and of 230 AMPs [the top management grade] ensure that 97 are *women* (there are currently 22)—is unrealistic. As a first step, therefore, our intermediate aim should be to ensure that we achieve the ratios for [three key groups]. These are achievable within the aims which Directorates have set themselves, and will be reviewed in 1996. (BBC, 1990, p. 4)

The equality officers I interviewed mentioned economic and pragmatic reasons for implementing equality goals. One said that programs designed to provide opportunities for women will actually bring the company good feedback and good publicity. Another said that companies can't afford *not* to implement such policies:

> We're not just talking about some woolly liberal notion, we're actually talking about working in a way which is nondiscriminatory so that we don't end up in an industrial tribunal. All right, OK, so there are fines, the fines are modest, but the reputation of [the broadcaster] is impaired.

Other organizational practices that may foster equal opportunities for women include short- and long-term training programs. These vary, but their overall impact is seen as highly positive. There are training programs for journalists, technicians, secretaries, clerks, managers, etc. Each has a different goal: to provide practical experience to complement college or other training, to enable a clerical worker to gain skills required for transition to a technical position, to encourage workers' personal development, or to create a greater awareness of equality or other issues. Other training opportunities include what are called "attachments," in which workers can be temporarily assigned to a different department, learn new skills, and perhaps prove themselves in nontraditional jobs.

The success of the training schemes, particularly the longer–term ones, cannot be ignored. Several women I spoke with had joined their organizations as trainees and have had quite successful careers. One joined the BBC 20 years ago, in the very first batch of journalism trainees. She now leads a staff of about 100. Another also got her start in the BBC's journalism training program and after 10 years is responsible for all national news coverage on BBC TV. A woman currently in a technical training program said, "I don't think I would have been able to get into television in any other way. I could not have just applied for a job."

Besides training programs, many broadcasters also offer women greater opportunities by creating a flexible working environment, through job sharing, flex-time arrangements, daycare facilities, maternity/paternity leaves, and the like. To the extent that such flexible arrangements are available, they clearly encourage skilled women to remain in the industry.

4. *Physical Issues.* Science is responsible for the two main physical opportunities for women in broadcasting: reliable birth control methods and the miniaturization of equipment. These physical-level opportunities actually represent the removal of longstanding physical constraints. "Some things have changed forever," one woman said when discussing the impact of the birth control pill. "If you have the capacity to control your biology, so that you don't need to bear children in a random way, then you own your own destiny.

And that has changed the role and status of women forever." (The significance of the Pill on women's lives and roles is something that can be difficult for younger women to comprehend, but if you ask an older woman about it, she'll tell you how revolutionary it was.) Another physical opportunity for women is that, given the development of lightweight equipment, the longstanding myth that women can't haul or handle heavy gear is simply irrelevant. According to one editor, this is "one great excuse [that] is rapidly being eradicated by clever men . . . on the outskirts of Tokyo."

5. *Individual Issues.* Two main types of individual-level opportunities for women take the form of receiving encouragement from a supportive manager and the ability to play by "a different set of rules." One woman I spoke with described how she was "pushed" by her boss to "go for my present job, which I would never have applied for, because I thought I had insufficient experience in that area. . . . I would never have put myself forward." As her boss expected, she's doing just fine. An editor told me, "A lot of [my success] was because I worked for at least three very good male bosses who pushed me, unwillingly, to the next stage."

Second, some women see opportunities just because they are women. As one department head said,

> The advantages are huge! I'm not expected to work by the same rules because I'm not expected to know the rules. Because I didn't go to those schools, I don't talk like that, I don't go to the male lavatories. I don't have to wear the same clothes, I don't have to have the uniform. The rules of behavior, I'm not expected to know them. . . . I'm not trapped in the tradition, because there hasn't been a tradition of a lot of senior women around.

This woman reveled in her ability to define a new way to play the game.

Encountering Barriers: Perceived Constraints for Women in British Broadcasting

1. *Societal Issues.* Several types of constraints operate at a societal level, many dealing with family issues. Some constraints involving the perception and treatment of women result from women's own attitudes. As one woman said, "The danger for women is that they sell themselves too cheap. They're so glad to be accepted that they will work harder and for less money than men."

Also, because some women put off their careers until their children begin to grow up, they don't have a record of working outside the home. Entering the job market without a work record isn't easy, and the skills involved in coordinating a household and raising a family aren't often valued by employers. Alternatively, women who begin careers before having children—or who don't want children—may find themselves being passed over by employers who don't want to "take any chances" on an employee who might leave, even temporarily. As one equality officer said,

> By the time a woman is old enough to have gained sufficient working experience to be getting into a position where she's credible and will be started to be considered for progression, she's entering those childbearing years. And whilst to some extent it tends to go underground, in that men don't say "this is the reason I'm not selecting this particular one," it is a consideration to them.

The women, therefore, aren't as likely to be promoted as men are.

Besides this, there are some women for whom the constraints mean not having children that they really do want. One department head said,

> I would love another child. If I had another child it would probably be the last one we would have. And I have a secret fantasy that I would have one last baby and actually stay at home for 2 years with the child, maybe until he or she was going to kindergarten, and I would absolutely love that.

However, this woman said that doing this would probably mean giving up her career:

> I don't think I could do that, stay home, and then come back as a senior manager. Because I think you get on a ladder, and that ladder works like an escalator. It progresses up. And if you step off, you can't go back in at the same level.

An additional constraint is acknowledged by many people who argue that women with children are faced with responsibilities that men with children are not. "A man does not have the problem of children," said one announcer. "He does not have the problem of running a family because generally there is a woman to do that." Finally, women with children find it difficult to attend business-related social gatherings. A department head said,

> I am asked to so many functions. And they're always at 5:00 or 5:30 in the evening. They're clearly designed for the busy male executive who will leave the office a bit early, drop in for a drink, be seen, and go home. And the dinner is on the table when he gets in at 7:00 or 7:30. I can't do that. I mostly refuse to go to those things.

She added, "I'm sure that goes against me."

2. *Institutional Issues.* Both formal and informal social institutions operate as constraints. One formal institution is the educational system. Several women said the traditional nature of British education, which distinguishes between appropriate careers for boys and girls, inhibits both men and women from realizing their full potential. One interviewee who'd graduated from Oxford University asked her college for career guidance and was told that as a women she shouldn't pursue a broadcasting career. Clearly, bad advice such as this can make it very hard for broadcasters who want to hire women. As one equality officer said, "There's still very few women entering into engineering and technical areas of work, and there's a big problem for us." It also makes it difficult for young women interested in nontraditional careers. A female broadcasting regulator I spoke with said,

> Your career advice is, "Well, you're not clever enough to go to University, so how about teaching." I mean, those were the options that I got. "Yeah, well, you can always go back to teaching, you might not like it that much, but it's always a good standby." Well, what kind of career advice is that? Nobody said to me, "Well, how about broadcasting policy regulation?"

A more informal constraining institution is the very strong male social network in the industry. Many people have acknowledged how much like a "men's club" broadcasting is and have noted that women cannot easily become a part of that club. One woman stressed how alone she felt when she began her career as the only woman on staff.

> One of the things I found really isolating was the fact that I tend not to go to the pub as a recreational thing. I'd probably go into town for coffee. And so, I continued to do that,

when I was first employed at a radio station. And I just found that I just didn't find anybody to relate to, at all, and, oh, I felt terribly isolated. And I suddenly twigged that everybody was going out to the pub at lunchtime, and that's where they were doing the feedback, that's where they were doing the chatabout thing. And I was left out. I mean, as a woman, I never thought about that. But there was no doubt about it at all. And I was not happy. I found I took a long time to learn the trade. And it all changed when another woman joined us.

Many women I spoke with lamented the lack of a strong peer group, and many felt they'd suffered as a result. Another way in which informal (male) networks constrain women is the word-of-mouth method of recruiting. If women aren't active within the networks, it's unlikely that a woman's name will spring to mind when there's a position to fill. One personnel controller I spoke with considered this one of women's biggest hurdles.

Finally, organizational cutbacks can present serious setbacks for equality. If layoffs are based on seniority, recent hires—including many women hired due to new opportunities—will be the hardest hit. Seniority is easily applied and in one way eliminates unfair dismissals. However, although it's widely supported by unions, at least one union officer would like to see that changed. She favors consultations between management and union regarding layoffs and argues that if layoffs were spread across all levels of seniority, some incoming talent would be protected while at the same time some of the more senior people would remain and could continue to serve as mentors.

3. *Organizational Issues.* Organizational-level constraints are seen as either the lack of some desirable attribute or the presence of some undesirable attribute. The people I spoke with mentioned the lack of career guidance, the lack of management sensitivity, the lack of qualified women to fill certain positions, and the lack of role models. The lack of career guidance contributes to a haphazard, nonproductive series of job transfers, as opposed to job transfers motivated by a desire to reach a certain post and attain a certain level of seniority. The lack of management sensitivity is most problematic when women are trying to enter a predominantly male stronghold. One department head said that when women enter nontraditional areas, "If they come into a department which is totally male, there are still difficulties, there's no question about that." Further, a lack of qualified women makes it difficult for people who wish to hire women. As one department head said,

> I have only one woman correspondent. I would like to have more women correspondents. It hasn't been possible to appoint them. Because there really haven't been any suitable candidates at all. And I arrived here saying, "Right, I am determined to appoint as many women as I can." And it just wasn't available.

Additionally, many women felt the lack of strong role models. One woman said, "You can count them on the fingers of one hand."

Other organizational issues serve as constraints due to their presence-these include the need for women to work harder than men and the perception that part-time workers are only partly committed to their jobs. The feeling that women need to work much harder than men isn't unique to broadcasting. Still, it's a powerful constraint. As a reporter put it, women must be twice as good as their male colleagues; however, "you can't whine about it; you just have to do it."

In addition, most broadcasting jobs are highly demanding, and many people believe that if you're not a full-time worker, you're not fully committed to the job. Leaving full-time status

> can be seen as a lesser commitment. If you're going to go off and have a baby, and maybe consider taking a career break, what sort of degree of dedication have you got to the area you're working in and the people you're working with?

While equality officers would like to see this perception altered, many managers buy into it. A personnel director said that it's hard to perceive a person as wanting to work as much as a promotion would require, when they're only willing to work part time. An editor said that job sharing "might be done, but on the whole, I would have thought someone who wanted to be a correspondent would want to do it as a full-time job."

Finally, one practice acing as a constraint is actually meant as an opportunity. Organizational goals and action plans for equality can be controversial. Opponents say it doesn't make sense to pass up a well-qualified man for a less-qualified woman, because they'd rather base the decision on who was the best person for the job at the time. They also think affirmative action programs can encourage doubts about the women's performance—namely, that women were hired because of their gender rather than their talents. In the worst-case scenario this might even cause a woman to wonder about her own qualifications and talents, thereby setting up a self-fulfilling prophecy.

4. *Physical Issues.* Two main physical constraints have already been mentioned, and to a certain extent have been counteracted by scientific advances. However, the very process of bearing children does constrain those women who wish to do so, and the perception that women can't haul heavy equipment persists in spite of technological advances. It's unfortunate, but an equality officer reluctantly acknowledged that women seeking broadcasting jobs might be well-advised to hide their pregnancies (or their intentions to become pregnant) from prospective employers.

5. *Individual Issues.* The main types of individual qualities that can constrain women from reaching their full potential in broadcasting are feelings of intimidation, lack of motivation, and lack of assertiveness. Several people I spoke with mentioned that women—who must accept some of the responsibility for creating their own opportunities—can be intimidated in the face of the status quo. An equality officer said that women must push their way through the door. However, she acknowledged that "If what you're pushing open reveals a sea of men, this can be a little intimidating." Overall, a lack of confidence makes it difficult for women to compete effectively with men in a male-dominated industry. One woman described the lack of women's motivation as "the Wow factor." She said,

> As a woman, you apply for, and you get, a job as a BBC producer. And you go, "Wow! Wow, I'm a BBC producer!" And you spend the next 5 or 6 years saying that. And if you're a man, and you apply for a job as a BBC producer and you get it you say, "Fine, I'm a BBC producer. What am I going to do next?"

THE BOTTOM LINE

While the opportunities described here are indeed helping women enter and advance in the British broadcasting industry, significant forces counteract them. Certainly, important progress has been made and should not be discounted. But until it is no longer possible to rattle off the names of the women in a certain department, or at a certain senior level, or filling certain technical positions, women in broadcasting will remain unique, somehow special, and in a sense separated from the rest of the industry. Women in broadcasting, when they are truly integrated, will cease to be obvious.

Even after years of effort, women are not progressing through all levels of management. This was particularly disheartening to the senior women I interviewed. As one said, "I'm looking at the women coming up behind me, and actually there are relatively few of them." In general, my interviewees believed that while progress has been made, there is still a long way to go. As one equality officer said when pondering whether the early years of the millennium would bring true gender equality to British broadcasting, "I just somehow can't see it. There's just a gut feeling that, I don't know, I just feel it won't happen."

IT'S YOUR TURN: WHAT DO YOU THINK? WHAT WILL YOU FIND?

1. What do you think are the strengths and weaknesses of affirmative action programs for the people they're designed to help? Are you in favor of such programs? Why or why not?

2. If a media organization is downsizing, how can layoffs be made other than on the basis of seniority? What are the strengths and weaknesses of the alternate system, compared to those of the seniority formula? What's really the most fair and equitable? What should result in the best media content?

3. I interviewed only people who had "made it" in broadcasting. How do you think my findings might have differed if I focused on people who tried to work in broadcasting but hadn't succeeded?

4. Working in small groups, creating a brand-new network morning show featuring news, sports, features, and weather. Consider all the media professionals you can think of. Who would you get to anchor the show? Who would your reporters be? Who'd do sports? Weather? After you make these selections, discuss why you chose these people. Who else did you consider, and why didn't you choose them? Reflect on the gender, race, age, and appearance of these individuals. What does that tell you about what viewers expect on this type of program? Reflect on how viewers have attained these expectations.

REFERENCES

BBC. (1990). *A Strategy to balance the gender composition of the BBC's workforce* [Draft version]. London: Author.

Steering Committee for Equal Opportunities in Broadcasting; Commission of the European Communities.

(1990). *Working document for committee meeting of May, 1990*. Brussels: Author.

8.4 AMERICAN JOURNALISM AND THE POLITICS OF DIVERSITY

Rodney Benson

> *The author critiques the extent to which one of the largest and fastest-growing journalistic professional organizations,* UNITY: Journalists of Color, *truly is a voice of diversity. He argues that UNITY focuses on a narrow racial–ethnic definition of diversity and is closely allied with corporate media companies and advertisers; with such a myopic perspective, UNITY cannot be a genuine force for diversity in news.*

What does it say about the state of the American news media that one of the largest and fastest-growing journalistic professional associations is *UNITY: Journalists of Color*? Many people would say that it's a positive development. After all, UNITY's mission is to increase diversity, and diversity has become nearly a sacred word in American political culture. Specifically, UNITY wants to increase ethnic–racial diversity in employment (more Black, Asian American, Native American, and Latino journalists) and in news representations (more persons of color in the news). I do not dispute the need to hire journalists with a broad range of backgrounds and perspectives, or the need to produce news that is ideologically diverse and represents the full spectrum of human experiences. However, in this essay, I argue that using the word *diversity* to refer only to reified racial and ethnic categories (or for that matter, to gender) is an impoverished use of the term. It also impoverishes the quality of American democracy and undermines efforts to mount an effective, organized challenge to increasingly concentrated and profit-obsessed corporate media power. To put my case in the starkest possible terms, as I hope to demonstrate: Because UNITY is focused on a narrow racial–ethnic definition of diversity, and because UNITY is closely allied with corporate media companies and advertisers, it is not a genuine force for diversity in news; in fact, quite the opposite.

DIVERSITY JOURNALISM

Today's Latino, Asian and Native American—as well as gender and sexual—identity politics are largely the legacy of the Black civil rights movement of the 1960s. The movement originally encompassed a complex array of organizations and political orientations, including protestors against neocolonialism, defenders of alternative lifestyles, and upwardly mobile middle-class professionals. In the end, not surprisingly, it was the latter who predominated, with groups such as the Ford Foundation–funded Mexican American Legal Defense and Educational Fund reducing the multifaceted "multicultural" movement to a simple demand for proportional representation in universities, governments, and corporations;

government benefits for perceived past discrimination; and public recognition of categories of persons—such as Asian American or Hispanic American—officially created by the U.S. Census Bureau in the early 1970s.

With the exception of the National Association of Black Journalists, founded in 1975, the other constituent members of UNITY began well after the struggle to define multiculturalism had been largely fought and settled as the recognition and defense of separate "communities" of color. The Asian American Journalists Association was founded in 1981. The National Association of Hispanic Journalists and the Native American Journalists Association were both founded in 1984. In 1988, all of these groups came together to form UNITY.

UNITY's annual conferences are generously sponsored by a virtual *Who's Who* of the world's largest media corporations and advertisers, including General Motors, Gannett, Bloomberg, Ford Motor Co., Toyota, Time Warner, Coca-Cola Co., and Microsoft. On the Web page advertising its 2004 convention (www.unityjournalists.org/DC2004/index. html), UNITY portrayed itself as "A Powerful Alliance, A Force for Change." There is little doubt that UNITY and its identity politics allies in corporations, universities, and foundations are increasingly powerful. But what kind of change exactly are they trying to achieve?

UNITY's first priority has been to increase the employment of journalists of color, and it has had some limited success in achieving this goal. UNITY has encouraged and closely monitored the kind of surveys conducted by the American Society of Newspaper Editors, for instance, that show employment of journalists of color lagging behind that of the general population: between 1978 and 2005, whereas the total population proportion of "people of color" increased from 19% to 33%, the proportion of newspaper journalists of color rose from 4% to 14%. In television news, the numbers are somewhat higher, with 21% of its workforce non-White. However, in both print and television news, only about 10% of editorial management positions are held by journalists of color (ASNE, 2006; Papper, 2007). Another major priority of UNITY has been to track the amount of coverage focused on various communities of color. In this spirit, the National Association of Hispanic Journalists (2006) offers a much publicized *Network Brownout Report*. In a study of 2005 coverage, the NAHJ report found that only 105 of 12,600 national television network news stories were exclusively about Latinos or Latino issues and that nearly one in five of these stories focused on crime.

In addition, UNITY has fought to change the language of race reporting, often successfully. For example, noting how public opinion poll results on race and ethnic issues vary sharply according to wording of questions (e.g., people tend to be against "quotas" but for "civil rights"), UNITY's Web site has provided a helpful list of "suggestions" on how to employ "the words that frame the issues." Instead of "quotas," UNITY suggests "hiring outreach," "goals," or "adaptable timetables"; instead of "illegal alien," "undocumented immigrant" or "new immigrant." UNITY members are always on guard to catch "culturally insensitive" comments, sometimes going to ridiculous lengths. In a 2008 column on the UNITY Web site, Native American journalist Michaela Saunders writes about her successes in convincing her newspaper, the *Omaha World-Herald*, to discourage the use of the word "powwow" in place of the word "meeting." As Saunders (2008) wrote, "We have a sizable Native community and several powwows—Native social dances—are hosted in the area annually. Why use the word in place of 'meeting' when it could be interpreted as a belittlement of Native cultures?" While this example seems relatively trivial, some language changes have clearly been for the better. At the *Los Angeles Times*, for instance, the in-house style guide has been modified to prohibit the use of dehumanizing terms like "illegal" or "alien" as nouns to describe immigrants.

Finally, UNITY and the larger diversity journalism movement have succeeded in making courses on media and multiculturalism virtually mandatory in most university journalism and communication programs. Conferences, colloquia, and reports on diversity and race have been sponsored by most of the major journalistic professional and educational institutions. The Society of Professional Journalists (SPJ), America's oldest professional organization of journalists, has issued a *Rainbow Source Book* (www.spj.org/divsourcebook.asp) to help "broaden the perspectives represented in the news media" (Diversity Committee, 1999, p. 46) meaning in SPJ's terms not an ideological broadening but simply providing names of experts from "groups that are historically underrepresented in the media: women, gays and lesbians, ethnic minorities, and people with disabilities" (p. 46).

Race and gender are "crude proxies for ideas," argued one participant at a journalism diversity conference. But if this is so, why has there been an increasing ideological narrowing, de-politicization and trivialization of American news during the same period when employment of minorities and women have increased (Rosenstiel, Forster, & Chinni, 1998; Weaver, Beam, Brownlee, Voakes, & Wilhoit, 2007)? And if racial and gender diversity translate into diversity of content, how can it be that the vice president of Gannett Corporation, publisher of *USA Today* and dozens of bland, mediocre newspapers, can truthfully brag that his company has "one of the best records for diversity in the work force among the mass media industries" (cited in Glasser, 1992, p. 133)?[1] The answer, of course, is that there is no necessary connection between physical and ideological diversity, and the gap between the two is widening as diversity journalism is increasingly allied to multicultural marketing and public relations.

VISIBLE AND INVISIBLE IN THE MULTICULTURAL VISION

The American news media have always been highly commercial. But in recent decades, the sale of family-owned companies to media conglomerates trading shares on the stock market has intensified profit pressures (Squires, 1993; Benson, 2004). Technological advances in the use of computer databases have provided one way to meet these increased profit expectations: instead of inefficient mass marketing, highly focused target marketing. Since the mid-1980s, census data have been used to target according to race/ethnicity (chiefly, Hispanic, Asian Pacific Islander, and Black) in addition to other "lifestyle enclaves" linked to age, gender, income, and previous buying habits (Wilson & Gutiérrez, 1995). The three major racial categories—Hispanic, Asian Pacific Islander, and Black—that guide the growing field of "multicultural marketing" are constructs that owe their existence to U.S. Census Bureau categories. Since the 1980s, the raw number of so-designated minorities has increased relative to the White population, but more important, thanks to the efforts of ethnic media activists and outlets, the self-conscious identity of dozens of diverse national origin groups have coalesced around these three categories. In other words, if an African American or Black identity was well entrenched in American life from the long history of slavery, segregation, and discrimination, a Latino identity bringing together Puerto Ricans, Cubans, Mexicans and El Salvadorans had to be "forged," as did an Asian identity joining Koreans, Chinese, Japanese, Indians, Vietnamese, Cambodians, etc.

Joseph Turow (1997) argues that the advertising industry, via its target marketing strategy, "affects not just the content of its own campaigns but the very structure and content of the rest of the media system" (p. 194). Chiefly, he maintains, target marketing favors the rise of "segment-making" media, those outlets that speak to ever-smaller slices of America, over "society-making" media, those outlets "that have the potential to get all those segments to talk to each other" (Turow, p. 3). Likewise, Wilson and Gutiérrez (1995) stress that media outlets and advertisers actively "look for differences in the audiences and ways to reinforce those differences" (p. 257). There is evidence that target marketing has not only favored the rise of "segment-making" media, as Turow suggests, but has transformed "society-making" media such as daily newspapers. The national television networks each have their own executive "head of diversity," and many major newspapers have in-house diversity committees, made up of journalists of color on staff as well as news and business managers. Against the American tradition that there ought to be a "wall" separating editorial and advertising departments, diversity journalism has in some cases aggressively undermined these distinctions. At the *Orange County Register*, reporters on the "Asian Cultures" team, in addition to writing about the growing Vietnamese immigrant population, have become scouts to help business staff identify the best distribution points and potential advertisers (Robertson, 2000).

Ultimately, what matters to advertisers is "class not mass." Minority readers are desired only to the extent that they are affluent (Cranberg, 1997). As civil rights activist Jesse Jackson (1999) pointed out, less than 1% of total U.S. consumer advertising spending is targeted toward the African American market, significantly less than their proportion of the population. Given African Americans' and Hispanics' yearly earnings in the hundreds of billions, "multicultural marketing . . . is not just another 'cause,'" Jackson argued, "it is good business" (p. 56). Maybe so. But what is surprising is that Jackson and so many other civil rights activists have put so much faith in the unadulterated workings of the market. What Jackson does not acknowledge is that if multicultural marketing is simply "good business," then the "cause" will be sharply limited by the needs and interests of major corporations.

Indeed, UNITY has done little that might offend its big corporate sponsors. Rather than criticizing or resisting the massive downsizing of quality journalism, UNITY has urged its members to adapt to the new economic "realities," which are portrayed as inevitable. Rather than work on behalf of all journalists whose interests increasingly diverge from those of management and stockholders—for example, profit margins in the media industry continue to exceed 15% or even 20%, even as greater job cutbacks are demanded—UNITY pits journalists against journalists, only concerning itself with defending the jobs of "journalists of color" (as evident in a 2007 column written by UNITY president Karen Lincoln Michel).

Some ethnic identity activists argue that diversity journalism and multicultural marketing have not gone far enough and have settled for bread crumbs instead of parity. But in fact the "movement" has succeeded all too well, in that it *has* helped equate diversity with "race" in the public mind and thus diverted attention from the increasing lack of broad *ideological* diversity in the American media—compared to Western European media, the range of ideas from left to right tends to be much narrower, and strong critiques of laissez-faire capitalism, in particular, are rarely heard. In this sense, diversity journalism is not so much a movement for racial justice as an agent of "racial mysticism." Racial mysticism promotes the idea of homogeneous non-White racial "communities" that in fact are sharply divided along class lines (Lind, 1995, p. 175). And thus, if the identity issues that the diversity movement raises are important for a segment of the non-White upper middle class, the racial mysticism hypothesis suggests that this focus on diversity (defined purely in terms of representation of semi-arbitrary racial categories) helps draw attention away from other pressing issues, such as widening income inequality and increasing job precarity for the working class. Not coincidentally, these are precisely the kind of class and economic problems that a globalizing, shareholder-profit driven media system would prefer to ignore.

"At stake today in local as well as global political struggles is the capacity to impose a way of seeing the world, of making people wear 'glasses' that force them to see the world divided up in certain ways," Pierre Bourdieu (1998, p. 22) has argued. "These divisions create groups that can be mobilized, and that mobilization makes it possible for them to convince everyone else that they exist, to exert pressure and obtain privileges. . . ." If diversity journalism and multicultural marketing are seeking to make visible, and hence socially "real," the 14.8% of Americans who claim Latino identities and the 5% who claim Asian and Pacific Islander identities, they are by the same token contributing to making invisible, and hence nonexistent, the 12% of American workers who belong to labor unions and the 12.3% of Americans who live below the poverty line (all 2006 data from U.S. Census Bureau, 2007a, 2007b, 2007c). Indeed, a number of studies have documented the nearly complete absence of coverage of labor unions and poverty issues in the corporate-owned media (e.g., Tasini, 1990; Alterman, 2000); in many newsrooms since the 1970s, the rise of the "race" beat came at the direct expense of the "labor" beat, which has virtually disappeared at most American newspapers today. In short, if problems of racial and ethnic discrimination have admittedly been under-covered or written about in simplistic, stereotyped ways, issues of economic and class inequality are all but silenced completely.

In this context, UNITY's push for more news focused on particular "communities of color" may be the last thing that is needed—even in order to improve race relations. More coverage of the "Whites" who are poor, who commit crimes (violent or otherwise), who lose their jobs, etc., could help dispel the almost automatic association many Americans make between non-Whites and social problems. As Gilens (1999) documents, since the 1960s the U.S. news media have tended to portray poverty as primarily a Black problem and to systematically portray the "black poor more negatively than the nonblack poor" (p. 6). Public misperceptions based on these media representations have helped to create support for drastic reductions in government social services needed by both the White and non-White poor and working class. More stories about systemic social problems, and more stories about these problems that don't link them exclusively to non-Whites, could do as much or more to combat racial stereotypes as, for instance, NAHJ's PR-sounding push in the *Brownout Report* for more stories about "the positive impact Latinos are having on the U.S. economy" or the "cultural stories about Latinos in their communities" (2006, p. 9). Moreover, UNITY's reification of artificially created racial categories undermines efforts to create more fluid cosmopolitan identities that transcend as well as tolerate differences and thus provide the basis for broad social solidarity.

DIVERSITY, OBJECTIVITY, AND THE MONEY EQUATION

Labor struggles, poverty, social problems that affect the poor and middle-class across "racial" lines—these kinds of comprehensive stories, largely missing from the U.S. media, are unlikely to be taken up by journalists focused on the fragmenting (and to listen to UNITY's own elected officials) even trivializing politics of identity. On a *Talk of the Nation* call-in show with UNITY leaders (National Public Radio, 1999), a caller from Minnesota asked, "Isn't news news? . . . are there different facts for different races?" Kara Briggs, a reporter for the *Portland Oregonian* and president of the Native American Journalist Association, responded to the caller with a lesson in geography:

> You know, I would submit to you that you being from Minnesota and me being from Washington state, we might say very different things are news. I might talk about the crisis in salmon. You might talk about the crisis in walleye fish. We just have different perspectives. . . .

When another caller brought attention to the "narrow class basis of all current journalists, regardless of race, sex, or national origin," Vanessa Williams, a *Washington Post* journalist and president of the National Association of Black Journalists, avoided the question entirely, instead turning to the need to

> look for nontraditional journalists of color. What about a person who's retired, maybe a homemaker who now—children are out of the house, looking for something to do, somebody who's committed to that community, who knows that community, who can be trained to be a journalist? A young person with a couple of years out of junior college. . . .

There are two major reasons for such confused responses. One is that the language of diversity is in tension with American journalism's professional credo of objectivity. Journalism is somehow supposed to be above the ideological fray. Hence the UNITY journalists are placed in the difficult position of criticizing the media for lacking diversity yet, in order not to seem ideological, forced to deny any substantive reason for such diversity. The result is this kind of tepid defense of diversity, defending the unique experiences or perspectives that journalists of color, or female journalists, bring to the news, while at the same time denying that such experiences or perspectives have any ideological content. There is an important critique that one could make of the practices of "objective" journalism—how these practices force the journalist to silence his or her own voice and privilege those of powerful official "sources" (e.g., Bennett, 1990; Pedelty, 1995). However, UNITY is not making this critique. As a result, even if media organizations hire more journalists with diverse racial–ethnic backgrounds—assuming that such racial–ethnic backgrounds really do entail diverse perspectives—the limiting strictures of "objectivity" will mostly prevent these journalists from actually expressing diverse viewpoints.

A second reason that UNITY journalists seem tongue-tied when forced to elaborate a defense of identity-based diversity is that at some level they probably know that bringing about change will require more than new hiring practices. A long tradition of social science research (e.g., Gans, 1980; Schudson, 2003) has shown that the news product is ultimately shaped far more by economic and organizational constraints than the personal characteristics—race, class, sexual orientation, or even ideology—of individual journalists. Even the editor and news director, whatever race or ethnicity he or she is, has little power to override the powerful economic constraints that ultimately shape news decisions (Entman, 2006, p. 27). The harsh reality is that persons of color and their specific concerns are under-covered in large part because they are disproportionately poor. They are less likely to be part of the affluent audience that media companies and their advertising sponsors care about reaching. Without changing the economic model that drives the entire media industry—stock market profit maximization pressures and advertiser funding—little will change. At most, a greater sensitivity to racial/ethnic identities will ensure more coverage of affluent audiences who also happen to be Black, Latino, Asian American, Native American. This would not be a bad thing, but it is clearly a very limited kind of diversity.

In the midst of major economic restructuring of the news industry, UNITY's race-based alliance with media owners helps cloak the latter's activities in the aura of a progressive cause. For profit-obsessed media corporations, a tip of the hat to ethnic and racial diversity costs virtually nothing. It's far easier to change the style guide than to hire more journalists (of all "colors") or to make a serious commitment to critical, in-depth reporting of the growing economic inequalities that underlie racial tensions. To admit this would both undermine UNITY's raison d'être and place the organization in the position of biting the hand of its corporate feeders. Yet only broad professional and economic structural reforms of the media system are likely to produce diversity that is more than skin deep.

NOTE

1. Gannett's links to UNITY are particularly close. At a Gannett-hosted dinner for the UNITY board of directors on March 19, 2004, UNITY president Ernest R. Sotomayor remarked, "There are few news media companies that, over the years, have consistently shown the level of support that Gannett has, and it has made a difference in the newsroom, and in coverage." (See "Remarks by UNITY President," 2004.)

IT'S YOUR TURN: WHAT DO YOU THINK? WHAT WILL YOU FIND?

1. I have argued that UNITY is not a genuine force for diversity in news but rather is quite the opposite. Do you agree or disagree? Why?

2. How would you define "diversity in news"? Do we have such diversity at present? How could we try to achieve your ideal of diversity?

3. Which is more important to you, "objectivity" or "diversity" in news coverage? Why? Do you see these two journalistic ideals as incompatible? Why or why not?

REFERENCES

Alterman, E. (2000). Still with us. *The Nation.* April 24, 12.

American Society of Newspaper Editors. (2006). *ASNE census shows newsroom diversity grows slightly.* Retrieved April 2008 from: http://www.asne.org

Bennett, W. L. (1990). Toward a theory of press-state relations in the United States. *Journal of Communication, 40*(2), 103–125.

Benson, R. (2004). Bringing the sociology of media back in. *Political Communication, 21,* 275–292.

Bourdieu, P. (1998). *On television*. New York: New Press.

Cranberg, G. (1997, March/April). Trimming the fringe. *Columbia Journalism Review*, 52–54.

Diversity Committee developing source book (1999, July/August). *The Quill, 87*(5), 46.

Entman, R. M. (2006). *Young men of color in the media: Images and impacts*. Washington, DC: Joint Center for Political and Economic Studies, Health Policy Institute.

Gans, H. (1980). *Deciding what's news*. New York: Vintage.

Gilens, M. (1999). *Why Americans hate welfare*. Chicago: University of Chicago Press.

Glasser, T. L. (1992). Professionalism and the derision of diversity: The case of the education of journalists. *Journal of Communication, 42*(2), 131–140.

Jackson, J. (1999). Rainbow imperative. *Advertising Age, 70*(39S), 56.

Lind, M. (1995) *The next American nation: The new nationalism and the fourth American revolution*. New York: The Free Press.

Michel, K. L. (2007). *UNITY president: Achieving diverse workforces should be key consideration in industry cutbacks*. Retrieved May 2, 2008, from: www.unityjournalists.org/presidents/przmsg_070507.php

National Association of Hispanic Journalists. (2006). Network brownout report. Retrieved April 28, 2008, from: www.nahj.org/resources/2006Brownout.pdf

National Public Radio. (1999, July 8). *Talk of the nation* [Transcript]. Livingston, NJ: Burrelle's Information Services.

Papper, B. (2007, July/August). Women and minorities in the newsroom. *RTNDA Communicator*, 20–25.

Pedelty, M. (1995). *War stories: The culture of foreign correspondents*. London: Routledge.

Remarks by UNITY president Ernest R. Sotomayor, March 19, 2004, at a dinner hosted by the Gannett Co.'s vice president and general counsel, Thomas L. Chapple. Retrieved July 21, 2004, from: http://www.unityjournalists.org

Robertson, L. (2000). Reporters who know the business. *American Journalism Review, 22*(10), p. 18.

Rosenstiel, T., Forster, S., & Chinni, D. (1998). *Changing definitions of news: A look at the mainstream press over 20 years*. Washington, DC: Project for Excellence in Journalism.

Saunders, M. (2008). *So many news gatherers, not enough news judgment* [Special UNITY column]. Retrieved April 25, 2008, from: www.unityjournalists.org/news/news031208saunderscol.php

Schudson, M. (2003). *The sociology of news*. New York: W.W. Norton.

Squires, J. D. (1993). *Read all about it! The corporate takeover of America's newspapers*. New York: Random House.

Tasini, J. (1990). Lost in the margins: Labor and the media. *Extra!, 3*(7), 2–15.

Turow, J. (1997). *Breaking up America*. Chicago: University of Chicago Press.

U.S. Census Bureau. (2007a). *Poverty: 2006 highlights*. Retrieved April 18, 2008, from: www.census.gov/hhes/www/poverty/poverty06/pov06hi.html

U.S. Census Bureau. (2007b). *Table 642: Labor union membership by sector: 1983 to 2006*. Retrieved May 2, 2008, from: http://www.census.gov/compendia/statab/tables/08s0642.xls

U.S. Census Bureau. (2007c). *Minority population tops 100 million* [News release]. Retrieved May 2, 2008, from: www.census.gov/Press-Release/www/releases/archives/population/010048.html

Weaver, D., Beam, R. A., Brownlee, B. J., Voakes, P. S. & Wilhoit, G. C. (2007). *The American journalist in the 21st century*. Mahwah, NJ: Lawrence Erlbaum Associates.

Wilson, C. C., II, & Gutiérrez, F. (1995). *Race, multiculturalism, and the media: From mass to class communication*. Thousand Oaks, CA: Sage.

EPILOGUE AND RESOURCES

Now that you've read these chapters, think again about some questions raised in the introduction to this book: Does the social scientific or the critical/cultural studies approach seem to make more sense to you? Why? What do you think are the strengths and weaknesses of each approach? If you were going to investigate media effects, how would you approach the subject? Which types of questions (narrow or broad) do you think are more important? Which do you think are easier to answer? Which methods provide more valid and valuable results? Is it possible to maintain one's objectivity while studying human beings? What is lost, and what is gained, by holding one perspective (social scientific) over the other (critical/cultural)? Can researchers borrow from both traditions? Should they? If so, how? What would be gained? At what cost? The answers to these and other questions will influence how you interpret the scholarship you engage as you continue through school, and beyond. As you ask these questions, you are being a critical participant in our academic system/tradition of scholarship and research.

Being a critical participant in our media system means constantly asking questions. The readings in this book have presented you with a kaleidoscope of questions to consider—questions about media production, media content, and media audiences. Which ones did you enjoy the most? Why? What additional questions did you think of? How have you seen your own media literacy increase as you thought about the issues presented here, and as you have brought the question-asking process to your own media use? How have you become a more active and empowered member of the media audience? How can you bring what you've learned to any future media production you might undertake?

Ultimately, the media in our lives constitute a powerful social institution—not the only one, but the one most of us spend most of our time with. What the media tell us about our social world has a profound effect on our understanding of that social world. Even though your time in this class has come to an end, never stop questioning the media and the image of our world they offer us, the way the messages are constructed and by whom, and the way we receive, interpret, use, and are affected by the media. The media do matter. And so does your ability to ask questions, to be a literate and critical participant in the media system.

FOR MORE INFORMATION

What follows are some resources you might find helpful as you continue your studies of media production, content, and audiences. As are all such lists, it's incomplete—in this case, limited by available space—but it's a starting point.

Books

Alia, V. & Bull, S. (2005). *Media and ethnic minorities.* Harrogate, North Yorkshire: Edinburgh University Press.

Allport, G. (1954). *The nature of prejudice.* Cambridge, MA: Addison-Wesley.

Alwood, E. (1996). *Straight news: Gays, lesbians, and the news media.* New York: Columbia University Press.

Ang, I. (1997). *Living room wars: Rethinking media audiences for a postmodern world.* London: Routledge.

Ang, I. (1991). *Desperately seeking the audience.* London: Routledge.

Barnhurst, K. G. (2007). *Media Q, Media/Queered: Visibility and its discontents.* New York: Peter Lang.

Beasley, M. H., & Gibbons, S. J. (2002). *Taking their place: A history of women and journalism* (2nd ed.). State College, PA: Strata Publishing.

Benwell, B. (Ed.). (2003). *Masculinity and men's lifestyle magazines.* Hoboken, NJ: Wiley-Blackwell.

Berry, C., Martin, F., & Yue, A. (2003). *Mobile cultures: New media in queer Asia.* Durham, NC: Duke University Press.

Browne, D. R. (1996). *Electronic media and indigenous peoples: A voice of our own?* Ames: Iowa State University Press.

Browne, D. R. (2005). *Ethnic minorities, electronic media and the public sphere.* Cresskill, NJ: Hampton Press.

Bobo, J. (1998). *Black women film and video artists.* New York: Routledge.

Bobo, J. (1995). *Black women as cultural readers.* New York: Columbia University Press.

Bogle, D. (2001). *Primetime blues: African Americans on network television.* New York: Farrar, Straus & Giroux.

Bogle, D. (2003). *Toms, coons, mulattoes, mammies, and bucks: An interpretive history of Blacks in American films* (4th ed.). New York: Continuum International Publishing.

Bonilla-Silva, E. (2006). *Racism without racists: Color-blind racism and the persistence of racial inequality in the United States* (2nd ed.). Lanham, MD: Rowman & Littlefield.

Braziel, J. E., & Mannur, A. (Eds.). (2003). *Theorizing diaspora: A reader.* Hoboken, NJ: Wiley-Blackwell.

Byerly, C. M., & Ross, K. (2005). *Women and media: A critical introduction.* Hoboken, NJ: Wiley-Blackwell.

Campbell, C. P. (1995). *Race, myth, and the news.* Thousand Oaks, CA: Sage.

Carstarphen, M. G., & Zavoina, S. C. (2000). *Sexual rhetoric: Media perspectives on sexuality, gender and identity.* Westport, CT: Greenwood Press.

Chambers, D. (2004). *Women and journalism.* New York: Routledge.

Chan, J. (2001). *Chinese American masculinities: From Fu Manchu to Bruce Lee.* New York: Routledge.

Craig, S. (1992). *Men, masculinity, and the media.* Newbury Park, CA: Sage.

Creedon, P. J., & Cramer, J. (Eds.) (2006). *Women in mass communication* (3rd ed.). Newbury Park, CA: Sage.

Cuklanz, L. M. (2000). *Rape on prime time: Television, masculinity, and sexual violence.* Philadelphia: University of Pennsylvania Press.

Curren, R., & Bobo, J. (Eds.). (2001). *Black feminist cultural criticism.* Hoboken, NJ: Wiley-Blackwell.

Dennis, J. (2006). *Queering teen culture: All-American boys and same-sex desire in film and television.* New York: Routledge.

Dines, G., & Humez, J. M. (Eds.). (2003). *Gender, race and class in media: A text-reader* (2nd ed.). Thousand Oaks, CA: Sage.

Dotson, E. W. (1999). *Behold the man: The hype and selling of male beauty in media and culture.* New York: Haworth Press.

Entman, R. M., & Rojecki, A. (2001). *The Black image in the White mind: Media and race in America.* Chicago: University of Chicago Press.

Everett, A. (Ed.) (2007). *Learning race and ethnicity: Youth and digital media.* Cambridge, MA: MIT Press.

Feng, P. X. (2002). *Identities in motion: Asian American film and video.* Durham, NC: Duke University Press.

Fiske, J. (1996). *Media matters.* Minneapolis: University of Minnesota Press.

Ghassub, M., & Sinclair-Webb, E. (2000). *Imagined masculinities: Male identity and culture in the modern Middle East.* London: Saqi.

Georgiou, M. (2006). *Diaspora, identity and the media.* Cresskill, NJ: Hampton Press.

Gilens, M. (2002). *Why Americans hate welfare: Race, media, and the politics of antipoverty policy.* Chicago: University of Chicago Press.

Gill, R. (2007). *Gender and the media.* Cambridge, UK: Polity.

Gray, H. (2004). *Watching race: Television and the struggle for "Blackness."* Minneapolis: University of Minnesota Press.

Gross, L. (2002). *Up from invisibility: Lesbians, gay men, and the media in America.* New York: Columbia University Press.

Gutierrez, E., Moreno, R., & Armillas, C. (2001). *Suave: The Latin male.* New York: Universe Publishing.

Hogg, J., & Garside, P. (2007). *Women, feminism and the media.* Harrogate, North Yorkshire: Edinburgh University Press.

Holtzman, L. (2000). *Media messages: What film, television, and popular music teach us about race, class, gender, and sexual orientation.* Armonk, NY: M. E. Sharpe.

Hunt, D. M. (2004). *Channeling Blackness: Studies on television and race in America.* New York: Oxford University Press.

Jacobs, R. N. (2000). *Race, media, and the crisis of civil society: From Watts to Rodney King.* Cambridge: Cambridge University Press.

Jensen, R. (2005). *The heart of Whiteness: Confronting race, racism and White privilege.* San Francisco: City Lights.

Jhally, S., & Lewis, J. (1992). *Enlightened racism:* The Cosby Show, *audiences, and the myth of the American Dream.* Boulder, CO: Westview Press.

Johnson, M. L. (2007). *Third wave feminism: Jane puts it in a box.* London: I. B. Tauris.

Johnson, P., & Keith, M. C. (2001). *Queer airwaves: The story of gay and lesbian broadcasting.* Armonk, NY: M. E. Sharpe.

Keever, B. A. D., Martindale, C., & Weston, M. A. (1997). *U.S. News coverage of racial minorities: A sourcebook, 1934–1996.* Westport, CT: Greenwood Press.

King, C. R., & Springwood, C. F. (2001). *Team spirits: The Native American mascots controversy.* Lincoln: University of Nebraska Press.

Kirkham, P., & Thumim, J. (1993). *You Tarzan: Masculinity, movies, and men.* New York: St. Martin's Press.

Larson, S. G. (2005). *Media & minorities: The politics of race in news and entertainment.* Lanham, MD: Rowman & Littlefield.

Lee, R. C. (2003). *Asian American.net: Ethnicity, nationalism, and cyberspace.* New York: Routledge.

Lehman, P. (2007). *Running scared: Masculinity and the representation of the male body* (New ed.). Detroit: Wayne State University.

Levin, D. E., & Kilbourne, J. (2008). *So sexy so soon: The new sexualized childhood and what parents can do to protect their kids.* New York: Ballantine Books.

Liebes, T., & Katz, E. (1990). *The export of meaning: Cross-cultural readings of Dallas.* New York: Oxford University Press.

Lipsitz, G. (2006). *The possessive investment in whiteness: How White people profit from identity politics* (Revised expanded ed.). Philadelphia: Temple University Press.

Lont, C. M. (Ed.). (1995). *Women and media: Content/careers/criticism.* Belmont, CA: Wadsworth.

Lotz, A. D. (2006). *Redesigning women: Television after the network era.* Champaign, IL: University of Illinois Press.

Mansfield-Richardson, V. (2000). *Asian Americans and the mass media: A content analysis of twenty United States' newspapers and a survey of Asian American journalists.* New York: Garland.

Marlane, J. (1999). *Women in television news revisited: Into the twenty-first century.* Austin: University of Texas Press.

Marzolf, M. (1977). *Up from the footnote: A history of women journalists.* New York: Hastings House.

MacDonald, J. F. (1983). *Blacks and White TV: Afro-Americans in television since 1948.* Chicago: Nelson-Hall.

Marciniak, K., Imre, A., & O'Healy, A. (Eds.). (2007). *Transnational feminism in film and media: Visibility, representation, and sexual differences.* New York: Palgrave Macmillan.

Marriott, D. (2007). *Haunted life: Visual culture and black modernity*. Piscataway, NJ: Rutgers University Press.

Mayer, V. (2003*). Producing dreams, consuming youth: Mexican Americans and mass media*. Piscataway, NJ: Rutgers University Press.

Means-Coleman, R. (2002). *Say it loud! African American audiences, identity and media*. New York: Routledge.

Meyer, C. J., & Royer, D. (2001). *Selling the Indian: Commercializing & appropriating American Indian cultures*. Tucson: University of Arizona Press.

Meyers, M. (Ed.). (1999). *Mediated women: Representations in popular culture*. New York: Hampton Press.

Montagu, A. (1997). *Man's most dangerous myth: The fallacy of race* (6th ed.). Walnut Creek, CA: AltaMira press.

Morrison, T. G. (2004). *Eclectic views of gay male pornography: Pornucopia*. New York: Routledge.

Nakamura, L. (2007). *Digitizing race: Visual cultures of the Internet*. Minneapolis: University of Minnesota Press.

Nelson, J. (1994). *The disabled, the media and the information age*. Westport, CT: Greenwood Press.

Noriega, C. A. (2000). *Visible nations: Latin American cinema and video*. Minneapolis: University of Minnesota Press.

Noriega, C. A., & López, A. M. (1996). *The ethnic eye: Latino media arts*. Minneapolis: University of Minnesota Press.

Nguyen, M. T., & Nguyen Tu, T. L. (Eds.) (2007). *Alien encounters: Popular culture in Asian America*. Durham, NC: Duke University Press.

Omi, M., & Winant, H. (1986). *Racial formation in the United States: From the 1960s to the 1980s*. New York: Routledge & Kegan Paul.

O'Riordan, K., & Phillips, D. J. (2007). *Queer online: Media technology and sexuality*. New York: Peter Lang.

Peach, L. J. (Ed.) 1998. *Women in culture: A women's studies anthology*. Malden, MA: Blackwell.

Peele, T. (Ed.). (2007). *Queer popular culture: Literature, media, film, and television*. New York: Palgrave Macmillan.

Pendergast, T. (2000). *Creating the modern man: American magazines and consumer culture, 1900–1950*. Columbia: University of Missouri Press.

Reichert, T., & Lambiase, J. (Eds.) (2005). *Sex in consumer culture: The erotic content of media and marketing*. Philadelphia: Lawrence Erlbaum Associates.

Riley, C. A., II. (2005). *Disability and the media: Prescriptions for change*. Lebanon, NH: UPNE.

Roberts, G., & Klibanoff, H. (2007). *The race beat: The press, the civil rights struggle, and the awakening of a nation*. New York: Vintage.

Roediger, D. R., & Cleaver, K. (2007). *The wages of Whiteness: Race and the making of the American working class* (2nd ed.). New York: Verso.

Ross, K., & Byerly, C. M. (Eds.). (2004). *Women and media: International perspectives*. Malden, MA: Wiley-Blackwell.

Roy, J. (2002). *Love to hate: America's obsession with hatred and violence*. New York: Columbia University Press.

Rush, R. R., Oukrop, C. E., & Creedon, P. J. (2004). *Seeking equity for women in journalism and mass communication education: A 30-year update*. Philadelphia: Lawrence Erlbaum Associates.

Signorile, M. (2003). *Queer in America: Sex, the media, and the closets of power* (3rd ed.). Madison: University of Wisconsin Press.

Shimizu, C. P. (2007). *The hypersexuality of race: Performing Asian/American women on screen and scene*. Durham, NC: Duke University Press.

Stecopoulos, H., & Uebel, M. (1997). *Race and the subject of masculinities*. Durham, NC: Duke University Press.

Sun, W. (2006). *Media and the Chinese diaspora: Community, communications, and commerce*. New York: Routledge.

Sylvester, J. (2008). *The media and hurricanes Katrina and Rita: Lost and found*. New York: Palgrave Macmillan.

Thorne, B., & Henley, N. (Eds.). (1973). *Language and sex: Difference and dominance*. Rowley, MA: Newbury House.

Trotta, L. (1991). *Fighting for air: In the trenches with television news.* New York: Simon & Schuster.

Turner, G. (1996). *British cultural studies: An introduction* (2nd ed.). New York: Routledge, Chapman & Hall.

U.S. Commission on Civil Rights. (1977). *Window dressing on the set: Women and minorities in television.* Washington, DC: U.S. Government Printing Office.

U.S. Commission on Civil Rights. (1979). *Window dressing on the set: An update.* Washington, DC: U.S. Government Printing Office.

Valdivia, A. N. (Ed.) (1995). *Feminism, multiculturalism, and the media: Global diversities.* Thousand Oaks, CA: Sage.

Valdivia, A. N. (Ed.). (2008). *Latina/o communication studies today.* New York: Peter Lang.

van Dijk, T. A. (1987). *Communicating racism: Ethnic prejudice in thought and talk.* Newbury Park, CA: Sage.

Walters, S. D. (2003). *All the rage: The story of gay visibility in America.* Chicago: University of Chicago Press.

Weston, M. A. (1996). *Native Americans in the news: Images of Indians in the twentieth century press.* Westport, CT: Greenwood Press.

Wilson II, C. C., Gutierrez, F., & Chao, L. M. (2003). *Racism, sexism, and the media: The rise of class communication in multicultural America* (3rd ed.). Thousand Oaks, CA: Sage.

Wolf, M. A., & Kielwasser, A. P. (1991). *Gay people, sex, and the media.* New York: Haworth Press.

Wykes, M., & Gunter, B. (2005). *The media and body image: If looks could kill.* Thousand Oaks, CA: Sage.

Zook, K. B. (2008). *I see Black people: The rise and fall of African American owned television and radio minority owned television and radio.* New York: Nation Books.

Zook, K. B. (1999). *Color by Fox: The Fox network and the revolution in Black television.* New York: Oxford University Press.

Journal Articles & Chapters in Edited Volumes

Beaudoin, C. E., & Thorson, E. (2006). The social capital of Blacks and Whites: Differing effects of the mass media in the United States. *Human Communication Research, 32*(2), 157–177.

Bonnett, A. (1998). Who was White? The disappearance of non-European White identities and the formation of European racial Whiteness. *Ethnic and Racial Studies, 21*(6), 1029–1055.

Brown, J. D., & Schulze, L. (1990). The effects of race, gender, and fandom on audience interpretation of Madonna's music videos. *Journal of Communication, 40*(2), 88–103.

Busselle, R., & Crandall, H. (2002). Television viewing and perceptions about race differences in socioeconomic success. *Journal of Broadcasting & Electronic Media, 46*(2), 265–282.

Caliendo, S. M., & McIlwain, C. D. (2006). Minority framing, and racial cues in the 2004 election. *Harvard International Journal of Press/Politics, 11*(4), 45–69.

Chiricos, T., Eschholz, S., & Gertz, M. (1997). Crime, news and fear of crime: Toward an identification of audience effects. *Social Problems, 44*(3), 342–357.

Covert, J. J., & Dixon, T. L. (2008). A changing view: Representation and effects of the portrayal of women in mainstream women's magazines. *Communication Research, 35*(2), 232–256.

Devine, P. G. (1989). Stereotypes and prejudice: Their automatic and controlled components. *Journal of Personality and Social Psychology, 56,* 5–18.

Devine, P. G., & Elliot, A. J. (1995). Are racial stereotypes *really* fading? The Princeton trilogy revisited. *Personality and Social Psychology Bulletin, 21*(11), 1139–1150.

Dixon, T. L. (2006). Schemas as average conceptions: Skin tone, television news exposure, and culpability judgments. *Journalism & Mass Communication Quarterly, 83,* 131–149.

Dixon, T. L. (2008). Crime news and racialized beliefs: Understanding the relationship between local news viewing and perceptions of African Americans and crime. *Journal of Communication, 58*(1), 106–125.

Dixon, T. L., & Linz, D. (2002). Television news, prejudicial pretrial publicity, and the depiction of race. *Journal of Broadcasting & Electronic Media, 46*(1), 112–136.

Domke, D. (1997). Journalists, framing, and discourse about race relations. *Journalism and Mass Communication Monographs, 164.*

Domke, D. (2001). The press, race relations, and social change. *Journal of Communication, 51*(2), 317–344.

Domke, D., McCoy, K., & Torres, M. (1999). News media, racial perceptions and political cognition. *Communication research, 26*(5), 570–607.

Entman, R. M. (1990). Modern racism and the images of blacks in local television news. *Critical Studies in Mass Communication, 7,* 332–345.

Entman, R. M. (1992). Blacks in the news: Television, modern racism, and cultural change. *Journalism Quarterly, 69*(2), 341–361.

Evuleocha, S. U., & Ugbah, S. D. (1989). Stereotypes, counter-stereotypes, and Black television images in the 1990s. *Western Journal of Black Studies, 13*(4), 197–205

Faber, R. J., O'Guinn, T. C., & Meyer, T. P. (1987). Televised portrayals of Hispanics: A comparison of ethnic perceptions. *International Journal of Intercultural Relations, 11,* 155–169.

Gaertner, S. L., & Dovidio, J. F. (2005). Understanding and addressing contemporary racism: From aversive racism to the common ingroup identity model. *Journal of Social Issues, 61,* 615–639.

Gentles, K. A., & Harrison, K. (2006). Television and perceived peer expectations of body size among African American adolescent girls. *Howard Journal of Communication, 17*(1), 39–55.

Gilliam, F. D., Jr., Valentino, N. A., & Beckmann, M. N. (2002). Where you live and what you watch: The impact of racial proximity and local television news on attitudes about race and crime. *Political Research Quarterly, 55,* 755–780.

Gilliam, F. D., Jr., Iyengar, S., Simon, A., & Wright, O. (1996). Crime in black and white: The violent, scary world of local news. *Press/Politics, 1*(3), 6–23.

Giroux, H. A. (1997). Rewriting the discourse of racial identity: Towards a pedagogy and politics of Whiteness. *Harvard Educational Review, 67*(2), 285–320.

Gorham, B. W. (2006). News media's relationship with stereotyping: The linguistic intergroup bias in response to crime news. *Journal of Communication, 56*(2), 289–308.

Gorham, B. W. (1999). Stereotypes in the media: So what? *The Howard Journal of Communication, 10*(2), 229–247.

Gray, H. (1989). Television, Black Americans and the American dream. *Critical Studies in Mass Communication, 6,* 376–386.

Harrison, K. (2000). The body electric: Thin-ideal media and eating disorders in adolescents. *Journal of Communization, 50*(3), 119–143.

Harrison, K., & Cantor, J. (1997). The relationship between media consumption and eating disorders. *Journal of Communication, 47*(1), 40–67.

Harrison, K., Taylor, L. D., & Marske, A. L. (2006). Women's and men's eating behavior following exposure to ideal-body images and text. *Communication Research, 33*(6), 507–529.

Heavner, B. M. (2007). Liminality and normative Whiteness: A critical reading of poor White trash. *Ohio Communication Journal, 45,* 65–80.

Henderson, J. J., & Baldasty, G. J. (2003). Race, advertising, and prime-time television. *Howard Journal of Communications, 14*(2), 97–112.

Hendriks, A. (2002). Examining the effects of female bodies on television: A call for theory and programmatic research. *Critical Studies in Mass Communication, 19*(1), 106–123.

Hooks, B. (1992). Representing Whiteness in the Black imagination. In L. Grossberg, C. Nelson, & P. Treichler (Eds.), *Cultural studies.* London: Routledge.

Iyengar, S. (1990). Framing responsibility for political issues: The case of poverty. *Political Behavior, 12,* 19–40.

Jane, D. M., Hunter, G. C., & Lozzi, B. M. (1999). Do Cuban American women suffer from eating disorders? Effects of media exposure and acculturation. *Hispanic Journal of Behavioral Sciences, 21*(2), 212–219.

Johnson, J. D., Adams, M. S., Hall, W., & Ashburn, L. (1997). Race, media, and violence: Differential racial effects of exposure to violent news stories. *Basic and Applied Social Psychology, 19*(1), 81–90.

Johnson, K. A. (1991). Objective news and other myths: The poisoning of young Black minds. *Journal of Negro Education, 60*(3), 328–341.

Kiecolt, K. J., & Sayles, M. (1988). Television and the cultivation of attitudes toward subordinate groups. *Sociological Spectrum, 8,* 19–33.

Kinders, D. R., & Sears, D. O. (1981). Prejudice and politics: Symbolic racism versus racial threats to the good life. *Journal of Personality and Social Psychology, 40,* 414–431.

Lind, R. A., & Salo, C. (2002). The framing of feminists and feminism in news and public affairs programs in U.S. electronic media. *Journal of Communication, 52,* 211–228.

Lind, R. A. (2002). Speaking of culture: The relevance of cultural identity as Afro-, Latin-, and Euro-American laypeople plan a television newscast. *Journalism and Communication Monographs, 3,* 111–145.

Lind, R. A., & Danowski, J. A. (1998). The representation of Arabs in U.S. electronic media. In Y. R. Kamalipour & T. Carelli (Eds.), *Cultural diversity and the U.S. media* (pp. 157–167.) Albany, NY: SUNY Press.

Master, D. E., & Stern, S. R. (2003). Representations of race in television commercials: A content analysis of prime-time advertising. *Journal of Broadcasting & Electronic Media, 47*(4), 638–647.

Mastro, D. E., Behm-Morawitz, E., & Kopacz, M. A. (2008). Exposure to television portrayals of Latinos: The implications of aversive racism and social identity theory. *Human Communication Research, 34*(1), 1–27.

Mastro, D. E., & Morawitz, E. A. (2005). Latino representation on primetime television. *Journalism and Mass Communication Quarter, 82*(4), 110–130.

Mazie, M., Palmer, P., Pimentel, M., Rogers, S., Ruderfer, S., & Sokolowski, M. (1993). To deconstruct race, deconstruct Whiteness. *American Quarterly, 45*(2), 281–294.

McIntosh, P. (2002). White privilege, color, and crime: A personal account. In C. Mann & M. Zatz (Eds.), *Images of color, images of crime* (2nd ed). Los Angeles: Roxbury.

Means Coleman, R. R. (2006). The gentrification of "Black" in Black popular communication in the new millennium. *Popular Communication, 4*(2), 79–94.

Monteath, S. A., & McCabe, M. P. (1997). The influence of societal factors on female body image. *The Journal of Social Psychology, 137*(6), 708–727.

Morgan, M. (2005). Hip-hop women shredding the veil: Race and class in popular feminist identity. *South Atlantic Quarterly, 104*(3), 425–444.

Myers, P. N., Jr., & Biocca, F. A. (1992). The elastic body image: The effect of television advertising and programming on body image distortions in young women. *Journal of Communication, 42*(3), 108–133.

Ogunyemi, O. (2007). The Black popular press. *Journalism Studies, 8*(1), 13–27.

Oliver, M. B. (1994). Portrayals of crime, race, and aggression in "reality-based" police shows: A content analysis. *Journal of Broadcasting & Electronic Media, 38*(2), 179–192.

Oliver, M. B. (1999). Caucasian viewers' memory of Black and White criminal suspects. *Journal of Communication, 49*(3), 46–60.

Parker, S., Nichter, M., Nichter, M., Vuckovic, N., Sims, C., & Ritenbaugh, C. (1995). Body image and weight concerns among African American and White adolescent females: Differences that make a difference. *Human Organization, 54*(2), 103–114.

Peffley, M., Shields, T., & Williams, B. (1996). The intersection of race and crime in television news stories: An experimental study. *Political Communication, 13,* 309–327.

Poindexter, P. M., Smith, L., & Heider, D. (2003). Race and ethnicity in local television news: Framing, story assignments, and source selections, *Journal of Broadcasting & Electronic Media, 47*(4), 524–536.

Pritchard, D., & Stonbely, S. (2007). Racial profiling in the newsroom. *Journalism & Mass Communication Quarterly, 84*(2), 231–248.

Railton, D., & Watson, P. (2005). Naughty girls and red blooded women: Representations of female heterosexuality in music video. *Feminist Media Studies, 5*(1), 51–63.

Richardson, E. (2007). "She was workin like foreal": Critical literacy and discourse practices of African American females in the age of hip hop. *Discourse & Society, 18*(6), 789–809.

Reep, D. C., & Dambrot, F. H. (1989). Effects of frequent television viewing on stereotypes: "Drip, drip" or "drench"? *Journalism Quarterly, 66,* 542–550, 556.

Reep, D. C., & Dambrot, F. H. (1994). TV parents: Fathers (and now mothers) know best. *Journal of Popular Culture, 28*(2), 13–23.

Seiter, E. (1986). Stereotypes and the media: A re-evaluation. *Journal of Communication, 36*(2), 16–26.

Sender, K. (2003). Sex sells: Sex, class, and taste in commercial gay and lesbian media. *GLQ: A Journal of Lesbian and Gay Studies, 9*(3), 331–365.

Shah, H., & Thornton, M. C. (1994). Racial ideology in U.S. mainstream news magazine coverage of Black–Latino interaction, 1980–1992. *Critical Studies in Mass Communication, 11*, 141–161.

Simpson, J. L. (2008). The color-blind double bind: Whiteness and the (im)possibility of dialogue. *Communication Theory, 18*(1), 139–159.

Ward, M. L., Hansbrough, E., & Walker, E. (2005). Contributions of music video exposure to Black adolescents' gender and sexual schemas. *Journal of Adolescent Research, 20*(2), 143–166.

Wong, W. (1994). Covering the invisible "model minority." *Media Studies Journal, 8*, 49–59.

Zimmerman, A., & Dahlberg, J. (2008). The sexual objectification of women in advertising: A contemporary cultural perspective. *Journal of Advertising Research, 48*(1), 71–79.

Web Sites

Adbusters. *www.adbusters.org/home/*
Asian American Journalists Association. *www.aaja.org*
Body Image Site. *www.bodyimagesite.com*
Center for Media Literacy. *www.medialit.org*
China Media News. *www.chinamedianews.net/*
Citizens for Media Literacy. *www.main.nc.us/cml/*
Directory of Media Literacy Sites Worldwide.
    www.chebucto.ns.ca/CommunitySupport/AMLNS/internet.html
Fairness and Accuracy in Reporting. *www.fair.org*
Feminist Media Project. *www.feministmediaproject.com/*
The Freedom Forum. *www.freedomforum.org*
Gay & Lesbian Alliance Against Defamation. *www.glaad.org/*
Hispanic Digital Media. *http://hispanicdigital.blogspot.com/*
Hispanic Trending: A Latino Marketing & Advertising Blog. *http://juantornoe.blogs.com/*
Index of Native American Media Resources on the Internet.
    www.hanksville.org/NAresources/indices/NAmedia.html
I Want Media: *www.iwantmedia.com/resources/index.html*
Jean Kilbourne (women & media). *www.jeankilbourne.com*
Media Awareness Network. *www.media-awareness.ca/english*
Media Matters for America. *http://mediamatters.org/*
Media Report to Women. *www.mediareporttowomen.com/*
The Media Resources Center of the Library at the University of California at Berkeley (films by and about people of color). *www.lib.berkeley.edu/MRC/EthnicImagesVid.html*
The Media Resources Center of the Library at the University of California at Berkeley (films dealing with gender issues). *www.lib.berkeley.edu/MRC/WomenVid.html*
Media Watch. *www.mediawatch.com/*
Media Education Foundation. *www.mediaed.org*
NAACP (National Association for the Advancement of Colored People). *www.naacp.org*
The National Association of Black Journalists. *www.nabj.org*
The National Association of Hispanic Journalists. *www.nahj.org*
The National Lesbian & Gay Journalists Association. *www.nlgja.org*
National Organization for Women. *www.now.org*
National Video Resources project called "Viewing Race: A Film and Video Project to Stimulate Community-Based Discussions on Race." See a list of resources at *www.viewingrace.org/*
Native American Journalists Association. *www.naja.com*
Out Front Blog. *www.fhoutfront.com/2008/03/gay-media-matte.html*
Poynter Institute. *www.poynter.org*
The Radio-Television News Directors Association. *www.rtnda.org*

Selected women and gender resources on the Web: *http://womenst.library.wisc.edu/*
Southern Poverty Law Center. *www.splcenter.org.* Also see *www.tolerance.org*
The Transnational Community Program (Oxford University): *www.transcomm.ox.ac.uk/*
The University of Iowa, Communication Studies Department (much information about gender, race, and
 the media). *www.uiowa.edu/~commstud/resources/GenderMedia/*
Women, Action, & the Media. *www.centerfornewwords.org/wam/*
Women in Media & News. *www.wimnonline.org/WIMNsVoicesBlog/*
Z Magazine Alternative Media Sources. *www.zmag.org/altmediaresources.htm*

Films/Videos (Distributors; date; run time in minutes)

The Ad and the Ego. (California Newsreel; 1996; 57)
The Beauty Backlash. (Films for the Humanities & Sciences; 2006; 29)
Bell Hooks on Video: Cultural Criticism and Transformation. (Media Education Foundation; 1997; 66)
Black Is . . . Black Ain't: A Personal Journey Through Black Identity. (California Newsreel; 1995; 87)
The Black Press: Soldiers Without Swords. (California Newsreel; 1998; 86)
Blue Eyed. (California Newsreel; 1996; 93)
Campus Culture Wars: Five Stories About PC. (Direct Cinema Ltd.; 1993; 86)
Casting Calls: Hollywood and the Ethnic Villain. (Films for the Humanities & Sciences; 2004; 47)
The Celluloid Closet. (Columbia Tristar Home Entertainment; 1995; 101)
The Color of Fear. (StirFry Seminars & Consulting; 1994; 90)
Color Adjustment. (California Newsreel; 1991; 88)
Deadly Persuasion: The Advertising of Alcohol & Tobacco. (Media Education Foundation; 2003; 60)
Dishing Democracy: Arab Social Reform via Satellite TV. (Films for the Humanities & Sciences 2007; 58)
Dreamworlds 3: Sex, Desire, & Power in Music Video. (Media Education Foundation; 2007; 55 [35
 abridged])
Enough Man. (Frameline Home Video; 2005; 61)
Ethnic Notions: Black People in White Minds. (California Newsreel; 1987; 56)
The Extremes of Fashion: Women's Couture and the Media (Films for the Humanities & Sciences;
 2006; 53)
The Eye of the Storm. (Center for the Humanities; 1991; 26)
Facing Racism. (Films for the Humanities and Sciences; 1996; 57)
Further off the Straight & Narrow: New Gay Visibility on Television 1998–2006. (Media Education
 Foundation; 2006; 61)
Game Over: Gender, Race & Violence in Video Games. (Media Education Foundation; 2000; 41)
Girls: Moving Beyond Myth. (Media Education Foundation; 2004; 28)
Hate.com: Extremists on the Internet. (Films for the Humanities & Sciences; 2000; 42)
Hate and the Internet: Web Sites and the Issue of Free Speech. (Films for the Humanities & Sciences;
 1998; 21)
Hip-Hip: Beyond Beats & Rhymes. (Media Education Foundation; 2006; 60)
Hispanics in the Media. (Films for the Humanities & Sciences; 1998/1994; 44)
The Killing Screens: Media and the Culture of Violence. (Media Education Foundation; 1994; 37)
Killing Us Softly 3: Advertising's Image of Women. (Media Education Foundation; 2000; 34)
Bollywood Bound: Finding Fame and Identity in India's Filmmaking Capital. (Films for the Humanities &
 Sciences; 2002; 57)
The Looking Glass: Inside TV News. (Films for the Humanities & Sciences; 1996; 60)
Media Literacy. (Films for the Humanities & Sciences; 2007; 35)
The Media and Democracy in the Arab World. (Films for the Humanities & Sciences; 1999; 45)
Playing Unfair: The Media Image of the Female Athlete. (Media Education Foundation; 2002; 30)
Race and Local TV News. (Films for the Humanities & Sciences; 1998; 21)
Racial Stereotypes in the Media. (Films for the Humanities & Sciences; 2008; 42)
Sexual Stereotypes in the Media. (Films for the Humanities & Sciences; 2008; 38)
Slaying the Dragon. (Women Make Movies; 2007/1988; 60)

Slim Hopes: Advertising & the Obsession With Thinness. (Media Education Foundation; 1995; 30)

Small Steps, Big Strides: The Black Experience in Hollywood. (20th Century Fox Home Entertainment; 1998; 58)

The Strength to Resist: The Media's Impact on Women and Girls. (Cambridge Documentary Films; 2000; 35)

Telenovelas: Love, TV, and Power. (Films for the Humanities & Sciences; 1995; 59)

This is Nollywood. (California Newsreel; 2007; 56)

Tongues Untied. (Frameline Home Video; 1990; 55)

Tough Guise: Media Images and the Crisis in Masculinity. (Media Education Foundation; 1999; 87 [56 abridged])

Understanding Media Literacy. (Films for the Humanities & Sciences; 2007; 35)

Who Is Albert Woo?: Defying the Stereotypes of Asian Men. (Films for the Humanities & Sciences; 2000; 51)

CONTRIBUTORS

Cory L. Armstrong is an assistant professor at the University of Florida College of Journalism and Communications. She has more than 8 years of professional journalism experience. Her research interests are influences on news content, media credibility, gender and media, and effects of news coverage.

Rob K. Baum is a senior lecturer and the chair of the Centre for Drama and Theatre Studies at Monash University, as well as the convenor of the International Dance Therapy, both in Melbourne, Australia. Her research interests include race/gender/identity politics, trauma and the Holocaust, disability discourse, and therapeutic movement practice.

Rodney Benson is an associate professor of media, culture, and communication at New York University. His research interests are immigration in the media, international comparative studies of journalism, cultural globalization, online news media, and methodologies of image and discourse analysis.

Emily Berg is a PhD student at the University of Minnesota. Her research interests include gender and politics, presidential public address, media bias, and political campaign discourse.

Adrienne Biddings is a JD candidate at the University of Florida Levin College of Law. Her main research interests are communications and media law, specifically legal issues in new media.

Katie Blevins is a master's student at the University of Florida at the College of Journalism and Communications. She specializes in media law. Her research interests include the first amendment and access law, gender in the media, media history, and media ethics.

M. Junior Bridge is president of Unabridged Communications, a research and education company specializing in media studies. She is an adjunct faculty member at George Mason University, where she teaches a senior-level media criticism course entitled Women and Media. Her research focuses primarily on civil rights, gender, and culture.

Dwight E. Brooks is a professor and the chair of the Department of Mass Communications at Jackson State University (Mississippi). His teaching and research interests include critical/cultural studies, diversity and media, media literacy, and media programming and management.

Patti Brown has a master's degree in social work from the University of Iowa, is a licensed independent social worker, and is finishing a master's in journalism at Iowa State

University. Her research interests are in social welfare, health care, and immigration policy and how those subjects are covered by the media.

Angie Y. Chung is an assistant professor in the Department of Sociology, University at Albany. Her research interests are race/ethnicity, immigration and the second generation, ethnic politics, community and urban sociology, Asian American studies, and gender and family.

Cynthia Conti is a doctoral candidate in the Department of Media, Culture and Communication at New York University. Her interests are community media, radio history, and broadcast regulations. Her dissertation will investigate the meanings, rhetoric, and application of localism as it is articulated in communication policy and enacted at licensed LPFM stations.

Cynthia A. Cooper is an associate professor in the Department of Communication Arts at Salisbury University. Her research interests are First Amendment law, hate speech, media regulation, and government policymaking.

David Cuillier is an assistant professor in the Department of Journalism at the University of Arizona. His research interests include the state of freedom of information and public attitudes toward open government and psychological influences in producing and perceiving news.

George L. Daniels is an assistant professor of Journalism in the College of Communication and Information Sciences at the University of Alabama in Tuscaloosa. His research interests include media management and the role of diversity in the media workplace.

Dave Decelle is a consultant at Cheskin Added Value. His interests include gender and sexuality in media, ethnographic consumer research, and new media trends and policies.

Gail Dines is a professor and the director of American Studies at Wheelock College, Boston. Her research interests are pornography and violence and images of women in popular culture.

Travis L. Dixon is an associate professor of communication at the University of Illinois at Urbana–Champaign. He is primarily interested in the portrayal of people of color in the mass media and the effects of these images on audiences.

Bradley W. Gorham is an associate professor in the Communications Department at the S. I. Newhouse School of Public Communications, Syracuse University. His research interests center around the reception and effects of media messages about social groups.

Leslie A. Grinner is a doctoral candidate in cultural foundations of education at Syracuse University and an instructor in the Women's & Gender Studies Department at Pace University in New York City. Her research interests include feminist cultural studies, popular culture, identity, and performativity.

Veronica Hefner is a doctoral student in the Department of Communication, University of Illinois at Urbana–Champaign. Her research interests are mass communication processes and effects in areas of romantic relationships and body image.

Nina B. Huntemann is an assistant professor of communication and journalism at Suffolk University. Her research and teaching interests include communication policy and history, political economy of communication, new media technologies, game studies, critical cultural studies, feminist media studies, and media literacy.

Ryan J. Hurley is a doctoral candidate at the University of Illinois, Urbana–Champaign. He is primarily interested in media effects and health communication.

Ralina L. Joseph is an assistant professor in the Department of Communication at the University of Washington. Her research interests include African American and comparative mixed-race representation in the media and literature.

Christopher S. Josey is a doctoral student at the University of Illinois, Urbana–Champaign. He is primarily interested in the effects of new technology and stereotypical portrayals.

Marjorie Kibby is a senior lecturer in cultural studies at the University of Newcastle, Australia. Her research and teaching interests are focussed on Internet culture, including the way that the Internet has changed the way music is acquired, stored, and consumed.

Jean Kilbourne is internationally recognized for her pioneering work on alcohol and tobacco advertising and the image of women in advertising. She is the creator of the award-winning film series *Killing Us Softly: Advertising's Image of Women* and the author of *Can't Buy My Love: How Advertising Changes the Way We Think and Feel* and *So Sexy So Soon: The New Sexualized Childhood and What Parents Can Do to Protect Their Kids*.

Minjeong Kim is an assistant professor in women's studies at Virginia Tech. Her research interests include global gender issues, international migration, Asian American studies, and the mass media. She is a co-editor of *Global Gender Research: Transnational Perspectives* (Routledge).

C. Richard King is an associate professor and the chair of comparative ethnic studies at Washington State University. He has written extensively on the colonial legacies and postcolonial predicaments of American culture, with special interest in the racial politics of expressive culture.

Rebecca Ann Lind is an assistant professor in the Department of Communication and Assistant Vice Chancellor for Research, University of Illinois at Chicago. Her research interests are race and gender in the media, audience studies, journalism, media ethics, and new media.

Cynthia M. Lont is a professor in the Communication Department and the director of film and video studies in the College of Visual and Performing Arts at George Mason University. Her research interests include women and media, women's music, and visual communication.

Amanda D. Lotz is an assistant professor in the Department of Communication Studies at the University of Michigan. Her research interests include gender on television and U.S. television in the post-network era.

Sheena Malhotra is an assistant professor in the Gender & Women's Studies Department at California State University, Northridge. She has worked in the commercial film and television industry in India and on documentary films in the United States. Her research interests are race, gender, and nation in mediated contexts, with a particular focus on India and the Indian diaspora.

Jon B. Martin was a graduate student in the Department of Speech and Communication Studies at San Francisco State University when he prepared his contribution to this book. The primary focus of his work in critical theory and communication and his research examines communication and identity at the intersections of race, gender, and sexuality.

Mindy McAdams is a professor of journalism and Knight Chair at the University of Florida. She teaches courses about online journalism. With more than 20 years' experience in journalism, she is the author of *Flash Journalism: How to Create Multimedia News Packages* (Focal Press, 2005).

Jody D. Morrison is an associate professor and the internship director in the Department of Communication and Theatre Arts at Salisbury University in Maryland. Her research interests include interpersonal/relational communication, communication education, and conversation analysis.

Sandra L. Nichols is an assistant professor at Towson University in the Department of Mass Communication and Communication Studies. Her research interests include mass communication and democracy, journalism, computer-mediated communication, and issues of race and gender in mass media.

Gwendolyn E. Osborne is the associate editor of *Black Issues Book Review*. She writes extensively about contemporary African American literature and popular culture.

Debbie A. Owens is an associate professor and coordinator of student internships in the Department of Journalism and Mass Communications, Murray State University. Her research interests include mass media and social construction, race, gender, and age in the media.

Robert A. (Bob) Papper is a professor and the chair of the Department of Journalism, Media Studies, and Public Relations at Hofstra University. His research interests include audience and local radio and television news, and he has directed the RTNDA annual survey of radio and television news for the last 14 years.

Janice Peck is an associate professor at the University of Colorado in Boulder, where she teaches media studies. Her research focuses on the place of media in U.S. culture and politics, media and social theory and philosophy, and the history of media. She is the author of *The Gods of Televangelism: The Crisis of Meaning and the Appeal of Religious Television* and *The Age of Oprah: Cultural Icon for the Neoliberal Era*.

Donnalyn Pompper is an associate professor and public relations sequence head in the Department of Strategic & Organizational Communication, Temple University. Her research interests are gender, ethnicity, and age in media representations and organizations.

Lea M. Popielinski is a PhD candidate in the Department of Women's Studies at the Ohio State University. She is writing her dissertation on feminist social movement involvement with HIV/AIDS. She also reviews films at http://crimsoncarpet.wordpress.com/.

Laura Portwood-Stacer is a doctoral candidate in the Annenberg School for Communication at the University of Southern California. Her research interests are identity, consumption, popular culture, and radical political movements.

Naomi Rockler-Gladen is a freelance writer.

Susan Dente Ross is a professor of communication and the Associate Dean in the College of Liberal Arts at Washington State University. An expert in media representation, peace journalism, and press freedom, she trains journalists around the world and publishes widely on issues of media, identity, and intercommunal and international conflict.

Jody M. Roy is a professor of communication and the Assistant Dean of Faculty at Ripon College. Her research focuses on pro-violence and anti-violence messages in media and popular culture.

Jaideep Singh is an assistant professor of ethnic studies at California State University, East Bay, where he holds the Sabharwal Chair in Sikh and Punjabi studies. He is also co-founder and director of the Sikh American Legal Defense and Education Fund.

Laura Stempel has had an eclectic career that includes teaching, university administration, consulting to nonprofits, selling art supplies, and writing for both scholarly and general audiences about literature, media, and gender. She worked as a TV critic for 10 years and currently lives in Chicago, where, among other things, she knits.

Susannah R. Stern is an associate professor of communication studies at the University of San Diego. Her research interests are located at the intersection of gender and electronic media uses and effects, especially the social contexts and uses of new technology.

Pamela J. Tracy is an associate professor of communication studies at Longwood University. Her research interests include studying identity and difference within the context of children and media interpretation, ethnographic audience studies, and media pedagogy.

Michelle A. Wolf is a professor of broadcast and electronic communication arts at San Francisco State University. Her research interests include representation of race, gender, social class, disability, and sexuality in media; audience studies; media power and control; and qualitative research.

Gust A. Yep is a professor of communication studies at San Francisco State University. His research, focusing on communication at the intersections of culture, "race," ethnicity, class, gender, and sexuality, has been widely published in international and interdisciplinary academic journals and anthologies.

ALTERNATE TABLES OF CONTENTS

ALTERNATE TABLE OF CONTENTS 1: BY RACE/GENDER EMPHASIS

Gender Emphasis

Race Emphasis

Both Race and Gender (some more "both" than others)

ALTERNATE TABLE OF CONTENTS 2: BY MEDIUM

Televison

Film

Audio Media

New Media

Print Media

General Media

ALTERNATE TABLE OF CONTENTS 3: BY ENTERTAINMENT/ JOURNALISM FOCUS

Journalism (includes advertising and public relations)

Entertainment